Katrosits - Art

MORE THAN MEAT JOY

Carolee Schneemann

COMPLETE PERFORMANCE WORKS & SELECTED WRITINGS
Edited by Bruce McPherson   **DOCUMENTEXT 1979**

Library of Congress Cataloging in Publication Data

Schneemann, Carolee 1939-
   More than meat joy.

   Bibliography: p.
   1. Schneemann, Carolee, 1939-
2. Performance art—United States.
I. McPherson, Bruce, 1951-   II. Title.
N6537.S356A4   1979   700'.92'4   78-15300
ISBN 0-914232-16-9

This publication has been assisted in part by a grant from the National Endowment for the Arts. Typeset at Open Studio Print Shop, a facility funded in part by the New York State Council on the Arts.

Manufactured in the United States of America.

FIRST EDITION

DOCUMENTEXT
New Paltz   New York

contents

Grateful acknowledgement is made to the following magazines and publications and their editors for the first appearance, often in substantially different form or version, of the following works.

The scenario and descriptive notes to **Meat Joy** appeared in Some/Thing No. 2, ©1965 by David Antin and Jerome Rothenberg, and in Theatre Experiment (Doubleday), ©1967 by Michael Benedikt and ©1967 by Carolee Schneemann. "Notes as Prologue" for **Meat Joy** is reprinted in facsimile from Some/Thing No. 2. Several texts appearing here as "from The Notebooks" appeared in different arrangement as "Notations 1958-1968" in Caterpillar 8/9, ©1963 by Clayton Eshleman, and in A Caterpillar Anthology (Doubleday), ©1971 by Clayton Eshleman. "Hormones Circling" appeared in Matter, ©1963 by Robert Kelly. The scores of **The Queen's Dog, Americana I Ching Apple Pie,** and **Schlaget Auf** first appeared in Parts Of A Body House Book (Beau Geste Press, Devon, England), ©1972 by Carolee Schneemann. "Woman in the Year 2000" was first published in Woman in the Year 2000 (Arbor House), ©1974 by Maggie Tripp. "Istory of a Girl Pornographer," a slightly different version of "Unsent Letter to Allen Kaprow," and the spoken text of **Interior Scroll** first appeared in Cèzanne, She Was A Great Painter, ©1975 by Carolee Schneemann. An earlier version of the scenario, description, and related texts of **Snows** first appeared in I-KON No. 5, ©1968 by Susan Sherman. An earlier version of "On the Making of Snows" appeared in Experiments in Art and Technology Newsletter, June 1967. The revised score of **Banana Hands** (1969) first appeared in Plays for Children to Direct, published by Heinemann, London, 1970. The notes for **Divisions and Rubble** were first published in a different version in Manipulations (Judson Publications), ©1967 by Jon Hendricks. **Road Animations for Reykjavik** first appeared in Súm: A Listaijatid I Treykjavik, Galerie Súm, Reykjavik, 1972.

Additional copyright information regarding photographs has been placed in the photographers' index. The publisher wishes to extend special thanks to the photographers, and to the contributors to the Festschrift. All rights are reserved by or for the individual photographers, artists, and authors.

My grateful thanks to all the performers and technicians whose participation brought the work to realization, and to those associated with us in generously providing space & materials. Thanks also to those artists, critics, writers and photographers whose responses were confirming and spread the intention of my work.

I had hoped to be able to devote more space to the network of friendships where so many areas of concern were shared and developed. This could only be touched upon in the individual works, and in the snapshot collages.

Many of the works would not have been possible without grants from the Benedict Arnold Foundation, Cassandra Foundation, Croton Press, National Endowment for the Arts, New York State Council on the Arts, Creative Artists Public Service Program. Help at critical times came from Walter Gutman, Victor Herbert, Harold Wit and Mary Kaplan.

Immediate thanks are due to friends whose encouragement helped this book along the way: Sharon Avery, Scott Bowron (who photographed the paintings and constructions), Mary Beth Edelson, Jaimy Gordon, Robert Haller, Eve and Harry Lerner, Mary Ellen Morrow, George Quasha, Sara Seagull, Lynne Tillman, Rosmarie Waldrop, Women/Artist/Filmmakers. To the Open Studio staff. To my parents, brother and sister. Especially to James Tenney and Anthony McCall. And to the memory of Kitch.

for Bruce McPherson

The edge of a tornado ripped through Sidney, Illinois in the summer of 1960. I was a graduate student in painting at the University of Illinois, living with James Tenney (a composer and pianist studying electronic music) in a ramshackle country house surrounded by trees. The tornado toppled our favorite Tree of Heaven, which crashed down on the insubstantial back roof. Its wide limbs blocked the wooden steps and pathway into the field. My attachment to particular trees is animistic and I was desolate over this destruction. Our cat Kitch, then four, quickly discovered that she could walk directly out her open kitchen window onto the tangle of branches and make a new and efficient journey down towards the stream. It is all ridiculously simple, but that is how and why I decided to use the fallen tree and flooded-out rock walls, the mud and broken branches, as an "environment"—a labyrinth—for a group of friends to proceed through one Sunday afternoon. I made a drawing of a possible course, the elements to encounter, and instructions based on what Kitch was doing: make a self-determined set of pathways around and through the obstacles, evolving the sorts of motions and actions which the obstacles propose; make contact with mud, water, high grass, the stream, the fallen tree; proceed from east to north to west and meet at the rock pile for a cook-out. The only "rule" was that no one outside of the journey was to observe the passage of others. Except myself—I returned to my small work room to watch through the window.

The week after **Labyrinths**, Liz Hiller, an actress and one of the participants, gave me Artaud's **The Theater and Its Double:**

> Beside this need for the theater to steep itself in the springs of an eternally passionate and sensuous poetry available to even the most backward and inattentive portions of the public, a poetry realized by a return to the primitive Myths, we shall require of the **mise en scene** and not of the text the task of materializing these old conflicts and above all of giving them **immediacy**; i.e. these themes will be borne directly into the theater and materialized in movements, expressions, and gestures before trickling away in words.

In my work the significance of Artaud became linked to the theories of D'Arcy Thompson, Wilhelm Reich and Henri Focillon—for example, Focillon's statement that "substances are not interchangable, but techniques penetrate one another, and at the moment of their doing so, interference tends to create new substances." This book is about that work in all of its unsystematic processual variety.

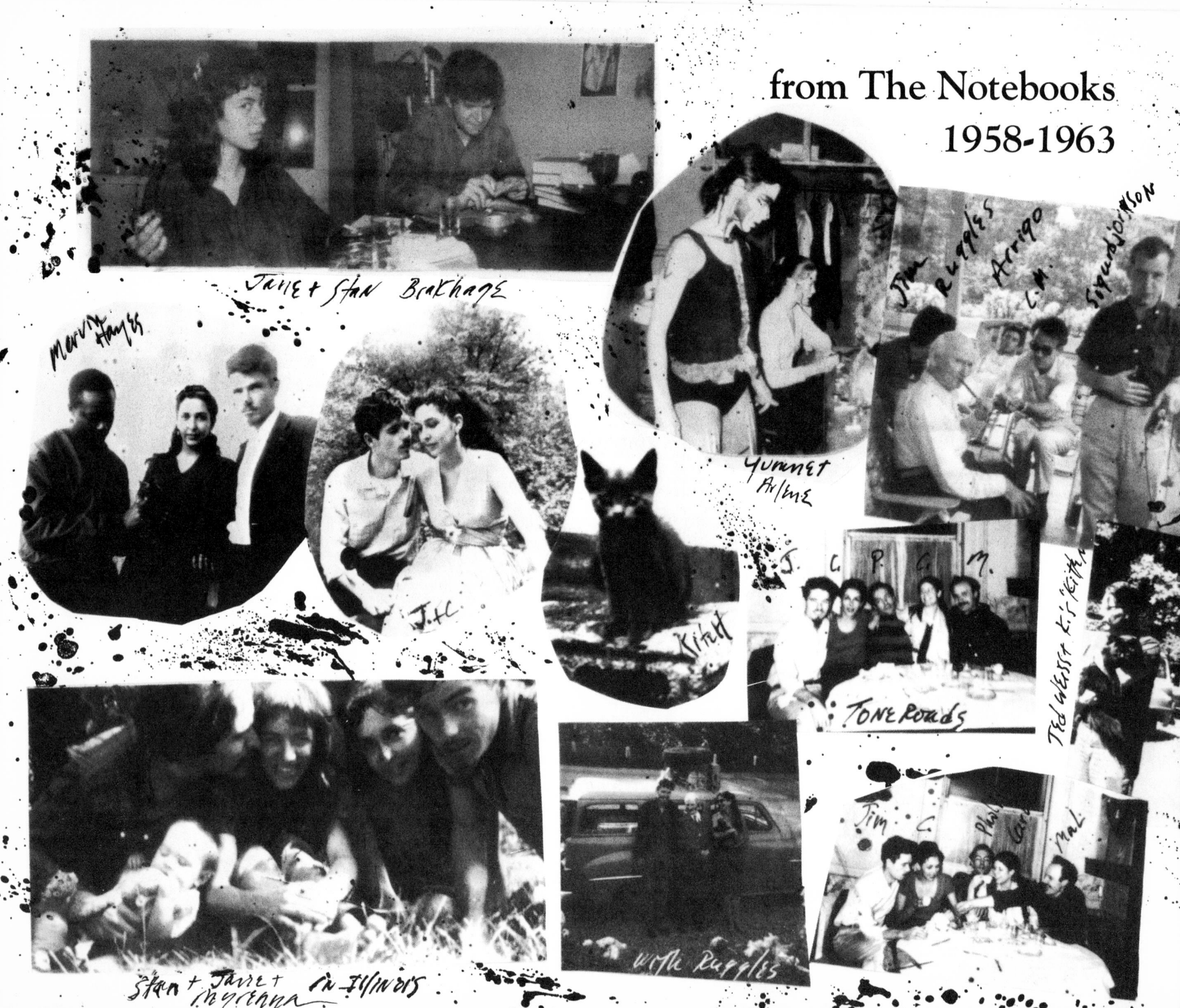

from The Notebooks
1958-1963

Janet + Stan Brakhage

Mervin Hayes

Jim Ruggles Arrigo C.M. Sigurdjonson

Yunnet Arlene

J.H.

Kitty

J C P G M
Ted Weiss t's Keith

Tone Roads

Jim C Phil Carol Mal

with Ruggles

Stan + Janet + Myrenna in Illinois

I assume the senses crave sources of maximum information; that the eye benefits by exercise, stretch, and expansion towards materials of complexity and substance; that conditions which alert the total sensibility—cast it almost in stress—extend insight and response, the basic responsive range of empathetic-kinesthetic vitality.

If a performance work is an extension of the formal-metaphorical activity possible within a painting or construction, the viewers' sorting of responses and interpretation of the forms of performance will still be equilibrated with all their past visual experiences. The various forms of my works—collage, assemblage, concretion—present equal potentialities for sensate involvement.

I have the sense that in learning, our best developments grow from works which initially strike us as "too much"; those which are intriguing, demanding, that lead us to experiences which we feel we cannot encompass, but which simultaneously provoke and encourage our efforts. Such works have the effect of containing more than we can assimilate; they maintain attraction and stimulation for our continuing attention. We persevere with that strange joy and agitation by which we sense unpredictable rewards from our relationship to them. These "rewards" put to question—as they enlarge and enrich—correspondences we have already discovered between what we deeply feel and how our expressive life finds structure.

Anything I perceive is active to my eye. The energy implicit in an area of paint (or cloth, paper, wood, glass...) is defined in terms of the time which it takes for the eye to journey through the implicit motion and direction of this area. The eye follows the building of forms...no matter what materials are used to establish the forms. Such "reading" of a two-dimensional or three-dimensional area implies *duration* and this duration is determined by the force of total visual parameters in action. Instance: the smallest unit variation from stroke to stroke in a painting by Velasquez or Monet; by extension the larger scale of rhythms directing the eye in a painting by Pollock—this which is shaped by a mesh of individualized strokes, streaks, smudges and marks. The tactile activity of paint itself prepares us for the increased dimensionality of collage and construction: the literal dimensionality of paint seen close-on as raised surface...as a geology of lumps, ridges, lines and seams. Ambiguous by-plays of dimension-in-action open our eyes to the metaphorical life of materials themselves. Such ambiguity joins in the free paradox of our pleasure with "traditional subject matter" where we might see "abstract" fields of paint activity before we discover the image of King Phillip II astride his horse (Velasquez)...or a rush of dark arcade concavities from which we learn, by his flying robes, that a saint is in ascension (El Greco).

The fundamental life of any material I use is concretized in that material's gesture: gesticulation, gestation—source of compression (measure of tension and expansion), resistance—developing force of visual action. Manifest in space, any particular gesture

All dates are completion dates.

All works collection of the artist unless otherwise noted.

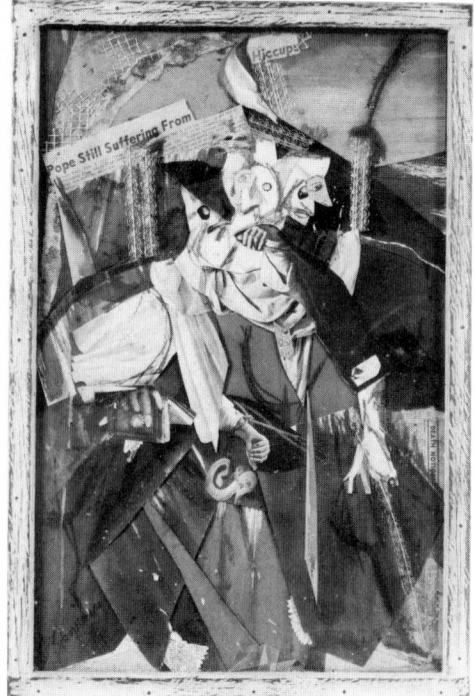

Pope Still Suffering   *1954*
First collage: paper, cloth, paint. 11½" x 17½"

acts on the eye as a unit of time. Performers or glass, fabric, wood. . .all are potent as variable gesture units: color, light and sound will contrast or enforce the quality of a particular gesture's area of action and its emotional texture.

Environments, happenings—concretions—are an extension of my painting-constructions which often have moving (motorized) sections. The essential difference between concretions and painting-constructions involves the materials used and their function as "scale," both physical and psychological. The force of a performance is necessarily more aggressive and immediate in its effect—*it* is projective. The steady exploration and repeated viewing which the eye is required to make with my painting-constructions is reversed in the performance situation where the spectator is overwhelmed with changing recognitions, carried emotionally by a flux of evocative actions and led or held by the specified time sequence which marks the duration of a performance.

In this way the audience is actually, *visually* more *passive* than when confronting a work which requires *projective vision,* i.e., the internalized adaptation to a variable time process by which a "still" work is perceived—the reading from surface to depth, from shape to form, from static to gestural action and from unit gesture to larger over-all structures of rhythms and masses. With paintings, constructions and sculptures the viewers are able to carry out repeated examinations of the work, to select and vary viewing positions (to walk with the eye), to touch surfaces and to freely indulge responses to areas of color and texture at their chosen speed.

During a theater piece the audience may become more active *physically* than when viewing a painting or assemblage; their physical reactions will tend to manifest *actual* scale—relating to motions, mobilities the body does make in a *specific* environment. They may have to act, to do things, to assist some activity, to get out of the way, to dodge or catch falling objects. They enlarge their kinesthetic field of participation; their attention is required by a varied span of actions, some of which may threaten to encroach on the integrity of their positions in space. Before they can "reason" they may find their bodies performing on the basis of immediate visual circumstances: the eye will be receiving information at unpredictable and changing rates of density and duration. At the same time their senses are heightened by the presence of human forms in action and by the temporality of the actions themselves.

My shaping of the action of visual elements is centered on their parametric capacities in space. In performance the structural functions of light, for instance, take form by its multiple alterations as color—diffuse, centralized, (spot and spill) mixture, intensity, duration in time, thresholds of visible/invisible. The movements of performers are explored through gesture, position and grouping in space (density, mass), color and their own physical proportion.

The body itself is considered as potential units of movement: face, fingers, hands, toes, feet, arms, legs—the entire articulating range of the overall form and its parts.

The performers' voices are instruments of articulation: noises, sounds, singing, crying, commentary on or against their movements may be spoken; word-sound formations are carried forth which relate to, grow from the effect on the vocal cords of a particular physical effort they experience. The voice expresses pressures of the total musculature so that we may discover unique sounds possible only during specific physical actions and which provide an implicit extension and intensification of the actions themselves.

The distribution of the performers in space evolves the phrasing of a time sequence: levels of horizontal, vertical and diagonal or the need for larger rhythms carried visually by an independent figure which moves in relationship to the overall environment— shifting dimensions, layers, levels. Every element contributes to the image. The active qualities of any one element (body, light, sound, paper, cloth, glass) find its necessary relation to all other elements and through conjunction and juxtaposition the kinetic energy is released.

My exploration of an image-in-movement means only that its realization supercedes (or coincides with) my evocation of it. This is *not* a predictable, predetermined process: in the pressure to externalize a particular sensation or quality of form other circumstances or "attributes" may be discovered which are so clear and exact that the function of the original impulse is understood as touchstone and guide to the unexpected. "Chance" becomes one aspect of a process in which I come to recognize a necessity—the way to unpredictable, incalculable advances within my own conscious intent.

1962-63

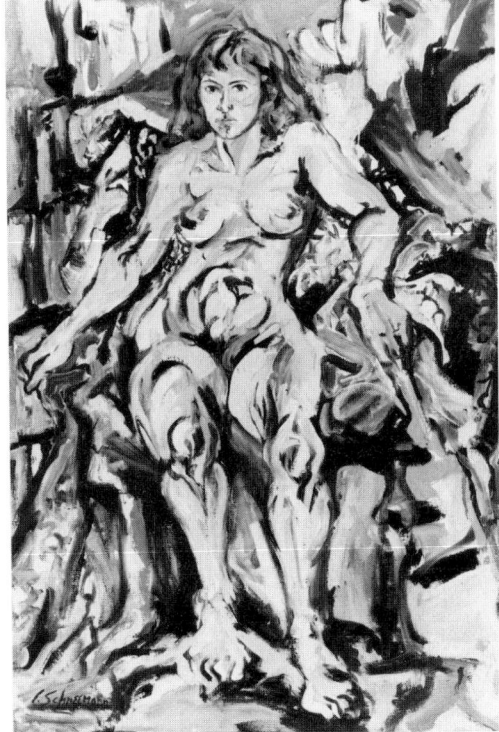

Portrait of Jane Brakhage   1958
Oil on canvas 46½" x 31½"

From a letter to Jim, written in a Museum.

My love I found two lovers: dancing stone each other. (A guard laughed to another; "there's a young lady copying a new way to do it in an old way".) I was drawing. Drawing on an embrace of forms: rolling, halting gestures of combination, of meeting. Complete, secretively convoluted, clearly tenuous: that something is happening, has happened and occurs again...uniquely, samely extending the mystery it conceals. An embrace emphatically conceived and lucidly sexual. What evolution of forms performs before the senses, repeats and then counters motion so that the figures hold all possible in stone space. I can find us, hear our hours of love, years enfolded,...(Shakti and Shiva, Bengal, Pala period)

Elsewhere: extensive compilations of gloom; shadowed light shafting art objects, frou-frou dying eternally—a provincial museum...rank leftovers, agglutinations...bad breath, heavy appetites. The Arensberg Collection is not enough to save Grace by—the Impressionist Collection is, but it has been shipped off to the Modern. (My little sun and shadow, a tiny watercolor study by Picasso for Les Demmoiselles which flies out of Cézanne's clear-eyed bathers.)

Ah, a Pontormo of a de Medici—strange, strange a door opens behind the looming, robed torso, a compelling head. Three fine frescos (a tiny Pieta of glowing strokes...made of glass) and the Titian where the seated Archinto peers through a curtain.

19 March 1958 Philadelphia

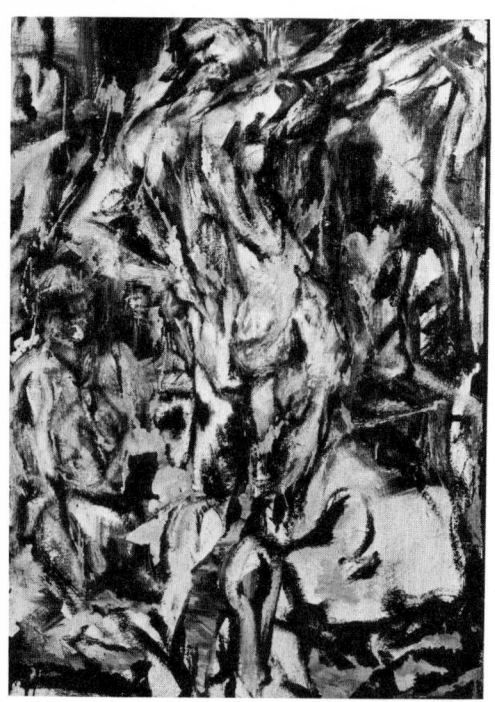

From Pontormo Drawing 'Nude Male Figures'
1957
Oil on canvas (incised layers) 32" x 45½"

When I was fifteen, a teacher with a surface regard for my temperment advised me to study the Expressionists...Kokoschka in particular. My eyes moved to Cézanne; the rigor of the action of paint in space was nowhere more demanding than in his works—my longing for the richness (engulfing all preconceived notions about what was an expressive image) and extensiveness of natural forms took courage and challenge from his experience. At this time D'Arcy Thompson's writing enforced my intuition to really build sight on natural forms and conditions. From childhood—without any break—I felt myself a part of nature; saw the world as animate, expressive, alive and sometimes responsive to my own desires; but always the natural world was intoxicating, giving my senses information which freed emotions for personal relationships which might one day have the rich wheeling of unpredictable qualities. My sense of my own physical life and of making things within the life were always united. I began to draw before I could speak and never stopped drawing.

1963

Earliest Drawings. Learning, all learning—the curve of the buttock as moon pushed to cloud. Learning remembering as the image opens worlds concrete, sensuous. There is no manipulating. I have been needing to retain, regain a beginning; the unwilled sight of sense, palpable being—an emergence of my own world forms free in the space of their expressive determination, of their desire to give light.

Drawings done when my first room maintained the clarity of its borders, of boundaries. Such drawings showed dramatic happenings! Before I had language I regained the changes of the first room with pencils and crayons on thick leafy tablets. The dramas developed in sequence: on the first page two vertical lines foretold a stage, cutting the paper plane into curtains. The second page: the two vertical lines were placed further apart; painfully in anticipation of subsequent revelations! By the fifth page a banana-like formation appeared beyond the boundary of opened curtain—a hand! The hand would fitfully grow on rapidly turned pages to find its body. The central dramatic action began. The pencil lines found the body a personality, knew its character. From the line of "stage right" another figure would develop and *the intensity of these presences grew over the pages in proportion to "their" desperation to manifest my expression.* The desperation drew on its recognition of illusory self; that a banana hand was not, could not become the alley arm from which it hung, nor the "I'll huff and I'll puff and I'll blow the house down" teeth which gnashed in a pencil lead head. One figure could attack another in space; in a fury of excitement the elements claimed space (through another twenty pages) and the sequence accelerated with an enormous mouth—a wavering moist sun, a toilet bowl, a cup of milk—until the lines pulled from left and right again vertical through four pages flipped over and over, to be drawn to a close.

Form is Emotion. The materials I use in a painting-construction or a concretion evade their usual utilitarian context; deflecting, reflecting, expanding relationships—these materials become ambiguous as prehensile tools. I work towards metaphors of sensation; a dramatization of loss and recovery, of movement in time and space. I want to find my work endlessly renewable, vitalizing the present but no longer the lineage, linkage between desires sought and fears captured.

My concretions provide for an intensification of all faculties simultaneously—apprehensions are called forth in wild juxtaposition. My eye creates, searches out expressive form in the materials I choose; such form corresponds to a visual-kinesthetic dimensionality; a visceral necessity drawn by the senses to the finger of eye . . . a mobile, tactile event into which the eye leads the body; a picture plane as dimensional as dream is, or landscape. Perspective is the over-all immediacy in which each area partakes of every parameter open to it. Horizontals, verticals, pressure, tortion, pulse and color move to sustain an image as a habitation.

The body is in the eye; sensations received visually take hold in the total organism. Perception moves the total personality to excitation.

Insight is a result of sensation's creative action on our capacity to experience and discover functional connections.

(We are a part of nature and of all visible and invisible forms.)

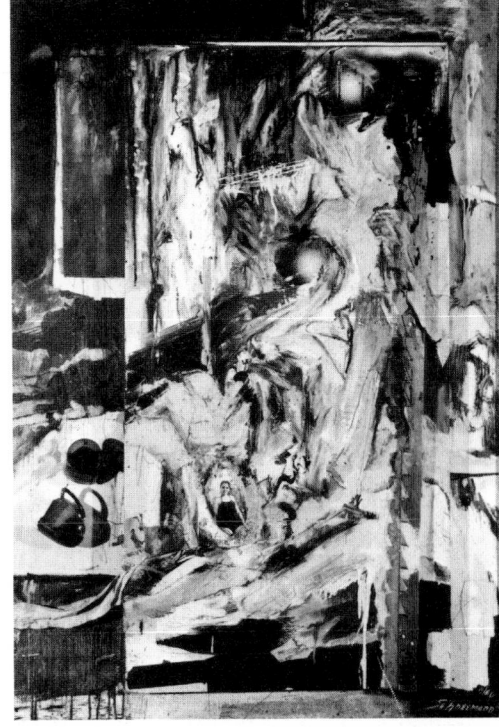

Quarry Transposed (Central Park in The Dark)
1960
Construction: masonite panels, wood strips, photo of N.L., red glass pitcher, nails, wire, paper, oil paint. 57" x 34¾" x 4"

Movement of the immediate present: "the human mind is only an executive organ of investigating, living plasma feeling out its environment"...W. Reich. *Organomic Functionalism, p. 291.*

1960-1962

That the friendship of men, boys is involved with masteries; the friendships of girls, women with mysteries. Substance for women of what you are: their alert curiosity for one another is personal. Men meet over what they do, the friendship itself balanced competitively: what will provide substance of friendship and who shall dominate, direct its passage. The figure of Hermes, dream-slowed motion eternally running, sprinting forward, movement of arms and legs bridging to future time. In the phase of friendship his hands carry scrolls, machines, messages. But with my women it is a confrontation — very direct and immediate of time present on which we then bring to bear movements of time past, future, spun from our experience. (Also a turtle slow, blinking image for a man, plodding, even will-lessly but ineluctably Forward. And the men care about what one another do while the women have a proportion more toward "Who are you" and "how are you that.")

This smidgen from conversations between J. and myself, about our friends, the friendships. That I become infatuated with women, they interest me to a degree that men do not. The men tending to bear bludgeons in private, close conversations, the staking of territories with this forward time sense I mention. The women share an arcana, a flesh sympathy and appreciation often; sharing our work within the world and the unique efforts we make there as material shared between us. The women themselves as material. Also — women relax together, while sexual excitation is a basic and alert measure between men and women.

1962

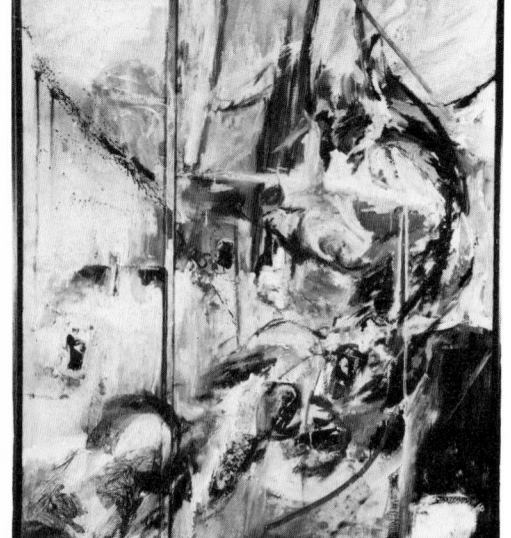

Tenebration (to J.T.)   *1961*
Oil on canvas: paper, wood strips, cloth, photos of Landowska, Brahms, Beethoven.

I don't work with "chance methods" because "method" does not assume evidence of the senses; chance is a depth run on intent, and I keep it open, "formless." "Chance method" is a contrary process for my needs and a semantic contradiction which carries seeds of its own exhaustion in its hand clasp of chance-to-method. Method as orderly procedure, way to classification, arrangement — like a bag into which gestalten insight allows chance to pour: what might happen, possibility, unpredictable agent, unknown forces...so corralled, netted, become a closing in. Depth run of it—"chance," is way of necessity to surface and tentacled riches are not captured by method.

Process with material/image leads exploratively, spontaneously. Change, recognition and insistence with discoveries *is* field of action. Visual-kinesthetic sources are not abstract-theoretical conceptions for my process. In bearing. Slug and release—fling it out and pull in the nets: expect to be surprised.

(Notes on the day Lolita Le Brun was sentenced.) January 1962

ABOUT CLAES OLDENBURG'S *STORE*

And one night did they say how they would like a big yellow cake to eat; and in the morning did she say "I don't know what to wear, I wish I had a ruffled blouse green gold and blue-black." So did he then envision to merchandise wishes, to pioneer an emporium of material banalities, fantastic from the pressure of actualities—not available—and of dreams exceeding the reality of existing objects. Yes! he did.

And the storehouse of mind play had absorbed life stores. The substance of necessity to be plaster and paint; to be tactile, sensuous, palpable with roaring color glosses. So began an enterprise which would startle, shake awake a world of objects transformed in shape, texture, taste and aroma.

Slapping, patting, kneading, twisting, chopping gave dough and cloth, flesh and metal, sugar and leather spontaneous, surprised cast. Cakes and pies, brides and flags, shoes and socks, suits and blouses astounded themselves emerging from an ordeal by paint. All grew larger than that precedence in worldly life which named them and by which we recalled them.

The tribal unit united amidst these relics which delighted their eyes.

If we had stretched out full length in Rauschenberg's "Bed," we found none of Oldenburg's clothes were anybody's size; each cup-cake and lamb-chop doubled bite-size its generic sister. We performed the wonders of body following eye's journey from minute slippery steps over enamel cleavings into brittle growth by which we felt the great brown jacket fall onto our shoulders.

If we went to the Store hungry, we left it belly full. If we were threadbare when we entered we departed skinned with glowing stockings, unmatched shoes, helmets and bathing suits. In our pockets transpositions of happy rectangles elicited candy bars, combs,

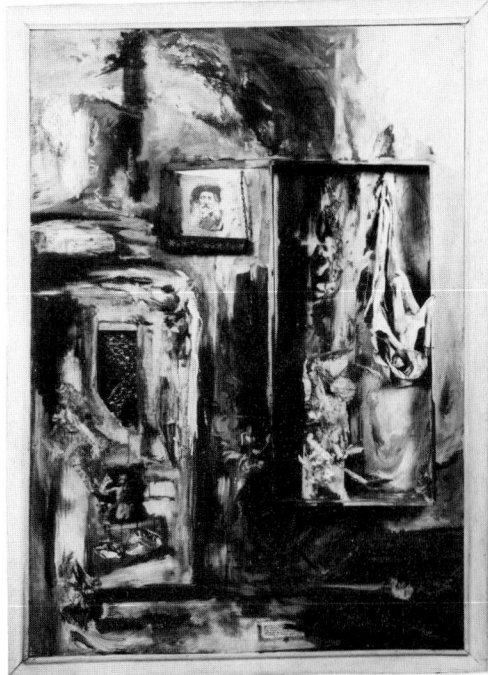

Sir Henry (Sir Henry Taylor 1800-1886) 1961
Construction: masonite panels, plaster sculpture, underpants, swing, glass, photo of Sir Henry Taylor by Julia Margaret Cameron, photos of nudes, glass, oil paint. 54½" x 39" x 6½"

prizes. What we needed we found.

(After: real cakes amazed us with their obtuse doughiness, their pallid colors which could never refract light, their soft compliance to be eaten up.)

Then did she say, "what do we wish to see next?" And he said "something more ancient, more private."

(Ambiguous and simultaneously persistent, insistent on their immediate nature. These objects state that we change; stretch and contract our own shape and size in appreciation of them.
—Can you say "brown suit"? NO say BROWN SUIT
EYE journey: Oldenburg—flat footed sensuousness. Direct, visceral; always enlarging upon and evading the intellectual structure which marks base, strata, for departures kinesthetic, psychological and painterly.

March 1961

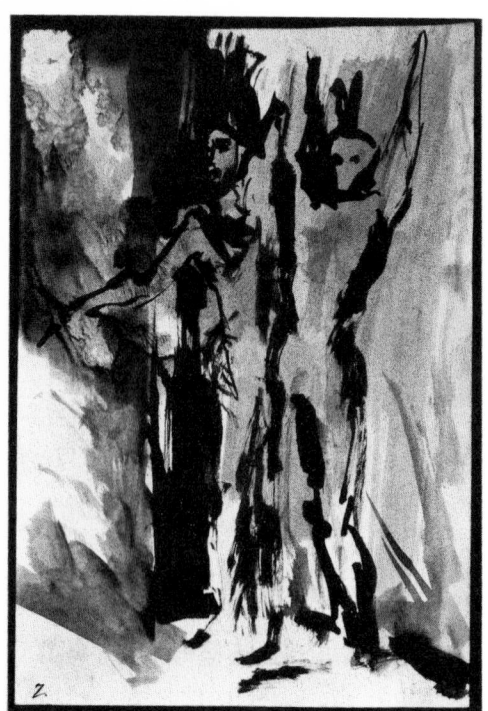

Partitions   1962
Ink & tempera. (Unperformed, for cubicles in a gallery space). 10" x 7"

Vertical table legs pound into horizontal tops; supporting planes, stable leverage—or search out their pressure on the floor—definition of ground and grounding always a beginning again, against. How a strip of wood plays recession and a plane-of-advance to its adjacent surface, being active with minute variations...light, marks, smudge, streak. The body moves through eyes recall, claim and disposition of its own measure (journey) in space.

GESTURE IS BOTH IMPLICIT AND EXPLICIT ACTION: STRUCTURAL FORM AND ACTUAL ACTIVITY.
Gesture is the envelope of unity; contains the impulse uniting various parts of an object or scene; assumes the dominant rhythmic forces. Gesture is three-dimensional in quality; it is neuro-muscular: remembrance and recognition are linked to basic kinesthetic identification. Gesture is in the spine; it is intangible and cannot be grasped without feeling it. First we feel the gesture of an object, then we may describe it.

Physiology of the Dancers
With the dancers I find two channels of movement occur:
1. a naturalistic attitude of the body in actual space.
2. involvement from *within* the body as projective space.
Gesture speech (theory of Sir Richard Paget) that the muscles of tongue and throat adopt a

position in conformity with the muscles with which an act is performed.
Instance: gripping, reaching, pulling, and mouth simultaneously grips, reaches, pulls. Then vocal response to body action—choral commentary; the implicit sound gesture and the conscious vocal release on physical act/gesture; here tension of performance and response (evaluation and perhaps psychological frontage..."what do you think of what you've just done"...so the dancers are free to rejoice, complain, protest, assert!)

I want the dancers to reach for extremes. The material I present requires breakthroughs in intensity, in emotive location...strong feeling for concentration on new movement... or familiar movement performed as if it were uniquely present for them. This demands resources of available psychic energy which may never have been called for before in their dancing.

Their bodies are capable of feats; in so far as possible they are—as a group—inquisitive, adventurous. Grounded in their implacable and moving traditions they scent clearly the forms which they must search to break clear of past traditions. It is not enough to see this necessity; only a few are held by an emotion desperate and strong enough to carry them through. Their own needs are in process; my visions of movement often upset them—they cry "impossible" just as a traditional cellist does when instructions call the bow to the bridge! I have to be able to perform all I ask of them.

Some of the dancers are armored vocally or facially; there may be particular body movements which are psychologically difficult for them to enact, but they are prepared to provide for such circumstances, while facial movements or vocal sounds can present areas of severe expressive dislocation. In *Chromolodeon* for the ending sequence of chicken cluster rehearsals were, in the beginning, set around ten minutes screaming together. I would begin and one by one those who were able would join in until the throat was open, flexible and the ears did not rebel at "chuckchuck, skreiiicckkh, chipppppchieepp, EIIIIIIIchummm, chuck chuck chuck turptruphtruph"....

1963

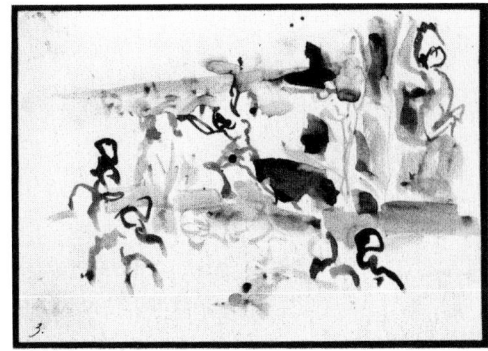

Partitions   1962
Ink & watercolor. 7" x 10"

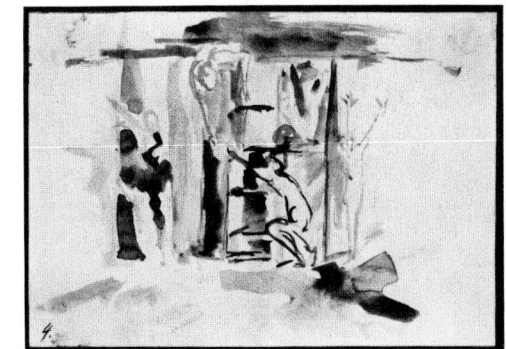

Partitions   1962
Ink & water color. 7" x 10"

WHAT IS A DANCER   a dancer has dirty feet, a dancer has poor little tight pants—ankles and feet are sticking out; a tight little top—wrists and hands and neck sticking out. Reaching for (new) heaven, pounding the floor...sweat beads across the forehead, a cheek muscle twitching.

A dancer bends, ass covered taut in stretch nylon; neatly folded balls and prick, sculptural breast mounds, pussy humps. They used to be encased in black...then pink, white... rainbow dyes until their second skins became stenciled, decorated like wallpaper with toes, fingers and head escaping flesh shards.

Expressionless faces—the body was their expression. Feet remained bare, bottom blackened.
Their eyes reached into space without touching it. They were alone. The distance between "art" and life. Space was anchored in their bodies, space was where they felt their spines. They didn't realize a radiator behind them equaled their mass, asserted verticals against their legs.

I want a dance where a body moves as part of its environment; where the dancer says Yes to environment incorporating or says No transforming it....where that choice is visual as a dancer is Visual Element moving in actual real specific dimensions. I want a dance where dancers can fall, can crash into a wall; aim movement beyond their line of spine INTO space, into materials, into each other—projective, connective! A dance where dancers can fart, can start and stop, are aware of the impulse, the necessity by which they move and its implicit diminution or contrary flow. A dance where dancers can leave the performance...and return...or not return.

1963

I say "I use materials" but I often sense that they use me as vision from which they re-emerge in a visual world which could not speak without them. At the same time in the art world today people often say "I'm only interested in what is *useless.*" The Fro-Zen, the expanse of slight sensation, the twist to existing conventions: not to be shocked, disturbed, startled, not to exercise the senses thoroughly...to be left as you were found, undisturbed, confirmed in all expectations. Not what is "useful" but what moves me.

1963

HORMONES CIRCLING

Something happens. I cannot foretell! THE HEAT WELLED UP over all thought, tided into substance—no consciousness beyond the interchange of body heat and

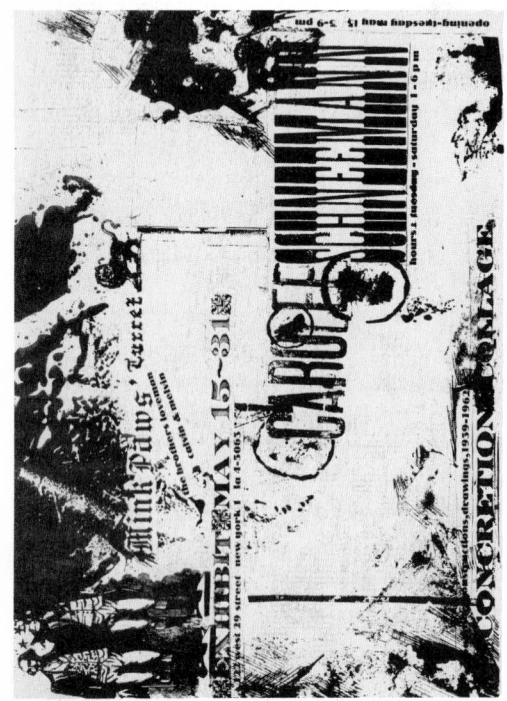

"Mink Paws' Turret"   *1962*
Flyer for first retrospective (1939-1962), NYC.
Printed paper.

atmospheric heat. (Who dies without leaving sign of a last fleet thought . . . a mark of feeling until the instant could no longer recognize body's sound; the high leaping of brain passing over body's protest and complaint.)

So in my sleep an image offers itself from sensation and is accepted for narrative journey shorn of source (his leg heavy over my own: an image of . . . bureau drawers; the sheet twisted beneath my foot: skyward flash, light incorporating a pair of dancers pulling a wagon past the place where I dress in burnt paper scraps.

Flesh shake a hand to thought: blood radiant,
bedeviling, churned by passage, changing chemistries,
traveling mysteriously to touch into the "past," to
light a light darkened over that child's bed . . . to reset
the bird (firmly) on the window sill.

DIRECTOR! WHO IS IN CHARGE?

. . . . here come estrogen, adrenalin . . . . . "evinced by such easily measurable factors as changes in temperature, in basal metabolism and blood sedimentation rate" . . . . . progesterone, pituitary, thyroid . . . . . again look! headed to CALCIUM and a shot of peristriate in the corners! RELEASE. Shade flapping stubbornly . . . no, there is no wind, oppressive, hushed . . . a storm slow in coming . . . or the GRAPE ARBOR, or the texture of the wicker bassinette—(that desolate place).

Wheel turning. (Possibility of total recall.) Reviving various sensory and motor experiences. "In the mental (brain) processes that go on between some stimulus and some response, we may arouse an image or memory of an earlier stimulus or experience."

Subject to Recall

The past informs itself freely: building is harkening. I rest against a total mosaic of experience and below, beyond the six points of recognition.

Glandular function stimulated by para-sympathetic at one time, by sympathetic at other times. When I write the sympathetic dominates: central tension high, streaming from periphery to center, "away from the world, back into the self": wrote Reich.

Or,

Epstein's study of epilepsy: that particular brain tissue which receives impression of terror may be altered by the reception of the experience; normal neural tissue may be altered by reception of painful experience and provide for later appearance of such an experience as "repetitive mental product."

Hormones circling endlessly—for "Love of God"! (Olaboga) Try and catch 'em . . . that is keep up to 'em. Tyrannies begin in the flesh. As they say: "No wonder!", meaning: "ALL WONDER"!

July 1963

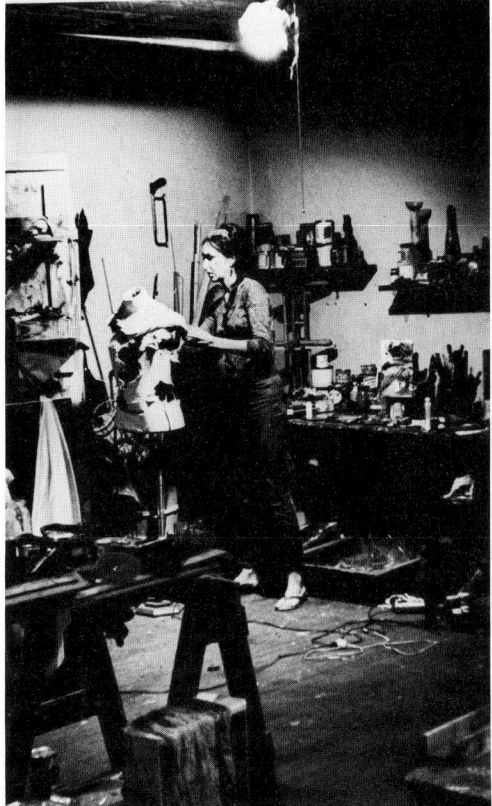

Leo Chaplin

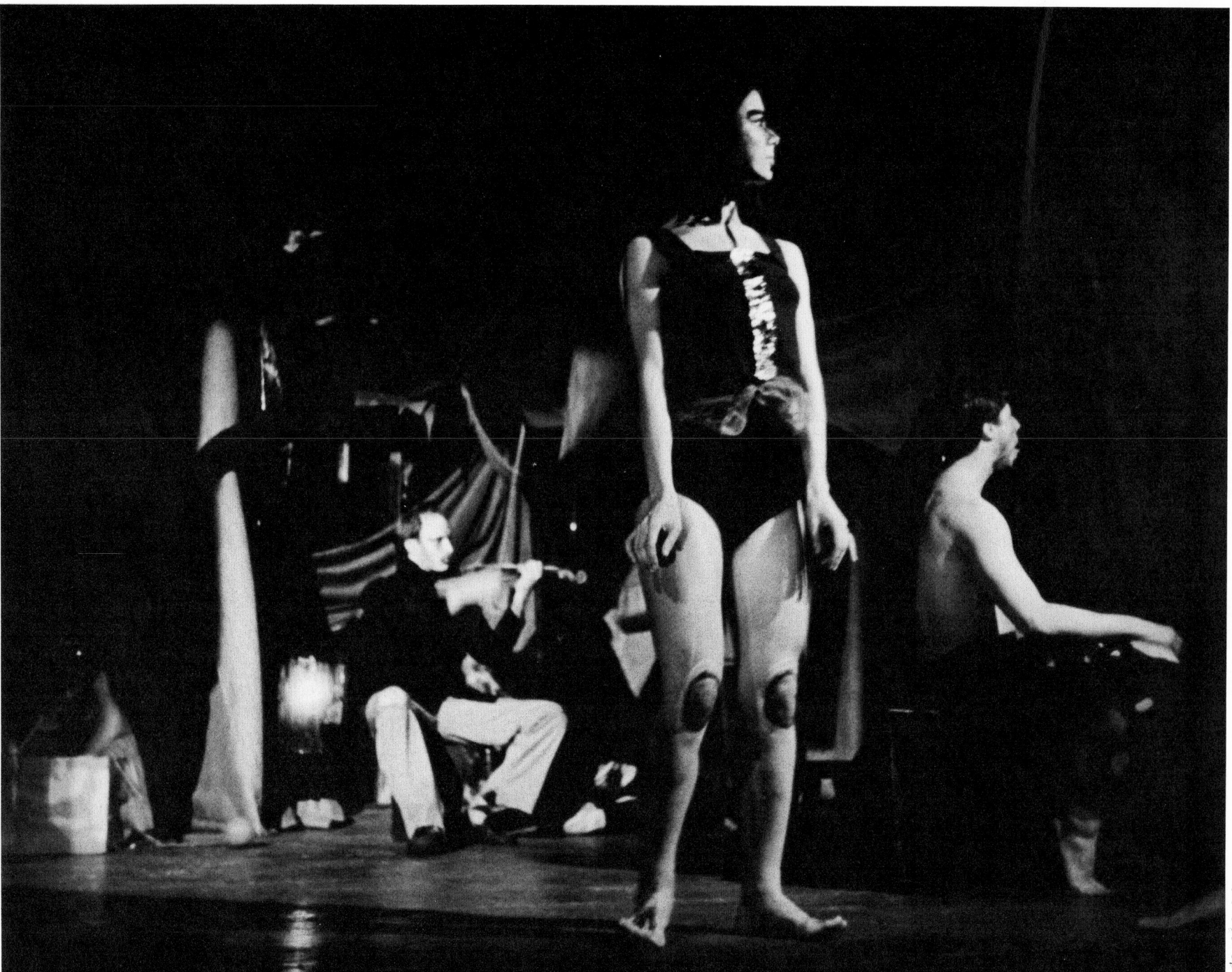

An evening of performance at The Living Theater was organized by Philip Corner and Dick Higgins. Philip invited me to take part, to explore movement, sound and visual conjunctions. My concept was that the environment would determine, and at the same time transform and integrate any action or gesture of performers and audience: an enlarged "collage," to break up solid forms, frames, fixed conventions or comprehensible planes, the procenium stage and the separation of audience and performer.

I collaged the stage with broken glass: mirror glass, safety glass, fused lumps of glass drilled and hung in clusters in varying planes across the stage. Shards and clusters of glass, some shrouded, some visible, were set so performers would produce sounds by striking against them as they moved. Large broken mirrors were positioned to reflect and refract portions of the performers' bodies.

My instructions were intended to allow everyone to find and develop personal motivations by immediate contact with materials and each other. Philip collaborated on the sound "score," extending his "Soft Materials" sound piece, which also occurred between the other events on stage, into the anteroom during intermission. Malcolm was a free agent, moving from stage to audience and back, playing a violin. I worked three high-powered flashlights both from the stage and the audience area, bouncing light through the performers' motions into the mirrors and into the eyes of the audience—drawing with light.

GLASS ENVIRONMENT FOR SOUND AND MOTION

May 1 2 1962 Living Theater NY

SCORE

Props
hammers to smash the wired glass, to sound on glass   nails—to be hammered in across the stage, to be scattered   a long bench   electric fan   baby carriage   large pink plastic ball   a long pole with silver strips   gourds   bells   violin   trombone   large cardboard box   a chair   high intensity flashlights

Sounds and Motions
All movements have the potential of creating sounds with the glass environment. Improvisations develop by attention to one another in which exchanges, duplications, initiations of actions are experienced as interrelated and mutually informing.

Performers write out lists of possible actions, spatial positions, interactions, work with props and forays into the audience. Props and objects as well as actions and positions are switched and exchanged—repetition, variation.

Durations of improvisation in "Soft Materials" and "Display" are controlled by the overhead stage lights (worked by Billy Linick). Actions are arrested when the lights go off. Each black out functions as a scene change, though a performer might simply shift from one leg to another. The changes are as discrete or extreme as each performer decides they should be. Billy scores the stage lights to go on and off in rotating sequences. No one group of lights will be on for more than three minutes; black outs do not exceed thirty seconds.

Basic Movements, Characteristic Sounds
Notes to performers conceived for the particularities and contrasts between types; each seen as vivid, distinctive.

Judy: small, round, compact, unself-conscious, innocence and efficiency of temperment. Graceful, calm.
Arlene: pressure outwards, controlled wildness, poignant energy—to be "pleasing", vulnerable, a radiance.
Yvonne: pressure inwards, strength, intensity; not to be "pleasing"; concentration, a severity, explosive.
Judy, Arlene, Yvonne; a slow shuffling walk—bend forward, fall onto hands, walk on hands, fall onto floor. Rest, rise up on hands, straighten back, slow shuffle walk, bend forward, fall onto hands, etc. . . .

Soft Materials
Judy seated on bench. Yvonne enters with shuffle walk, flaps arms, makes the sound "umbah, umbah, UMBAH." Judy, spinning, reaching, touching out, sits down (hums). Repeat. Arlene contracting and expanding as she rolls into a ball and flings arms and legs wide, exclaiming. Yvonne standing still turns head, bending, exhaling; vocalize muscular tensions. Andre, prolonged, sustained efforts: push-ups, a repeated phrase on trombone from a fixed position, extending tongue at a mirror. Exclamations. Arlene rolling on her back slowly, back and forth from behind the drapery. Philip on his back; holding trombone, slides slowly forwards; breathes, coughs into trombone. Malcolm from stage to audience, through the aisles, walks on empty seats playing violin. **Black out.** Judy takes Malcolm's violin, plays it ineptly while spinning in wide arcs. These arcs impinge on Andre doing push-ups; he rolls into Arlene, they embrace and roll across the stage into drapery and

Costumes (light shadow reflection)
Judy (clown ballerina): red rose cheeks, enlarge eyes, whiting on face.
Arlene (shadows): blacken neck so head "floats"; sew dots of silver foil on black leotards—specks of light; black dots on cheeks.
Yvonne (seismograph): stripes of black grease paint down middle of face, arms, sides of bare legs; strips of silver foil around torso, down back.
Andre (satyr): black leotard pants, bare chest.
Philip, Malcolm (wandering musicians): normal clothes, black shirts or white; blacken eyes, cheeks.

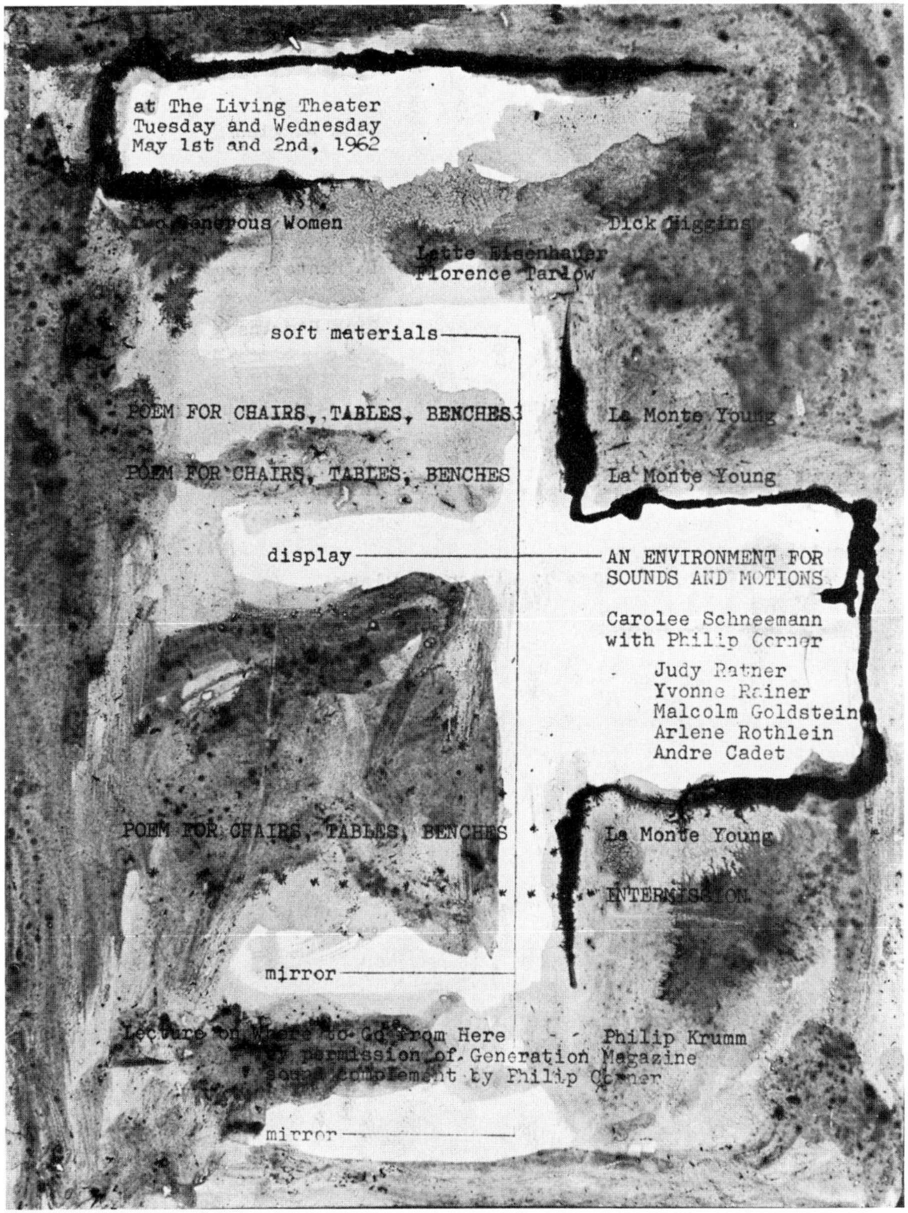

at The Living Theater
Tuesday and Wednesday
May 1st and 2nd, 1962

Two Dangerous Women   Dick Higgins
        Lette Eisenhauer
        Florence Tarlow

soft materials

POEM FOR CHAIRS, TABLES, BENCHES3   La Monte Young

POEM FOR CHAIRS, TABLES, BENCHES   La Monte Young

display   AN ENVIRONMENT FOR
                                       SOUNDS AND MOTIONS

                                       Carolee Schneemann
                                       with Philip Corner

                                         Judy Ratner
                                         Yvonne Rainer
                                         Malcolm Goldstein
                                         Arlene Rothlein
                                         Andre Cadet

POEM FOR CHAIRS, TABLES, BENCHES   La Monte Young

                                       INTERMISSION

mirror

Lecture on What We Can From Here   Philip Krumm
   by permission of Generation Magazine
   Sound complement by Philip Corner

mirror

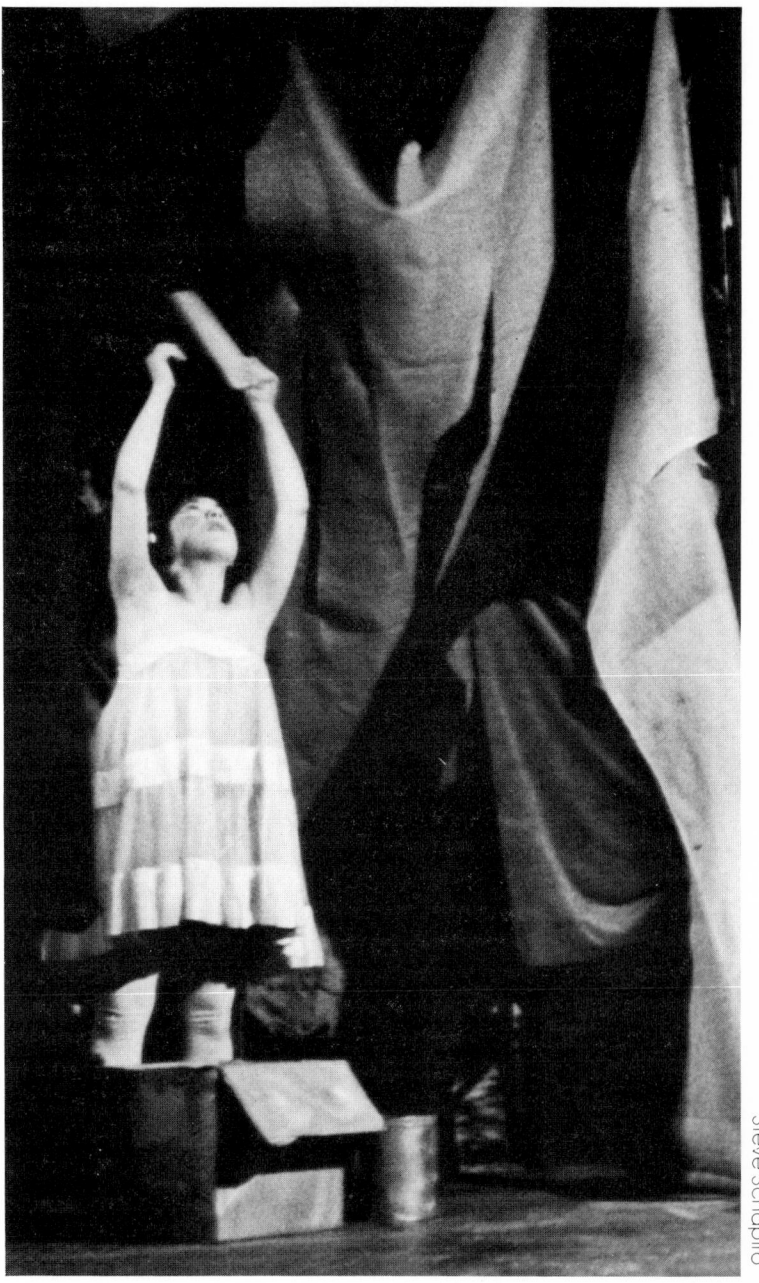

Steve Schapiro

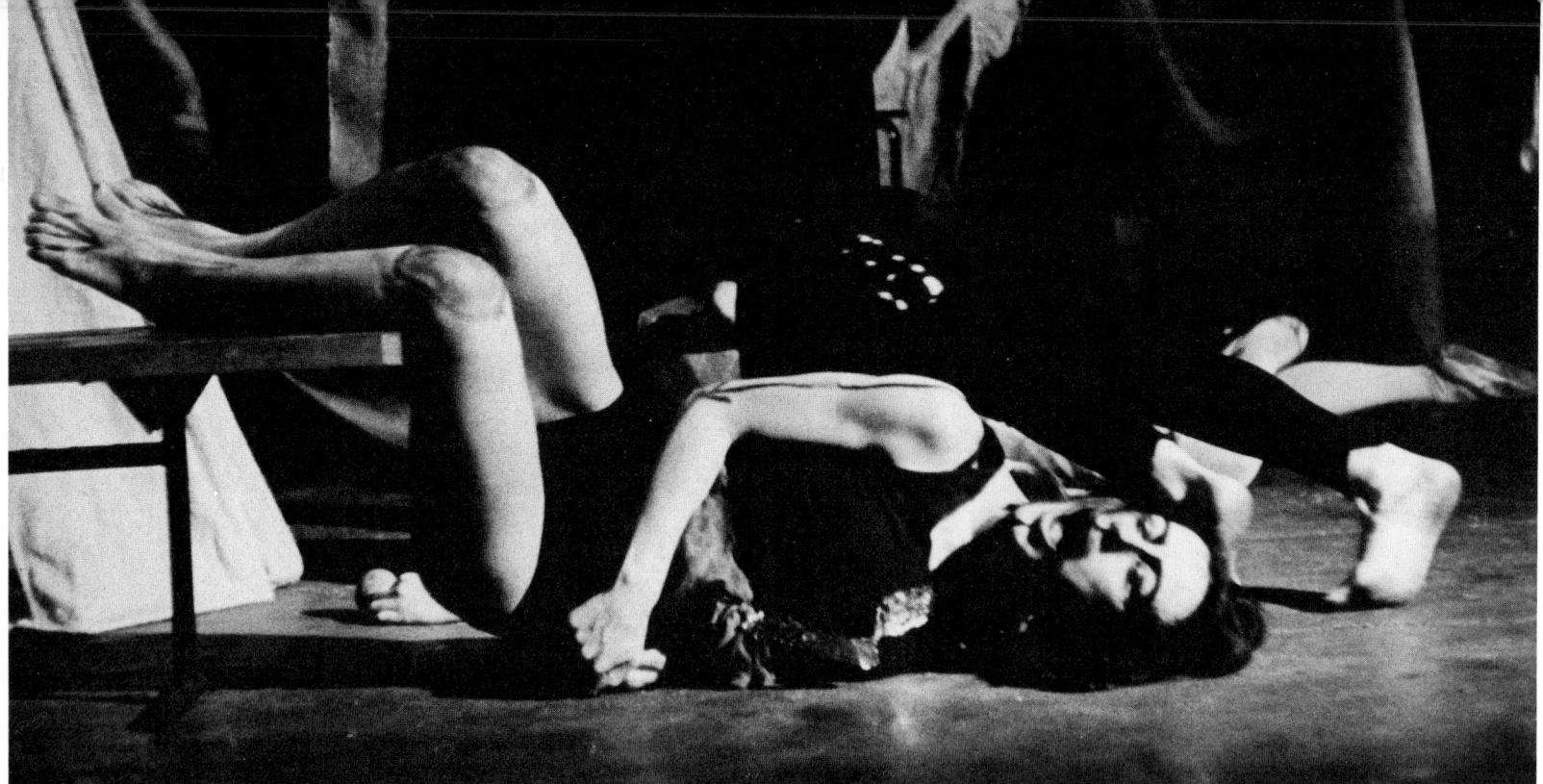

back out. Andre takes trombone from Philip, plays it directing notes to bits of hanging glass as if to bounce the notes, sets off resonance; Malcolm responds to the timbre of clinking glass and trombone with staccato strokes on the violin. Yvonne throws out her arms, swings torso, bleats. **Black out.**

Display

Everyone walks around asking "what's next?" Arlene goes and sits among the audience. Judy puts her head in the cupboard box and beats her fists on it. Yvonne lies on the floor, extending arms and legs, shrieks. Arlene rolls the silver pole over her. **Black out.** Nails are hammered in across the stage; gradually

one person replaces another completing the task. When the last nail is hammered in place everyone becomes still. Malcolm walks on the empty seats among the audience, plays one sustained note on the violin as long as possible. Philip on stage facing away from the audience, into a mirror, whispers long sustained hiss into the trombone. **Black out.**

Mirror (I)

Judy wheels Arlene back and forth in the baby carriage, doing movements of expansion, contraction on her knees. Judy's legs are wrapped in foil; as she spins the foil falls off tangling around her feet, she continues spinning. **Black out.**

Philip stands in the foil striking the hanging glass with the violin bow. Arlene dumps over the baby carriage. Judy spins back and forth carrying an electric fan, hitting against the glass. **Black out.**

Mirror (II)

The movements are slow, prolonged. The only source of light is from the flashlights which I work from the audience area. In rhythmic sweeps and arcs, and fast on-off bursts, fragments of bodies are spot lighted, still or in motion. The light strikes mirrors at different levels within the stage, blinding the audience; performers' gestures and reflections of the audience are momentarily arrested in the beam.

BANANA HANDS

Original score 1962
Revised score 1969
Performed March 23 1970 New Milton
Drama Center   The Castle,
Winchester, England

A creation of the world/of the senses: water, fire, mud, snow, wind. For twelve performers with extensive props: ape suits, barrels, masks, draperies, fans, hoses, ropes, a trapeze. Sound score calling for "Roll Out the Barrel," circus music, rock 'n roll, train noises, screams, dialogue.

An obsession in the form of drawings, notations, moving imagery during my first two years in New York; it was never performed. At the time of its conception **Banana Hands** must have been too much for me to produce. In 1970 the second, edited version (1969) was presented by a children's theater group in London.

Re-reading the original script I see elements of a personal iconography, including childhood fantasies, which would appear in **Chromelodeon, Meat Joy, The Queen's Dog, Cooking with Apes,** and to some extent **Water Light/Water Needle.** Lormay Boo and Pete Jo were the names I devised at about age four for the female and male genitals. They appeared in the guise of invisible human friends for whom I made tea parties. The derivation of the name "Lormay Boo" is from the French children's song I later understood to be "Frère Jacques, Frère Jacques...dormez-vous"

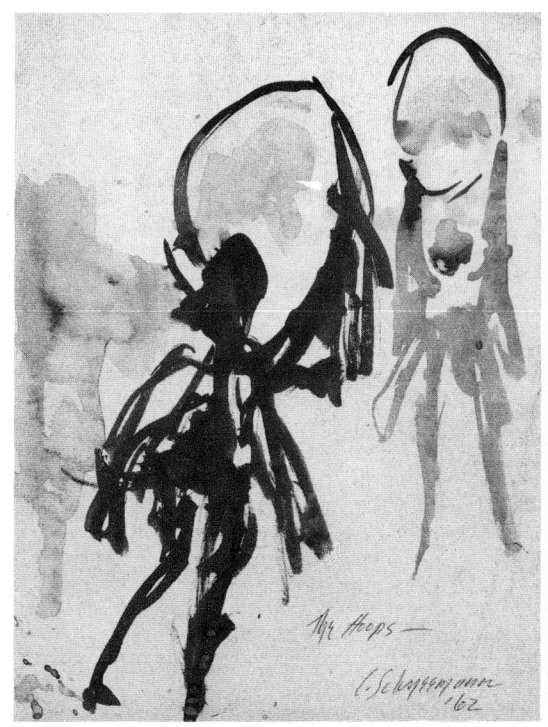
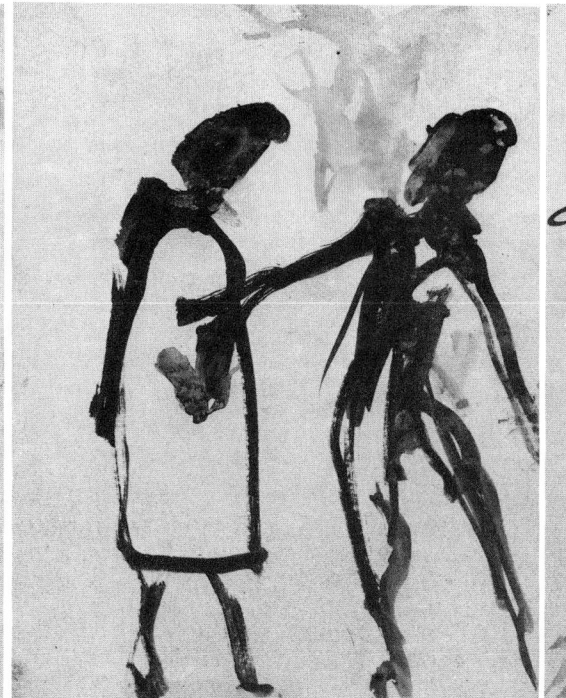
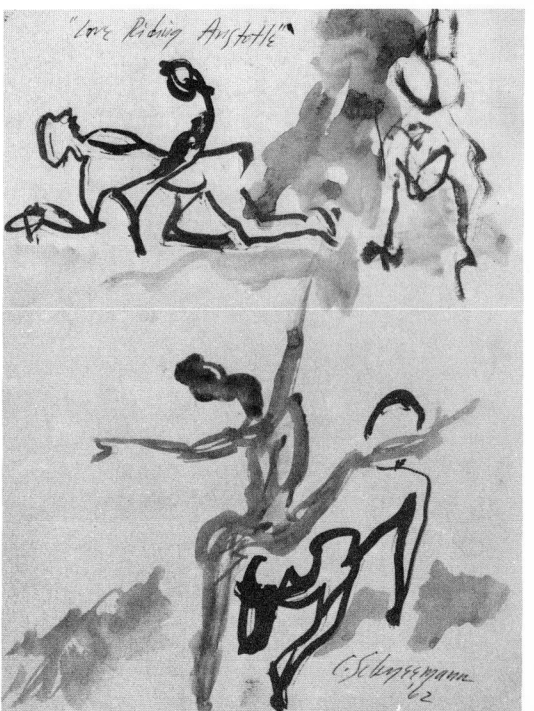

Score (1962)

dedicated to Valda Setterfield and David Gordon

I. Divisions and Rubble

PRELUDE:
Who is that swinging a starry sky: Michael of Central Park. Mary in storm shadows arranging pebbles. Black...blue-black. Flicker lights begin—stars stabby. A spot—white light—searches out Michael. He stands trapeze stanced, self-absorbed within a sea of confetti stars. He peels a banana. All else in darkness.

He eats the banana...so slowly. The light finds him: flame feathered fur, a Urangatang of an Ape. Mary the same.

The painful music
Rolling barrels: The Red and Blue Fat Men...rolling barrels at random. Music: "Roll Out the Barrel"
The Painted Girls run after, at random, conflicting directions, cover space hungrily, distractedly.
Banana peels thrown through the air. Plenitude of garbage or flower peels.
Lights dim on peels falling every which where?

Glimmer of white: The Sheet Which Falls.
The Painted Girls inundated: choreographic struggle of bodies under sheeting—lights plays convolutions. Rocks. Landscapes.

The snowfall falls. The fat men are crawling in and out of barrels. Love rides Aristotle through the audience.
Simultaneously: Red Light.

Screen of Cloths, Screams of Cloths: ripping, tearing—improvisation out of sight.
Sorrow to fabrics.
Wind: The Painted Girls are blown about. Sound of rain into white noise: ear shatter.
Lormayboo runs through blowing screens of cloth...sound increases. Cries from audience: "Cut it out! OK, OK, quit it!"

Black out—ominous
suspend time of space

ENTRANCE:
The 19th minute. Circus Twist Music.
Michael and Mary by trapeze determine their actions: what to play.
Turning lights—kaleidoscopic and full strength. (A headache.)
The large entrance formation: stoic thighs. Crevasse Hoar as door all jump through from behind where are raised stairs.
High music: Applause.
Jumping as they can, tossing balls, banana peels: Lormayboo and Petejo, Love and Aristotle, Two Fat Men, The Painted Girls... tumbling, falls, steps of forgotten dances. A clumsy bunch.

Love and Aristotle drag on the small false stage. Lormayboo and Petejo fall (are pushed) into it. All others freeze.
Lights out.

The waltzing couple, treading on audience hands & feet; five times in and out of audience until they are "shot" by people in the audience holding play pistols. At the same time the girl on the Zebra is crying "gallop, trot, faster, jump jump": Zebra performs all this while remaining in one spot. Song: "Pencil, Pencil, Pennsylvania". Dervish girl wrapping and unwrapping herself in whirls across stage in grand american flag: "Stars and Stripes Forever" comes in over football song.

BANANA HANDS:
Lights up: slowly pulsing green-gold. Silence. Growing electronic sound. Apes and others watch the false stage. (It is necessary to have a stage to destroy it!)
Lights
the closed curtain
lights out
lights on
the curtain opened one inch
lights out
lights on
the curtain opened three inches

lights out
lights on
the curtain opened six inches
lights out…repeated eleven times or until the parted curtains reveal:

s.l.: a banana hand—   s.r.: glimmer of
  propulsive, static.   paper knife
            Thus emerging Lormayboo and Petejo.

II. **The Power of Indulgences**

Petejo and Lormayboo in their stage. Draperies blow, flashes of white light bleach image, cast shadows played. (A Haiku, a delirium…solemn, slow creation of sexual attributes).
  Sound: Illinois Hog Market Report and trains coupling.
  Love rides Aristotle through the audience.
Lormayboo raises yellow banana hand, collage-face forward: the face has never been written on. Petejo presumes inscriptions. True and false innocence. He extends green banana hand holding circle breast and carefully pins it to her dress; faces forward, smooths his moustache. Breast, belly, fur. Slowly. Now they turn, formal motions.
  The fat men are rolling their barrels through the audience;
  they crawl frantically in and out of them, they switch barrels.
Petejo and Lormayboo shifting hands-dance—one to the other. Whisperings. Spots circle them. Sound of cat howls rises over Hog-Train sounds. Petejo raises the cardboard knife. Lormayboo's arms rise in butterfly shape. She turns away, he follows behind the hollow stage…THE PURSUIT: through the audience, where they will, random and sustained.
  Lights out.

  Flickering spots over Michael and Mary, beneath their swing
  they ape a drama of desire: very fast in flicker lights.
Petejo chases Lormayboo into false stage…collapsing. Lights out.
  Michael and Mary.
Petejo stabs Lormayboo with luxurious, grandiose gestures. Love and Aristotle, the Two Fat Men, stand by to squirt her with red paint. She dies. She awakes—a fit of giggles. Petejo and Lormayboo

and the Fat Men begin a wrestling match as the lights dim. Love and Aristotle and The Painted Girls grab the small stage, drag it away kicking at the wrestlers who lie where they fall.

PICNIC:
Love and Aristotle lay a cloth around the fallen wrestlers; the Painted Girls carry on picnic baskets and generously pile bananas, herrings, sausages, tin cans, etc. on the cloth. Slides projected above the picnic area of Illinois horizons. Sound of Hog Market Report and trains coupling. Lormayboo and Petejo, Michael and Mary, Love and Aristotle, The Painted Girls, and the Fat Men eat. They eat quickly and slowly, they pass things and grab things as they talk continuously.

The sheet falls over them.
They continue eating under the sheet.

Lights out.

January-December 1962

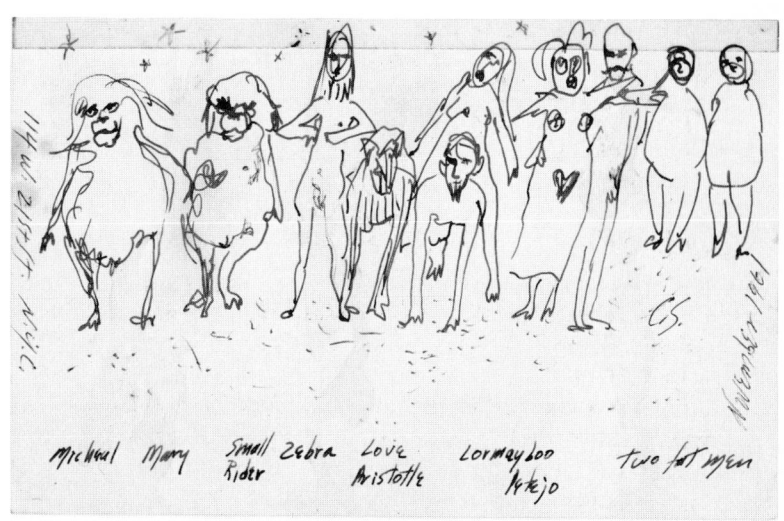

Michael Mary   Small Zebra Love   Lormayboo   two fat men
                 Rider   Aristotle Petejo

BANANA HANDS!

A Pudding Mix and Media Event for Some English Children

London 1969

(adults admitted only by o.k. from a child)

Unsolicited comments have come to our attention from people who have Not Even Seen **Banana Hands: evil and foul, peww (fwhew)**

"Banana Hands!" is rated "worse than X, we will try for Y or Z."

"It is obscene."

From a jockey in Kent: "Bloody awful, bloody outrage!"

From a brewer in Camden Town: "The bloody thing had no beginning, middle or end, far as I could see."

From a mother in Highgate: "If I had any idea of such goings on I would never have let Charlie come all the way down the hill."

"A disgrace to British parents which they cannot afford to miss." **Evening Star.**

From a performer, 11 years old, "My participation in **Banana Hands!** was the most creepy thing ever happened to me, **EVER!**"

What is a "de-rehearsal?" That's how you learn to perform in **Banana Hands!**

"Schneemann is a monster of unquenchable perversity: the authorities should never let her near children." A father, Kensington.

"Jolly good show." **Sunday Times.**

"Sure, I like a bit of good clean fun...but what was the meaning of all that flying about in the air?" Petticoat Lane, Butcher.

Michael and Mary, the Apes
Four Fat People
Lormayboo and Petejo—our hero and heroine (in reverse order).
Crawling Feathers—eight or ten of 'em.

(Parts are inter-changeable on demand: continuity will be sacrificed to emotion.)

"I can't understand what drove normal young people to behave like that"; a mother.

"Mind you, actually I was more excited than when the Luftwafte fell on our roof."

From a gravel crusher in Bushy Park: "Bloody cheek muckin' about so."

"Mind you, I wouldn't want them put away." A ticket taker, Circle Line.

"Bleeding awful"—Northumberland gate keeper.

From an Oxford Don: "I rather felt it's rather bizarre fetchingness brightened a rather melancholy stretch you know..."

This is the way my mind is working this morning anyway... how is yours going? But first of all we must agree to have a director; when the whistle is blown, everything stops.
When we feel most enchanted we will be correct.
Each participant will have a chance to do what they are best in; then they will do what they are worst in...
(You guys (chaps) are really nuts (batty)).
Running, saying: Oh no   Oh yes
        Leave Me Alone   Leave Me Alone
        Leave Me Alone
        I won't   I won't   I won't

Elements will include: earth, sky, stars, water, fire, bananas, rope, barrels.

"Makes Democracy safe for us." **The Guardian.**

"I believe in realizing realizable potential...perhaps that is what they are aiming at." Public School Mistress, Mayfair.

"These kids won't be dropouts—they can't get any lower." **Daily Sketch.**

"Dreadful little cannibals, I'd say." Jellied eels vendor, Piccadilly.

"Rubbish!" "Rhubarb!" **Daily Mirror.**

Two phonographs will be available during the play and will be used one at a time or simultaneously. Records should include: "Roll Out the Barrel," "Playmate Slide Down My Cellar Door," "Why Don't We Do It in the Road," "Hey Buffalo Bill" (also known as "Hey, Bungalow Bill"), "All Things Bright and Beautiful."

A Tape-recorder for a tape of animals feeding at the zoo would be good.

If possible the children will learn to make their own slides and will organize the moments of their projection.

Props: 4 Burlap sacks
       many pounds of newspaper
       2 rope swings
       2 whistles
       1 large pink blanket
       1 paper dagger
       2 wooden barrels
       a lot of feathers
       several dozen bananas
       ketchup
       hamburgers and buns
Costumes: feathers, masks, funny old clothes, 2 small ape suits, 1 white dress, a black suit, 1 moustache (or a few?), a paper yellow wig.

Prelude: Wonderful music. The stage is dark, the curtains are open. Twinkling little lights begin. Michael and Mary, two Apes on their swings against a starry sky. They swing gently and make gentle ape sounds. Below them we see a big lumpy pink blanket spread out. All the children are hidden under this blanket which almost imperceptibly begins to lift as the children take hands, slowly rising, circling. As the blanketed circle shifts we see they have been covering a big pile of bananas. One arm reaches out of the blanket, grabs several bananas and hands them up to Michael and Mary. They chew contentedly, laconically. The blanket shifts about in performance area, quivering a bit. The stars go out. In the dark the curtains close. The music stops.

Children with flashlights appear in front of the audience; they shine these lights onto the closed curtains which begin to part slowly, slowly, slowly. Inch by inch, the curtains part, nothing is seen; terrible suspense. (Suspense music? noises very low in the throats of the lighters?)

In the flashlight beams we suddenly see on each side of the curtains a pointed shape!

The curtains continue to inch open and we can identify a dagger peeking from behind one curtain, a finger peeking from the other. Bit by bit we see the arms, then the bodies of Lormayboo and Petejo. She is dressed in a big, white dress; he is in a black suit. Their faces are papier mâché masks: his is sinister, with a droopy black moustache; hers is innocent with huge eyes. For hair she has a fall of yellow paper curls.

The stars come back on. Michael and Mary on their swings watching.

Petejo begins a slow motion pursuit of Lormayboo around the stage. It is like a dream. As they move, four children (who have left the flashlight group) come onto the center of the stage dragging two huge sacks. They signal to children in aisles for a change of music and for slides to begin. From the sacks they dump out two other sacks and

Hampshire

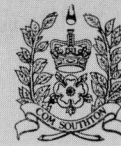

R. M. MARSH, M.A.,
County Education Officer.

THE CASTLE, WINCHESTER. Tel.: 4411.

Please quote: CM/ACT/JS   Your ref.:   Telephone enquiries to: Mr. James   Ext.: 469

Dear Miss Schleeman,   3rd April 1970

Sorry you were not able to get to the production of "Banana Hands" at the New Milton Drama Centre on the 23rd March. It was an interesting performance which took about three quarters of an hour. The audience were seated in squares and rectangles, with the action taking place amongst them and between them, rather as the attached plan. The performers were the junior section of the local Youth Theatre Workshop. That is to say young people of about 12 and 13 years of age.

The proceedings were somewhat as follows:-

The cast rushed in and busied themselves talking individually to members of the audience, asking where they had come from and why they were here etc. The producer then called them to their places to start the play. This they refused to do, giving various criticisms of the play. After some argument an amicable settlement was made. The cast were to do anything they thought they were best at and then they would do the play. They proceeded to do what they were best at. A member of the cast nearest to me mixed and baked a cake, out of the corner of my eye I saw a conjurer and out of the other eye an explosives expert. That being completed the producer called them to order. Again they refused, giving more criticisms of the play. Again a settlement was made, this time they were to do what they were worst at and <u>then</u> they would do the play. They proceeded to do what they were worst at, mine was a ballet dancer. I was so involved in holding her up that I could not see what else was going on.

At the end of that there was another argument, the cast still refusing to do the play. They agreed to take a vote amongst the audience. The audience voted to see the play. A metal framework was uncovered showing two monkeys hanging around. The others got under a sheet and hands emerged throwing bananas at the monkeys. From then onwards things went more or less as indicated in your script. The ultimate crime was throwing rubber bananas to the monkeys. There was some confusion about the sentence but I believe the guilty party was thrown to the monkeys.

My two favourite moments came from the young people stuffed with paper. One went along my row planting real daffodils between our feet. A second followed watering the daffodils. A third followed picking the daffodils. This led to argument and argument led to fight. One tore paper out of another and there was a terrible scream. Amidst terrible cries of hatred and agony the two tore each other to pieces.

What was not accomplished in the time available for rehearsal was the mixed media aspect of the work and there were no slides, films, placards etc. Purely the work of the cast and some music specially composed (if composed is the word) for the occasion.

A cheque for £2. 12s. 6d. is enclosed, as agreed with Mr. Shields.

Miss C. Schleeman,   Yours sincerely,
17a, Belsize Park,
LONDON, N.W.3.

All communications should be addressed to the County Education Officer.

County Adviser for Speech
and Drama.

mounds of crumpled paper. (Banana mound and paper mound). They dress each other in the sacks which have holes for their feet to stick through, and frantically stuff the sack-clothes with the papers. In this way, they become the Fat People. Being so stuffed they can do wonderful movements. They explore the possibilities of pushing each other over, falling, bouncing, rolling, shoving; finally falling off the stage (if it is not too high!). They may continue to roll, bounce, carry one another about in the aisles.

During de-rehearsals we will study the way spontaneous communication, messages, information, cries and calls can work with the physical actions.

Lormayboo and Petejo reappear gliding slowly; perhaps they have switched roles with two others; in which case they have a different quality indeed. The Feathers have been released among the audience. They wear bands of straggly feathers tied on their heads and hands: they crawl slowly through the audience tickling their legs.

Petjo catches Lormayboo in a slow embrace; she never struggles! He holds her away from him and stabs her gently with the paper knife. She sinks to the floor. Does she make any exclamation at all? Michael and Mary, having observed the proceeding, jump from their swings, scurry over and pour ketchup on her, making excellent ape noises.

The Feathers run in and out carrying paper plates full of hamburgers and buns. Michael and Mary have spread the pink blanket and placed Lormayboo on it. She may give them directions as they do this: "Don't knock my hair off... you're hurting my ankle, smooth out my skirt," &c. The Players settle down in a circle around "the body" for a picnic and discussion. Slides of animals eating in the zoo.

They must decide if a murder has been committed. "We must fit the punishment to the crime!" Yes. First you must have a crime! The nature of the crime will be explored. Who is guilty? Of what? Is Petejo a killer? Is Lormayboo a provoker? Why don't they switch roles?

Lormayboo and Petejo stand up and exchange masks.

They sit down and join in the discussion. Perhaps the crime is that one of the Fat People pushed another too hard, or stepped on a Feather accidentally. Is the play real? Or playing in it?

At any rate they agree to find someone guilty of some offense or crime and they plan a punishment. The punishment must be agreeable to the one to be punished. In de-rehearsals they will explore various possibilities from which they now select one on the basis of its imagery or drama.

By this time there may be a lot of grabbing and pulling. The Fat People will surely be about to lose their stuffing, the Feathers, their feathers. There may be a lot of screeching.

The Fat People will leave off to go and roll in their barrels. "Roll Out the Barrel" is put on the phonograph. They will end up rolling barrels through the aisles as "the punishment" is brought to its conclusion.

The audience will be given the bananas to eat.

Jolly good show   rhubarb   there's only one England   G.B.H.
fairy soap it was

NEWSPAPER EVENT

January 29 1963 Judson Dance
    Theater NY

Spine (Arlene Rothlein)
Legs/Face (Ruth Emerson)
Shoulders/Arms (Deborah Hay)
Neck/Feet (Yvonne Rainer)
Hands (Carol Summers)
Head (Elaine Summers)
Fingers (John Worden)
Free Agent/Crawling (C.S.)

for eight performers
a few benches, stools or small chairs
a pile of newspaper stacked at least
    four feet high

Not long after the Living Theater collaboration Yvonne and Arlene invited me to join a group of dancers who were meeting to explore new ideas and processes which had originated for several of them in the workshops of Bob Dunn. Jimmy Waring offered the use of his studio on Second Avenue, and various people assembled to share experiments and work together. Valda Setterfield, David Gordon, Elaine Summers and her husband Carol Summers (a painter), Deborah Hay, John Wordon (an actor) and Lucinda Childs were among the people I remember in our first sessions. (And soon after, Barbara Lloyd, Trisha Brown, Steve Paxton, Fred Herko, Ruth Emerson and Judith Dunn).

I was too self-conscious and unpracticed to perform publicly but participated in the workshop experiments and felt no restraint as a painter who had in effect enlarged her canvas, to prepare movement events based on the physical qualities of the others present. I was intrigued by the particularities of the performers in the group; I thought of them as a sort of physical "pallette". They inspired the Body-Parts of **Newspaper Event.**

Movement, exercise, physical work, dancing were always a part of my visual sense of things; I needed to feel my body as active, responsive much as the eye was. I was a devoted square dancer when we lived in Vermont; and I discovered in high school that I saw better before I painted or drew if I warmed up to music—(usually Bach). When my early Kinetic Theater works were first reviewed in the press and I was described as a dancer, I was annoyed, believing that the visual density of the works was the logical outgrowth of a painter's sensibility—and this was obviously different from that of a dancer's.

After a few months in the Waring studio Yvonne and Steve Paxton arranged a concert at the Judson Church; the workshop now met in the gym at Judson, a much enlarged group assembled. By the end of our first six months based at Judson other visual artists joined us from time to time: Robert Huot, Chuck Ross, Bob Morris, Robert Rauschenberg.

Newspaper Event was an experiment I presented to the group while we were still in the Waring studio. It built on improvisational and physical contact ideas begun in the **Environment for Sounds and Motion.** Aside from the visual emphasis, the crucial deviation from existing performance investigations had to do with introducing risk, uncertainty—reliance on reactions and inter-relations which could be immediate, impulsive and sensitive. The dancers had been developing randomizing processes, chance methods, and natural movement, where each person tended to realize instructions or tasks as an independent, self-reliant unit/entity. I wanted touch, contact, tactile materials, shocks—boundaries of self and group to be meshed and mutually evolving. **Newspaper Event** was a first attempt to provide specific instructions through which contact and improvisation could activate neglected thresholds of awareness. Individuals would create their own activity and its momentum, while responding to and incorporating the "intrusions" and unexpected conjunctions with others. Any particularized area of focus could be absorbed directly into a collective unity. There was no underlying basis of abstract structure or rule, no pre-determined movement patterns. Unpredictability permitted the audience to respond exactly **as and when** we were responding.

I was thinking of an organism interchanging its parts (phagocyte). I noted five principles: 1) the primary experience is the body as your own environment. 2) the body within the actual, particular environment. 3) the materials of that environment—soft, responsive, tactile, active, maleable (paper...paper). 4) the active environment of one another. 5) the visual structure of the bodies and materials defining space.

The specified part or parts of the body indicate a source of concentration from which all other movements would arise; the source of emphasis, of internal focus and projective insistence, was to determine all functions or actions in relation and contrast to the overall movements of the body. Phrasing, duration, repetition, the "scale" of gesture, would all be improvised within the centralized and overlapping movements generated by the instructions. The ruminative, meditative attitude evoked in working concertedly, in making something with the hands seemed a basic sensory value rarely explored publicly. The activity of each performer with the materials of the environment was undertaken in personal terms of invention, concentration. Resistence or lack of interest was a personal option as well, to be discovered then and there.

SCORE

The overall shape is circular, centralized. Lights focused only into the performing area with no spill by the audience. The profusion of newspapers is sculptural—a varied ground on which/with which the bodies are active. The audience is seated in a curve on the floor. The back wall facing the audience must be considered visually in relation to the performers and newspapers. It could have objects, signs, words on it. The performance should not take place in a room of textured, strong colored materials; it should not be performed on a procenium stage. It could be performed outdoors in the grass, or in the snow.

Entrance
The seven performers carry cartons of newspapers. The Free Agent carries on the benches, small chairs or stools; these are placed toward the rear and center of the performing area (triangular apportionment). The seven performers unfold and throw newspaper cascades in the central area, fast as possile. Thickest amount of paper in the center, then outward toward the edges in a circular sweep. Cartons are thrown off to a side. (Every portion of the floor they will use must be covered with papers).

INSTRUCTIONS

1. SPINE. You need to disappear in a horizontal effect. You strive for this physical illusion: 1. by contrast—from vertical, assertive stances to horizontal positions, limp to rigid. 2. by willfulness— flatten yourself under newspapers; find someone who will roll over you; stretch out over others, becoming as flattened as possible. When you speak it is clear and spontaneous.

2. LEGS-FACE. Your effort is to become horizontal in space. a) propulsion b) suspension c) the impossibility of it. All you can muster for a struggle against gravity. Chairs, benches to be used as you will. You may attempt to elevate yourself by climbing on someone and balancing across their back and shoulders. Punctuate your physical efforts with facial expressions which comment on your actions. Do not ignore the illusory possibilities of your effort.

3. SHOULDERS-ARMS. You have a refrain to use in any way: "I'll huff and I'll puff" or "huff and puff." Use this as an extension by breath or voice of actual energy exerted. (Quiet motion, quiet "huff & puff", etc.) Walk around, crawl a bit... follow someone...you feel lonely ("huff & puff"). If you see someone trying to fly assist them. You can be helpful. Sometimes you feel like running a little. You could stand on your hands. You are a link in space between various performers; find and be aware of the

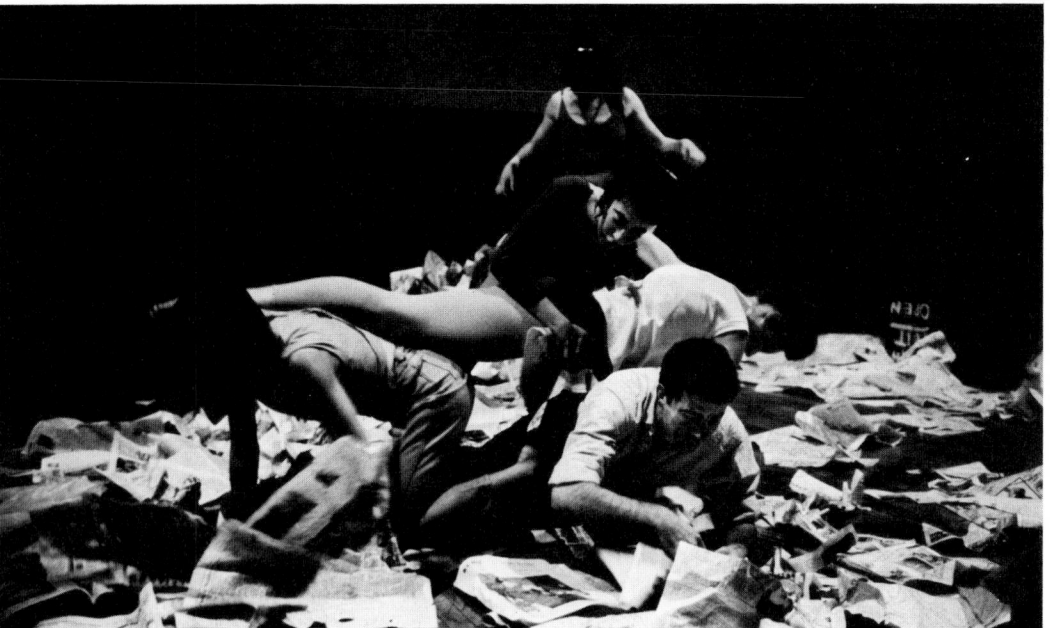

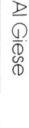

Al Giese

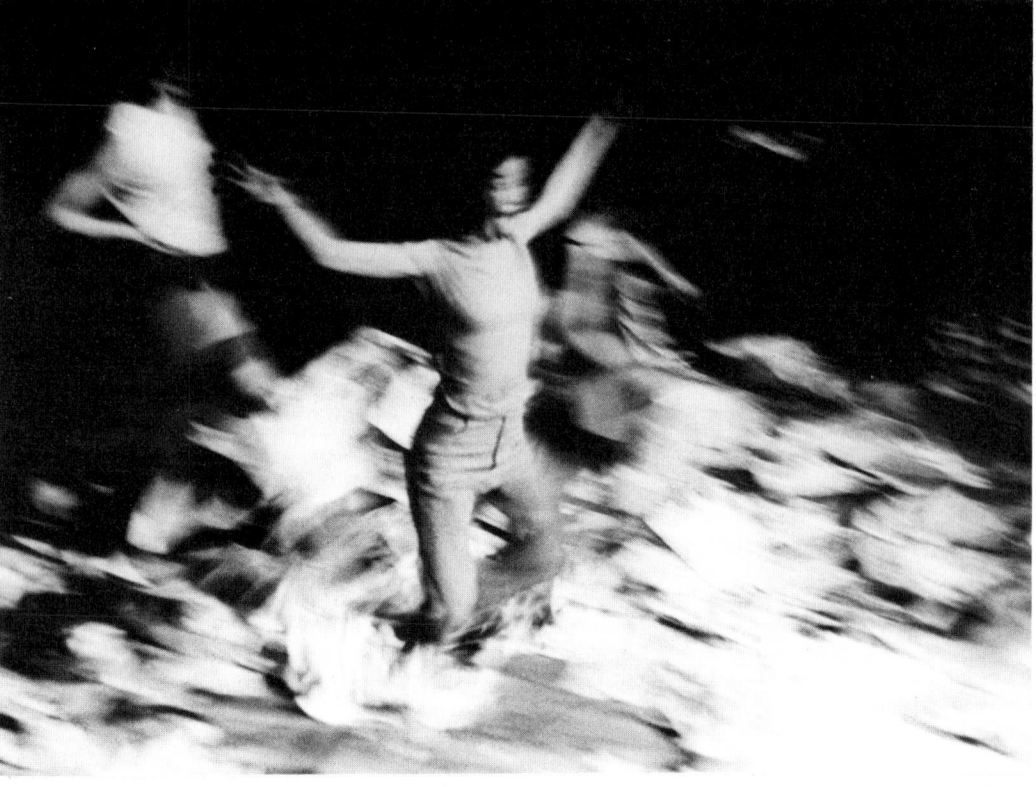

Al Giese

34

tension between self-absorption and your alignment/juxtaposition with others. Work towards extremes in variation of gesture coming from shoulders and arms, (sometimes very intense, outward in impulse—almost grotesque).

4. NECK-FEET. Push newspapers around until you've made a shape to stand on (pinnacle, ludicrous proportions). Become as small as you can be—then as large. A monster in fact. ENGULF someone...something. Lie down to rest. Then repeat the above. Energy compression is your focus and how you release gesture in space, the spacing between your actions; concentrate on specific area of generation...neck and feet, where you are.

5. HANDS. Make yourself a little something to wear from the newspapers. Move about until the object is completed. Wear it. Roll across the floor until you encounter an obstacle. Stop. Make something else to wear. Roll across the floor...stop...when you've made an article you can hold it up and say "that's beautiful." Hands and Head should interrelate their dressing, crawling, rolling.

6. HEAD. Same instructions as for HANDS: make clothing, wear it, roll. But your refrain when an article is completed is, "I need breakfast" or "I need some breakfast." Concentrate on your head as movement source—all its variations, as

counterpoint to your hands.

7. FINGERS. This day has been endless. You can be good to yourself; you should be indulgent. Do not move about as the others do. Sit by yourself; make a little something amusing from newspapers... do not show it. If anyone comes too close you call them "you little prick" or "you dumb ass," in an impersonal way. Your world remains private; sustain introspective quality. Your fingers are almost constantly moving; your body shifts slightly—its own balance re-positioned. Explore finger gestures as representation for your character, feelings....

8. FREE AGENT. You know the piece should not exceed ten minutes; you have a watch and a whistle. You have

several small flags of your own country. Sit on the floor by the audience and watch carefully. There will be a time when you will see the necessity to plant a flag on a performer getting high into space; anticipate this...crawl as fast as you can with the flag in your mouth. If you are too late plant the flag on another performer—quietly, discretely. You are like a slow line in space tipped with color. Return by another route, still crawling (slowly) to your watching place. When the energy diminishes for the others, blow your whistle and slowly crawl forward into the group. Touch each one to signal the conclusion of the event.

The performers need not know each other's parts when they rehearse.

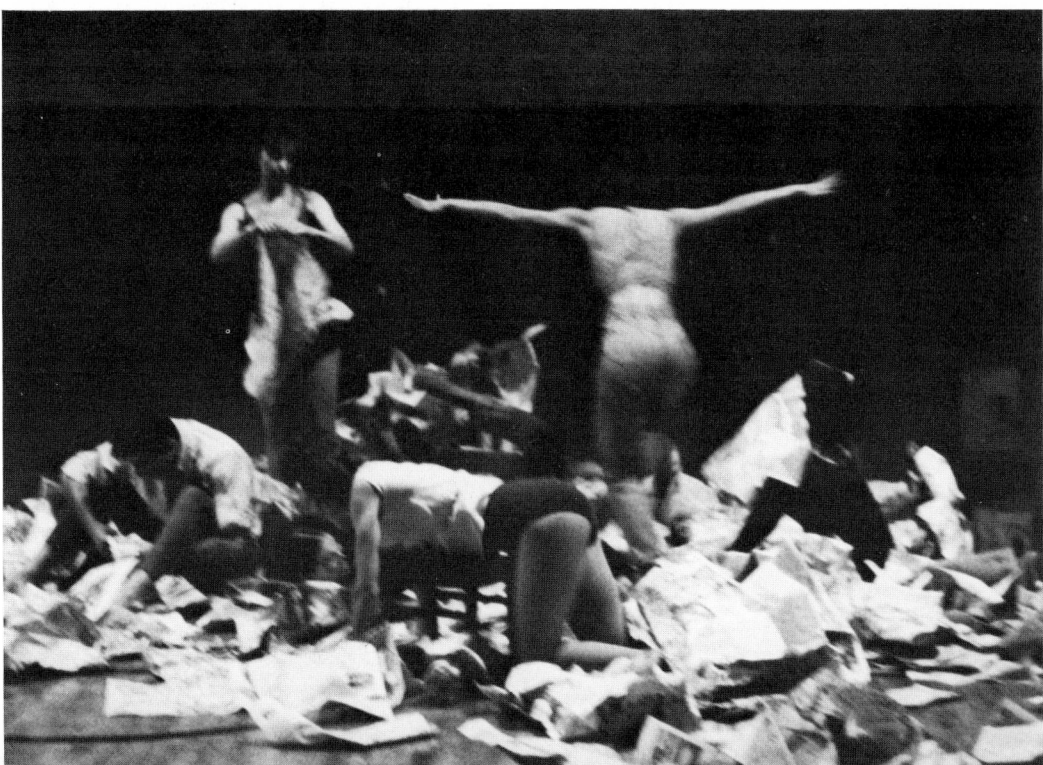

Robert McElroy

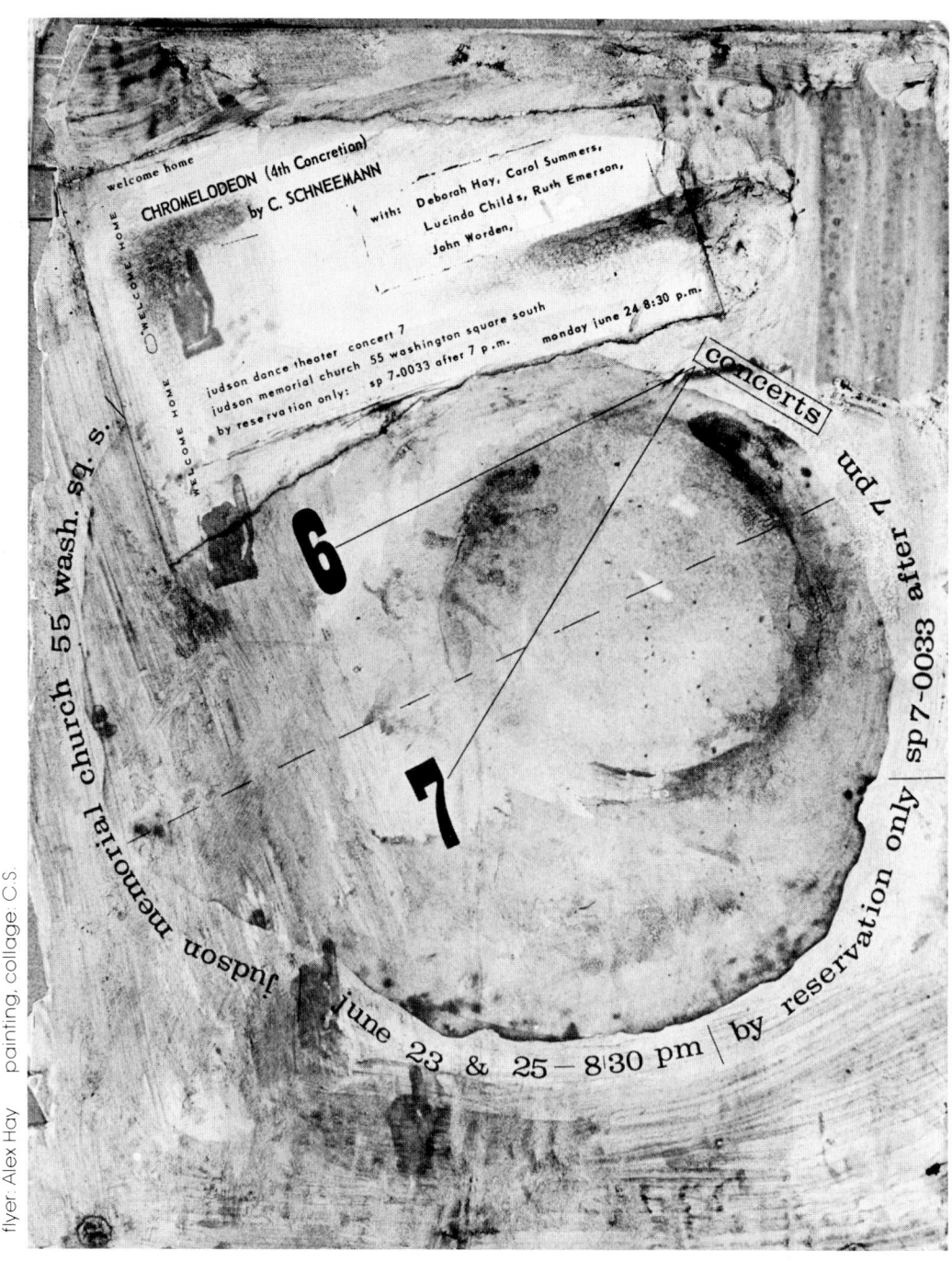

welcome home

CHROMELODEON (4th Concretion)
by C. SCHNEEMANN

with: Deborah Hay, Carol Summers,
Lucinda Childs, Ruth Emerson,
John Worden,

judson dance theater concert 7
judson memorial church 55 washington square south
by reservation only: sp 7-0033 after 7 p.m.   monday june 24 8:30 p.m.

concerts

6

7

judson memorial church 55 wash. sq. s.

sp 7-0033 after 7 pm

june 23 & 25 – 8:30 pm | by reservation only

flyer: Alex Hay   painting, collage: C.S.

36

This was the most completely "scripted" work before **Meat Joy**—the movement sequences were based on diagrammatic drawings of criss-crossing patterns, and were coordinated to layers of sound and lighting changes. "Chromo: combination of forms, colored vision. Chromatic: having notes not included in diatonic scale, admitting notes marked with accidentals."

The texture of the work is contrapuntal. The movement is a set of object equivalences, consisting of three sorts:

> a) Spins, leaps, pushes, runs, whirls: all from and returning to center points. These spiral patterns have a correlative in the body's balance on its central axis while at the same time its energy is released, spun like a centrifuge. A toy top (in which a handle is pushed down like a piston against the weight and balance of the top) was the precise object correlative for the movements: the "tops," "whirling," and "struggle-to-rise."

> b) Set against, cutting across these gyroscopic movements is the silent, dark, heavy slice of "the pursuit." Debby's squeals and shrieks were aural equivalents to the final sounds evolved in the "chicken cluster." The pursuit motions reiterated the centrifugal movements, but pulled them all into a single line: two performers facing each other, focusing and tracing the energy.

> c) The chicken cluster is the resolution of the piece: conceived as a rooster solo for Yvonne Rainer (and inspired by her **Three Seascapes**), it became a group movement when she dropped out of the work. Chicken cluster pulled in, and tightened all the open lines, curves, the momentum of drops and leaps; straightened the body axis down into the fixity of feet taking all spatial information from the ground.

Barrel organ ("nickelodeon") music and the Aria Duetto of Bach's **Cantata#78** were collaged live by Jim from three tape decks, both during rehearsal and performance. During one rehearsal Ruth and Cindy had climbed into the choir loft and began to play the church organ—we discovered they could manage a wonderfully crude and sonorous four-hand version of the **Em Fugue,** and it worked perfectly for the performance. The third tape was made by Jim: a computer-generated bass pulse, like a heart beat; a unifying and consistent thump or clunking which acted as a bridge between the bass ranges of the barrel organ and Bach.

CHROMELODEON

June 24 1963 Judson Dance Theater

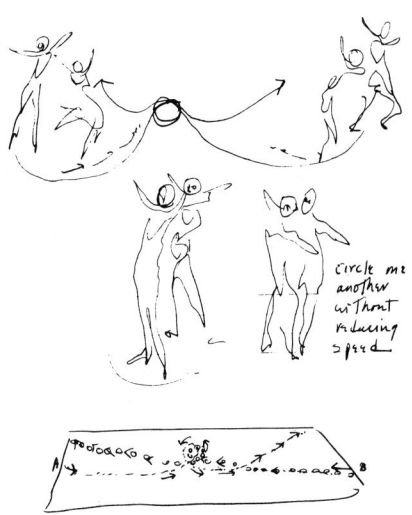

circle me
another
without
reducing
speed

Allusions to old movies are an obvious aspect of **Chromelodeon**: the use of flickering lights and exaggerated running, the melodramatic pursuit by a wolfman after a heroine trapped in a sensual dream of inevitable capture. The barrel organ music refers to the music played in movie houses to accompany silent films, and with the movement it evokes circus bigtops and ice skating rinks.

SCORE

Darkness. Noises from the balcony: banging, clanking. Electronic-tones tape **Dim vertical light centered**. John appears in the balcony, drops horizontal poles hung with costumes, hats, cloths to the floor; additional pile thrown down. Carol at edge of curtains. Barrel organ music, low. . .rises into collage John calls to him, climbs over balcony onto his shoulders—Carol spins him quickly off, runs to pile of materials. John follows. They are in colored underwear, proceed to dress themselves from clothing on the floor (all smeared with paint and singed or scorched). Barrel organ **Flickering light**. John and Carol exit running (exaggerated slow motion). **Back lighting, golds and blues**. They return dragging an open crate—Debby and Cindy (wearing underwear) are half-hidden among various cloths and blankets. Men slowly dump crate contents onto the pile of materials. Ruth

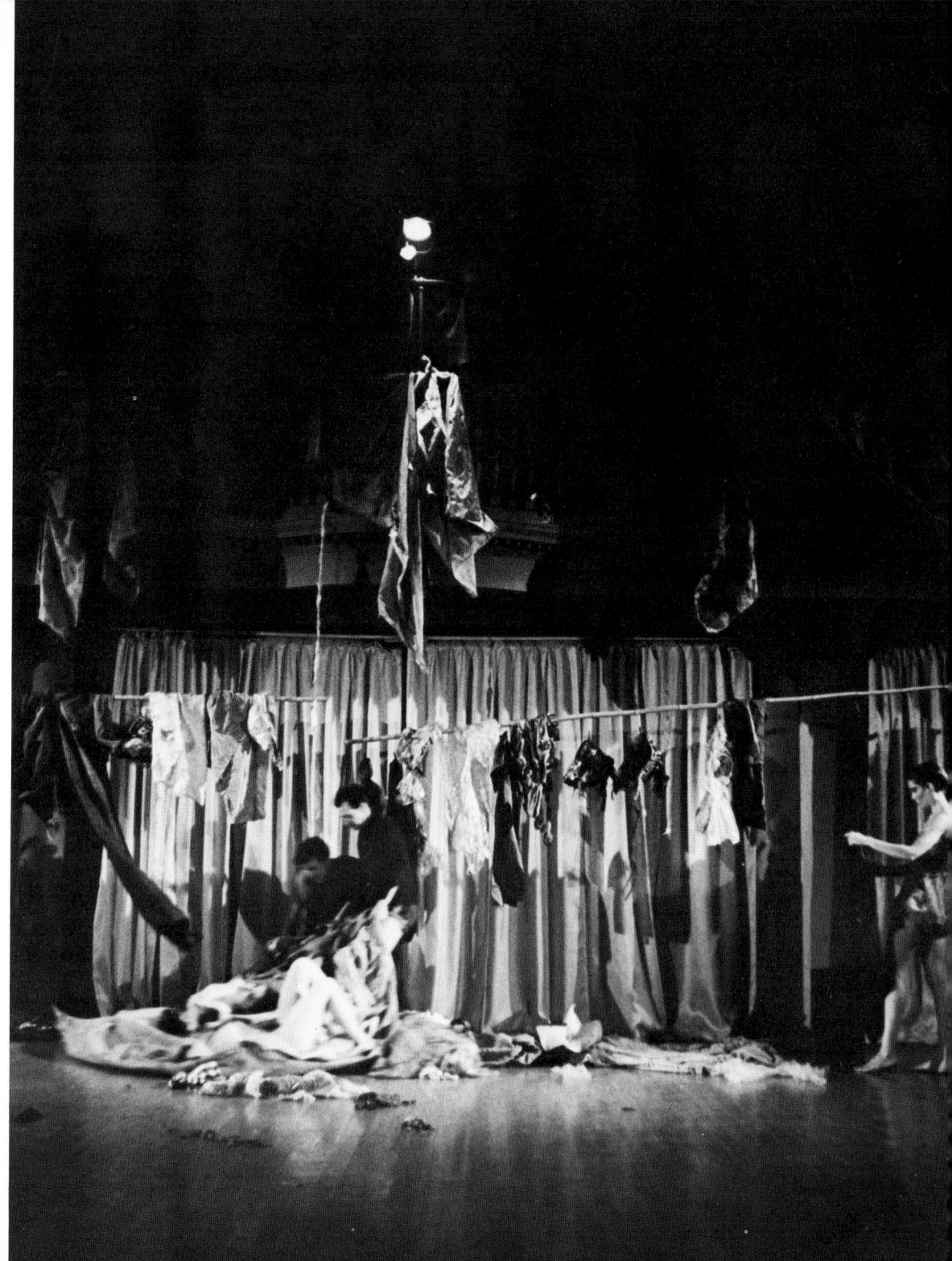

enters with a ladder, positions it on right, exits. Debby and Cindy dress themselves while emerging from the pile. John and Carol sort and handle additional fabrics on the horizontal poles above and behind them—their motions are short, frantic, they run back and forth. While dressing, Cindy and Debby begin to talk, and paint each other's legs.

Gold/white lights fan out from above. Wearing singed yellow and blue ''capes,'' the women are stood up by the men and turned to spin off into dervish whirls, enlarging their area, making whirring sounds. **Fast changes of bright lights, many colors.** Barrel organ collage…into Aria Duetto. (The whirls: arms pumping in and out, centrifugally). John and Carol drag out a huge pyre of brown paper to the side of the ladder. Ruth enters with a violin case, climbs the ladder, and hands down make-up jars to the men, who are sitting in the paper. The men paint each other's faces, then legs, with quick, intent strokes. Ruth goes to the clothes pile and takes off her leotard (a 1930's bathing suit underneath).

Cindy exits whirling through the center curtains. **White lights, centered.** Debby falls whirling, continues spinning slowly on the floor until she ''runs down.'' Cindy enters walking backwards and turning: to begin writing ''LOVE,'' ''LILLY,'' and other words with her body and a long yellow ribbon: sharp and linear—

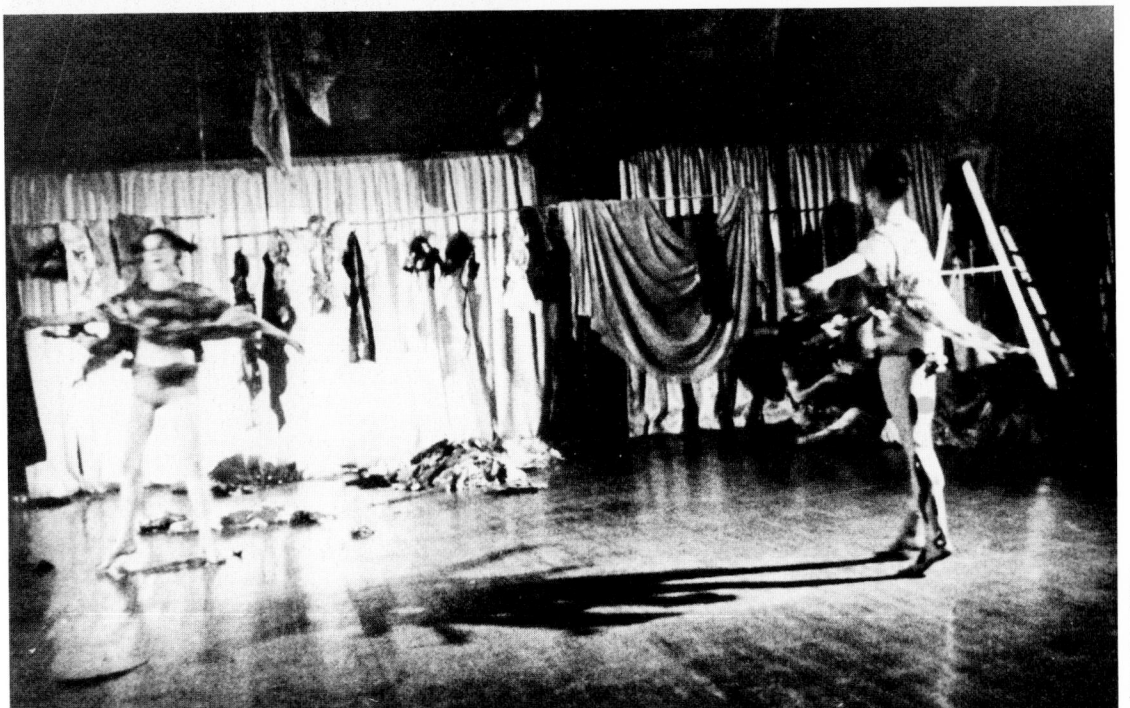
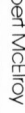

Robert McElroy

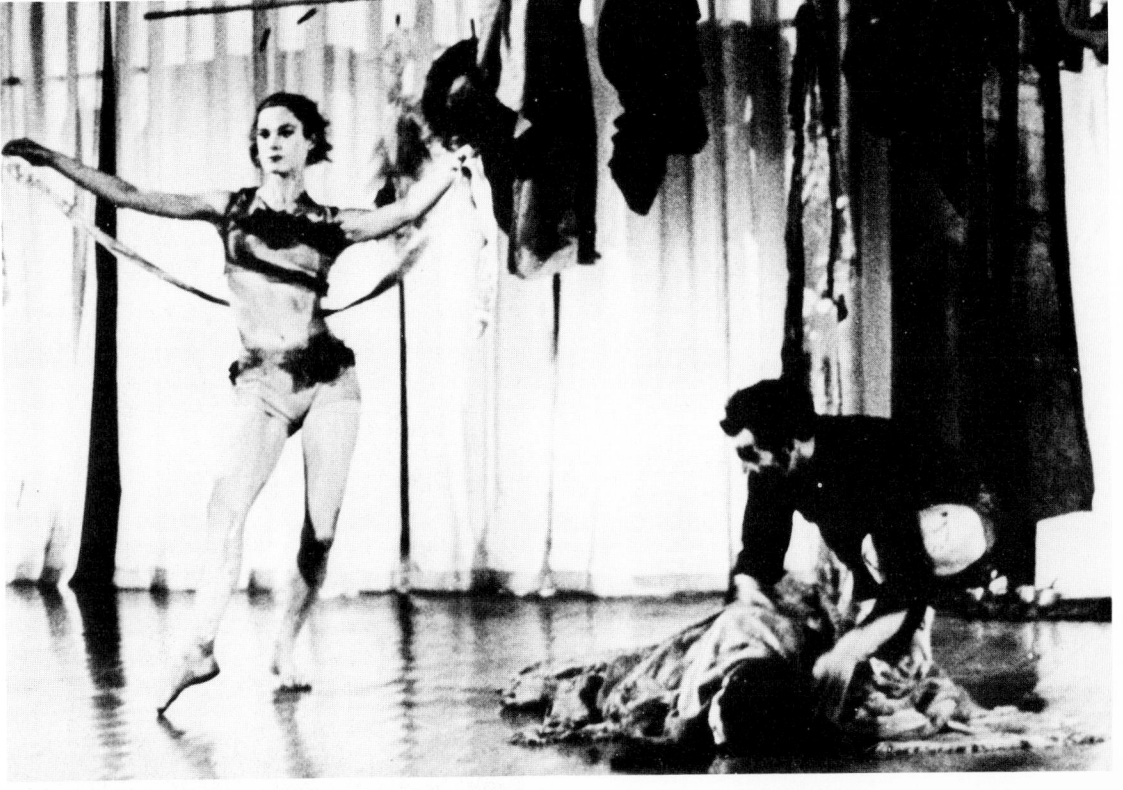

Robert McElroy

verticals, horizontals, diagonals against the floor. She announces each letter while chewing gum; collapses after completing a letter. Collage and Aria Duetto, low...fading. Carol runs with a large blanket over to Debby, covers her, says "Now go to sleep, you're good as gold, you're my girl, I want you to dream..."; he moves away distracted several times during what follows, always returning to Debby, patting, pulling, un-covering and covering her up again. John completes streaking his own face. Ruth returns to the ladder. Barrel music, low behind collage tape. **Steady blue light.** John moves to Ruth, brings her from the ladder, and "pushes" her off into grand jetés across the area; he beats time and yells "Grand Jetty!" When she reaches far right, **lights out.** Ruth runs back in the darkness, joining John in the paper pyre, which they make into a "house". **Lights.** Aria Duetto. They watch Cindy. John is seized with nervous con-fusion, gets up. Ruth exits. John begins to run back and forth, his cap and pants are slipping off; he turns, runs, slips, reaches finally for an overcoat to throw around himself, and exits. Immediately he returns pulling Ruth.

Bright to soft, slow tonal shifts—rose, violets. As Cindy completes her letter writing, John begins "turn-body" with Ruth, soon joined by Carol. (Ruth in stiff angular positions as the men turn her over and over, sometimes lifting her, shifting her, resting, consulting, turning her again.)

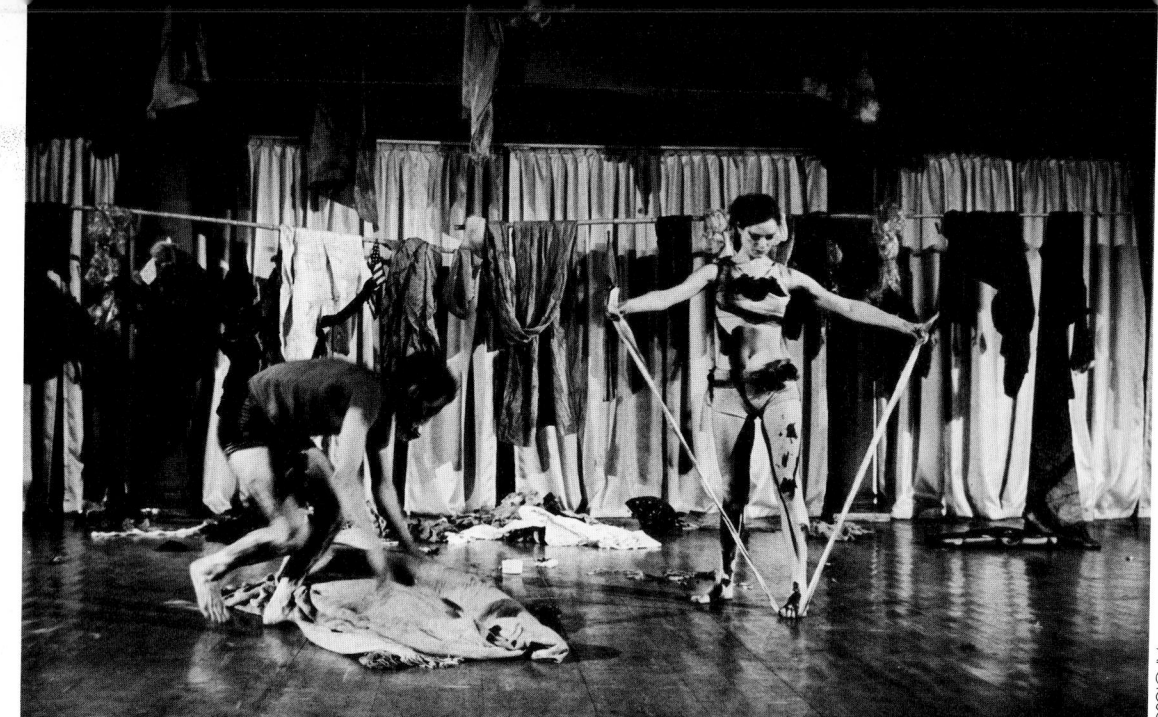

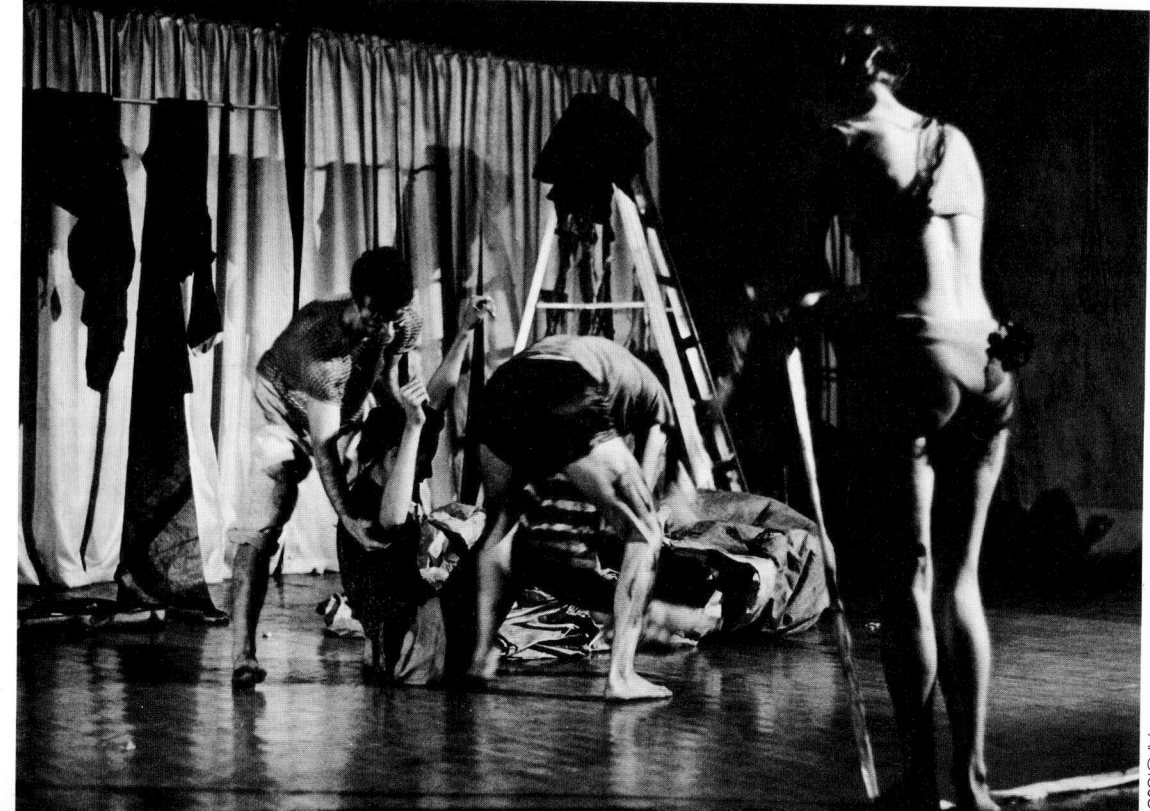

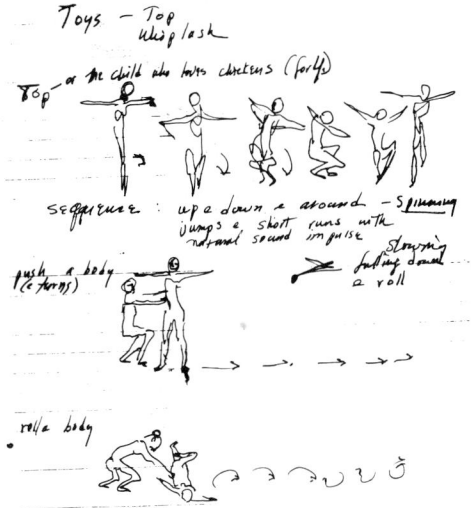

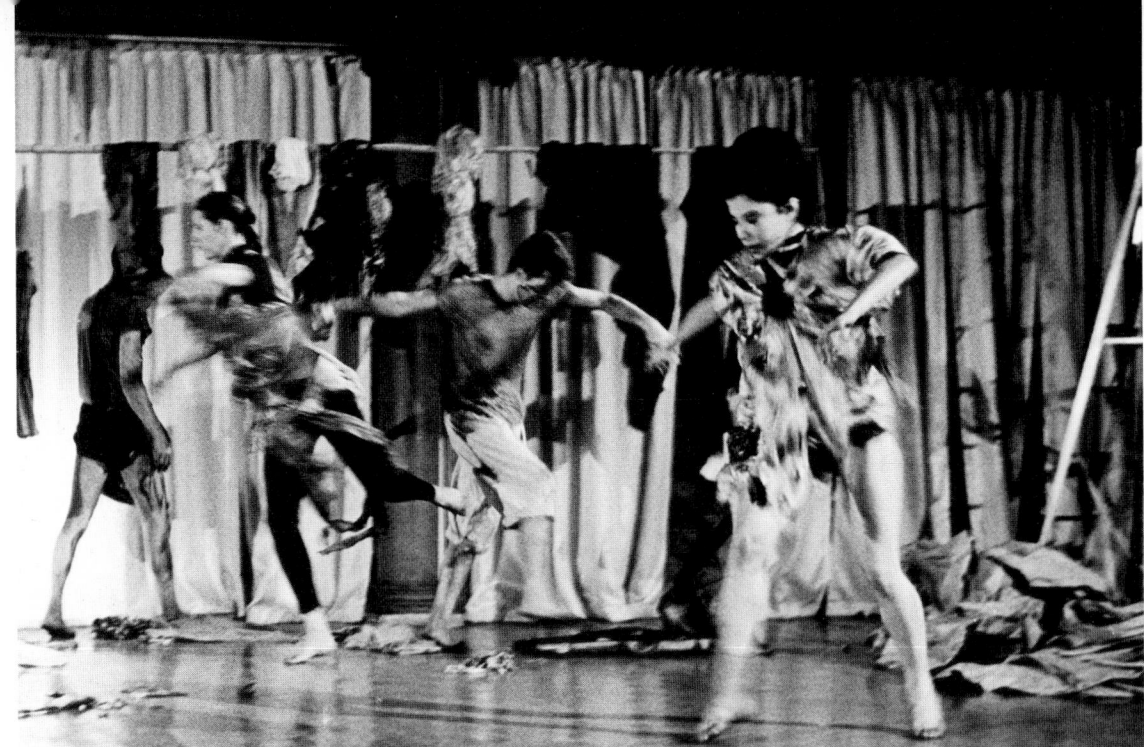

Barrel organ. **Spill light around ladder.**
Cindy handstands over to Debby,
uncovers her. Together they rise slowly
underneath the blanket; twists and turns
over to the ladder. Fade out.

John ties blue silk strips onto Ruth. Carol
calls Cindy and Debby in Japanese.
They come down from the ladder. Carol,
John dress Cindy, Debby from the
hanging clothes, adding scraps. Carol
begins counts in Japanese numbers
loudly; John quickly spins Cindy, Debby
and Ruth into "tops" which wobble and
twirl (feet close together). Barrel Organ.
John and Carol sit on the clothes pile
clapping, calling. The wobbling tops
collapse, John and Carol slowly re-
group them together—**dim spot
light**—cover them with a massive red
blanket.

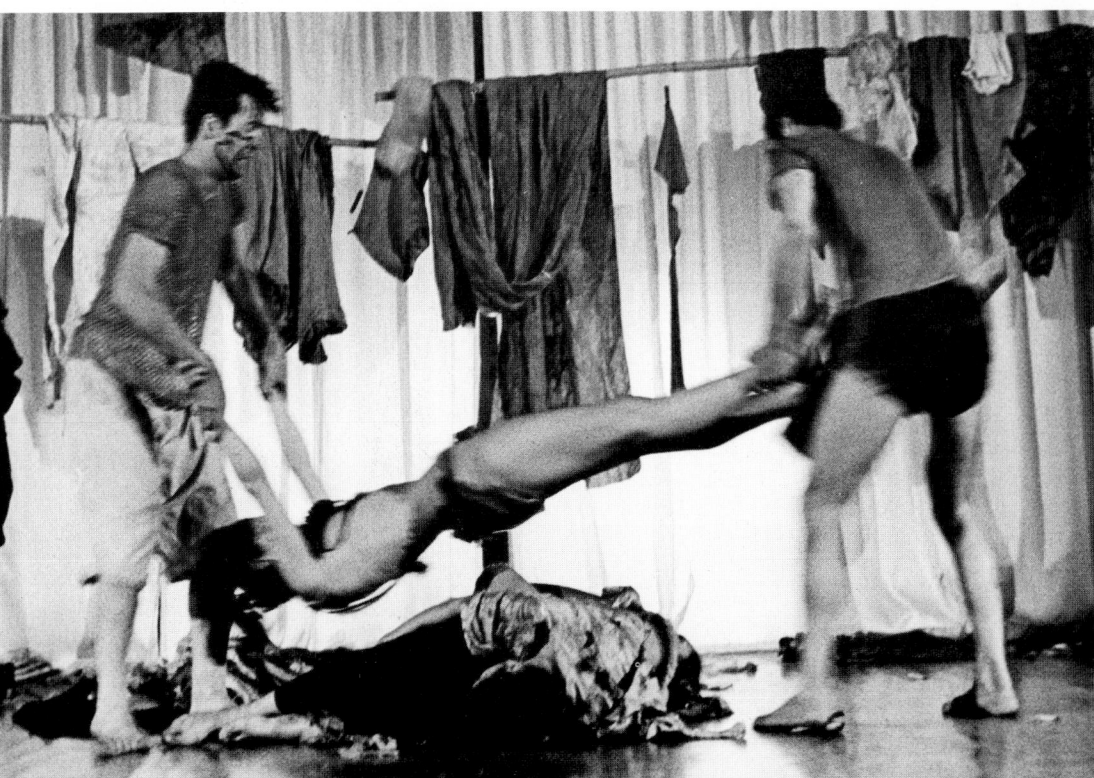

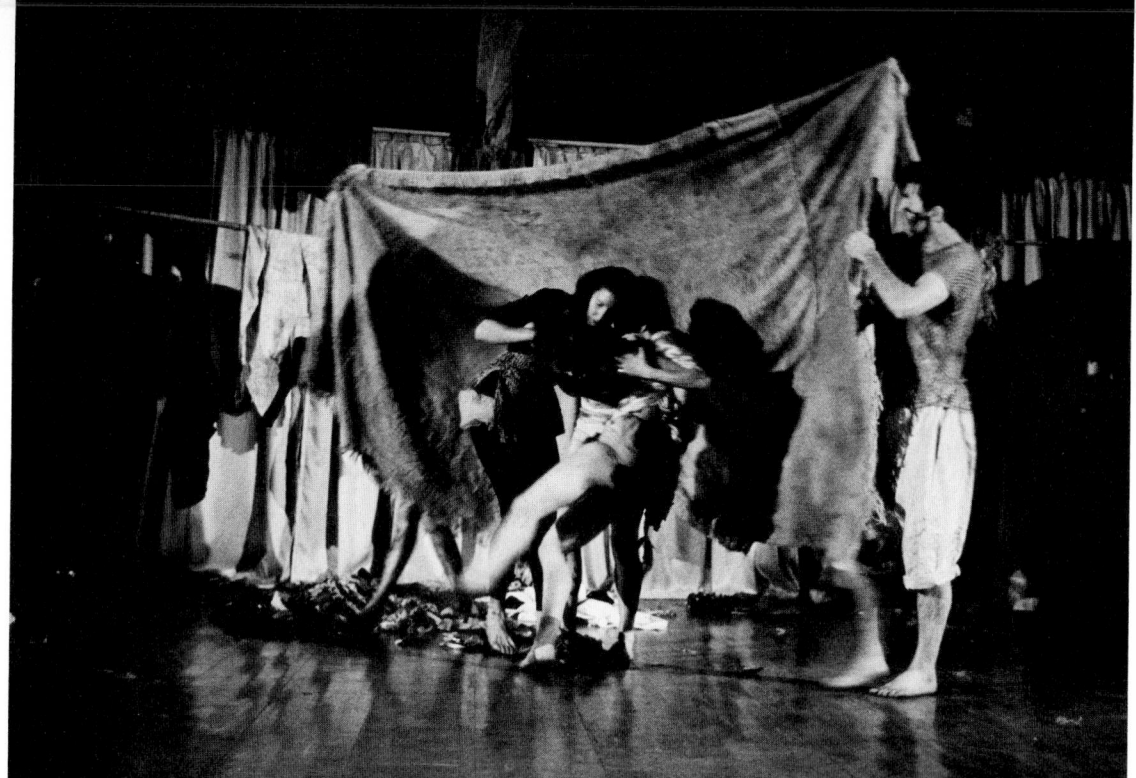

Silence. **Masked spot light.** Struggle-to-rise sequence. The women, hands on shoulders, push each other down and up like pistons, pushing to rise. The men are pushing them down from outside the blanket. Choking, coughing sounds. The swaying struggle continues; eventually men become entangled, the blanket covers them, the struggle reverses, and as the men try to rise the women push them down. **Black out.** Exit all.

Ruth and Cindy re-enter left, in darkness, and carry a lantern to top of the ladder. Barrel organ low They climb up into the balcony, begin to play Bach Em Fugue. **Balcony spot.** They play "together," syncopating the organ (open valves) to the barrel organ tape. John enters right, carrying food in an American flag "apron"; throughout the next sequence he watches the movement as he methodically eats.

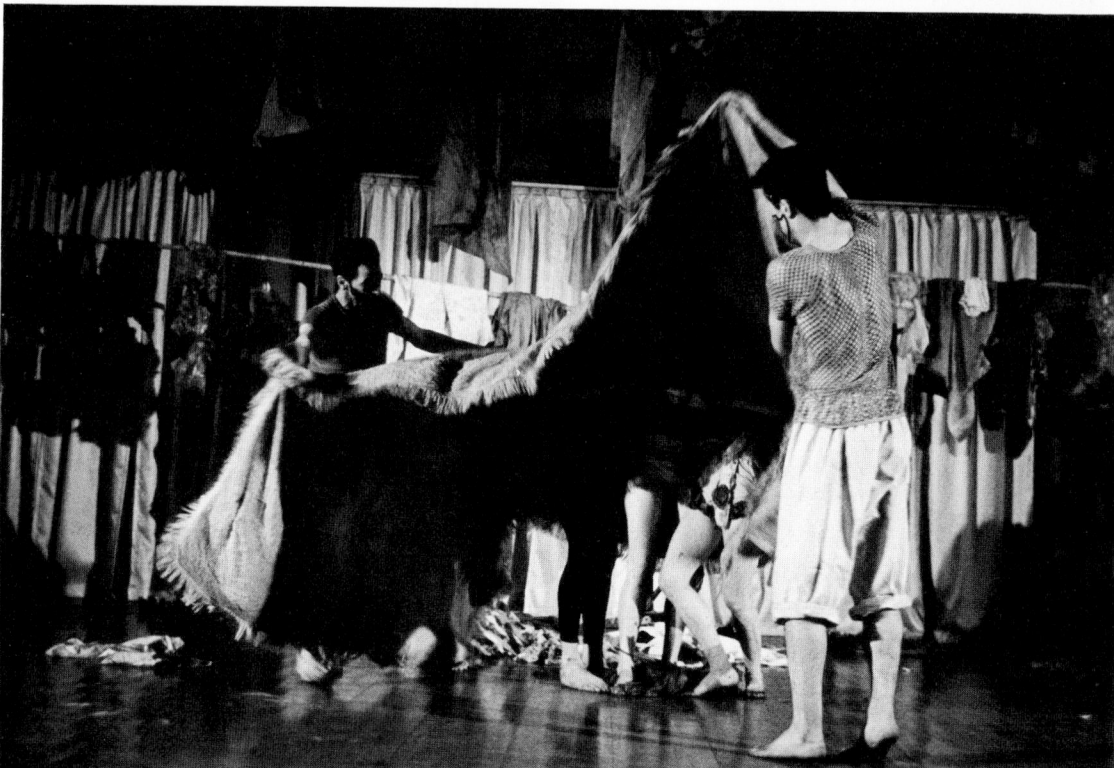

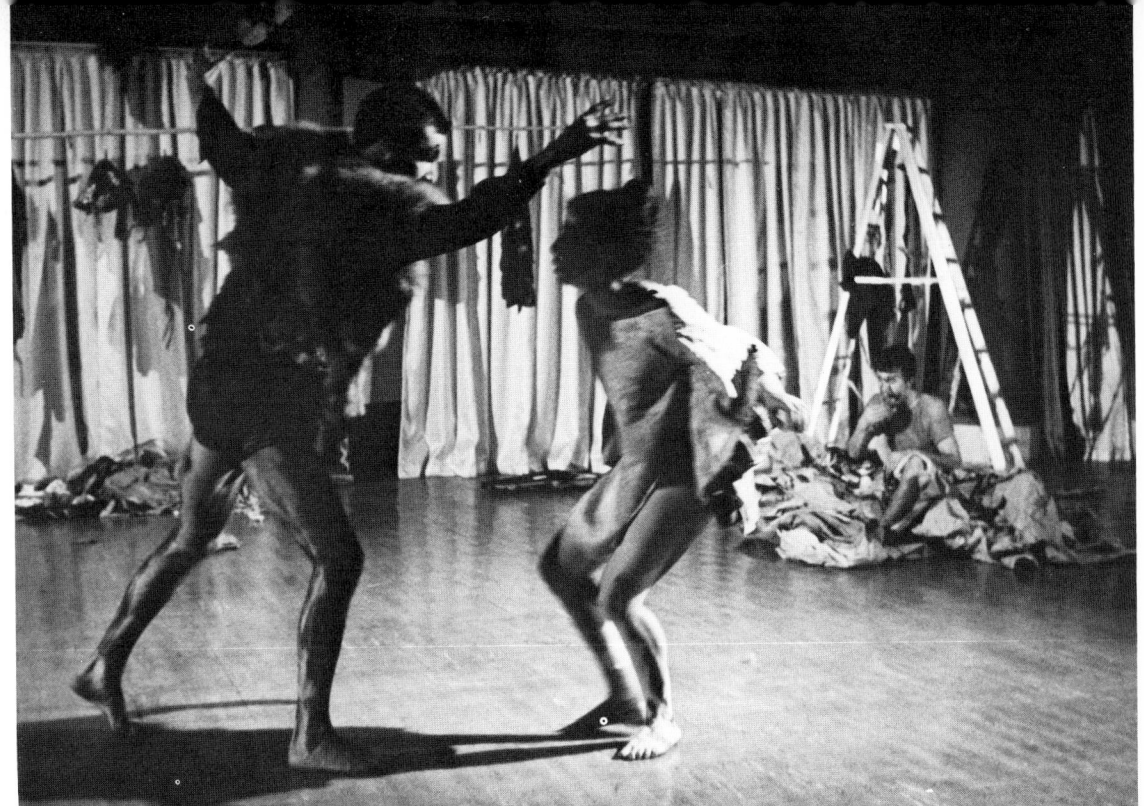

The Pursuit. **Dim, ominous flickering light from side towards center.** From between the center curtains Debby appears, in alarm, walking backwards. She is pursued by Carol (wearing a "wolfman" cape and fur scraps). Em Fugue fade out Slow dream. He "surrounds" her, motion barely visible as they advance through space. An "endless" walk circling across the floor—she faces him throughout. Suddenly drops to her knees...retreats backwards, staccato, stands, walks backwards, drops to her knees...Carol arms raised—monstrous, growling, grunting—**lights up, slowly, colorless, diffuse**—nightmare pursuit; she shrieks, slows, Carol catches Debby on his side and over his back: swinging, growling, her legs wing out from his back, shaking. Debby repeats unvaried shrieks. Falling forward on his knees, they drop over in rolling, entangled, single form...separating, she rolls past him, gathering momentum, both roll through the back curtains. Rolling, she reappears first—he rolls in pursuit, over her, almost into the audience. He lies over her—silence—rise up, sink down together...slow rolls facing each other, back to the clothes pile.

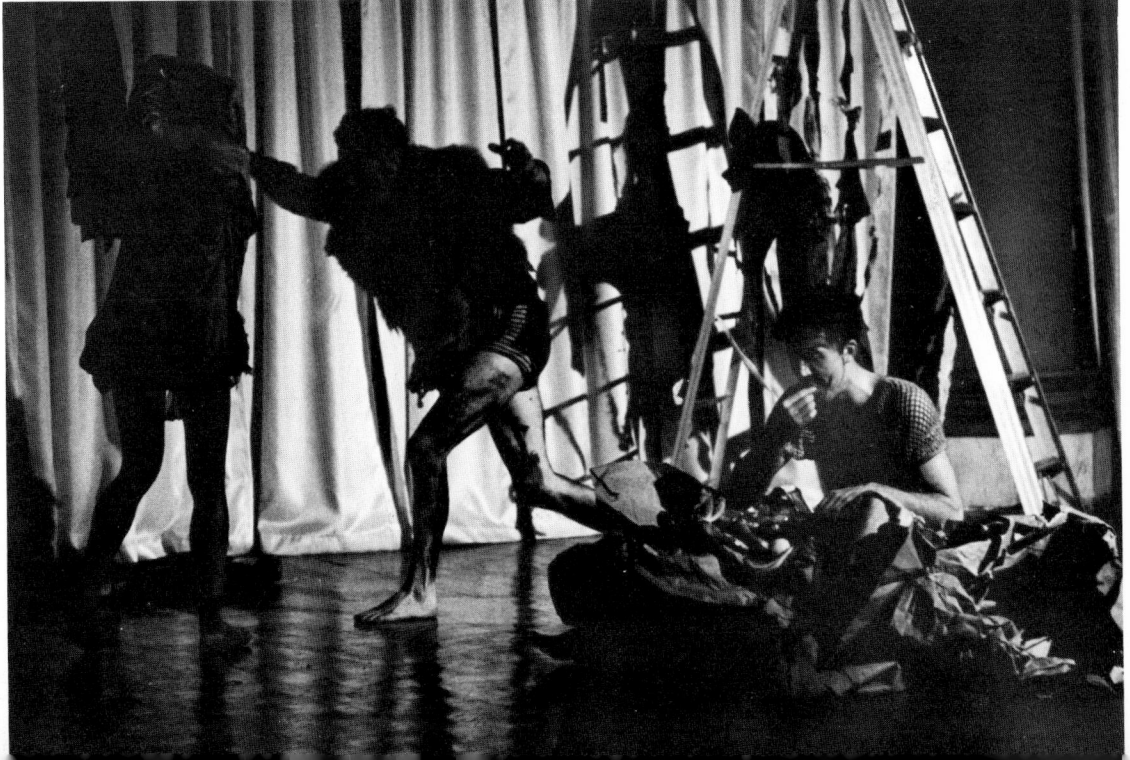

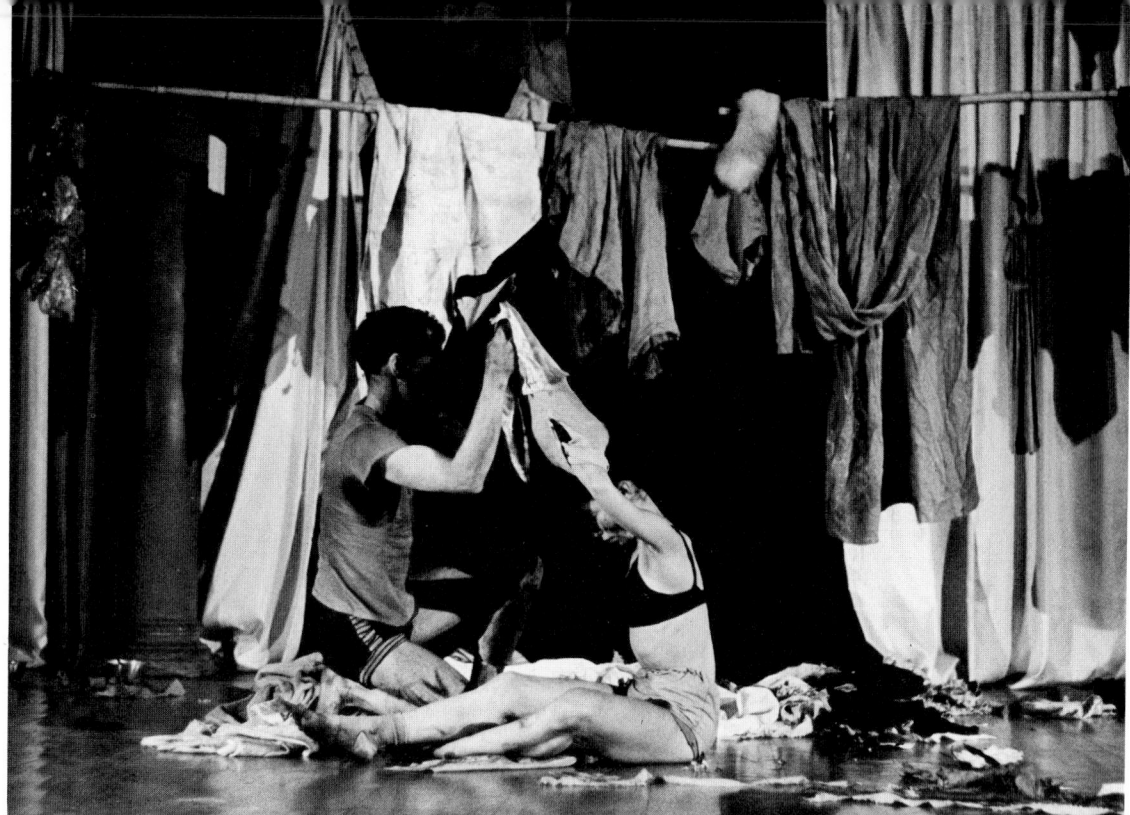

Al Giese

Lights slowly up—magenta and yellow—to flood center stage. Carol takes off cape and furs, puts on shirt, slowly removes Debby's clothes. Collage and Aria Duetto. Dresses Debby, choosing from the hanging array.

Intermittent mix with collage. Debby is dressed and standing. Carol leaves, returns with a small bench, which he places upsidedown near her feet. **Bright shifting golds and yellows.** He puts her inside the bench, and begins to push the bench. He stops to change her position, and pushes again. All very slowly. They hold eye contact and discuss the movements. With Debby like a statue, the bench is pushed in a full circle around the performance area.

44

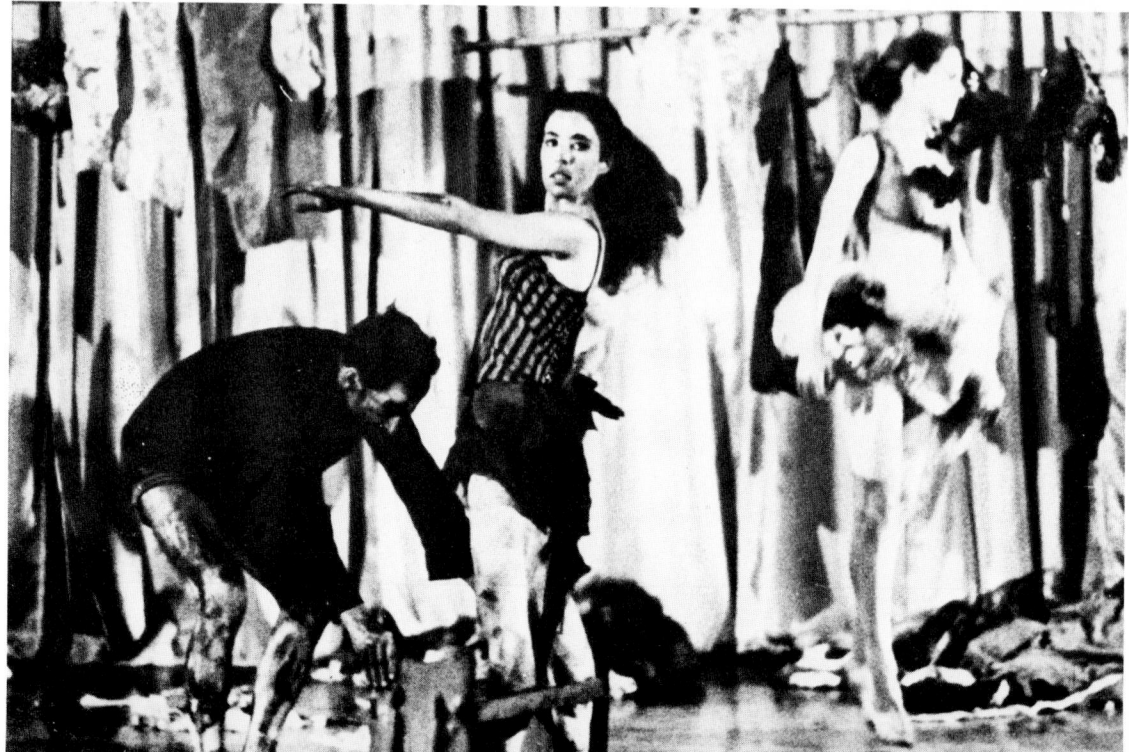

Robert McElroy

When John has finished eating he rises and distractedly flings peels and crusts into the audience. **Bright yellow, green, blue.** Ruth and Cindy enter in bizarre tutus of curtains, making *grande jetés* twice around the floor, to John upstage. *Music fades out.* John calls out through a megaphone, reading from a list of ballet steps. (Midwestern pronunciations). Cindy and Ruth figure out what he's saying and perform these precisely, one at a time, while John imitates their steps:

reel levy (relevé)
tan do (tandu)
change meant (changement)
pass de cat (pas de chat)
pass de ducks (pas de deux)
please (pliés)
tour jetty (tourjeté)
balancey (balancé)
brush sess urbley (brush cesseurblé)
pass de burry (pass de boureé)
coupy (coupé)

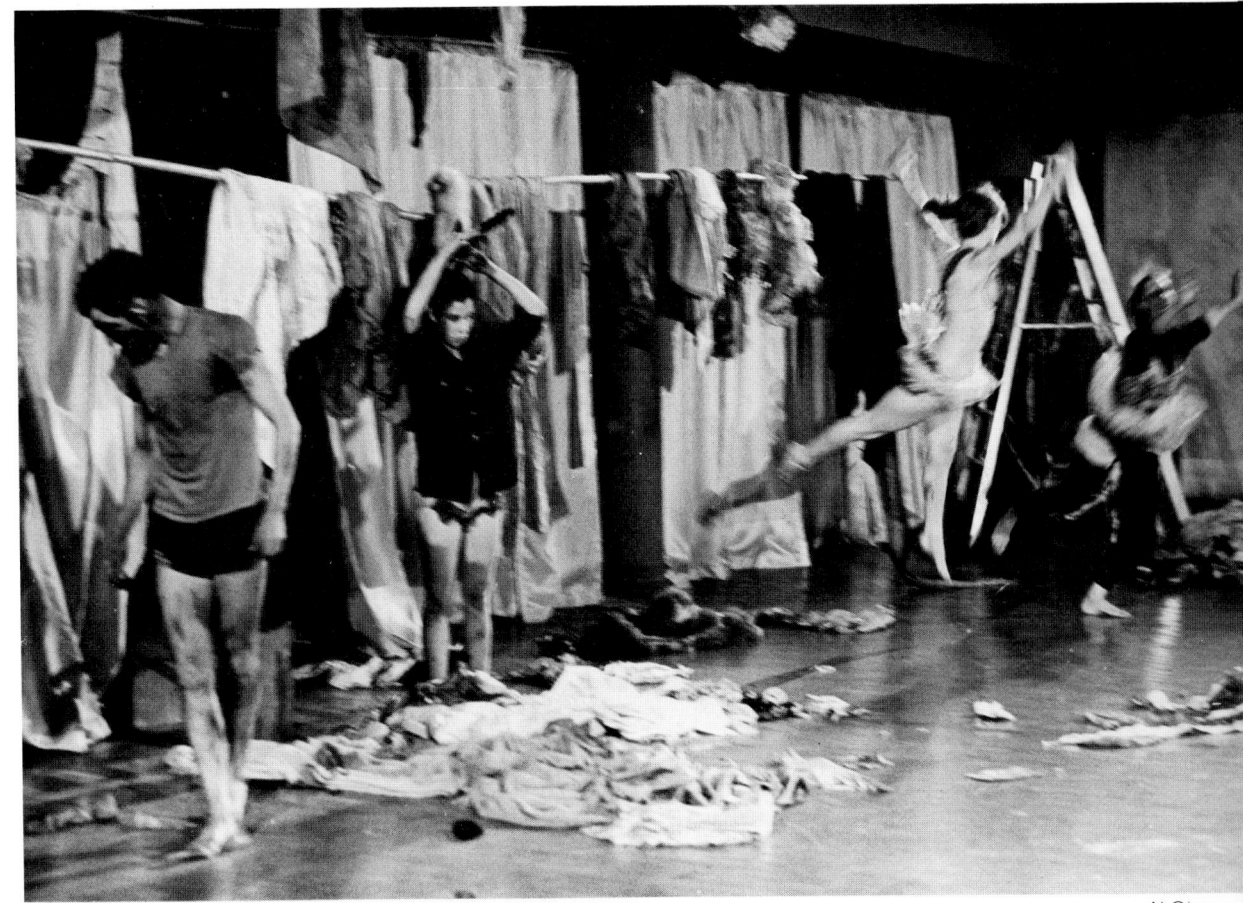

Al Giese

Barrel organ collage fade in, with Aria Duetto line. Carol and Debby begin "chicken cluster"—attempting to become chicken-like from the feet/claws up, emitting squalks (natural to arched diaphram). **Lights dim slowly.** Cindy follows. **Spots center, blue, green, yellow.** John reads four more ballet steps. Ruth follows. Cut Aria Duetto line. John reads five more steps, then follows. Collage fade out to silence. Random contact. All chickens. No exits. **Lights out.**

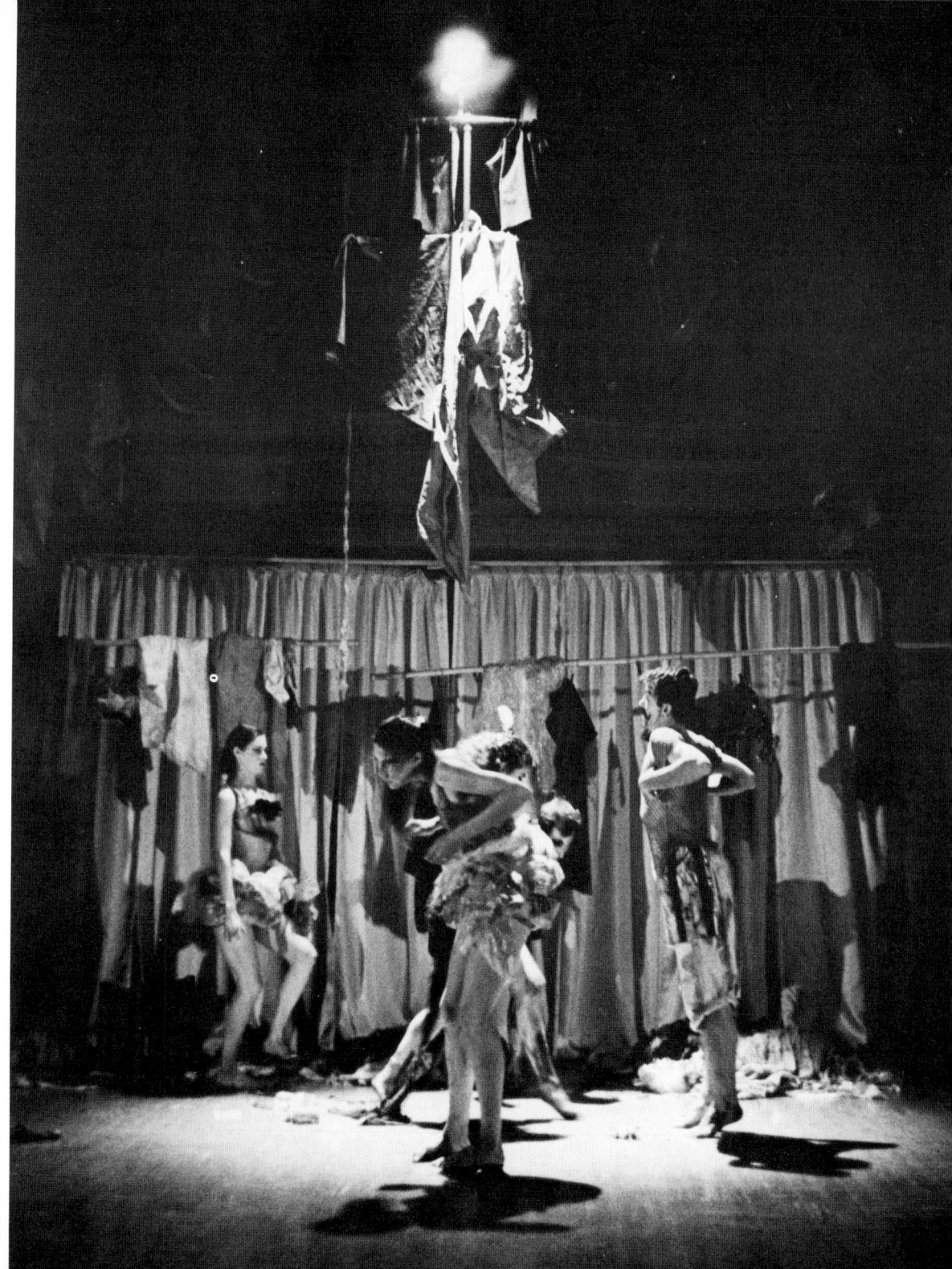

Al Giese

LATERAL SPLAY

November 19 20 1963 Judson Dance
Theater NY

An event repeated throughout Judson Dance Theater Concert #13, within an environment by the sculptor, Charles Ross. Ross had made a mountainous slide of steel folding chairs which flooded one corner of the open floor up to the balcony. This sculptural pile remained a constant while during the collaborative works a variety of metal scraps and odd props were introduced: bed springs, steel bars, ropes, brooms. Performance works consisted of solos, duets, teams and a massive tug-of-war. The thirty participants included dancers, writers, painters, musicians, actors, sculptors.

Lateral Splay functioned as an explosive and linear refrain, a propulsive jet of movement cutting through the sequences of other works and the materials of the environment. It involves a maximum expenditure of directed energy; in rehearsals we practiced with the sense that the runners were particles bombarding space. Four basic runs were made at highest speed by twelve runners:

1) backwards run (spot direction by turning head from side to side, spine straight)
2) forward run (head high, free, intense, clear forward focus)
3) low crawl-run (knees bent, relaxed shoulders, arms swing)
4) turning run with falls (turning as you run, sharp falls, rise immediately, continue turning run, or after fall choose another run)

The audience was seated in wedges forming a complete circle around the floor space. Three times during the evening the Lateral Splay runners positioned themselves behind the audience seats and unexpectedly shot out across the floor. Runs were also done in the balcony over the heads of the audience where steel sheets had been laid, making tremendous thundering noises as the runners passed over them.

Rules to Performers included: SPEED—fast as possible. DURATION—long as possible; any action taken to exhaustion. DIRECTION—random. VARIATIONS—climbing, swinging. PERFORMANCE—stylized, severe, maximum energy in runs; collision embraces are natural, abandoned.

In order to stop a run the rule was to collide with an obstacle. The obstacles were the walls of the church, the audience, the steel girders, the mountain of chairs, and the other runners. When collision occurred, the runner had to meet the obstacle at full speed, merge with it, and fall down. Rests lasted until the impulse

Violent, expulsive energy—a single impulse. Inspired by/in reaction to the formality and grace of certain works by Merce Cunningham.

For twelve to fifteen runners in a large open space. The spectators should be seated in a circle or semi-circle cut through by several aisles. Balconies, doors, or low windows which might lead into the main room will be used by the performers.

Clothing: big sweat pants in various colors, worn low on the hip. Men are bare chested. Women wear small tops which leave midriff exposed. (During a rehearsal for the Judson performance I had imagined soft lengths of colored material to be tied around waists and legs; the next morning I found a carton in front of my loft filled with long strips of blue and green velvet.)

to run again. Because the runs were exhausting, the sequences could last for only three minutes.

Variations on the rules were realized in the following ways:

"Begin with **any** of the runs until you encounter an object, wall or other performer. At an encounter you may 1) switch to another run; 2) drop down immediately and rest; 3) you may gain a rest by colliding with another runner intentionally, grab them (support them, **they** will be off balance) and fall down in an embrace. They cannot get up until you get up. Then you begin one of the runs again at maximum speed. 4) If someone collides with you accidentally you may grab them, fall in an embrace and rest. 5) If you run into any resting performers you may fall down by them and rest also. 6) If you run up against a wall or an object you may engage in some maximum energy activity until you fall down under or by the object to rest. Remember, a person who has fallen down to rest counts as an object and you may direct your run towards them to gain a rest or engage in a maximum activity with them. Whatever you do to them, they remain relatively passive, or they jump up and begin another run."

I was convinced that proper concentration—an instantaneous yielding on impact, rather than resistance—could prevent us from injury.

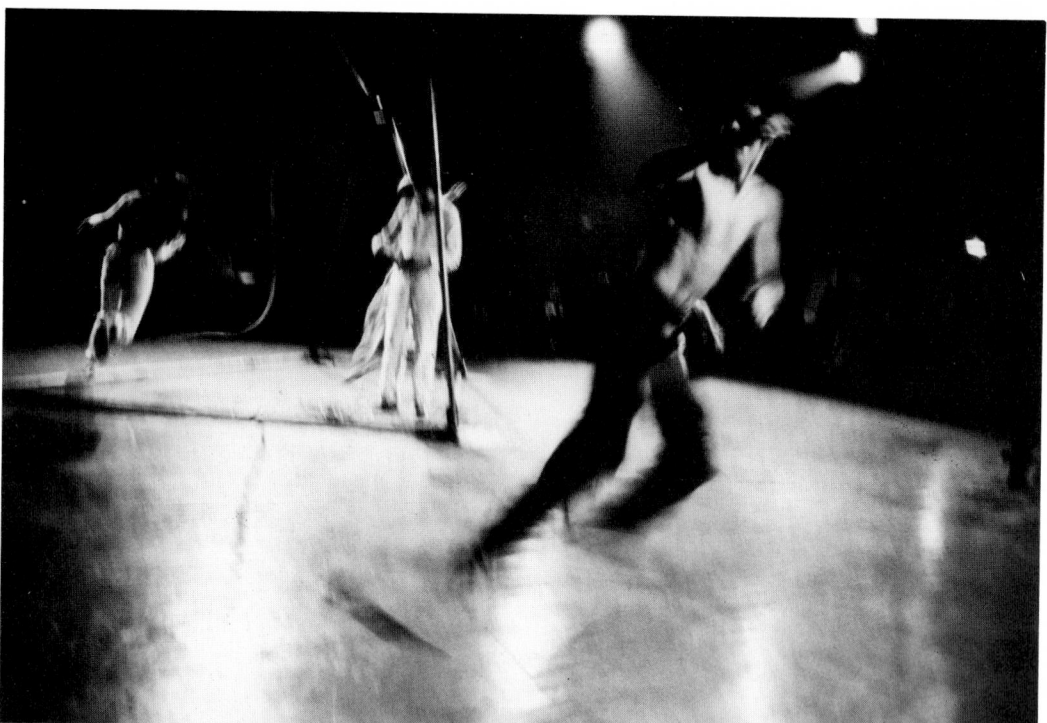

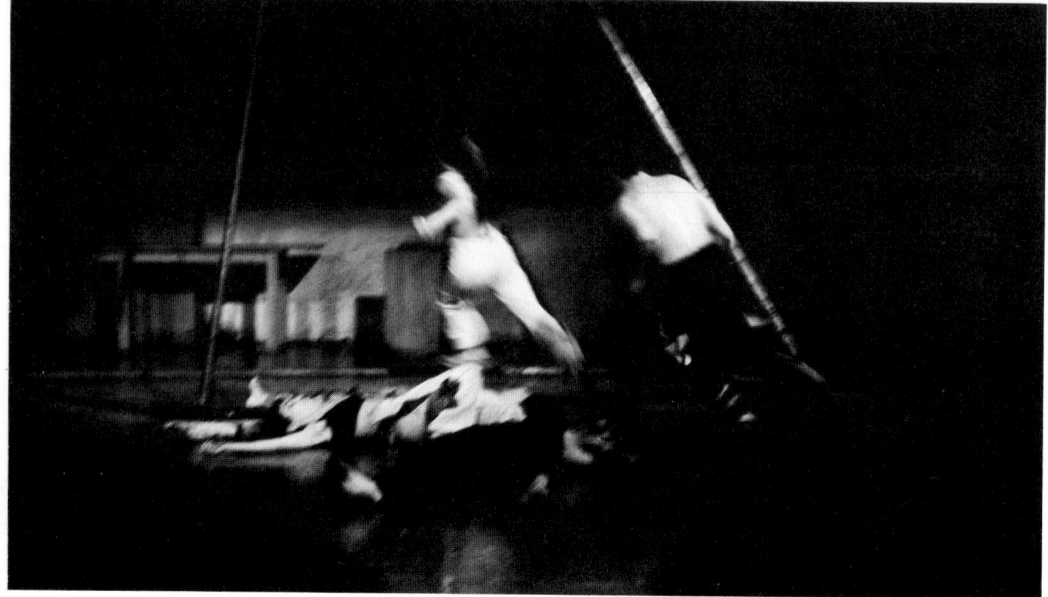

Several special exercises were necessary to secure peripheral vision and spatial memory: **a) blindfolded in a close heap, keeping constant bodily contact, we crawled over, under and between each other's arms, legs, bellies, backs; b) blindfolded we walked alone through the space of the church, exploring the performance area, balcony, halls, closets; c) open-eyed fast walks, constant directional shifts with awareness of every other person moving.** These exercises enabled us to absorb the sense of one another's physical presence as part of a unitary organism, and to slowly assimilate distances of the spaces which would be compressed in the runs. The speed of the blindfolded walks increased gradually as we felt familiar with the dimensions and variations of architectural space. Another exercise, "Grabs and Falls," which recurs in many of my works, began here. Two people knees slightly bent, feinting, just out of arms reach, concentrate on the weight and shifting position of the other's torso, until one person takes the dominant impulse to pull the other down. The point of the exercise is to lose any sense of opposition or resistance when grabbed, and for the grabber to take an instantaneous responsi-

bility for their mutual fall, spontaneously directing the musculature and weight of both. Exercises of collision and impact were practiced over and over again until we actually felt secure and free crashing into one another.

Performers:

Judith Dunn	Larry Siegal
Deborah Hay	Tony Holder
Deborah Lee	John Quinn
Elaine Summers	Jerry Howard
Sally Gross	Alex Hay
June Ekman	John Worden

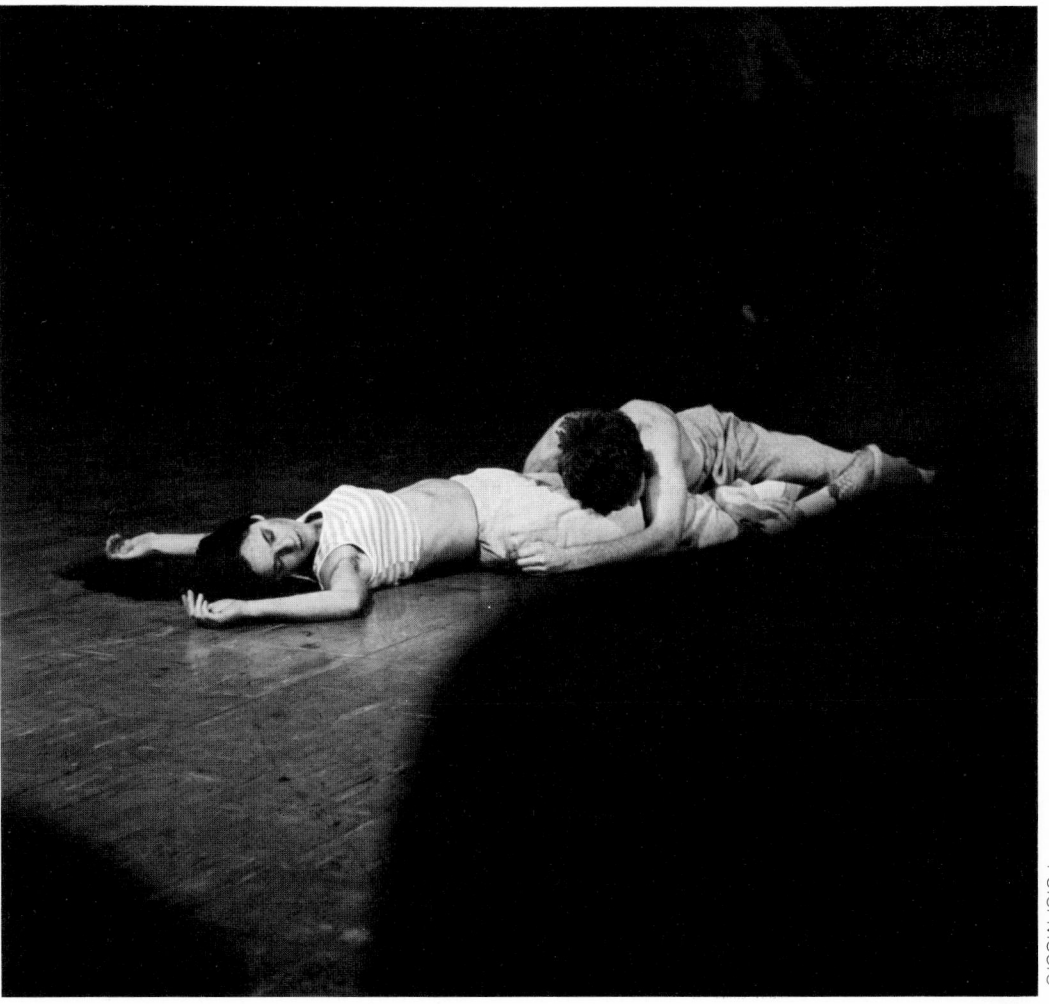

LOOSELEAF

January 21 1964 Judson Dance Theater
Workshop NY

June 8 9 1966 Bridge Theater Festival
NY

A brief "didactic" eating-event made around a text composed from earlier essays and notes about perception, the body, along with thoughts about my transitions from painting to environment to performance. Two identical sound tapes were played, one slightly in advance of the other. Each tape is a superimposition (with shifting dominance) of the texts being read with racous music of Harlem teenagers, singing, drumming, chanting. Jim and I recorded the high school students at the invitation of a friend, the writer Naomi Levinson, who had said if we really cared about new music we should hear these kids.

Looseleaf was organized as a set of discrete interference patterns, requiring the audience to choose between contrasting and antagonistic audial and visual material. It was performed only once. Performers: Mark Brusse, Philip Corner, C.S. The following actions took place for the duration of the tapes:

I wear an apron. I bring a card table into the performance area; a trunk, a large mirror. The table is set upright. The trunk dragged behind it so that when the mirror is propped against the trunk, the table is perfectly reflected in it.

I bring a stand to the left of the table; place it ten feet away. On the stand I place: a table cloth, napkins, paper plates, knives & forks, candles, glasses and a pitcher of water, and cakes.

I attach a whistle to the apron band; it has a long chain.

I bring two chairs to the table.

Philip and Mark come to the table from the audience; they sit down.

The tape begins.

I set the table. Lights are out. I cover the table with the cloth, place candles, napkins, cups, utensils. Then I bring a plate of small, gooey, many-colored cakes to Philip and Mark. "Here are your cakes." "Thank you."

They eat slowly, vacantly. At first they use the forks. Then they pick up pieces of cake with the knives.

They finish the first plate of cakes and I come to take them from the stand, where I wait attentively, with a fresh plate of cakes.

I ask them if they would like some water. If they do I bring the pitcher and fill their glasses. At any time they may ask for more water or more cakes.

The second plate of cakes they eat with their fingers; absorbed & quiet, they pay no attention to one another. (The candles flicker, their images waver in the mirror.) They are a little messy; some icing gets on their chins and cheeks. They like that feeling. They stick their fingers in the cakes. Their tenor remains reflective, quiet against the din of the tapes.

I bring the third plate of cakes. They can barely stand to eat cake. They put their fingers in the cakes and break them apart. They put some cake in their mouths. They take filling on their fingers and slowly reach across the table and smear, streak, smudge one another's faces. Slowly, each at his own pace. Back & forth, stop & start, accepting the gestures impassively, openly.

The tape stops. They wipe their hands and faces with the napkins. They leave. I walk to the table and blow out the candles.

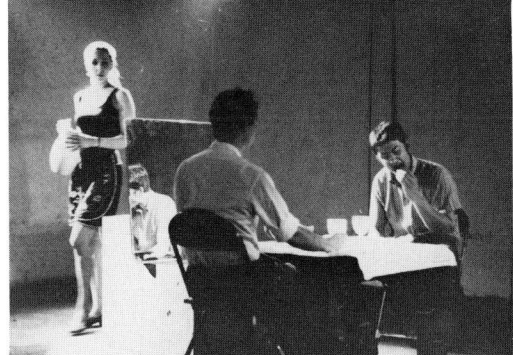
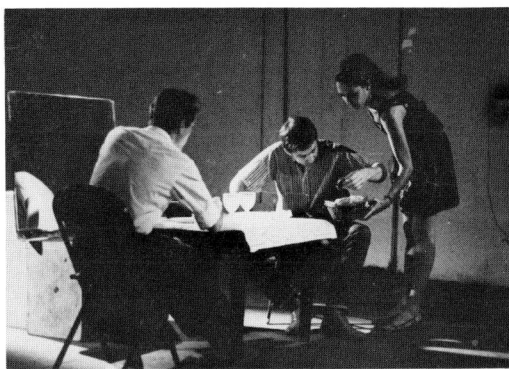
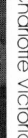

Charlotte Victoria

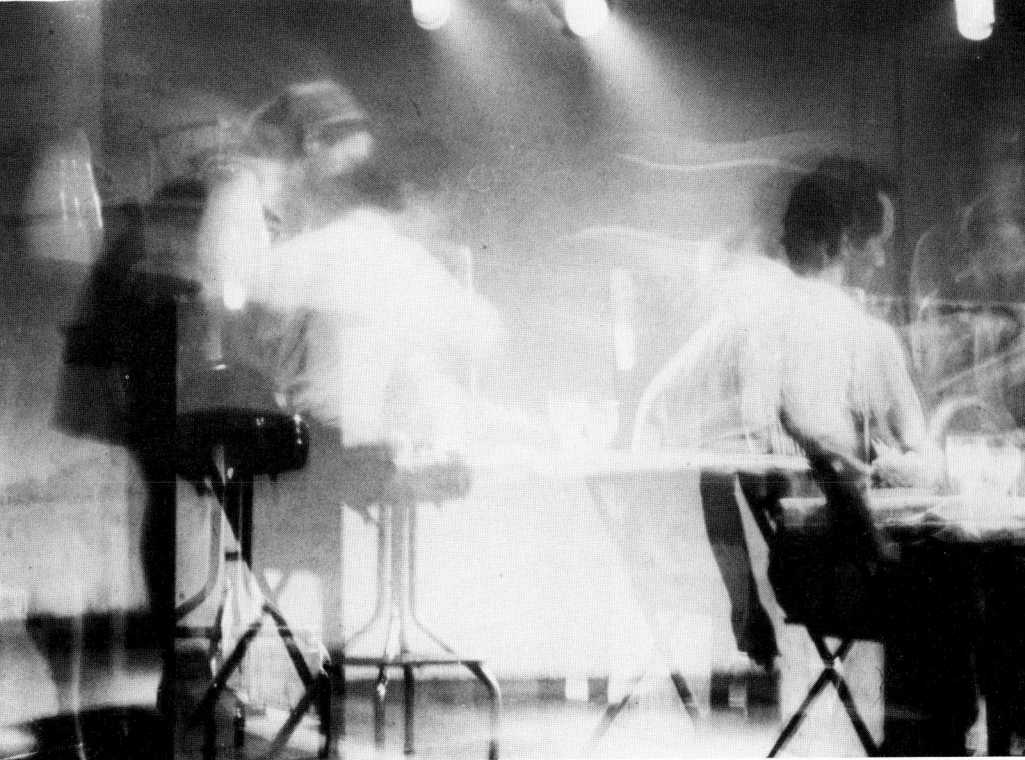

Herbert Migdoll

EYE BODY

December 1963 NY

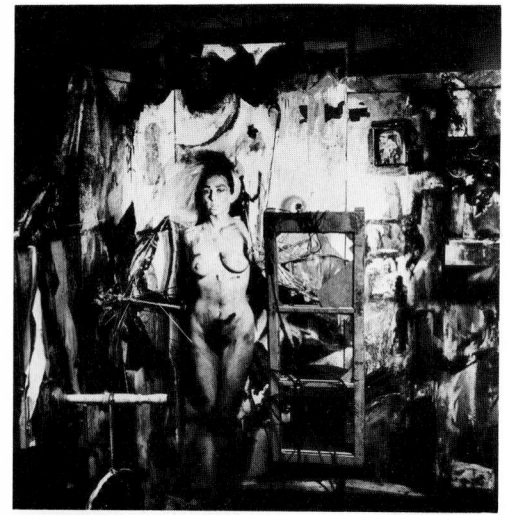

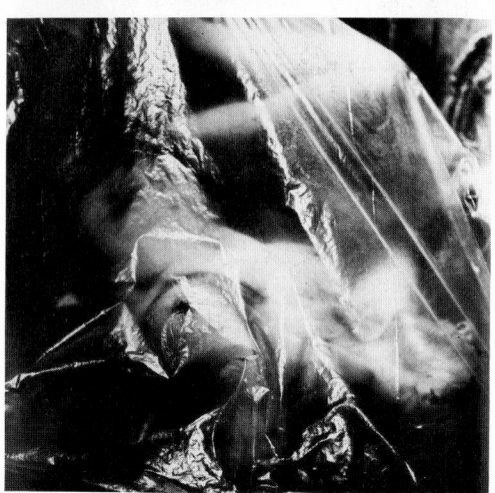

In 1962 I began a loft environment built of large panels interlocked by rhythmic color units, broken mirrors and glass, lights, moving umbrellas and motorized parts. I worked with my whole body—the scale of the panels incorporating my own physical scale. I then decided I wanted my actual body to be combined with the work as an integral material—a further dimension of the construction...

In December of '63 I was encouraged by my friend Erró (the Icelandic, Paris-based painter) when I told him I wanted to do a series of physical transformations of my body in my work—the constructions and wall environment. I thought the ritual aspect of the process could put me in a trance-like state.

Covered in paint, grease, chalk, ropes, plastic, I establish my body as visual territory. Not only am I an image maker, but I explore the image values of flesh as material I choose to work with. The body may remain erotic, sexual, desired, desiring but it is as well votive: marked, written over in a text of stroke and gesture discovered by my creative female will.

I write "my creative female will" because for years my most audacious works were viewed as if someone else inhabiting me had created them—they were considered "masculine" when seen as aggressive, bold. As if I were inhabited by a stray male principle; which would be an interesting possibility—except in the early sixties this notion was used to blot out, denigrate, deflect the coherence, necessity and personal integrity of what I made and how it was made.

In 1963 to use my body as an extension of my painting-constructions was to challenge and threaten the psychic territorial power lines by which women were admitted to the Art Stud Club, so long as they behaved **enough** like the men, did work clearly in the traditions and pathways hacked out by the men. (The only artist I know of making body art before this time was Yoko Ono.)

The nude was being used in early Happenings as an object (often an "active" object). I was using the nude as myself—the artist—and as a primal, archaic force which could unify energies I discovered as visual information. I felt compelled to "conceive" of my body in manifold aspects which had eluded the culture around me. Eight years later the implications of the body images I had explored would be clarified when studying sacred Earth Goddess artifacts of 4,000 years ago.

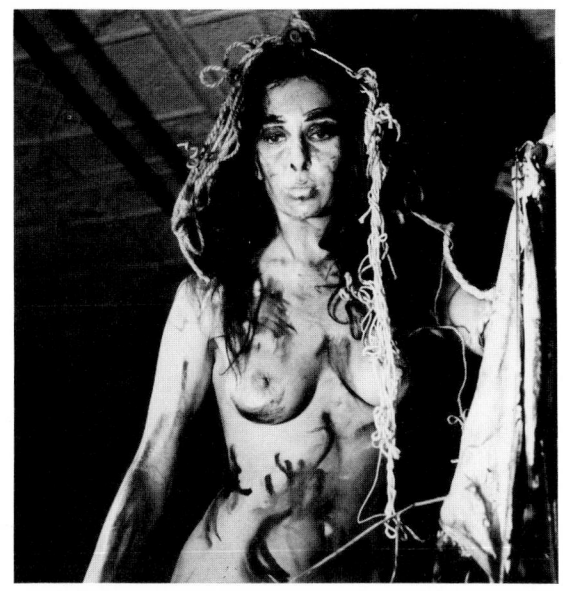

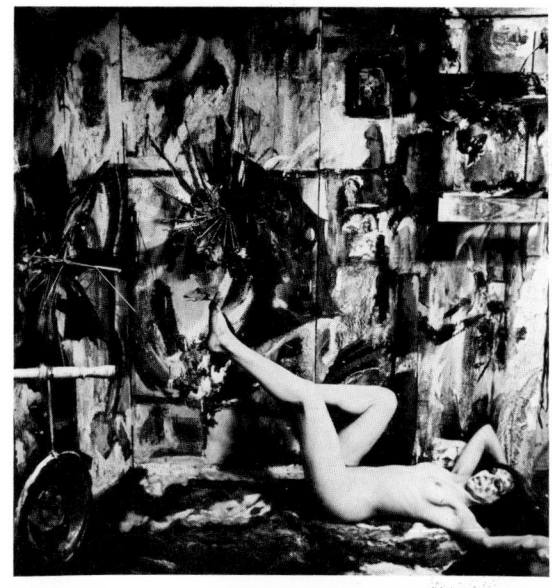

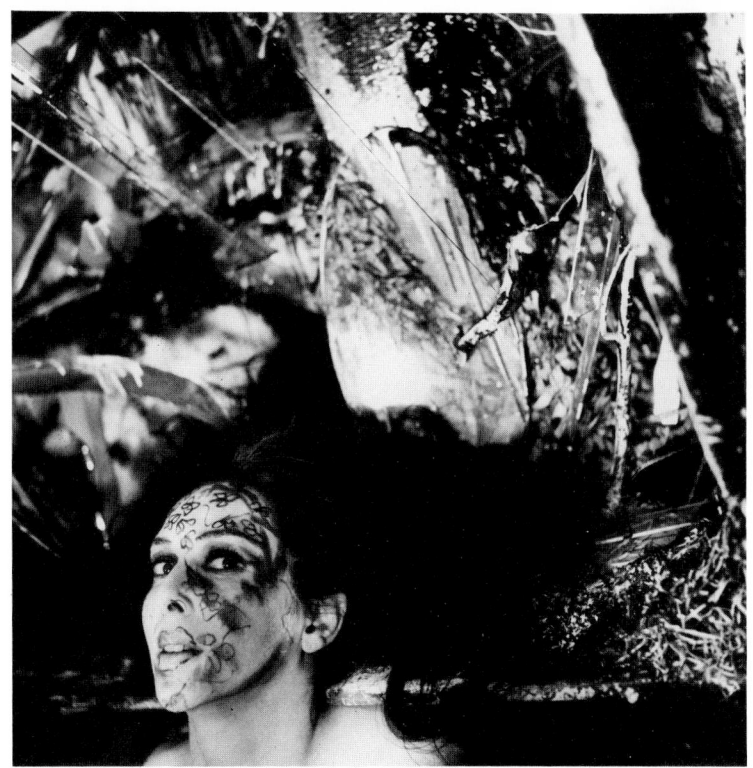

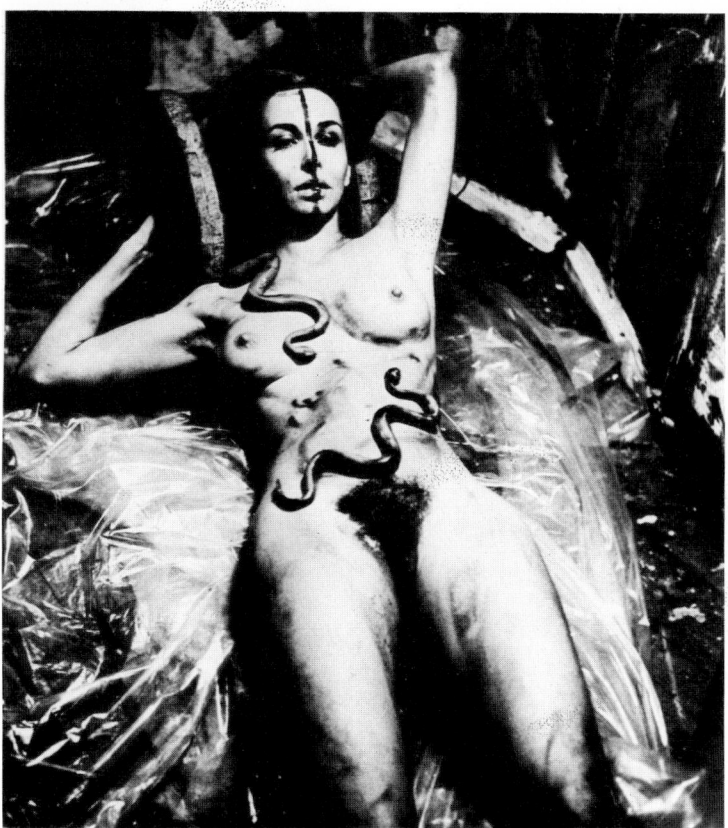

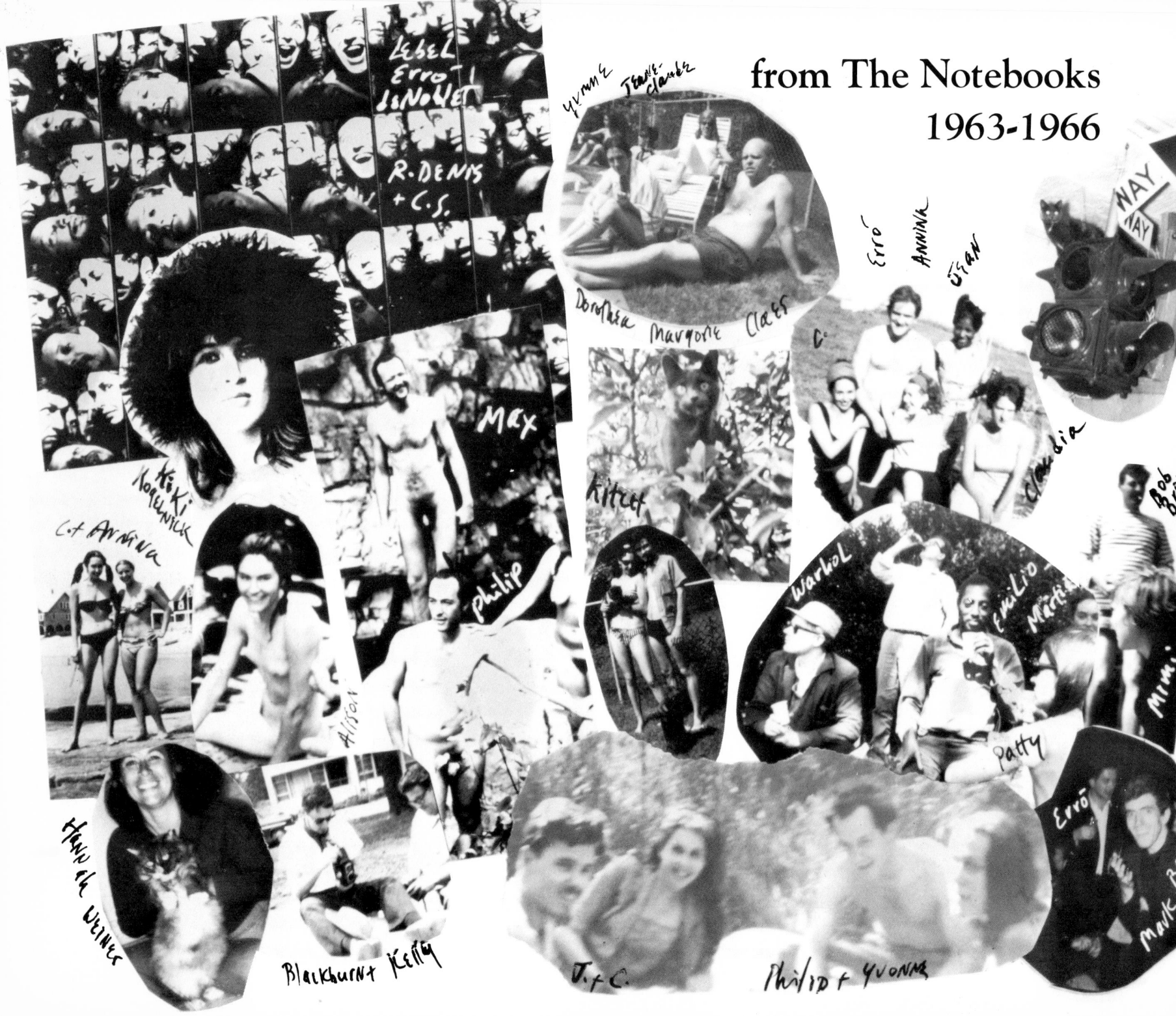

from The Notebooks
1963-1966

I can remember orgasm, the tree rustling at my window, a particular woven blanket and the crib I was in where my own experience of my body sensations gathered. I decided my genital was my soul . . . that is what my parents' explanation of soul led me to believe. Soul was "true and most perfect, when the body died the soul lived in the stars" . . . the soul was some essence of being! Conscious!

1963

Principle: one in need is assisted by the other . . . most imminent need—no matter how slight—is one provided for . . . in this way we never "leave" one another.

1963

---

our relation to Nature—(my work and Brakhage's)

while I've not worked microscopically, smallest open eye unit activates full range of actual eye activity; scale in our works rooted in natural phenomena, visual immediacy as I find no where else.

Duration (Zukofsky pointed out in "Northlight" and other boxes) is that of landscape; compressed, transformed—the total vitality of any one area to another. . . . Blue vesicles: basic organic shape force, direction of life energy pulse. Bion the simplest notation of a rhythmic impulse (stylized in Paisley, ancient Eastern gold ornaments, flower, tendril, hair, nostril, navel, cunt, mushroom flange cock head, flute, mandolin, scrolls, scripts, cello, guitar, basket! And a cat stretches, a monkey leaps, a bird darts upward.)

(Exceptions to note: hard edge patterns, tactile reductions. . . . out of finger into the mind, systematic; impulses of reverential severity—to be put away from nature: Aztec, Nigerian, Mayan . . .)

Take arrowhead, horn, tooth, half-moon, yin-yang, take a snake! Take basic stroke of hand nerve pulse to brush, eye to hand, paint to canvas as related, integral organic rhythm: Monet, Velasquez, Rembrandt, Pollock, Joan Mitchell. Event. Particle of universe action. Microcosmic movement building a world moment by moment, motion by motion!

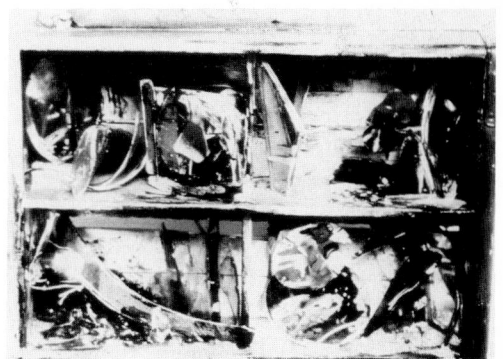

Northlight   *1962*
Construction: wooden box, clocks, mirrors, glass, oil paint. Private collection.

Fluid energy shapes immobilized in Ainu, Jo mon comma shaped jewels and sculptured figures. Take Crete! Serpent of Aesculapius protector against disease! The cure and curve of Lotus, Lyre, spiral instruments, adornments. Keep us on our way as one with what we perceive.

1963

Our lives themselves as material, stuff for our art or our lives as art containers/or life the way we shape or discover it being a form of art, the happening an intensification of our actions in life. The distinctions here swinging between intellection/perception/action.

It is not a part-time, compartmentalized (studio) activity: it is as if we are launched in some wondrous banal boat whose very motion transforms the landscape it moves through.

Notice this insistence on Motion. We cannot capture, hold a moment (impressionism), repeat the moment's verbal content (theater), capture the action itself (futurism): we intensify the perceptions of change, flux, and release them in juxtapositions which grind in on the senses.

It is intimate and intense. Happenings: raw, direct, no intermediate crafting, fabricating. Kaprow's works stream mythic, socially edged by ritual process; Oldenburg's are netted in private memory as environment through which we re-focus, discover strands of our own past time-relations; strong cultural and nostalgic roughness. Whitman's performances the most interiorized, tactile, plastic-poetic, evolving a less specific time-space than Oldenburg's. Whitman leaves the audience as discrete, perceiving agents; Kaprow physically engages them, moves them in a mass of linear participation. While Oldenburg uses the audience as physical material, packed in around, surrounding, holding the frame on an irregular rectangular performance-environment. Hansen's Happenings are loose, rangey, arbitrary, open to impulse; the audience hangs raggedly to anticipations, shifting conjunctions. (And Dine the first man to use explicitly personal material—his psychoanalytic tape, uncensored self-exposure. . .just the voice in the dark. The audience didn't approve of that much actuality! A turning point for me. He had stripped it all down to bare desire, anger, the lived life. Audience didn't get it or couldn't stand it.)

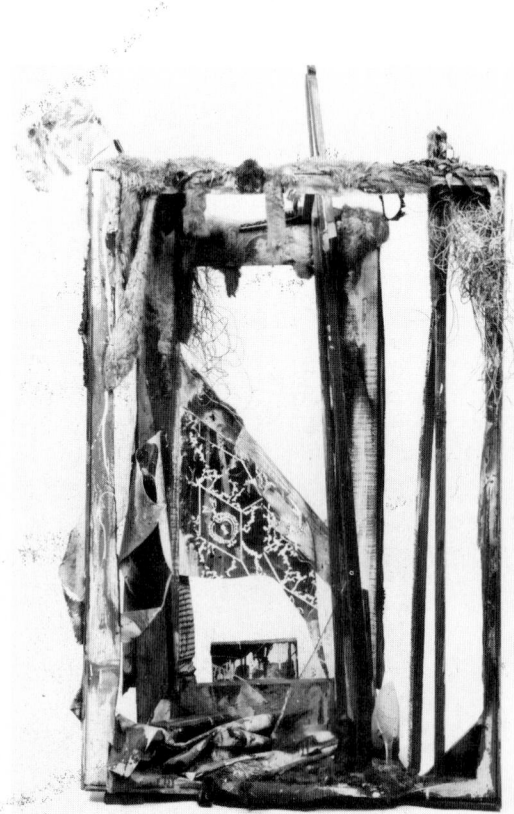

Colorado House   1962
Construction: wood, mirrors, glass, bottles, fur, gloves, cut up oil painting, oil paint, flag. 45" x 32½" x 17½"

Image—Whitman
Atmosphere—Oldenburg
Concordance—Kaprow (audience/participant must agree to his procedures)
Restraint, slowed durations, collectivity—Dewey
Social action, aggression, attack—Lebel
Comic strip, populist Americana—Grooms, Gross
Guilt and transfiguration—Vostell
Sensation and memory is tactile, plastic, palpable for painters—not verbal, musical or conceptual. Sensation and memory evade the grasp of traditional media.

Note for *Fuses:* cut Greek white seduction into turning backside....

"The trouble with Yoko Ono's pieces is that she wants to make you feel what she felt, to feel like her, and I don't think I want to do that," said Higgins tonight.

December 1965

Capacity for expressive life and for love are insolubly linked; that was my understanding when I taught; saw immediately facing the individuals in a class what their chance for expressive work was and its direct relationship to their social/sexual and emotional life

1963

Sexual damming is expressive damning.

Do not assume that what you think is "natural" for you is just. He says "what she expects of me is not natural for me!" She said "things he wants to do with me seem unnatural!" How they fear sensation, pleasure; starvation drives them to an embrace which is a shadow to expression they repress.

When I said LOVE I meant EROTIC love; deep transforming bounty one imparts to another reciprocally; it assumes...all! To celebrate, illuminate respect, tenderness, trust, passion and regard...to joyfully put all we are into one another's hands...all contact, touch, expression possible, desired.

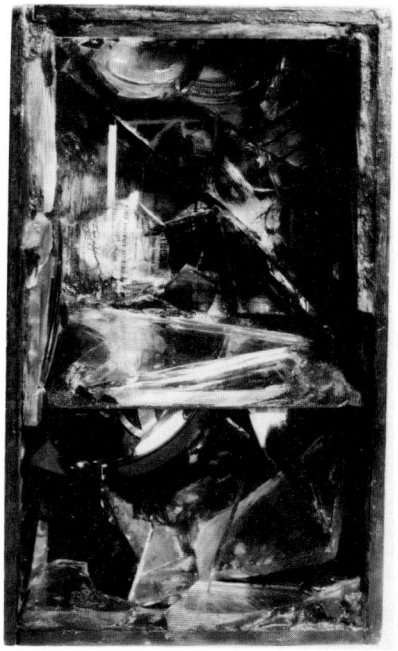

Romer's House (for Julia Smolinski   1962
Wooden box: metal, mirrors, glass, oil paint.

These women are fastidious: the living beast of their flesh embarrasses them; they are trained to shame...blood, mucus, juices, odors of their flesh fill them with fear. They have some abstracted wish for pristine, immaculate sex...cardboard soaked in perfume. Many of them imagine that in giving birth they abandon themselves to flesh life—drugged and desensitized as they may be. But they've been taught that here is their physical worth, moon fed, streaming process...let the gift of the child ennoble and redeem the intricacies of their bodies.

Your own language calling you to change and assert your deepest personal image addresses you by *inclusion!* (Ever say: "Woman and husband"?) *"Men* should be freed, healed, and cured, not adjusted" (McClure). Is inclusion an emotional generosity? How can you even know? ("*Men* revolt outside in Universe World Air by acts of personal nobility; they refuse themselves as usable articles or objects." McClure.) Are you still turning to Freud as sexologist—he who at the end of his life admitted (from the patriarchal summit he struggled upon) 'woman...it is true I have always dealt with them in terms of men.' Or, Jung who raises his arms in benediction over *I Ching* where the world is tipped topsyturvy, where the sequence of earlier Heaven or Primal Arrangement is broken, where moon which was the second daughter becomes the second son! Then when we asked the *I Ching* to speak about itself...what we saw had occurred in its life as a book: our form endlessly falling asunder and coming together again.

1963

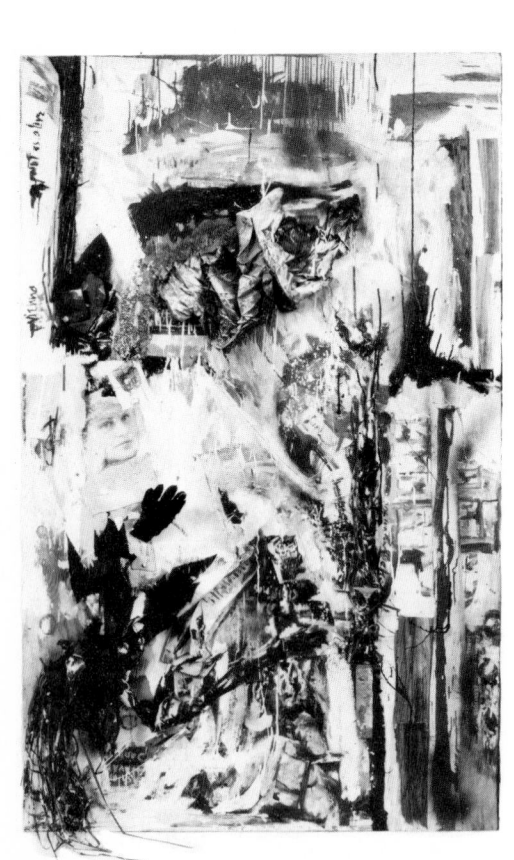

IS it   too dog   or too loved? ?
Is IT more delicate   after you've loved?
Is the DOG too delicate *or* beloved?
Is it too—delicate   to be loved?
Is it too dog to love?
Is it too love to be dogged?

1966

One Window Is Clear—Notes to Lou Andreas Salomé 1965
Masonite panel: photos of Salomé, Rilke, Nietzche; cloth, recording tape, paper, gloves, canvas, oil paint. 69½″ x 47½″ x 4″

Vision is not a fact but an aggregate of sensations.

I want evocation—SPACE (a place) between desire and experience

1966

these Americans
hard, stiff, cold, repressed; brutality and sentimentality
moving into icy psychic technological "cool"
when they are falling in love they can be beautiful; they are full
of hope and fearful emotion

they do not have charm; they do work with charms in the world
everything dies under their hands and they don't know why

they blame secretly and indulge themselves in substitute/second-
hand pleasures

they have energy for work and materials; but they are not loving, abandoned, childlike
and convinced that joy can be in them. Cut off in their emotion their relations to
materials, objects and each other become brittle; they keep moving; they are accepting of
what surrounds them lacking interior self-confidence to change and be changed. Giving,
going over feeling is most difficult—they enjoy masks, costumes, festivities which reveal
them slightly. They are hot or cold—they do not stream in their flesh. Many stream in
their mouths, out of their mouths; and so they confuse shit with material, shit and sex;
excretion with excess gifts with taking—that is losing essence, so bewildered are they as to
what essence is in them. They manage certain intellectual breakthroughs; they are never
dumb; they are stupid about their own natures. But then, cosmopolitan Nature is remote,
antique...perhaps for sports or specific periods of play and pursuit of health or frail
dreams mixed with glamour.

Wild things/wild life confuses them, makes them uneasy: bugs, birds, snakes. Mud, dirt
and dust discourage their control over the world—In this way their insecurity increases;
they are guilty, cast-out, and full of anger and impatience. And this obstructs their
pleasures. Egoistic, guarded, jealous of their effectiveness they feel crowded in their need
of one another; they proportion and ration contacts; they measure and judge endlessly,
narrowly, they even frighten themselves and wonder why; being distrustful and distrusted;
open and naive. The myth, the dream which they do not meet.

1966

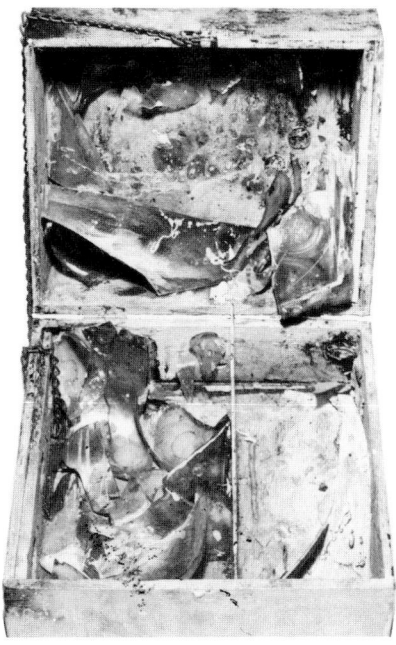

For Yvonne Rainer's 'Ordinary Dance'   1962
Fire Series (controlled burning): burnt wood,
glass, mirrors, paint.

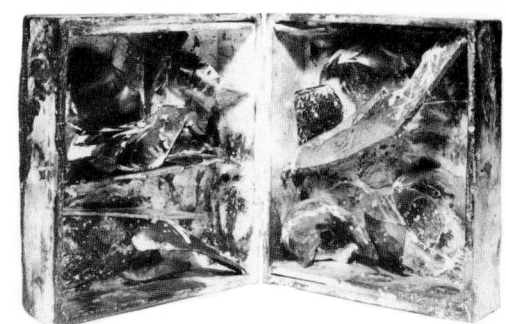

Darker Companion   1962
Fire Series (controlled burning): burnt wood,
glass, mirrors, paint.

from Diary 1965: Memoranda

Lively irony that I developed theater to do for me in moments, what I wanted words to do infinitely: to provide compression, spring-board to senses....Very complicated...evades statement....being surprising to me, but I know the experience I sought to *hold* with words I now use gesture-action to release...where vision can move most freely.

A despair with language re-enforced by its social-sexual action. When I am saying what I see, men find it difficult to hear that *I* say it—they take it away, use my words as their own because a female source of illumination registers negatively....(not so with Jim, of course), but very often *they need what I say* but not from me—a peculiar withdrawal, (absence) or aggressive twisting to what is most possibly fine and fat as interchange—two people speaking *to* (not "at" or away from) one another. To some extent this also occurs in regard to my Happenings, Kinetic Theater pieces. So—definitely—in its brief new life here—a man's enterprise, that I get a sort of wavery regard, as if my work is a vagary, dismissable, *because* my aggressions, anxieties are not those the male community recognizes, prizes.

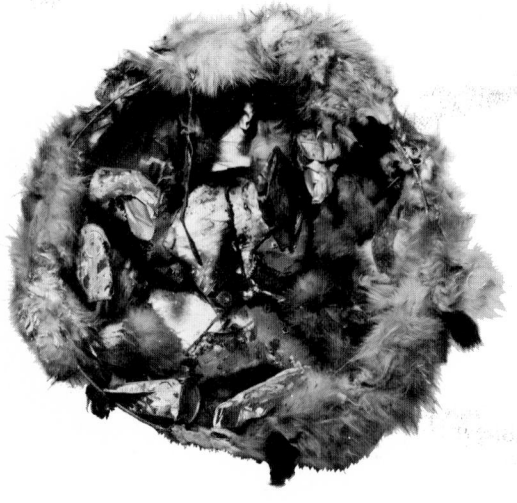

Fur Wheel   1962
Construction on lamp shade base: fur, tin cans, mirrors, glass, oil paint; mounted on turning wheel. 19" x 19" x 11½"

you can't tell an idea STOP   i'm not ready for another idea yeats—you can ignore it put it out of your head but a real impulse insight zooming in try and stop it you'd be mad   or to stop voluptuous mad will organic desire lust superimposition dream breaking yr eyeballs open   never mind

all the things this generation has individually discovered, defined, hewn, structured as unique, personal, will become a spectrum of interchangeable elements, freely available and subject to new uses and certain commonplace understandings.

what we want we want everyone else to have a chance at—it insures our gains, affirms their importance, gives us an enlarged "community." WE've pretty much got sex cleared into natural, intense, flow exchange; we're working on pot, LSD and "black power" which will mean a liberation of old white-spirit energy and the clarification of sick white autocratic ambivalence towards woman.

1964

BE PREPARED:
to have your brain picked
to have the pickings misunderstood
to be mistreated whether your success increases or decreases
to have detraction move with admiration—in step
to have your time wasted
your intentions distorted
the simplest relationships in your thoughts twisted
to be USED and MISUSED
to be "copy" to be copied to want to cope out cop out pull in and away
if you are a woman (and things are not utterly changed)
they will almost never believe you really did it
(what you did do)
they will worship you they will ignore you they will malign
you they will pamper you
they will try to take what you did as their own
(a woman doesn't understand her best discoveries after all)
they will patronize you humor you
try to sleep with you want you to transform them with your energy
they will berate your energy they will try to be part of your
sexuality they will deny your sexuality/or your work they
will depend on you for information for generosity they will
forget whatever help you give they will try to be heroic for
you they will not help you when they might they will bring
problems they will ignore your problems a few will appreciate
deeply they will be loving you as what you do as what you
are loving how you are being they will of course be strong in
themselves and clear they will NOT be married to quiet
tame drones they will not say what a great mother you would
be or do you like to cook and where you might expect understanding and appreciation you must expect NOTHING then
enjoy whatever gives-to-you as long as it does and however and
NEVER justify yourself just do what you feel carry it strongly
yourself

1966

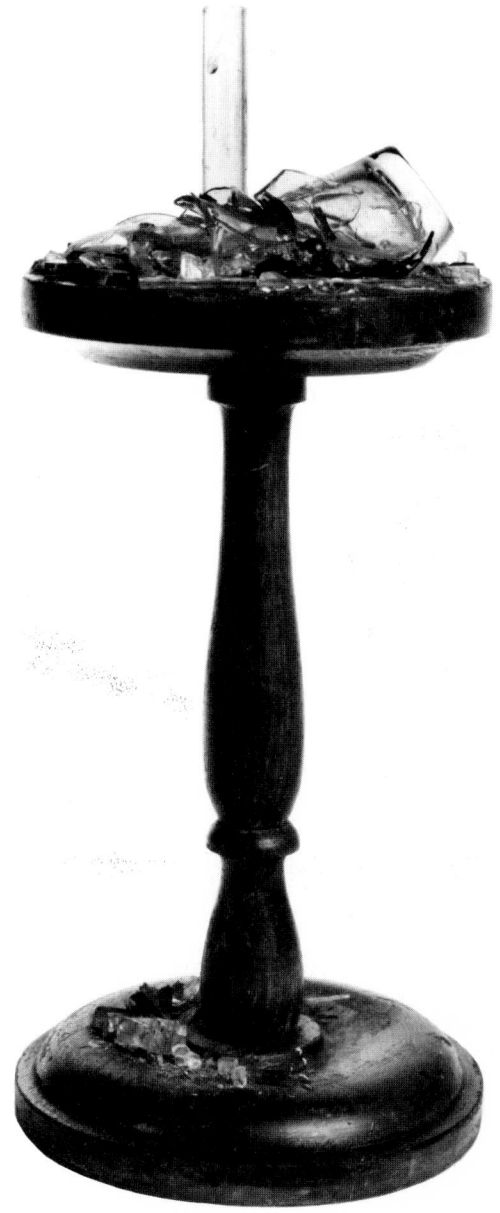

Hat Stand   1965
Object: wood, glass. Private collection.

From a letter to Jean-Jacques Lebel,
February 1964, responding to an
invitation to create a "happening" for
Lebel's Festival of Free Expression:

There are now several works moving in minds-
eye...tentatively identified as MEAT JOY, and
DIVISIONS AND RUBBLE;...MEAT JOY shifting now,
relating to Artaud, McClure, and French butcher
shops—carcass as paint (it dripped right through
Soutine's floor)...flesh jubilation...extremes of
this sense...may involve quantities of dark fabric
and paint drawn from performance area outward
into audience to become inundation of all available space—action and viewing space inter-
changed, broken through. Smell, feel of meat...
chickens, fish, sausages? I see several women
whose gestures develop from tactile, bodily relationship to individual men and a mass of meat
slices. Specific sequence of collision and
embrace...a rising, falling counterpoint to
bodies...very dark (very bright). Hand-held lights
spotting color cover movements.

My work can take substance from the materials I
find...this means that any particular space, any
debris unique to Paris and any "found" performers...would be potential structural elements for
the piece. I've been working a great deal with the
Judson dancers for love of their non-dance movement and their aggressive, expansive interest in
changing the very physical traditions which have
given their bodies extraordinary scope and
strength; and my pieces impose space relations
for them, provoke personal responses which will
work inclusively with any chosen or found environment. I do not require or want any specially pre-
determined "set-up". What I find will be what I
need.

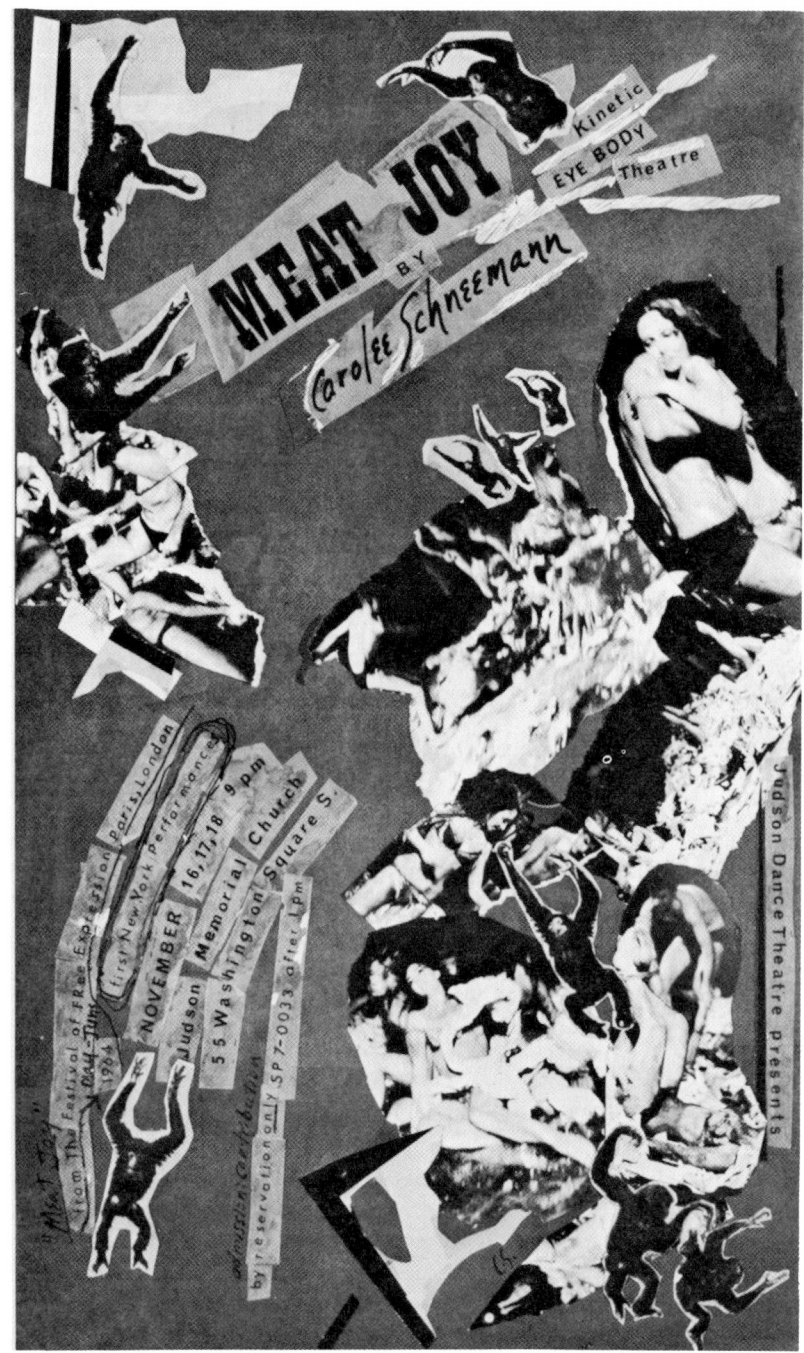

MEAT JOY

May 29 1964 Festival de La Libre
Expression, Paris

June 8 1964 Dennison Hall, London

November 16 17 18 1964 Judson
Church NY

Meat Joy developed from dream sensation images gathered in journals stretching back to 1960. By February '64 more elaborate drawings and notes accumulated as scraps of paper, on the wall over my bed, in tablets. I'd been concentrating on the possibility of capturing interactions between physical/metabolic changes, dream content, and my sensory orientation upon and after waking: an attempt to view paths between conscious and unconscious organization of image, pun, double-entendre, masking, and the release of random memory fragments (often well-defined sounds, instructions, light, textures, weather, places from the past, solutions to problems). I found the transition between dream and waking, envisioning and practical function, became so attenuated that it was often difficult to leave the loft for my job or errands. My body streamed with currents of imagery: the interior directives varied from furtive to persistent: either veiling or so intensely illuminating ordinary situations that I continually felt dissolved, exploded, permeated by objects, events, persons outside of the studio, the one place where my concentration could be complete.

The drawings of movement, and notations on relations of color, light, sound, language fragments, demanded organization, enaction, and that I be able to sustain the connection to this imagery for an extended time—through the search for space, performers, funds, during painstaking rehearsals, the complexities of production down to the smallest details—all to achieve a fluid, unpredictable performance.

Meat Joy has the character of an erotic rite: excessive, indulgent, a celebration of flesh as material: raw fish, chickens, sausages, wet paint, transparent plastic, rope, brushes, paper scrap. Its propulsion is toward the ecstatic—shifting and turning between tenderness, wildness, precision, abandon: qualities which could at any moment be sensual, comic, joyous, repellent. Physical equivalences are enacted as a psychic and imagistic stream in which the layered elements mesh and gain intensity by the energy complement of the audience. (They were seated on the floor as close to the performance area as possible, encircling, resonating.) Our proximity heightened the sense of communality, transgressing the polarity between performer and audience.

In precisely determined patterns, vertical, diagonal and horizontal shafts of movement and lighting cut through the overall circular structures of **Meat Joy**. The popular songs occurring throughout most sequences are "circular" in their thematic and rhythmic three-minute disc-spun durations, and they introduce a literal, istoric time—popular "ritual" sound centering the sensory flow. Tapes of Paris street sounds were superimposed: the cries and clamourings of Rue de Seine vendors selling fish, chickens, vegetables and flowers beneath my hotel window where I first composed the actual performance score. These shouts dominate a layering of traffic noise, and displace the songs' recognizable continuity, interfering with their associative range.

Certain parameters of the piece function consistently. Sequence, lights, sound, materials—these were planned and coordinated in rehearsal. Other components vary with each performance. Attitude, gesture, phrasing, duration, relationship between performers (and between performers and objects), became loosely structured in rehearsal and were expected to evolve. For instance, "The Paint Attack" was rehearsed as a **projective** exercise with brushes and dry sponges: the actual paint, fish, chickens, hot dogs introduced during performance came as a visceral shock.

Lighting is keyed to the larger rhythms of the work—sound and action—by washes and sudden

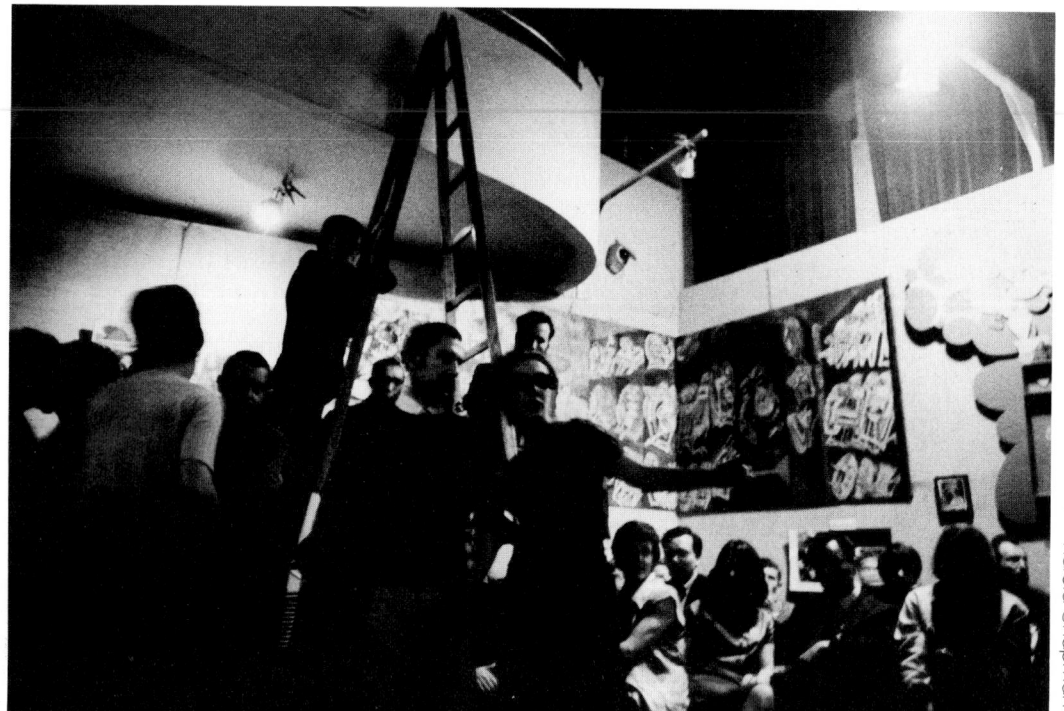

Seating audience, with Ben Vautier. Free Expression visual exhibit in background.

Harold Chapman

concentrations of strong illumination on energy clusters. Here again, within certain determined bounds (I knew when I needed, for example, "a muddy light in a pool over there which then turns to diffuse gold" or in another place, "something blue and wet-looking with a blast of green") the lighting and sound technicians were free to improvise. They followed formal cues but had to be able to make choices relating to energy shifts of both performers and audience. Four black-outs were used to compact or shatter sequences, to

insert a **blank** in which perception is halted and the imagery settles into the mind.

As the audience enters, the tape of "Notes as Prologue" begins: a collage of my voice reading the written notes formative to **Meat Joy** (so that the work is verbally revealed before it begins, including discarded unrealizable imagery), beginning French exercises (from a book titled Look and Learn and a dictionary), a ticking clock, the noises of the Rue de Seine.

MEAT JOY NOTES AS PROLOGUE

Voici la tête d'un homme
DREAM WORK February 14th 1964 Images
from Jim's dreams (I'll form it this way to theater)
Voila la tête d'une femme
a couple enter darkened room slowly
as if on ice together lifting off each other's
clothes gliding gestures they lay each gar-
ment on the floor carefully repeatedly until they are naked
they take covers from a bed & continue covering
the floor when it is covered they lie down together
on it & begin a slow embrace rolling

TRAVAIL / TRAVAUX *voici les hommes* *TRAVAUX FOUS*
SCENARIO GREY FILM no black & white
si loin proche voici l'homme **TRAVAIL / TRAVAUX /**
extremes of grey a permeation the
train angled rush slow slow & wild against
the skin heavy thick figures rushing in the darkness
from above to an entrance myself from below
towards that platform (others pulse by me) they are
the soldiers my arms are full of hard boiled eggs
I shift them as I run reach the platform
move onto the steps

TRAVAIL / TRAVAILLER / TRAVAILLEUR / TRAVAILLAIT
THROW OUT THE DOG murky particles of grey
/ TRAVAILLONS *TRAVAIL DUR*
clarified to the rotting wide porched house a very brief
set to image of it open swung porch details of
debris (childrens toys-household implements-carriages-wheels-
broken posts-clothes-rags-cords-rusted metal) flow around the
door across the steps & fan out over the front yard
two tall feathery trees the light does not increase a small figure moves out the door a
child holding a round shape in her arms she heaves it
quite suddenly forward it flies off the porch into the yard
at our eyes the small dog unwinds in the
air **THROW OUT THE DOG** **THROW OUT THE**
DOG

les yeux sont dans la tête *cette femme a les yeux ouverts* *j'ai*
les yeux ouverts je suis engagée dans *c'est que j'ai besoin de*
UNDER HIM circle of the balls slow
de boire *le droit* *doit être faux cette femme a*
rush down the legs up the cock cock of love
les yeux fermés *il faut que j'apprenne un bon français* *cet*
follow its head into arch of hairs all as I do see him
homme a les yeux ouverts *j'ai les yeux ouverts* *FICHEZ MOI*
when he raises me on his arms over me the belly
LA PAIX / FOUTEZ MOI LA PAIX *il a les yeux fermés*
circle & muscle ridges bounding it leading to a sky
VA TE FAIRE FOUTRE *j'ai les yeux ouverts* *quel voit?*
of chest close on arm muscles precise as ap-
elle me voit *je la voit* *il a les yeux* *FICHE LE*
ples his neck

CAMP / FOUT LE CAMP *elle a les yeux fermés* *elle ne*
voyait pas *elle ne me voyait pas* *je parle difficilement le*

francais *un homme a deux yeux* *j'ai deux yeux* *voici*
mes yeux

In March

A SOLO FOR MEAT JOY
tearing hair / painting self / slipping falling over plastic
cloths / fall into a water trough // jump up running wringing
il emportera les souliers *ecoutez-moi* *regardez cela*
hair // slide turn smearing body with grease
vous me suivez? *ça c'est chouette* *ça me plait* *les*
turning rocking hair/head thrown back
mains sont sales *les mains sont propres* *cette serviette est sale*
& forth done until collapse

je l'ai dans la peau
ça me rappelle *je ne vous oublierai pas* *quelle*
est la fonction du nez *cette femme tient une fleur à la main*

or beating on garbage lids cans inter-
minable
elle sent la fleur *quelques fleurs sont parfumées*
figures crawl very quickly over the floor lights flash
before them

elles sentent bon *d'autres fleurs n'ont pas de parfum*
raw meat raw fantasy not as things are wished but
voici de l'herbe *l'herbe n'a pas de parfum* *il sent bon*
how they feel no justification / no impulse censor
no explanation

the nude flips like a fish

ces fleurs sentent bon *voici les cochons*
1. wrapped in rags bang the fish around frantically
as if to smash if & then suddenly sit brush hair back
legs open take a cigarette & smoke 2.
voici des cochons *j'en suis marteau* *je suis marteau*
take a fish & slowly follow the contours of the reclining nude
with it tenderly sustained the nude jumps up
grabs the fish & frys it all gather to eat
(the fish is dipped in paint) they are naked
quelques cochons sont propres *vois la page un deux*
cinq *des cochons sales ne sentent pas bon* *ils sentent mauvais*
half-naked in rags splattered with paint
bright glorious & worn

voici de la fumée *il y a de la fumée qui sent bon*
cet homme fume une pipe *torque / tort / avoir tort / toupion*
touret / tournée *d'autres cochons sont propres* *bien*
end with clearing cleaning washing each other closely packed
tournée *voici les noms des couleurs* *vert / bleu / blanc*
dull light one two men carry a woman to table for painting
lay her out on plastic Claudia in apron with a basket (tran-
/ rouge **ELLE EST BETE** **ELLE EST BETE** *rouge /*
sitions) with a flashlight to collect the chickens & fish & to
replace them

jaune / vert / bleu / blanc / gris *quelle est la couleur de l'herbe*
ROLL CALL

et des feuilles au printemps *l'herbe et les feuilles sont vertes au*

& the vision which cannot be repeated I take vision
printemps *je suis prête* *quelle est la couleur de cette*
not as fact but as an aggregate of sensations I want
jeune fille
evocation space & place between desire & experience

(and blow it open!)
high sound—go to—
low sound—go to—
screech . . . go howl . . . go
a very short work of smash conjunctions NO BUILDING
painted figure: utterly shaped in silence TENSEGRITY
call it Lateral Splay?

Interception; transformation of intention / impulse
Action with materials: gesture from activity of tearing
pushing gluing rumbling ripping rubbing scratching spilling

tiffany glass mexican glass broken in layers
did someone say SIN or SORROW?
corn on their doors & wreaths pumpkins on
steps ancient connecticut tribes which observe the ritual
having lost the original commemoration of fervor & appeal
now decorating the passage of impassive months
spread secure in the regulated observance of haunting pleasures our house old/fierce/forlorn/stone/staunch
/forgotten abandoned where no one wants to live

ugly piece
assistants give paint in various containers fury of throwing hurling non-determinate color / aim / direction of impact the figure charging thru alley aisles

a tray of substances soft & cake-like balanced
fast movement & the tray slips off his shoulders the
objects fall over the audience movements of rising falling contained between heap of debris & an immense saucer
of water body wrapped in rags strings cords

ces lèvres sont rouges *le ciel est bleu*
IN THE PYRE
they drench me with sponges full of paint they drench
all the women all the women are drenched with paint
we throw the sponges we grab the sponges
we drench one another

oser / ôter *est jeune* *quelquefois* *quand le soleil se*
couche ôté ôtez-moi *cette épine du doigt* *les belles choses nous*
font plaisir *quand elle se voit dans la glace elle est belle Mona Lisa*
ête-vous belle? *peser petite mon petit* *elle a un sourire*
pourquoi ce sourire *pourpre* *vous êtes belle?*
quand elle sourit elle ne fait pas de bruit *fait des phrases*
pis piscine à peu après tant pis plaindre se plaindre *voici*
un beau tableau par Léonard de Vinci *s'il vous plaît*

MEAT & PAINT

painting of sex of each other by couple (interlude section
myself bandaged head   cut up the chicken
stand over it   on my lap   between my
legs   matter of factly)   build to amore-paint inundation   close focus inward / mirror behind

this feels better
for my right hand now
it may be alright from   from
or this is better is this better I get more turn or pace
why it is better I don't know but it is better than this is
try this
a fine point is dreadful
a gold point is rigid
after a couple hours

cela est certaine   Lisa est-elle belle   cela n'est pas certain
from certain sequences marked new york march 1964
couple painting exchange   mixture   figures charging thru alley aisles   slipping
        1. woman hacking plucking throwing the bird
        2. tearing hair / painting self / falling running rocking
poissons policier polisson pollen
group 3   the fish banging smashing follow a body's flight
        wild pig meat   slapping caressing rising falling
between heaps of debris   naked bodies all wash in bowls
drying each other   closely packed dull light banging on

j'ai mon idée de beauté   se moucher   il a son idée de
garbage lids   hammock   painted figures painted
beauté   nos idées de beauté ne sont pas sûres   miroir mouchoir
at   water guns   begin clothing stapling to floor

*mouvement   Lisa est-elle belle   il n'a pas de mesure pour
la beauté   sourire de femme   mouvement   est-ce que la
femme est belle   cela n'est pas certain   les plaisirs et la*

NAKED   MATERIALS   TEARING   INSTRUMENTS—POWER
TOOLS   CONSTRUCTION—BUILT IN PERFORMANCE: GLUE
PAPERS DOWN INTO STANDING PANELS: RUB ON THEM RUB-
BINGS   GLUING PAPERS & RUBBING: BLOOD / SEX CON-
CRETELY: THE CITY / THE BODY   SUCKING PULLING IN
GRAB HOLD

*douleur sont des sensations   voilà des plaisirs   voici des
plaisirs ensuite   la balle   il est au bord de la mer   il est
couché sur le sable   il entend le bruit de la vague et il regarde
la mer   voilà des plaisirs   il prend un bain   simple
simplement   impresse   nager   plaisir*

MEAT JOY (certain instructions)
The images are realized by a process which unites visual obses-
et un concombre   sans encombrement encombrer concombre cul
sions and spontaneous physical action.
encombrer
The sequence developed by my partner and me will be counter-
thrust in their relation to actions of the other performers. We
should provide a focus which brings to extremes the qualities
of the other performers—extremes of intensity, in the range of
speeds and actions—from dream frame slow motion for virtual
frenzy, and in concentrated presence.

*essai étable étalon   le plaisir et la douleur sont des sensations
étaler   le plaisir   le plaisir et la douleur*
The focus is never on the self, but on the materials, gestures
& actions which involve us. Sense that we become what we
see, what we touch. A certain tenderness (or empathy) is pervasive—even to the most violent actions: say, cutting, chopping,
throwing chickens.

*apprendez   on pose le doigt sur un objet   on a des sensations
on a une sensation de toucher de chaleur et de froid   cet
homme touche un morceau de bois avec ses doigts   attirer*

Series
upper torso evolutionary naked covered with dark paint
ce bois est sec   ce bois est dur
smeared lower torso work pants rolled up shave legs
        FEET FOCUS under curtain or plastic
        3. debris pile on which I perform eye/body
les objets ne font pas plaisir
        4. spreading of clothing
        5. meat/ running / slapping against self & objects
        6. kissing rolling couples to exhaustion
        7. sewing & being costumed
        8. leg choreography in debris
fleuves   nous font plaisir   un attrait   cet attrait nous
        9. sponge drench
attire   cet attrait nous plait   nous ne cherchons pas plus
        10. running tray of objects falling involvement slow
motion random juggling
loin   nos desirs peuvent nous changer
        11. painting wrapping then the painted ones roll to-
gether
        12. blowing bubbles
        13. bouncing balls
        14. from the balcony lowering cloths & materials plastic
        15. the love paint exchange
        16. the chickens / hacking / plucking / tearing hair /
painting self / rooms / falls
        17. naked bodies all washed in bowls drying each other
        18. banging on garbage can lids
        19. crawling
        20. hammock bed figures / jumping / painting at /
water guns
        21. the fish dance on the self / or / the nude follow-
ing contours
        22. performers behind plastic staccato touching
        23. group under within plastic rising falling angular
musculature
        24. figures wrapped in plastic like presents rolling &
effréné effrénées ce regard égarer égayer égide églantier   silence
jumping running
silencée   à demain   église   mais nos désirs peuvent
        25. reclining lovers   the independent space
nous changer   il y a certains désirs qui sont plus forts que d'autres

        26. women on boards

*le bébé voit le chat et il voit la balle   il a le désir de prendre
le chat   il a le désir de jouer avec la balle   lequel des deux
prendra-t-il   si son désir de prendre le chat est plus fort que son
désir de prendre la balle il ira vers le chat   il est allé prendre le*

*chat   crasser   nous désirons les choses qui nous semblent bonnes
les désirs ne sont pas toujours bons   nous pouvons avoir les
idées fausses   cuir cuire cuisine cuisinier cuisse   il pense à sa
balle   cuistrerie   il donne un bon coup a sa balle   dessous*
FEET FOCUS
curtain slightly raised   stage illuminated   choreography for feet
destinée destrier désir   il a le désir de jouer avec la balle
debris pile drag on   from which & in which I can perform eye/body
upper torso naked covered with dark smeared paint
workpants rolled up to knees   shave legs
remove the pants   turn back   white flesh bottom
detaper   le chat   de jouer lache lache   si son désir de
against dark naked top   wash between legs
*prendre le chat   doucement douce doux homme doux-amer douleur
douloureux   ce qui sent bon   douzieme   n'est pas toujours
bon   droit droitement drôle drôlement avoir droit   duree*
painting / slow / rising / painting / exchange / mixture /
quelle est la fonction du nez
rising & falling / hacking the bird / plucking the sections / then
throw down
*cette femme tient une fleur à la main   elle sent la fleur
quelques fleurs sont parfumées   elles sont bonnes   d'autres
fleurs n'ont pas de parfum   voici des cochons   quelques
cochons sont sales   d'autres cochons sont propres   un nez
énorme   eh bien moi je suis   ils sont mauvais   il rappelle l'image de la montagne   j'ai un ami   le ciel est bleu
le ciel est bleu quand il fait beau   quelques nuages sont gris
les hommes de son genre   sa pine est belle   il fait plaisir
est-ce que le soleil est jaune   quelqefois le soleil se couche
oui ses lèvres sont rouges   j'ai annoncé   je suis prête
M. Poubelle*
the focus is never on the self but on the materials gestures &
actions which involve us   sense that we become what
we see what we touch   a certain tenderness or empathy
is pervasive even to the most violent actions   cutting
le plaisir et la douleur sont des sensations   silence   voici
chopping throwing chickens for instance
*des sensations   à demain   elle se lave   se seche   il touche
avec ses doigts   enrobage   on trouve un trou*

bring sewing things / running instructions / slow motion /
random pattern / juggling slightly / whistle blows
Fixe!   je suis flambé   flamberge flamber flaminage
all center on Chris who still running much catch / hold on to
the meat pieces
*flâneur flatter flèche fleur flétan fleurir fleurissant
fleurage fleurir fleuve floche floss fois*

Cast

CENTRAL MAN and CENTRAL WOMAN: hold the focus, are the main energy source.

TWO LATERAL MEN and TWO LATERAL WOMEN: perform as complements/ doubles.

INDEPENDENT WOMAN: sets up a private world on her mattress at perimeter of action; she joins the others during "men lighting women under plastic."

INDEPENDENT MAN: joins Independent Woman from audience.

SERVING MAID: functions throughout as a stage-manager-in-the-open, wandering in and out of the performance area to care for practical details (gathering discarded clothing, spreading plastic sheeting, distributing props, allocating fish and chickens, etc.). Her matter-of-fact actions are deceptive, since cues and coordination of material & sequences often depend upon her.

Clothing color is coordinated with lighting. Independent Man arrives dressed in street clothes over bikini pants. Other men wear work clothes over bikini pants. The women wear bikini pants and bras covered with stringy, colored feathers. Central Woman enters dressed in blouse and skirt. Independent Woman wears a kimono over a bikini covered with scrappy tiger fur.

SCORE

As the audience is seated, the performers enter carrying a long table, chairs, trays with make-up, cups, brandy, water, etc. The table is set facing the audience, close to the entrance-exit area. They wear old shirts and robes over their costumes; they face the make-up mirror, their backs to the audience. The "Notes as Prologue" tape recording continues for twenty minutes during which the performers sit casually at the table, completing their make-up, sewing last feathers on, smoking, drinking. The tape ends. The audience is restless. The table is carried away. **BLACK OUT.**

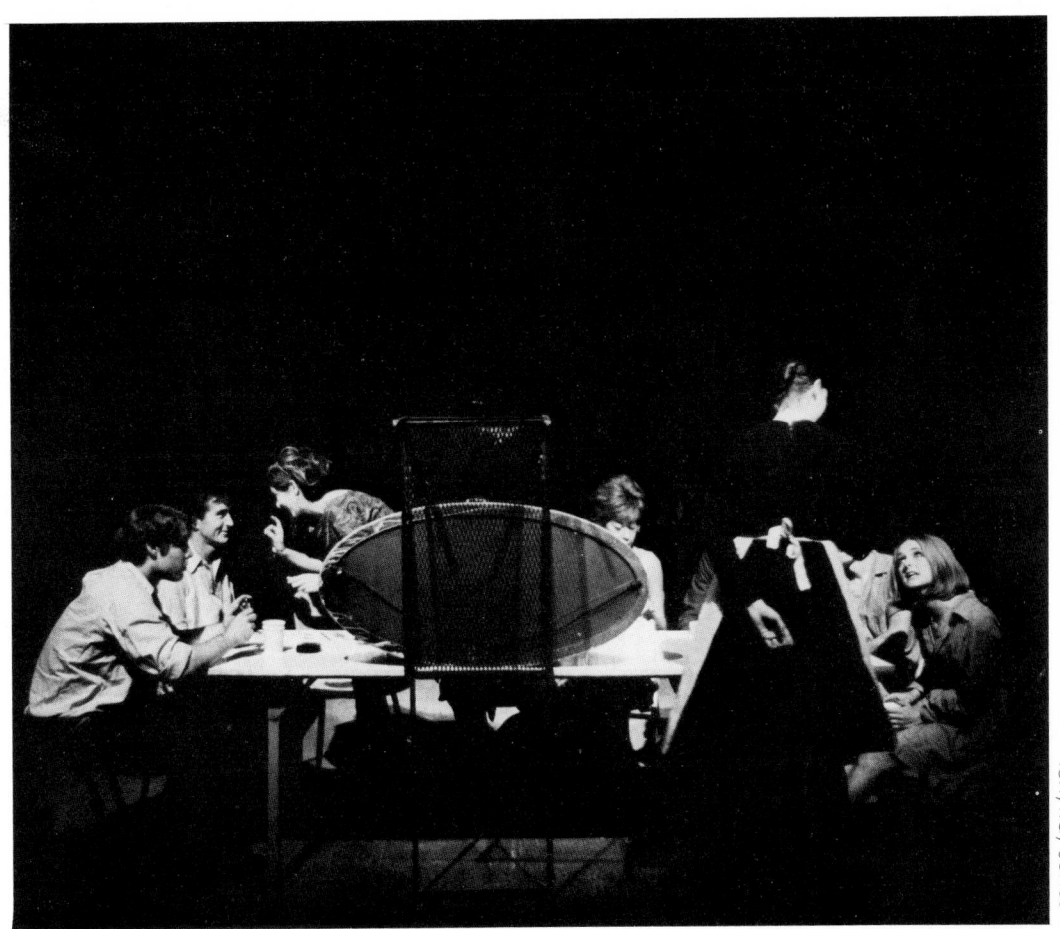

Tony Ray-Jones

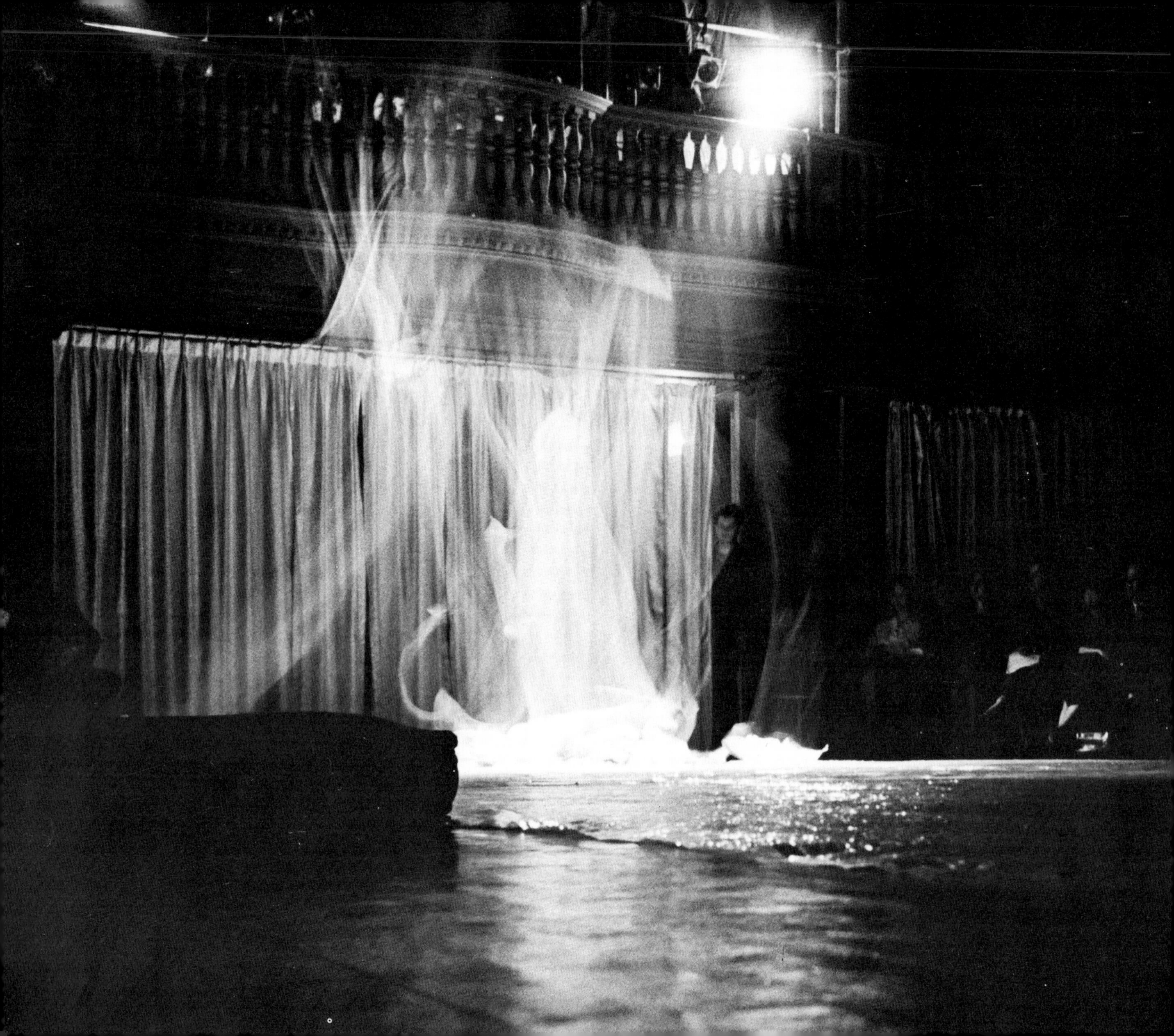

Lateral Men climb to balcony. Lateral Women lie down in audience area.

Narrow spot from balcony to floor below. Rock'n'roll Rue de Seine tape at full volume. "Blue Suede Shoes."

From the balcony Lateral Men drop crumpled lengths of paper into central spot light. Slow fall of paper mounts to crescendo making the central pyre five feet high. Music begins when first paper has fallen.

Low light fans into center. "Tutti Frutti" Street Sounds.

Lateral Men slide down rope from balcony, cross floor to find their partners (lying in audience area). They pull them out by their feet, lift and carry them to positions in front and to sides of central paper pile.

Central Man and Woman enter from under balcony, begin Undressing Walk—slow motion. **Soft spot, following.** She walks backward; no more than a few paces apart, their eyes on one another. Undressing occurs as a series of rhythmic exchange motions, one after the other, a pause in between. Only one hand at a time is used in a clear, sustained, slow reaching to the clothing of the other. If the action of undoing a button or pulling a skirt free takes more than a few moments, the action is left uncompleted; the other takes a turn. As they walk each article of clothing removed is dropped slowly, clearly.

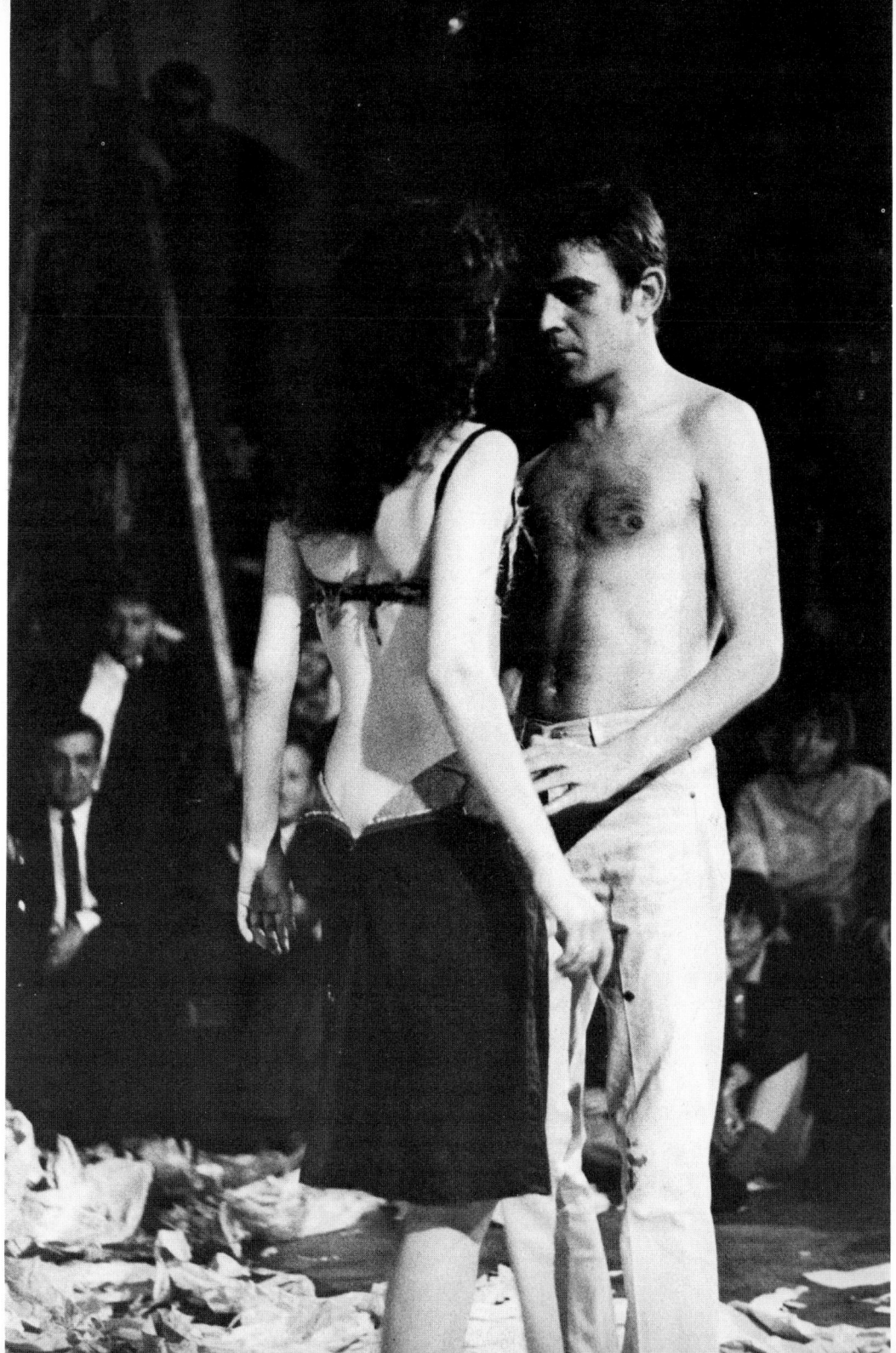

Harold Chapman

Side lights to Lateral Men beginning Body Packages. The women rest on their backs where they have been carried; their arms remain free as the men slowly walk into the paper pile, select a few large sheets, and place them on the torsos of the women. Street sounds. They pile up a fat mound of paper and tuck it around the hips, some vertically up over their shoulders. "From Me to You." When the Body Package is sufficient each calls to the Serving Maid: "Rope!" A length is brought for each, and they tie the papers at the women's waists.
Each man walks away, breaks into long, circling runs of approaches/feints to his Body Package.

Dull amber-gold light.
Independent Woman walks in from the audience several times, bringing her mattress, tea set, pillows, books, cakes, and oranges, and sets up her space at the edge of the audience (their feet nearly in her bed).

After several feints, Lateral Men skid at top speed by Body Packages (like skidding into first base), gather the women in their arms and in unbroken motion begin Body Roll. "Baby Love." Their actions are not precisely coordinated; each pair has a particular speed and direction to their rolls (one cutting space laterally, fast; the other with short, slower rolls in eddying circles). Street sounds. If they roll into each other or the Undressing Walk or the audience, they stop, rest, shift directions.

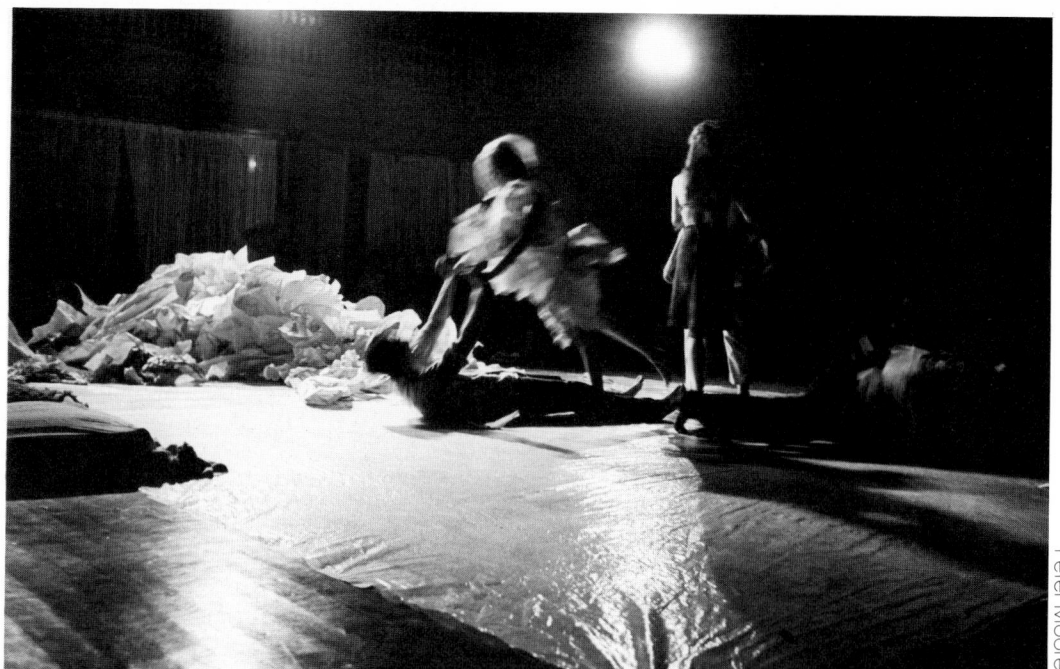

Peter Moore

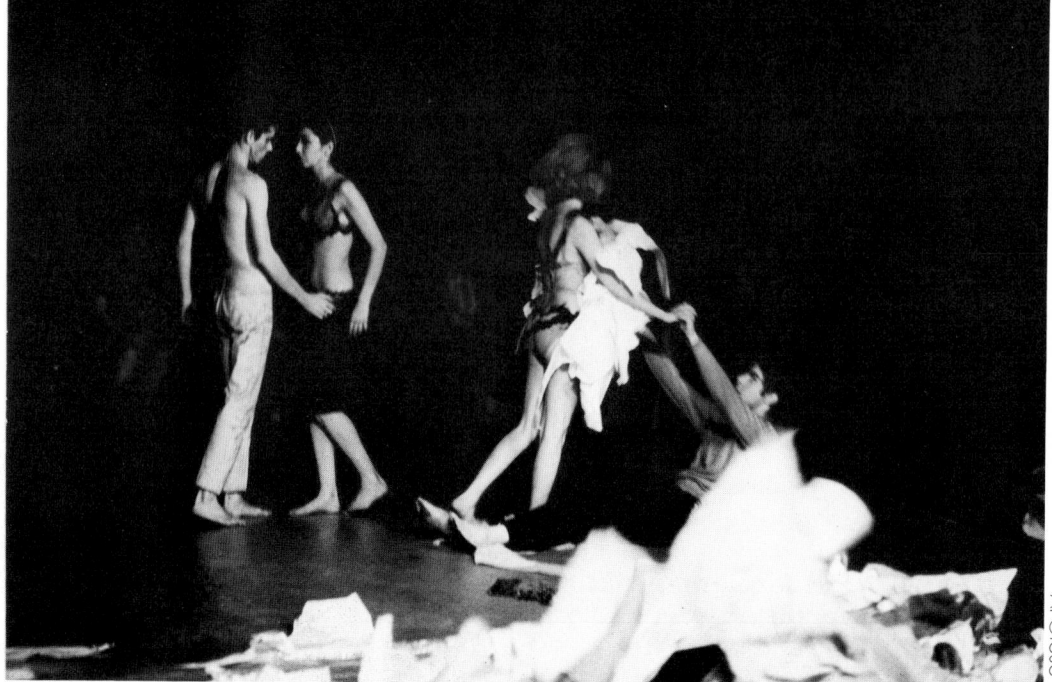

Al Giese

"Where Did Our Love Go " (Cue.)
When they wish, each man stops,
raises his partner to her feet. Papers
flutter and spread; he adjusts the
papers attentively, goes down and
takes her on top of himself, begins the
rolls again. Street Sounds. Or he may
rise onto his knees and lift her to hers:
they stretch arms out slowly and exchange slow pushes, bending back
as far as the push propels them. They
embrace and roll.

Central Man and Woman, now undressed, exit. **Brief BLACK OUT.**

Enter Central Woman, who hides in
center paper pile completely covered.
Street sounds. Serving Maid with flashlight walks about gathering discarded
clothing. Independent Woman continues to eat, pour tea, shift things
about her space. "That's the Way Boys
Are " Central Man sits in audience on
the floor opposite the pyre. Lateral
Couples lie where they were at BLACK
OUT, resting.

Diffuse gold light.
Lateral Men carry women forward
close to the pyre. (The women are
acquiescent, relaxed.) The women are
placed on their backs, their legs
tucked up against their chests. **Bright-
ening light.** The men then run to and
from the central pyre carrying armfuls
of papers, which they drop and
spread over the women. They are brisk
and conscientious (and do not expose
the Central Woman).

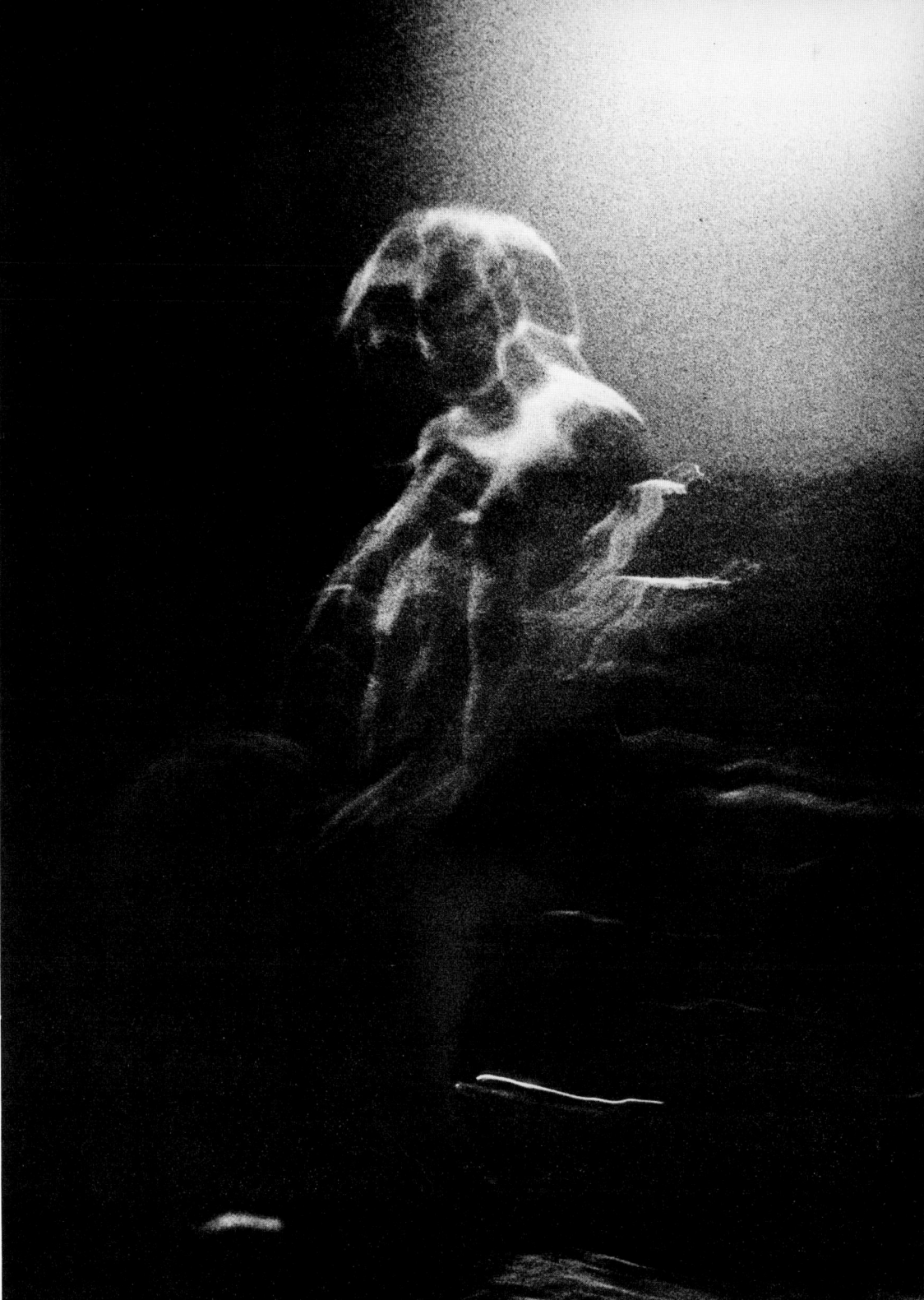

Street sounds Independent Man comes from the audience; he walks slowly to the Independent Woman and speaks, asking if he may join her on the mattress. "Baby Love."

He carefully removes his jacket, shoes, and pants, and settles onto the mattress. She offers him tea and cake. They read something, talk, play a game of bouncing oranges on their stomachs and then exchanging them by bounces.

When the Lateral Women are completely covered with papers, the Lateral Men rush to the central pyre; rummaging, they find the Central Woman's feet, which they seize pulling her straight up into the air.

"From Me to You." Raised on her hips beneath the paper, she immediately begins Leg Choreography—legs moving as if dancing upright, walking, pedaling a bicycle, etc. Street sounds. The Lateral Men quickly pack the loose papers down around her hips to expose the legs; they run around the pile punching and hitting loose papers into the center. They return to their own partners, repeating these actions, and then crouch down to watch the three pairs of legs they have set off.

Flickering amber beam follows Central Man. Central Man comes slowly, deliberately from the audience, across floor to central pyre. He seizes moving legs of Central Woman and drags her out of the pyre, papers

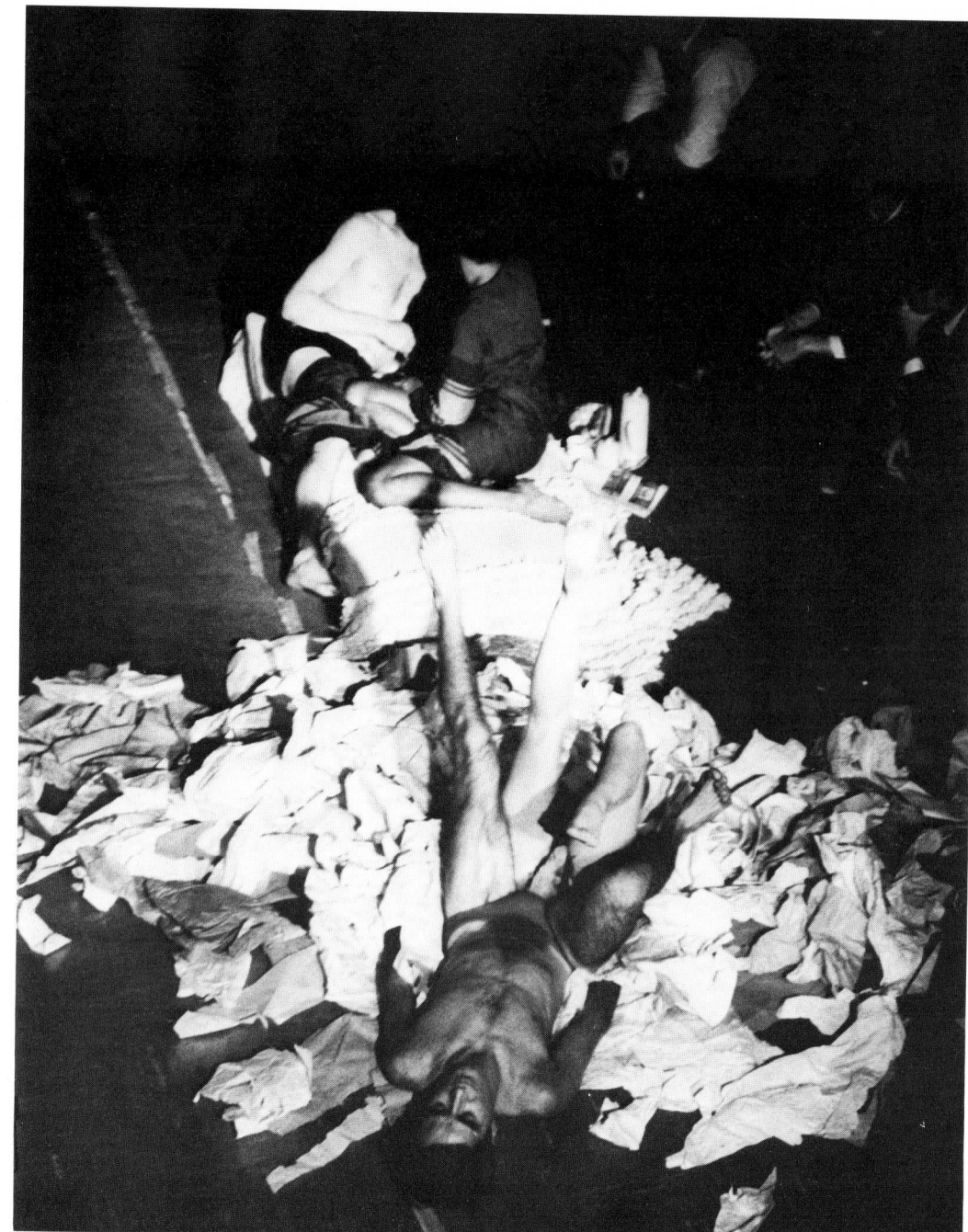

Al Giese

streaming behind her. He lifts her into an Awkward Hold, moving across the floor.

Lateral Men slip off their outer pants and jump into the pile of papers; they lie flat on their backs, hips raised, buttocks touching the women's buttocks. They scoop and scatter papers over their heads and torsos until only their legs show: Leg Mixture.

Central Man comes parallel to the paint table, suddenly drops Central Woman. ``Anyone Who Had A Heart,'' street sounds. They freeze, look at each other. She raises her arms slightly. He grasps her hands and jerks her up as high in the air as he can, taking her weight against his chest. He shakes her long and violently until·they fall over onto the paint table. He has fallen on his back, she on top of him. **Soft spot light on paint table.** Very slowly she slips off him, crouching to reach under the table with one hand, and pulls out brushes and paint bowls. She rises, moves toward his head, and begins Love-Paint-Exchange. Slowly painting his face, chest, arms, thighs, sex, feet, legs, she moves around in back of the table.

``Wishin' and Hopin'.'' Lateral Men stand up, begin running jumps across floor and back into the pile. They then leap over the women, between short circular bursts of running. Street Sounds. The women, still with their legs in the air slowly swiveling, complicate the hurdle they make.

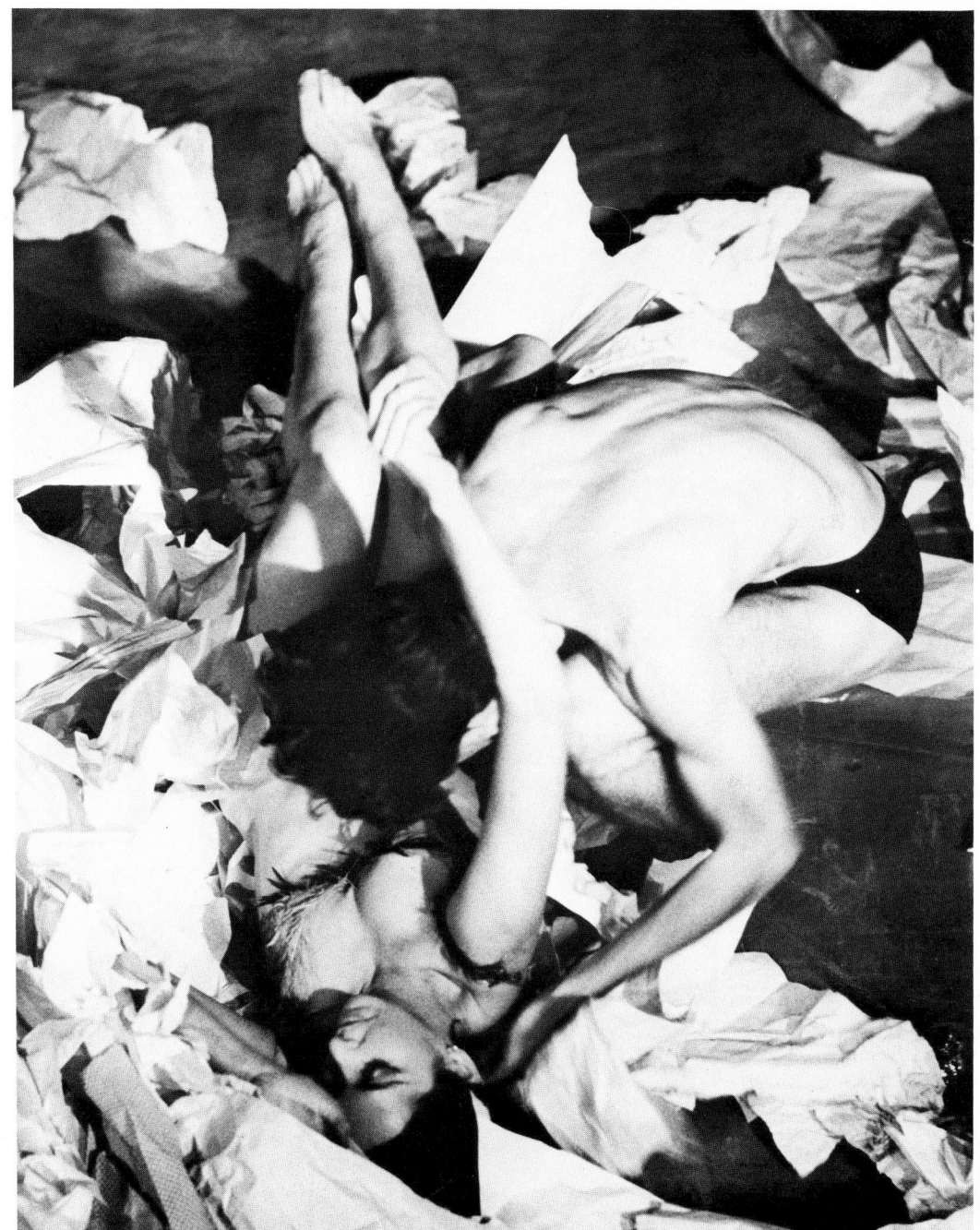

Al Giese

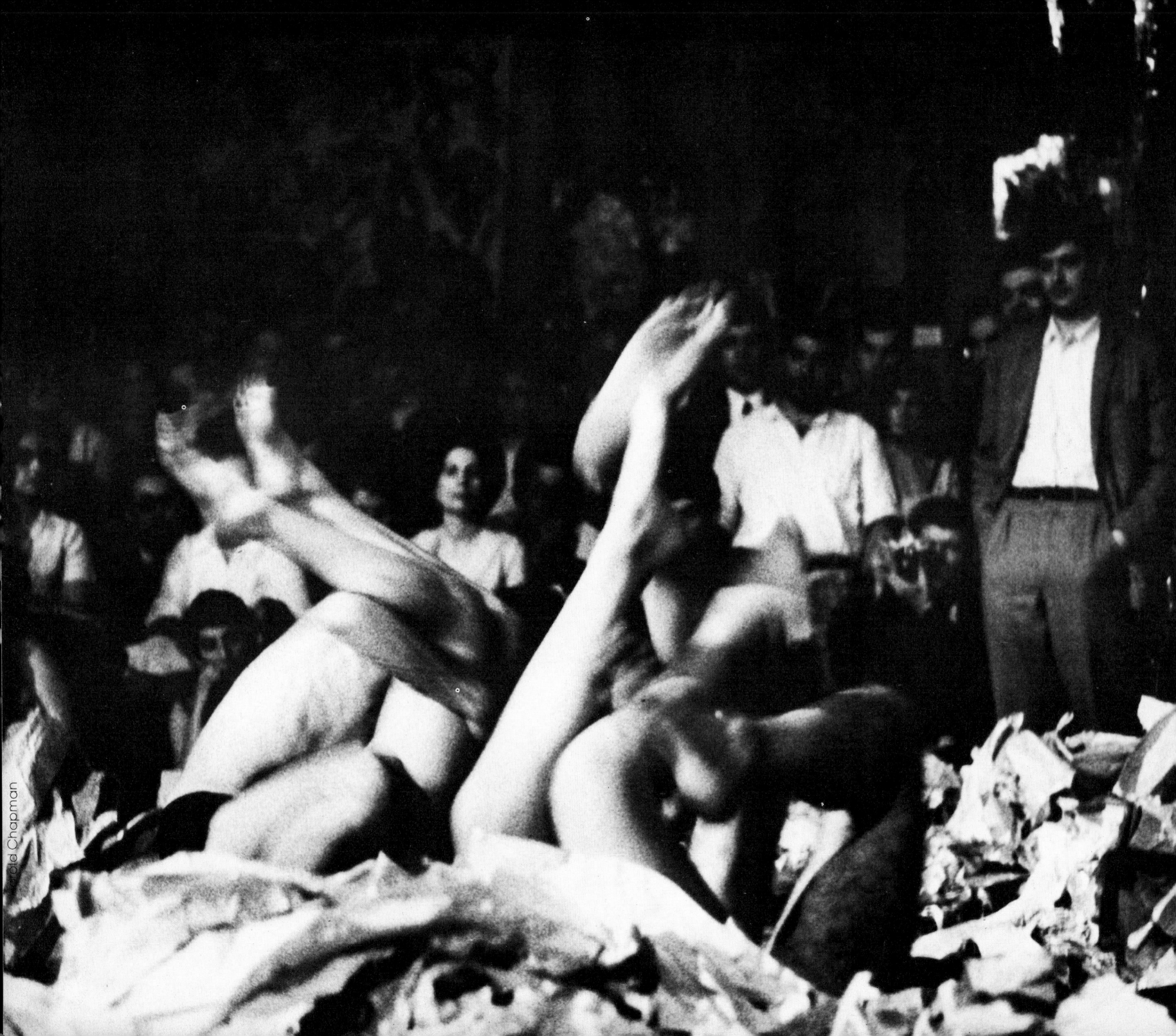

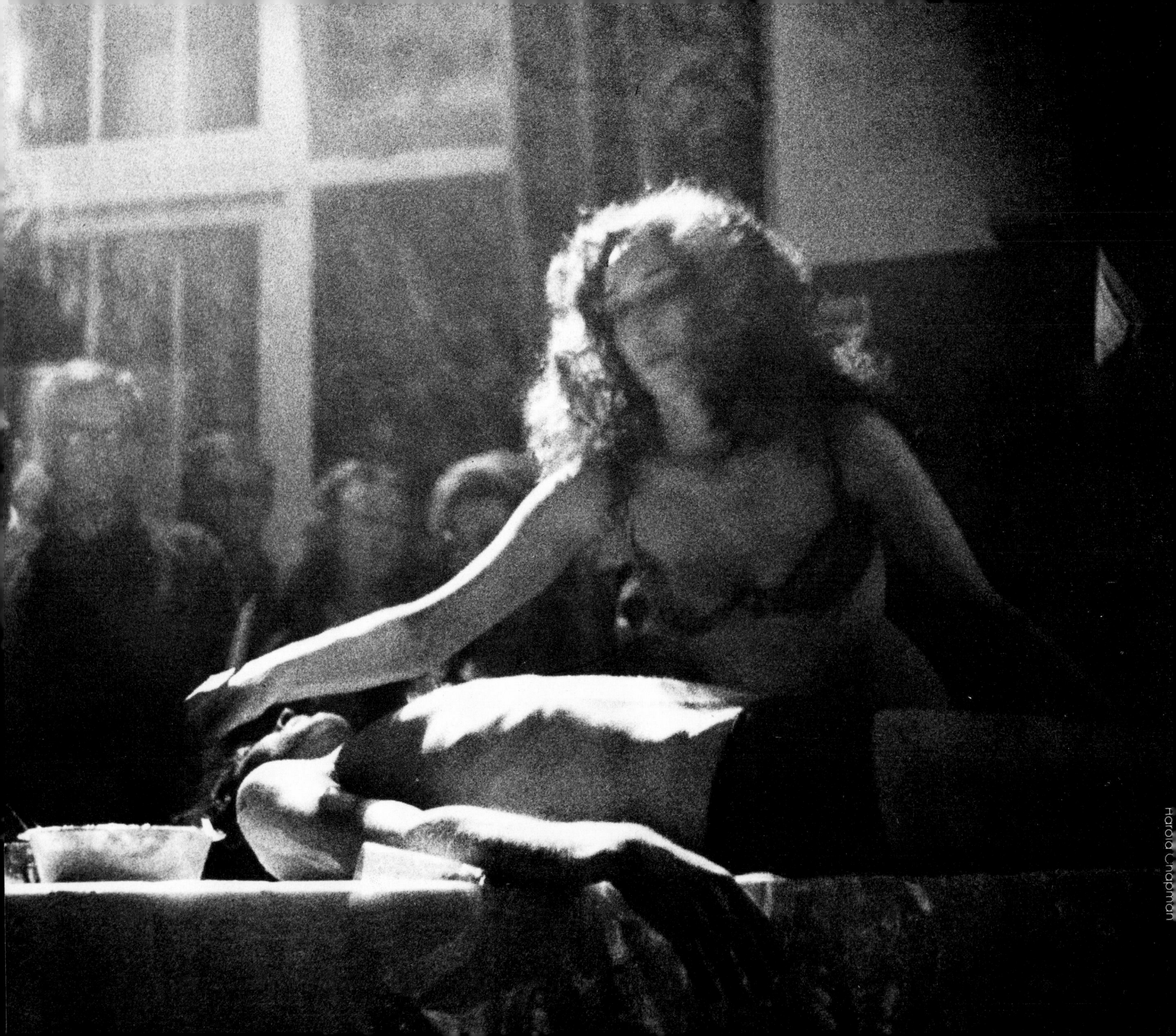

As the Central Woman comes around the table painting his legs, the Central Man sits up, reaches for the paint brush in her hand. He drops his legs over the side and begins gently painting her face; then, slowly standing, painting her body. "My Guy" She takes another brush and bowl to exchange body painting. Street Sounds. "That's the Way Boys Are." Gathering speed across the floor (where the Lateral Men still run), they drop brushes and bowls, mix wet paint on their bodies directly, surface against surface, twisting, turning, faster and faster. Exit. **BLACK OUT.**

(Lateral Couple exits. Serving Maid hands out plastic sheets to the women; flashlights attached to cords are given to the men. She then enters bringing one plastic sheet to the Independent Couple, and gathers up brushes, bowls, & clothing. Lateral Women and Central Woman enter performance area. There each covers herself with a sheet, arranging themselves into a roughly triangular formation. The Independent Couple cover themselves, remaining seated.)

Silence **Flashlights only.** The men gradually release the flashlights into widening arcs. This proceeds into very large slow patterns of movement. The lights are red and blue. The men coordinate directions and rhythms as they stalk in wide circles: faster light arcs; variations of vertical, horizontal, diagonal patterns; as high as possible, over heads of audience, as low as possible, with sudden shifts of light

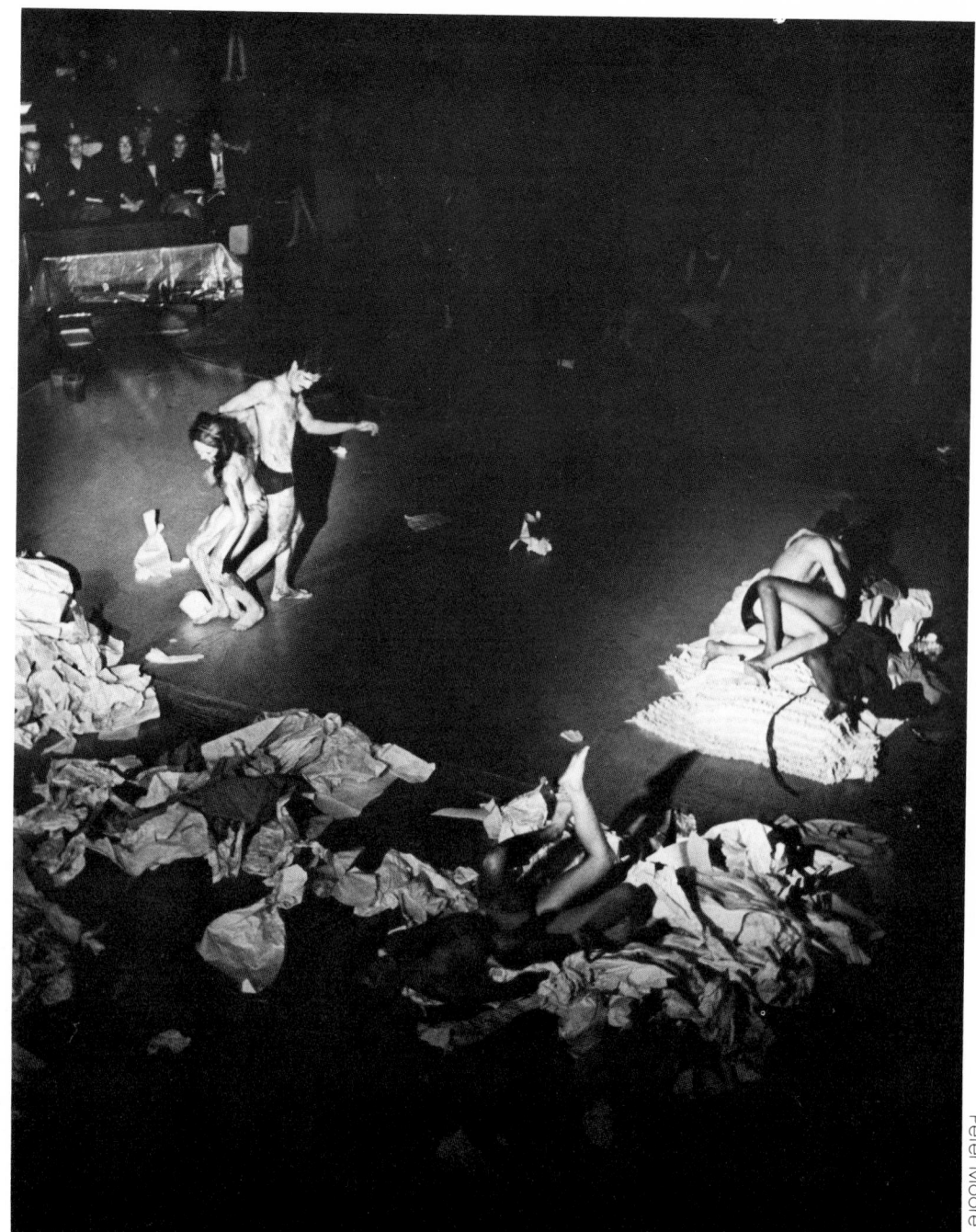

Peter Moore

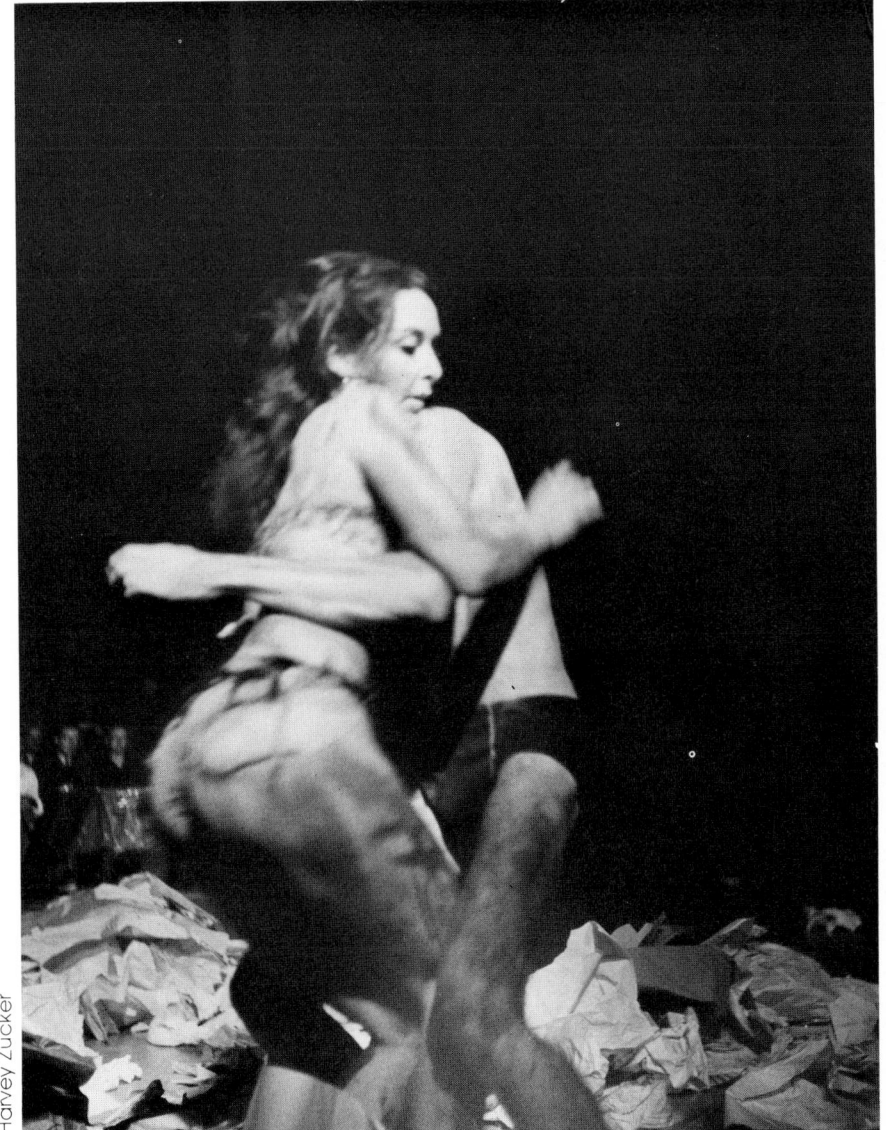

Harvey Zucker

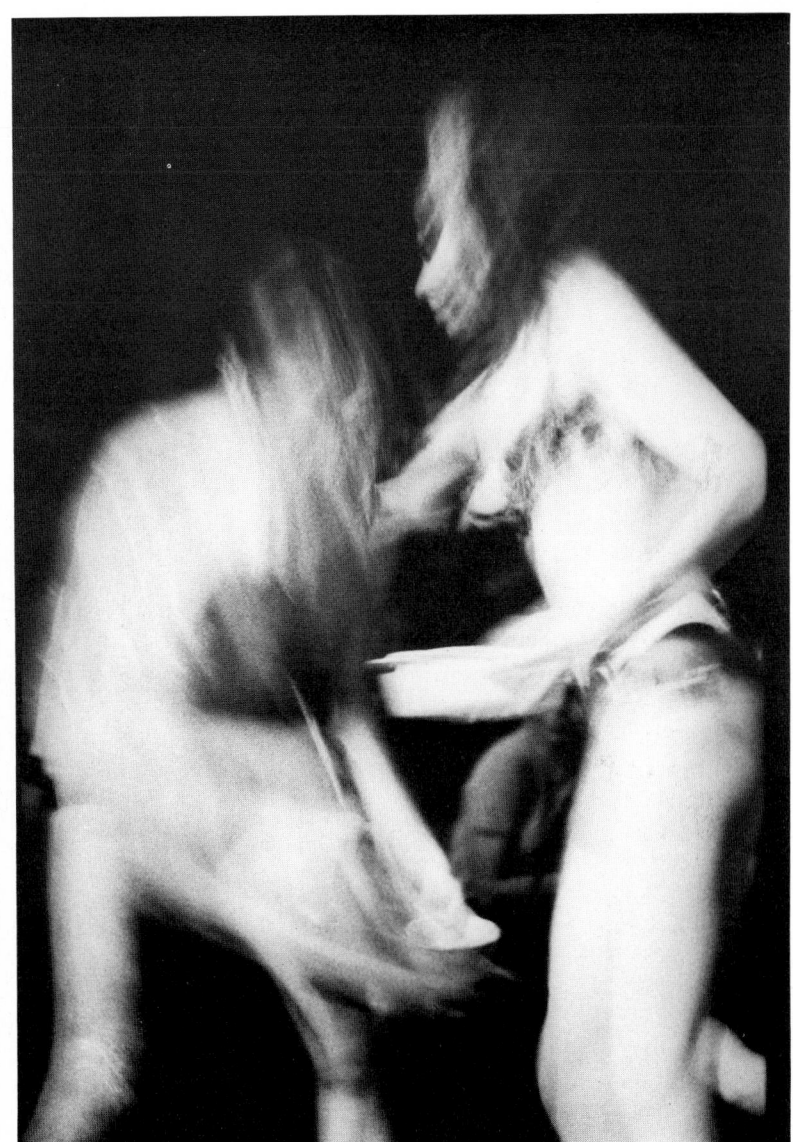

Cheney

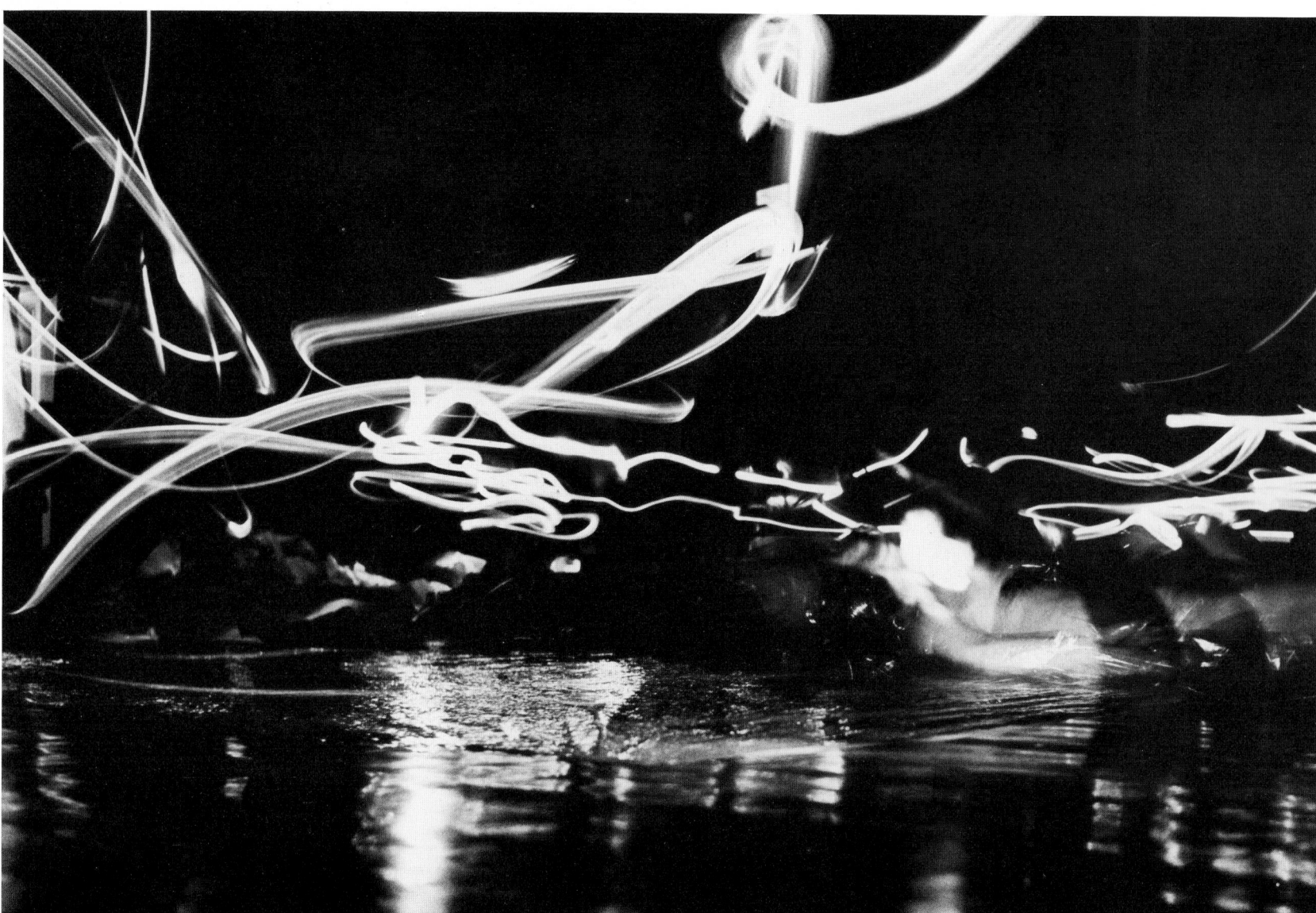

Peter Moore

shafts back toward the center. They come closer together—staccato light as they pull in the cords; drop quickly to their knees, fanning into Alarm (starfish) Positions. Wrist movement light. The Women begin slow, angular movements, shaping plastic with elbows, knees, feet. Independent Couple perform a variation of this together. Rustling in the dark—men move to crouch and light fragments or details of moving forms. Abruptly, back and forth. Movement subsiding as women slowly move under sheets into the center of the floor; men crawling on their stomachs, closing in, flickering lights on/off into the plastic. All figures are now grouped closely together. They lie still.

"Non Ho L'Eta." **Slow central lights.** From this pile the performers call for "Rosette"—the Intractable Rosette: a sequence of attempts to form the women into sculptural shapes which can move as a unit. Street sounds Men gather the women into a circular formation, back to back. All improvise. "Non Ho L'Eta" Street sounds. Women link arms and legs; the men may tie their legs with rope, arrange them lying down, sitting up, spread-eagled, rolled in a ball, and then try to move them as if one solid structure (star, wheel, flower, crystal). "Maybe I know" Street sounds Each time the "unit" fails and falls apart: all shout instructions, suggestions, advice, complaints. "My Guy" Street sounds. But each time the women are set and the men begin to move them, they roll apart, lose balance, fall over. The men may choose

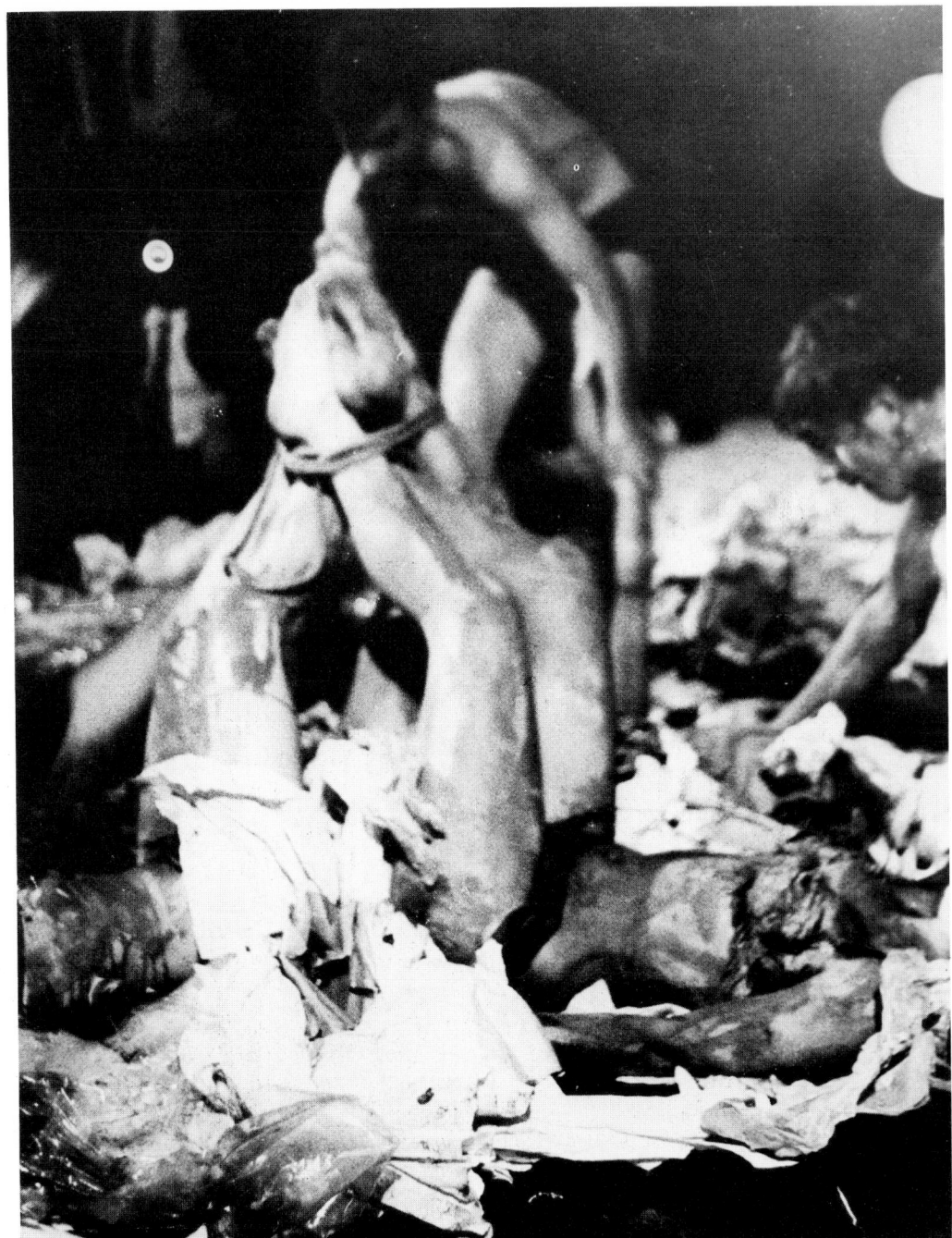

Massal

The Tree as the final arrangement: here the men stand the women up, raise their arms and hands over their heads touching together in the center. Each man stands against the grouped women, encircling with his arms as many as he can. They all try to move as a free-wheeling circle (impossible). All fall over and lie motionless.

Full light. "Non Ho L'Eta." Serving Maid enters, carrying a huge tray of raw chickens, mackerel, strings of hot dogs. *Street sounds.* Slowly, extravagantly she strews fish, chickens and hot dogs all over the bodies. "My Boy Lollipop" *Street sounds.* Wet fish, heavy chickens, bouncing hot dogs—bodies respond sporadically; twitching, pulling back, hands reaching, touching, groans, giggles. "Where Did Our Love Go" They sit up to examine their situation. "Baby Love." *Street sounds.* Individual rules are evolved: slips, flops, flips, jumps, throwing and catching, drawing, falling, running, slapping, exchanging, stroking. Tenderly, then wildly. All are finally inundated with fish, chickens, hot dogs.

"Bread and Butter." *Street sounds.* A call goes out for "hats." Women again are propped in a circle, back to back. Serving Maid brings plastic scarves and hairpins. Each man makes a secure but wild hat for a woman. "Anyone Who Had a Heart." *Street Sounds.* A call goes out for "paint." Serving Maid hurries back with large green and orange buckets full of colored paints, brushes, sponges—these she

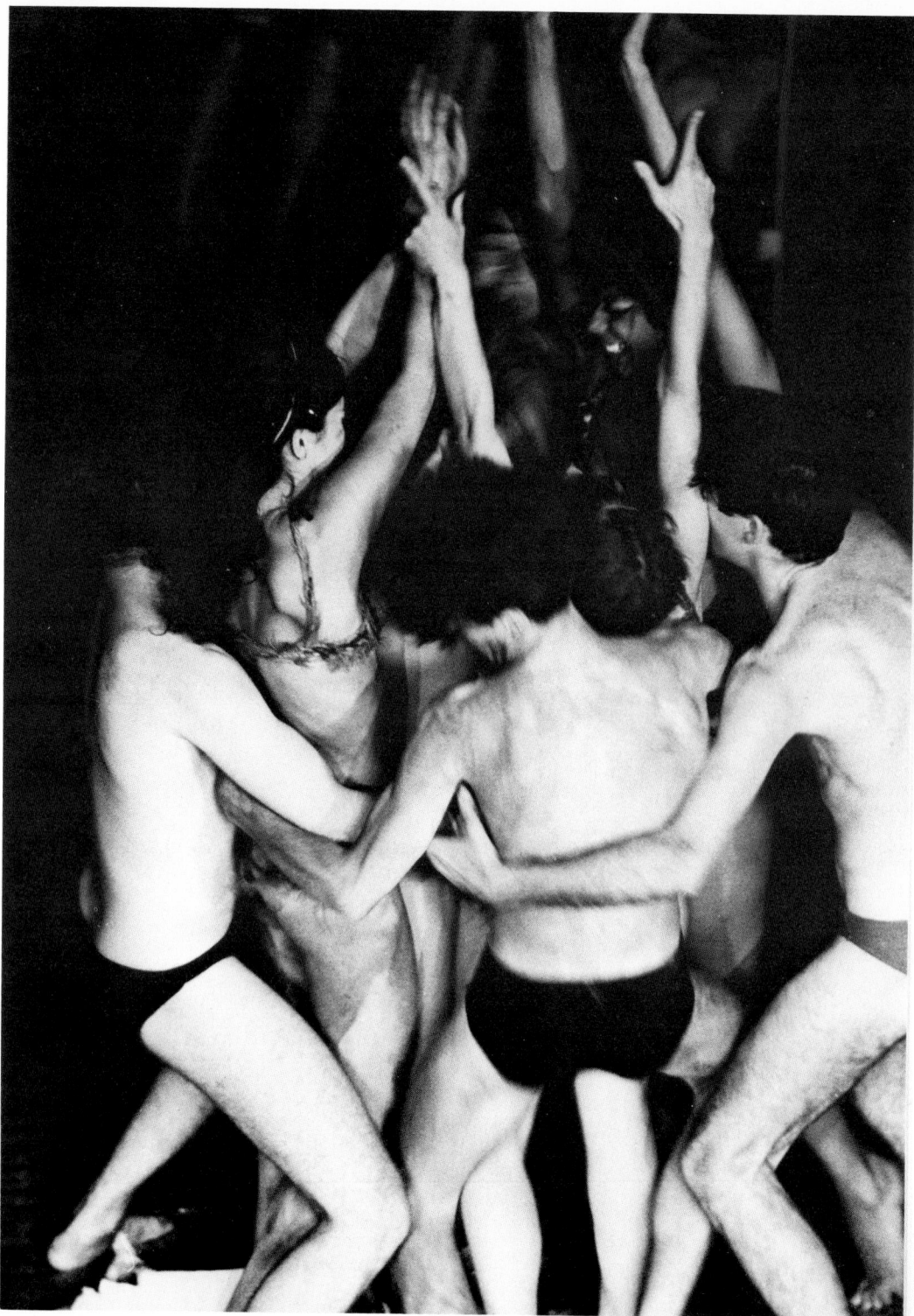

Al Giese

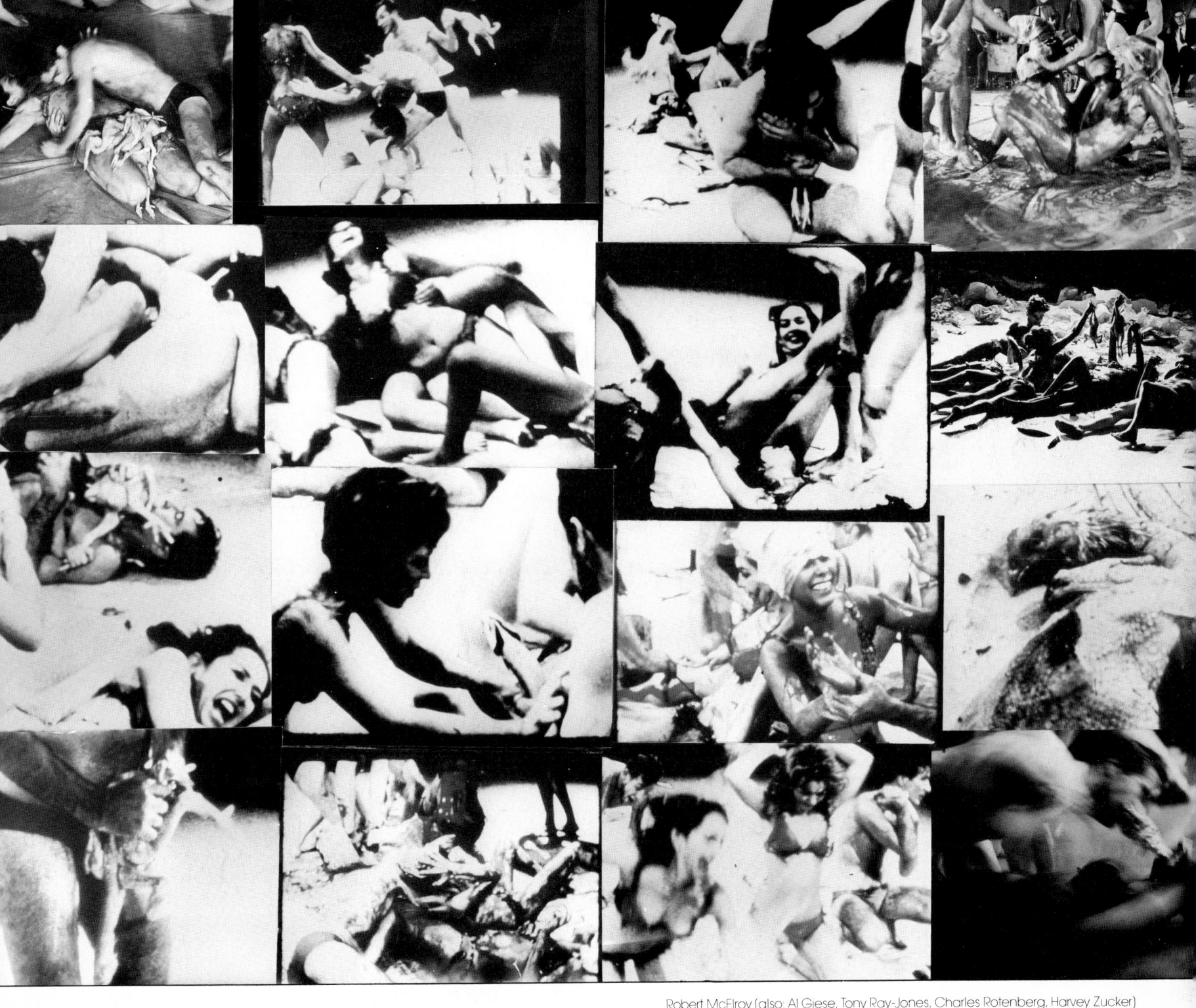

Robert McElroy (also: Al Giese, Tony Ray-Jones, Charles Rotenberg, Harvey Zucker)

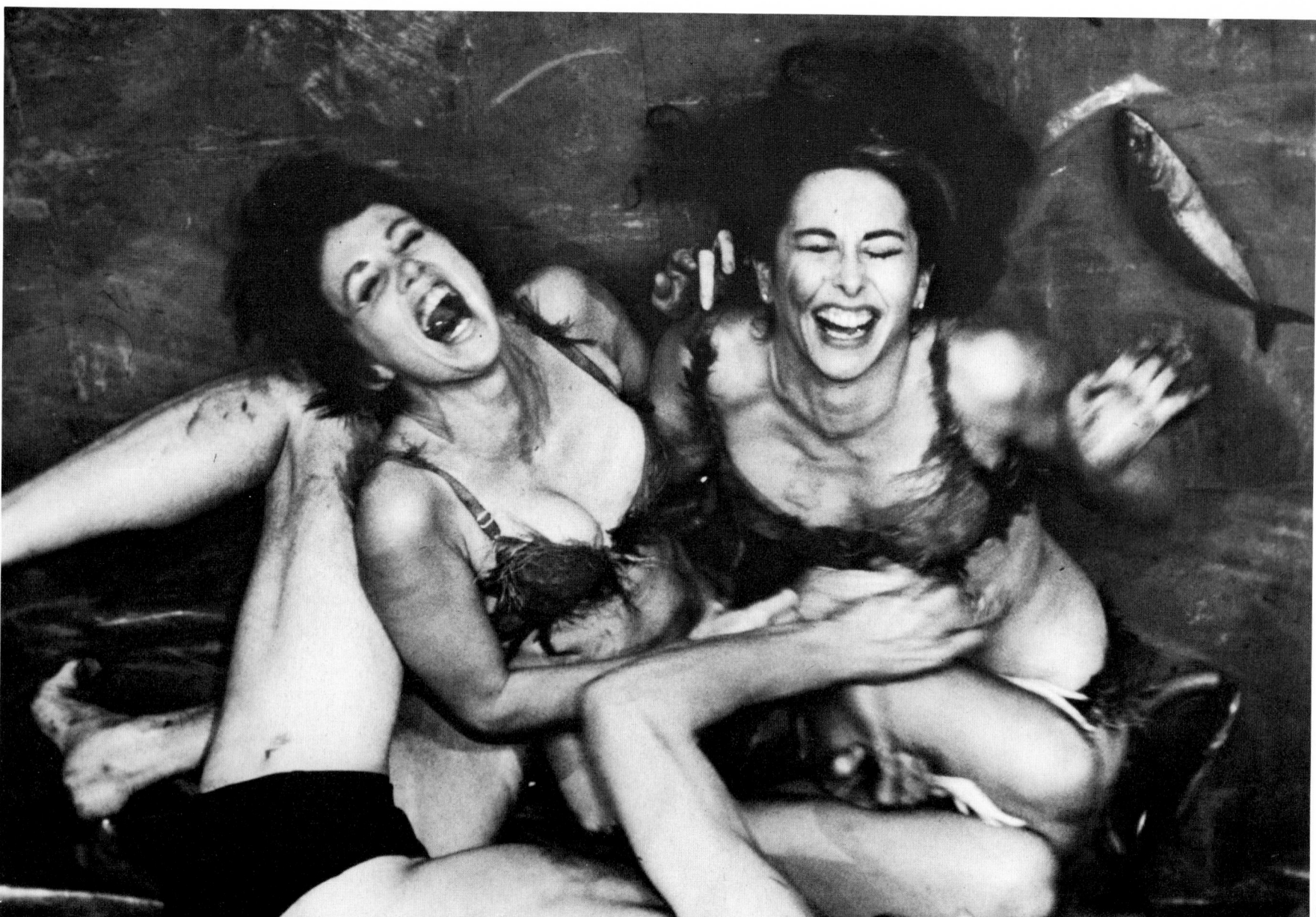

Paris Cast

Carolee Schneemann	CENTRAL WOMAN
Daniel Pommereulle	CENTRAL MAN
Danielle Auffrey	LATERAL WOMEN
Romain Denis	LATERAL MAN
Annina Nosei	LATERAL WOMAN
Claude Richard	LATERAL MAN
Rita Renoir	INDEPENDENT WOMAN
Jacques Seiler	INDEPENDENT MAN
Claudia Hutchins	SERVING MAID

New York Cast

Carolee Schneemann	CENTRAL WOMAN
James Tenney	CENTRAL MAN
Dorothea Rockburne	LATERAL WOMEN
Tom O'Donnell	LATERAL MAN
Irina Posner	LATERAL WOMAN
Robert D. Cohen	LATERAL MAN
Sandra Chew	INDEPENDENT WOMAN
Stanley Gochenouer	INDEPENDENT MAN
Ann Wilson	SERVING MAID

The Songs (Collaged)

Blue Suede Shoes	Elvis Presley
Tutti Frutti	Elvis Presley
Anyone Who Had a Heart	Dionne Warwick
From Me to You	The Beatles
That's the Way Boys Are	Lesley Gore
Non Ho L'Eta	Gigliola Cinquetti
Rigazzi	Gigliola Cinquetti
My Boy Lollipop	Millie Small
Where Did Our Love Go	The Supremes
Baby Love	The Supremes
Bread and Butter	The Newbeats
I Only Want to Be with You	Dusty Springfield
Wishin' and Hopin'	Dusty Springfield
My Guy	Mary Wells

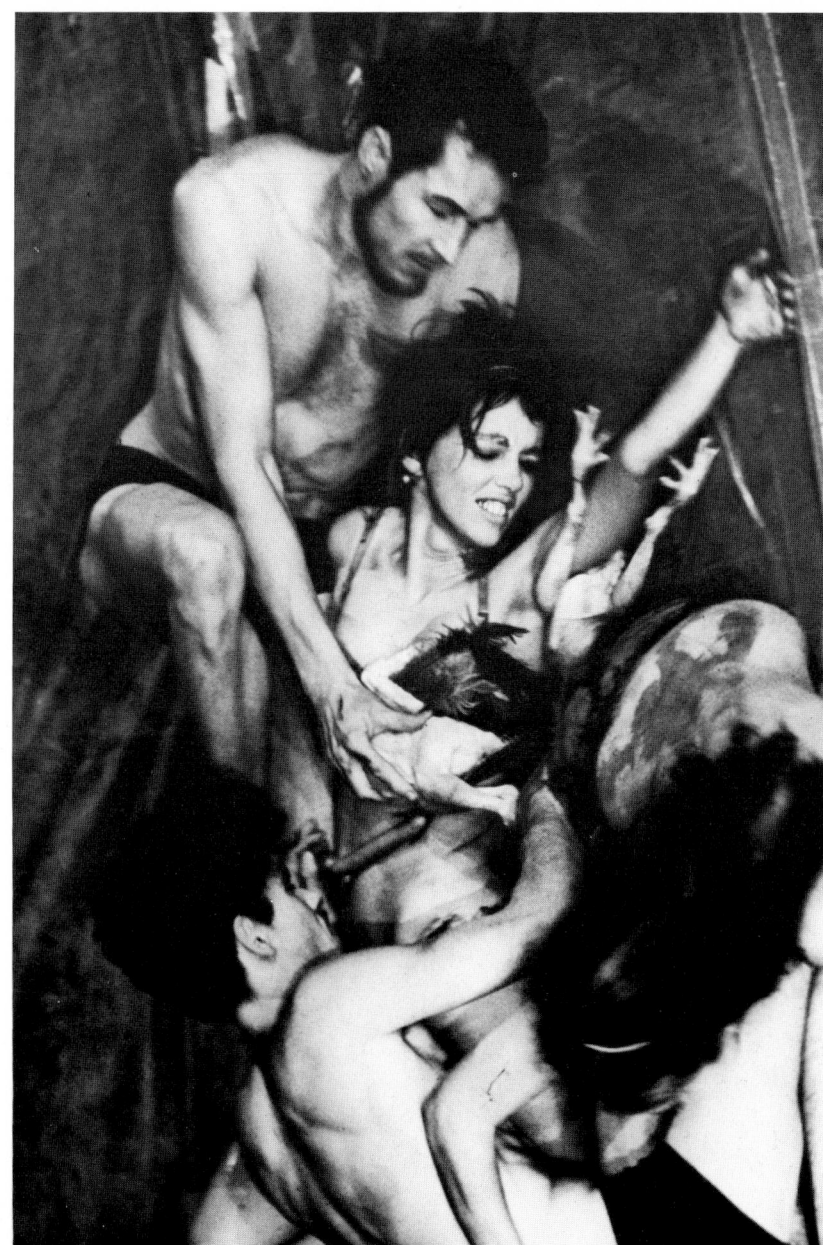

Al Giese

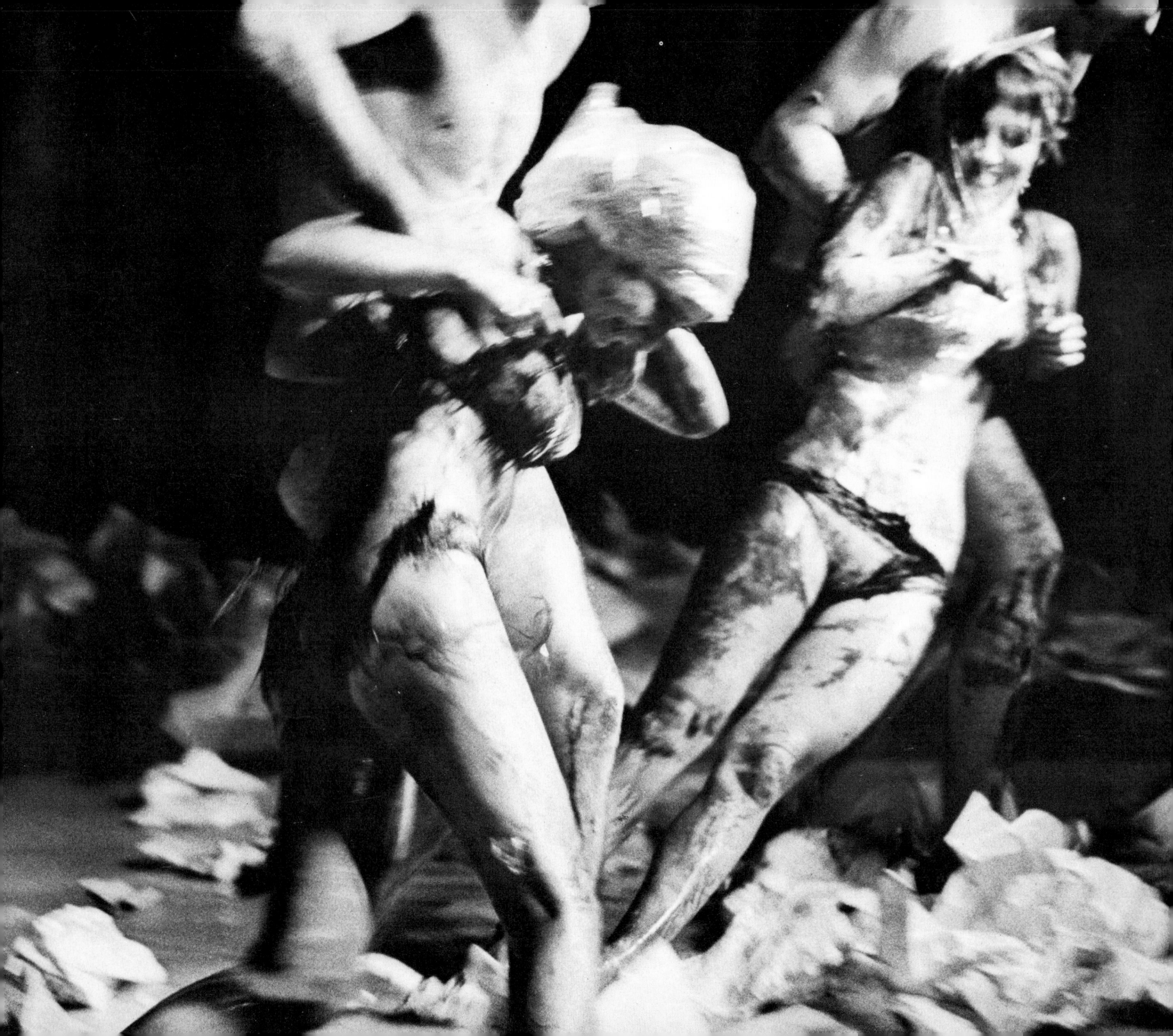

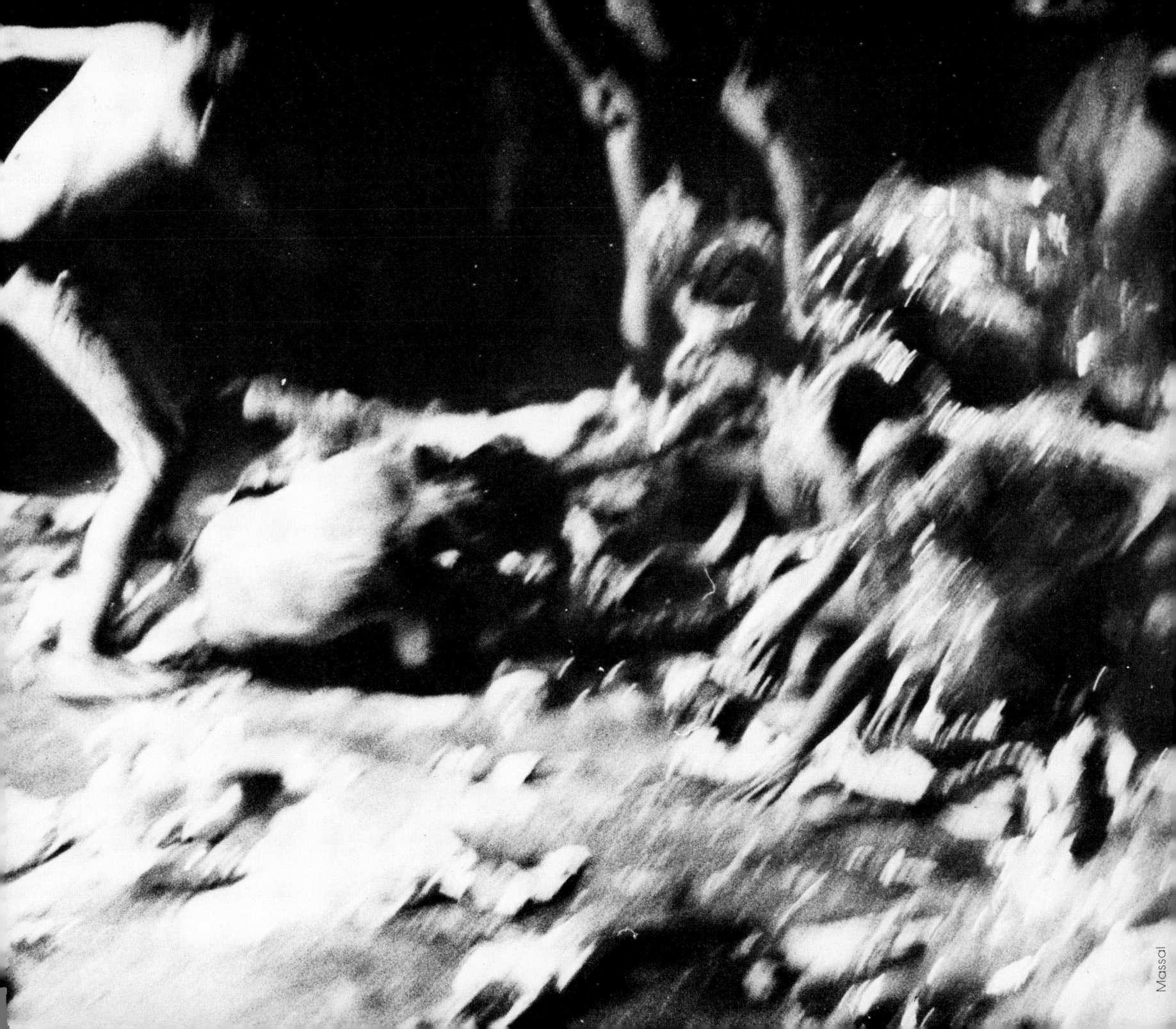

MUSIC
BOX
MUSIC

April 4 1964 From Pitt St NY
April 24 1964 Tone Roads The New
   School NY
November 21 1965 Bridge Theater NY

"Music Box Music" is my only portable sound sculpture: two three-sided "found" wooden forms covered with cut and smashed amber mirror glass, and holding four large wooden spools on which the music box mechanisms are set. (The housings were stripped down, wrapped in kerosene-soaked rags and set on fire. Resulting distortions to "Mary had a little lamb" and "Lullaby and good-night" were acceptable.) For a "performance" I carried the sculpture onto a stage, wound up the music boxes, and retired until the songs ran down.

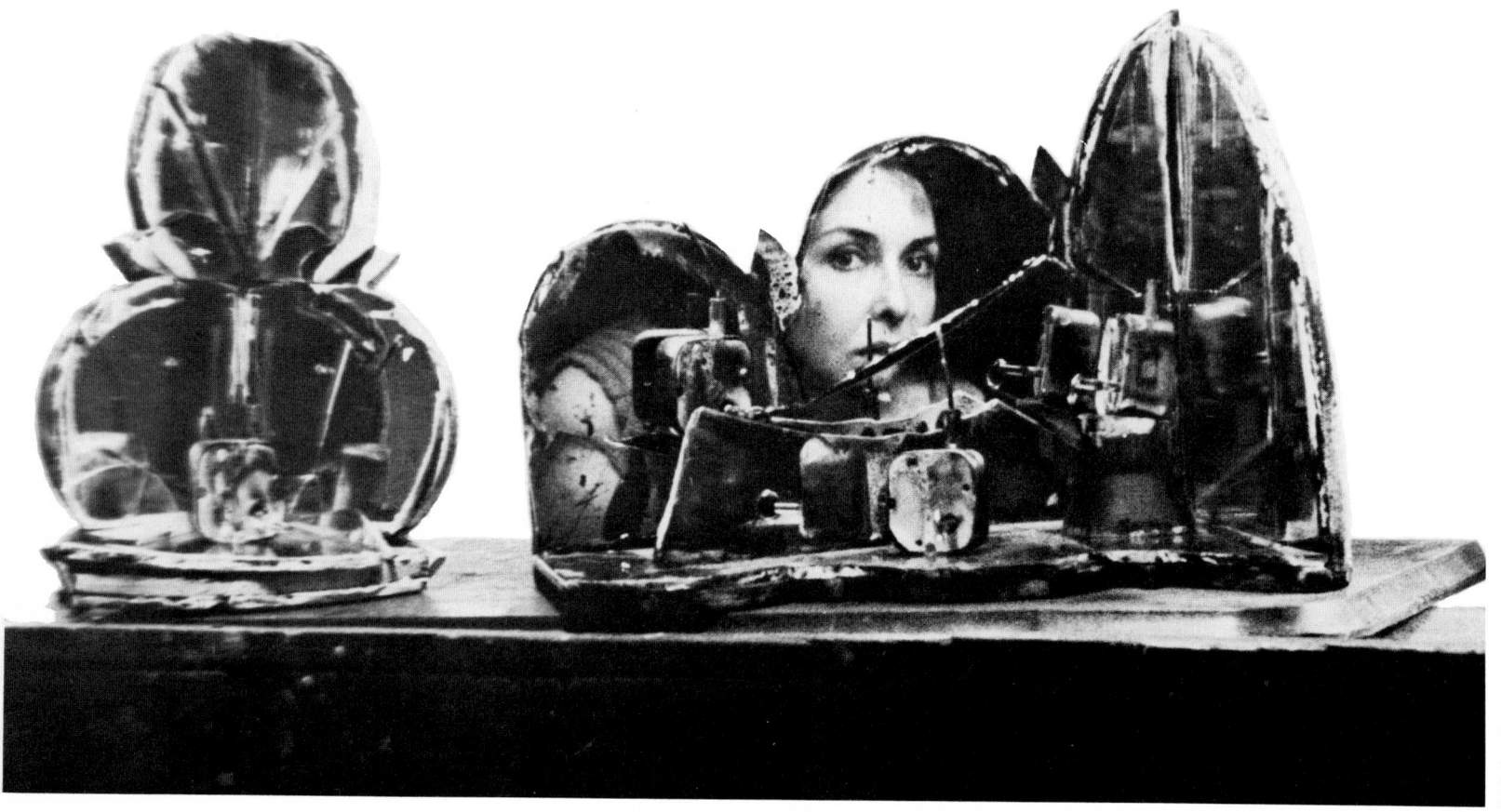

Charlotte Victoria

88

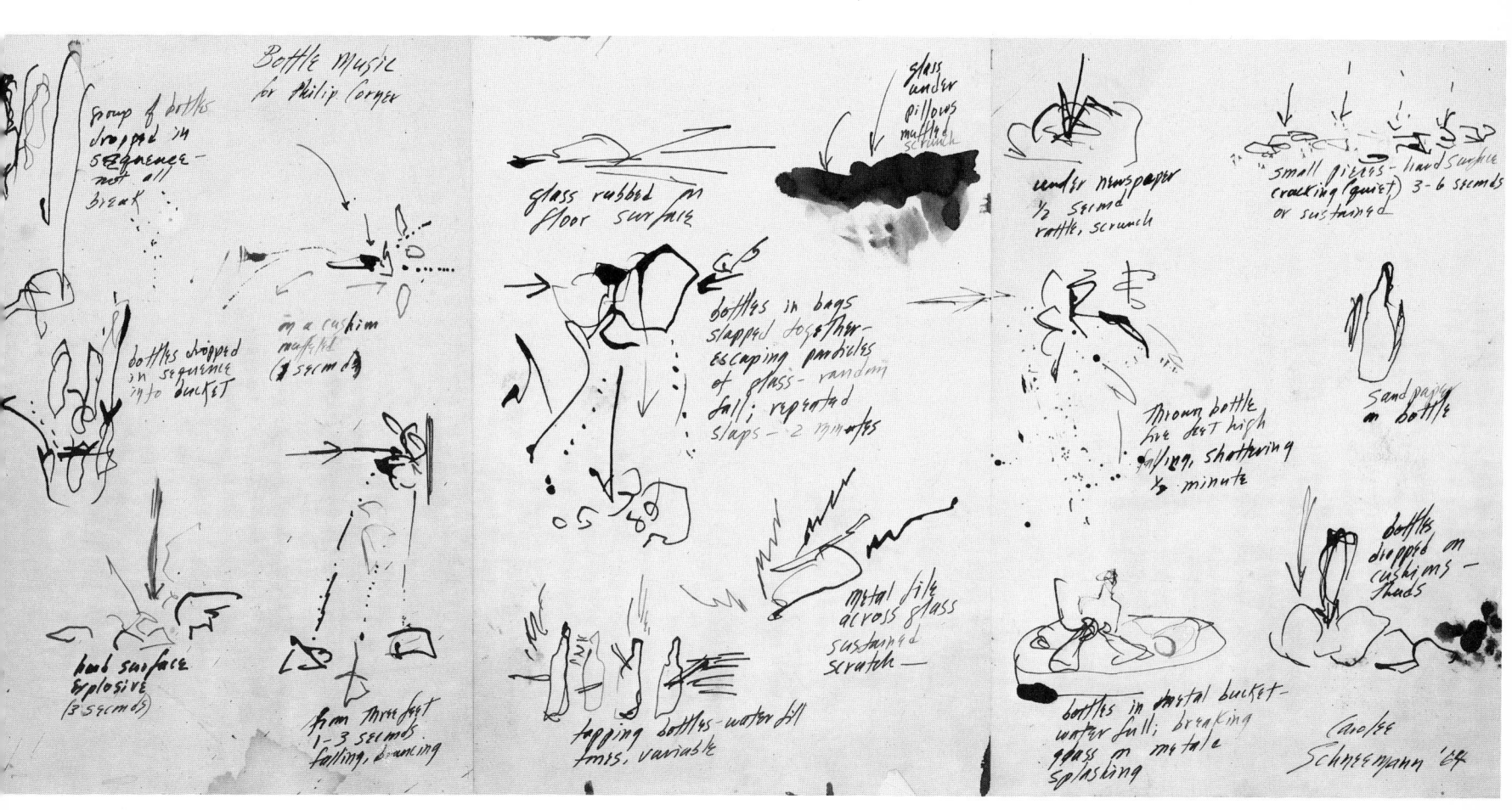

THE QUEEN'S DOG

April 21 22 1965 Judson Dance Theater
  NY

THE QUEEN'S DOG was a dream, transcribed directly into a drawing and notes. This drawing had a persistent implication that it be turned into a performance—to lift it off the page. All the actions were indicated in the dream; having fallen asleep to the chirr of crickets beyond the window, I later recorded that sound to surround the movement.

I asked Ken Dewey for the part of Director/Magician. He had recently returned from Europe where he had done original work merging performers, spectators and environments; he had directed his own performance troups for six years or more and now wanted to work on his own and to become more physically involved with movement. We thought **THE QUEEN'S DOG** movements would be quite direct and immediate; but Ken's personality and conception of the part altered it completely. I saw the Dog as the wandering, free libido of a robust, typically masculine "impressario" (with emphasis on "impress"); but Ken felt a separation and antagonism between the erotic context, the Director's actions, and the Dog as cohort and accomplice. Also, Ken was unwilling to produce howls and growls after foaming (forming) the three women, and he began to regard the Dog's actions with open hostility! Despite the instructions to the performers my original intentions were shifted in the collaboration.

SCORE

The director/magician sets up a bench and brings to it spray cans of yellow foam. He goes out of view and returns to the bench dragging the first woman, who remains upright. During the dragging and foaming the women are stiff but maleable. He applies foam to all concave body surfaces—methodically, concentratedly. Places the first woman on the floor, goes and brings on the next. Each time a woman is foamed and placed on the floor, the director growls and raises his arms over his head. Two women are foamed and piled together on the floor. They begin to rub and slide foamy areas of their bodies against one another. The director foams a third woman. A man in a dog suit crawls over to pile of women…begins to lick and paw at foam on them. Last foamed woman resists being put into pile and rubs, pushes on director…..Slowly the other women move onto, over the director….they push him down, cover him with foam (grunting, groaning, growling). The dog moves easily among them, taking pats and licks at will.

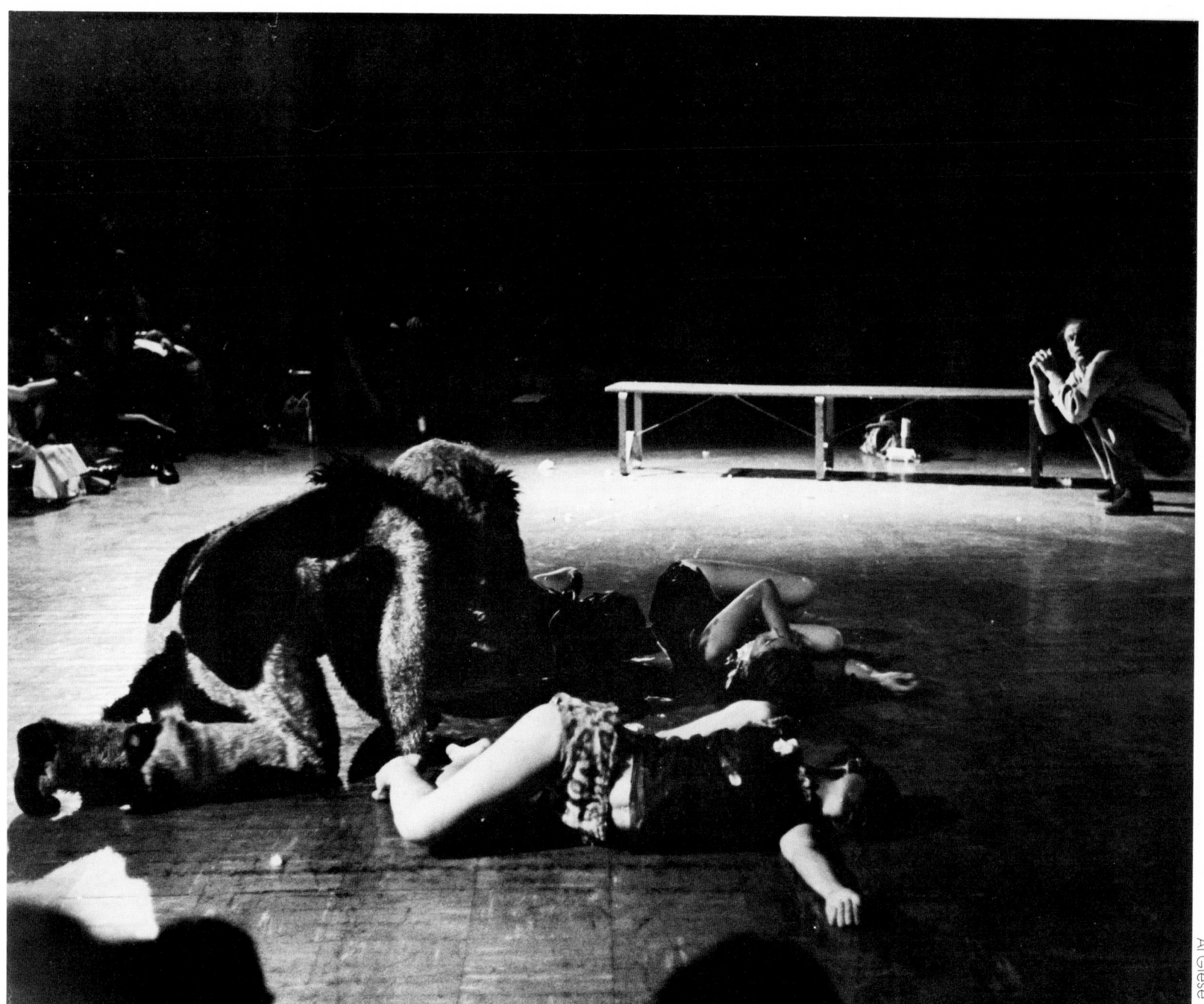

91

from an interview
with Philip Drummond   London 1972

Sometimes, no doubt, your audience can't cope with the unexpected kind of freedom you allow them. What kind of responsibility does that place on you?

There are always special probabilities to take into consideration—they change from place to place (from country to country), they change within differing time spans. What I learn from an audience is also unexpected. The first time I did an event which was to be turned over to the audience it became a disaster. Allan Kaprow asked me to "direct" an event for audience called **Push and Pull** as part of Charlotte Moorman's Avant-Garde Festival (at Judson Hall), following an intermission after a John Cage piece. I requested the audience to use a forty minute break by going out to 57th St. to bring back soft materials with which to construct an environment of two rooms. The artists at the festival erected two three-sided rooms with windows cut in them while the audience was away. The next thing I knew someone was running up the back stairs yelling "There's three paddywagons out front and forty police coming up through the box-office." The audience had gone on a rampage, dragging trash cans from alleys, pulling hubcaps off cars, tearing at neon signs. To give people permission to do something we considered inventive and constructive was for them the freedom to attack the ordinary fixtures of their culture. They

streamed back past the police—with whom we were negotiating a truce—with all this crud, and there weren't ten out of eighty able to cooperate on building anything at all. Or, if two people started to put materials together in some shape, five others would kick, slam, chop, tear it apart. There was one rather old woman in a yellow linen suit balanced on broken two-by-fours, just banging away with pots and pans and bits of debris. The artists were in terror. All the wild avant-gardists were huddling behind the stage wondering how to stop it. I finally had to black out the hall.

But isn't that how it should be? Or is at least bound to be, if you genuinely invoke a spirit of freedom and a certain kind of anarchy?

That sort of license wasn't my intention or expectation. What I realized I had to do was to find ways to sensitize people so that contact with each other, with environmental materials, was not an aggression but an extension of a sensitive, relational self. That meant I had to construct situations which they could destroy but that the destruction would be experienced in terms of primary feelings and an awareness of them. I began to consider the effects of sound, lights, the physical sensations of a space; what sort of tactile materials would induce physical interactions so that space would be examined as an extention of our own physical nature rather than a challenge or affront to it.

kaprow's
∠PUSH AND PULL

NOISE BODIES⟩

Week of Avant Garde Festival...Friday August 27th: electronic music concert, Jim's "Phases." Went up at 2 p.m., tangled pile of my clattering "costumes" for "Noise Bodies"; setting up for rehearsal, chaos—everyone running around, carting cables, testing amplifiers, speakers, dancers practicing...hollering for quiet. Good rehearsal; simple, clear shape of piece carries directly; but Jim resisting re-formation, definition of sequences. Helping Charlotte and Philip.

Saturday August 28th: heat blasted city; Jim practicing Ives songs. To Judson Hall 4:30 with last minute supplies. Beverly Schmidt and I go over lighting for our pieces. **Noise Bodies** so uncomplicated—just Jim & me—own body sound system. Crazy dressing each other in all the metal parts; hooking on the refrigerator tubes, ice trays, carburator vents around our legs...balancing the noise squeakers, flashlights, tea pot top "breasts"...Joe Jones rushes into lounge says Judith Dunn is sick and no sign of Lucinda! Beverly's "Interiors," and we're on! Moving in the black out, slowly the indefinable clanking, stacatto percussion of the metal costumes as we walk the length of the darkened hall...audience an intense mass, heat of them, silence...the two spots flash on—the audience roars. We begin to touch and "play" the sound of our "debris bodies." Furious, cacophonous exit totally concentrated on pitch and timbre of our strikes, moving fast through tripods, crouching photographers—applause over our din. Meredith, Yoko, Malcolm and Elaine useful comments, approval. We recruit Yvonne from the audience to do version of her "Satie" while we're taking off our debris. See the McDowell-Waring "Lecture-Demonstration" which is droll.

Sunday August 29th: Back to Judson Hall for the "Ensemble Concert"; Charlotte in usual frantic last minute preparations; ticket collector disappeared, singers and musicians warming up in barnyard chorus of polyphonic squeals, scales, tunings, runs, chords, screeches...Jim's "For Two Gently" by Charlotte and Paik....

Tuesday September 7th: Kaprow-Cage program. I direct "Push and Pull"....

Wednesday September 8th: First call from Paik—CONCERTS ARE CANCELLED! Shock & confusion, anger moves to a sort of relief—we'll be free of the mad, relentless work. But feel I have to act, am directly responsible. Alison calls: "do nothing"; possibility of a suit for damage to hall. Higgins speaks to me, says "keep your name out of it." Charlotte calls—says, "don't go to loft, stay in Jim's apartment, let him answer the phone"; she is with lawyers and managers of Judson Hall....

Actions performed on floor level

1. bodies completely costumed in sound making debris; penlights and squeekers on both of us.

2. in the dark we circle the space, lighting ourselves briefly (like fireflies); sporadic noises of the metal and squeekers.

3. slowly move towards each other in the dark, beginning very rapid (staccato) lighting of the debris.

4. circling about six feet apart; a spotlight goes on in the center between us.

5. keeping eye contact we each pull out a gear cable from the assembled costume parts (from an old car, they look like wands); constant circling of one another.

6. slowly reach out and begin to play each other, first very lightly striking the bells, then striking the tin cans; circling each other more quickly in rapid exchange of strokes; increasingly cacophonous: metal pieces clang and crash together as the speed quickens (percussive, rhythmic).

7. a spotlight suddenly illuminates a large suspended metal wheel (bicycle rim) of "junk"; we begin to interpose strokes on the hanging wheel between strokes on each other.

8. one lifts the wheel down and begins to spin it as the other is striking debris on the wheel; the wheel is thrown in the air, caught by the other, and amidst a crescendo of shattering noise and strokes we exit.

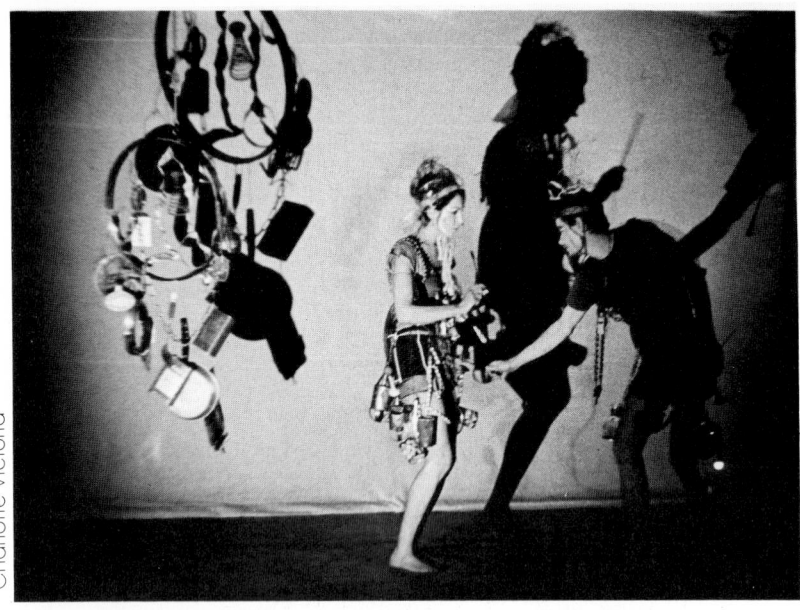

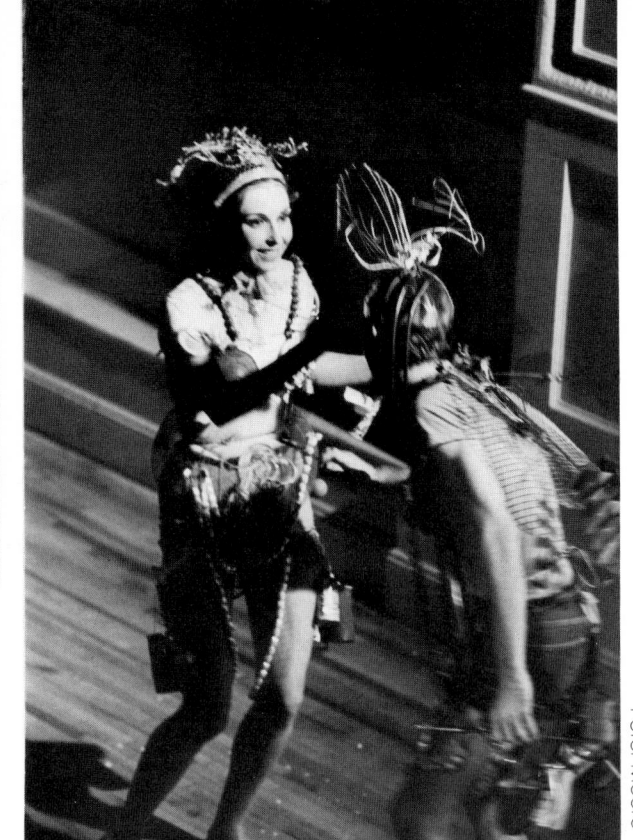

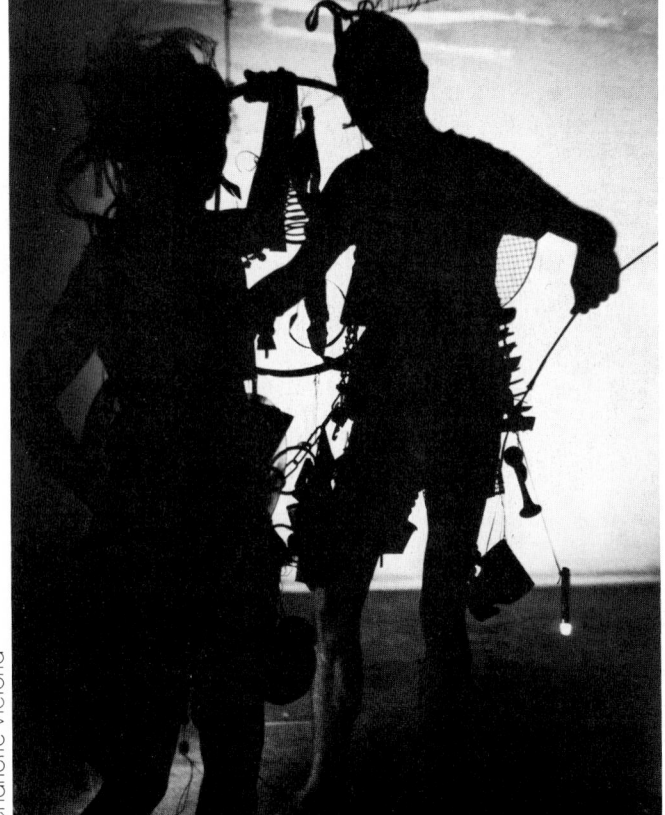

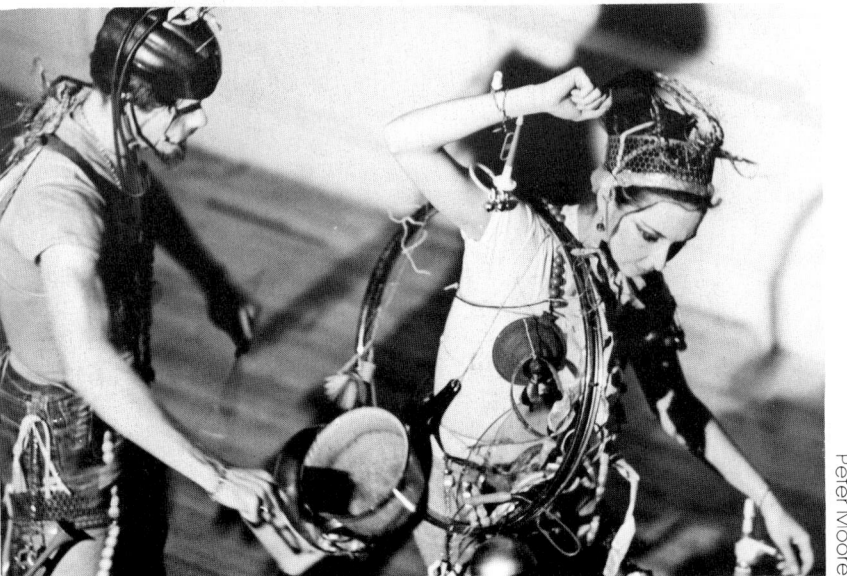

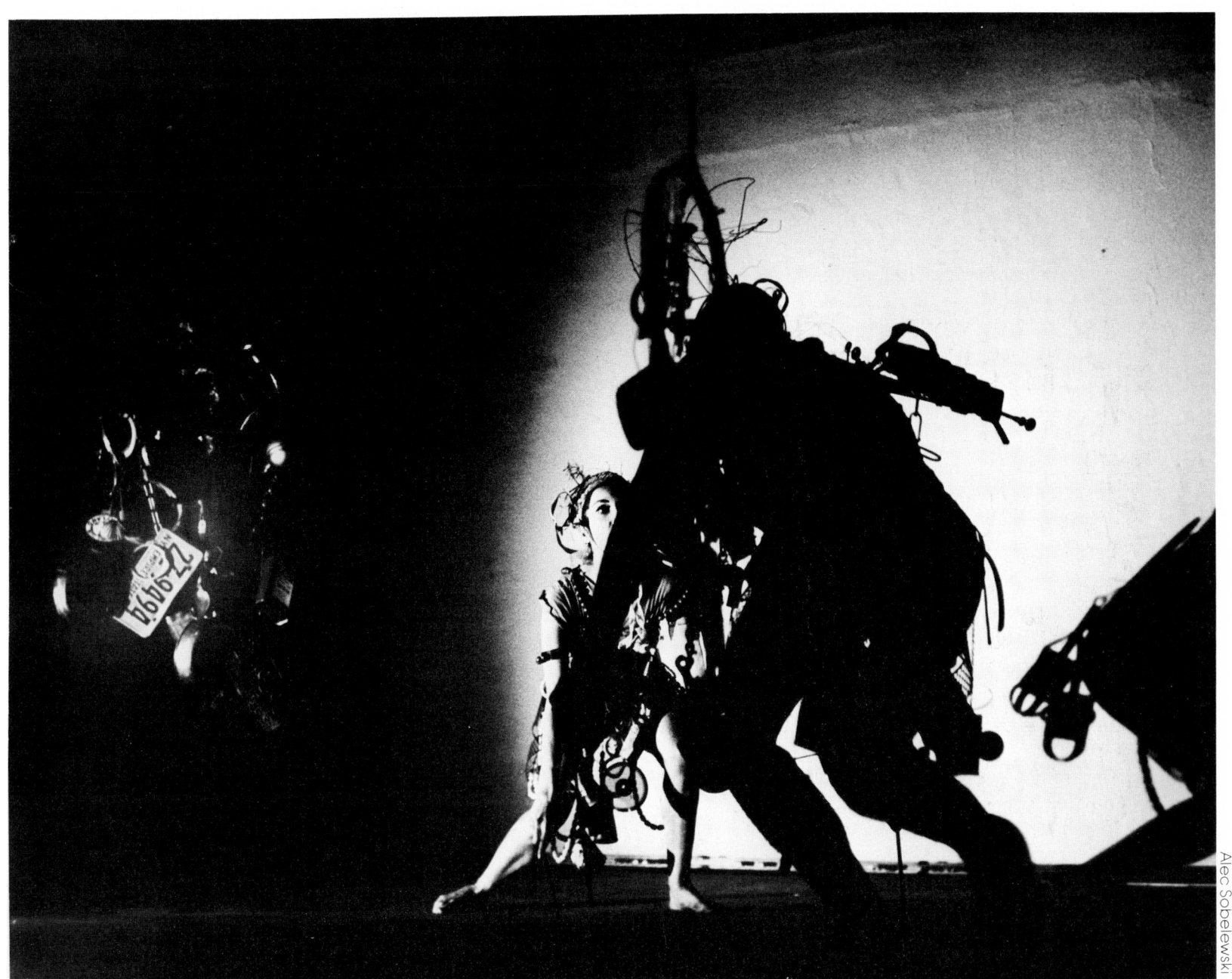

95

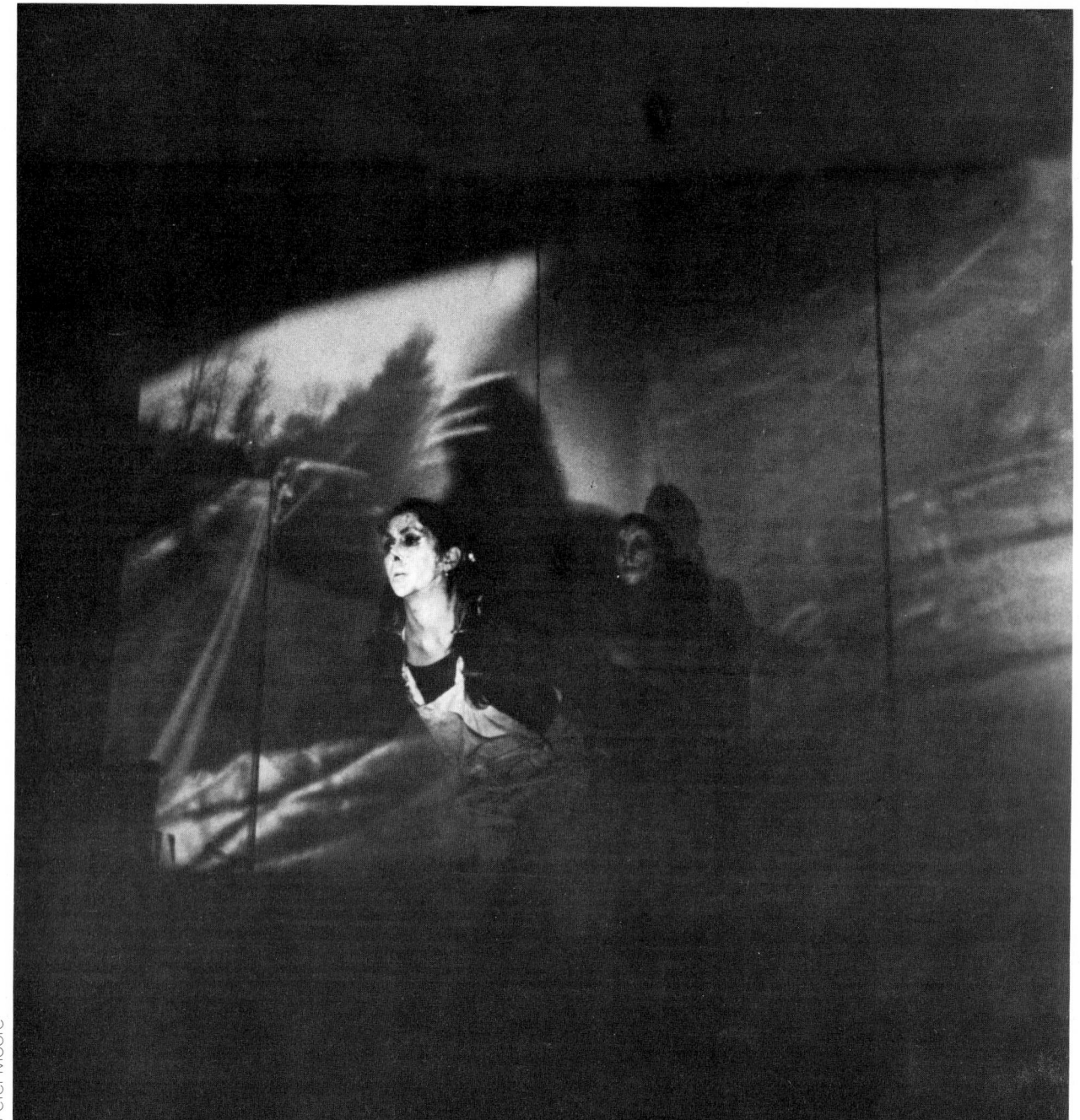

My first performance to incorporate film—film as a material element—began when Gerd Stern asked me to collaborate with USCO* on a film/performance event for the new Cinematheque, where Jonas Mekas had arranged a series of special evenings. The year before I had started to edit the first footage of "Fuses" in my loft: at some moment I projected the film onto a wall of irregularly-shaped rectangular white boxes which I'd made as a sectional bridge between two floor-to-ceiling panels of a construction. Until that time I'd considered filmmaking only as an independent, discrete, self-contained language. But studying the film as it was split into multiple moving images and planes shifted my reticence about including film in performance. "Fuses" was structured to emphasize my concern with impacting and intensifying the focal plane, the illusory spatial dimensions—while at the same time "breaking" the frame by scratching, dying, bleaching, cutting and gluing frames, layering and collage. Because of its visual complexity a film such as "Fuses" couldn't become part of a performance. But I saw the way film could be activated by literal, formal properties into a material equation with the constructions: increasing the ambiguity of the focal plane of film into actual space; extending, compounding repetitions and variations of color, rhythm, texture and literal imagery from film into environment and performance.

The electronic systems USCO was using in 1965 were advanced and original: strobes with film and slide projection, alternating currents for projectors on tilting bases and fitted with macro and micro lenses, cathode rays . . . and other systems developed by their community. Gerd screened the films for me and we agreed to the collaboration on the understanding that I would work **against** the physical integrity of the films. The USCO films incorporated real time or established image-sets of specific things—highways, signs, symbols—and several films were not too complex to preclude live performance.

What I proposed (Gerd consented) was to dominate the films perceptually with

---

*USCO (us company) was composed of artist/technicians working and living cooperatively—variable number of men and women who, like guild artisans, did not want to be individually identified apart from the group. Stern asked me to work without my name being used, though he was well known as the director of USCO. As a painter I stubbornly identified with the signature scrawled on my canvasses since I was fourteen. As a young woman, the world was constantly trying to absorb me, rename me, and define my functions. It was all very well for men to choose to be anonymous! I was aware I was fighting for my actual functional identity by insisting on attribution by name.

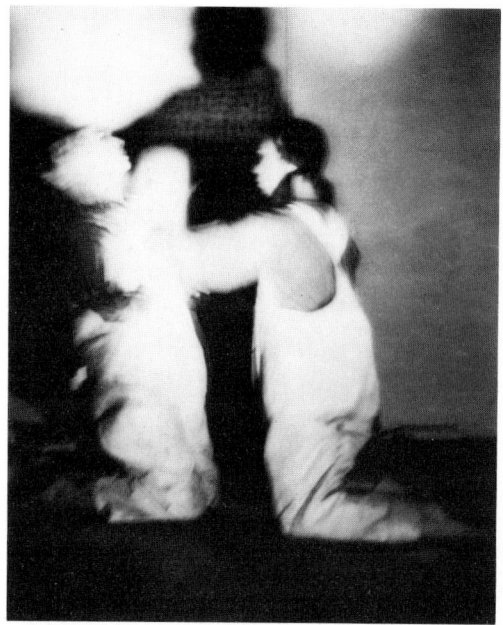

Peter Moore

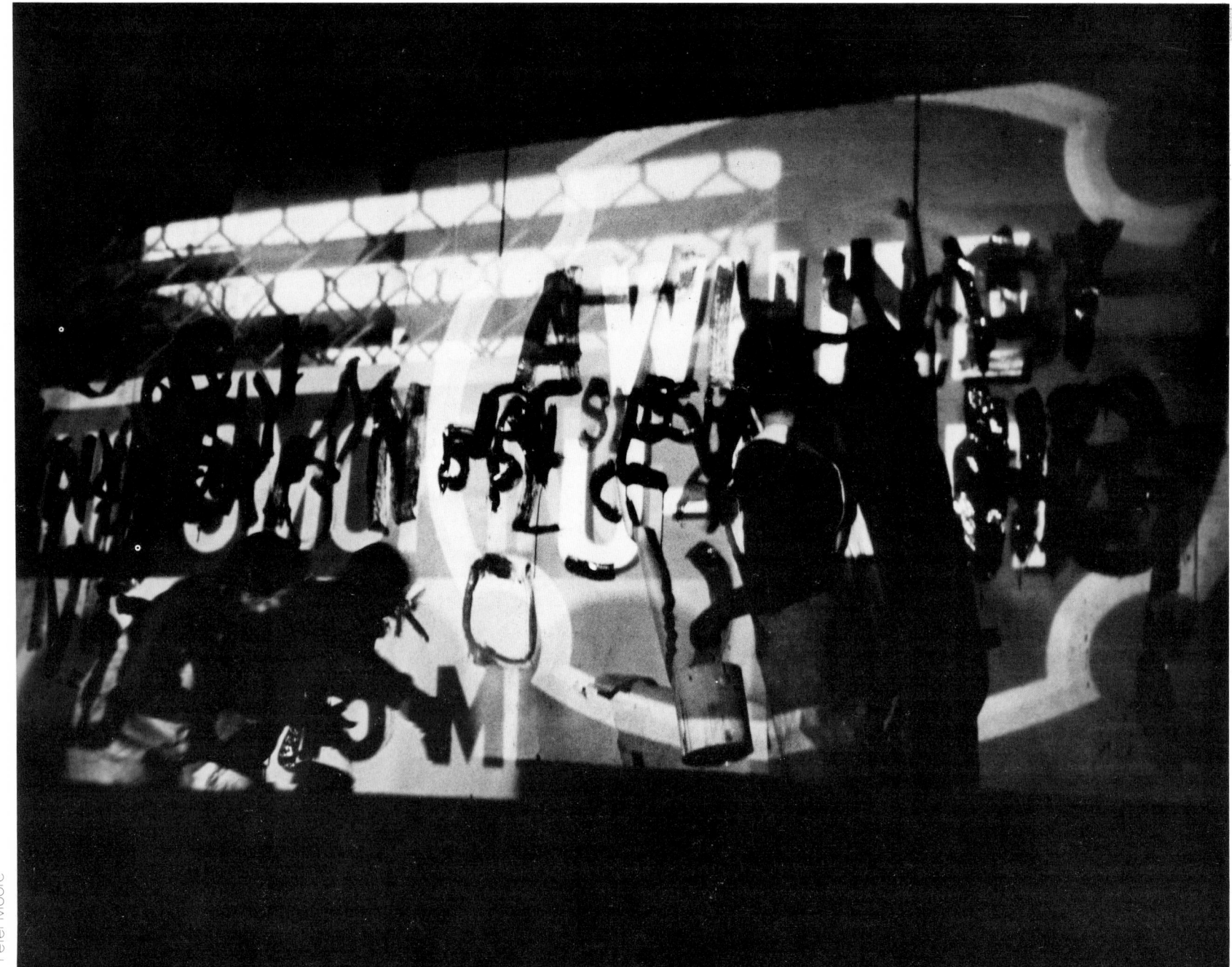

physical activity. The performance presumed the films antagonistic, that the two performers would spread action in literal dimensions **away from** the fixed-screen illusions of image, depth, speed, rhythm, direction, duration. It was that or have a performance embellishing and ancillary to the films—a stylization.

Ghost Rev (I took the title from the final film) was a curiously calm but intense performance—the first time I made a work for just myself and another woman, and it had a deep intimacy and mystery. Phoebe Neville has always been a rare dancer, one whose training never interferes with her ability to take physical risks in unrestrained improvisation, and one with whom I was always able to freely extend my most fluid, untried ideas. We stained our bodies with whiting under painter's overalls (worn to de-emphasize our body shapes). Our props included buckets of red and white paint, large brushes, knives, small flashlights on cords, ropes, iron and ironing board, whistles and brooms—a strange combination of transposed painting and domestic implements.

SCORE

1) HIGHFREETHRUSAFEWAY

Centered in the projection beam, Neville and I slit layers of paper screen away with knives until the images are intersected with wavering lines; slicing finally through the last layer the film imagery dissolves into the dark back wall.

We blow the whistles (against the soundtrack of a motorcycle), crawling slowly down ladders we have tipped from the stage onto the first row of seats; we crawl across shoulders and laps of the audience, film projected on our overalls. We reach into pockets and give the audience bubble-blowing jars, blowers. As we approach the rear seats and turn to crawl back, we drape strings of flashlights around ourselves. Soap bubbles blown by the audience shine in the projection beam.

2) Y

We crawl up the ladders to the stage, lift and position them in front of new screens which we unroll from large cores of paper. With brushes and buckets of paint we "attack" the multiple projection of filmed words—one of us "catching" strokes of circular letters, the other vertical letters—as they flash on. Quickly we move back and forth. The "frame" edge begins to blur as shreds of piled paper and glimmers of splattered paint accumulate on the walls and stage.

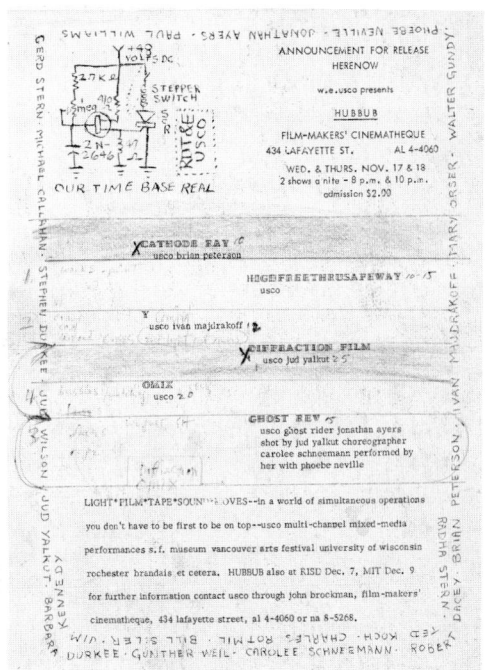

During Jud Yalkut's DIFFRACTION FILM we disappear.

3) OMIX
Phoebe enters with an ironing board, sets it stage center, and in the flickering light begins to iron white shirts. They are hung on hangers onto the ladders. She irons and calls to me: Where are you... come on out here...bring the ropes... where are you?...I enter and remove the iron; Phoebe tips the ironing board against a ladder; we turn slowly, go down on our knees, crawl forward to each other with arms extended. We touch one another's shoulders and begin a slow exchange of pushing, falling back, rising, pushing, falling back. We carefully unbutton our trousers, pull out a length of rope, lean forward to tie it around each other's waist—a coil of rope in each of our pockets. We rise swaying against the tension of the rope and begin a sequence of roping each other in and out—letting our full weight pull against the rope the other holds, so that at times we are almost reeled out into the audience, off the edge of the stage. As we are reeled back and forth we call out the words seen in rapid cuts in OMIX: go do don't won't can't ow no now how our your us let hold on high up want blow. **Black out.**

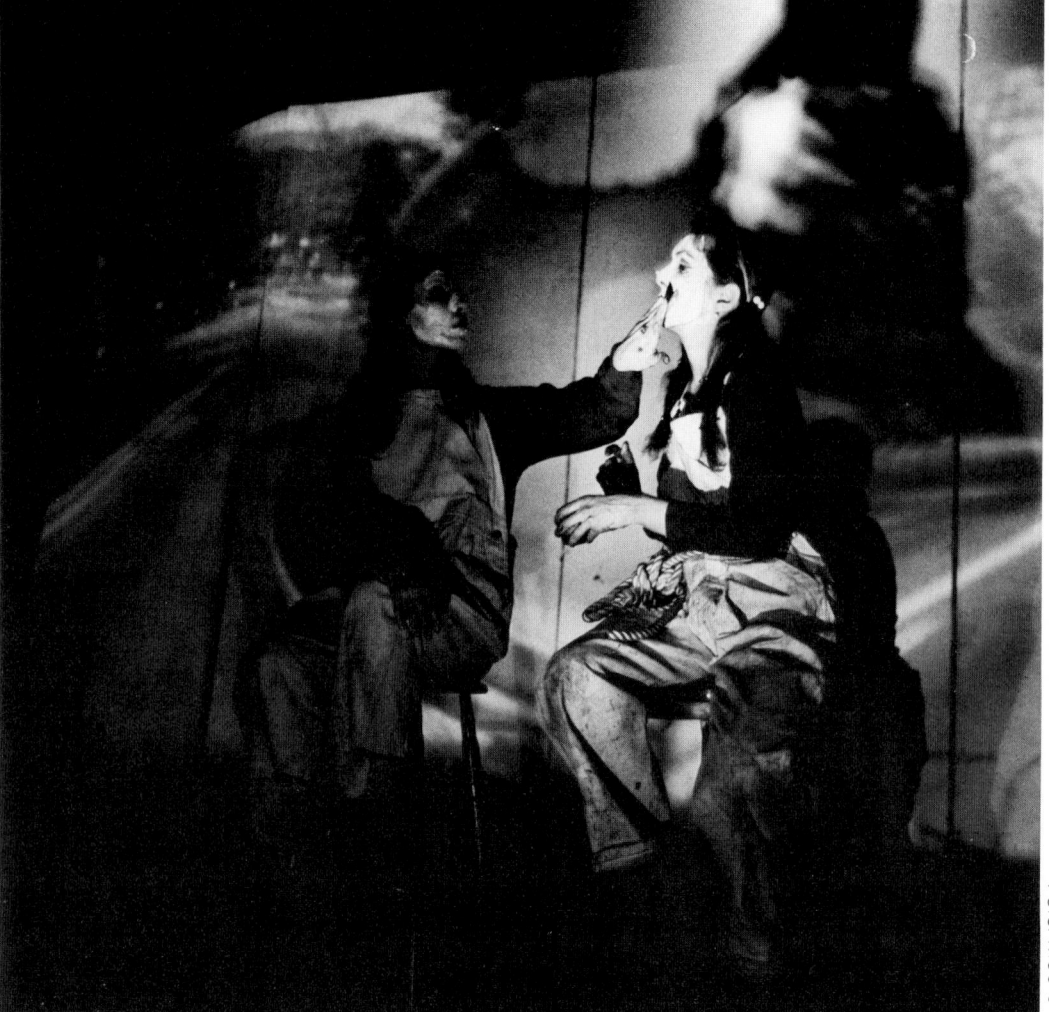

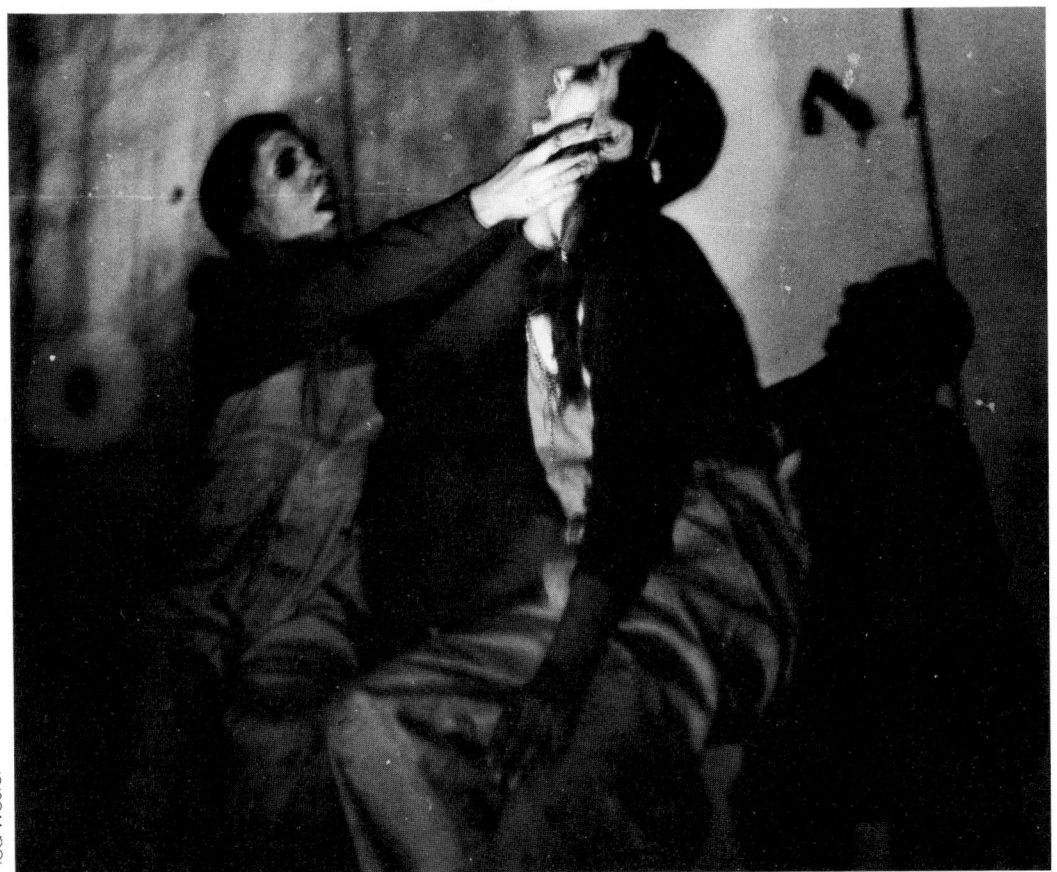

Ted Wester

4) GHOST REV

Creation of Faces. We are seated side by side on stools, facing out slightly towards the audience, the film continuously projecting across us onto the screen behind. We cannot see the audience, we sense their shapes: shadows as boundaries within the light. Slowly, looking directly at each other, we smear white grease paint on one another's faces in a sustained exchange. The whiting is buttery, applied thickly with the fingers, full arm awareness with the touching strokes.

With one or two hands the first woman reaches out to the face of the other, slowly pushes her cheeks, brows, nose, chin, lips or jaw into an expression, and withdraws her hands. The first woman watches the "face" she has created... and its transformation. The woman receiving the face finds that it creates emotion, evokes memory, assumes character...She allows her facial muscles to relax and the face to fade away. Certain created faces (the most ugly, painful ones) will not fade, as if they possess our muscles and have to be **broken;** we seek some counter muscle movement to dispell the rigid face by opening the mouth wide, shifting the jaw up or down, or slowly shaking the head.

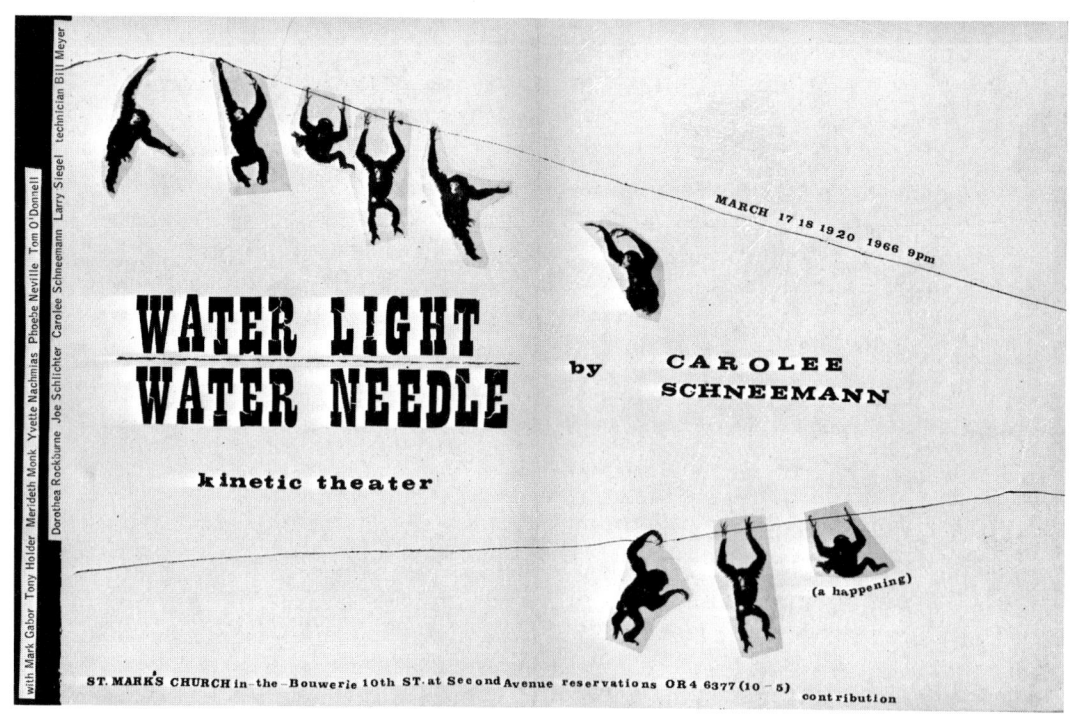

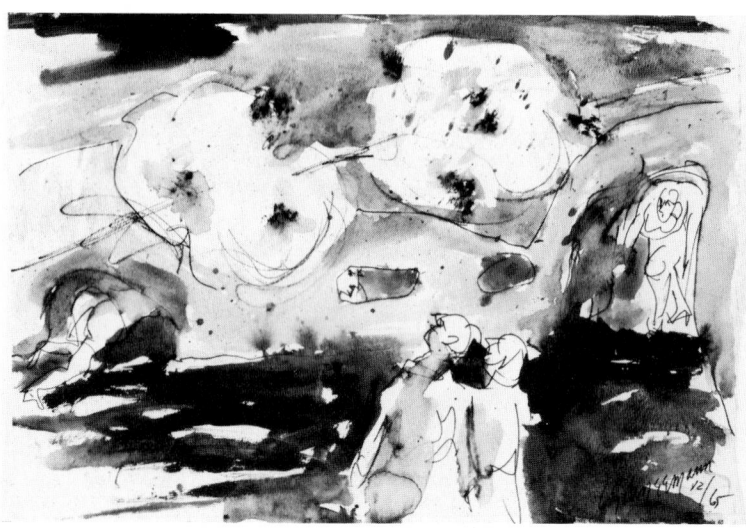

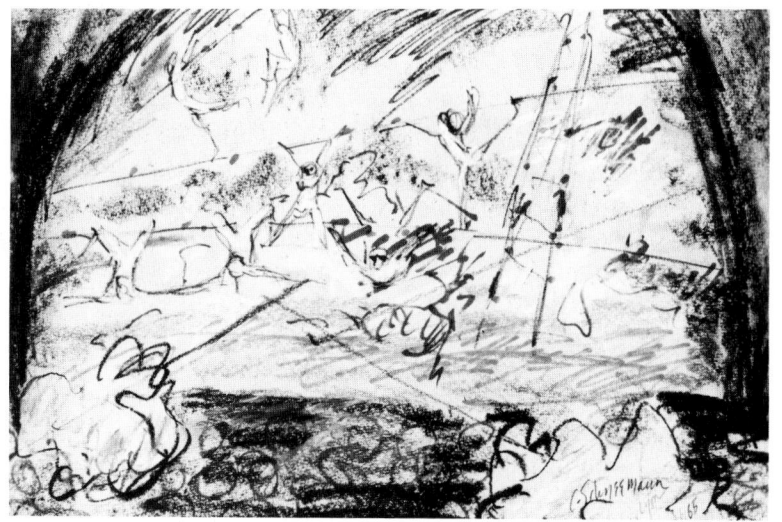

To celebrate the success of **Meat Joy** in Paris, my friend Francois-Bernard Mâche gave me a train ticket to Venice to attend the Biennale '64. I walked off the train and across the station into startling reversals of figure and ground, water and stone, dazzling light and shadow, solidity, transparency. It seemed musical, contrapuntal: echoing footsteps in narrow alleys, the surge of bodies, the constant unexpected appearance of water lapping at the side of a street, the recurring verticality of steeples, spires, posts, masts, and the human figure itself—cubistic, spatially ambiguous. Palaces rose out of the water—closed, impenetrable, or festive with lines of blowing clothes. Moving fluidly by vaporetto along the irregular canals induced a sensation of floating, suspension.

It was as if I had physically entered my own mirror constructions where focus will converge and splinter depending on the angle of observation; like the fragmented mirrors the waterways shaping Venice enlarge detailed optical effects, merging and duplicating whatever is "outside," including the viewer. The network of waterways and the mirror constructions arouse a sense of "rising out of", rather than "being upon" a fixed plane. Sensory disorientation led to new conceptual considerations over the days of my explorations of Venice (including the frenetic international "art world", reunions, the drunken parties and receptions, hours on the beach, sleeping under an equestrian statue in Piazza Academia lacking money for a hotel room): the inclusion and transformation of subjective response to environment, the city as a model of fixed transience. The accumulation of visual and sensory effects was more extensive than any of the observable components would indicate of themselves.

Venice and the Illinois prairies are the opposite extremes from the rolling, dense Pennsylvania and New England landscape I know best. If Illinois had been an "empty stage," Venice was full, a constant performance arena of operatic proportions. In Illinois my own verticality and frontal vision centered as a hub in a wheel, or plumb-line positioned in the unvarying expanse; only the details of forms close to the body shifted scale. In Venice water is "ground," duplicating, reflecting the repeated upright rhythms—whatever is above the horizon line is also below the horizon line mirrored in water.

Underpinning the incredible Baroque details of Venetian architecture was this basic grid: scattering light on waves, on glass, the moving colors of crowds, the continual horizontal pulse of vaporetti, speedboats, gondolas. Sounds them-

WATER LIGHT
WATER NEEDLE

March 17 18 19 20 1966 St. Mark's Church NY

May 29 1966 Havemayer Estate MahWah NJ

March 17 18 19 20 1966

St. Mark's Church-in-the-Bowery   10th St. & Second Avenue N.Y.C.
presents

WATER LIGHT
WATER NEEDLE   Kinetic Theatre by   CAROLEE SCHNEEMANN

with-

Mark Gabor Tony Holder Meredith Monk Yvette Nachmias Phoebe Neville

Tom O'Donnell Dorothea Rockburne Joe Schlichter Carolee Schneemann

Larry Siegel
****

Guides--Michelle Stuart Linda Sampson

Exterior Sound--Philip Corner with Ferdy Buonanno

Interior Sound, Organ_-- Aldis Lagzdins (Fri. Sun.) Larry Leitch (Thurs.Sat.)

    William Meyer -- Rigging Lighting Technical realizations
    Joe Forn -- Stage Manager Technical assistance
    Phoebe Neville -- Technical assistance
    Joe Jones -- Cloud light realization
    Bernard E. Kirschenbaum -- Architectural advisor
    Bernard Olderman -- Roustabout

****

    Rope - Mr. Schenk Paper - Harry Lerner Ribbon - Stylecut
    Trucking - Ed Iverson Fans - David Stone

    Mailing: Emmett Williams Alison Knowles Judy Vyssotsky Mrs. Allen
    Phoebe Neville Jonathon Altman Max Neuhaus Horatio Szwarcer
    Al Hansen Valerie Hansen Pat Cook Ralph Cook Barbara Harris

    Detail work: Judy Vyssotsky Marta Minujin Ann Charters Mark
    Brusse Jonathon Altman John Brockman Barbara Harris Jack Agueros
    James Tenney Alex Sobolowsky

Very special thanks to Ralph Cook, Rev. Allen and the St. Marks's staff and
parish, who made these performances possible by providing us with time, space
production costs and good will.

Grateful thanks to William Meyer, Phoebe Neville and Joe Forn who volunteered
their invaluable help for over three weeks.

****

No photographs may be taken of the performance without permission from
Miss Schneemann.

selves were lifted and mixed in the air, their physical origins deflected. A tissue of light seemed to be the source of color, form, the substance of matter. Added to this was the relative invisibility of the domestic and social lives of Venetians apart from their services to tourists.

Water Light/Water Needle was conceived as an aerial work for ropes rigged across the canal at San Marco. I proposed "Acqua Notte" to Leo Castelli at the Biennale. Later that year I re-designed it for L'Opera de Lyon, the director's son, Humbert Camerlo, being intrigued with images of performers gliding on pulleys stretched for 500 yards between the highest balconies and the stage. I built a model with dolls in harnesses on pulleys (which I subsequently destroyed as the rejections for this "impossible" proposal accumulated). The images of suspension, floating effortlessly, continued to be confounded as I tried to produce the work in New York. It seemed I was dedicated to a structural fantasy. There had to be walls to which steel supports could be anchored, steel pulleys and fittings which would accommodate 3/4 inch manilla rope: thinner rope would cut performers hands and legs, fatter rope was impossible to grasp for periods of sustained time.

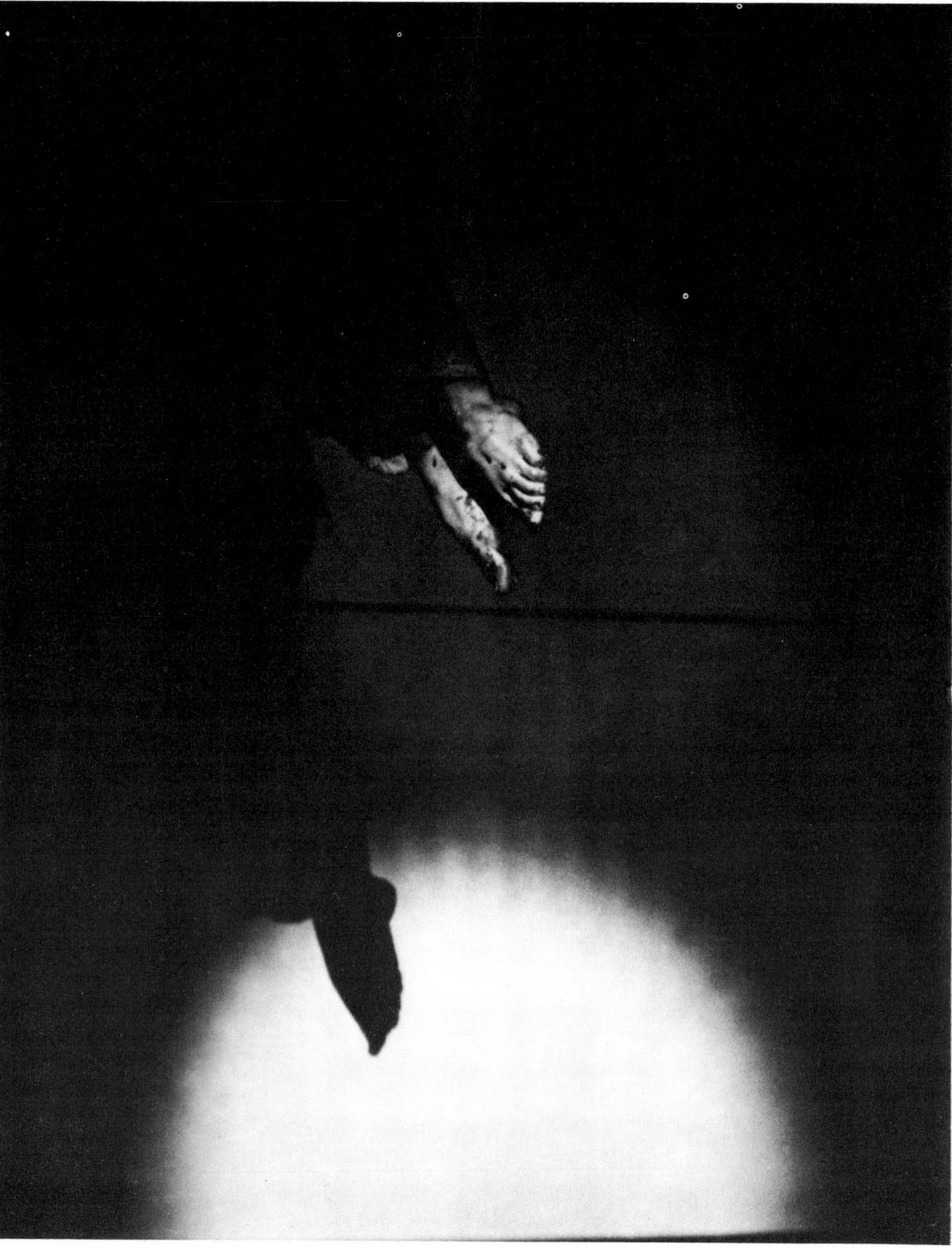

Peter Moore

Metal fatigue, rope tortion, knotting, braiding, the hardware of rigging dogged my dreams of a possible space. And the image insisted on an open rigging of interdependent ropes—not placed against a wall or anchored behind a stage.

Water Light/Water Needle was finally realized within a large open room at Saint Mark's Church in the Bowery (Venetian name sake!), then later rigged in a grove of trees to be filmed. The transparencies of Venice still motivated the actual aerial arrangement of ropes which enclosed or surrounded the audience seated below.

Discovering that the two delicate fluted pillars twelve feet apart in the middle of the St. Mark's parish meeting room were indeed made of steel seemed a religious miracle worthy of the Venice cathedrals. The side walls of the rooms were solid enough to be braced with steel supports. Reverend Allen and Ralph Cook would risk performers falling onto an audience. And they would pay for the mailing and provide production funds of $200.

The next physical paradox was human: "effortless" movement on the ropes was exhausting and painful; we had to slowly build cal- louses on our hands, feet, behind the knees. To raise ourselves and to hang from the ropes we had to sustain "muscle memory" which required a minimum of working out on the ropes for three hours every other day. Missing one rehearsal was starting all over again.

The sculptor and architect Bernie Kirschenbaum generously gave structural advice. The sculptor Bill Meyers single-handedly built the steel wall supports, designed pulleys and rings. I somehow convinced a shipyard to contribute a hundred and fifty feet of 3/4 inch manilla rope. Joe Jones, Flux musician and sound sculptor, worked with me constructing the "clouds" which floated on adjacent pulleys under the ceilings down into the audience; filled with twinkling lights the clouds signaled the beginning and end of movement sequences. The church gave permission to open the choir loft where a volunteer organist would play the Bach-Vivaldi A minor concerto—which flooded in at the conclusion of **WL/WN**, the performers barely visible in near darkness, slowly moving back into the row of white cupboards against the wall from which they had originally burst out. The window above these cupboards faced into the church courtyard. A firescape was behind them.

The interior sounds were the swooshing of the "clouds" on pulleys, the threatening clanks and bangs of the steel rigging as the ropes were traversed, and the calls of the performers to one another. Outside in the courtyard Philip Corner evolved a score of seemingly random noises, peripheral and threatening.

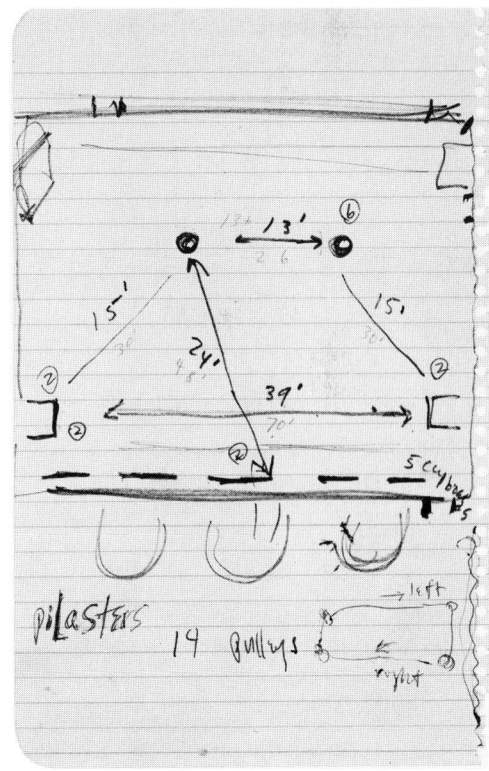

NOTES 1

Character of movement: NOT acrobatic
                      NOT balletic
always functional: you are always consciously involved with gravity, your precarious, variable journey on the ropes: your partners are each other, gravity, ropes.

Concentration on contact with the ropes: balance, stretch, the continuous slight sway of the ropes strengthens and relaxes the motions of the body; the facial expressions are natural. The balancing and stretching opens the diaphram; sounds which echo in your chest/throat from muscular pressures can be emitted. The tendency in current performance to tone down both facial and vocal expression should be avoided (half of you have performance experience): relax your throats—the breath carries the energy of each motion—permit the spontaneous impulse to sound. Range of grunts, groans, exhalations, exclamations, panting (by the time you're on hand-over-hand hangs), and cry out if falling—we'll all need to know.

Signal vocally to other performers when you are going to change the tension on the rope they are using; when on a higher rope and swinging down and for jumps from one rope to another.

You must not pass another performer on the ropes without physical contact; each independent journey will be temporarily suspended, deflected or changed by an encounter. Each presence should be treated as contact—combinations of bodies remains an extension of the ropes which support us, a unique spatial configuration. Encounters of more than two people will change the movement rhythms of individual journeys by tightening their sections of the rope. Our awareness of each other stretches the entire length of all rope levels.

When passing on parallel ropes above or below another body, try to make contact with it.

The basic rope walk is hand over hand: frontal, back and forth, sideways, forward and back. Impulse to change the basic walk is taken from the tensing or slackening of the rope dependent on the motions of everyone else.

1 March 66

NOTES 2

Phrases of movement build by individual body's energy duration; relational shifts between one another.

(visual verbal tactile genital—action flow stream impulse to each other sparking a harmonious collusion)

Preparatory exercises to rid the men of competitiveness, muscular feats, unnecessary exploits on the ropes, risks which become dangerous to others—not being sensitive enough

For everyone: more intensity, concentration; greater visual focus on where you are in space; don't take your body movement for granted and don't predetermine it—feel the motion as part of the ropes, flow into it (sway of the ropes like an ebb and flow of water)

Reminder: this work is actual, functional movement and evocative. No gesturing, funny, mechanical or acrobatic "effects." We are a unitary system; your own energy and the position of the ropes expands, vibrates and extends each motion. Every movement and every moment is *relational.*

Think of the ropes as flesh extension—conveyance. Concentrate on "feeling" HERE—not a literal emotion but a sense of connectedness. In beginning rehearsals we will work alone, stay alone until we begin to flow into someone else, an object, the floor, the ceiling, lining of our stomach, weight of our wrists stretched out above our heads...

...each particular moment contributes to the total time in space—every individual body unit is in relation to the environment and to any other body which leads us to a full peripheral awareness...

The freedoms we have in this work exist within the unique conditions of the rope for which we mutually assume responsibility for ourselves and each other.

You are the imagery and you are not the image.

5 March 66

RULES

I. Entrance & Approaches

On your first entrance from the cupboards and after each rest, decide which rope you wish to move to; go and make contact with it and immediately leave the rope—turn away, move in another direction before returning to the rope you have chosen. Or, having turned away from the rope, you may change your mind; pick another, go to it, make contact, turn away...or choose a third rope...turn away...return.

Moving directly onto a rope you've chosen slackens your time impulse; the turning away and returning builds the energy with which you finally mount the rope.

II. Contact

1. Low ropes: frontal and hand-over-hand movement. When another performer is met on the ropes, each frees a hand from support on the rope to turn the head of the person encountered; the turns are slow, deliberate, sensitive; may be done simultaneously, from face to face, from behind. At times there may be three or four almost simultaneous head-turns. Each person continues their movements with the meshing of their bodies.

2. Low and Mid Ropes: frontal and hand over hand and lying across ropes. At each encounter a head turn is exchanged and the bodies combine, impinge on each other's movements; these combinations alter the specific directions and forms of individual movements. The performer situated on the rope to accept the weight of the other may

carry them along in their motion; there is never a struggle; the balance of each on the ropes regulates the possible combinations.

3. Low and Mid and High Ropes: knee hangs, arm hangs, swings
Encounters effect the head turns, body combinations, carries and lifts.

III. Rests

1. Voluntary—at any time you choose you may leave the ropes and go to the cupboards, the shelf, the center area. You may rest as long as you wish.

2. Slips from the ropes—if a slip from a rope (or a fall) puts you on the floor in a position from which you cannot simply reach out and re-establish contact with a rope, you must take a rest for a few moments.

3. Enforced—the clouds will be pulled along their pulleys at specific intervals; when they reach the end of their cord—descending into the audience area—the Guides signal the immediate start of the enforced rest by shattering glass bottles with hammers. If your position on the ropes is not comfortable for a rest there, drop down to the center area, to the cupboards or to the shelf. You must rest a minimum count of two minutes.

The first person to begin moving on the ropes after an enforced rest is left alone for a minimum count of sixty seconds. The duration of the enforced rest depends on the impulse to move of one person.

4. All rests—at the conclusion of any rest, performers must pause at the grease crayons and apply a smear of crayon on their face.

The white workclothes as they get dirty will model the shapes of our bodies; the crayon smears have the effect of modeling our faces—toning the face as the white clothes become toned.

The character of our rests should be as relaxed as a resting animal; experience the fatigue and muscle strain; we almost completely give up contact with the activity of the others still on the ropes. A completely experienced "rest" can convey the consistent and unique muscular activity which—on the ropes—looks "effortless"—by its actual loss of effort. The selfless absorption of an animal resting. If you go to rest in an area where someone else is already resting, curl up on them...be comfortable (it is a nesting).

10 March

REMINDERS

Signal changes from one rope to another; speak to each other whenever necessary: for help, coordination of movement, to adjust position, for the pleasure of it...

All sounds occurring from your physical actions are part of the sound environment (the noises from outside, noises made by the audience, the constant clank and metalic rings of the rigging...)

The minimal physical exchange would be when the person who is either first or able, takes one hand off the rope and carefully moves the head of the encountered person to another angle or position. Instantaneous decisions as to who is first to free a hand or hands: you may have to support your partner. If a third (or even a fourth) performer comes into contact with two others, all suspend intended movement until the relay of contact exchange is made. The quality of the head-shifts is always intimate, sensitive, intense...

After a face shift you may evolve more complex body encounters...or you may pass on. The person whose face has been turned lets the position gradually relax before continuing.

When you come up behind someone on a rope you must imitate their movements until you overtake them—not as a game but to echo their rhythm so as not to throw them or forcibly change their motion.

Secret instruction to the women: take more physical risks, chances with the men: hang on them, leap on them, embrace them, creep up on them, give your full weight to them.

In the beginning when we are locked in the cupboard shelves use the isolation to find your real attitude for the time; we'll be under great pressure—try to come in contact with it—tired, anxious, fearful, high, pleased, anticipatory, blank...Work that into the silence, the sense of all our bodies in proximity through the walls. Unity, conspiracy, warmth, potential action; the strange but familiar world we share waiting...edged by the energy of the spectators...feeling them also through the cupboard walls...spectators as definition and containment of our unique focus, our coherence.

Our closest moment should be in these separate cupboards. Each sends their full energy stream forward to the person in the next cupboard. Wait until you do feel connected to one another...wait as long as necessary. Concentrate until all of us sense linkage through the walls as clear as the ropes waiting outside.

There will each time be one of us who gathers the energy increment of all of us and explodes the cupboard door open.

(During this time the tension may provoke disturbances among the audience. For instance one man started yelling "What is this, a sacred ritual or something? Where's the action?" One of the guides went to him with the previous instruction to touch him with her pole, kneel down and whisper in his ear "just be patient" or "I'll lead you out now if you want to leave." It was usually only men who made disruptions, any aggressive response intensified theirs, we anticipated that the guides (Shepardesses) would have a calming effect.)

SCORE

I.

9:00-9:20

The audience is led in by Guides (carrying shepardess staves) in twos and fours; settled in semi-circle of crumpled papers around ropes. Two house lights, soft, murky (green & blue).

The Guides ask the audience groups to read their programs while they fluff the papers around them, which they do repeatedly, adjusting the papers around the accumulating groups. A row of seats against the walls is reserved for the old, infirm or fearful.

Performers are all hidden in a row of open cupboards behind a curtain. We relax in the cramped positions and concentrate our energy through the cupboard partitions.

Musicians: Philip and Ferdi are in back room waiting to go outside by rear door.

9:20-9:30

House lights out, Xmas lights on. Carolee and Larry enter from the kitchen carrying trays of crumpled paper; we go through the audience to the fans, kneel down, turn them on, listen to them. . .begin to drift papers in front of the blades slowly, finally filling the center aisle with blowing paper heaps.
Silence. Musicians wait.

II.

9:30-9:40

Turn off the fans. Push fans to side walls. C & L exit behind curtain, close all the cupboards quietly and each choose a vacant shelf for themselves. Joe and Bud walk through the audience and slowly roll up the huge curtain, revealing closed cupboards, unoccupied space. Exit with curtain.

9:40-9:50

Emergence from cupboards. The performers have concentrated on passing their energy to each other through the five cupboard partitions. The audience becomes anxious. The first performer to feel that the energy of all has centered in their cupboard bursts it open, shattering the hinges. The others wait until they individually feel the cumulative impulse to emerge.

The first performer moves onto a low rope slowly after hesitation/choice. If two performers arrive at ropes simultaneously, one waits in position for the other to move for two minutes; each performer counts two minutes before moving onto the ropes after another.

III.

9:50-10:10

Walking/Encounters/Carries—all performers. **Low & Middle ropes.** Musicians begin soft noise clusters outside the windows. Guides send up lighted clouds on the pulleys which traverse from audience level to ceiling on opposite walls beyond the ropes. The clouds are brought back down after fifteen minutes. Shatter glass to signal first enforced rest, 10:10-10:13.

IV.
10:13-10:30
Clouds pulled back up. After first performer has begun to move again on ropes for two minutes, the Guides count for fifteen minute sequence.

Go directly to rope you want, face it, touch it, turn away and return, or turn away and lift anyone still resting and carry them to a position on the rope; they in turn face the rope, touch it, turn away and return or turn away and lift a resting performer, and drag or carry them to rope…After each rest, enforced or chosen, smear a streak of blacking on face. Climbs/Hanging. **Middle & High ropes.** Broken Line Relay.

Guides bring clouds down through audience. Smash glass signalling enforced rest. Turn off cloud lights. Gold spot light on. Joe ready on ladder. Organist up to choir loft. Musicians outside silent.

V.
10:30-10:34
Lights out, flashlight beams on. Performers climb onto cupboard, huddle together, decide in whispers which four will go out onto the ropes in the dark, following flashlight beams directed by Joe. Two figures remain standing on top of the cupboard; two others sit or lie down there.

10:34-10:42
In the darkness the two teams slowly follow light beams guiding their movement. The lights shift from one team to the other: a start-and-stop series of hand-over-hand walks and carries on the **middle ropes.**

10:42-10:50
Xmas side lights up on floor. Side doors open as Organist begins Bach-Vivaldi A minor at full volume. The other performers slide from shelf onto floor…moving on low ropes in the minimal light. The two teams are on the high ropes—they return to the floor, or make an exchange with two others on the **low ropes,** or with one another on the **high ropes.**

10 50-10 57
Organist continues…first movement of the Bach-Vivaldi over and over. Performers slowly touching, shifting contact with each other, begin to draw back into cupboards—falling, dragging, lying, sitting in the open shelves. Joe and Bud enter with the long curtain and spread it over the back rope…the cupboards disappear from view. Side lights out. House lights on. Guides signal the organist to stop playing as the audience exits.

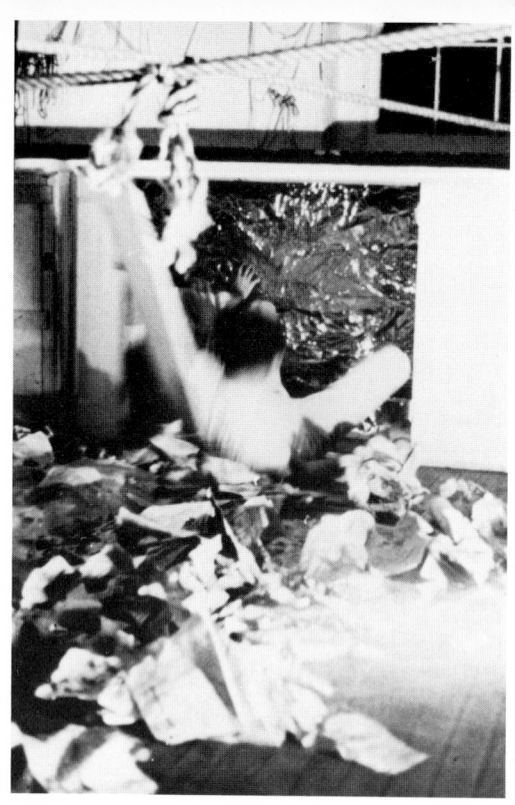
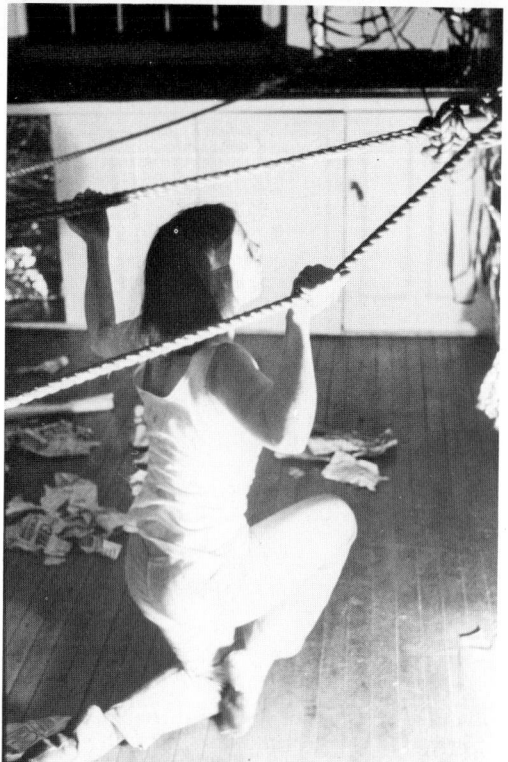
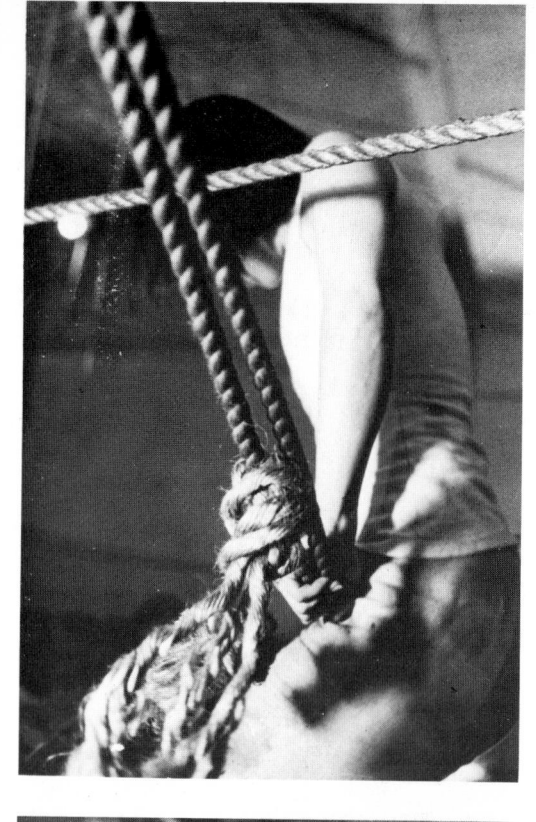
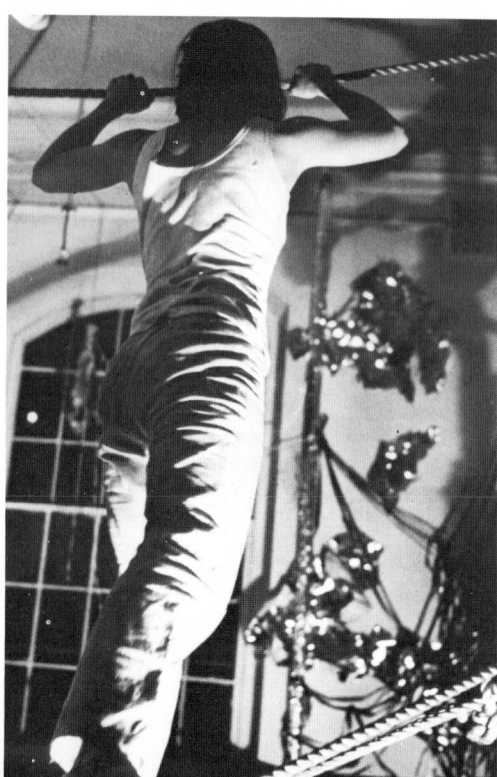
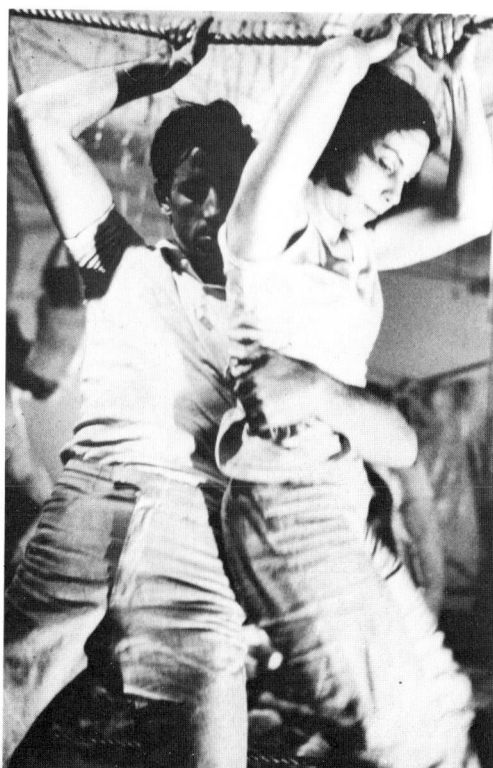
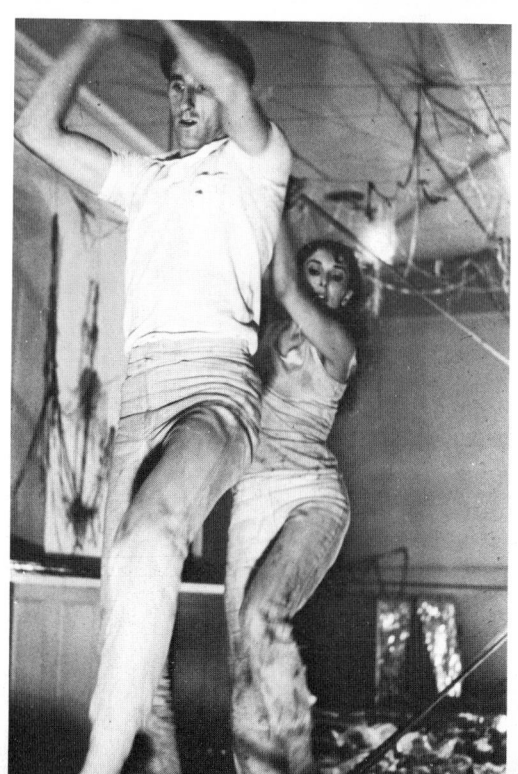

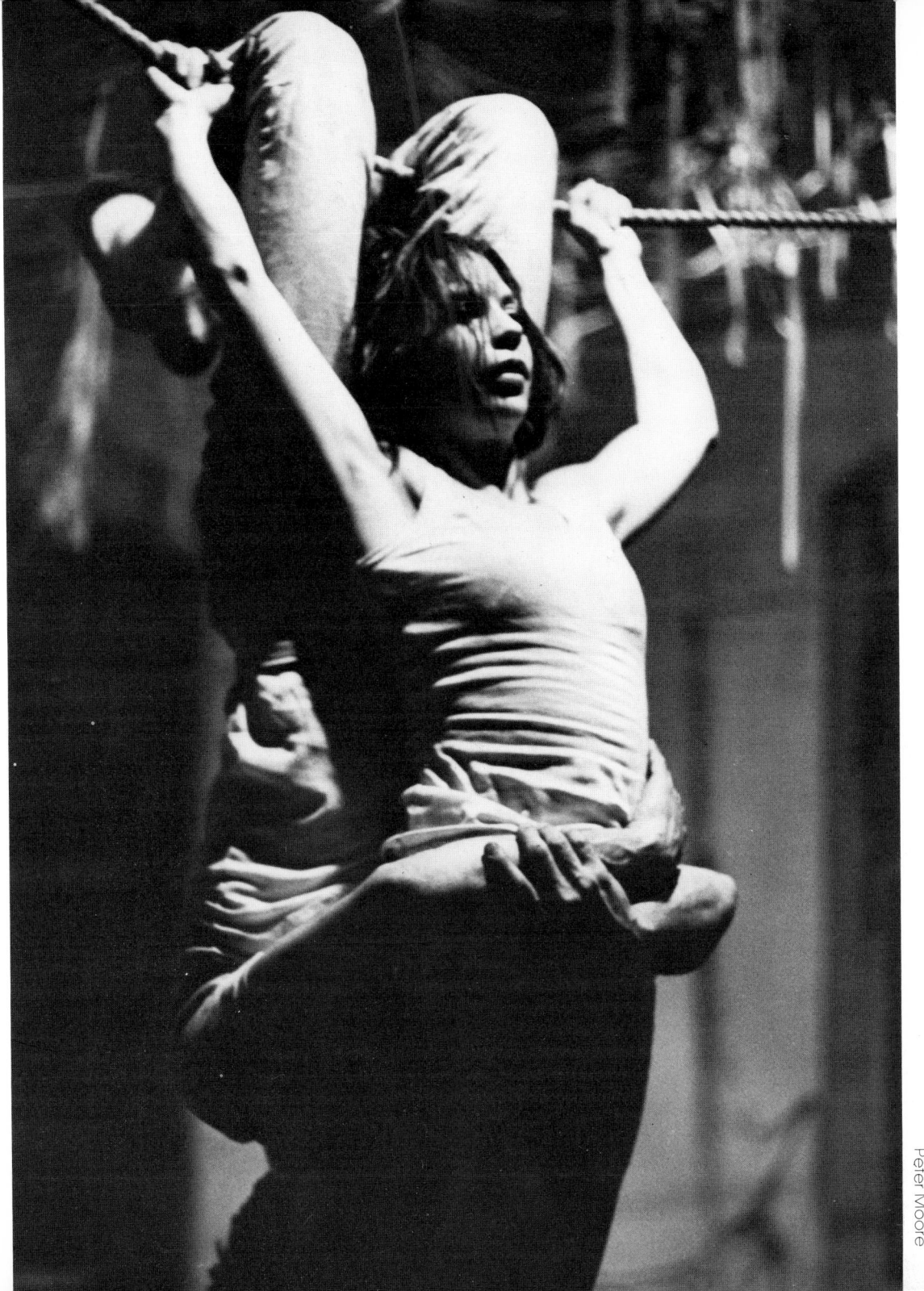

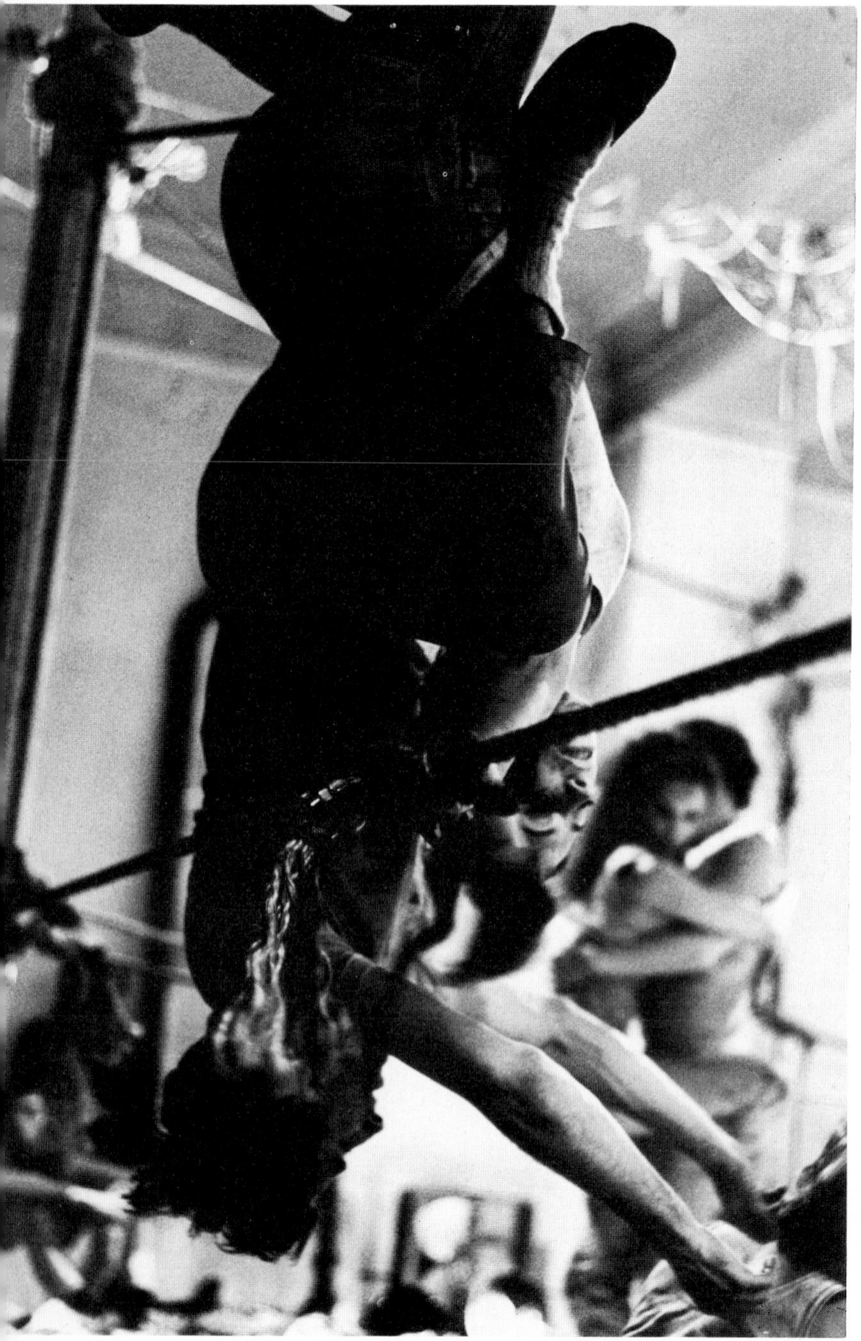

Terry Schutté

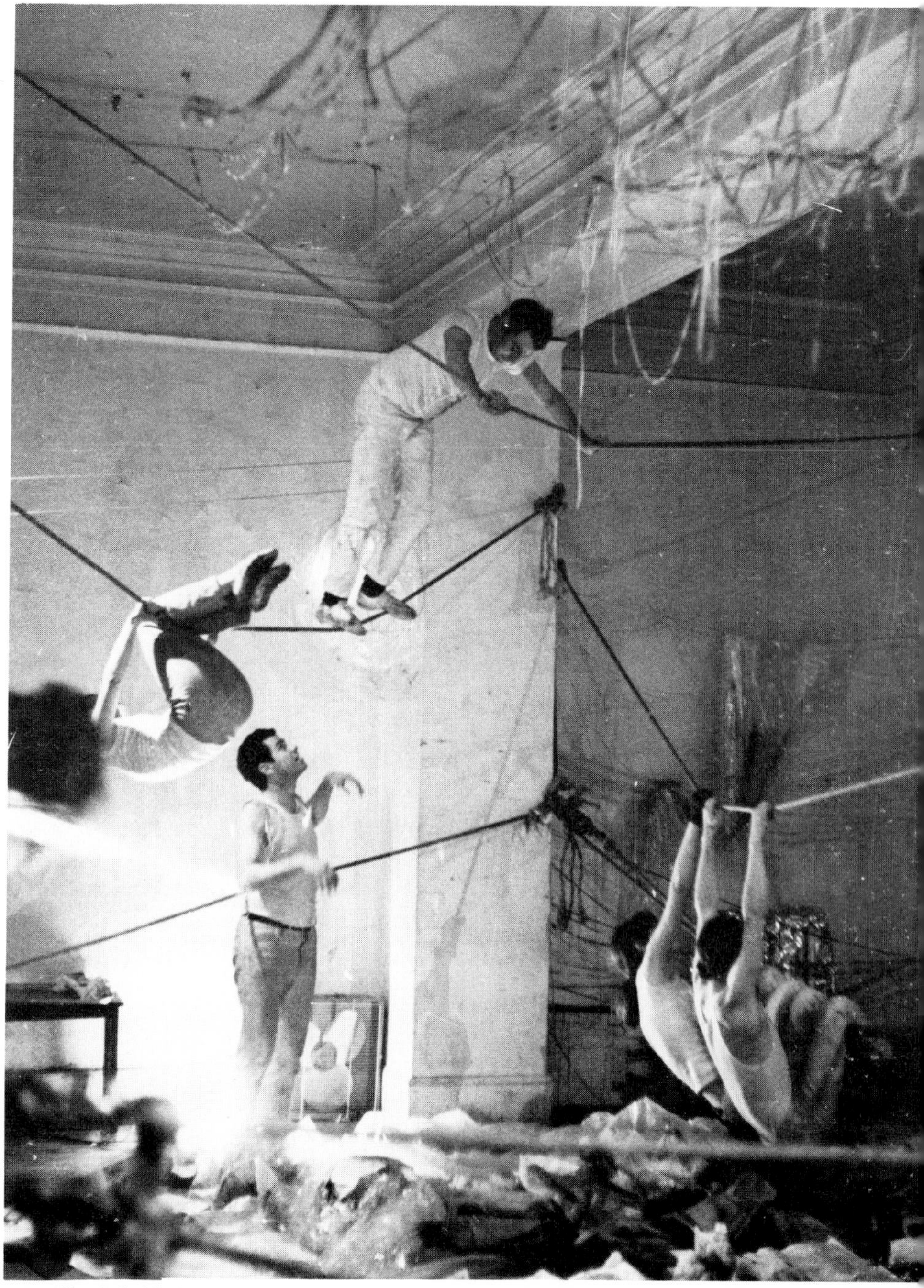

Charlotte Victoria

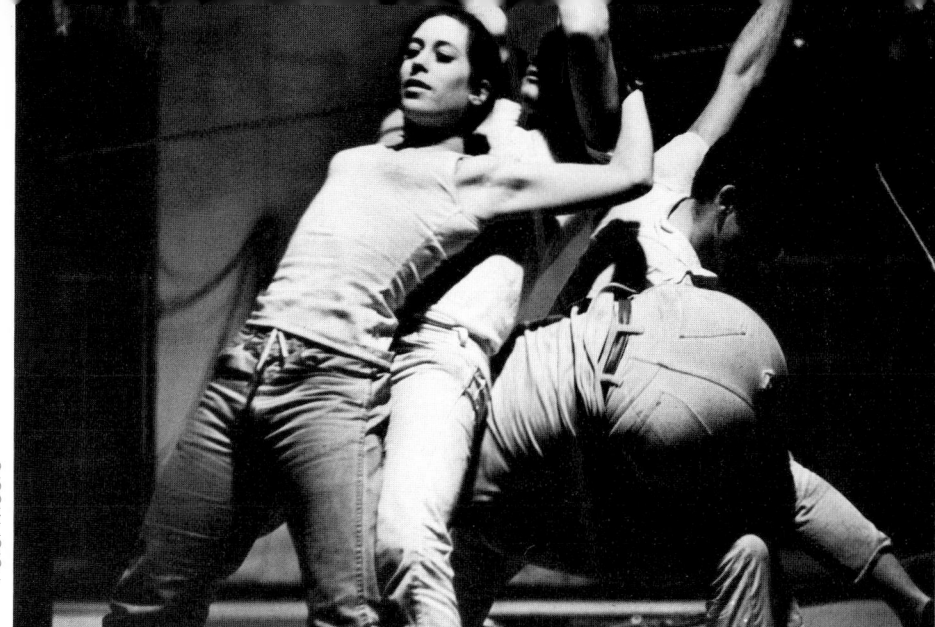

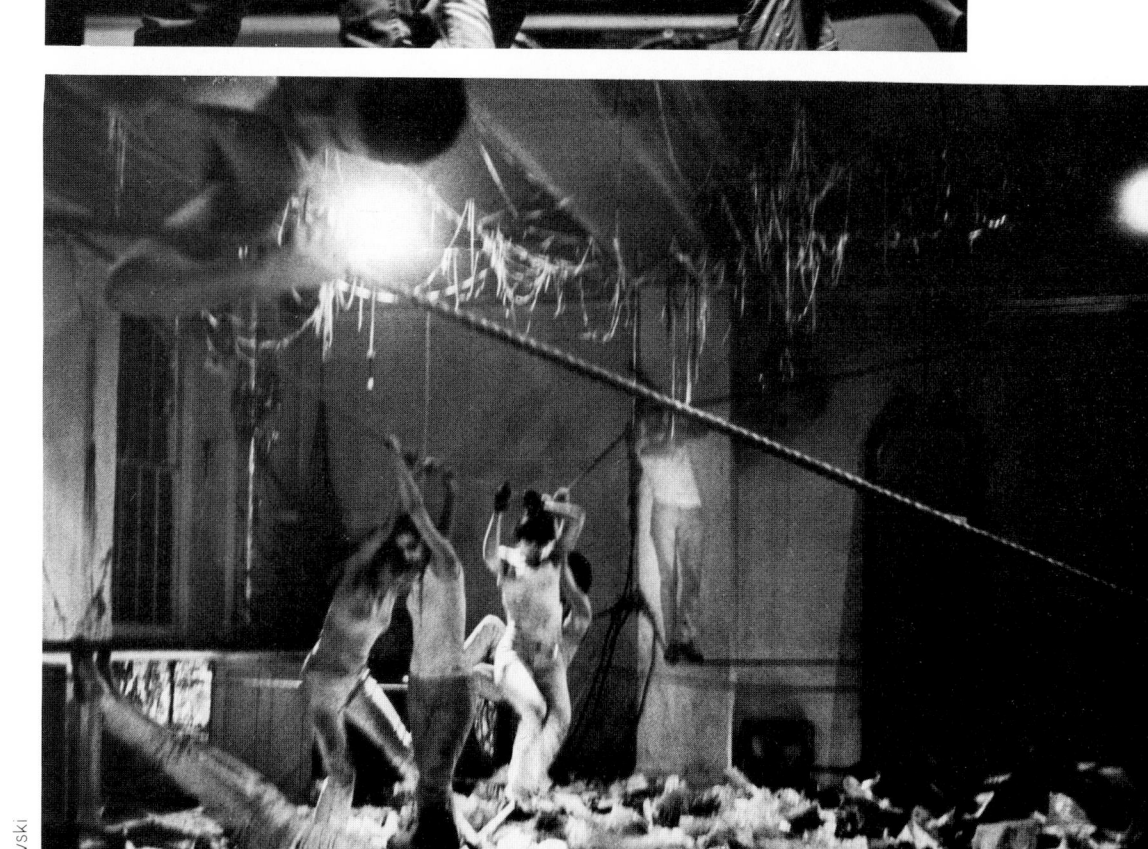

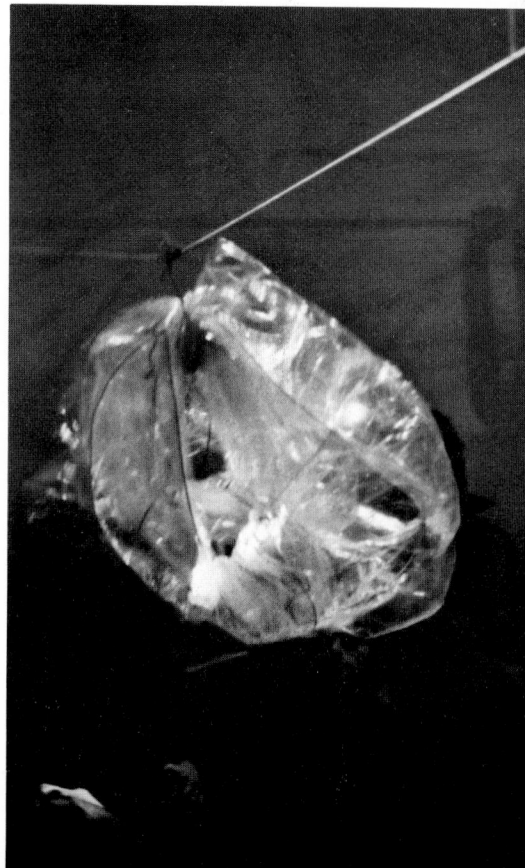

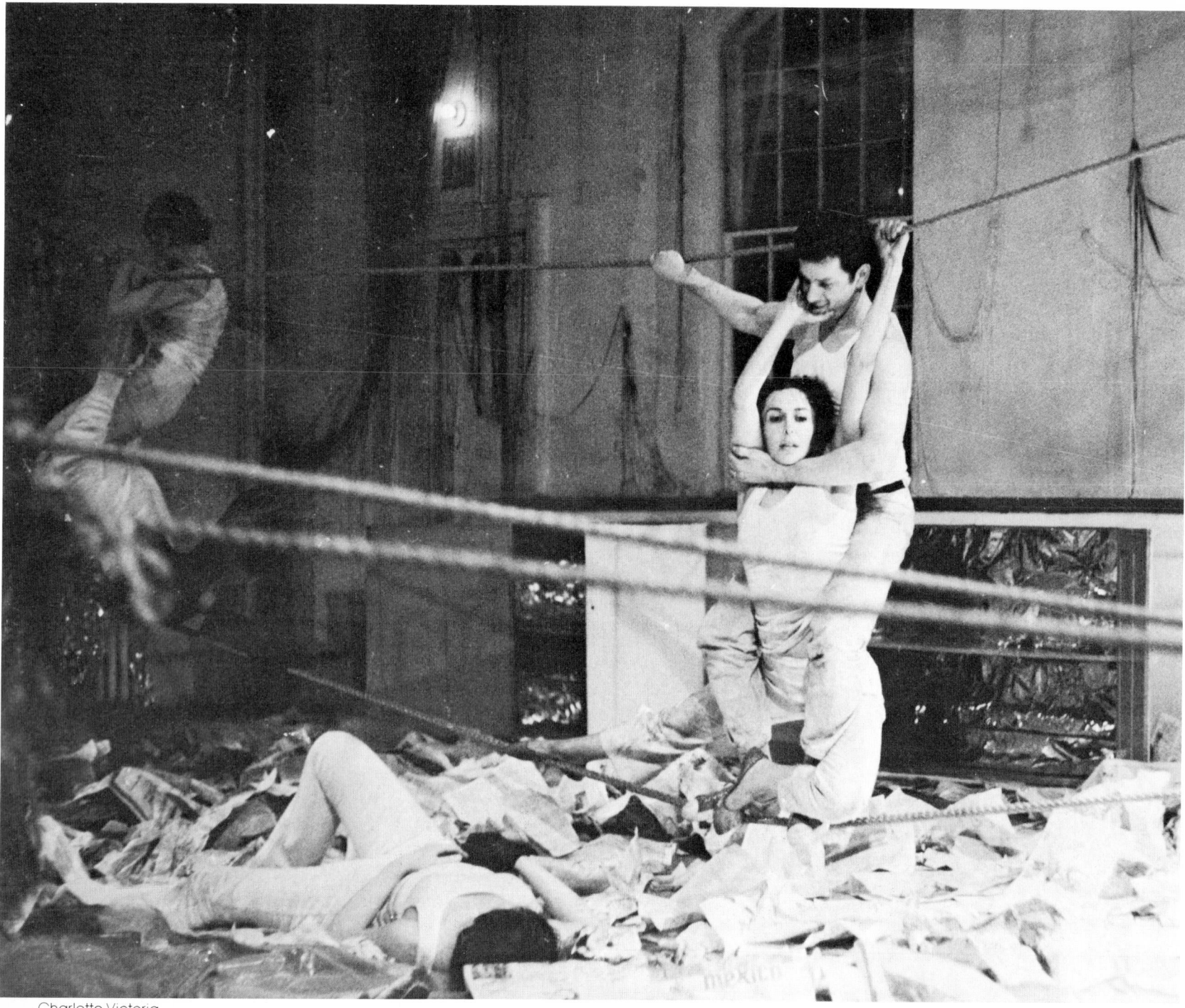

Charlotte Victoria

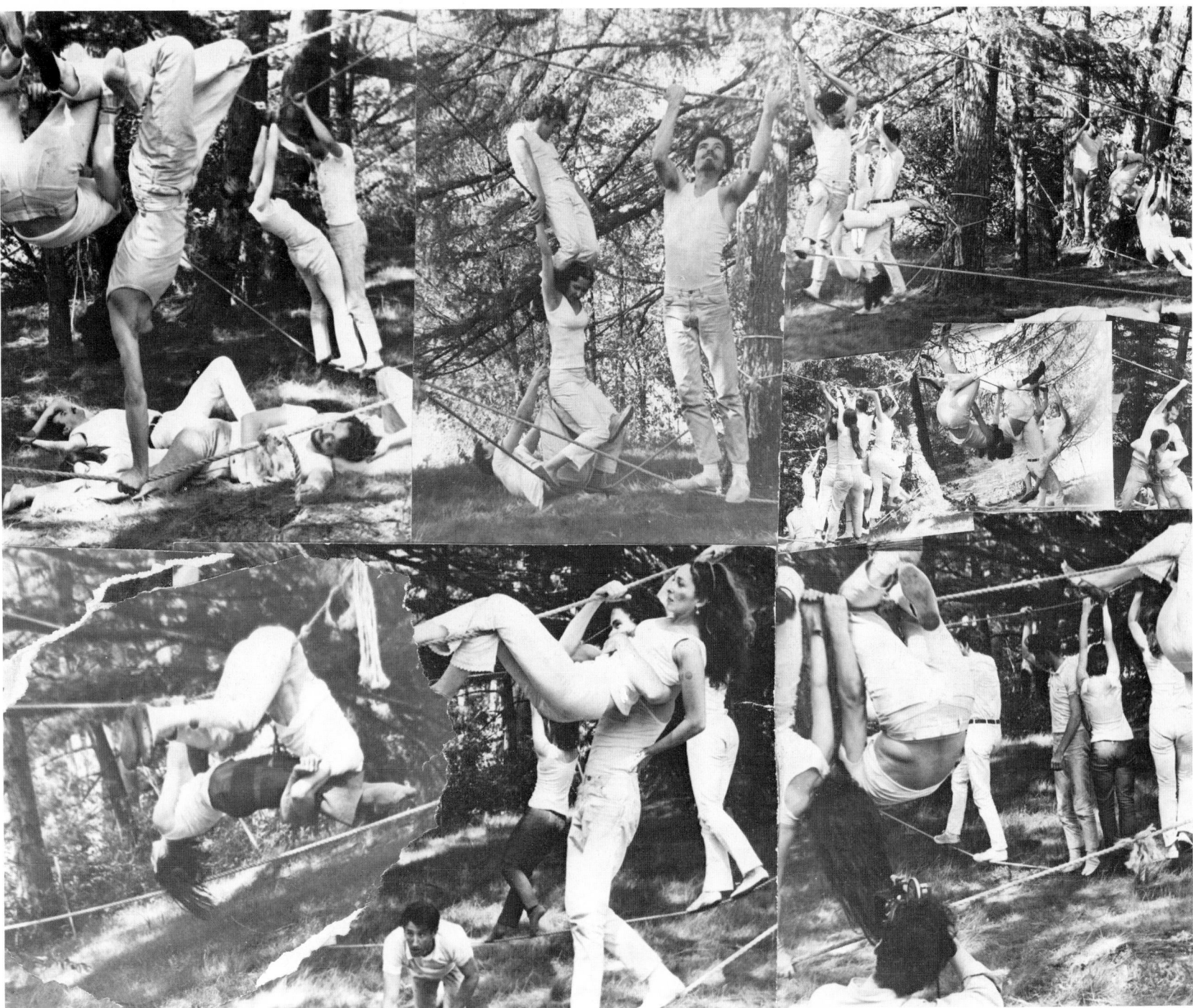

Charlotte Victoria

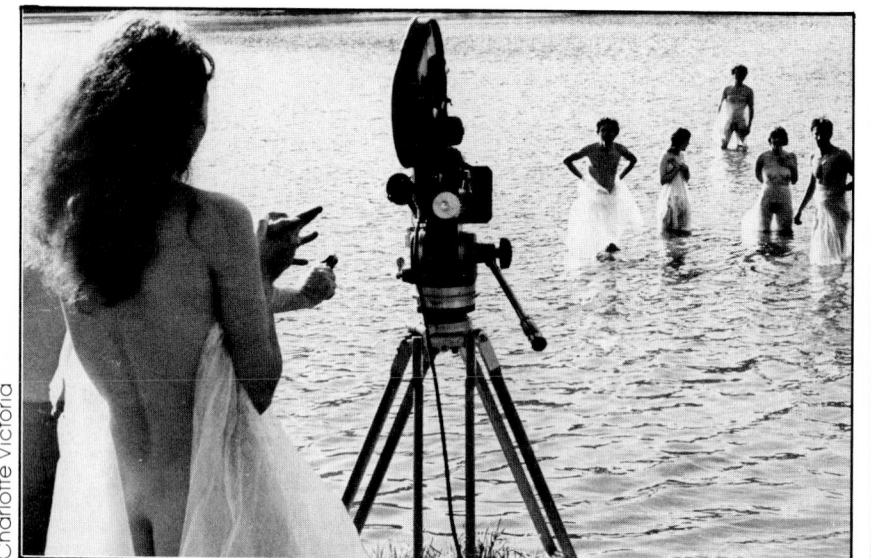

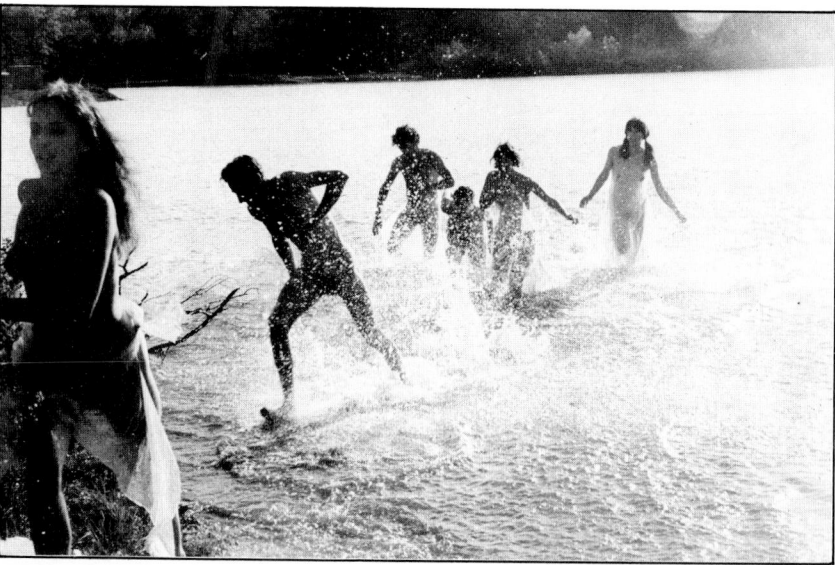

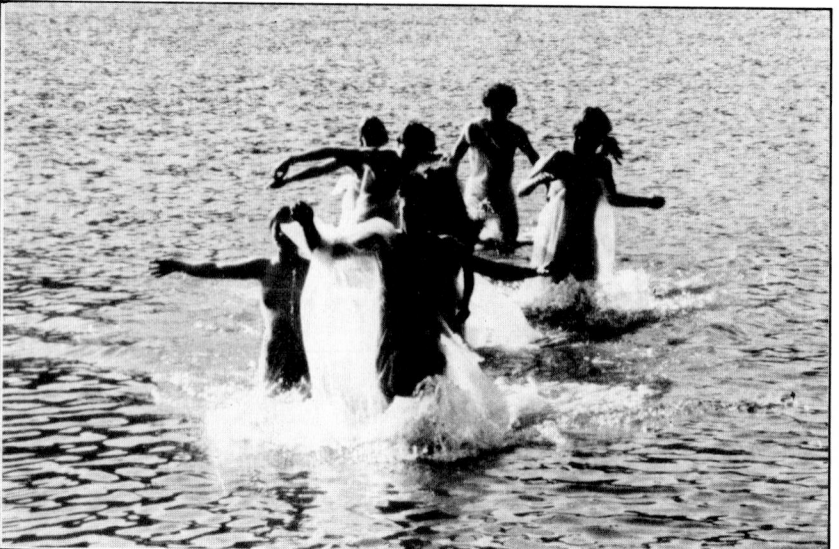

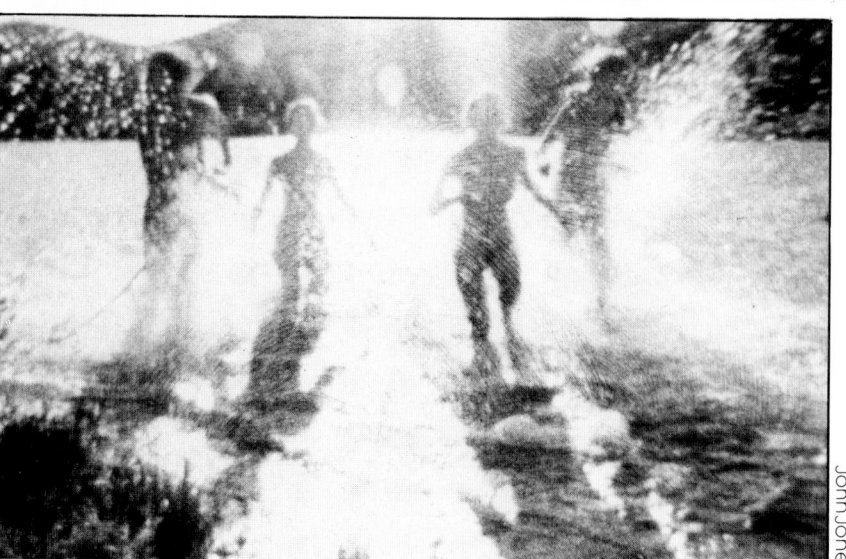

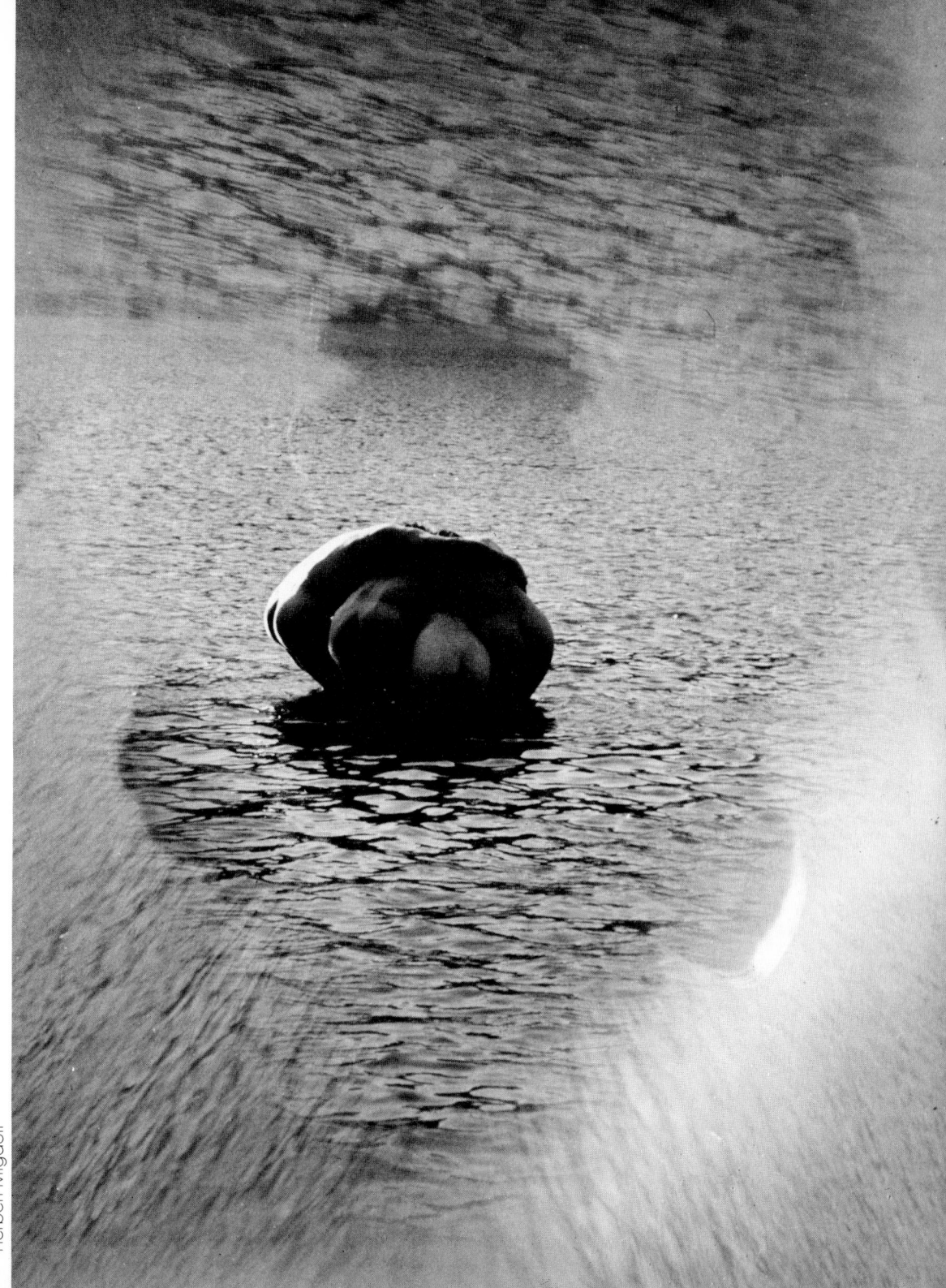

All of us wanted to continue with the piece; its formality was engrossing, involving, in ways we felt could go on indefinitely. I now wanted to try **Water Light/Water Needle** outdoors, approaching the original conception. Ferdi Buanano had assisted Philip with the outdoor cacophony at St. Marks. He said he knew of a place in the country where we could rig the ropes and perform undisturbed for filming. It seemed unlikely: we required a grotto of trees strong enough to take our combined weight, at least twelve feet between them, no obtruding lower branches. We would need a sunny day, transportation for all the performers, technical help, filmmakers, photographers.

A further series of magical conjunctions ensued. Ferdi's father was from Venice, negotiating the purchase of an abandoned estate. Most incredibly for me it turned out to be the old Havemayer Estate. Their distinguished and extensive collection of Impressionist works had been acquired through the persuasion of Mary Cassett, a close friend to a Havemayer daughter. The first Impressionist works I'd ever seen were those of the Havemayer collection in the Philadelphia Museum of Art—the Monet's of Venice! My roots past and present were completely tangled, ending up through the intricacies of the Venetian imagery in the perfect circle of Havemayer pine trees, overlooking a mirror clear lake.

The Saturday morning we organized for MahWah began with a torrential rain, forecast to continue throughout the day. I put my entire will to it...we set off in the downpour, and as we reached the gates of the estate the sun broke through.

Herbert Migdoll

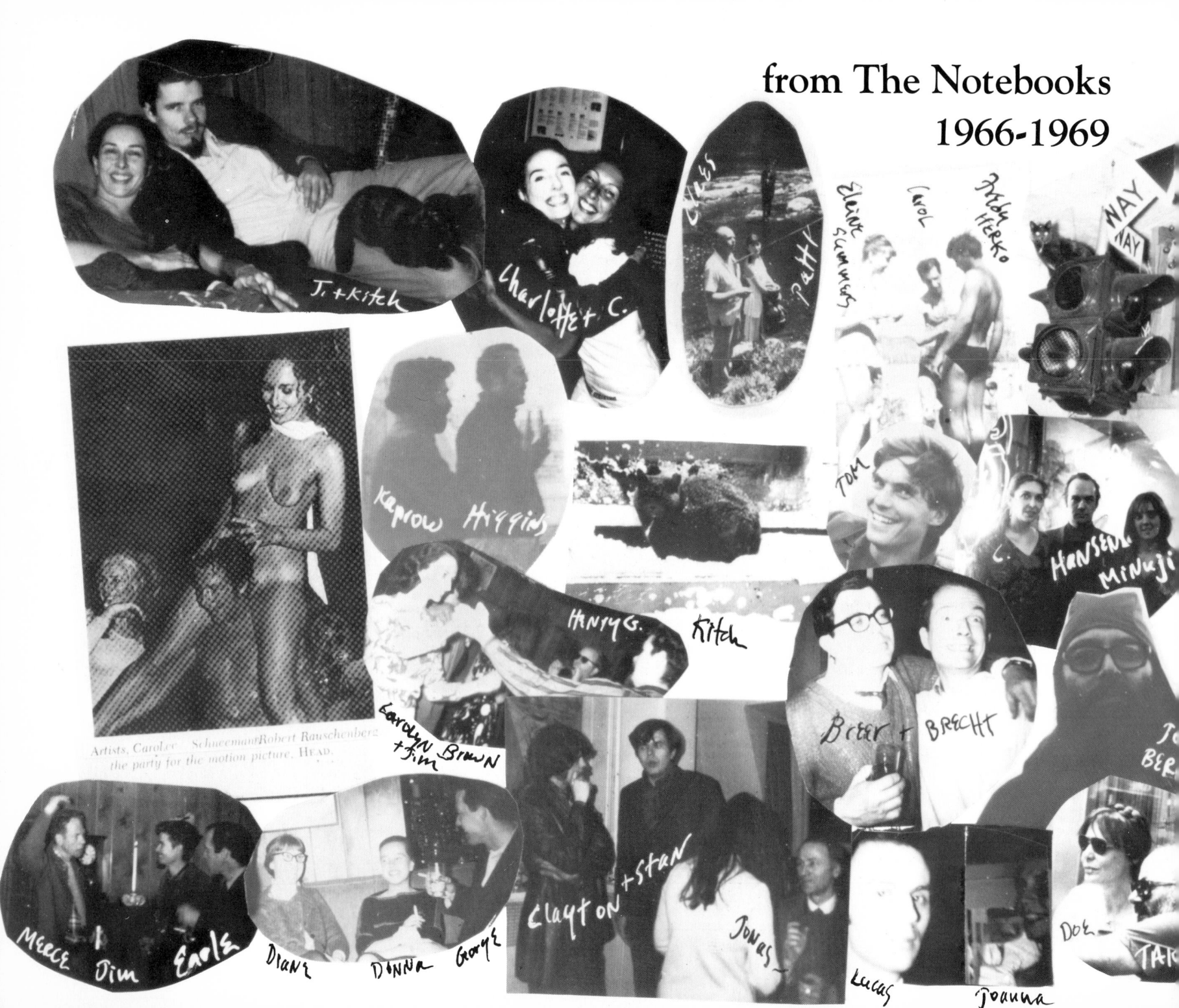

from The Notebooks
1966-1969

122 West 29th
N.Y.1, N.Y.
7 February 1966

Dear Jean-Jacques:

It's been a slow, hard year . . . getting better now. Last spring, so broke, had to sublet my loft, go away to a free-for-all quiet place in the country. Things brightened to hysteria for Charlotte's Festival (EVERY year EVERY one saying no, no never again and every year we all are drawn in and out). I did a new work for myself and Tenney—bodies completely encased in metal debris/a debris wheel falling from the ceiling/playing our sounds and each other's with metal rods . . . in the dark, little lights flashing on our junk-bodies. I directed Kaprow's "Push and Pull" with Paik—and provoked a riot. Utter destruction of the environment we built: old ladies, collared, hairless business men astride cracked two-by-fours, beating each other and the remains of the environment with objects I had asked them to go into the streets and bring back to furnish the environment. Police, paddy wagons, riot squad. Then endless interviews . . . . "yes, that was a possibility, but not my intention." Lawyers calling to tell me to disappear, the Festival cancelled, then reinstated with bonds, conditions . . . ! Violence and pent-up rage exploding in the grey ones—as you well know—but here it was the first such manifestation.

Then in December all the grand people started dying: Varèse, Kiesler, Cowell . . . the plumber's mother, Higgins' step-mother, somebody's father (under his tractor) . . . on and on like a rain around us.

The news from Europe all garbled. That you had married; that you were living in the south of France, going to Russia. And with Joyclyn the misunderstanding about "the book"—Erró tells me about *your* book; Joyclyn wrote that HE was writing a book on your festivals; he didn't answer when I wrote that I was broke and asked if his publisher would pay for the photos here . . . . What you are doing and single-handedly is fantastic; perhaps now "they" are ready; here we are beginning to be treated differently—invited to panels on theater (!) and such; the press ready to eat us alive and belch out some capsule synthesis . . . to break down the distinctions we found by heart, nerve, funny guts. The press is hip, anxious to capture and render-harmless. I can't imagine that process ever breaking over your head, and that finally the tension, resistence and insane, hungry response Paris can produce will keep your energies ferocious, determined. Something soft happens here . . . like the helpless, apathy over, what is now, our Dirty War; there is almost no motion towards political engagement, statement, by the advanced artists here . . . . Warhol's Velvet Underground giving a week of live performances: "Fairies I Have

Known".....a perverse, charming melt into chic; the normalization of terror, sadism, masochism become a popular consecration...almost homey and warm and friendly in character. One end of the spectrum, spectre.

The "Season" here was incredibly dull—dull in the sense of diminished finish, shine, patina, light interchange cut down. Exceptions being performances of new pieces of Oldenburg, Whitman, Rauschenberg at Cinematheque. Each with a beautiful piece; a mastery, fineness, and calm; clarity marking some point in our time of acceptance/ accepting that is completely new. I'll have four nights at St. Mark's in March for a new work—all in the air, performers over heads of audience; strange objects. (Imagery begun in Venice into Vietnam.) I'll enclose a scenerio and also the issue of *Some Thing* documenting *Meat Joy* in New York—how it changed from Paris. Did you see Hansen's *Space/Time Happening Primer?*

Erró is fine here, happy with Mary—more than I've ever known him to be, working very hard. We'll all be at Marta Minujin's Environment tomorrow—going like wild-fire, perils of Pauline. Erró and Restany suggested I send you a list of my Happenings— Theater Pieces and their materials for your exhibit. I expected you would write me. Why not? Hey?

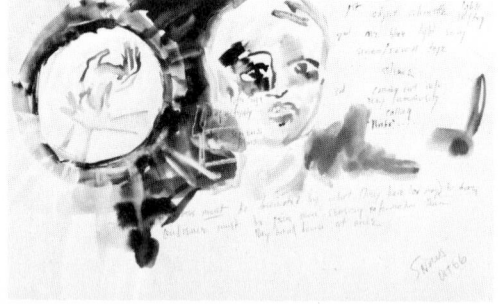

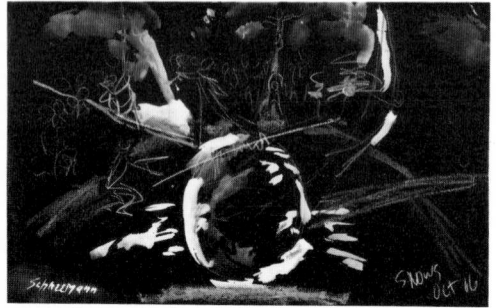

Snows   1966
Drawing: inks, chalk, watercolor. 12½" x 18"

NOTES ON AND AROUND *SNOWS*
 Vietnam a vegetable culture which leaves no garbage.
Misery America ------ ------ been gone wild vogue of nuclear power plants pollution delirious cut off from ecology from living relations between organic parts: the new sex book ("definitive"), Dow Chemical earnings, "mass art," when there is no "mass"; fragmentations, de-sexualization, de-sensualization and they're going crazy alone together, take shine and plastic onto into their half-starved bodies. Feeling low between "highs".......
and some of us work, scramble, clear ways to unity, joy a plateau.......

Can only tell it from where I am, what I do see and how, just here.

Tenderness of Charlotte's and Paik's performance (the T.V. Bra); the melodramatic brutality of cops arresting *her* (the "nude")....rotten theater: everyone playing a predictable role out of conditioning or preparation/anticipation. Cops jumping on the stage in their "plain clothes," flashing badges: "WE'RE THE POLICE—YOU'RE UNDER ARREST." The invited audience become stoney, watching. I began yelling "Boo, Fascists" and then all of us   yelling, running onto the stage; utter confusion; angry humiliated

Charlotte, struggling for her cello, waving the bow, searching for her lost wedding ring which she always parks on the music stand....loss of propriety, freedom to work—the arbitrary circumstance...trying to move and being trundled away. We should have all of US stripped stark naked then and there.

My life is sweet and my skin is crawling.

Handful of thirty artist/activists in and out of jail; all lying in monster belly shaking it as it shits its poison its contempt for life process for brown black red yellow white flesh dancing agitating the rotten belly confounding its monstrous stupidity where we can.

Charlotte and Paik child-like. Mixture of naiveté, the wisdom to trust themselves completely, courage and simplicity to share, expose, indentification with form, materials. Their gifts out of the presumptuous, bungling, rigid belly which wants to devour them... slowly, inexorably, blundering tape red/worm

Country without vital nerve center: cut, chopped, lobotomized in self-interest-greed. Consciousness hacked into paranoid bits of shifting evil...turn on yourself—monster, show your violence, impotence—bombing, flaming game ritualized machine that you become: your "culture" as vapid, paternalistic, frenetic and corrupt as your angry lusts....

Sweet mold in midst of it, rises bitter-sweet, ferment: finding the ways quietly, by internal necessity, integration of emotion/action, so simple becomes thunderous: sky falling flowers filling....And the *patrons* of art ran to the doors, to escape! Their henchmen. They needn't live the esthetics but simply defend, stand in place of their desire—which is us—uphold our need to form and manifest which is their need.

Movement   Mass   Murder   Vietnam   Peace   Parade   Committee   Commitment
1966

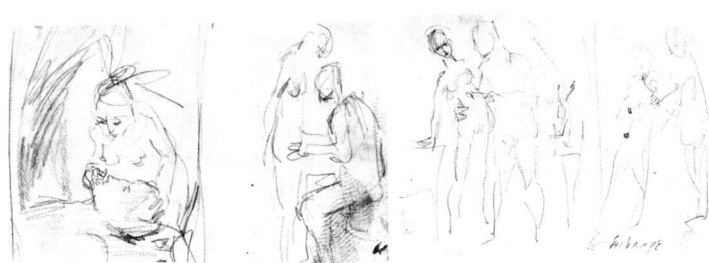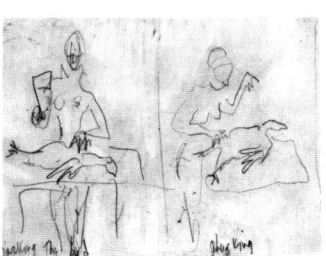

Meat Joy   1964
Drawings: pencil.

Alice Uber Alles   Aurora Uber   Alles   Unter Uber   SNOWBALL (Cool Clear Courage)

15-30 July - London, "Round House". 8 August - Franconia, N.H. "Love Games"
(Jim's). 24 August - NYC, Judosn Church, "Torture Environment - Ordeals".
8 Sept - Montreal, Expo '67 "Night Crawlers". 28 Oct - NYC, Goethe House,
Napalm piece? ----- Mexico?......N.Y. State Council Grant Environmental Arts?

will be a sensory expression of certain of the conditions explored verbally
by the Congress....NOn Verbal get them into their senses

22 words all Joseph Berke 4 St. George's Terrace London NW 1 keep reservation early July send date nothing available here lack plane fare
love carolee

POUNDS OF CREAM **** BELLY SLATHER EACH OTHER   june

xxxxxxxxxx pushing down

1) stand centrally blow whistle 2) run down among spectators begin sorting
piling on materials blow whistle..couples 3) pushing other rolled into a
ball into spectators 4) body sculpture walking around each woman moves between men -- when they have been positioned 4 times they position next on
over (who will not necessarily know they are 5th mover) they in turn accept
"shaping" 4 times and then take initiative.

IMAGE dividend/increment what I'm after -- that dislocation (it dissociates,
I compound, it insists on itself, grips senses, expands recognition into
unknown relations)

cover body with grease and stick plastic to it

use up old images XCLEAR OUT!   66666 posture crawls screams

naked figure plastic against body other figure holding fan blowing and they
walk   face to face   some are standing lifti ng their hands SCREAMING

Happening as basic psycho-social guerilla life-fare
as form is life-like or interchangable with life circumstances (not explained
beyond language which has been coercive, negative, excluding, devisive, pulling
apart where integration should be....)
1. organization 2. form   3. frame or focus   4. intensification of all
elements (action) 5. response(intensity of awareness) appropriatness of
reaction 7. unpredicability within the structure 8. immediate adjustment
to circumstance - percpetion. ALL slapped in on senses without obstruction,
convention, pre-determination. SOCK IT IN OUT

(take someone's hand a person close to you   and sit down please everyone
just sit down where ever you happen to be sit down and be comfortable

and hold someone's hand)   May

Think of this huge round high space as an arena of shifting focus: u nleash
spatial variations....like a telephoto lens -- figures fly in and run out --
groups rush forward and receed, ebbxxxxxxxx, flow, great speed to it.
                            1 July

I'v thought of it for years SPLAT
You never thought of it before SPLAT

revolving light bicycles ropes have them GROWL ropes film flood space

   journey   ride   drive   American trips car held highways dancing &
stops in the snow exhausted little hotel in Indiana nobody there multi-
layered collage-like percpétion endless passage an IMAGE persists
all my theater pieces structured like a ride cross country I realize
know the beginning the probable or possible end points of arrival   in
between and all passage dense compacted fluid straming on

I come to a microphone in filthly mens underwear.....good evening......
I would like to explain about the action of visual Gestalt' SPLAT...lorry
pulls up piled with crushed metal fragments, piles of bodies; men come and
dump over lorry infront of spectators: crashing metal, falling bodies, flesh
and metal lumped, sprawled. I go and kick debris around...silence...kicks,
clanking...scraping........
                          with Jim awaiting flight departure to London....
our farewell, Scotch and ʷideCars, Principes of form! 2nd law of thermo-
dynamics/entropy of universe is continually increasing Heisenberg inde-
terminancy cant simultheously determine velocity and position of particle...

special theory of relativity "in a frame of reference (closed environment)
which is moving uniformly (in a state of uniform motion) all laws of physics
will operate the same as with frame of reference at rest". No absolute
frame of reference   in a moving train moving evenly you can't tell.....
landscape or train moving!

whitehead russell 1910? in a logical language there are certain axioms which
are basic to this language but these axioms can never be proven in this language itself but in a "meta-language" assumed but Hot proven become circular
have to go xautk outside to demonstrate it.
action-readtion astronomy apple falls to earth earth moves a little bit
to receive it!

Parkinson's law amount of work to be done expands to fill available time

Brownian motion -- random collision of particles and what particles are
suspended in --- romparable smallness comparable

anything designed to transmit (derive) information will create a corresponding
entropy increase in environment in which it is carried out   Brillouin's Law

Jim's ideas for telephoto: figures run forward they have a banner folded
between them unfolding it as they advance (enlargement).......

the waitress.........?
the airline...........?
the heiress..........?
the hostage.........?
the steward..........?
HOSTESS STEWARDESS....!

need powerful projectors sound-sharp loud to hear reverberations:
clapping stam,ping

with the carts -- just keep loading and unloading bodies (some jump & run away

"The brick a brac is es ential to the inner form". J.   12 july

IF YOU'RE GOING TO CHANGE THING YOU'RE GOING TO MAKE A MESS every housewife
knows that! But the condition of dislocation/random configuration which arise
in changefull process is where we find the new possibilities and where me
may find relations we were not previously aware of   or even in favor of!

Suddenly (6:05 one hour in the air) they are all moving about like barnyard
animals a concurrance of reaching for blankets pillows heading off to the
toilets smoking vomiting passing cookies changing shoes exchanging newspapers (from another continent content conterment) and religious tracts.
I'v wrapped up in ax pink pale organe blanket which says HSIRI upside down;
it smells of scones; I'v found two tiny lemon colored pillows which keep
slipping back onto the feet of a woman behind. It is cold. And strange.
This Irish choice of citrus colors, provoking while whizzing through inter
stalactite space disembodied murky colorless floating through space nuzzling
infiniate air. Touched only by scraps of wool and linen.   Encapsulated.
No human expression to equalize suspension between...through the AIR
destination destiny determination. Held   captive given over -- entire
anonymous flock of us -- to "controls"...with my guts exploding, turning
tumbling I admire relish all this bizarre organization....we're IN the AIR
uh oh now we're stopped somewhere in mid-air...over

Announcements...yelling Shut Up! someone something ruffling my hair
spitting scratching pulling stuff out of huge overalls speaking again
distractions.......scratching

At the Round House. Begin running around balcony (dirty splintery wooden
boards grand iron arches cascading up to glass dome) running collisions
hollering keep it there a huge mass of us   stops   and starts

One figure appears downstairs in the dark flash of light   others in
the dark   shifting in the dark   ominous   slowly increase densities

.......little bunched bells ring in the balcony as he walks

NEVER NEVER AGAIN -- if I get another chance! Impingement terrible my sense
of mortality -- crowded crammed into this plastic urethra this hurtling
tin of sardines who chew gum......

Finally off: sprinkling light, delays.   Somewhere in the mass of little
figures against a railing he watches. I weep bitterly: what the hell am I
doing in here, where is Jim? his grace, shape I can't tell it from any
other human dot......scratching on the window pane, twisted in this weird
space to see through: tears, moisture, blurs, on window fog shine on pulsing
lights now heaving, squealing motors; dizzy spin temendous push against
gravity -- the wind swell bounce motions outside on my insides pound the
stick of plastic metal.   MUSIC! For Christ's sake -- wired for sound, calm
the beasts: "Sheep May Safely Graze"!   That really breaks me up....theme
song camp HSIRI

thunderous heave rolling....off we went (my love among a hundred headless
shadows...going to the car him going now where back empty lone)

we are promised drinks dinner "orange tea or coffee" in one hour fifteen
minutes that is heartening -- our invisible path is programmed with comforts

Over the wing again (revenge on an old chicken farmer): how is it stuck on?
what's in the secret underbelly? (can it be singed & plucked?); how much
pressure is "pressurized" (pasturized); while my ears are filling, dull
heavy roar from below from above a streamy hisssing, bleeps of sound escape....
release belt o.k. smoke o.k. find pen o.k.....looking around. Deadened,
blank, hapless, ugly creatures strapped to their seats reading, sucking
candy drops passed out by the sinister hostages trained to distract us from
what is REALLY going on. I'v clawd through the stems of the rose Jim gave
me....sucking sugar drops.... reach for the newspaper...IRISH............

A young fisherman sits next to me-- really. I want to tell him to put aside
his insane fishing pole and let me sit on his lap.....

Up and down the aisle priests meander, peristently offering literature litergy
to prepare the soul for God before Dublin. Oh dire dour drear bargain tour.
(Dr. Joe this is a trying sort of joke to start off with......)

(Ed Sanders on 86th St. day before leaving said he cant bear it either. Turn
on and sleep through he said. But I'v got to pay attention, see what they're
up to.)

A RAG MAN HORSE AND CART Eastwood Plastics little striped plastic tents
on construction sites...red and white....Westbourne...Shepards Bush.....
women in knit dresses big streets trees like Raspail...Holland Park Avenue
W. 11 Embassy Hotel...Bayswater Road...The Swan Watneys Clear Cool Courage
Sussex Gardens W.2...where are we going in this incredible fat black taxi
that Joe says is his "car"?

Do the OBVIOUS. The obvious is never traditional. Work out of where you
really are.

One group running. Another throws out pink plastic mats runners can fall
on mat or rest leaping when one is tossed in front of them.

polite honest careful patient tolerent fair its warm here not cool
shoes are sandals mostly beards saw a POLICE MAN WITH A BEARD Shamlessly
Poet directing traffic on Sunday vast numers of young people pushing prams
walking great distances pets on buses and tubes big sofa seats in subway
not knifed slit smoke o.k.

YES END RUN with banner slight split in top and they tear them apart fall over
as fabric rips apart until all fallen body mass group rushes on horse and
cart slowly to enter pile them up and take them to under screen of rags
for Viet-Flakes film Rock and Roll group goes directly into fragment tape
as cart is driven away...mass group in the rubble, spectators escape from
ropes to dance in debris

cascade build-up from balcony? tape scrap? paint mud styrofoam

I'm sick and tired of thinking about COLOR - "black and white"...I think
about tones pigment green blue vermil_ion orange umber yellow burnt sienna
and MIX THEM US we're going slow among ourselves show among ourselves
longing and terrors of ADMIXTURE its obvious we do it as a matter of priv-
iledge -- like regular meals or shelter -- that's just human beings turning
on to what moves them beyond pigmentation.........

.......and after; it is those elements, fragments which for any reason do
stay in memory, burn your senses....which are the IMAGES

catch from behind full head turn (like chicken)

like coming to a vast new city and watching the transportation of people,
the unfamiliar signals, signs, indicators, traffic events: all without clear
order and non-comprehensible as system but you know that an order, a structure
fulfills specific necessities (to get from here to there), and you yourself
a center point within which the pattern and configuration turns....

Just show what is possible. They forget they function through older forms
fulfilling describable roles (male) towards new principles (leaderships).
I can't accept the form of their proceedings for myself but I don't deny
it for them....

they are rather gentle stringy warmblooded but awkward curious but
reserved a certain wild childish abusive humor integrity none of our
paranoia ("we can work it out") politically keen -- what David and his
friends organized at Essex -- students taking over the University, run it....

1) push up and down 2) slather 3) reshape the flesh

Our response-ability to our lovers is to share our sexual strengths, to express
our greatest intensities, value need, desire. It's perverse destructive to
fragment our own bodies or anothers loves loving is inclusive not measured
proscribed and everything that contributes to sensation is to be used yes
woman dpends on the man for type quality or orgasm -- his rhytms in her
genital character shape pressure impulse dominant its a dreadful mistake
sophisticated oversimplification "equalitarians" to equate female and male
sexuality woman is simply orgasmically more complex a sensitive lover
feels his own desire intensified by hers   the joy of his powers in
exchange both transforming each

call to the audience: we need thrity seven volunteers
bring them to bath of dough which they kneed

seared fire light (we wasted weeks I didn't know) unsuspected spontaneous
exquisite...it happens...or not...no way to control xpuxx provoke out
of our minds...flying around each other...simplest things charged balls
of fire pass between us......

I'd like a time-mind machine: the next thing. To travel between generations.
Returns and extensions. Tune in on Mme. de Stael the day Constant came
back. Where are you originally from? The drop off of memrory-generation.
Remembering that three hundred years ago this mix of nationalities, races
in flux was uncommon. One came from where one was. (How far could a woman

dream to travel?) And because we are capable of simultaneous ideas, curios-
ities and desires with the time-mind we will grant each other the right and
help in discovering utilizing simultaneities. (Not literature).

First day at the Congress seminar I explained the shift in art-life attitudes;
that many of us rejected being "outside society -- "alienation", "neurosis",
not making-it, troubled relations, mythification or life, fragmentation as
basic to creative process, "role of the artist". That we worked from communality, integrations, trust or self and each other, shared process, abandon,
certain joys, pleasures (as well as darker forces to be grasped) -- but
emphasis has shifted. Old romanticism, neo-Freudianism was not where we
pivoted. The older people didn't believe me; the younger ones didn't know
what I was talking about.

Lying in the grass together: the sun spills a web o Bach flute, birds,
regular hammering, bees; heavy roses, orange cats moving close by. Melted
in one each other to...such a short time, Takes my hand. Too strong, don't
understand it. Need time, a softening proportion...too soon to leave. Misery.
He's joyous, sad, bedeviled, comforting. Driving again...Brompton Road. I
love you London and goodbye. Return to beloved Jim and my evil country.
Wrung out...waiting...coffee...whiskey. Holding to each other once more...
into dreadful bus, wet down my thigh. Lucky Jim he said. Empty sky through
the window...he watches...I watch...we are moving inside out....hands to the
window...backwards...

PLEASE HELP TO KEEP THIS BUS TIDY "By not getting on", someone had scrawled.

I'll collect you now MIND THE STEP   MIND THE DOOR   As hard as bloody nails
overtaking (passing cars) guess they must do well hang about hang on
Thrupence Opera   It doesn't smell half bad (it stinks) super messing around
Irish confetti (broken glasses in the pub)   I'm a bit short of the ready
I'm a bit short of the green and foldable (upper class) stand on me!
(I'M astounded) carsey bog loo slashouse doxie (toilet) HOLD TIGHT DUCKIE
Miss, he fancies you

expose exposure demystification yes get rid of old deadly mysteries
women women our genital and our pronoun new mysteries waiting for us
get it all out tell and show

fear of genital pleasure fear of woman terror of life process will to dominate inability to feel to be in relation to immediate moment to let go
use generously inability to realize full range of sensations/emotion starv-
ation-atrophy and a dull remote anger a vague awareness of deprivation
but so armored its expressive depth masked hostility so things "don'T work
out", are not seen, go against themselves of the person who provokes deeper
appetites, desires
BLACK OUT
blow whistle tape of drums resonating
bodies on ropes   slowly slid down from balcony
bodies on ropes slowly dragged through the aisles
begin mixing mud and silver foil

luminous flying transparent wings
feathers prisms of fire light   London   july '67
cold stiff paralysing light

Jan 21 22 27 28 29 Feb 3 4 5 1967
Martinique Theatre
32nd Street and Broadway, NYC

Paul Libin presents

S N O W S Kinetic Theater by
C A R O L E E   S C H N E E M A N N

with SHIGEKO KUBOTA   TYRONE MITCHELL   PHOEBE NEVILLE
      CAROLEE SCHNEEMANN   JAMES TENNEY   PETER WATTS

* *

            revolving light sculpture -- Laurence Warshaw

        lights & sound controlled light system -- Robert Schultz

            technical coordinator -- Ralph Flynn

                sound collage -- James Tenney

entire environment, "Viet-Flakes" film, flyer -- Carolee Schneemann

            projectionists -- Karl Schenzer Jack Agüeros

* *

technical assistance -- Robby Robinson   Per Biorn   Mike Yareck

builders -- Karl Schenzer Peter Watts Jack Agüeros June Ekman
          James Tenney Per Biorn James Finney

snow machine -- Jack Agüeros

roustabouts -- James Carroll   James Finney   Jim Kuo

* *

SNOWS is dedicated to poet friends.

SNOWS supports and is one of the events of Angry Arts Week.

grateful thanks to: Foundation for Experiments in Art & Technology
                     Consolidated Aluminum Reynolds Aluminum
                     Thomas Morley Alphonse Schilling Judy Kass

taking of photographs is absolutely forbidden

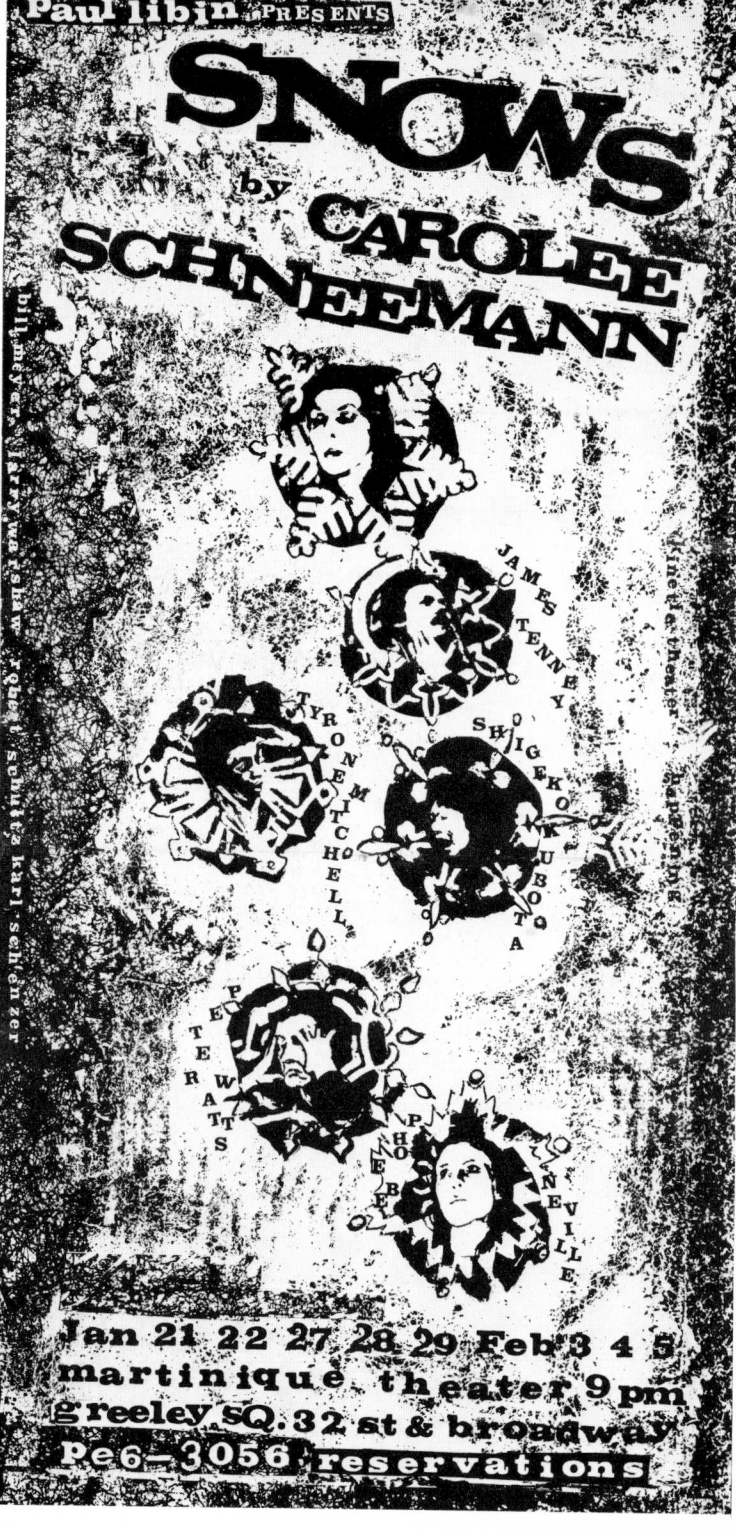

January 21 22 27 28 29. February 3 4
5 1967   Martinique Theater NY

SNOWS: to concretize and elucidate the genocidal compulsions of a vicious disjunctive technocracy gone berserk against an integral, essentially rural culture. The grotesque fulfillment of the Western split between matter and spirit, mind and body, individualized "man" against cosmic natural unities. Destruction so vast as to become randomized, constant as weather. Snowing...purification, clarification, homogenization.

Snows was built out of my anger, outrage, fury and sorrow for the Vietnamese. The performance contained five films whose related content triggered juxtaposition of a winter environment and Vietnam atrocity images. Of all the films "Viet-Flakes" was the heart and core of the piece: a source of confirmation and insistence from which movement and related imagery spilled onto the "snow-bound" audience.

As in **Ghost Rev** I wanted to use film as integral to performance while emphasizing it as a contrasting visual language—handled as tactile, palpable material. I saw film as a conveyance—a passage of realistic imagery—a powerful spark to memory—but film interested me also as a textural and structural element extending the visual densities of the Kinetic Theater works.

With film I could introduce literal information in rhythms spread spatially through performed movement sequences—the tension of live and celluloid "frames" of action. I didn't want to insert film as subordinate image concentrations; nor did I want image juxtapositions apart from the overall spatial texture. Each element (movement, film, lights, sound) was created to hold its defining edge and to merge with surrounding units.

Each film spilled out of its fixed frame, projected onto surfaces throughout the theater: spread, pulsing, centralized to have as much physical stretch and shift as the performers themselves. It was as if film could be projected back into/onto film, a collision and absorption of images like the collisions of our bodies. Dual projectors swung 360° across space. The structural intervals and gradations of light and darkness, the paper-layered walls, the water-lenses and revolving-light sculpture, the performance movement, the highly visible technicians: each element was drawn into a vortex of increasingly disturbing energy.

I prefer my work process to be as exposed as possible, while equally disguising the motivating source, the "textual" content. If I had told the performers that

Snows would be a work based on Vietnam atrocity images they would have had to assume a particular method and attitude. Without being aware of the central metaphor the performance movements were able to evolve with spontaneity, suspense, immediacy, both directly and in-directly, from the related films and tapes. The cultural discrepancies were constantly in mind: our inability to act directly on a situation where we humanly wanted to intervene, to make a difference. The evidence of the personal experiences of the Viet-namese was reaching us at a great remove, through reproduced photographs: the unknown outcome of the situations depicted and the ambivalent role of the photographer (whose life was also threatened) "taking pictures," as people burnt, bled, fled, were tortured.

With one exception none of us was formally trained in theater or dance. We discovered the nature of our work together by experiencing and creating it. Although sequences were fixed, durations were determined in performance: light cues for partnered actions and group convergences were always varied, made unpredictable by audience-activated electronic

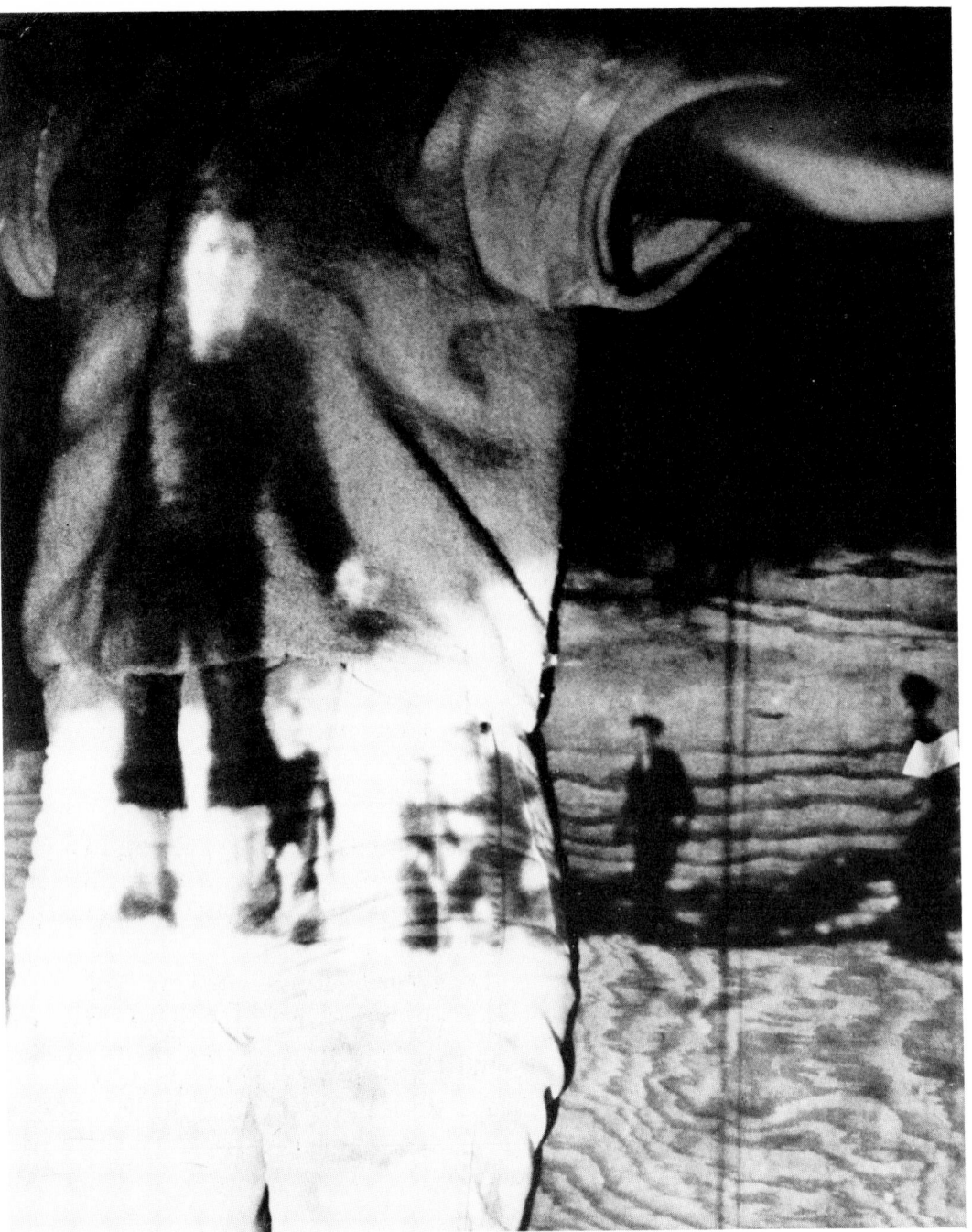

systems. We were actually frightened in **Snows**—the experience was enveloping, we were conscious of the audience as an extension of ourselves, but not of ourselves in self-conscious presentation. Walking the planks was actually dangerous, and the central imagery of "Viet-Flakes" once fully apparent, was so dire and agonizing that our own pleasurable expectations and collaborations within the glistening white environment were confounded.

"Viet-Flakes" had been made a year earlier from a collection of Vietnam photographs clipped from papers and magazines over six years. I used a close-up lens and magnifying glasses to "travel" within the photographs giving the effect of a rough animation. In broken rhythms, in and out of focus, abstract motions and shapes converge into the terrified frozen expression of people burning, dragged, drowning; a pointillism of falling black specks with focus becomes bombs dropping; the blurred face of American soldiers emerge leading girls from a shadowed hiding place; "a Rembrandt ink drawing" is a burning house . . .

The film which begins **Snows** is a five minute 1947 silent newsreel of one catastrophe after another. I found this film by "closed-eye vision"; that is, I stood in front of a rack of old remaindered newsreels in a camera store waiting to feel some impulse to let my hand be attracted to the packet which seemed to "speak." Projected at home the film justified my hopes; it begins with a ship exploding, then a sequence of tiny figures massed in a "riot," cut to tiny figures of "red" Chinese being shot by nationalist guards; then the Pope blessing crowds, a volcanic eruption in Bolivia, peasants running through a broken landscape, an American Legion parade in Philadelphia in a snow storm, an automobile race, car crashes, explosions. Amazingly, I had already used an image in "Viet-Flakes" from precisely this newsreel, which I had found in a book.

During the early sequences of our actions, two projectionists at the edge of the performing area each have a swivel head 16mm projector with which they direct two films over our figures and around the theater by hand. Both films are of Bavarian winter sports, made during the Second World War. Later, an 8mm color film is projected on the torsos of the three women leaning against the white "moon" disk. Images from a winter diary I'd shot flash over us: the neighborhood of my loft, the Martinique Theater, Gimbels, Greeley Square Park in a blizzard, driving through the whitened city out the West River Drive, into the night and country landscape.

James Tenney made the sound-collage for "Viet-Flakes" by breaking music sources we selected into sound fragments so small that they became recognizable only cumulatively, in time: Mozart Piano Concerto #20; Bach Cantata #78 (Aria Duetto); Bach Partita; Bach Alleluia from Christmas Cantata; The Beatles' "We Can Work It Out"; Jackie de Shannon's "What the World Needs Now"; Question Mark and the Mysteriums' "96 Tears"; Vietnamese Folksong; Laotion Love Song; South Chinese Folksong.

The other tape used in **Snows** is a collage of trains shunting, whistling, moving in and out of an Illinois depot, overlaid and juxtaposed with sounds of orgasm.

The performance imagery is finally ambiguous: shifting metaphors in which performers are agressor and victim, torturer and tortured, lover and beloved, as well as simply themselves. We set each other on fire, we extinguish the fire, we create each other's face and body, we abandon each other, we save each other, we take responsibility for each other, we lose responsibility for each other, we reveal each other, we choose, we respond, we build, we are destroyed.

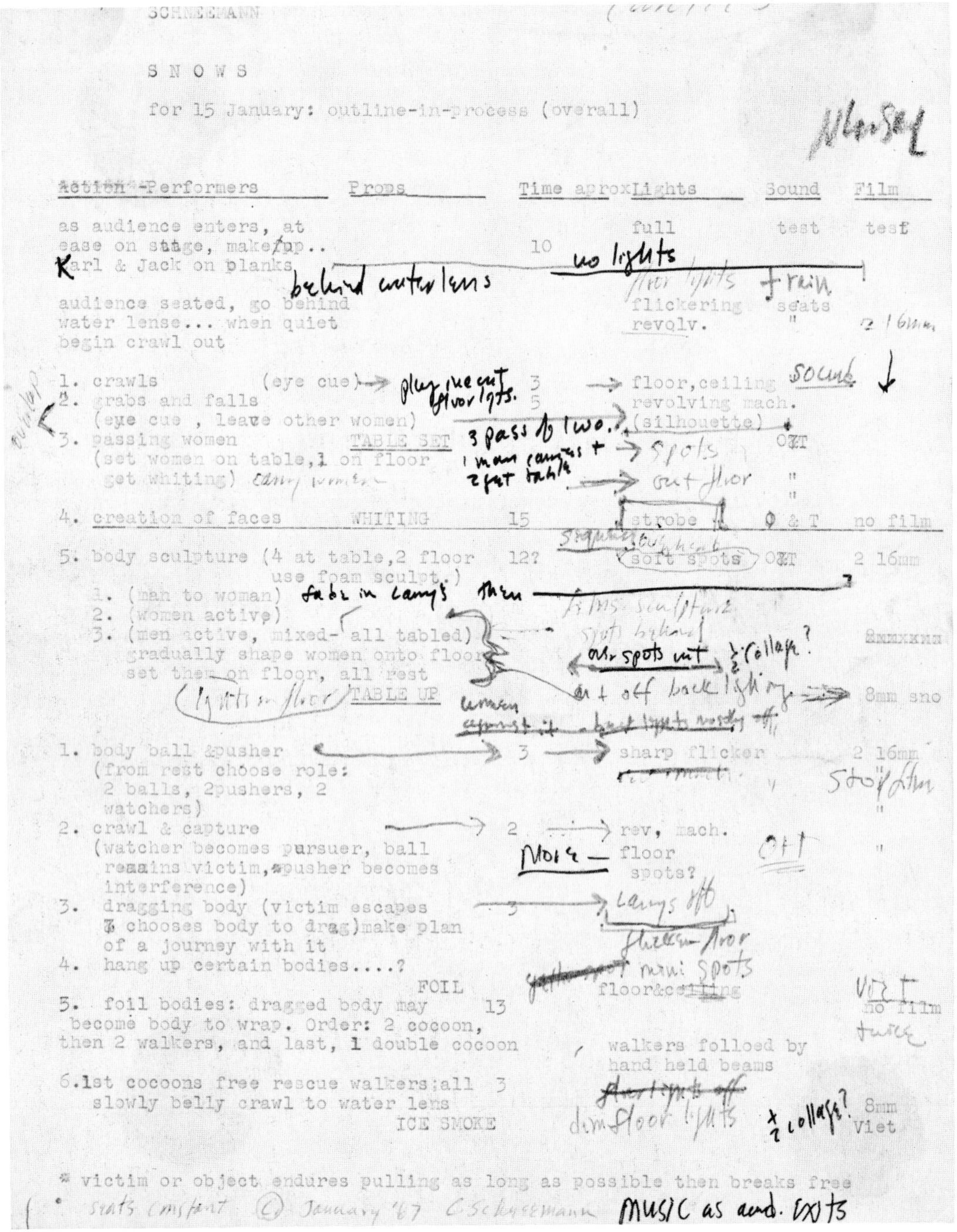

The image at left is a typed performance score with extensive handwritten annotations:

SCHNEEMANN

S N O W S

for 15 January: outline-in-process (overall)

Action—Performers	Props	Time aprox	Lights	Sound	Film
as audience enters, at ease on stage, makeup.. Karl & Jack on planks		10	full	test	test
audience seated, go behind water lense... when quiet begin crawl out			flickering revolv.	seats	2 16mm
1. crawls (eye cue)		3	floor, ceiling		
2. grabs and falls (eye cue , leave other women)		5	revolving mach. (silhouette)		
3. passing women (set women on table, 1 on floor get whiting)	TABLE SET		spots out floor		
4. creation of faces	WHITING	15	strobe	Q & T	no film
5. body sculpture (4 at table, 2 floor use foam sculpt.)		12?	soft spots		2 16mm
1. (man to woman)					
2. (women active)					
3. (men active, mixed- all tabled) gradually shape women onto floor set them on floor, all rest	TABLE UP				8mm sno
1. body ball & pusher (from rest choose role: 2 balls, 2 pushers, 2 watchers)		3	sharp flicker		2 16mm
2. crawl & capture (watcher becomes pursuer, ball remains victim, pusher becomes interference)		2	rev, mach. floor spots?		
3. dragging body (victim escapes & chooses body to drag) make plan of a journey with it					
4. hang up certain bodies....?					
5. foil bodies: dragged body may become body to wrap. Order: 2 cocoon, then 2 walkers, and last, 1 double cocoon	FOIL	13	mini spots floor & ceiling		no film
6. 1st cocoons free rescue walkers; all 3 slowly belly crawl to water lens	ICE SMOKE		dim floor lights		8mm Viet

walkers followed by hand held beams

* victim or object endures pulling as long as possible then breaks free
(C) January '67 C. Schneemann

SCORE

"The large arena stage of the Martinique Theater is covered in silver and plastic sheeting. Bare white branches hang down from overhead. The rear wall is flaked with large ragged sheets of white paper. Even the seats are festooned with white plastic scallopings; unoccupied, they look in the dark like receding ranges of snowy mountains. The lighting is icy: chill greens, blues, lavenders, with sometimes a flash of fire or sunlight. Two movies of skaters, skiers and related scenery are projected here and there on the set. At the rear is a large double construction; up to eight or ten feet, white outlined squares of varicolored plastic and open space on top; and a revolving light sculpture by Laurence Warshaw—flickering, reflecting, moving, shading colors and intensities within striations of plastic. It is very beautiful and surprisingly, not at all cold."

Michael Smith, Village Voice

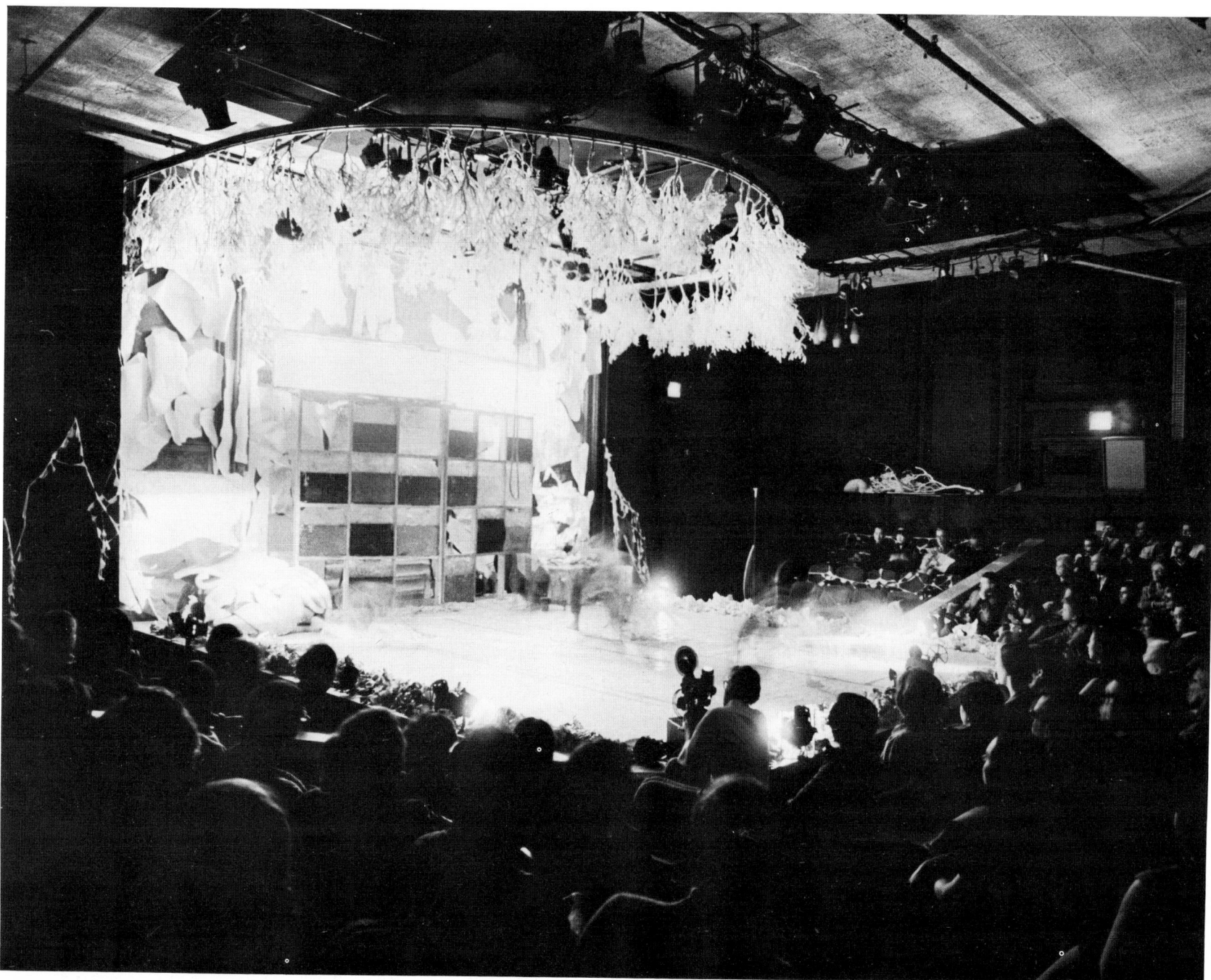

The audience has been led into the theater through the backstage door. In the dark they squeeze through two floor-to-ceiling foam rubber "mouths" and crawl over and under two long planks which stretch from the stage to the rear wall (across aisles and over the seats). Technicians rest on these silver planks—assisting the audience or not. The performers, wearing grey shirts and work pants, are sitting in a basic Oriental rest position, (squatting).

The Red-Newsreel begins. Train & Orgasm sound-collage A woman sweeps snow debris along the stage. The performers watch the film; when it is over they disappear behind the water-lens.

The light machine flickers dimly. Silhouettes of the performers appear—shifting shadows—behind the water-lens construction. They crawl or fall through empty apertures, and begin a slow animal-intense crawl toward the audience, some partly onto the planks. Turning back, they meet in the center of the stage and form a knot, crawling in, through, and out of one another's bodies.

Blue floor lights. Snow Speed and Winter Sports are projected across the ceiling, then center on side walls at varying levels.

The performers move apart. Crouching, staring at one another, they begin Grabs

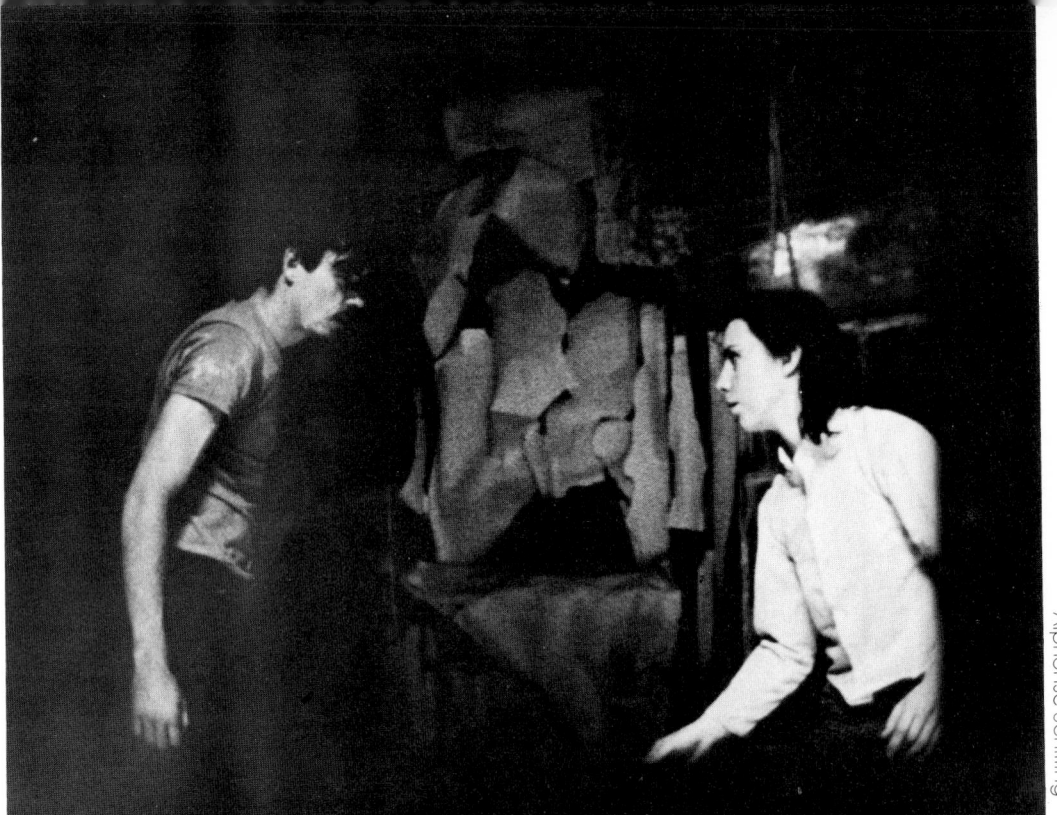

Alphonse Schilling

Alphonse Schilling

& Falls. Bodies thunder onto the stage; instantaneous collisions, a giving over of weight and impulse upon impact.

After an unspecified series of alternating encounters, a man about to enact a grab with a woman instead lifts her. The two other men stand, leaving their partners where they have fallen in snow, foil, foam rubber debris. Passing Woman: in clumsy walks and holds the men pass and carry the body until one of the men at last places it on the white horizontal disk.

After passing the remaining two women, all are seated on the disk and begin Creation of Faces. **BLACK OUT. Strobe begins.** T & O tape.

In pairs determined by the preceding sequence, each partner begins to cover the other's face with clown-white, silently responding to the other in a series of exchanges. When both faces are covered, one partner begins to shape the other's face, which takes on whatever aspect is pushed and prodded into the musculature—a transformation inducing a corresponding but unpredictable emotion. The created face turns toward the audience until the muscles relax by themselves and the expression fades.

Simultaneous overlappings of faces among the six are caught in the **flashing strobe.**

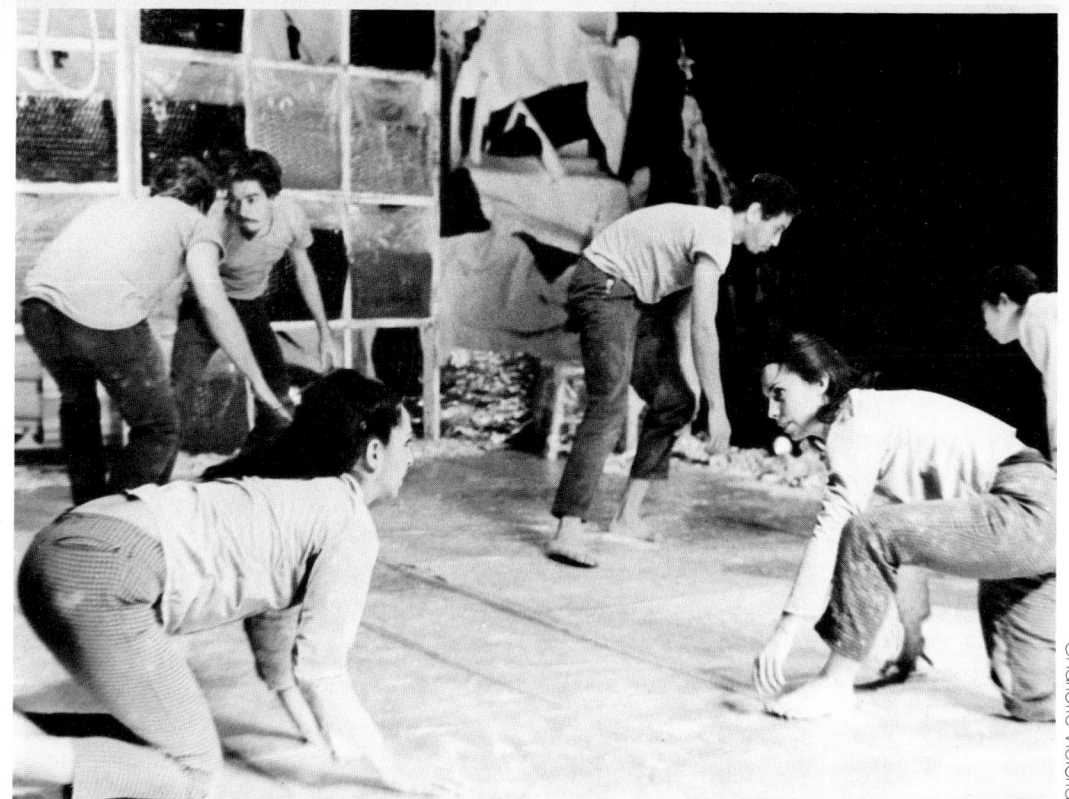

Charlotte Victoria

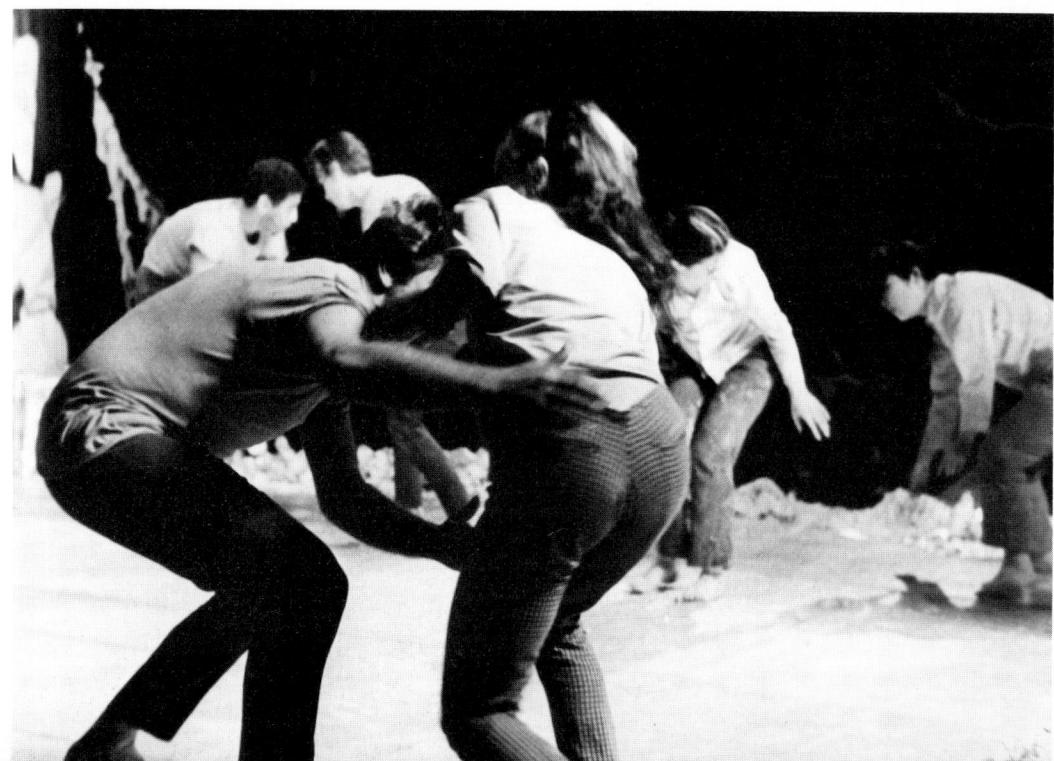

Charlotte Victoria

After an unspecified series of face-creations, one person will begin to move another (not necessarily the face partner) into *Body Sculpture*.

As the audience shifts, settles, they trigger the **lights overhead which slowly brighten.** T & O tape. **Films.**

Initially the men shape the women, who accept and hold whatever position they are given. Suddenly one of the women being sculpted will grasp the hand shaping her: the shaper freezes his action and becomes the one to be sculpted.

After the series of Body Sculptures the men center the women on the white disk; they are gradually sculpted onto the floor. Here they hold the positions, immobile.

Having raised the white disk vertically the men carry the women and prop them against it. A **color film** of a snow storm outside the theater is projected against their torsos. Lying on the stage, one of the men watches the film; the other two climb onto the water lens. On signal from the watcher, they slowly spill piles of "snow" over the women, who sink into a heap.

Audience motions are monitored and **the sculpture lights flicker sharply. Then flashing blue side lights.** Scrambling across the floor, two performers fall and

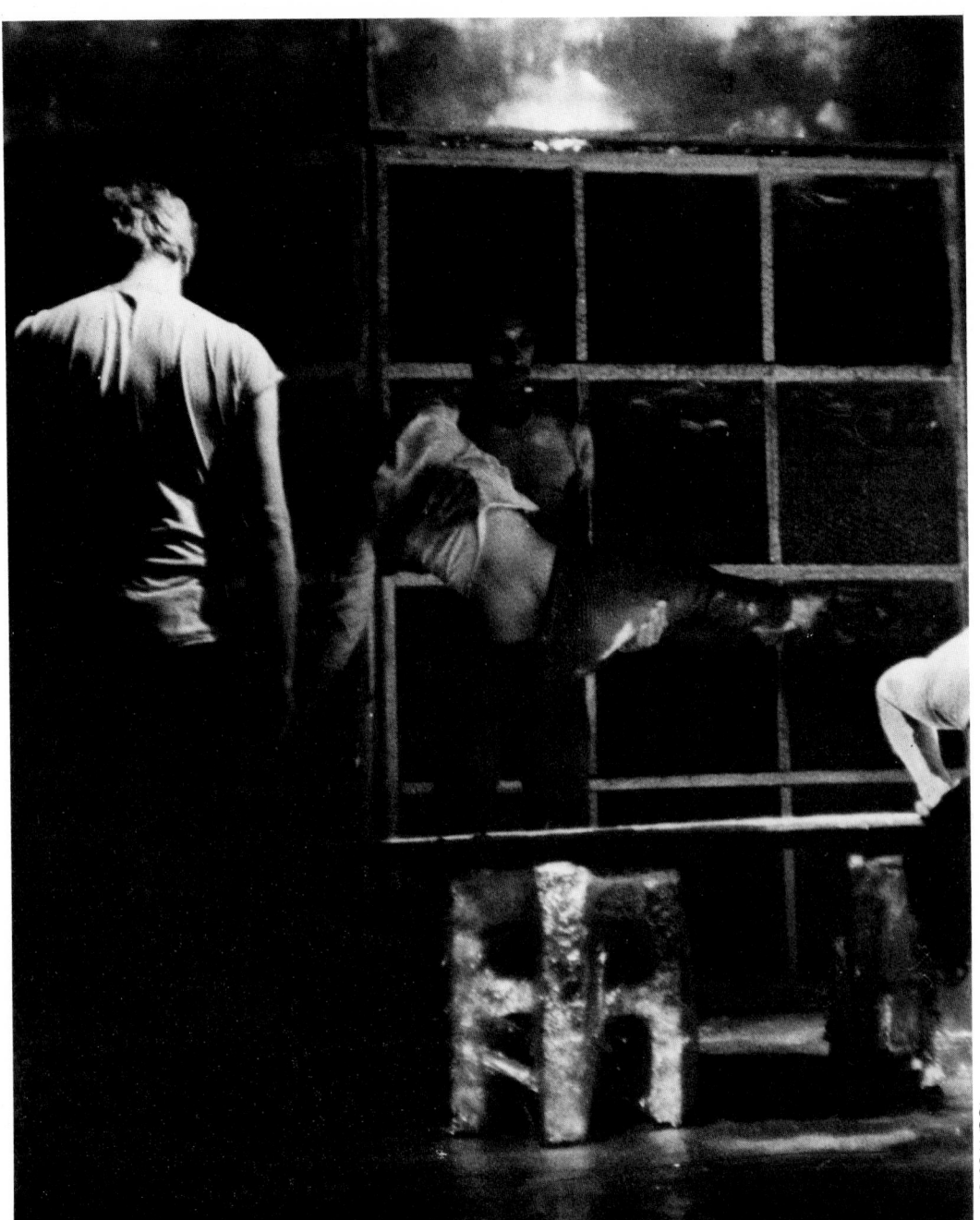

Ted Wester

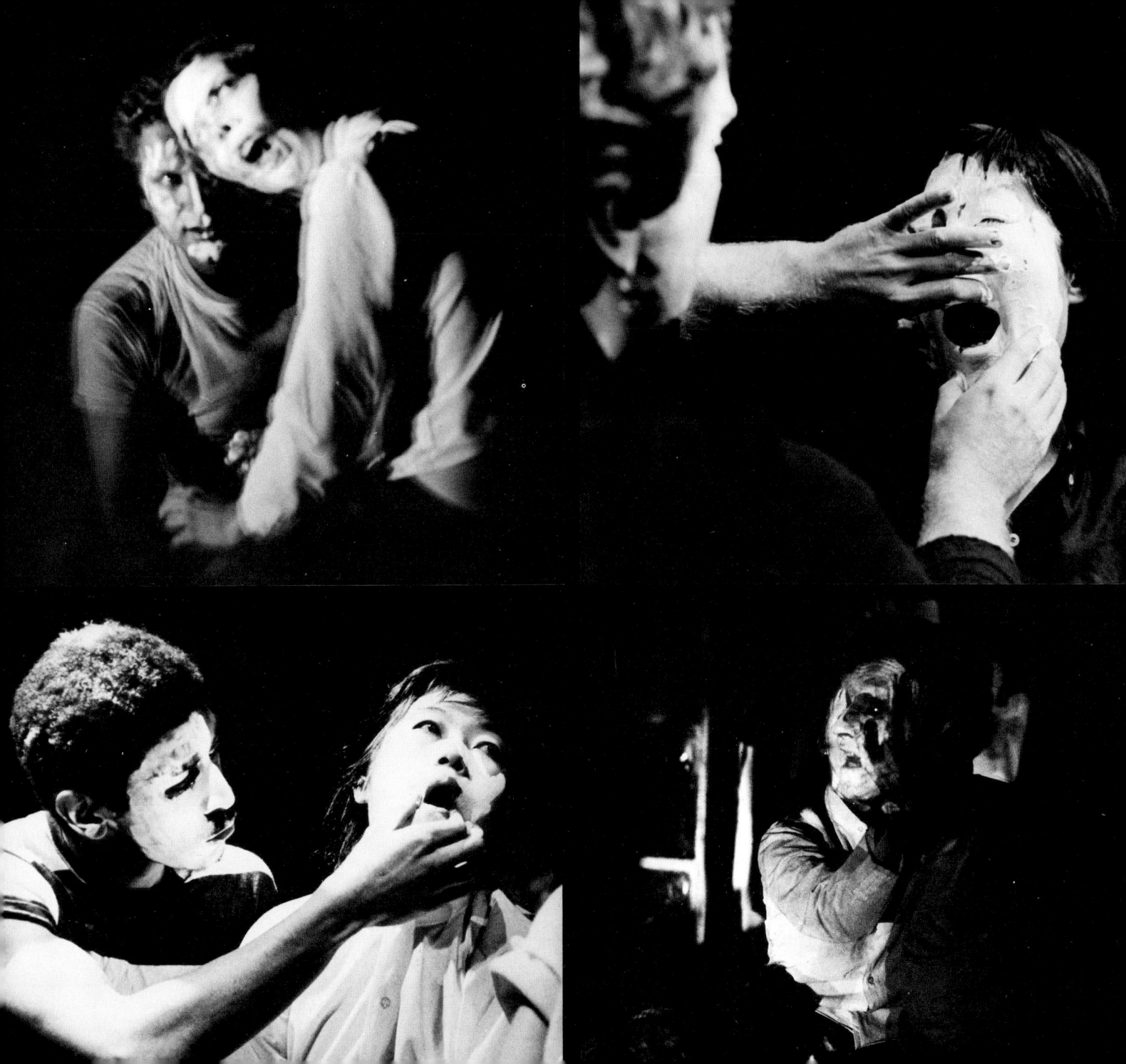

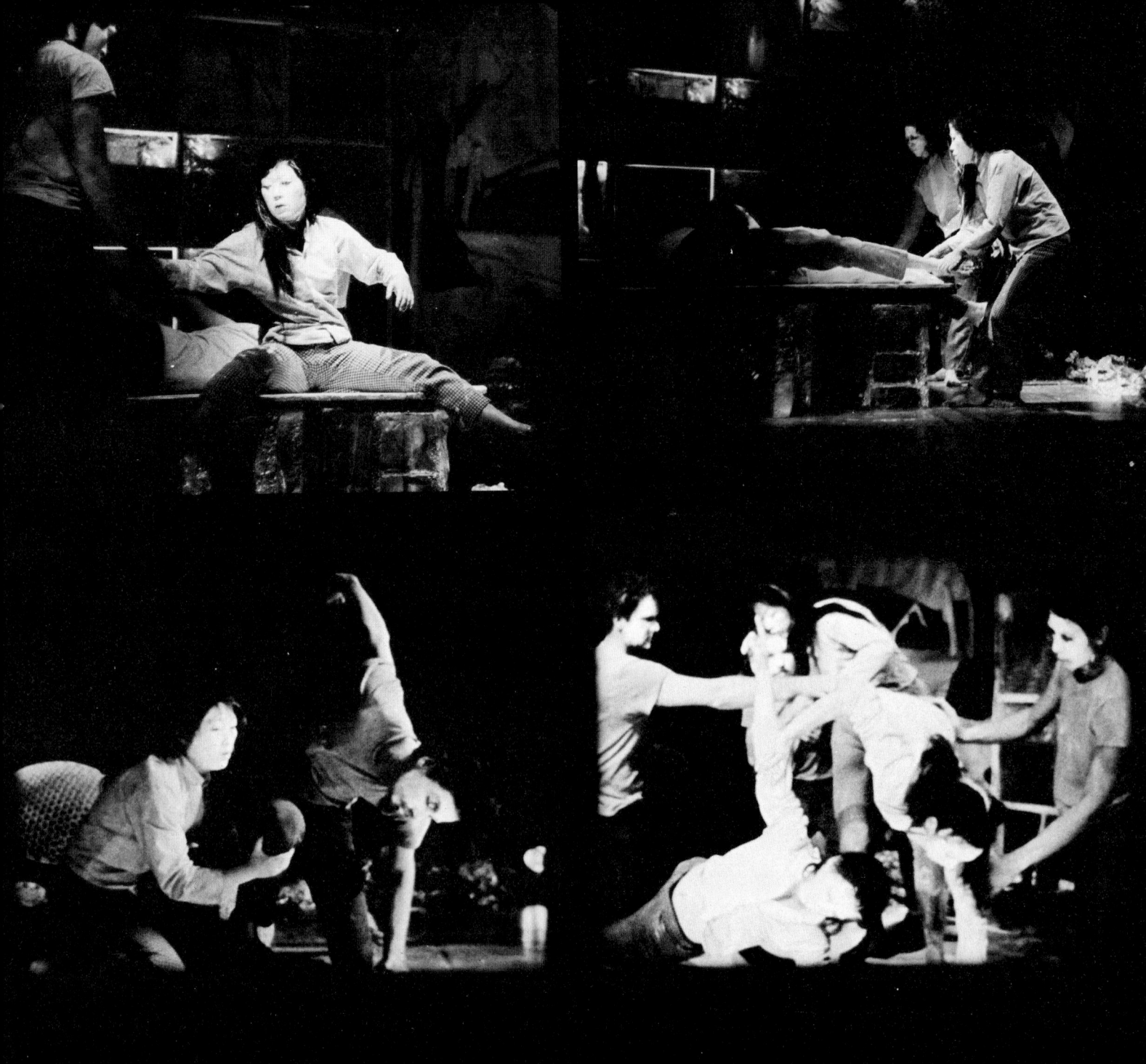

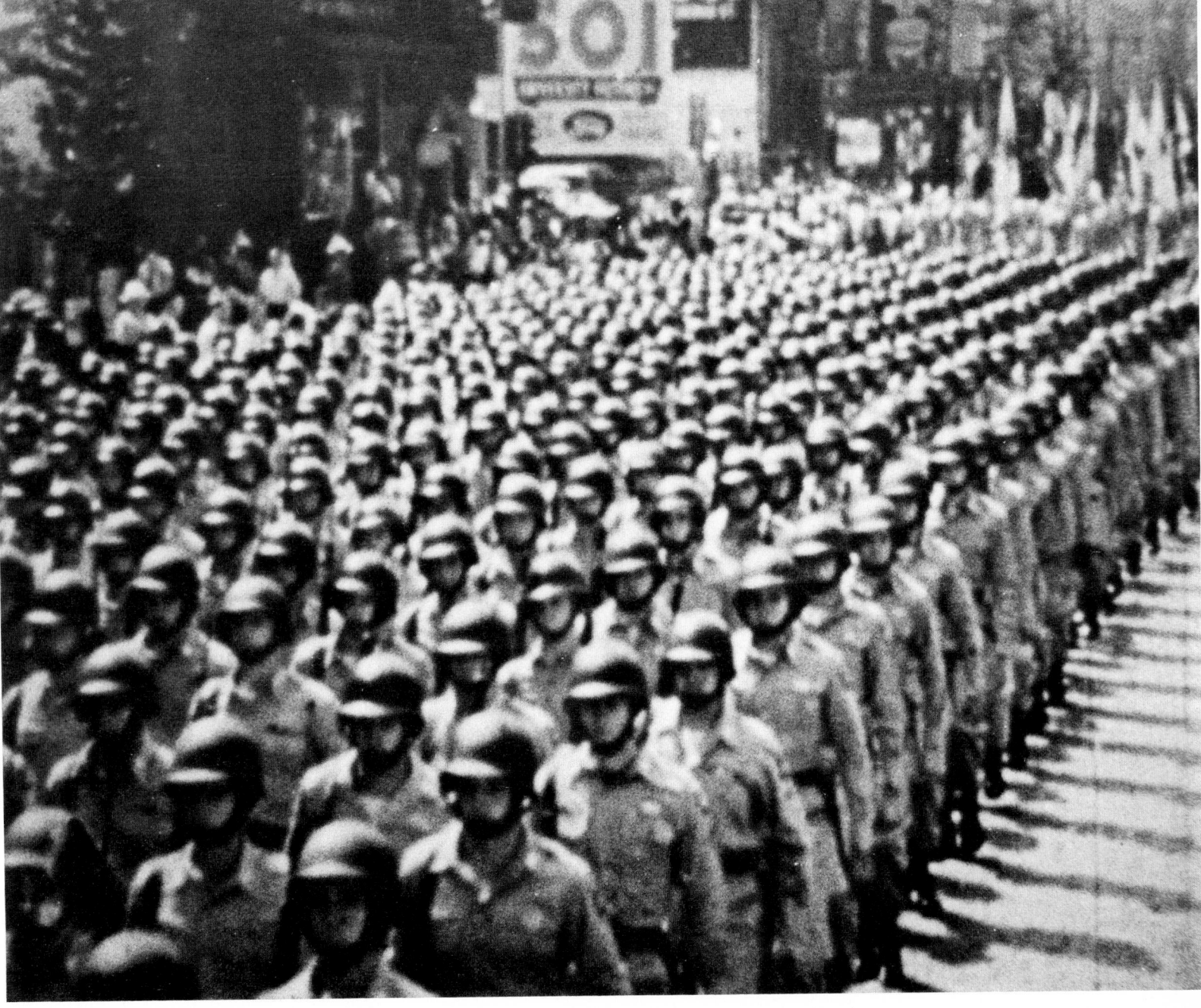

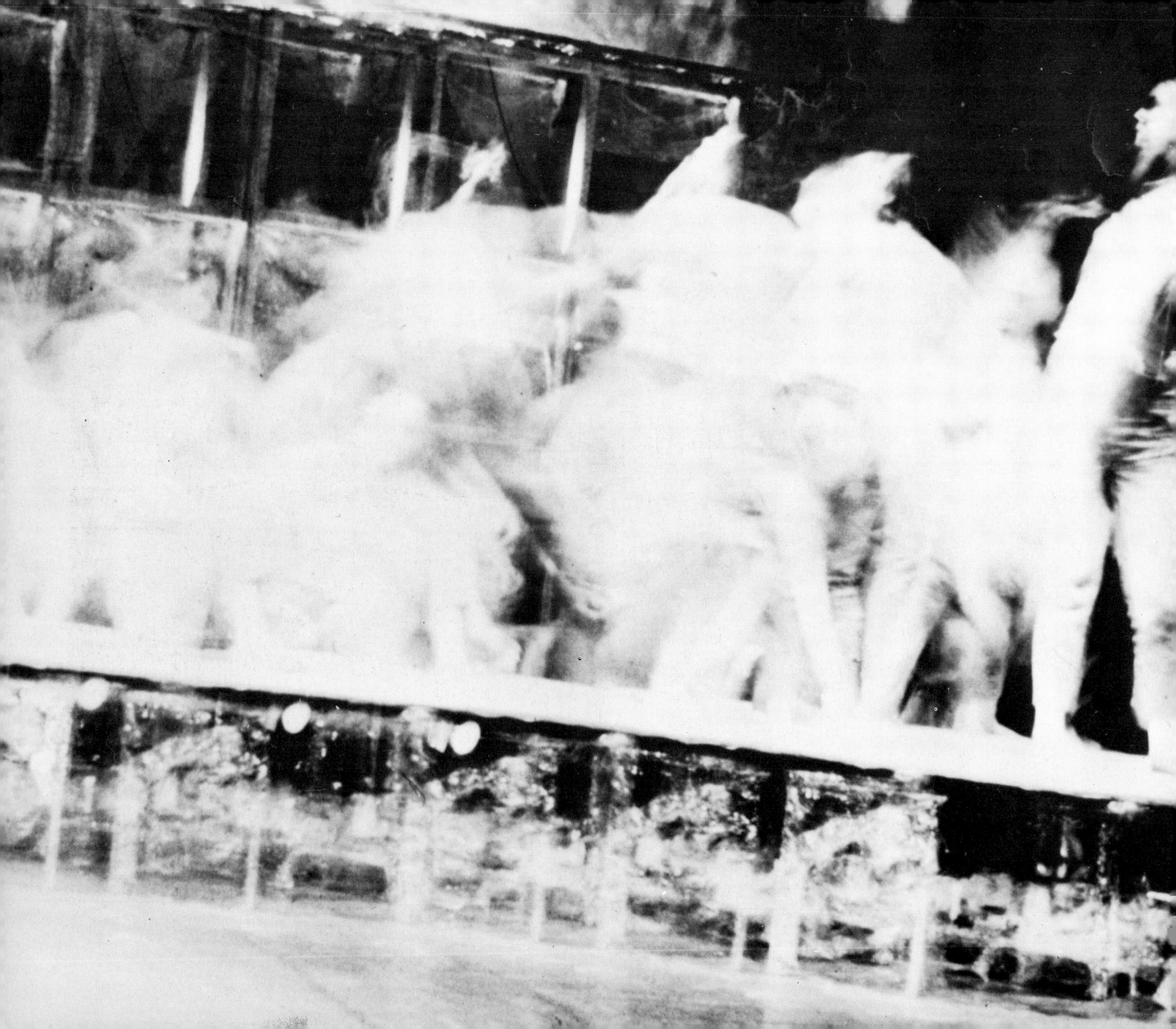

roll, choose to be the "body balls"; two standing become the "pushers"; the two remaining are "watchers." The Body Ball is pushed, rolled, and shoved in an uncertain journey by the Pusher, who may not use hands.

Quickly, they begin Crawl & Capture: body balls become "victims," watchers become "pursuers," pushers become "interference."

Flat on the floor the Victim crawls to escape the Pursuer, while the Interference hangs onto the Pursuer's ankles. When the Pursuer catches the Victim, the Interference moves suddenly to grab from the other end: a tug of war. (Usually each victim can gather enough force to leap from the grips of both tormentors:

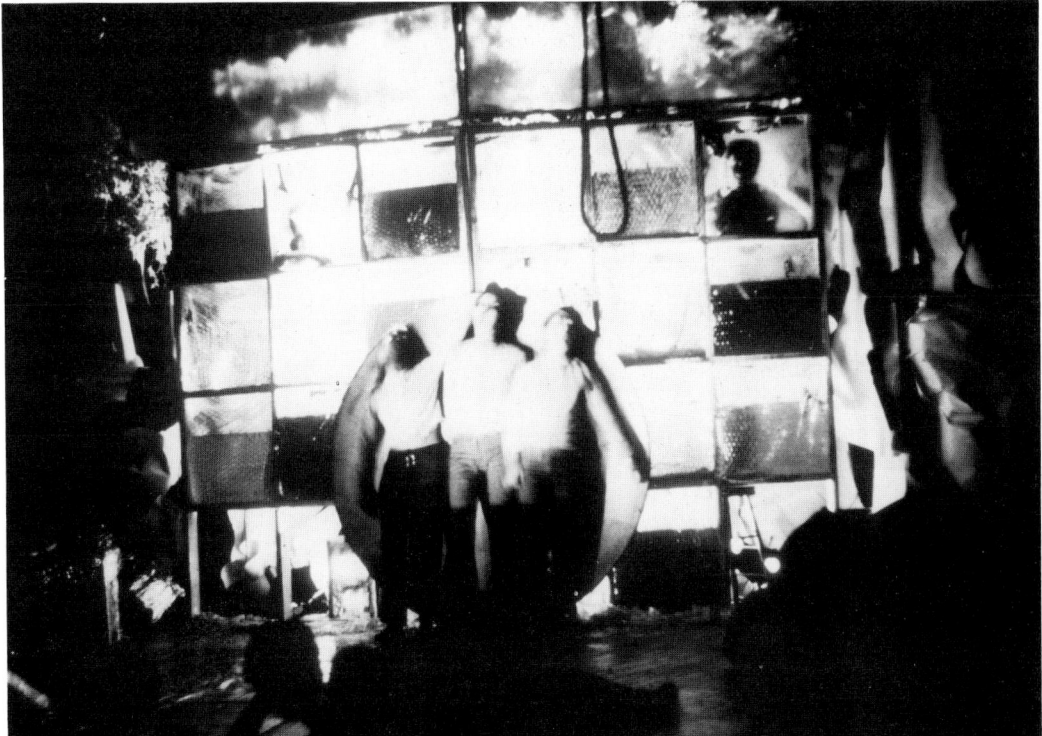

Herbert Migdoll

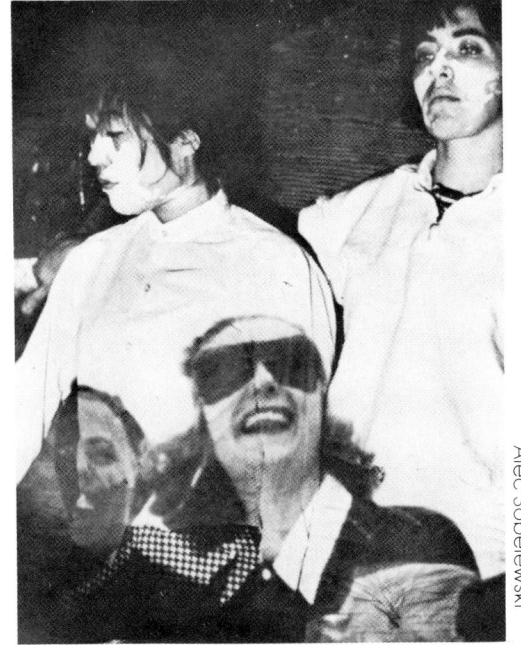

Herbert Migdoll

Alec Sobelewski

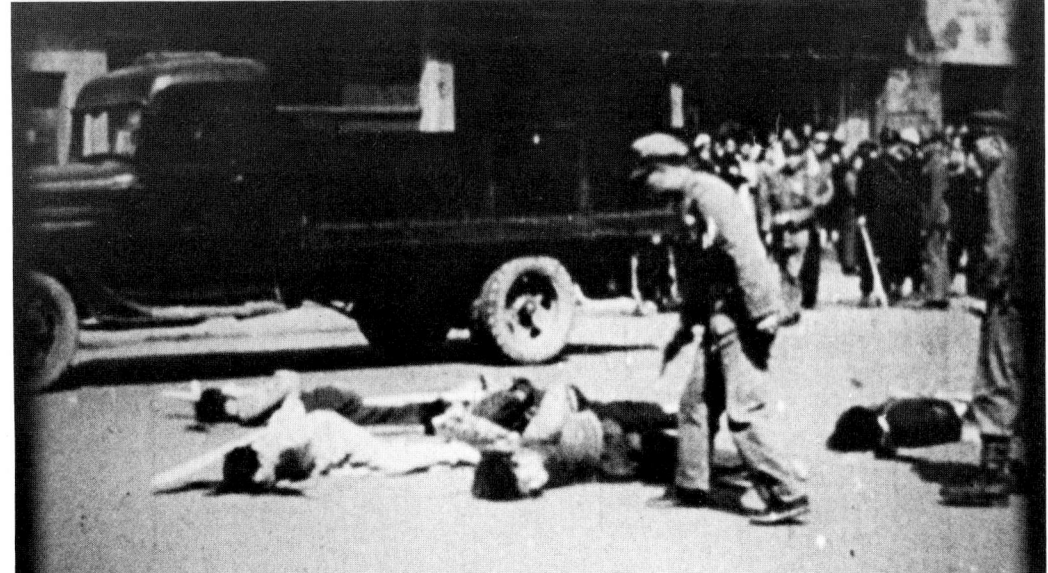

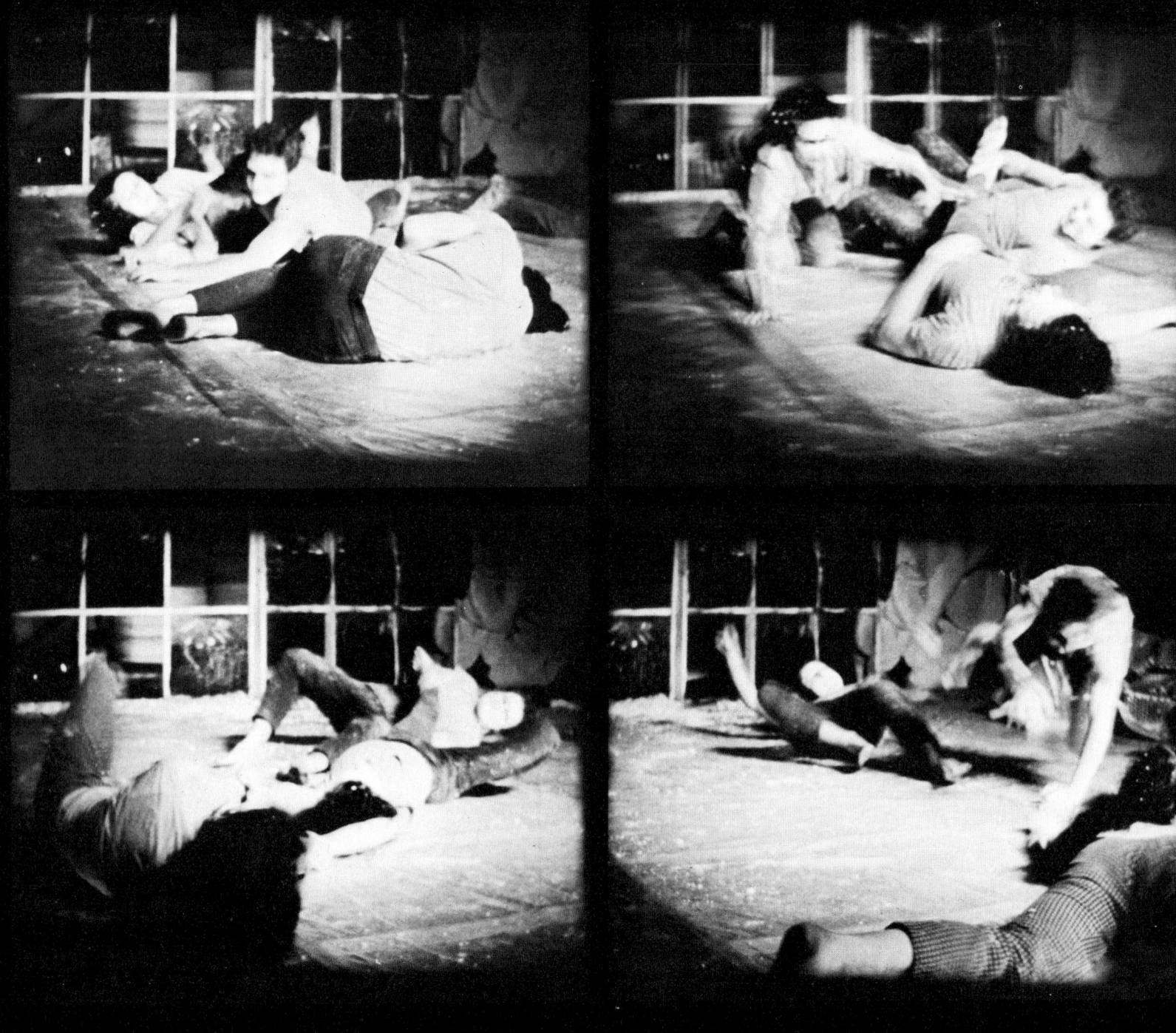

the leap and cry stops any movement of the other two.) Audience reaction triggers **sudden flashes of blue floor lights.**

Victim now chooses between pursuer and interference, one of whom becomes the Dragged Body (to be dragged and then hung from the looped rope). Gathering foil, two persons completely cover the first body hung; two others cover the second Dragged Body.

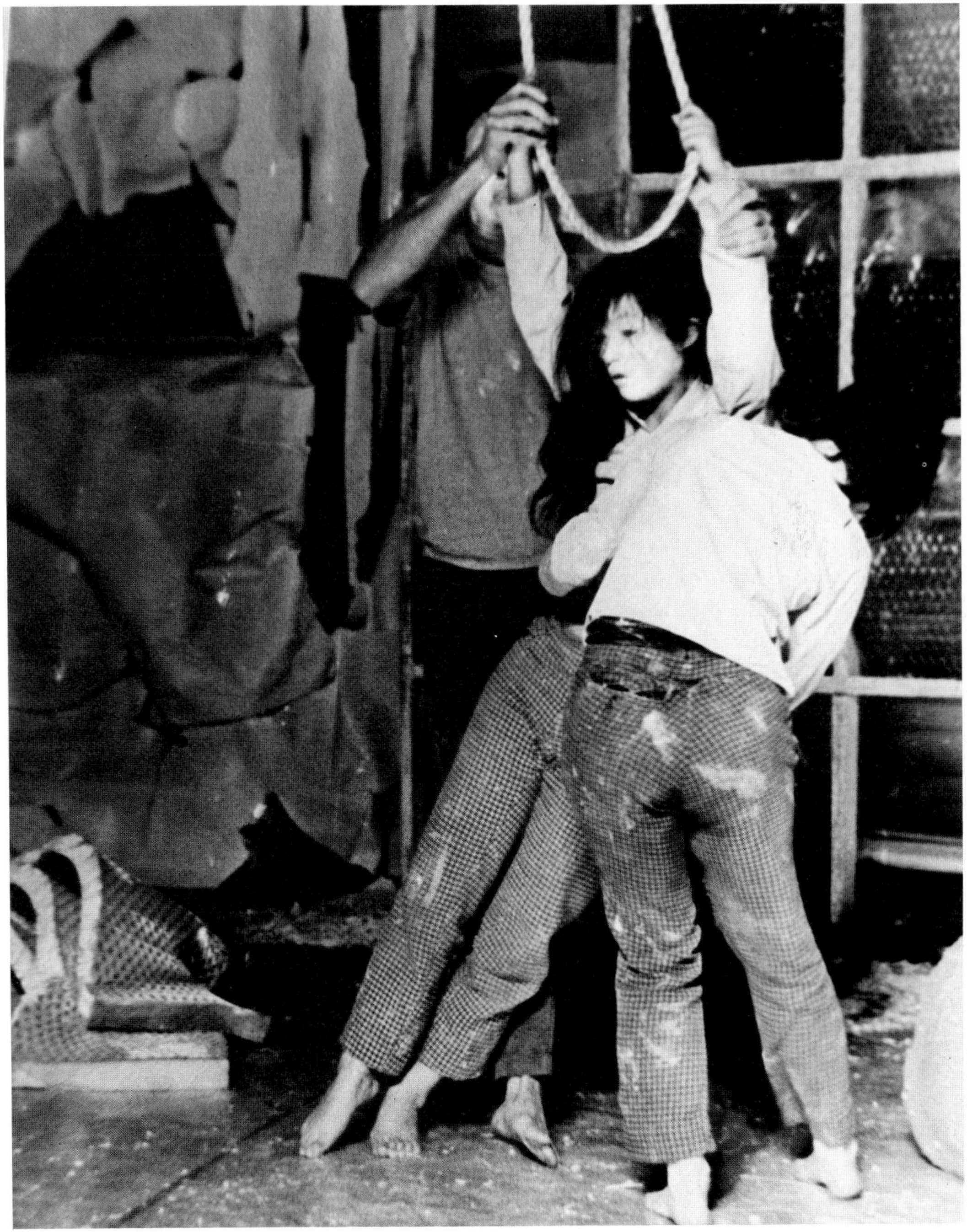

These bodies will become the two Silver Walkers. The remaining four become two Cocoons and a Double Cocoon (the last two unwrapped performers cover

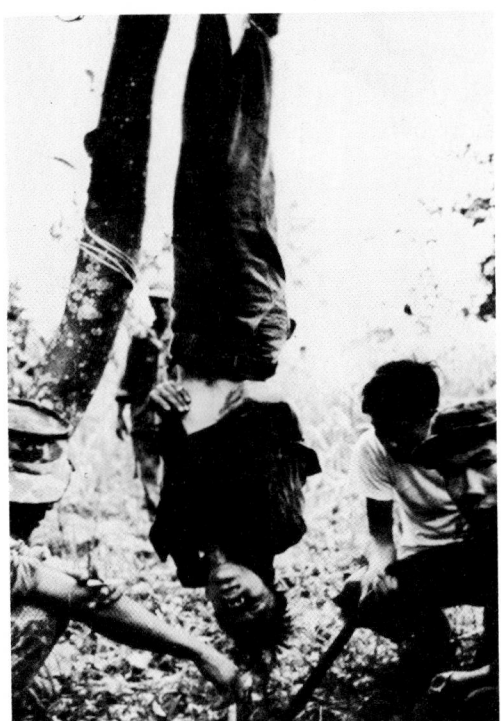

each other as one form, falling together when wrapped).

The fallen cocoons slowly, slowly twist from their silver wrappings without using their hands. Silence, but for the crackling foil. The silver walkers, nearly blind in their wrappings, walk out onto the planks into the audience area; projectionists with blue flash lights guide them. The planks are slippery and slope upward—the walkers precariously make their way to the end, where they sink into the sitting position.

The first freed cocoons become Rescuers.

As **Viet-Flakes** begins against the white disk, a rescuer—sensing danger—crawls up the plank, and drags a walker down.

The walkers are corpse-like, nearly unmoveable. The other freed cocoons wait prone at the end of the planks to assist the rescues. Together in desperate struggle and clumsy haste they gather in a pile, collapsing under the film projection. The snow machine begins—snow falling, filling eyes and ears, covering all.

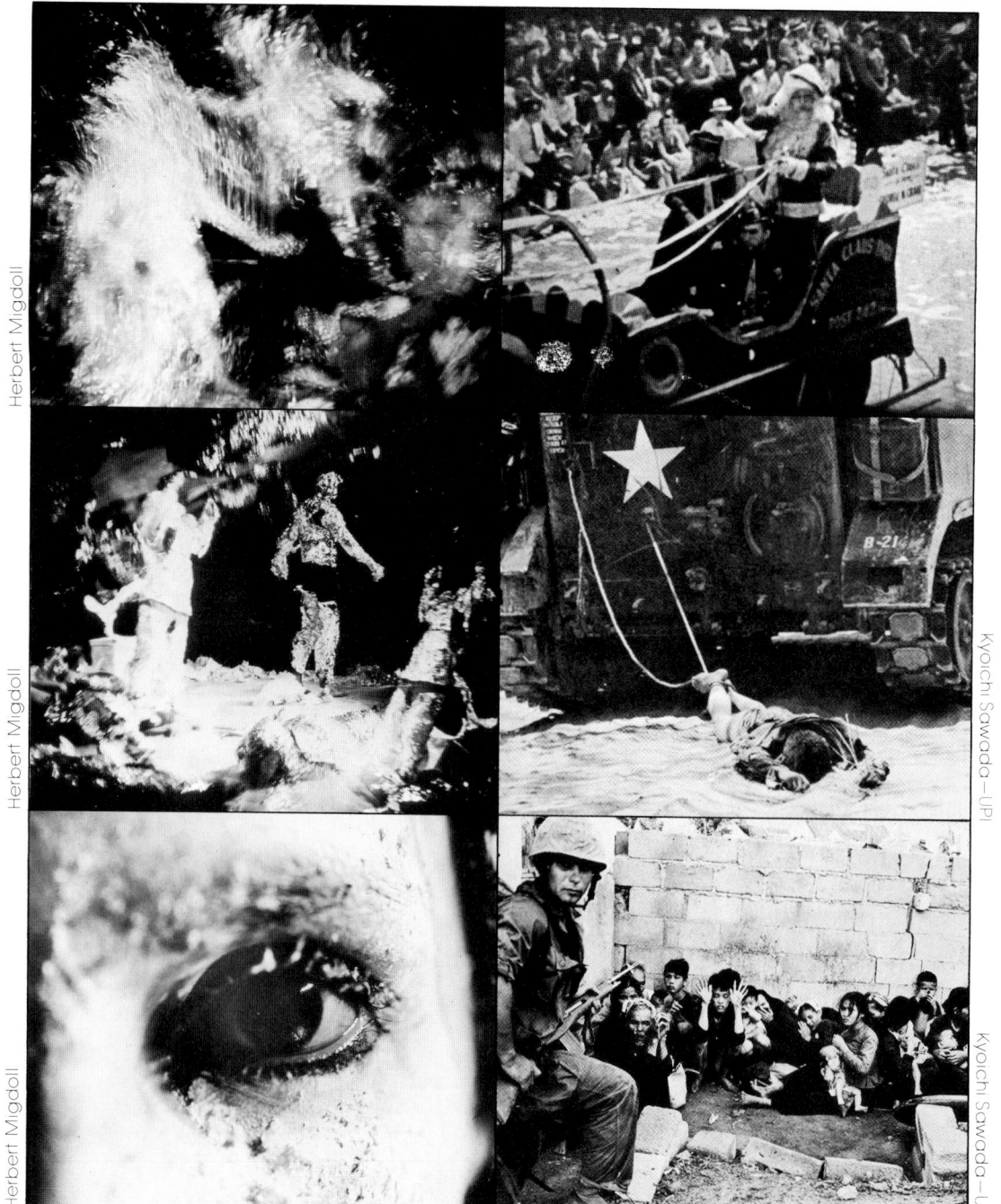

Herbert Migdoll

Herbert Migdoll

Herbert Migdoll

Kyoichi Sawada—UPI

Kyoichi Sawada—UPI

On The Making of SNOWS

I've always had great difficulty in asking for help and in believing it could be a source of satisfaction for someone to be of aid in accomplishing my work. I understood this as one of those twisted female inheritances, "Don't take up too much room!", against the social assumption "You have a right to all you need." This sort of conflict has hindered the smooth or efficient passage of my work into the art world maelstrom, but as well has made the energies and congruencies of collaborations on my work especially vivid and personal. The people I worked with all shared a devotion to our processes and the sense of bringing the work through against all odds. Essential to the risks and psychic submersions, the strains of personal daily efforts and preparations for a public work, was the emotional core, the interchange of ideas and the ballast of a shared life with James Tenney. There was always a direct flow between the confirmation of my work and personal life. Because there was the one person with whom I felt integral and whole, I could risk myself in public, and felt free to pursue forms of creative work for which I had no "special" training. Because Jim was a composer, pianist and conductor, the range of concentrations, tensions—working to a deadline, organizing groups, periods of abstraction, neglect of daily routines, had been endured by us both since the time we were college students. In the summer of '66 Jim was witness to hallucinations I suffered in the country, of Vietnamese bodies hanging in the trees; the kitchen stove became a miniature village, smouldering—seen from above—and I was afraid to bake in it. I was editing "Fuses" (16mm) and began making super 8 film from Viet-nam atrocity photographs; gradually drawings and notes formed a sinister reverie building towards a theater piece.

In 1960 when Jim and I had graduate Fellowships (his in electronic music, mine in painting) at the University of Illinois, we had met a young woman Vietnamese poet, through his composition teacher Wen Chung-Chou. She told me about the deep and pervasive traditions of poetry among all the Vietnamese; that reverence for nature and for ancestors was shared by rural and urban settlements, that the French had long been a disruptive presence there controlling oil, tin, rubber and opium; that American military forces were subverting the economy and were destroying farming villages, building barbed wire encampments for farmers, radical professors, intellectuals. We had heard nothing of this before. This fragment fit with other astonishing stories we had heard from artists who in their free-wheeling travels had told us of underground military installations in the New Mexico desert, where they had been brought to do a concert; or of passports withheld, of a relative dying from germ warfare research, etc....and also fit with an uncanny paranoia we felt to be the unraveling fabric of the cold-war and McCarthy pursuits. It related to humble health food stores in Illinois receiving bomb threats; to the firing of Prof. Ivey—head of science research at the University of Illinois for his espousal of Krebiozen as a cancer cure; to the death of Reich in prison; to the bizarre notification from the Urbana bank informing us that in the event of a nuclear attack we should mail in our checks rather than come in person!; to a theater director friend in Chicago who discovered his phone was tapped when the mechanism broke down and replayed his conversations as he dialed. And then there were the periodic newspaper reports from Kankeekee, Broadview or Tolono farmers, of spaceships landing in their corn fields, helmeted figures taking a pumpkin pie and pitcher of water from their kitchen tables before whirling away in silver disks.

In September '66 Paul Libin called to offer the use of his Martinique Theater for a series of "Angry Arts" performances relating to the Viet-nam war. I had the rough beginnings of **Snows**—a range of images which might incorporate complex technologies. I could "see" the atmosphere of the work, I knew I wanted the audience to somehow control the performance cuing systems, and I was obsessed with the contradictions I wanted the work to effect. But I didn't want to present **Snows** on a stage—even the low circular one of the Martinique. Libin generously wasted three weeks with me, searching for permission to perform on a boat as it circled NY harbor, or to use a cavernous ruin under the Brooklyn Bridge, or the Greenwich St. piers. We were in each case refused a "permit to assemble."

A performance work requires that antagonistic states of being co-exist and become mutually re-enforcing. A physical space has to be found; this becomes a formal reference, a basic structure on which the environmental and movement images take form. I have to mentally "dwell" there. I have to invite/provide for a para-normal state of "envisioning," becoming a vehicle through which the energies of the work will pass; in dreams and "abstracted" states I pay attention, concentrate for unpredicated relations, sudden elements running concurrently which may synchronize into a forceful sequence, an idea of film or equipment or a gesture... It's necessary to be strong physically: rehearsals are grueling, the body has to find the thoughts in concrete forms, to propel the collaborations and search in improvisation during rehearsal; then it is necessary to build, carry, cart, run around the city all day locating materials, deliver copy, films. Things go wrong, the strains increase. It is impossible to get ill, to miss a day, once a performance is set.

The conception of **Snows** began in the summer; the production was underway only a month and a half before the performance dates Libin provided. During this time I was working part time as a standby figure in a cocktail dress for unmemorable porno films; and I taught

"art" to a Unitarian Sunday School class in Queens. Jim travelled every week to his job in electronic music research at Yale; I scrabbled for the $85 a month loft rent and we travelled back and forth between the loft and a country place, sustaining our belief in brief times apart—that we continually "choose" each other. Production chores were my singular responsibility, combined with domestic concerns for two places—I struggled for undisturbed time to work in my constructions, light boxes, and the drawings and films which were crucial to **Snows**—and we had an active round of events in the art world.

Diary Notes during the week before the opening of **Snows**:

12 Jan. Worst day of all...no money, no breakfast, rehearsal.notebook lost, no lens on camera I rushed to borrow...too much to do! Films at Phila. lab may not get back in time. Aluminum is coming free! Talk with Paul Libin. Rehearse at 4:30 half of the piece...rough and ragged. The group is fantastic together. Delight with them. Ralph at work on electronic wiring, Larry rebuilding sections of light machine. Jim goes to work. Rush down to get lenses and look at 8mm o.k. Work with Jim on tape, it's coming wonderfully exactly what I hoped for...analogies and almost imperceptible transitions of sound sources.

13 Jan. Jim brings in eggs, a real breakfast. Wishing to stay quietly in one place together. Alphonse comes to check out Bolex for me—lenses all wrong. Go to 5 & 10 for magnifying glass. No good on Bolex; tape it onto 8mm Nikon. Re-do Voice ad. To Willoughby's trade my 16mm Craig editor for an 8mm. They give me $15. Finally shoot the (new) Viet images over again. Jim takes me to Max's for hamburger. No world but

the theater these weeks. Finish Voice ad. Cut super 8 films; Kitch happily on my lap, cat hairs in the viewer. Talk with Jim on phone over an hour! He's so with me on everything, real joy to do the piece, go through it together.

17 Jan. Filliou Happening at 8:30. Calling to locate projectors; mad wild rehearsal. Karl and June work on covering floor. Collaging walls. Collapse on floor middle of spreading foil, plastic...too much.

19 Jan. Wake up full of plans, errands to do, become hysterical...we go back to bed for loving. So, everything changes. Messy angry rehearsal; technical things still unresolved, unrealized...and I've got to insist. Change ending of piece...middle section altered.

20 Jan. Pick up projectors; programs typed for theater, good rehersal; projectors working with contact mikes and speaker placement set. Finally clear. Shaking with exhaustion. Jack and Karl finish a "snow-bucket" machine. 4:00 am both dead asleep, Shigeko calls...she cannot perform!

Week of the 21st—**Snows** opening

Yves Klein memorable opening Guggenheim; May Wilson exhibit; Gypsey dinner—Rotraut & Phillipe; Claes; Alphonse Shilling films; Brakhage films; call Victor P. for a job...feeling sick, kind of ghastly, sweet last hours in the theater....

I had presented Paul Libin with one of my typical $500 budgets for: 8 performances, six performers, five technicians, a complex environment to be built by my crew; I would design the flyers, print, address, mail them; I asked a guarantee from him for sandwiches, brandy and carfare for the troupe during rehearsals, a promise of ten complimentary tickets each night for friends who couldn't afford the $2.50 ticket...It was impossible to tell if Paul was accustomed to working this way but his faith was evident. He arranged to keep the theater empty for us for two weeks, understanding my need to construct the work in its physical environment.

From the beginning certain images for **Snows** had formed around Jim and Phoebe Neville; fortunately both found time to work with me again. Peter Watts, a sculptor, saw an earlier work and asked to be involved; I found Tyrone Mitchell, also a sculptor, in a store and knew immediately that I wanted to work with him—I convinced him right then to give us a try. I knew Shigeko Kubota only slightly—she lived then with the composer David Behrman, a friend of Jim. My friend and neighbor, June Ekman, the dancer, agreed to stand-in for me during later rehearsals.

I had designed a reflective prism across the back of the low horseshoe stage; the glass or lucite necessary for this refractive surface was beyond my means. Instead, an open grid of two by fours evolved into which I wanted to place heavy sacks filled with colored water; at either end of the structure I envisioned vertical rectangles of moving lights. (And I had to sacrifice my plan for a transparent plexi-glass floor cut with circles through which lights would shine.)

At this point the collaboration of sculptor Larry Warshaw became crucial; Larry proposed a light machine in a horizontal span across the "water lens," composed of many small motors driving mirrors and colored foil at speeds which could respond to the audience's mo-

tions. Through Deborah Hay, Larry had worked with Robbie Robinson on the "Nine Evenings" performances under the auspices of Billy Klüver's Experiments In Art and Technology. In order to realize the complex technical aspects of **Snows,** Larry contacted Robinson and Klüver for assistance. Klüver had created EAT to provide artists with access to equipment and technicians. He had been a friend to Jim and me when we first came East, when Jim had become composer in residence at Bell Labs developing music programs for the computer systems that Klüver was also involved with. It was Billy who had introduced me to Oldenburg, Rauschenberg, Brecht, de Maria and Breer, and who formed a vital nucleus of artists in association. I submitted my proposals to EAT, and **Snows** became the first occasion that EAT turned its resources over to a single artist.

One bitterly cold morning Jim and I drove through light snow with Robert Schultz and Larry Warshaw out to Bell Labs. Robbie Robinson (who, with fellow bell engineer Ralph Flynn, worked out the overall technical requirements of **Snows**) took us to an equipment house where EAT materials were stored. As if at a jumble sale, we pick and choose "these transistors, those cables, let's have this SCR system." We loaded up the station wagon, barely squeezing ourselves in...I'm told we're carting about $4,000 worth of cable, wire, power amps, transceivers, photoresistors, preamps, mikes, contact mikes, speakers,

and motors...a pile of stuff representing 10 times the budget of the whole performance piece!

My ventures with technology had been concrete and personal; my difficulties with working with technicians who knew the possibilities and limitations of machines had been mechanical. I could not be sure whether my technological systems would be ridiculous or inspired. With the help of Warshaw, and EAT's Ralph Flynn, Robbie Robinson & Per Björn, new perceptions were made possible.

Six years before, people had been disturbed by my having transformed the function and look of mechanical parts—lights, clocks, motors—including them in constructions where they no longer resembled what they "really" were. Now I also wanted all the mechanical parts exposed, edging (the stage) out of their boxes, jackets, casings. I wanted the pile of cables filling the aisles, to be walked over and around, but fire laws and the fragility of the electronic elements prohibited these ideas. The machines which finally did function visibly were the light sculpture, the snow machine, hand-held beams, the two noisy swivel head 16mm projectors, an old 8mm projector, two large strobe lights, and floor mikes sticking up in the silver foil on the stage.

I wanted the mechanical gestures of machine parts to equal performers' movements—exposed as part of the total environment to which they contribute particular effects. Whenever possible I wanted the technicians to be interchangeable with performers: the work of technicians an overt parameter—clearly embedded within the overall forms. Everyone took part in rehearsal exercises. I held a double reign: visual images and physical impulses which are enacted, in action. My performers are natural "objects" whose personal attitudes, gestures and responses move within a generative dream-vision source—meshing the fantastic and actual. And I had the wish that technicians and machinery could actively evolve their roles by discoveries of functions that the "personality" of the machines, and the emotions of the technicians could realize in active relationship with performers—a total sense of the situation which they shape; the process of collaboration freely transforming their presumed use.

In the thick of rehearsals the media began to take form. Karl Schenzer, Jack Aquiros, James Finney were building the "water lens" late into the night and offering overviews as the performed aspects grew and shifted. Robert Schultz was building a color organ to be operated by sound sources. Larry Warshaw's Light Machine, placed on top of the lens, was constructed and re-constructed until the final form consisted of:

Ten spot lights, mounted on two 5-foot frames, covered with colored gels and connected to the Schultz color organ. Aimed away from the screen of the frame, the lights were reflected off foil-covered spinning drums and refracted through the diamond patterned plexi-glass screens, pulsing according to sound intensities and manual controls. The machine had been inspired by works by Nicholas Stoffer, and the motor systems were designed by Per Björn.

The seats of the audience were to be wired with contact microphones feeding into an SCR switching system to which all other motors would be connected. I began a cue sheet to incorporate all the variations in our electronic equipment which could be altered by the unsuspecting audience:

3 16mm projectors—
five films: direction, speed, light intensity, grouping of films, on/off

3 sound tapes—5 speakers
volume intensity, on/off (variable speakers)

light machine—
speed, variation of motors, brightness intensity, on/off

color organ—
specific areas to be illuminated, colors, on/off

floor lights on stage—
randomized illumination, intensity, on/off

contact mikes on stage—
randomized active/inactive

performers cues—
durations of actions, sequences linked to the tempo, occurrence, position, of the above elements

Finally the magical coup for the environment:

Gimbels Department store is two blocks from my loft; I go there to get warm when the landlord turns off the heat. The Martinique Theater is directly across Gimbels at Greely Square. In December, Gimbels is decorated with acres of hanging white branches, imitation snow-fluff covering the stems. I need these branches. I call to speak with the decor-ator; the branches are to be taken down Saturday night and tossed into a garbage truck. I invent some story—that I am teaching children to build things by hand and need the branches. Wednesday, December 28th at 9:00 p.m., Carl, Jack and I arrive at a side door; bundles of branches carried on our shoulders across 6th Ave. to the Theater. It is snowing! We need 150 feet of heavy duty aluminum foil. Call all the companies—it is too expensive. I invent some story—we are a charity church group making a Christmas party for orphans. A huge package of foil is sent ot us!

Snows was performed eight times to capacity audiences. We lived in it, dwelled there so deeply, it could have continued many times over without becoming repetitious to any of us. Libin would have liked to extend it, but had booked another theater group, "Viet Rock" by Meegan Terry, directly after us. It's difficult to describe the audience reactions. People had wept unashamed. Involved and stunned, there was never applause at the conclusion. At that moment in time the work shattered indifference, confronting the weary outrage and hardening of our senses. And yet was transcendent—taking us, audience and performers, through another door of self and community. We were connected to each other through the metaphors enacted. The final night, February 5th, the city received "blizzard warnings"; again there was standing room only.

1966/1977

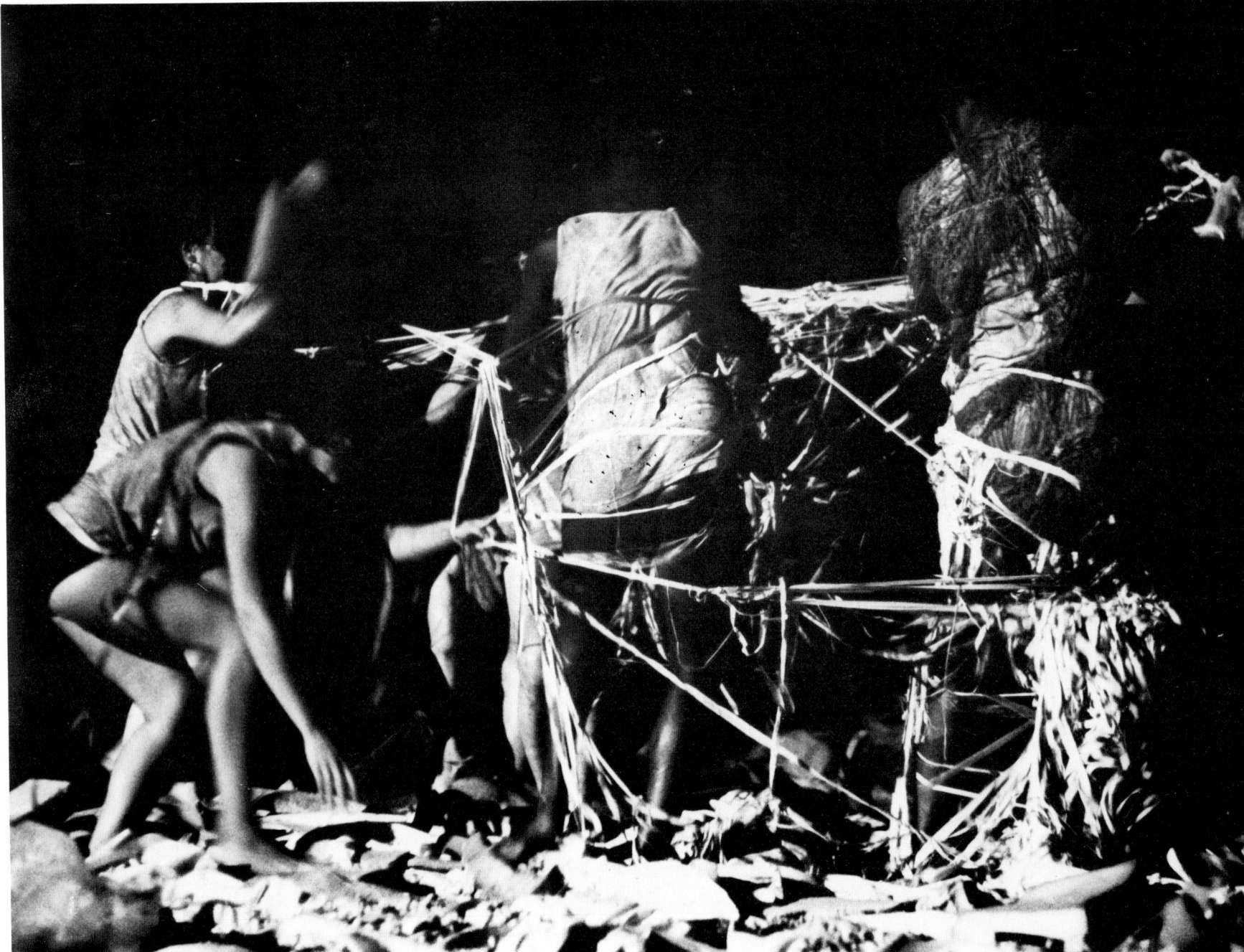

Come to London, I order, beseech, implore, tell, ask, direct command...let the Congress extend itself beyond the space/time of words...*Peace News* says the Dialectics of Liberation will be the greatest intellectual event of the decade...But the body speaks louder than the word and you understand... what must be done.

This in a February letter from my friend, Dr. Joe Berke—psychiatrist, organizer of the first Free University (NYC), friend of the Fugs, of poets Calvin Hernton, Susan Sherman—by then in London practicing work in Anti-Psychiatry with R.D. Laing, David Cooper, Jules Henry, and later to author a handbook of the '60's, *Counter Culture*. (And to marry the American writer Roberta Elzy).

A clipping from *Peace News* (London) came with the letter, and I read this projective evaluation:

> What is required, then, is a long-term project of *subversive re-education*, backwards to first principles! And this is why the congress of "The Dialectics of Liberation" is so important. All the *men* involved with the July congress are seeking to "demystify," which is to say, to demonstrate the mutilations which our regimented technological rationality inflicts upon *man's* apprehension of reality and of *him*self. They are not so much concerned with providing solutions as with arousing consciousness." (my italics)

Since the featured participants were "some of the most brilliant but unclassifiable thinkers in the world today"—sharing a deep commitment to clarify political consciousness, risking professional stability for a radical, reconstructive vision— since that was true—was it also possible that many of them would resent the participation of a woman, in particular a young woman, whose contribution would be a sort of "unclassifiable" physical extension, a sensory equivalence to energies explored/released in the course of the congress? The quotation, now ten years past, clarifies the bias underlying the actual hostility, ostracism, and sabotage which my work received. A few years ago, when I lived in London, I met another of the psychiatrists who organized the congress. He told me:

> I always felt we owed you an apology...but the disillusioning fact seems to have been that we didn't welcome a woman taking an equal space among ourselves, we distrusted a theatrical form, and we certainly didn't want a very young woman putting on a performance which incorporated our own words with a countering physicality...

ROUND HOUSE

July 29 1967 Congress of the Dialectics of Liberation London

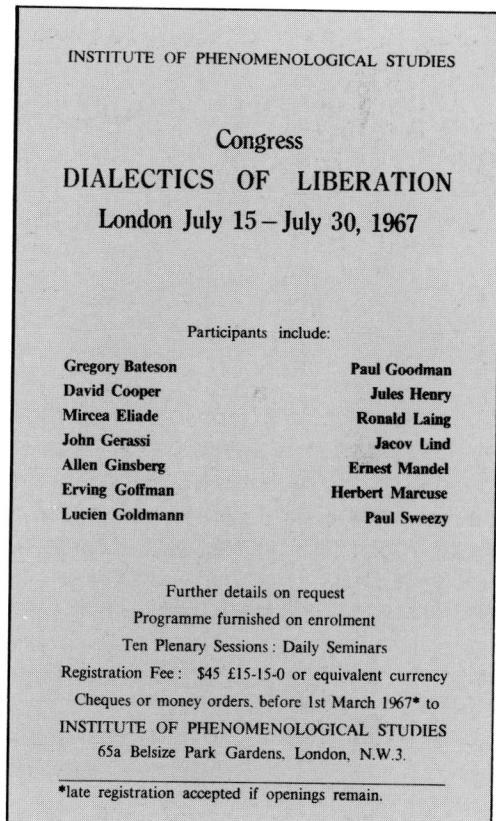

INSTITUTE OF PHENOMENOLOGICAL STUDIES

Congress
DIALECTICS OF LIBERATION
London July 15 – July 30, 1967

Participants include:

Gregory Bateson	Paul Goodman
David Cooper	Jules Henry
Mircea Eliade	Ronald Laing
John Gerassi	Jacov Lind
Allen Ginsberg	Ernest Mandel
Erving Goffman	Herbert Marcuse
Lucien Goldmann	Paul Sweezy

Further details on request

Programme furnished on enrolment

Ten Plenary Sessions : Daily Seminars

Registration Fee : $45 £15-15-0 or equivalent currency

Cheques or money orders, before 1st March 1967* to

INSTITUTE OF PHENOMENOLOGICAL STUDIES
65a Belsize Park Gardens, London, N.W.3.

*late registration accepted if openings remain.

THE DIALECTICS OF LIBERATION

ALL men are in chains. There is the bondage of poverty and starvation: the bondage of lust for power, status, possessions.

A REIGN of terror is now perpetrated and perpetuated on a global scale.

IN the affluent societies, it is masked. There, children are conditioned by violence called love to assume their position as the would-be inheritors of the fruits of the earth. But, in the process, they are reduced to little more than hypothetical points on a dehumanised co-ordinate system.

FOR the rest, terror is not masked. It is torture, cold, starvation, death.

THE whole world is now an irreducible whole.

THE properties of this whole world system force us to submit to the fatality of Vietnam, the starvation of the third world, etc.

IN total context, culture is against us, education enslaves us, technology kills us.

WE must confront this. We must destroy our vested illusions as to who, what, where we are. We must combat our self-pretended ignorance as to what goes on and our consequent non-reaction to what we refuse to know.

WE experience what is and what is being done through the filter of our socially approved lies. But what is. is not the limit of what is possible.

WE shall meet in London on the basis of a wide range of expert knowledge.

THE dialectics of liberation begin with the clarification of our present condition.

Carolees   26 July

TIME	ACTION		LIGHTS	FILM	SOUND	MATERIAL
	CORE	MASS				
930	hidden	guides	events	xx	organ? O+T organ?	plastic strips ....
945	wagon enters	back lights	central	xx	xxls	xx
	x waits	s hovel		Newsreel	I read the news today. "good morning" double Beatles	xx
	emerge debris clearing	balcony run	central			
	grabs & falls	run growls	sihouette			
	passing women (pile foam)	down hum				
	creation of faces	xx	strobe	xx	xx	whiting
	up & down push grease body	M.+C. read		Slides Fuses	Beatles O+T Beatles	grease
	body sculpture-	shake walk (down ropes)	slides			
	ru n/catch mud crawl into circle	throw mud corner	" " central	" "		mud
	central foam animal play shoot down	spill foam down/runs	Slides	xx	x x	Afran foam
	foil wrapping cocoons/walkers hand lift screams rescue	lights	blue,low	xx		foil
	into pile	quiet b. run	xx	Viet Flakes " "	collage " "	silver bits from all around
	loaded on cart cart them away	loaders	low	xx	double B.	xx
					Social Deviants	

boys clean up   Social Deviants

Nevertheless, Joe Berke, organizing secretary for the congress at the Institute of Phenomenological Studies, put through an official invitation with airfare, board, performance date, and a miniscule budget for materials, (though he couldn't manage to have my name included among the others).

The invited guests were to raise topics, present papers, deliver lectures each morning followed by discussion seminars; and there would be evening and weekend events of poetry readings and workshops continuously for two weeks.

On opening day there was a gathering in the vast Round House, to welcome and introduce the invited guests to those attending. Amid a blur of auspicious culture heros my turn came and I was introduced by Dr. Burke. I described the idea for a closing night performance work which would be developed in the coming days, incorporating dominant issues and elements of the congress, and asked for participants from those attending. I would work with a core group of eight or ten people: workshops in movement, physical exploration of the Round house, sensitization, improvisation, etc. An additional group of twenty or thirty people would function like a "Greek chorus" enlarging aspects of movement and text.

Paul Goodman sprang up from among the audience and announced that he objected to this event, that it would be intrusive and "we weren't consulted about inviting her... why in the world would we want her to do this sort of thing?"

The following night there was a welcoming dinner for the invited guests. From my diary:

> July 16. Excluded from the dinner party; told to arrive after the dinner at East Elsham Street—hour away in a workers' district; party at West Elsham...once there, no one speaks to me...deadly, impenetrable atmosphere...the men in huddles passing wine to each other. One other woman there. Finally Joe arrives; David Cooper and Mason are friendly. Talk with Jules Henry and Bateson about animals...

The overwhelming work of evolving a ritual performance form in two weeks for a vast space (originally a Victorian railroad turn-about station) with sixty participants, kept me from most of the lectures and discussions I wanted to attend. But those I did observe consistently described the malaise of "Western Man" in the

Performers:
Bob Harrison   Neil Hornick   Michael Kustow
Henry Martin   Brenda Dixon   Mary Hanna
Jean Michaelson   C.S./
Mass group: Conrad Clark   Tony Woodward
David Cronin   Adrian Harman   David
Triesman   Peter Davey   Bill Schliffer   Roger
Gottlieb   Martin Siegel   Seymour King   Jim
Lesch   Elizabeth Robinson   Shamey Maxwell
Hugh King   Susan Triesman   Peter Payne
Anna Kohela   Mary Armstrong   Steven Allyn
Thomasina Bodker/
Assisted by: Craig Gibsone   David Gibsone
David Jeffrey   Brian Kahin   Bernard Mathieu
Ron Geesin   Steve Dwoskin   Eve Turner
Craig Nichols   Tom Bushnell   Peter Stowell
Hugh Cutler   Steve Levinsky   Alex Stowell/
Roustabouts: Danny Hewoy   Tony Slingsby   Ian
Barr   Michael Campbell   Jimmy Bartlett

International Congress
DIALECTICS OF LIBERATION

HAPPENING

created by

CAROLEE SCHNEEMANN

"ROUND HOUSE"

at the Roundhouse, Chalk Farm Road, London, N.W.1

Tickets 48 hours in advance from the Roundhouse, Indica, Betterbooks 10/-

SATURDAY JULY 29th 1967

at 9.30 p.m.

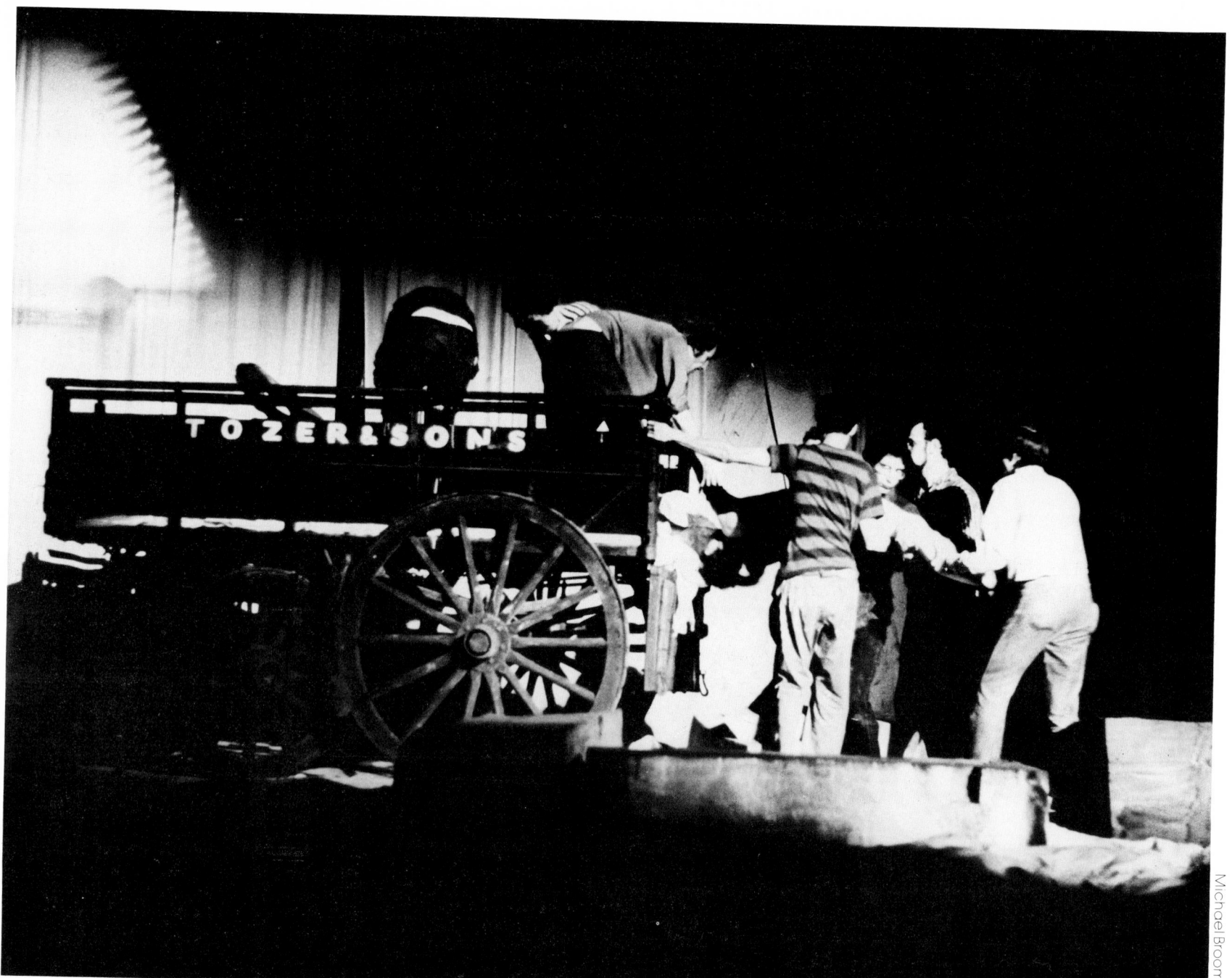

154

exclusive masculine gender. The splits and fissures of male/female, culture/nature, spirit/body, rationality/passion were grammatically inculcated, sustaining the proscriptive assumptions and patriarchal perogatives which characterized the dis-ease of cultural and social forms supposedly being "de-mystified." I was a participant among men who validated each other's work—each other's transgressions of established culture and myth—but who at the same time implicitly mythicized the female as auxiliary, adjacent. That is, woman was included under a set of standards and concerns auxiliary to or in implicit conflict with her own experience.

Just as men buried the immediacy of certain emotions (especially their vulnerabilities) and forced them to be transformed into disproportionate, distorted, or formidable channels (editing/censorship of self), they expressed a philosophical plaint against the exploitation of nature, of creative resources. Art, nature, the body, sensuality, became tropes for the missing women, the active female powers. And while they suffered this fragmentation, the inclusion of actual, contributing, "de-mystifying" women remained an exceptional consideration. The men who helped and furthered my work often did so at the expense of an uncomplicated relationship with the other men.

The rehearsals with the performers were constantly impaired by a group of students who felt that what I was doing was "Imperialistic," "individualistic"; that no particular group had a right to define itself within the congress. They stormed through the area where we meditated, stole our props, banged on tin cans while we struggled to concentrate on sensitized movement and contact improvisations. The paradoxes would not be unraveled, only experienced head on. Among the performers were economists, Trotskyites, Marxists, social workers, doctors, artists, an heiress escaping her family. The only actual working-class participants from the neighborhood of Camden Town were five young boys who became our "roustabouts". I had a room in a private house on Abbey Road with a garden full of roses—shared with an English writer, a Swedish sociologist, and a political exile from Greece. The separation from Jim was especially painful; the daily work and density of people and issues at the conference was chaotic.

I was able to function and proceed with this impossible work because the subtle and unanalysed exclusions sparked some instinct that I did need to be present and active, that subsuming my role was a way to elevate its relevance. And I was

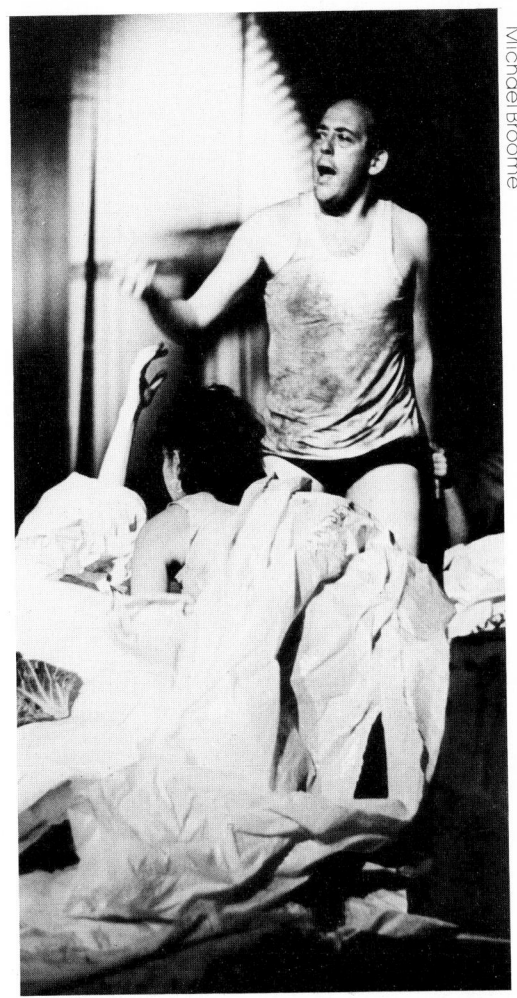

Michael Broome

WILL YOU JUST LET ME FINISH?....I'M NOT FINISHED... YOU'RE NOT LISTENING...CAN YOU HEAR ME?... YOU'RE NOT LISTENING........

IS IT POSSIBLE TO DEVELOP A SEPARATE SYSTEM IN WHICH WE CAN LIVE OUR LIVES COMPLETELY OUTSIDE OF THE EXISTING SYSTEM?.....IS IT POSSIBLE TO DEVELOP A SEPARATE SYSTEM COMPLETELY OUTSIDE OF THE EXISTING SYSTEM?........

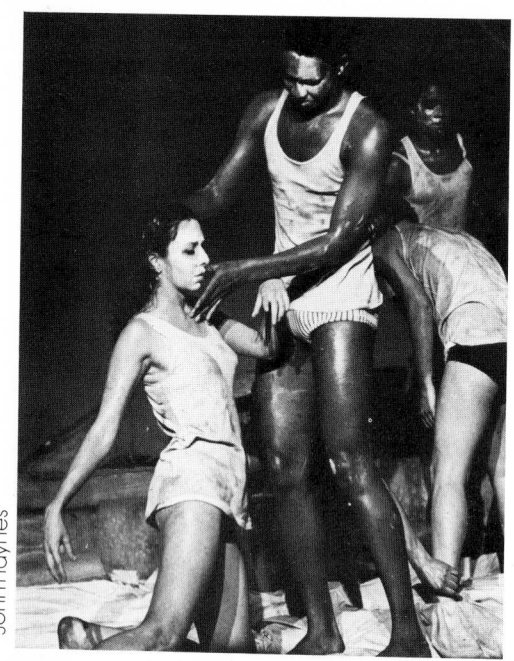

John Haynes

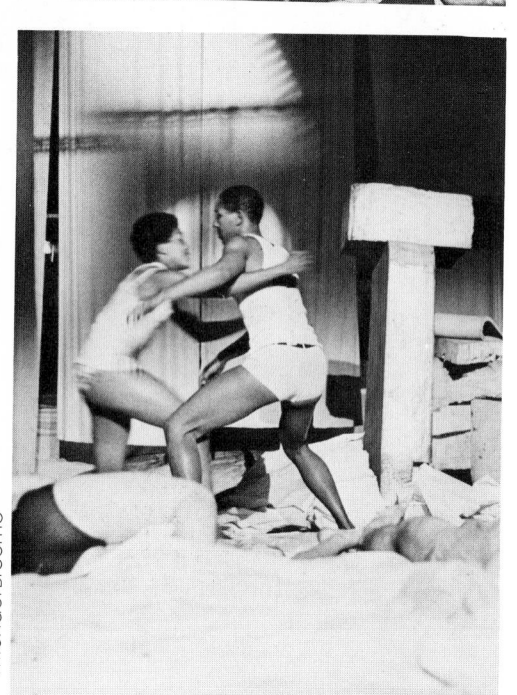

Michael Broome

fascinted with the space, with the conference issues, with the extended sort of movement and reactions required. The core group working intensively together was a vivid contrast to many of the congress discussions, which broke down into shouting matches. And there was the last minute arrival of Stokley Carmichael, pinpointing the alienation of London's black community from the congress itself. Since at this time there were no "feminist issues" as such, my very participation was something of a vague anomaly. The conventions of intellectual address presume a man's point of view. I would not presume to the contrary to present "a woman's point of view." Rather, a personal view. My inclusion in the congress as a woman only meant my experience must be exceptional—but the fact of its particularity and disparity served to illustrate and define the constructs and expectations of male culture admitting a female exception. The performance participants became aware of this.

As **Round House** progressed I decided to show "Fuses" within the context of the performance. Joe Berke, Ronnie Laing, and the lawyer for the congress called a sudden meeting with me outside by the railroad tracks. The lawyer said I could show the film, they did not want to prevent it...but they could not come to my defense, that I must be prepared to go to jail! Joe and Michael Kustow thought of a way around this: entrance would be by "membership," tickets would have to be purchased in advance. A dozen people had to run around London penciling in this addenda to the posters. Even after this ploy the lawyer repeated his advice.

There was no reason why the film which I considered a sorely needed reference to dismantling the structures of rationalized power—"de-mystified" or not—in a clear imaging of erotic intimacy—the farthest point from pornography—should be offered at the risk of my ending up in a London prison. But I decided it was a silly and unlikely issue, that I would simply project the film as part of the visual media with no further discussion.

During these weeks Michael Kustow and Joe Berke were unstinting in their help and efforts. Michael was in the core group; a writer, theater director, and editor of a theater journal, he was able to work on publicity, find technical help, and actively gather textual material from the seminars and discussions. Friends of the participants arrived to help with locating and hauling materials; the composer Ron Geesin, filmmaker Steve Dwoskin, Barbara and John Lathem, poet Bob Cobbing, photographer Jennifer Pike, all provided special help. Susan Sherman and

Jerry Rothenberg arrived at the congress to give poetry readings, and their appreciation kept me on keel as well.

The core group's developing closeness spread into the actions of the mass group. We were evolving not simply a "performance," but a microcosm of creative inter-relations. Despite harassment and shortness of time, we were discovering a concrete clarification of the actual social situation, and a full self-identity within a group process.

The night of the performance a rainstorm made it necessary to cut out "the rope journey" (leading the audience in by small units). Five hundred people settled themselves in a huge semi-circle; the atmosphere was testy, aggressive, or passive during **Round House.** Our final "rescue" by the mass group—piling us into the cart—was a relief from heckling and catcalls. As we were trundled away in a heap Jean muttered through the refuse: "Carolee, I'm glad you had the foresight to get us out of here."... The band, The Social Deviants, plugged in their amplifiers and began to play; finally the audience got up and danced in the debris.

The events at the Round House were indeed an impetus to shift directions. The next works would turn the environment and movement relations directly over to the audience. Later, in 1970, while directing another work here my intentions would be altered, when my final audience-activated work would be swept away in a sabotage of Acid punch.*

The Round House itself sits high on its hill at the edges intersecting three vivid districts of London: the northern end of Camden Town's narrow row houses—a working class section; the bottom reach of Hampstead Hill, leading up to tree-lined streets and Georgian houses long associated with its history of scholars, artists, and "liberals"; and the forked bridge leading west to Primrose Hill, mystically imbued, the highest point in London. In 1967 Arnold Wesker had taken on this abandoned space as a home for his theater group, and oversaw a restaurant, a bar, a gallery of sorts, community events and incredible rock concerts, all approved by the London Council, saving the Round House from ruin.

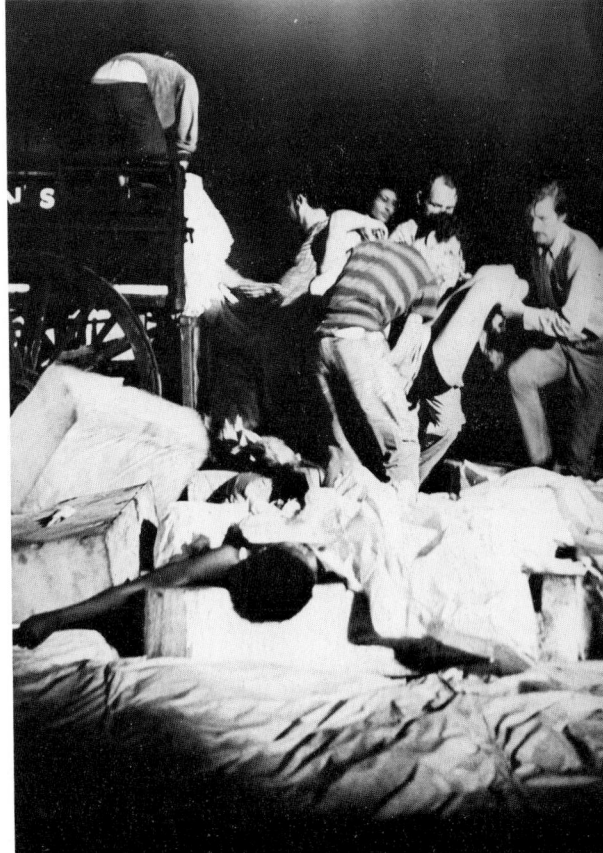

Michael Broome

*See: "Play Power in London," Cott, Jonathan, Rolling Stone, March 19, 1970.

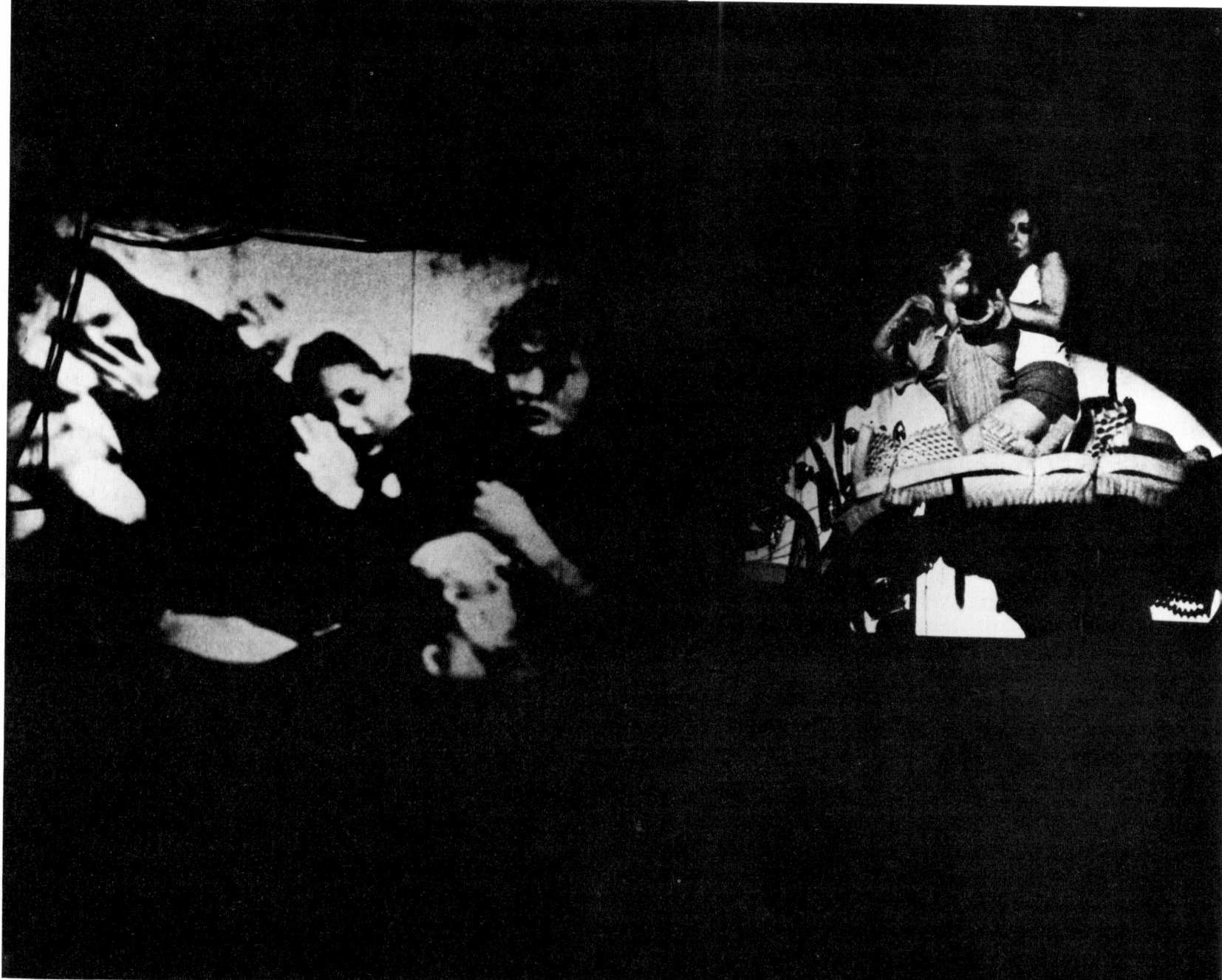

Shunk-Kender

NIGHT CRAWLERS

September 8 1967 Expo 67 Pavillon de la Jeunesse, Montreal

When I lived in Vermont we crossed recrossed the vague borders for nights of square dancing in Canada. Vermont and Quebec met at the edges of farm land where international borders are chewed over by grazing cows. A fish from the northern estuary may be hooked on a line by wriggling rampants de la nuit, or three miles along succumb with a night crawler in its mouth. Frame houses, trailers down the road—perhaps the vestigal territory of native americans who hang out a notice "Worms." Now we were to cross the border as performers invited to the Pavillon de la Jeunesse—organized by young French artists as an alternative to theater and media presented by official governments at Expo '67. La Jeunesse staff advised me that every bit of material transported for the performance must be recorded by them in advance to provide official papers to customs officers and border police searching for draft resisters and political stuff. We looked suspicious enough: Jim Tenney, Mitsou Naslednikov, myself in the old station wagon stuffed with six bales of polyurethene foam, films, tapes, ropes, food, bedding, our cat Kitch hidden under the front seat, and a three foot mound of pink foam rising from the top of the '52 Plymouth.

SCORE

In the darkened circular performance area Mitsou and I, dressed in ungainly overalls, move through the audience making physical contact with each person. We crawl across laps, stand balanced on shoulders, slip down knees; they are immediately engaged in helping or resisting us, watching their neighbor, wondering what contact we might make with them next. The pockets of our overalls are stuffed with candies, gum and fruit—everyone is offered a little something to eat. Because the audience is bilingual we speak to them and to each other in both French and English: May I stand on you? Would you pass this fruit?... Help me across. They quickly respond to us in French and English.

Black out.
Mitsou and I appear in front of a large screen of white paper in the light of the film "Red News." We attack the flashing images with brushes loaded with red and white paint. (The movement is based on part of **Ghost Rev.**) She strokes vertical forms and I circular ones of the film imagery. The screen is composed of multiple layers and we rip them open, continuing to paint, moving back and forth in front of the screen.

"Red News" concludes with a speedway race, sudden collisions in which cars burst into flames and rocket off the track. As this imagery occurs the tremendous noise of an automobile engine is heard and Jim drives a Volkswagon directly into the performance area. Mitsou rips the painted layers of screen down to a clear surface. The film "Viet-Flakes" begins with its sound collage. Jim emerges from the car, climbs onto the roof which is covered with large thick sheets of pink polyurethene foam. I come to the front of

Notes from then and now:
to make contact through us   may contact themselves   not telling audience what to do but where openings can be taken in on and beyond the event (shift the dangerous blocking) from where imagery evocation makes concrete link to actions breaking into certain barriers   putting that sudden awareness into actual time an inevitable expression of communality reorganize rage violence guilt   not atomized   moving together towards unknown qualities undefined unproscribed   why the responses could be so full   not agress the audience   some other performance groups put me off   even their sensitivity exercises competitive   foolish idealization loses the track   we were crazy and shrewd   the craziness worth attention of government "research"   middle class fodder identified with the victims this time enough anxiety to the right clawing in our mail   slipping through our telephones and formal requests for notification of our "performances" (government stationery) realizing the direction my work was going

implication of another dimension to share the privilege and practical physical knowledge "Night Crawlers"/"Rampants de la Nuit" ironic title in Canada the refuge for thousands of draft resisters "Rampants de la Nuit" and "Thames Crawling" titles about displacement relocating combining complete break the disillusionment of prolonged war student strikes of '69 200 colleges close down Bruce saying a contact of a shaping nature juxtaposed to the institutionalization of information sensuality and cruelty simultaneously in film of atrocities and the movement of Jim and me produced a crisis of identification participation of the audience a covenent sensitivity to be enacted first of the series merging perceptual field fulfillment of a direction implicit in previous work now expored two years human body/object equivalence human body/environment equivalence insistence on organic quality car expands breathes with bodies (contrast to Vostell's hard objects in confrontation material aspect to material aspect or Yvonne's body-as-object concern for objectness of the body) life requiring action our passivity enforced to realize parameters of the action psychological and physical response direction the work or event has to go interior dynamic releases itself functional statement any art work will be interpreted believability is invited physical experience sensory permission discoveries made between performers extended to include the audience.

1967-77

the car and climb up to join him. Mitsou moves to the side of the car and begins to pull out bales and bales of polyurethene foam; she continues unstuffing the car and filling the performance space as Jim and I develop contact improvisation on the body of the car.

Standing on top of the car, he unhooks my overalls and pulls them down. We begin a series of contact exchanges, balancing on the surfaces of the automobile illuminated within the shifting Vietnam atrocity images: turning, pushing, holding, shifting our weight in a continual series of embraces and separations. Our motions edge us down over the front of the car, finally sinking into the floor in the foam.

·At the conclusion of the film we lie exhausted on the floor. The overhead lights are raised dimly and flicker. Five friends in the audience have exited and return carrying pink cotton candy sticks from the fair ground. Mitsou, Jim and I go to the audience and choose a person to carry into the central spread of foam. We ask each person in French and English, "May I carry you?" Sometimes Mitsou and I crawl with our arms around a man too heavy to lift. When the first people are brought to the center we then ask them to go and bring another person back with them. In this way an unbroken relay unfolds. People who at first may have refused to leave their seats now consent to join the others. The distribution of cotton candy continues to the audience in the foam. A tape collage of animal sounds is mixed with the Viet-Flakes tape; the lights continue to flicker dimly. The participants now begin to spontaneously construct and arrange the foam piles.

Jim drives the car out of the room and the three of us go into the sound and lighting booth; the participants discover the elements in the room which were not used in performance. There are three levels of rope pulleys on which foam sheets may be rigged to fill overhead space with moving shapes. There are cans of paints and brushes in front of the paper screens. When the first screen is painted and torn down they discover another with the word **PROCEED** painted there. They "proceed" through about a dozen layers of papers, groups painting cooperatively or singly.

In the sound and lighting booth we can modulate the scale of audience activity: when someone gets out of control, rolling, leaping in the foam, tossing other people over, we create a black out, increase the volume of the tapes. When a group begins to build and construct in the space we increase available light. Our performance began at nine p.m.; at ten-thirty we were ready to leave.

Mitsou and I jump into a fountain and swim until the police call us out. At midnight we return to the Pavillon: the "audience" remains! Some are asleep in each other's arms, others have built and rebuilt mounds and structures on the pulleys. The walls are painted in arabesques, with figures and animals, poems and slogans. The following day the Expo staff tells us people stayed through the night. We see lumps of the pink foam high on a flag pole, floating in a moat, stuffed in corners of the Media pavilion, circling the shoulders of a monumental female statue from Poland...

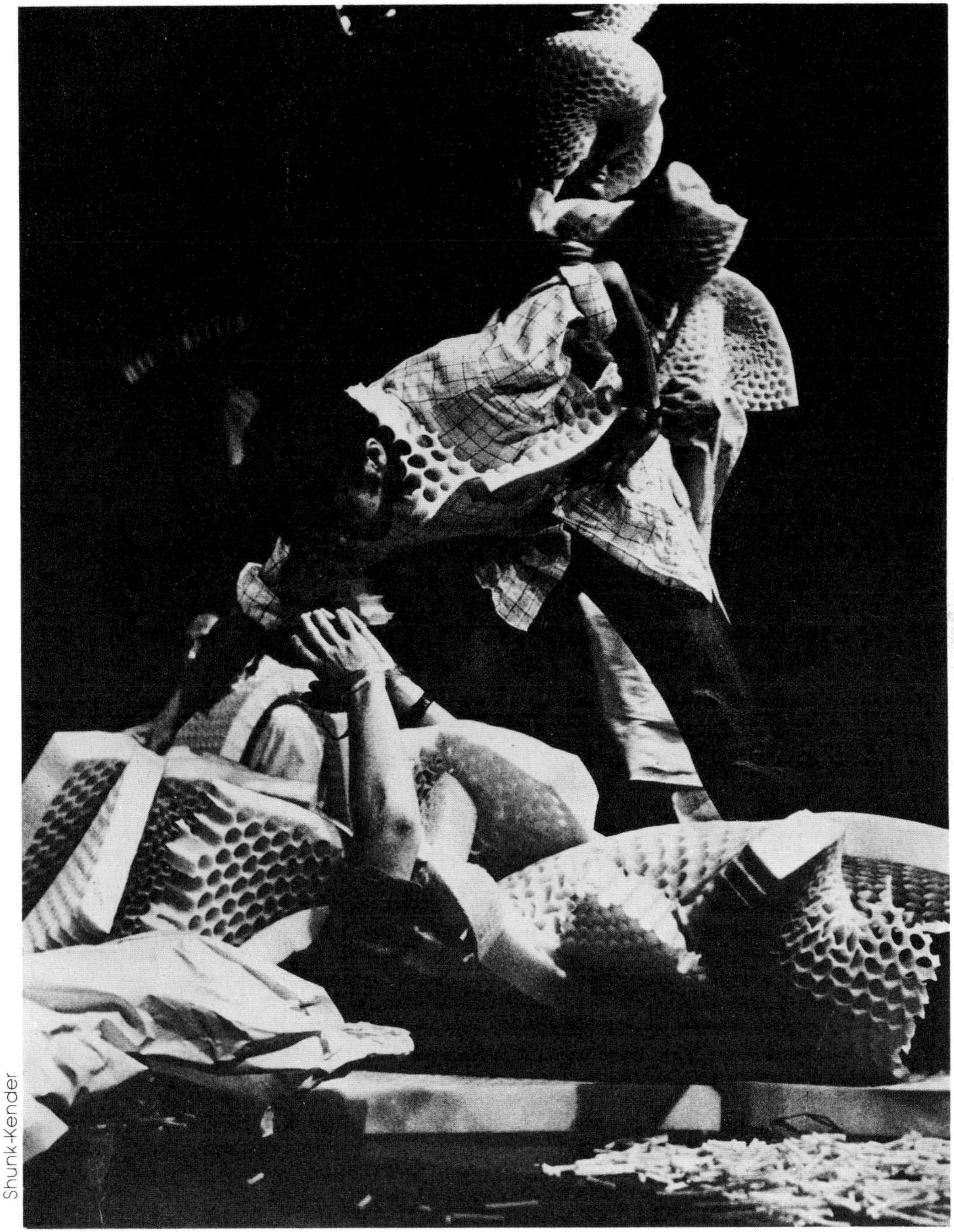

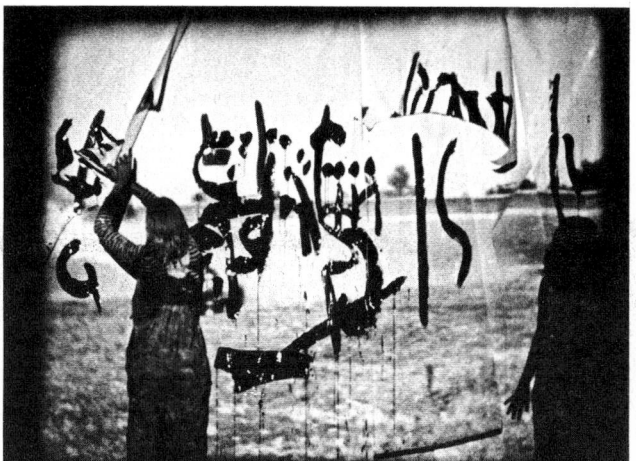

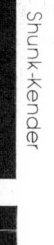

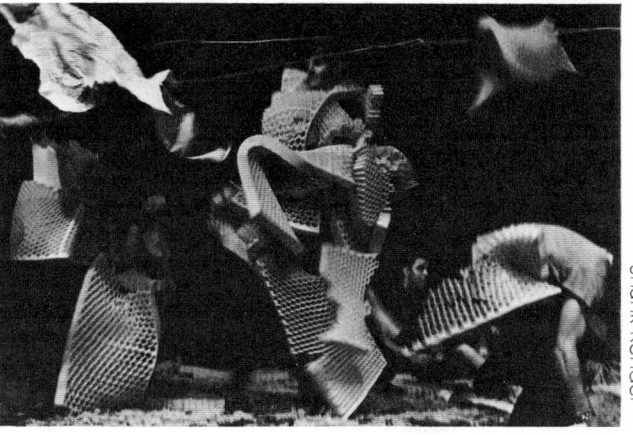

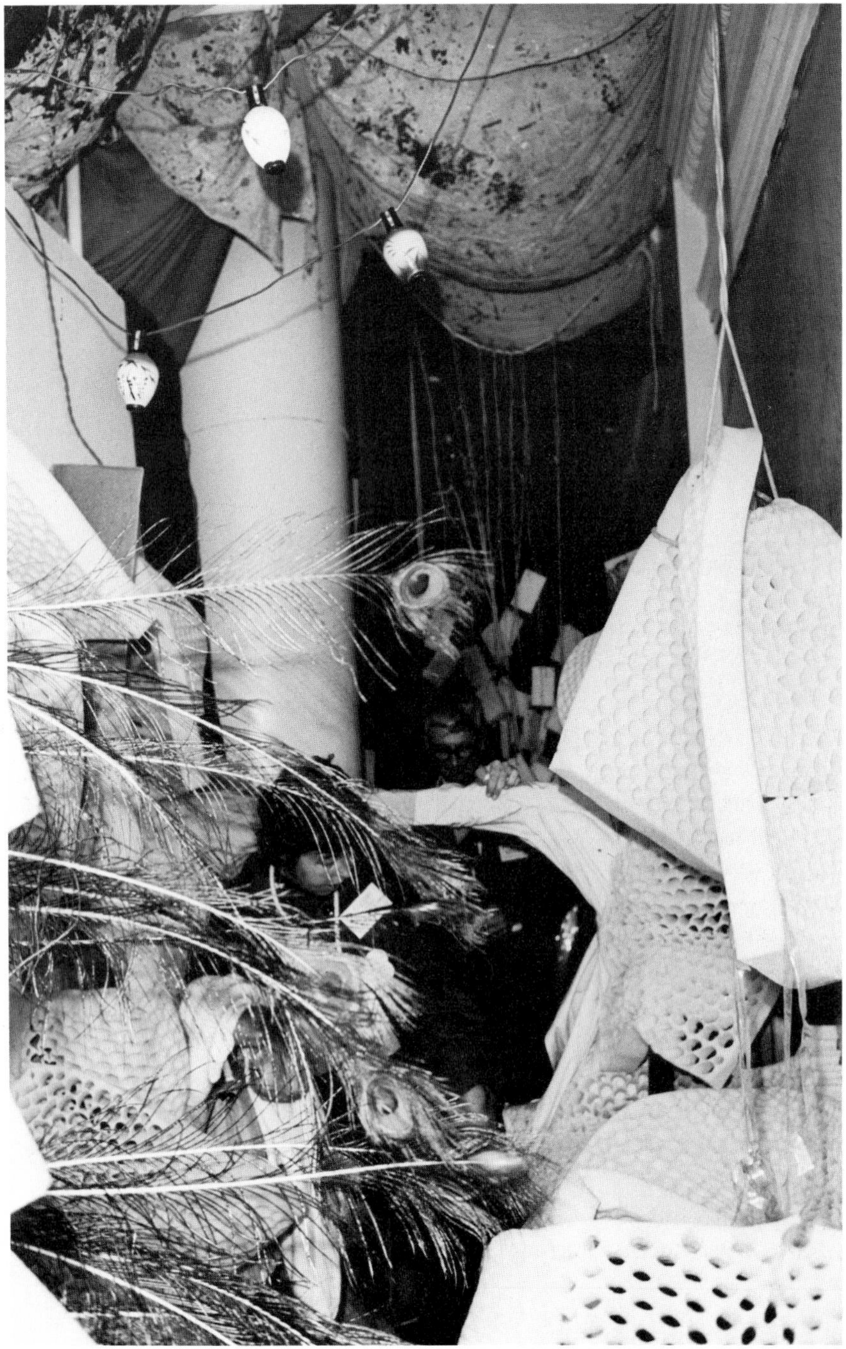

Peter Moore

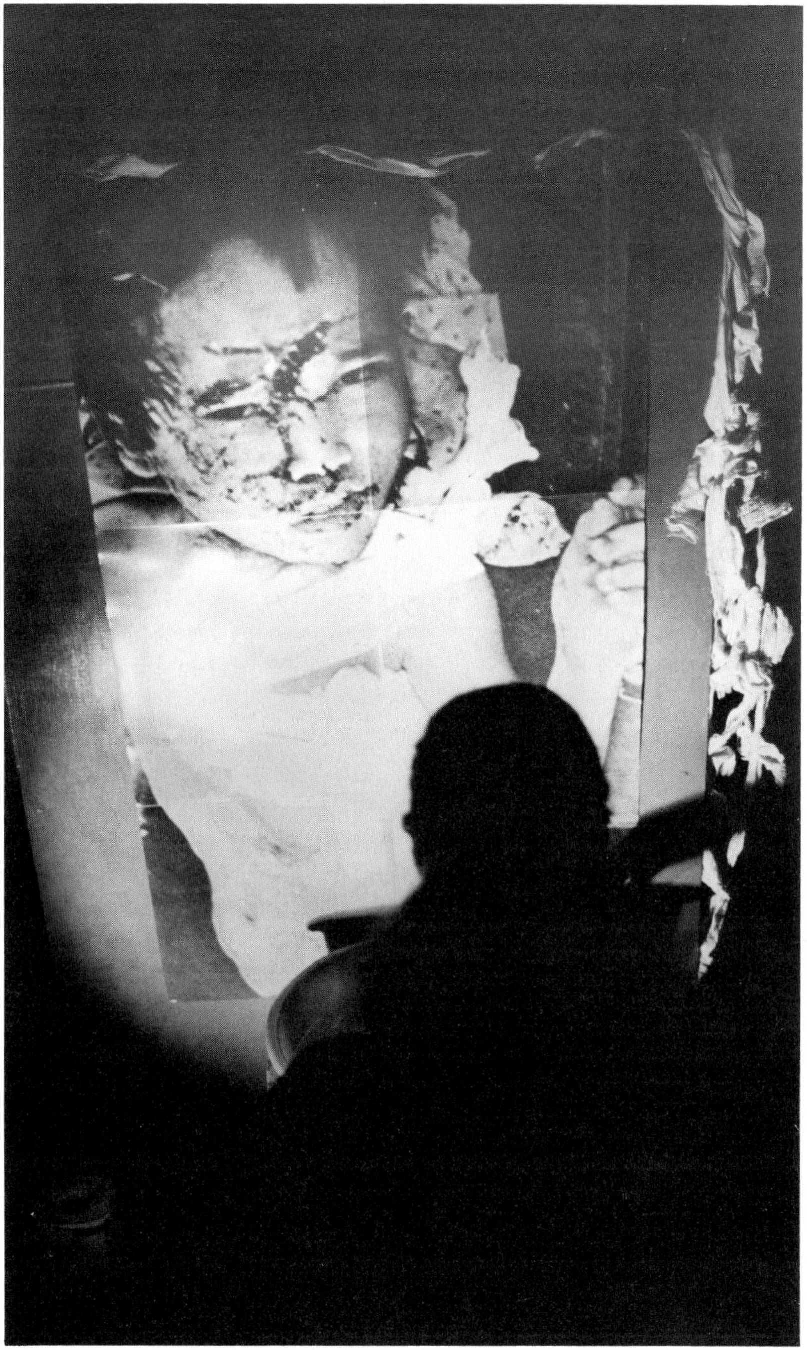

Peter Moore

An environmental work, **Ordeals** took its labyrinthian form after a conference of architects asked Al Carmines and Lawrence Kornfeld if they would present information on new environmental ideas in the arts. The "idea" became an individual and collaborative event which would activate all the very unexpected and complex areas of Judson Church itself. For a long time I had harbored a plan for a "journey" piece through the Church. Carmines, Bici Hendricks (Forbes), and Kornfeld took various sections of the church, altogether involving seventy-two collaborators and performers. My environmental areas were two: the basement gym (where the first Judson concerts had been given before we overran the sanctuary) and a far aisle running the length of the meeting hall. It was a friendly and frantic cooperation in which we all helped one another with materials, sequences, and assistants. Unfortunately, in the welter of efforts to organize my environment I never saw the other events to which my audience was also subjected.

Vietnam was our theme and I remember that Bici had organized a hospital, that I received my participants sometimes bandaged and heavily painted with mercurochrome, and that on leaving my foam area they had to obtain a medical certificate in a dressing room near the final exit door.

Upstairs I constructed a torture tunnel into which each architect was pushed as they exited from the previous "ordeal" area. The tunnel was covered in black cloth; behind these cloths were electric fans blowing through slits in the fabric onto lines of wet sponges which slapped at intervals on the person walking through. Long feathers tapped their faces and bodies; it was utterly dark and boards at various angles obstructed their passage. As they advanced down the tunnel blue lights flashed around them; ahead were huge illuminated slides of Vietnam atrocity images. Old raw fish hung overhead.

When they started down the stairs to the gym, blinding lights were flashed into their eyes. Assistants grabbed them, carrying the women, dragging the men, into the dark sea of polyurethene foam. In the face of the implied violence and spatial disorientation, the participants became extremely sensitive to the tactile material around them and began to touch and handle one another. Others struggled for footing or to sense bodies already moving in the foam (or asleep— one architect was found wrapped in foam and snoring after the church had closed).

TWO ENVIRONMENTS
1.ORDEALS

29 August 1967 Judson Church NY

2. DIVISIONS AND RUBBLE

October 19 1967 Judson Gallery NY

```
              12 EVENINGS OF MANIPULATIONS
              JUDSON GALLERY
              239 THOMPSON STREET
              4-7 P.M.

THURS. OCT. 5  RALPH ORTIZ   ( DESTRUCTION ROOM )
FRI. OCT. 6  BICI HENDRICKS  ( DETERIORATIONS )
SAT. OCT 7  JEAN TOCHE  ( ART EXPERIMENTS IN SENSORY DEPRIVATION )
SUN. OCT 8  ALLAN KAPROW  ( REARRANGEMENT )
THURS. OCT 12  AL HANSEN  (              )
FRI. OCT. 13  GEOFFREY HENDRICKS  ( SKY/CHANGE )
SAT. OCT. 14  MALCOLM GOLDSTEIN  ( STATE OF THE NATION )
SUN. OCT. 15  STEVE ROSE  ( ART DEMONSTRATION; HEAVY YOGA )
THURS. OCT. 19  CAROLEE SCHNEEMANN  ( DIVISIONS & RUBBLE )
FRI. OCT. 20  LIL PICARD  ( CONSTRUCTION-DESTRUCTION-CONSTRUCTION )
SAT. OCT. 21  KATE MILLETT  ( NO )
SUN. OCT. 22  PHILIP CORNER
              FRED LIEBERMAN
              CHARLOTTE MOORMAN
              YOKO ONO
              NAM JUNE PAIK  ( SOFT TRANSFORMATIONS )
              THOMAS SCHMIT
              KEN WARNER
```

Basic image: An environment which people will have to destroy to enter, to move in it: means of action altering action / means of perception altering perception. An exposed process. . . . Any materials left from previous manipulations could be incorporated. A discomforting labyrinth, cubicles, closures all through it, of paper or fabric which participants would first have to cut and tear their way through. Grim, dark and dirty. At first points of entrance, flashing slides seen through networks of remaining cloth/paper enclosures. Focus becoming clearer as subsequent cloths are torn away. A turn to a group of false doors, pushed, banged open. Those three words I wanted, thought well that's a start (or an end?), let's not forget "by their garbage you shall know them". . . not having a prescribed beginning it would have no defined end—that appealed to me. I was hoping for an undefined irritable sort of destructiveness enacting/transforming the environment by its own nature, but the people were thoughtful, quiet, slowly cutting, carefully pushing, avoiding the floor switch which shot off the photos (finally plugged the fans in directly), tapes of crying cats.

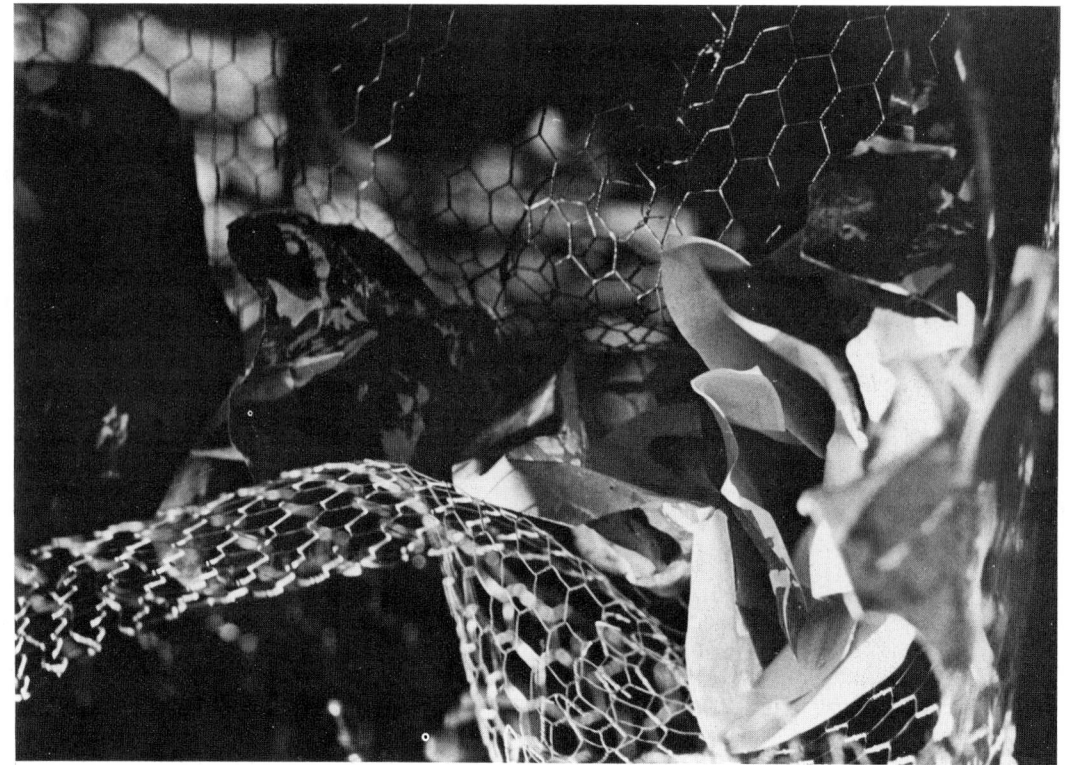

A rehearsal or movement event from which I hoped to discover an image to carry the central visual metaphor of **Illinois Central.**

I invited Gideon Bachmann to film the sequence in 16mm, and Peter Moore, Michael Benedikt, and Fred McDarrah to shoot stills. They would "document" the event in exchange for prints of the image I hoped to find.

I shredded a roll of white printer's paper and filled a bucket with wall paper paste and molasses. My intention was not simply to collage my body (as an object), but to enact movement so that the collage image would be active, found, not pre-determined or posed. When I had covered myself with glue I ran back and forth around the pile of papers until the momentum of the runs provoked a fall into it. Once there I rolled heavily to attach the papers to my body in random shape and proportion.

Standing up led to an impulse to fly. I stood on three iron steps leading from the loft to the fire-escape, my arms moving up and down like wings until I "took off" in a flying-run down the steps. The figure poised on the steps, the sense of elevation and lightly attached papers produced a propulsion, an alighting.

Six years later I was searching in a high library shelf for stillife reproductions. An old Art News Annual (1960) toppled down, falling open to an image of "Cretan Toreador." The **Illinois Central** running image is a double to this figure.

BODY COLLAGE

December 20 1967 NY

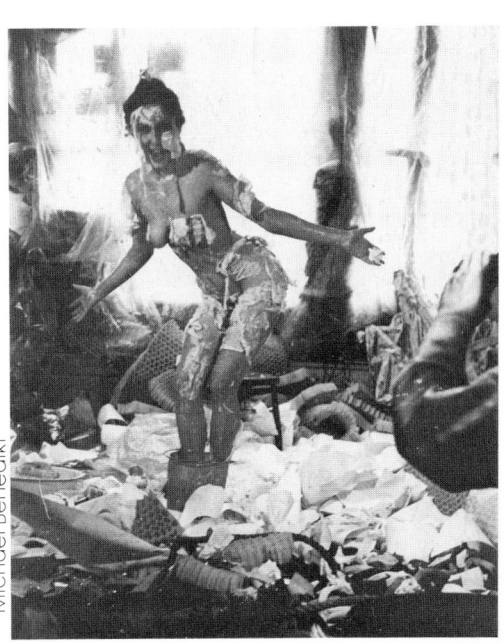

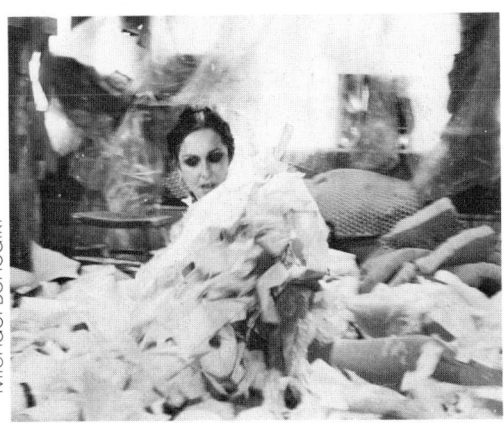

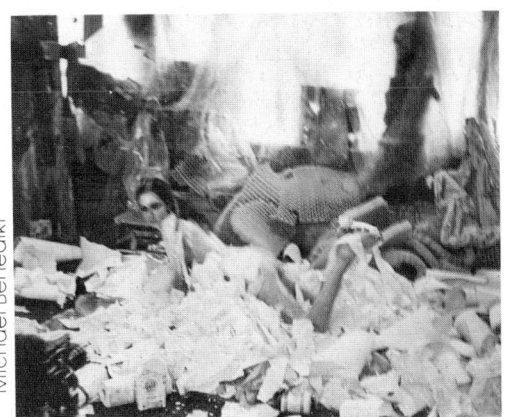

Michael Benedikt

Michael Benedikt

Michael Benedikt

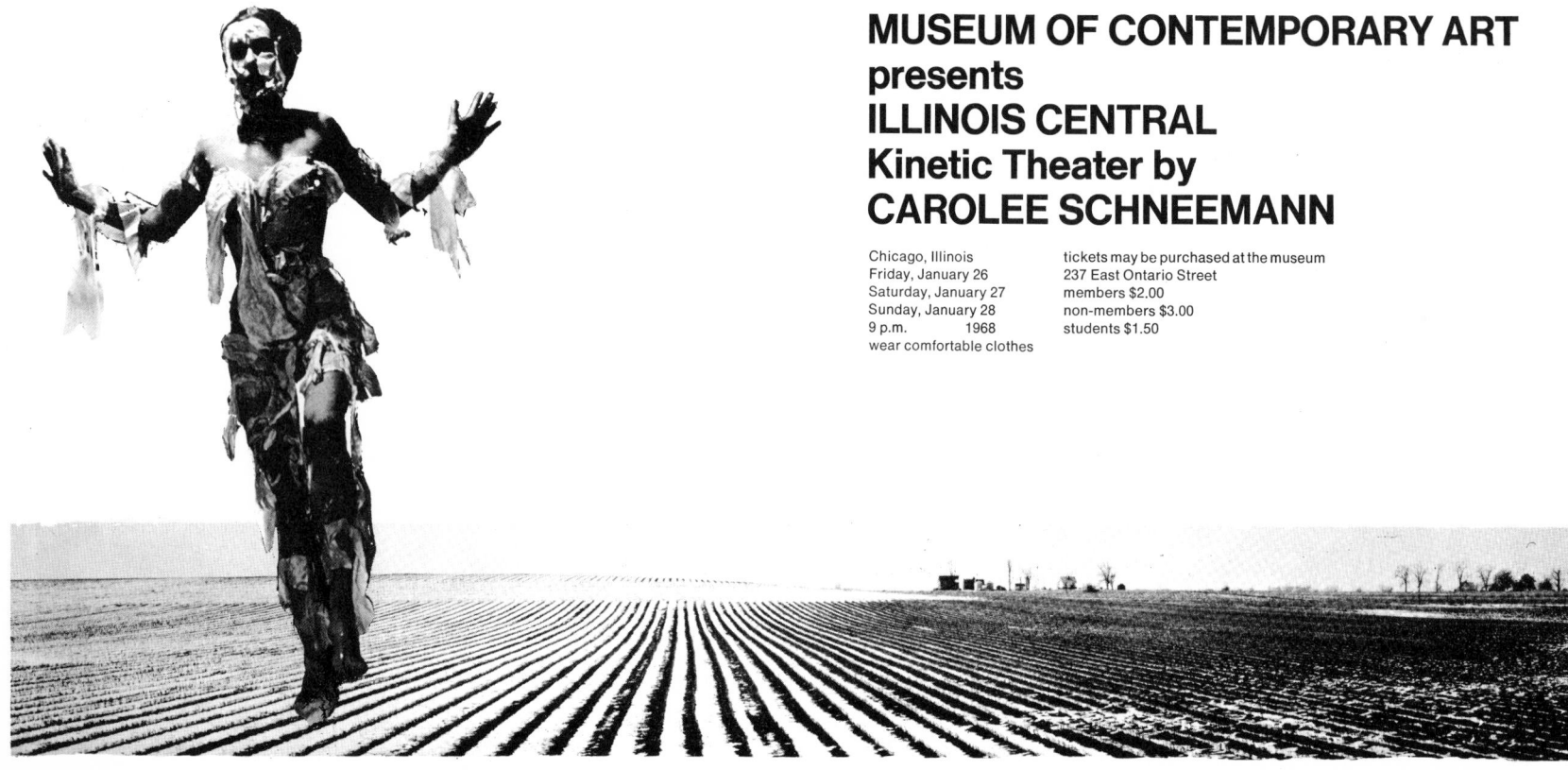

MUSEUM OF CONTEMPORARY ART
presents
ILLINOIS CENTRAL
Kinetic Theater by
CAROLEE SCHNEEMANN

Chicago, Illinois
Friday, January 26
Saturday, January 27
Sunday, January 28
9 p.m.   1968
wear comfortable clothes

tickets may be purchased at the museum
237 East Ontario Street
members $2.00
non-members $3.00
students $1.50

"Body Collage" photo by Fred W. McDarrah   Montage by C.S.   Midwest Landscape #34 photo by Art Sinsabaugh
courtesy of The Village Voice   Collection Museum of Modern Art

I think of this work as an exploded canvas, units of rapidly changing clusters. A flow of energy which makes an active audience inevitable and necessary—not to mimic the performance but to absorb relations within the space and between one another—to be correspondent to the materials and imagery, grasping a conscious and realizable wish to replace the performers with themselves.

The central imagery of this work is The Tree; the absence of the tree as characteristic of Mid West landscape and the transformation of the tree into paper. Our paper environment is in material contrast to the photographic landscape environment (landscape as dream territory (skin) meanders into view holds still we measure distances what is seen a scene wrapped around the body).

From the prairies Native Americans had been driven West; the high buffalo grass gradually cleared for roads, homesteads, farming. Tree planting became a measure of domestic and agricultural order: shelterbelts, wind barriers, water retention, erosion protection. Decades later the agri-business expanded acres of corn, soy beans and wheat; the trees once marking the boundaries of small farms were cut down as if an effluvium, inviting soil erosion, floods, destroying natural cover, the ecology of wild life. The destruction of the intensive, traditional farming in Vietnam meant the ruin of a coherent agricultural system, defoliation, the diabolical intention of "paving over the jungle with concrete."

The intimate and at times violent imagery is anchored in a tension of contrasting focal planes linking the exposed Illinois landscape to the devastation of Vietnam. If there was a mythic association between human body and tree, there was as well a tactile and sensory extension of flesh into paper—maleable, expressive, sculptural. The scrap paper we used in Chicago was bales of cancelled bank checks—Illinois trade representing millions of dollars—completely shredded. The absence of a dominant foreground, a landscape of frontal physical expanse (which is where I decided in 1960 that "painting is dead"), the openness an implication of visual paradox.

Because of the metaphoric political content—overriding language, polemic, propaganda, abstraction—I could never determine whether the difficulties in producing this work, and its reception, were random or somehow inevitable, coming at a time when even the length of people's hair was taken as evidence of their politics. The difficulties were extraordinary, though Illinois Central was the

ILLINOIS CENTRAL

January 26 27 28 1968 Museum of Contemporary Art Chicago

Illinois Central Transposed
February 20 1968 SUNY Stony Brook L.I.

March 8 1968 Brooklyn Academy of Music

March 16 1968 SUNY Rochester

March 18 1968 SUNY Buffalo, Spring Arts Festival

March 26 1968 SUNY Nasseau L.I.

16 March 1969 The Ark Boston

most extensively performed of my theater pieces. In the course of five months it was adapted to six different spaces and realized with six different groups of performers and technicians: originally for the Chicago Museum of Contemporary Art, then for John Brockman's Intermedia '68 tour.

The sound and visual elements had to do with precise tensions in scale—what they were as sources in themselves, what they meant in juxtaposition, and their triggering effect binding multiple perceptions. Slides were planned in collaboration with Art Sinsabaugh, whose photographs of Illinois horizons and prairies had introduced a previously ignored scale, one which in series suggested a continuous image. I envisioned a wrap-around span of touching horizon lines formed by multiple slides of landscape—an unbroken line which could shift the landscape details to include distanced visual minutiae which characterize the open Mid West horizon—trains, isolated farms, silos. Sinsabaugh's slide environment was projected along two walls half-surrounding the audience uninterrupted across 160°. He programmed five second slide projections so a moving panorama would be created with varying rhythms, according to the density of detail coordinated in the recurrent and simultaneous slides. To the left on the central area, at intervals, a single tree was projected—an image I'd specified to cue movement sequences.

The film "Viet-Flakes" intermittently projected onto the slide panorama; a tape of the Illinois Hog Market report; the rapid vertical movements of the performers cutting into the huge open performance space: these were the essential and divergent units. And finally the complete exposure of the body, being naked*, being covered in glue, collaged with paper, remnant of tree, becoming ourselves "tree."

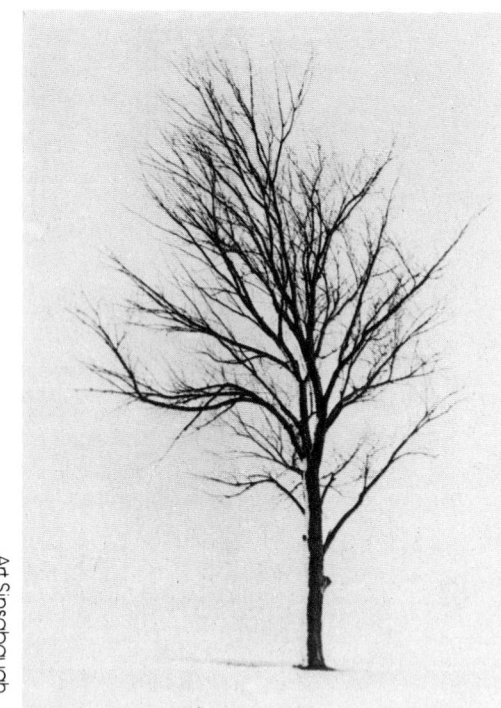

Art Sinsabaugh

The sound tapes and the slides are not auxilary to the movement; the performance movement is an extension of the media and its associative range, taken
from specific, actual Illinois environments. The Hog Market Report, for example
was recorded from the Illinois Farm Hour; broadcast daily at noon, it is of vital
importance to the farming communities, reflecting investment structures which
ultimately regulate agricultural practice. That distinctive—and initially incompre-
hensible—rapid droning market reporter's voice recurrs in one's daily life in the
Mid West, an aural motif in the luncheonette, gas station, grocery store, bank. The
speed, musicality and nasal twang of the voice is marvelous as it chants the rise
and fall of commodities, stocks, liquid assets, and the survival or decimation of
the small farm families I knew listening to the radio in their kitchens.

In Chicago there were several false starts in locating a performance space. The
Museum flew me out in advance for several days and I began work in an open
area in conjunction with an exhibit of paper products; I began choreographing
movement lines, designing a lighting and sound system. When I returned later in
January with one week to find and train performers, gather materials and props,
construct in the space, I found the paper corporation representatives had seen

---

*The clothing we wore was comfortable: yellow and orange dyed underwear and the oversize striped overalls.
Had we performed Illinois Central naked it would have seemed peculiarly erotic—inhabitants of an Ingres
Turkish bath fleeing a paper hurricane. (In Meat Joy nudity was appropriate for some rehearsals, and was my
intention for the performance, but the audience's perception of the overall rhythms and interrelations would
have been diverted in natural fascination for each body's particularity. They were seated as close as possible
to us.) The law at this time stated that persons could appear on stage naked without moving—that is, if they
become statues. Movement or physical contact between nude persons was criminal. At the Brooklyn Academy
of Music when the glueing began audience agents provocateurs started yelling "strip! take it off!" Other
audience members yelled to us that police were at the doors, and shouted "Plant, plant! Show your behind or
your badge!"

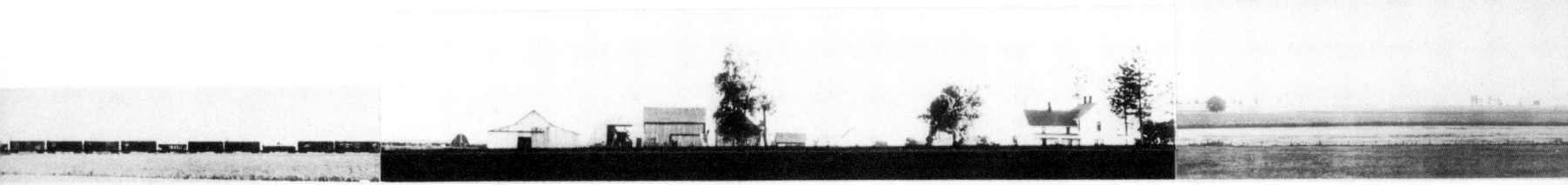

Art Sinsabaugh

preparatory **Body Collage** photographs in the Village Voice and wanted nothing to do with my metaphors enacted in their space with their paper products. Jan van der Marck and David Katzive of the Museum managed to secure the use of an immense filthy abandoned loft—formerly a bakery centrally located on Wells St. By herculean effort this space was cleared, cleaned in two days; lighting, sound, projection equipment was brought in and organized as simultaneously I found and began to rehearse with performers and technicians. After one ecstatic performance we were invaded by a contingent of Chicago Fire Marshals and forced to close down as the audience assembled at the door. Two nights later we managed to perform in a remote and clinical T.V. studio.

At Nasseau College, male students in the audience went berserk over the physical contact between the men (performing): they screamed obscenities, threw basketballs and cups of water at us. Rochester University was less contentious; there a student packed his bags, walking out of his life and into our van to continue the tour with us. Boston was buried under a foot of snow, disasters occurred. We were woken the first morning by a desperate call from New York to one of the performers; the woman he lived with had been raped, their apartment robbed, he had to return immediately. Rushing out to locate a new performer we discovered the tires on our rented van had been slashed. Next day at the Ark, the ten foot lighting/sound/projection deck collapsed, injuring an assistant and ruining several projectors. And there were hectic meetings with Legal Aid, since once again we were advised that plainclothes police would be present to arrest us if there was any nudity. At the Buffalo Arts Festival the audience went wild, carrying their participation in the glue and shredded paper environment through the Commons building.

The devotion, dedication and flexibility of each performance group made it possible to continue, to persist in taking the work fully into its own dimension. And we also had wonderful times. One of the premises of our touring was that we stay together as a group and have time with the people who had invited us. Hotel rooms were refused and we bedded down on sleeping bags and mattresses in the homes of people who wanted to house us. We brought assorted food for the various dietary inclinations of the troup, we cooked and cleaned for our hosts. A network of people helping in each performance situation was built out from this unofficial and personal base. They found rehearsal spaces, located materials, assisted with the complexities of setting up for each performance, and shared their own work and concerns.

For each performance the surrounding walls were collaged with large strips of torn white paper, with layers of crumpled paper piled at the base of the walls, so that the entire area was texturally active and a complete projection surface. As the audience entered a single slide of the bare tree in the snow was visible (there were 2 tree slides 5 1/2 feet high). The sound tape "Trains and Orgasm" was amplified through the speakers, resonating in the space. (The trains are of Illinois Central cars shunting at the Champagne-Urbana station; recorded at 4 a.m. one winter morning, 1960. The "Orgasm" tapes were made in 1964 when I began filming "Fuses" and kept a tape recorder by the bed. "Fuses" of course remained a silent film).

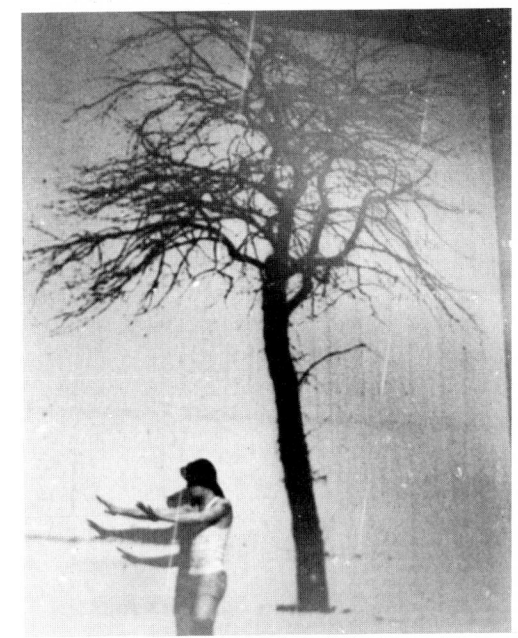

Charlotte Victoria

Art Sinsabaugh

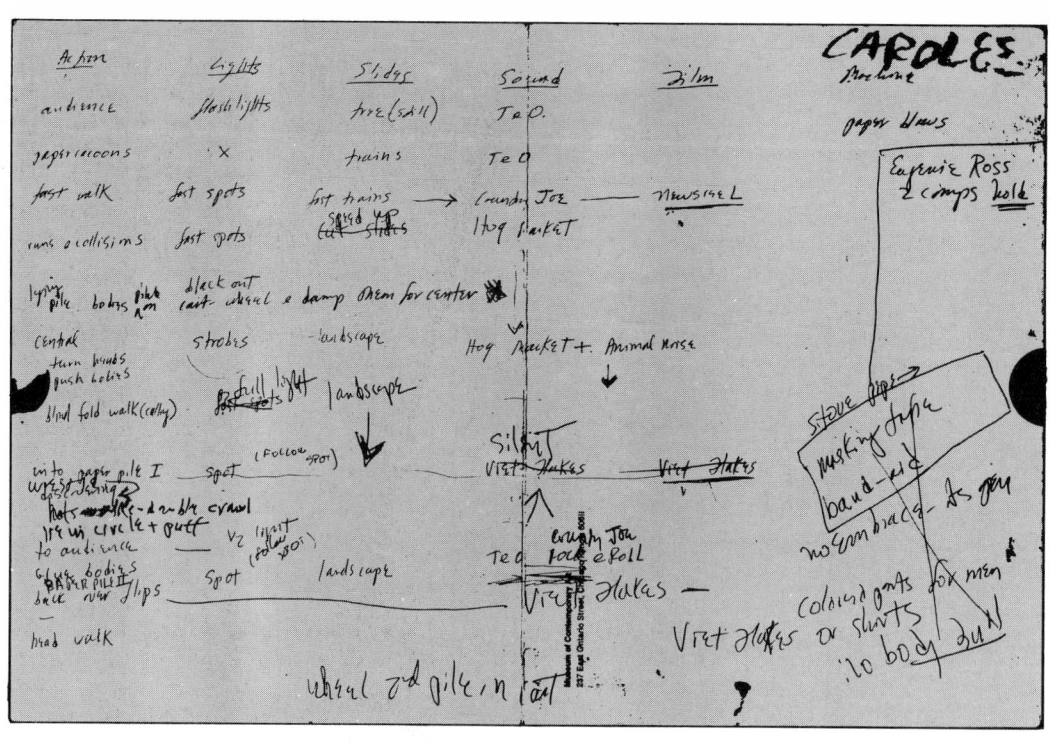

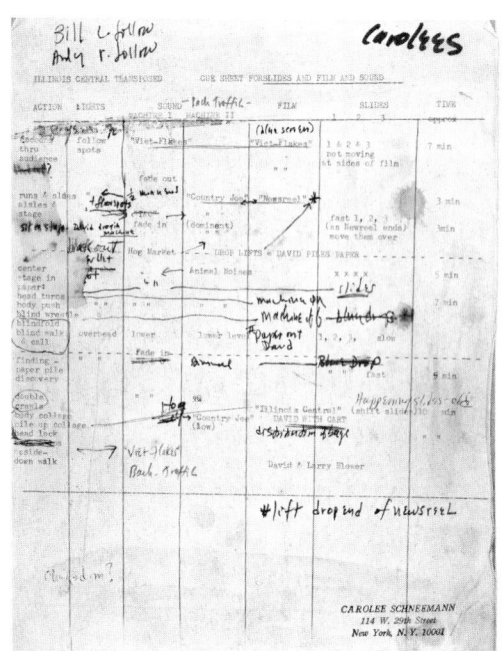

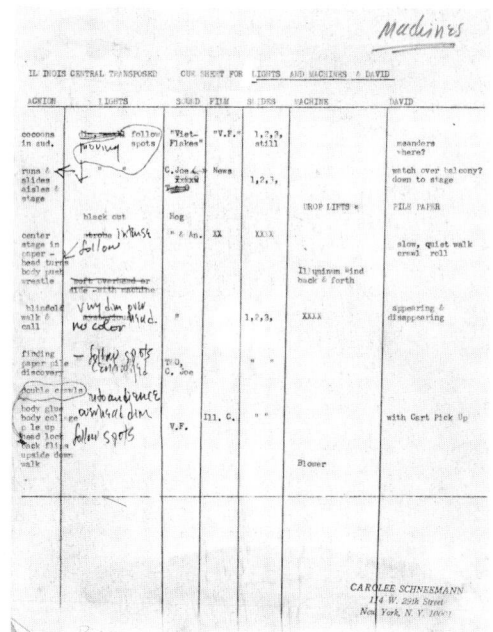

172

SCORE

There is an evident relay of inter-relation and response between the media and performers' actions. Certain parameters of sound, film, slides are subject to improvisatory decisions by technicians responding to actions of the performers, who in turn take sequence cues from changes in the media.

In the darkness the cocoons spread out slowly among the audience. The paper wrappings are tight around the body, with holes only for the eyes and the hands. Frontal vision is limited and the exposed hands function like whiskers, touching the audience, informing us of obstacles as we move in small steps. At some moment each cocoon traverses the light of the projector, centering the tree image on its column of white wrapping.

Technicians simultaneously begin: fast relay with overhead spotlights, the 160 degree span of slides of trains on the horizon of the Illinois plains, the film "Red News", and the sound of Country Joe and the Fish's "Viet-nam Rag"...the cocoons break into a very fast walk, exploding our wrappings. The walking corresponds to geometrical patterns of the overhead lights—determined for all participants by our various beginning positions when the fastwalk is cued. As each moves from directly under a light to directly under another light, that light is activated from "off" to "on." If necessary in the relay of lights, a performer will

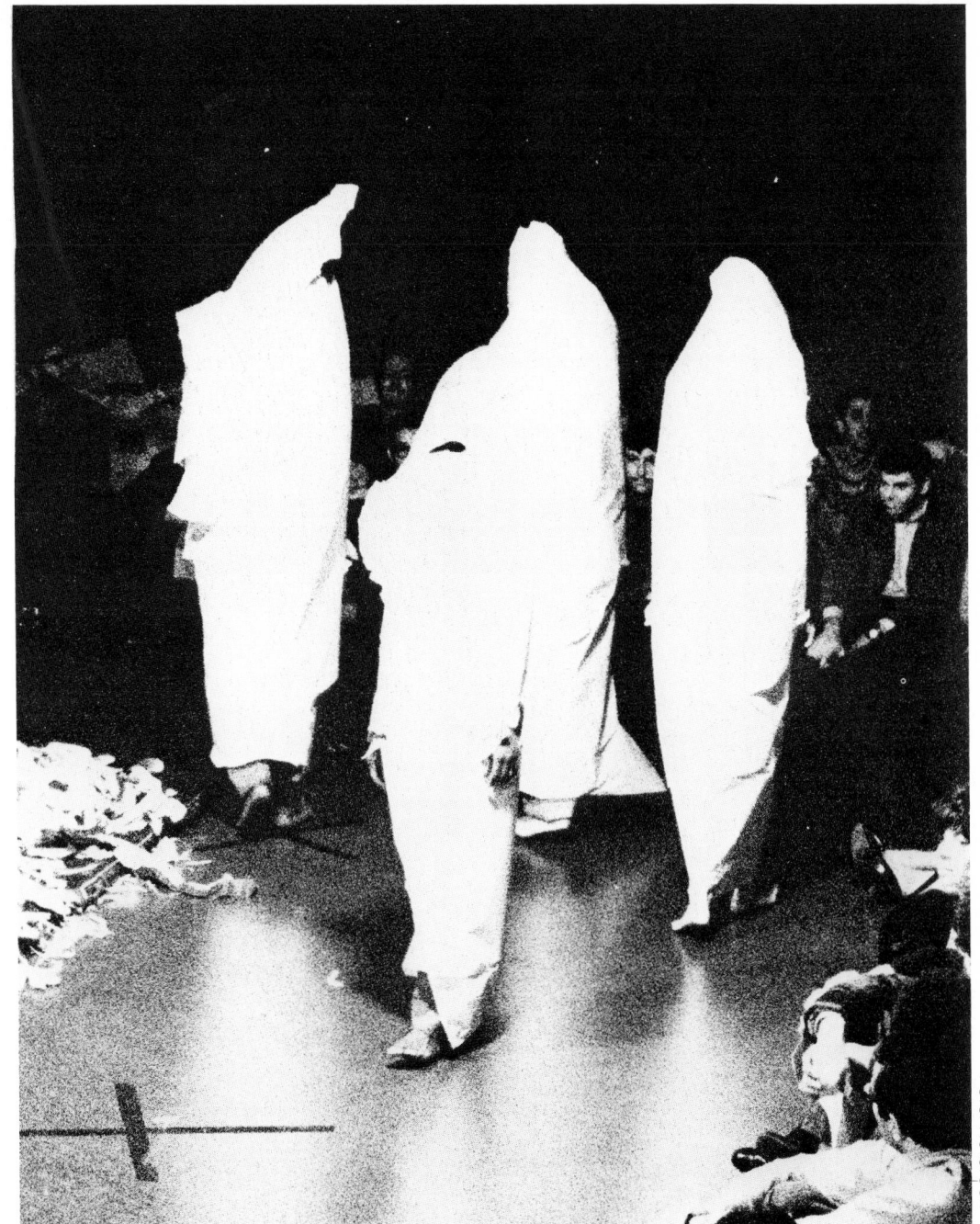

Peter Holbrook

173

raise an arm to signal the lighting response. The fast, fluid walks back and forth across the open space are punctuated by these vertical gestures and the "on"/"off" of the lights. The train slides are rapidly changing on the surrounding wall, and as they accelerate, the tape of the Illinois Hog Market Report fades in. The performers break into full speed runs (much like those developed in **Lateral Splay**). We collide with each other, fall together, rise up, shift direction, run at full speed, collide, fall and rise up—until, at the conclusion of the Hog Market Report, there is a black out.

The performers shed their overalls during the black out. We fall into a heap where we rest on top of one another. Roustabouts—also in striped overalls—wheel in a low cart, shooting flashlight rays over the audience: they drag the performers onto the cart; we stand facing one another, arms encircled, and are wheeled back and forth before the wall of continuous landscape slides. The Hog Market Report fades in, double tracked with animal noises recorded at the Chicago Zoo. The cart is wheeled to the center where strobe lights flash on the circle of performers as they begin a slow exchange of touching and turning each other's body. By exchanges of pushing, turning, yielding, performers gradually slip off the platform onto the floor. The cart is pulled away. We blindfold each other. As each person is blindfolded, she or he stands and slowly walks into the open area, hands extended, turning (to become disoriented).

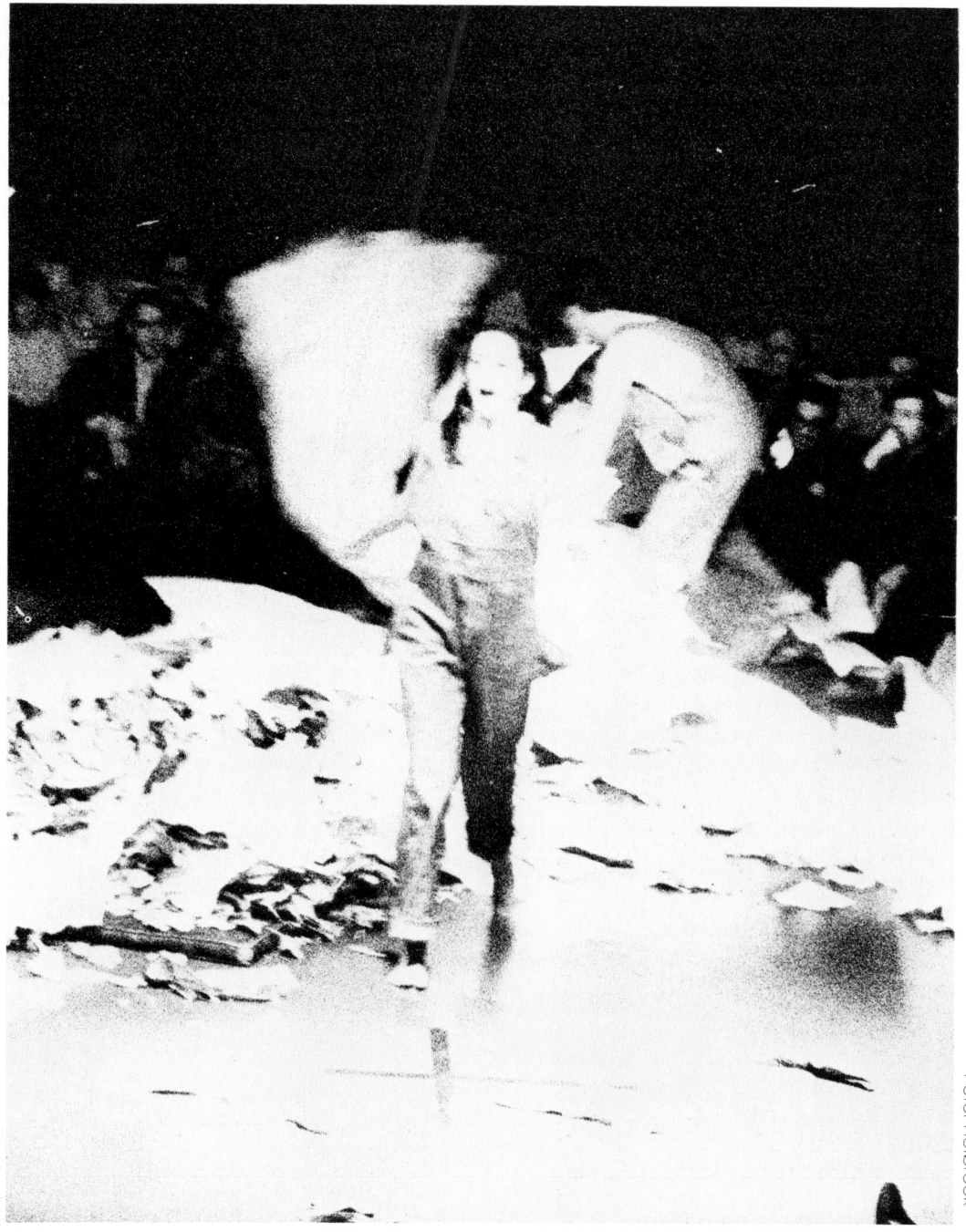

Peter Holbrook

174

Sound out. Full overhead lights on. Performers listen intently as we move through the open space or audience area, concentrating on finding the edge, the far walls. The figures randomly pass in and out of the landscape of slides. One of us eventually calls the name of another. The one called responds with the name of the person calling. By this sole vocal cue we move blindly towards each other. Other pairs continue to exchange names, until all eight of us are moving in uncertain paths towards one another. When the partners reach each other they move to locate the central pile of paper.

The landscape slides continue in programmed rhythms. A spot light centers on the performers seated in the pile of papers as we remove blindfolds from each other. From touching each other's face in removing the blindfold, sequences of contact improvisation begin: an exchange of turning, tipping one another's heads; holding one another's shoulders in a gradual slow wrestling in which each turns from one partner to another (from left to right), letting the push taken rebound slowly into a push given, rising finally onto our knees, back and forth. Balance becomes elastic—vulnerable to falling over into the paper, into the audience.

Once in physical contact with one or more persons of the audience, each performer turns to look among them, asking for a volunteer to join us in the center where the roustabouts are un-

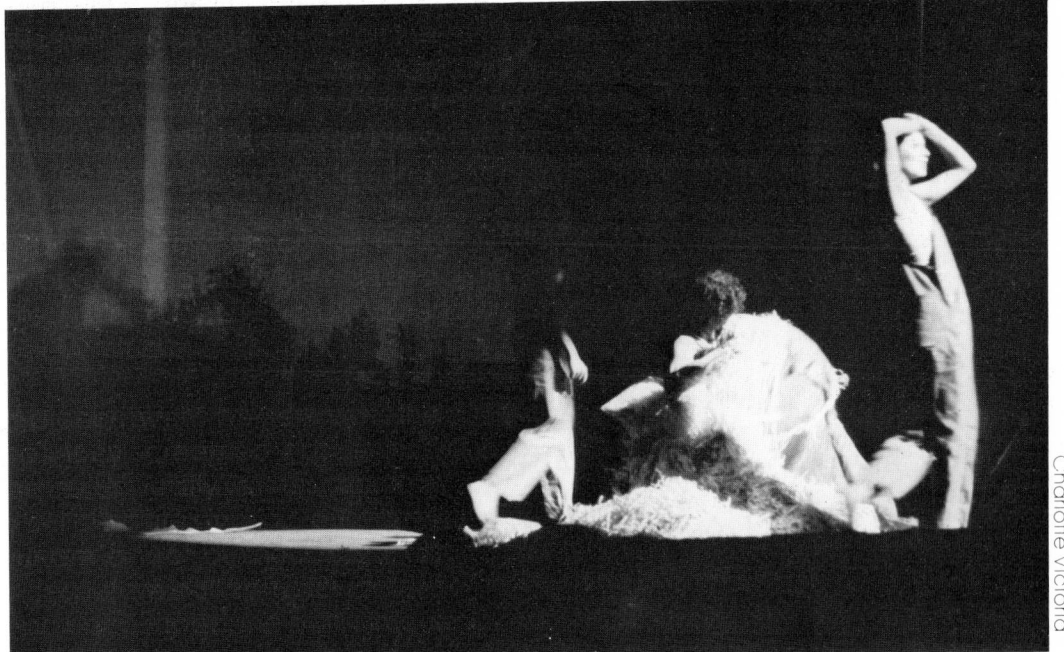

Charlotte Victoria

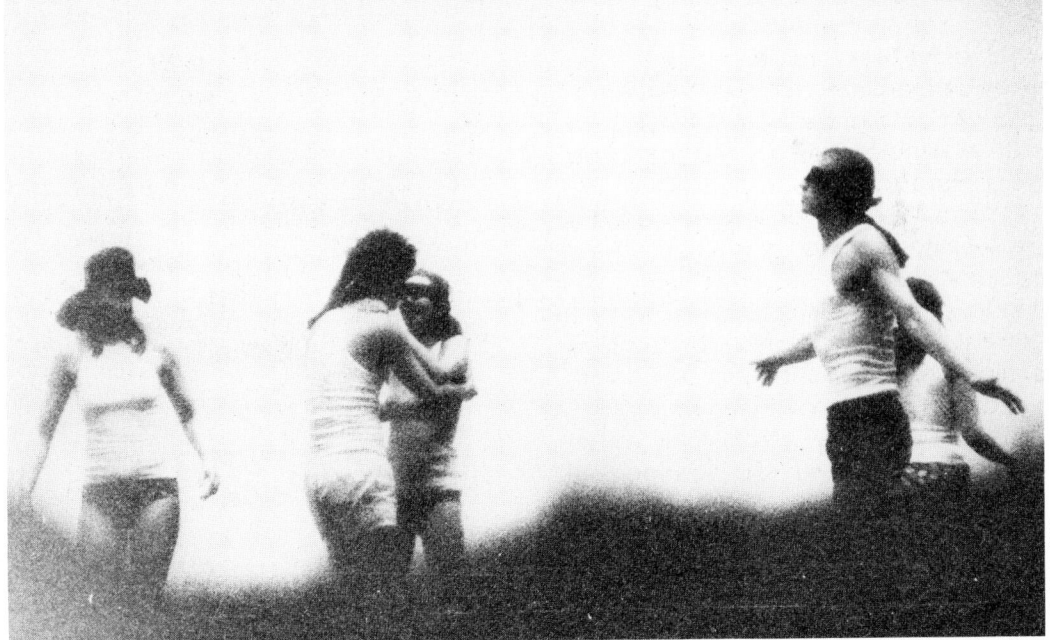

Ted Wester

175

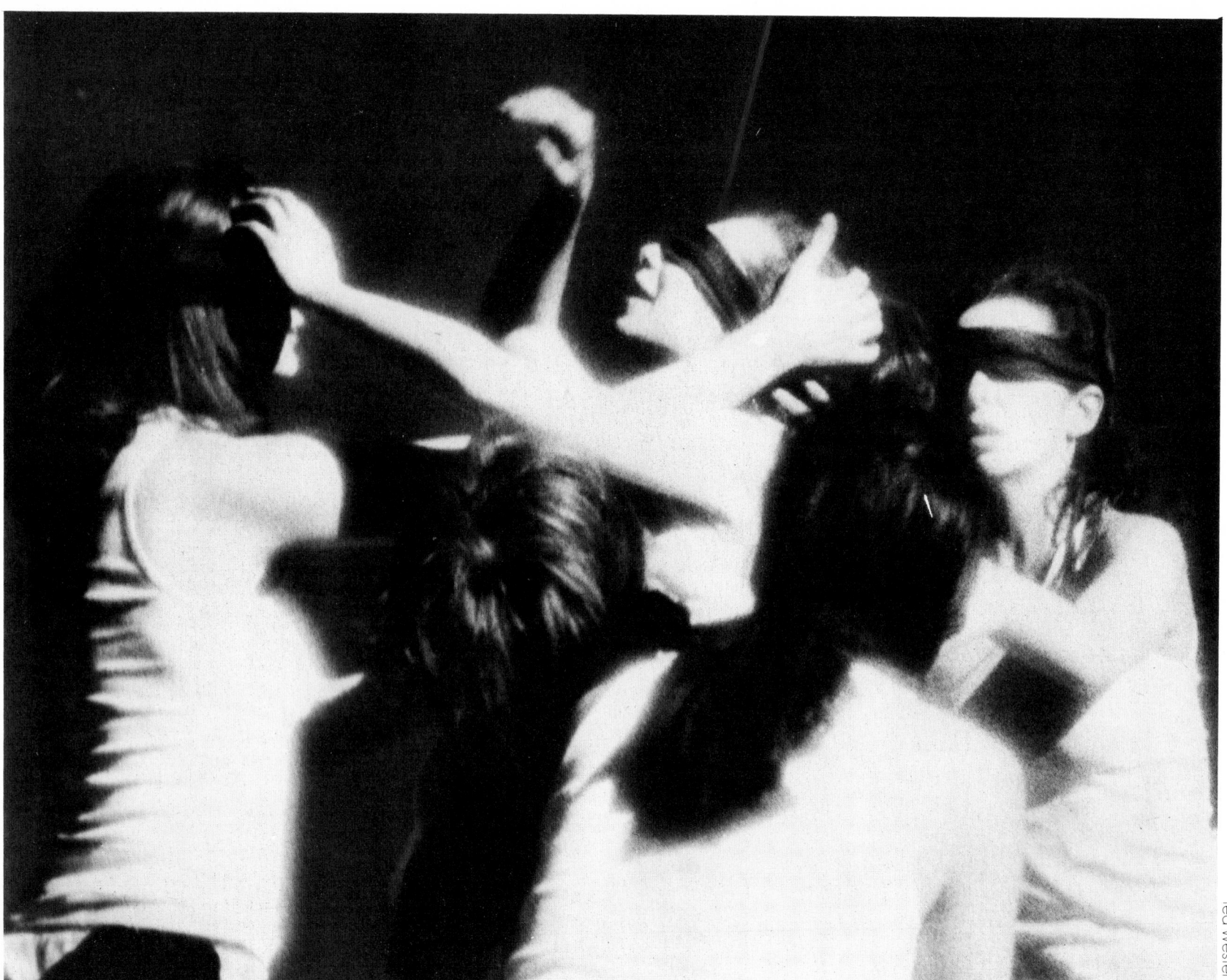

loading bales of shredded paper and positioning glue buckets and brushes. Willing audience members become our partners, taking up glue bucket and brush; we encourage them to glue our bodies with as much vigor and velocity as they wish. Once we are drenched in sticky paste the audience volunteers retreat and we slip and slide back onto the cart, turning in circles against one another until we slip or leap off into the bales of shredded paper. We flip in the papers—becoming "collaged"—back-flips, sit-ups, which toss up clouds of paper. We grapple towards a partner and position ourselves into the upside-down walk, silhouetted against the landscape slides and the walls of collaged paper. The film and tape "Viet-Flakes" begins on the central wall as we exit in zig-zagging upside-down walks. The audience begins to move into the shredded paper piles...

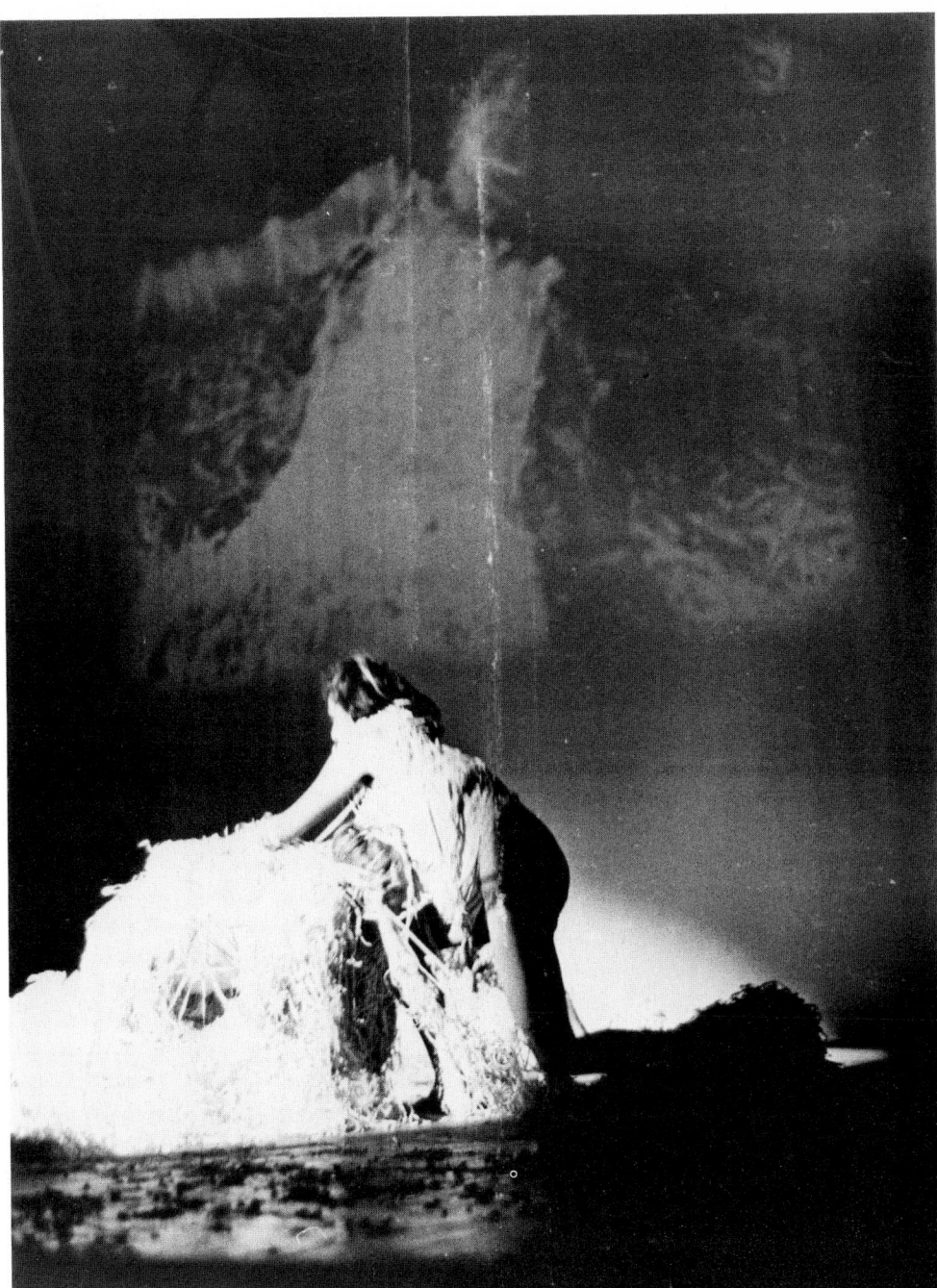

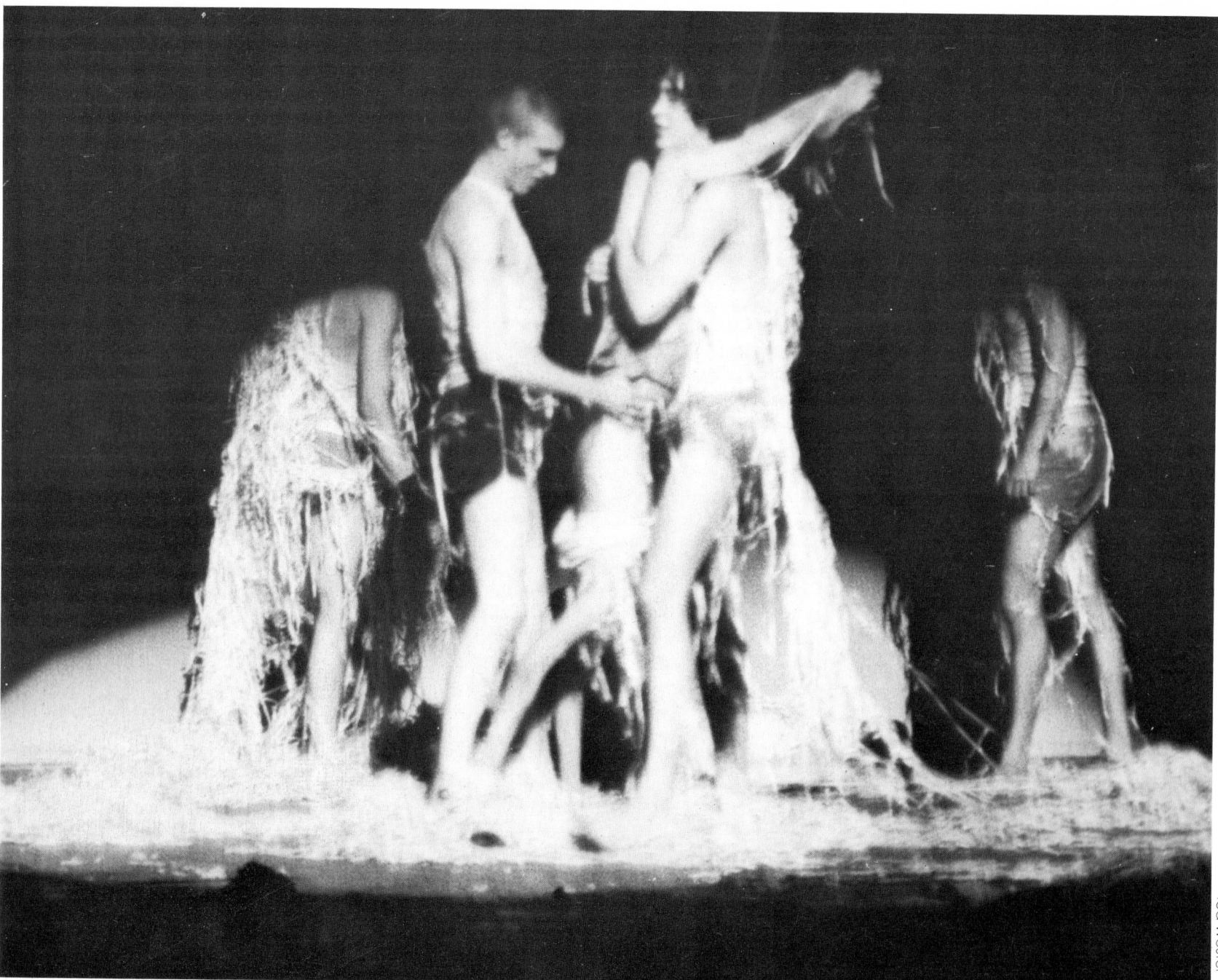

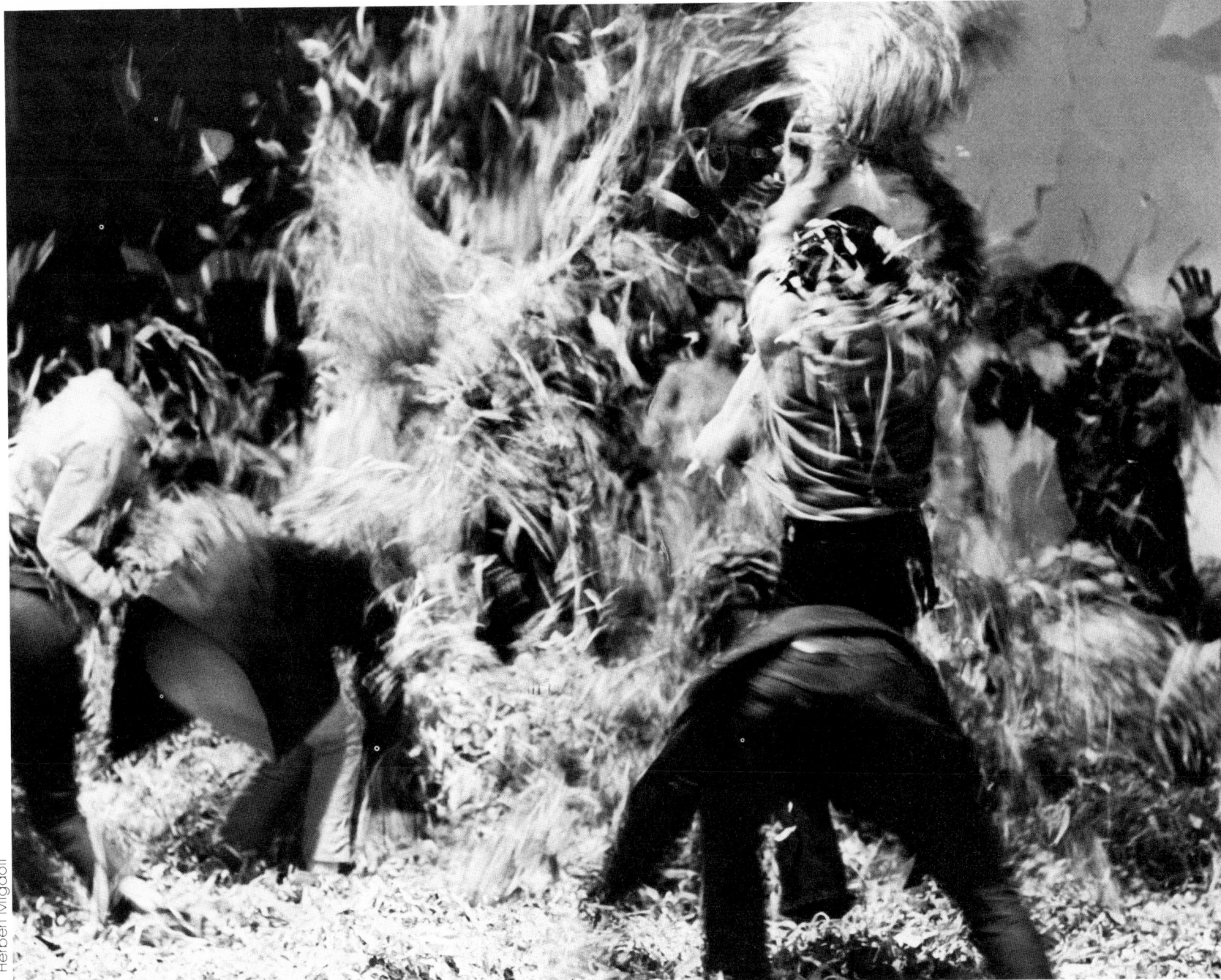

Herbert Migdoll

NAKED ACTION LECTURE

June 27 1968 Institute of Contemporary
Art London

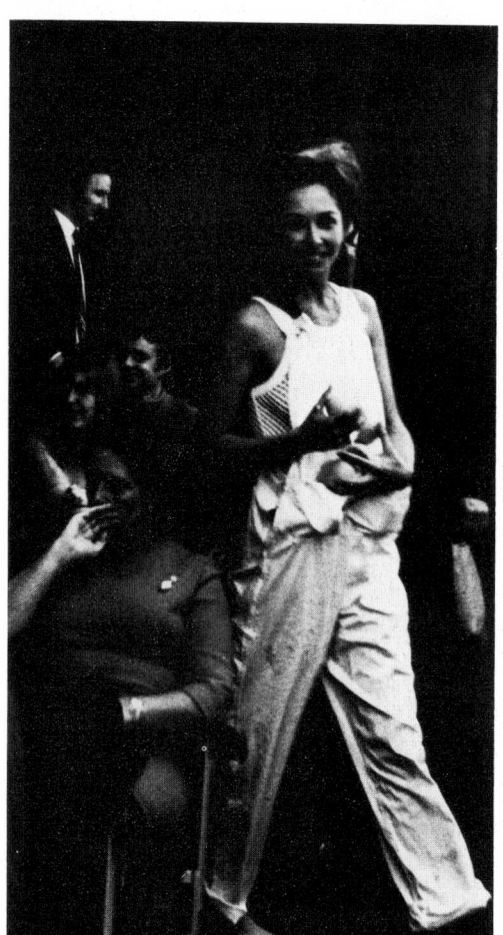

Naked Action Lecture was arranged by the director of the London Institute of Contemporary Art, Michael Kustow. I lecture on my visual works and their relations to antecedents in painting while both dressed and undressed, dressing and undressing.

Naked Action Lecture asked the questions: can an artist be an art istorian? Can an art istorian be a naked woman? Does a woman have intellectual authority? Can she have public authority while naked and speaking? Was the content of the lecture less appreciable when she was naked? What multiple levels of uneasiness, pleasure, curiosity, erotic fascination, acceptance or rejection were activated in an audience? (This work also prefigured **Schlaget Auf.**)

When the audience was seated I walked among them describing the sets of slides to be shown; I wore the string undershirt and oversize overalls from which I distributed a quantity of oranges. When all oranges were passed out, the lights dimmed for the beginning of the slides and I went to the front of the room and began my lecture. In the course of the thirty minute lecture I undressed and dressed and walked back and forth with a pointer, discussing aspects of perception and spatial organization. I took questions from the audience if they related directly to the content of the lecture. I continued dressing and undressing for the duration of the lecture and questions. At the conclusion of the slides I went on to the stage and asked for volunteers from the audience to join me in demonstrating a principle of collage; we would all undress, cover each other with paste and leap off the stage into the mound of shredded papers. Two volunteers came forward, young men, strangers. We undressed each other in the light of the slide projector, liberally applied the glue to one another, did a few practice jumps in place and finally lept—one after the other into the mound of papers, twisting and turning. We regained the stage and I finished my lecture with a few points about collage process and gestalt patterns now made clear by the three examples.

A black out. We left the stage for the showers upstairs. "Fuses" began.

3 slide carousels:

a) slides of my paintings, constructions—an istory
   projected on left abutting wall

b) slides of Kinetic Theater works
   projected on right abutting wall

c) slides of collage light boxes alternating with performance slides, to
   demonstrate rhythmic organization
   within the frame, gesture, texture,
   light sources, color saturations: relation to Cezanne, Monet, Morisot,
   Velasquez, Ryder, Marin, de Kooning, Joan Mitchell.

1 16mm film projector
   ("Fuses" to be projected at conclusion of lecture)

2 bales of shredded white paper

3 buckets of wall paper paste & 3 large
   paint brushes

1 pointer

two dozen oranges

oversize white overalls, (man's) string
   undershirt

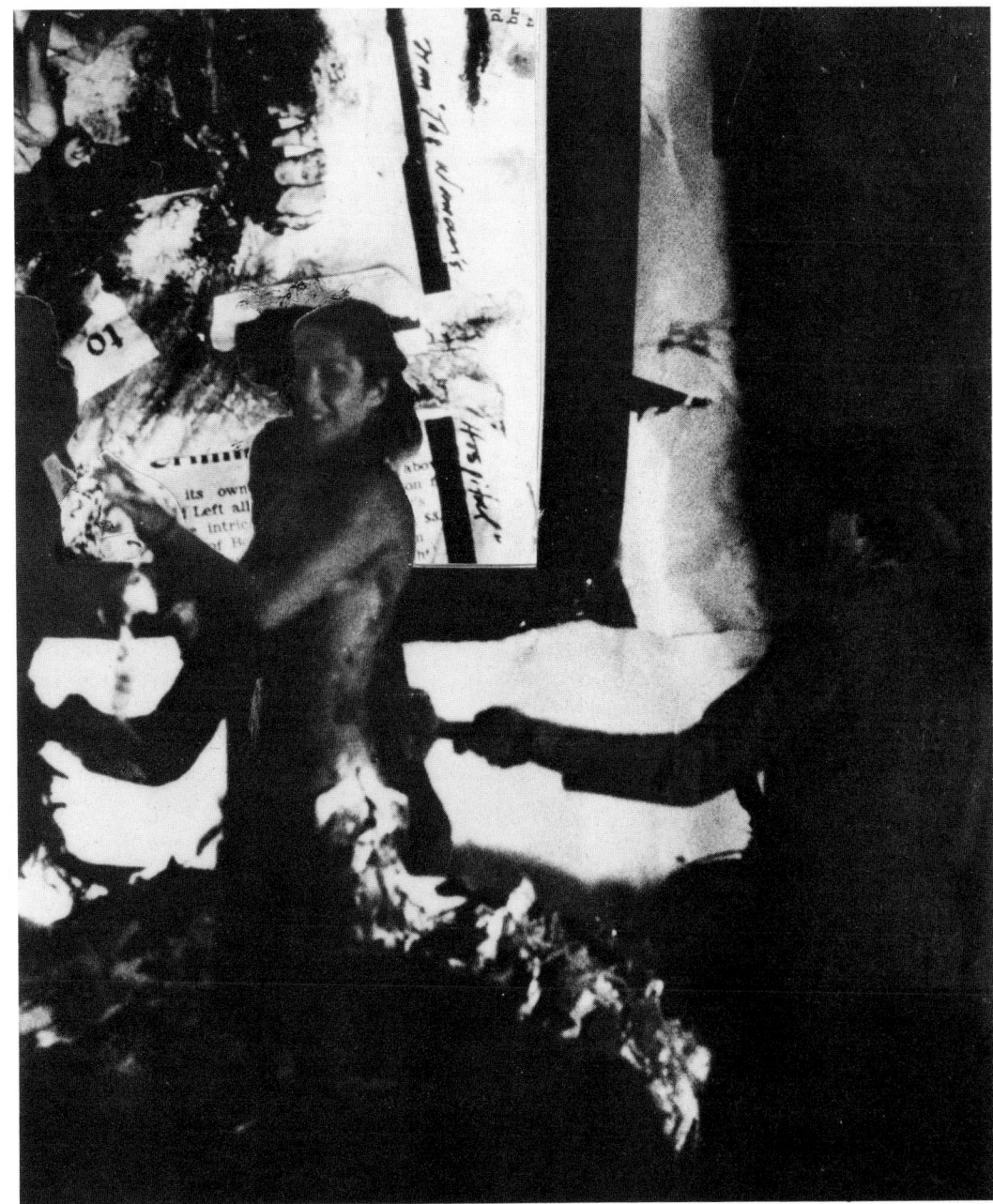

EXPANSIONS

April 24 1969 New Poets Theater NY

I'm surprised by a smiling photograph taken at the time. I was falling into the long slide of disorientation and despair. In a few days I was leaving NY for France; a friend had bought me a plane ticket to Cannes after finding a letter in my unopened mail detailing the selection of "Fuses" for a special jury presentation. I had no idea of where I would go, how I would support myself after the film festival. I could grasp only one day at a time, with difficulty. **Expansions** was made for Joachim Neugroschel's "poetry and events" given in a small performance loft on West 22nd St. (ironically next door to the loft where I had begun filming "Plumb Line").

I had this image for a symbolic hanging; "hanging up" the old self publicity...to inspire a transformation, to demonstrate a "hang-up"? The sense of this action was ambiguous, tragi-comic. **Expansions** was based on demonstrating the properties of certain soft materials. Two bales of compressed, pink polyurethene foam lozenges were carried in front of the audience. Dressed in shapeless overalls, I told the audience I was preparing an exorcism and that we would first observe the action of the foam. I formally cut the metal bands containing it with shears. For several minutes we watched as the lozenges slowly expanded, rose, popped, and spread themselves around our feet. They were inviting to touch and people grabbed handfulls and distributed them in various directions on each other, around the room. The second bale was cut open, and the room was flooded with layers of the pink foam. With a broom I swept large mounds around a chair facing the audience. I climbed onto the chair and dropped the overalls. Under them I had sponged whiting on my body in the exact shape of a leotard. A transparent nudity. A noose hung from the ceiling above the chair. A spot light. I put my head, arms, upper torso through the noose, let my weight fall onto the rope, kicked out the chair. For an instant I swung there. The lights went out.

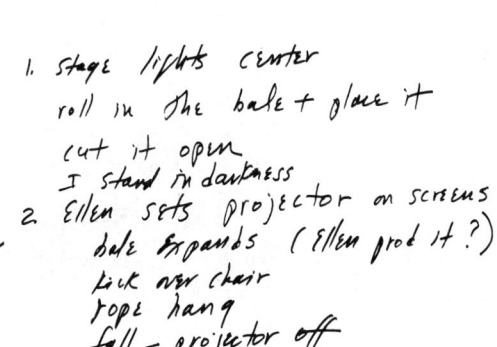

1. stage lights center
roll in the bale + place it
cut it open
I stand in darkness
2. Ellen sets projector on screens
bale expands (Ellen prod it?)
kick over chair
rope hang
fall – projector off

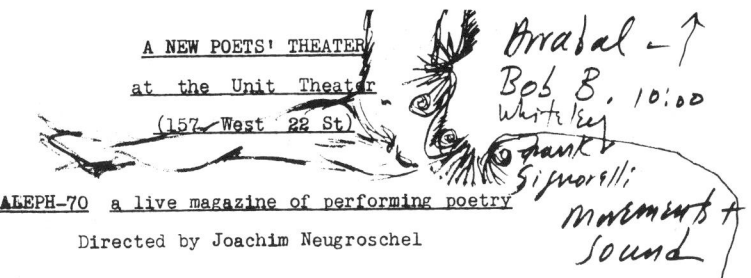

A NEW POETS' THEATER

at the Unit Theater

(157 West 22 St)

Brrabal →
Beb B. 10:00
Whitley
Frank
Signorelli;
Movements +
Sound

ALEPH-70 a live magazine of performing poetry

Directed by Joachim Neugroschel

Issue #2:   OBJECT LESSONS

April 24, 1969 (Thursday) 8:30 & 10:00 p.m.

Ronald Gross	Fold-out poems
Vito Hannibal Acconci	Untitled
Gary Dubosen	Graphics
Marvin Cohen	Object Dialogues
Tom Wasmuth	TAG DISTRIBUTION

Schuldt	LA POÉSIE CONCRÈTE VAINCRA
Dick Higgins	IT'S A POEM
Carolee Schneemann	EXPANSIONS

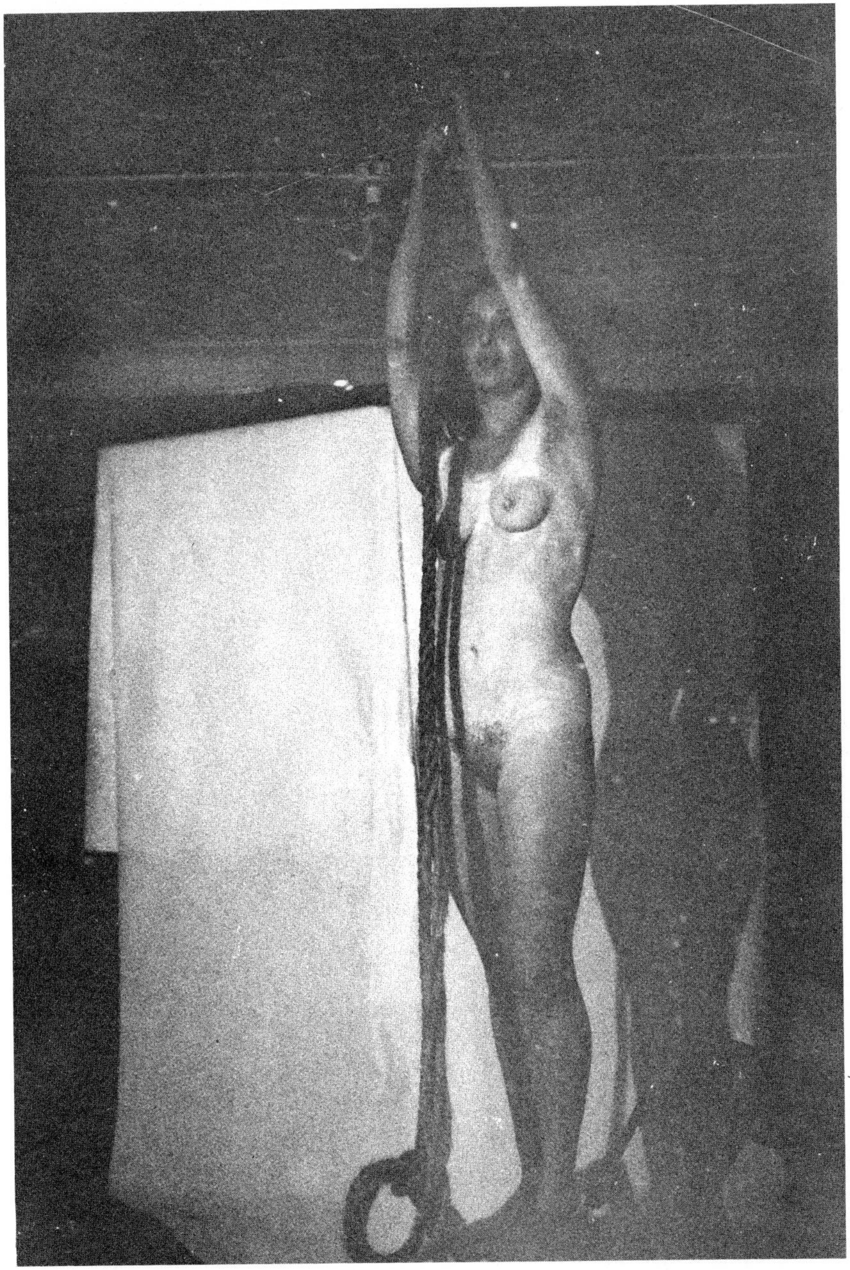

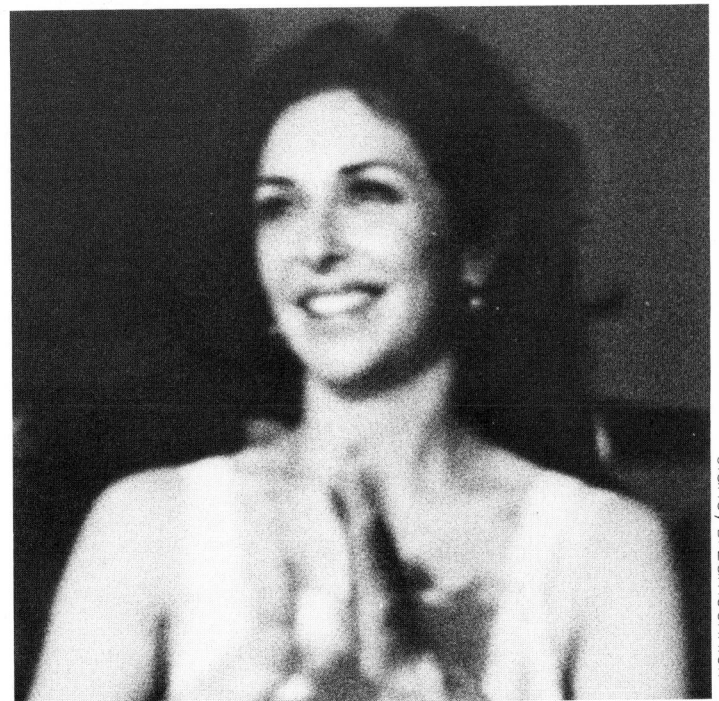

Sidney B. Zamochnick

Sidney B. Zamochnick

183

ON 'PERFORMANCE'

The character of the group works had so much to do with the spontaneous creation of movement and gesture by the performers that it would have been impossible to fully score them in advance. While I avoided stylized or exemplary movement, each particular work took a great deal of training for us to reach a fluid physical inter-relation, one that isn't inherently part of our culture. In order to discover a unitary function we had to experience personal transformations in terms of the group process. The thoroughness of our mutual awareness and the degree to which that heightened an "ordinary self," enabled us to move publicly with the real pleasure we evolved in rehearsals. I developed exercises on contact improvisation for each session—the imagery I sought becoming centered on the qualities of each person in the group. Out of these exercises the freedom of the group and the vitality of the work meshed.

Thames Crawling was my last group performance work.

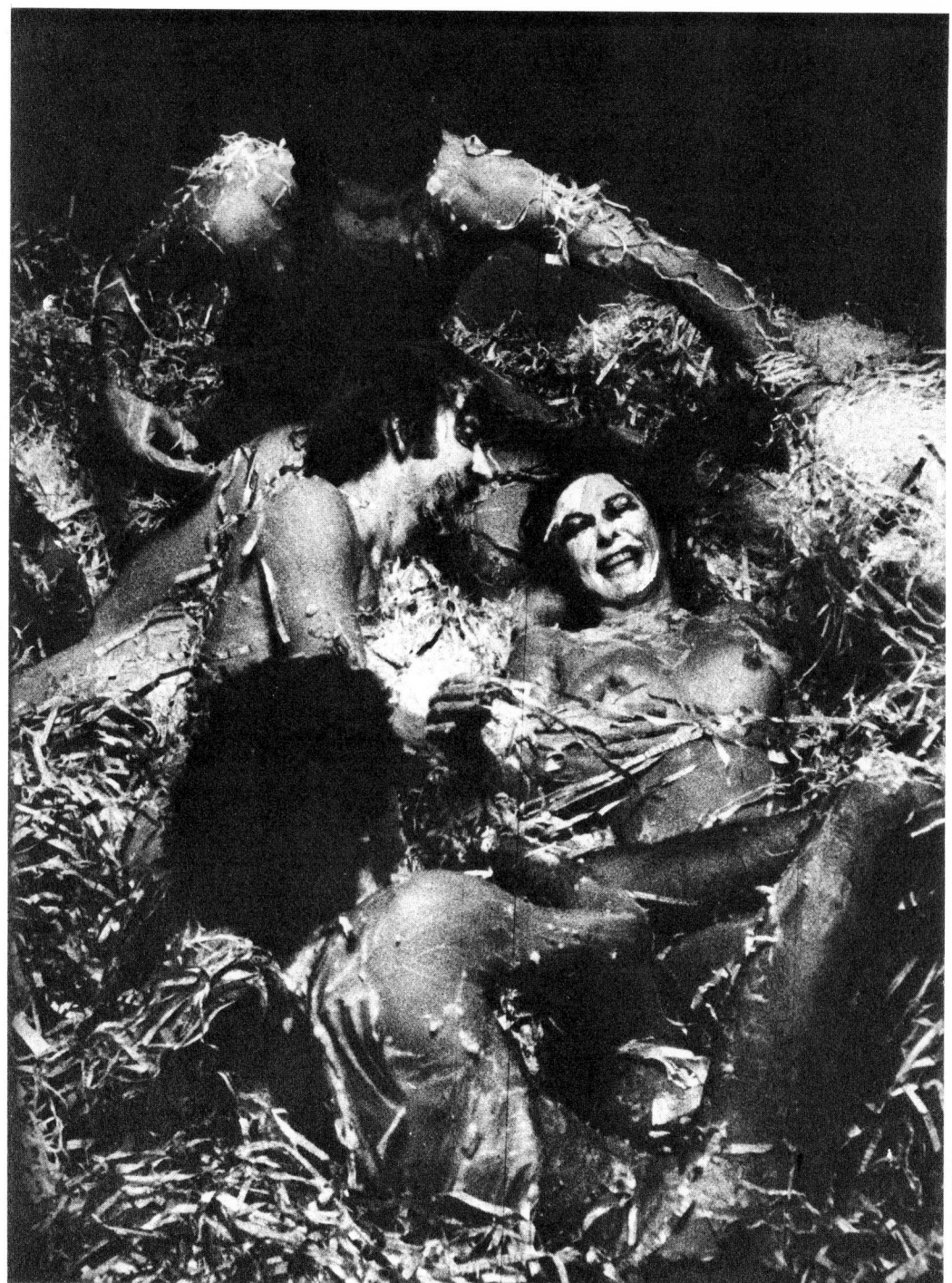

Max Waldman

184

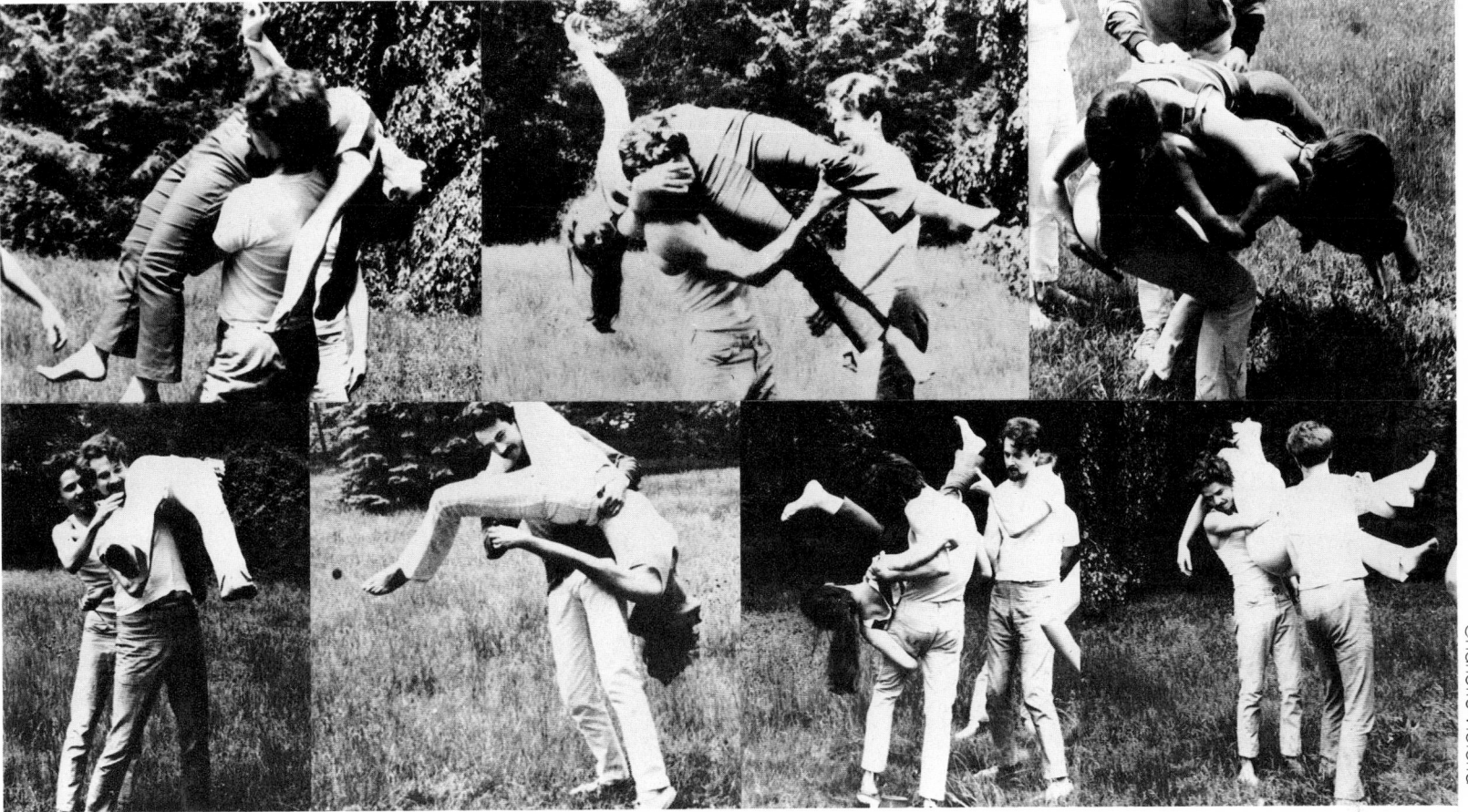

Charlotte Victoria

From Notes of Motion 1966-68

. . .Physical Action is an assertion of coherent function of place time commitment of gesture posture coordination. . .posture itself a total envelope statement of the organism. . .gesture is a biological istorical compendium of intention. . . an involuntary confession intention to communicate. . .we tell everything essential to our natures by stance posture gesture. . .we pretend we've forgotten how "to read" the information to allow masks social confrontations. . .to establish counter-gestures protective acceptable ones illusory wishful but to realize gesture perception is to free your intuition for what IS. . .responses to presence to present animal swift appraisal a natural thing
. . .equity
recent question as to the sexual differentiation in certain actions; the holds and carries for instance in which the women were lifted and carried by one man and passed to the arms of another—it would take two women to lift and carry one man, although we performed this action as well,it was less frequent. Why emphasize the muscular disparity, use, movement, in which the women seemed "passive", the men "active"? The experience is unitary; the person carried becomes the complement to the one carrying; her yielding, trust and relaxed body is an active response to the muscular effort of taking her weight onto his own. The carrier participates in the act of the carrier, just as the carrier absorbs the essential experience of being carried in doing so. We used all the variations between us in strength, duration, balance, quickness of reaction. In rehearsals all the actions of partners were exchanged; for instance the crawl and carry was relatively simple for the men on men, women on men, men on women, women on women in quick relays in which the weight was given in developing awareness of how it was to receive

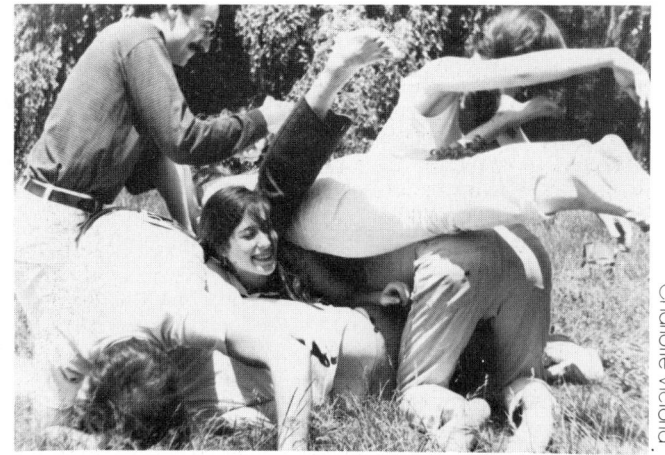

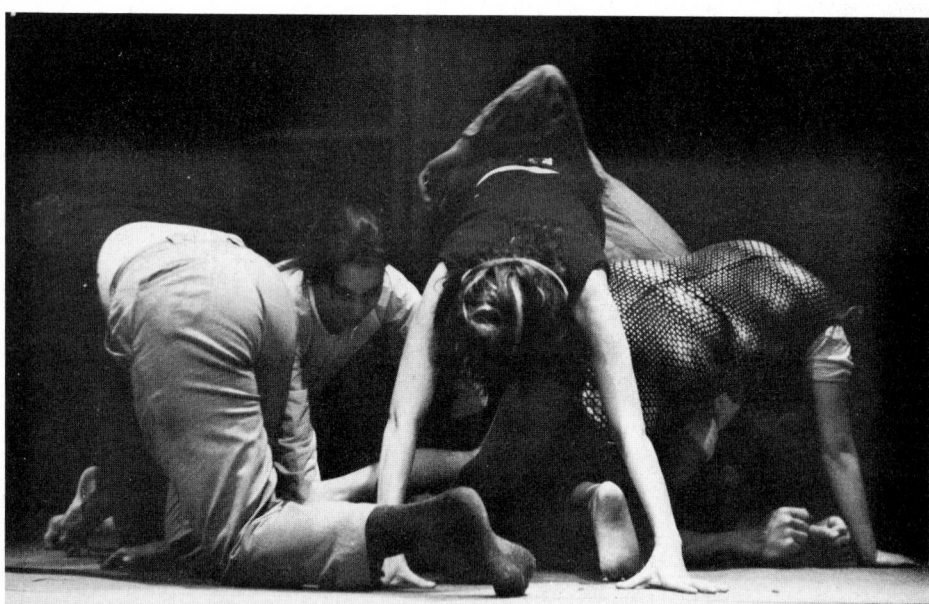

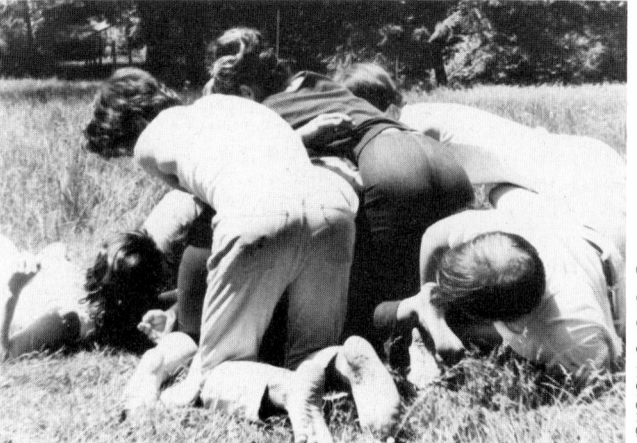

the weight and continue the movement. If a man in a sudden relay found he was in line to go onto the back of a woman, and that his weight would impede or make her movement forward impossible, he would take just enough of his own onto his feet or hands so that they could advance as a unit. The point was adaptability, adjustments which made the action possible.

To watch a person carrying another is to partici-pate in both situations simultaneously; empathically to be both the carrier and the one carried.

Then there are exercises which seem to be pure fun, but they serve other purposes. For instance everyone lines up flat on the floor, in a tight row, shoulder to shoulder. The person at the end starts to roll over everyone, followed immediately by the next person, rolling over all the bodies. The rollers may be afraid of hurting the prone bodies, the rolled-on people afraid of the weight and that much direct physical contact...everyone flat out...so that your breasts and pussey and cock and balls are all momentarily in contact. But you don't know who is who—its personal but general-ized; it goes very fast and everyone has the same experience and makes instantaneous shifts so

they don't get hurt...

Olfactory aspects of contact improvisation were important once we had full body contact. People in close contact are most uncomfortable about smells (particularly their own): mouth, feet, cunt, cock, ass, underarms. The smell taboo in our culture is particularly internalized. So there are exercises in which we seem to be doing one thing about movement but it is really about breaking down olfactory taboos. For instance the "body ball" where we have to crawl through one another's arms, legs, under the belly, around the head, concentrating on keeping a unitary shape in constant, smooth motion. If anyone had any resistance the entire shape loses its flow, you fall get crushed or stuck. But the unitary feeling of the motion is so pleasurable and mutually inter-dependent that the physical intimacy is absorbed into the larger action. Without ever mentioning an olfactory taboo people would eventually express their relief in jokes, "you really washed for this session!", "whose feet was I stuck on?"

...Initially simple exercises done in partners... you would pick someone who seemed attractive or not threatening...it could be a woman with a woman, a man with a man. You begin to learn something about mutality of rhythms, timing, re-sponsibility for one another's motion. We might start on the floor with contact of hands (not taboo), then contact of back to back, pulling one another over and upright, back and forth...so that in effect you are giving whatever you are receiving, then exchanging. Partners would be switched...suddenly a small woman would be pulling over the man who looked like he'd crush her...she's instantaneously adapting and so is he.

...P. came to me and said she was afraid of doing grabs and falls with D.; he was not only the tallest person in the group and muscular but she felt so much tension in his body she was fearfull of being hurt. He saw himself as being hurtful to others (and expected to get hurt in return.) In this instance, with a minimum of discussion, we all agreed that those who felt willing would begin a series of grabs, falls, tackles with Denys. His defensive expectations dissolved in the repeated falls and collisions once he found no one got hurt, that he could both yield and take responsibility for impact.

...The symbolic act "don't depend on me" might be enacted by dropping a partner; the fear of being "let down" might be enacted by falling out of lifting arms—we learned to fall like a cat and to hang on to imbalanced weight. Adjustments in trust and risk were exposed and communally ex-perienced as an essential relatedness.

...Our need for non-sexual physical contact...

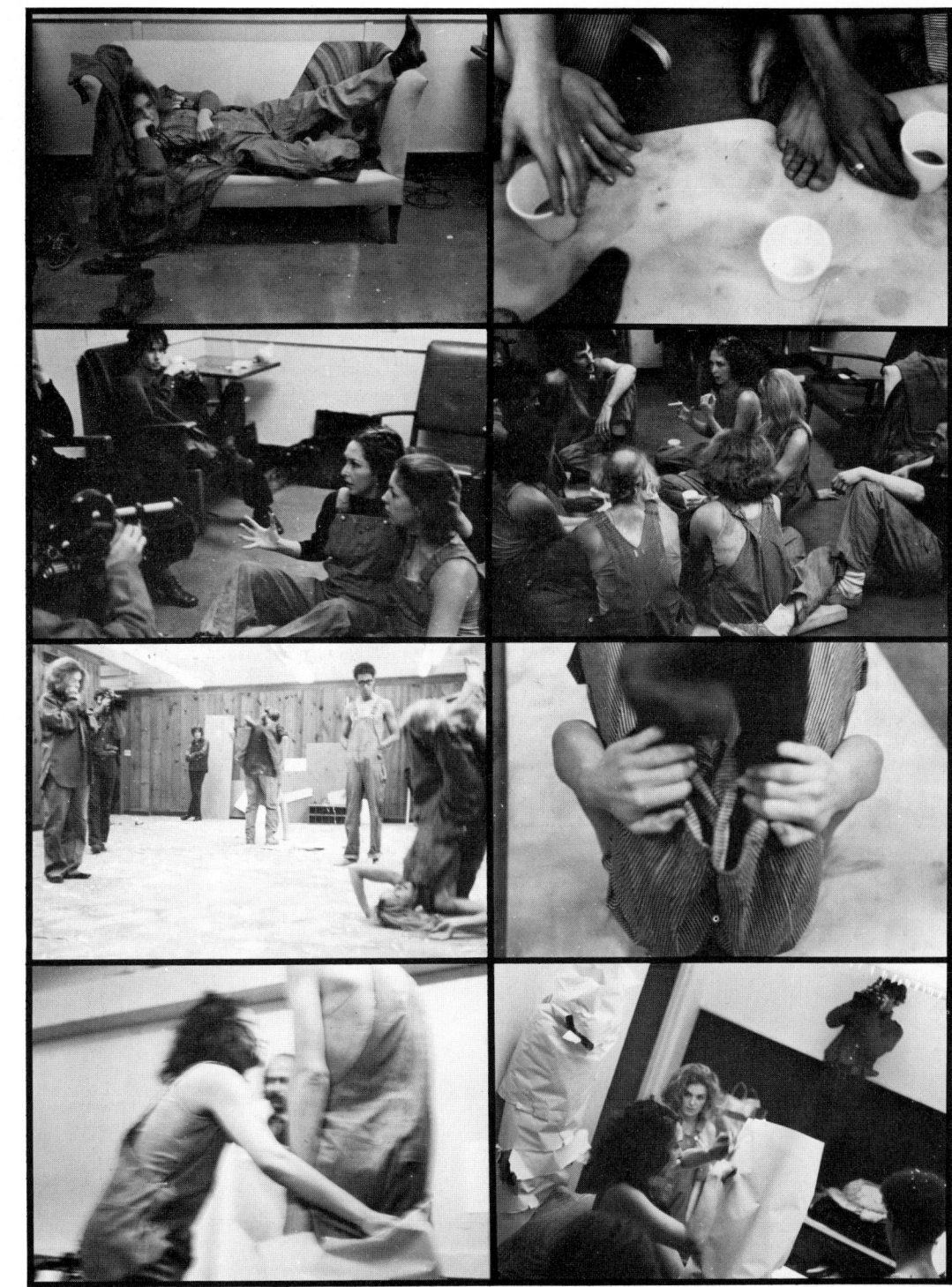

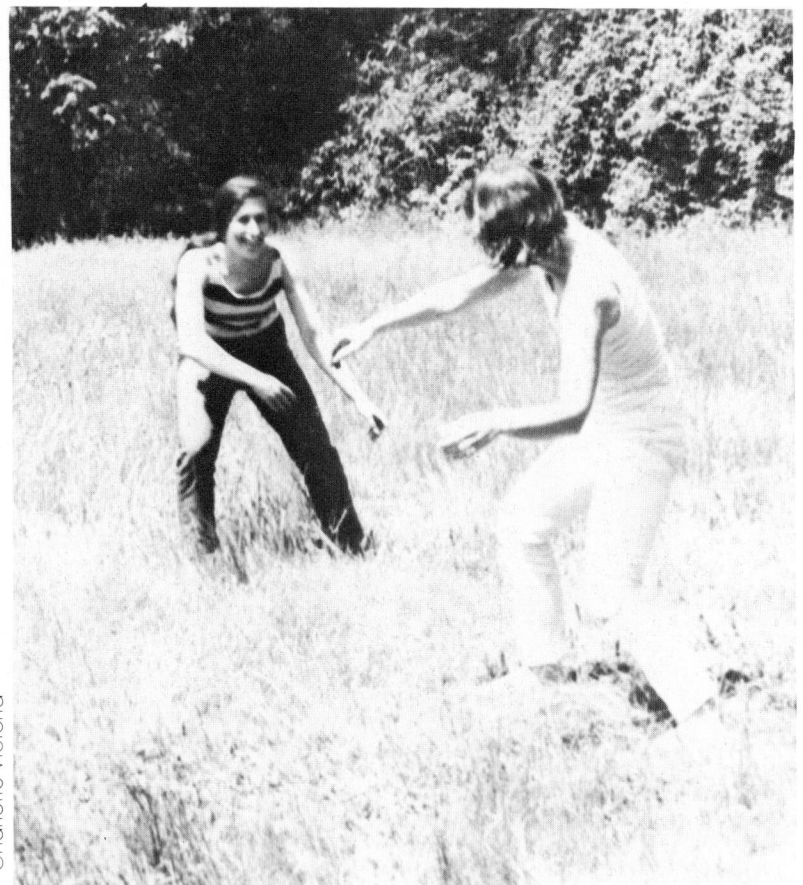

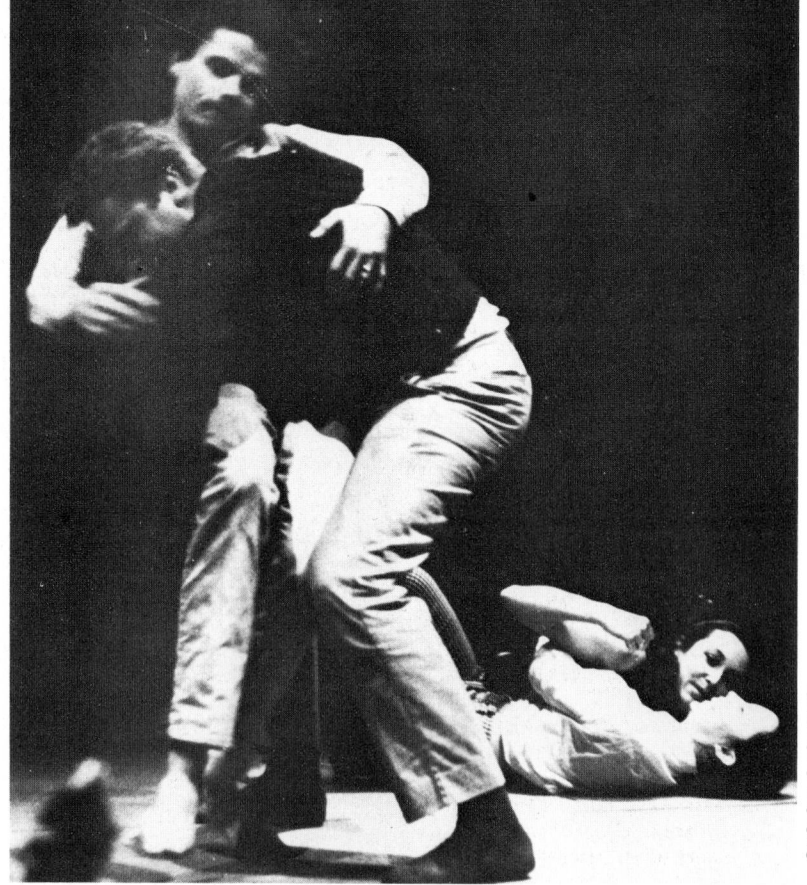

Charlotte Victoria

Charlotte Victoria

the confusion between sensual contact and sexual contact in reactions of audiences...we were asked if the intensive physical contact during performance resulted in "having to" make love. (The sensual satisfactions of contact confused with sexual desire.) Sensual contact as enacted by us became a form of privilege, a vicarious enrichment which had something to do with my turning later performances over to the audience. Their identification with us enabled them to put themselves in our place...

...taking risks—distinguished from agression as power/imposition/fear/constraints—exercises of

agression and assertion had to unravel emotional conditionings which would interfere with our muscular coordinations...

...the individual asserts responsibility appropriately...the information was in our bodies in a positive form...being aware of and responsive to one another did not restrict or inhibit our own explorations.......

...the insufficiency of our abilities to move co-operatively, instinctively to protect one another (and self) was vividly apparent in the charge of rigid police flanks against the Grand Central

Station Yippie celebrants...(and at the Pentagon)...our responses were helplessness, confusion, victimization....the cultural symptoms of frustration and anger over the Vietnam war increased as we confronted the unsuitability of our own behavior to the conditions affecting us... in '67, '68 I did a series of public workshops with the expectation that what we learned in theater could be of use in mass actions......

...I rejected standards of perfection, excellence, endurance exemplified by a leader or principle. My performers could develop quixotic and individual aspects within a work so long as that sensi-

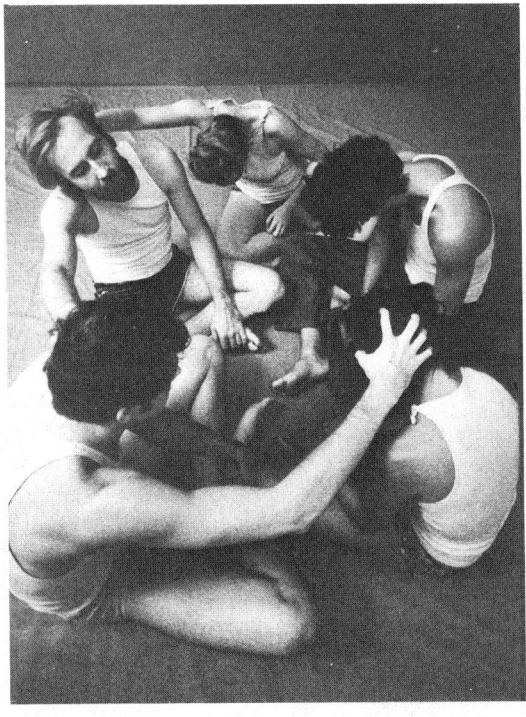

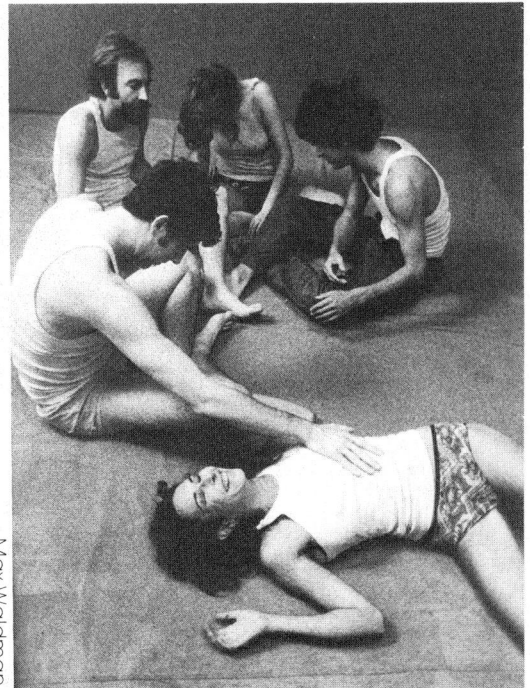

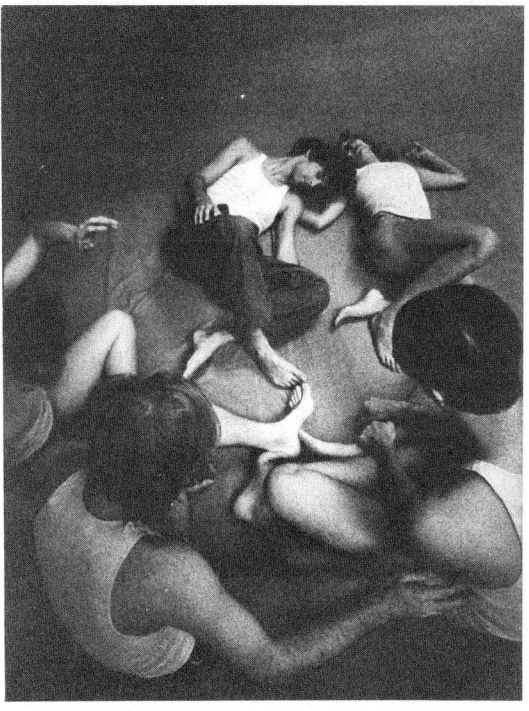

Max Waldman

tive and mutually accepting tissue was overtly there between us. . .for instance Tommy O'Donnell at moments had the tendency to bite! Not hurtfully or agressively, but unconsciously furthering the physical bonding he felt as bodies were embraced, held, and adjusted their motions to one another. . . . .or S. going limp during carries. . . or in my own case often being so absorbed in a sequence that I had no idea what happened next. . . . .

. . .being individually irreplaceable and as well interchangeable. . .the devotion and value we felt for one another had to do with this acceptance of particularity—each became a complement and extension of any other. . . .secure in how we were who we were. . . .

. . .if Mark and Joe were comfortable on the highest ropes this was not a standard to be imposed on others who were not facile on the high ropes. . . .the fact that some of us could work there satisfied the physical potentiality of the use of the environment and left the others free for those actions which were most natural and available to them. . . .

. . .centering and breathing. . .being able to move with a full breath lightens and energizes the body. . .but I wouldn't teach it directly. . .each one could discover this in themselves,

. . .Concentrating on tactile material as a convey-ance of our energies—projective, physical, sustained in time as work must be. . .and taking time for each to find their particular way into the shared efforts. . ."efforts" not in the sense of being effortful, but of application to a study which strengthens. . .to trust the exploration and exposure of neglected capacities of the self which a communal situation can bring to the fore. . . .

. . .each work exists in its own right but contains a method or potentiality that is then taken by others in different directions. . .I let it go. . .many of the performers used this interchange and discovery as a touchstone for themselves and took steps to alter their own lives. I didn't want to keep a constant troupe together but to let each move on with what we had explored. . . . . .it wasn't like a school, a company, a fixed practice. . . .it was in its particularity that it had its vitality, its richness, and the fact that Kinetic Theater could keep changing, letting people go on, and absorbing disasters and mistakes. . . . . . .

. . .reorganizing patterns of times and space. . . when you shift the predictable perceptual base, you begin to unlock structures in the social and political spheres as well. . . . .it might be through something very obvious that simply hasn't been done before. . . . .

189

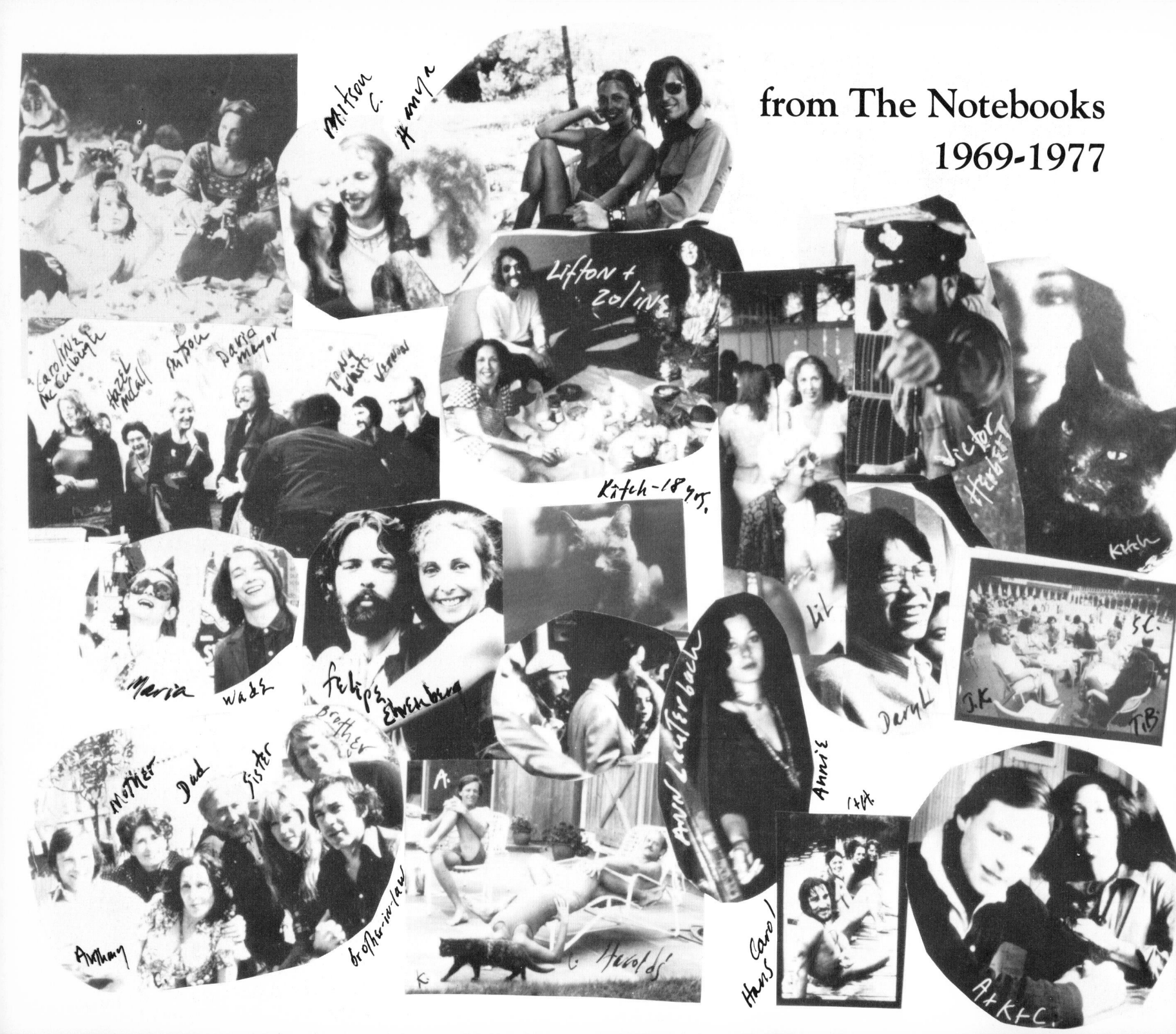

from The Notebooks
1969-1977

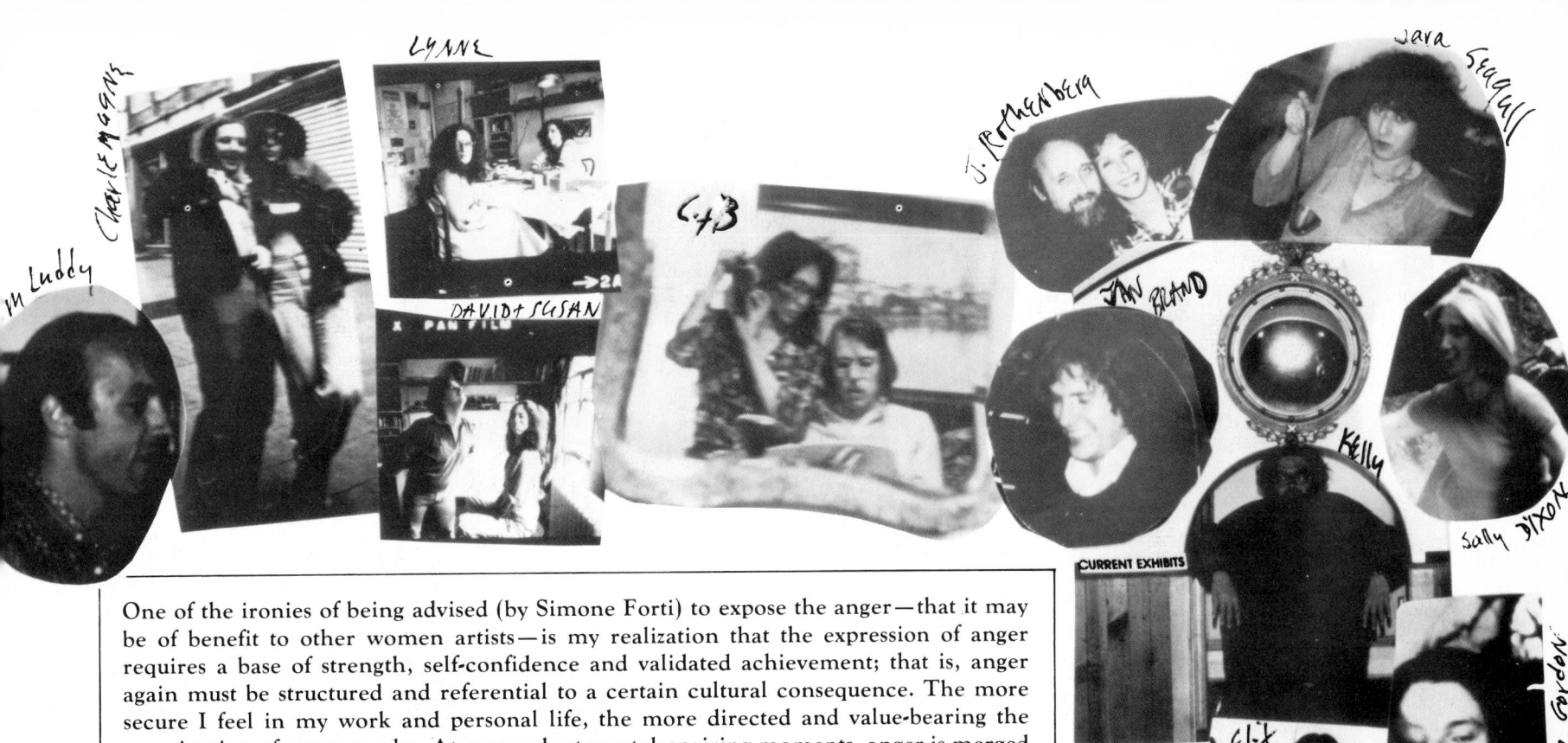

One of the ironies of being advised (by Simone Forti) to expose the anger—that it may be of benefit to other women artists—is my realization that the expression of anger requires a base of strength, self-confidence and validated achievement; that is, anger again must be structured and referential to a certain cultural consequence. The more secure I feel in my work and personal life, the more directed and value-bearing the examination of anger can be. At my weakest most despairing moments, anger is merged in a hopeless stew of guilt, self-blame, enclosure........it is important to remind myself that I *was* flipped out for several years—and if this is a representation for the implosion of my generation at a certain time ('69, '70), I still alone had to struggle to fight back into relevance, coherence, the unities of functional behavior. And that the total loss of a functional self has not only to do with the excesses of social and esthetic determinations— the materials and energies of the sixties—but of the individual who faces, endures, an hourly state of dis-location, dis-orientation, fears, ineptitudes and a sinister transformation of all ordinary things, objects and actions. If it takes an hour to get out of bed, and putting on socks has the confusing complexity of launching a battle cruiser, constructive anger and political insight are no longer available tools.

It was symptomatic that in our atomized social relations one had to find a special guide or personal aid—a psychiatrist—and pay them for healing, when a group with a collective awareness is the obvious solution to, and avoidance of the beleaguered self.

1977

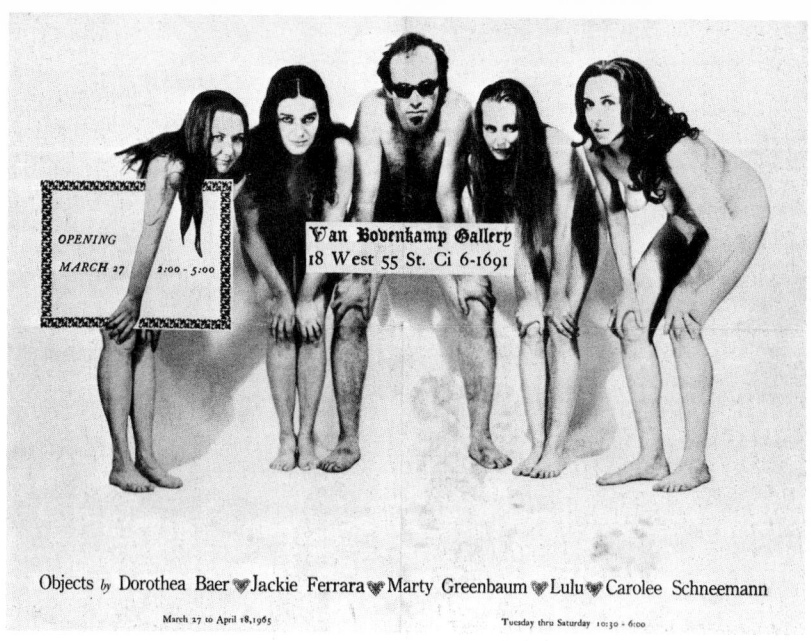

Objects *by* Dorothea Baer ♥ Jackie Ferrara ♥ Marty Greenbaum ♥ Lulu ♥ Carolee Schneemann

March 27 to April 18, 1965   Tuesday thru Saturday 10:30 - 6:00

ISTORY OF A GIRL PORNOGRAPHER

On the poster for the van de Bovenkamp exhibit, "Objects by Five": the usually "dignified" artists appear naked—four women, one man; hands on their knees as if poised for a skirmish (the image I had clearly envisioned, to which the other artists gradually became committed as well. The woman on the left holds a sign across her body inviting you to the opening, because her husband had insisted her naked body—only ink on paper—not pass into public domain.)

(1965)

Exactly one of the motivating factors in my determination to integrate the nude body in all my work: performance, Kinetic Theater, film, paintings, photo-collage, events. The others:

1. To confront the paradox that we deal with created images—painted, sculpted, performed—as "reality." As if paint, plaster, celluloid, stone, paper, exist to convince us of a life force as vital as our own flesh and blood . . . . and *subject to our social moralities!* This is as child-like as spanking our dolls for making imaginary pee-pee; and shelters an unconscious, debased primitivism—surrounding, endowing inanimate objects with projections of our repressed vitality.

[*"Istory" has been my solution to the History/Herstory tug and pull. Whenever possible I use a neutral noun or pronoun instead of a specific gender. A few years ago Clayton Eshleman asked about my use of "Istory": did I know Olsen's reference to "Istorin" in the Greek as "the root of history?" Eshleman explained an ancient conflict: Thucydides defined Istorin as "history as facts"; Herodotus defined Istorin as "the personal search for the real."*]

2. To bridge the conventionally public/private areas of experience.

3. For a painter no part of the body should have been considered taboo, relegated to a sub-physical "actuality"! As a student I painted self-portraits using my entire body as one which stood for all/or any human shape from which I would learn. I was free to study, perceive my own genital shape and form—as well as my ears and elbows.

My art professor told other students this study was narcissistic. I was dumbfounded. I thought I had "objectified" my own fragile, but concrete reality in a stream of istoric image-making. Further, this small co-ed liberal arts college did not have live models for its art students. The male students doing their endless self-portrait studies were not considered "narcissistic." But then they did leave out their bodies!

4. In the early sixties when I came to N.Y., a few artists were introducing real and literal materials to an extended canvas (or picture plane). I had been making constructions, light boxes, collages. In 1962 I began a room environment built of huge panels interlocked with rhythmic color units, glass, mirrors, lights, moving umbrellas and other motorized parts. I worked with my whole body, the scale of the panels incorporating my own physical scale. I decided to be combined with the work as an additional "material"—real & physical. To let my body be a further dimension of the tactile, plastic character of the construction. I did this by treating myself in a series of "inclusions"; with paint, sand, powder, flour, grease, glue, rope, fur, crayons etc. I concentrated on moving as an extended part of the structure. These movements were then photographed to become a variation of the environment itself, *Eye Body*.

Throughout college I was receiving the message: "of course you can/don't you dare." My family were interested to know if I had "dates," not that I was working in a lost encaustic process. My teacher said: "You're terrific kid, you could really go far, but don't set your heart on art, you're only a girl." Did all this have any connection with my English teacher insisting I not do a thesis on Virginia Woolf—"trivial and obscure" (but not to me!), but Proust would do instead? Or my philosophy teacher objecting when I wanted to do a paper on DeBeauvoir, advising me that Sartre was where my attention should be instead?

Not only were my creative energies constantly under question, subject to issues which contradicted everything the learning situation and my own abilities should have supported, encouraged to flourish, but my "right" to excel was in doubt.

Somehow the tremendously repressive culture around me had not effected a separation between my creative energies and my erotic energies. It came as a great shock when during my second year review, my painting and drawing were given highest honors but a committee told me to leave school for a year, that I had committed "morally

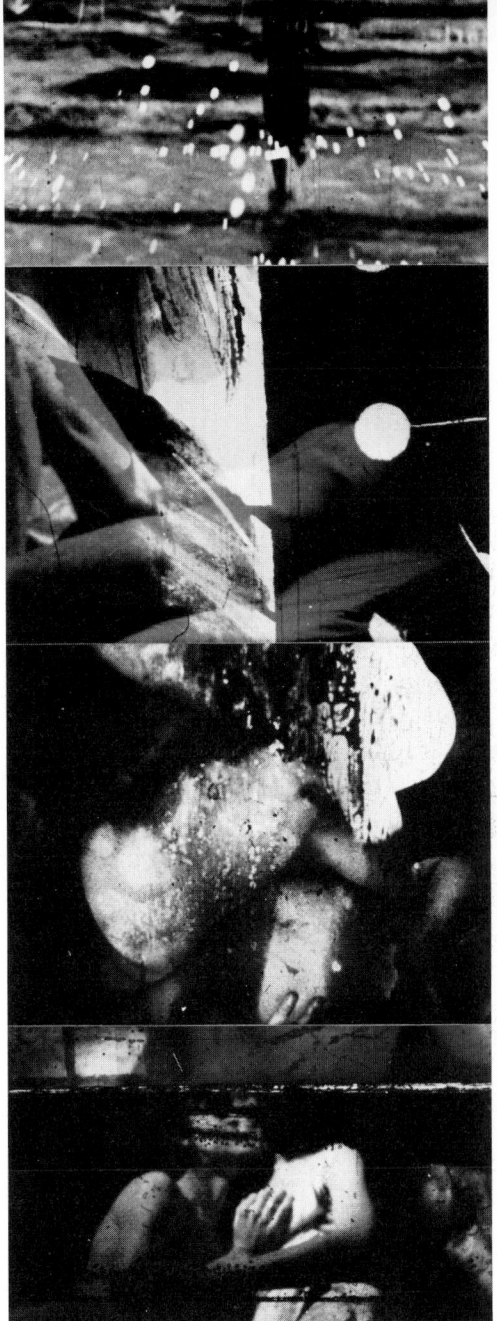

Stills from *Fuses*, 1964-1967.

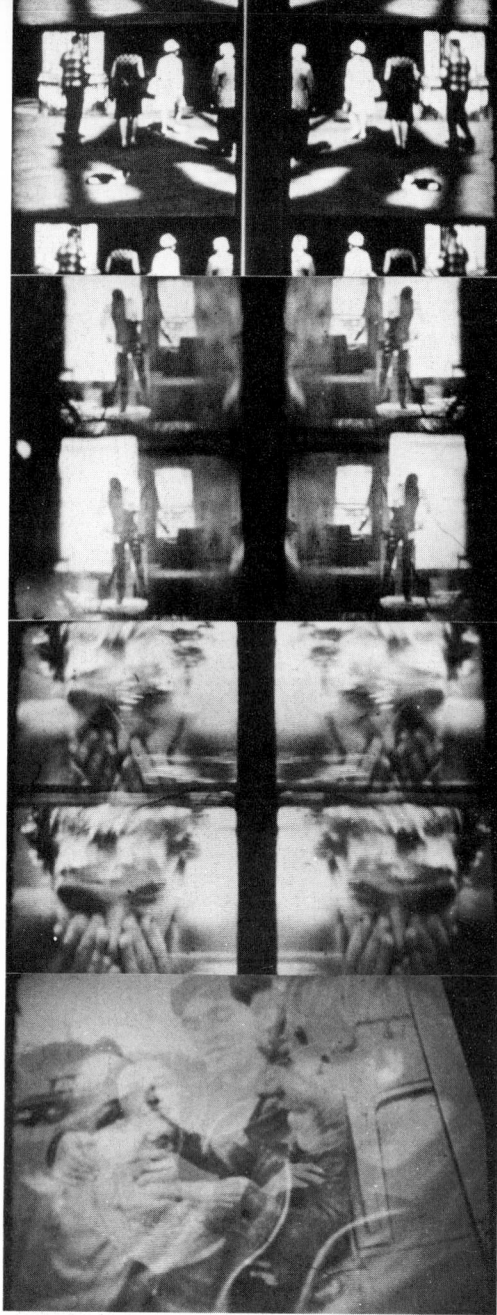

Stills from *Plumbline*, 1968-1971.

offensive acts": someone accused me of making love with my boyfriend under a tree! (He was not asked to leave, nor did we ever remember such an incident...) I was on full scholarship, this banishment created an uproar—one of the first that I would unwittingly generate throughout the years.

In the early sixties I felt quite alone in my insistence on the integrity of my own sexuality and creativity. There were many reasons for my use of the naked body in my Kinetic Theater works: to break into the taboos against the vitality of the naked body in movement, to eroticise my guilt-ridden culture and further to confound this culture's sexual rigidities—that the life of the body is more *variously* expressive than a sex-negative society can admit. I didn't stand naked in front of 300 people because I wanted to be fucked; but because my sex and work were harmoniously experienced I could have the audacity, or courage, to show the body as a source of varying emotive power: poignant, funny beautiful, functional, plastic, concrete, "abstract"; the key to related perceptions of our own nature as well as the organic and constructed worlds with which we surround ourselves. Alienation from our physical joys, constrictions in the scope of our own physical natures, meant endless disasters, acts against our own deepest needs.

In some sense I made a gift of my body to other women: *giving our bodies back to ourselves.* The haunting images of the Cretean bull dancers—joyful, free, bare-breasted, skilled women leaping precisely from danger to ascendancy, guided my imagination.

The use of my own body as integral to my work was confusing to many people. I WAS PERMITTED TO BE AN IMAGE/BUT NOT AN IMAGE-MAKER CREATING HER OWN SELF-IMAGE. If I had only been dancing, acting, I would have maintained forms of feminine expression acceptable to the culture: "be the image we want." But I was directing troupes of performers, technicians; creating lights, sound, electronic systems, environments, costumes—every aspect of production, and then physically moving in what I had created. Some people wanted to constrain our actions as seductive, provocative, obscene, but the tenderness, boldness, spontaneity and pleasure which the performers communicated forced them to question their own attitudes. After a time the audience stopped yelling: "Is this art? Is this sex? Is this some religion?"

Still, I was astounded when in the midst of *Meat Joy* a man came out of the audience and began to strangle me. Steeped in the writings of Wilhelm Reich I understood what had affected him but not how to break his hold on my neck! And I was terrified that the audience closest to us would think it part of the performance. No one made a move. Even if I could have squalked the din of the continuing performance was overwhelming. I was saved by three middle-aged women, who may have had no previous experience of the excesses of the avant-garde; they simply *felt* I *was* being assaulted apart from the often violent performance. They threw themselves as one onto the man & dragged him off me.

Again I had a shock when the Institute of Contemporary Art in London invited me to screen *Fuses* and talk about how it was made. The space was comfortable, the projection smooth. But the audience sat stony, rigid, as if commonly subject to deadly paralysis. At the conclusion of the film there was silence, no rise of conversation, applause. In the front row, a huge, red-faced man in the uniform of a Colonel, clutched a walking stick in one hand, a portly woman with the other, and BOOMED "Come My Dear! Away from what only a Deranged Frigid Nymphomaniac could make." So much for the questions & answers session. A young critic (close to my own age) rushed up to me and snarled: "Madam you have assaulted my sexuality." The critic from the more liberal paper shook my hand saying "I'm afraid we deserved that film."

1974

---

from an unsent letter to Allan Kaprow, June 1974

Dear Allan:

you have written me three letters recently—one of welcome back from England and an appreciation of *Fuses;* the other in regard to my coming West, perhaps to perform, show films or teach. I've decided it is interesting to try to say (to myself and you) why your letters, whose tone is of one contemporary—one associate—to another, are so peculiar

essentially I have stood alone for too long, having been methodically *repulsed* by those with whom I felt affinity

at the time when our gang was getting recognition & help in the 60's I received recognition, and poportionately no help whatsoever. You see I understand *men helping me to sustain what I had but not to enlarge its scope or join them in their world.*

The clearest example is not so far past. At Cologne*, Vostell assured me a publisher was coming who could save the day. I was penniless—unable to get myself and my collaborator back to London. I had understood we would have a living stipend once in Koln; but Szeemann reminded me that any stipend I had had was included in funds already spent on materials for my exhibit-process.

*Happening and Fluxus Retrospective at the Kolnischer Kunstverein, Cologne. November 1971.

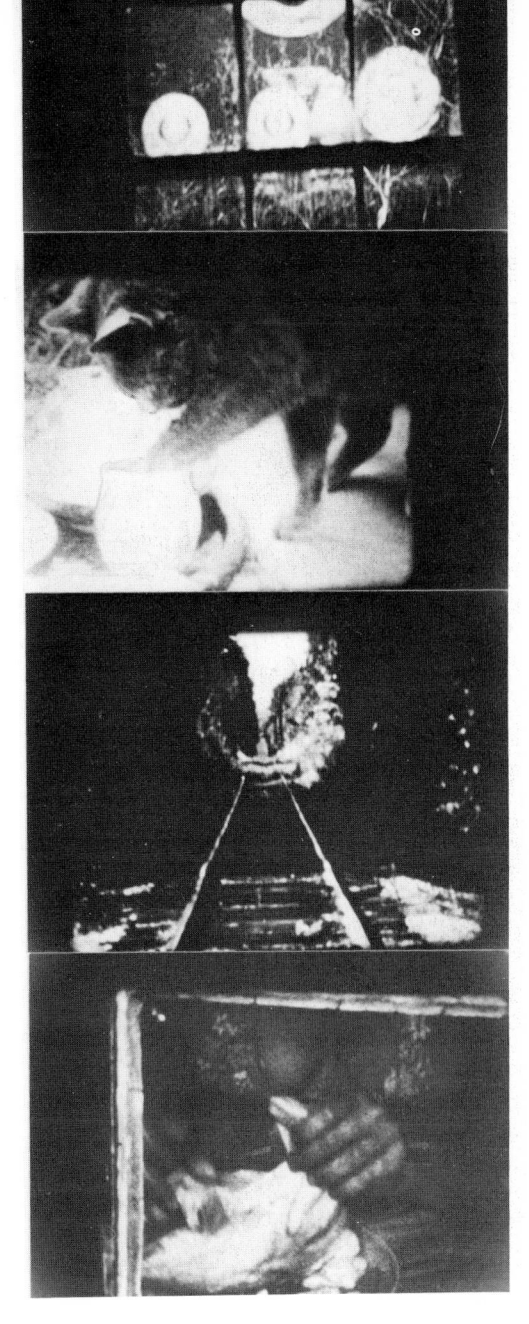

Stills from *Kitch's Last Meal,* 1973-1977.

My wits (ego) are sufficiently intact (somehow) to know, to assure myself that it is no great affront for me to ask you if there is work for me when I'm in the area on another job. But I couldn't tell any one of the "old" friends that we had nothing to eat. Yet the artists from Cologne whom we had never met before helped us unstintingly—with food, with bedding, some high drinking/smoking times and loans of small sums to get us from one day to the next. Strangers bought our meals as we sat among friends. I can only explain this to myself as a strange phobia on my part; I cannot ask for help; but I cannot ask for help because those whom I trusted to respond found that impossible—with no equivocation. What was my position among you then? My own title private title iron ironical title was "Cunt Mascot". Cunt Mascot on the men's art team. Not that I ever made love with ANY OF YOU NO! I didn't feel perceived by our group—not even sexually. As a female thing, yes, as a questionable element since I could never play your games your ways, which meant *I might stand in judgement* as well as need! the treacheries annoyances of slaves children servants witnesses who are not participants

so Vostell each day we asked Vostell when the publisher was coming. He was delayed. On the seventh day I knew indeed "he" must have arrived because when I crawled out of my tent it seemed you were all lined up in front of Wolf: 1. Kaprow 2. Higgins 3. Filliou 4. Hansen 5. Nitsch 6. Schmidt 7.......Wolf said I still must wait another day while arrangements were being organized.....that meant funds, commitments for printing work, advances.......what did you arrange? I was offered 15 marks on receipt of a layout! Nothing at that moment. Did they (I don't even know his name) do a book?

Charlotte* and I helped each other, called for each other at times of stress, materialized in the wings year in and year out with missing scores, safety pins, tampons, telephone numbers, ambulances, food, dollars.....that was the real sisterhood in the stud club. Bici was desperate and the tunnel wind men momentum blew us always apart hands extended in some confusion of pain & satisfaction, (and Alison and I close through the orbit of the men we lived with.....Dick, Jim.)

I thought my associates didn't care for my aesthetics, kept me among them for those successes tangential to their own efforts.....perhaps they liked me as a token of?

You were unusual—from time to time you *asked* what I was doing; you came to some of my Kinetic Theater works at Judson, and St. Marks....I was excessively pleased. None of the other men ever asked me what I was doing, thinking, or spoke about my work. It went in

*Charlotte is Charlotte Moorman; Bici is Bici Hendricks Forbes; Alison is Alison Knowles

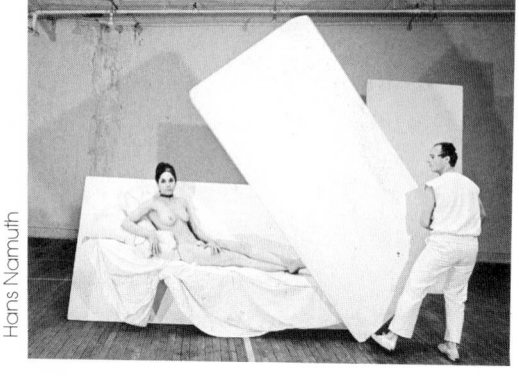

Hans Namuth

Site by Robert Morris, 1964. (Photo courtesy R. Morris.)

one direction: I asked them about their processes, events. I knew that a mutual exchange was normal! I observed you among yourselves: explaining, writing, introducing, meeting, making projects, plans . . . . . placing articles, lining up reviews, dealers, dinners . . . .

The European artists and I could share our work with great enthusiasm. Was that part of a tradition of accepting exceptional women? Or, that I was only visiting their turf? Or a social-political determination: that there was enough psychic space for all of us? That "capital gains" would be a vagary & imposition, rather than the heroic prize. We shared food, photos, tales, contacts; enjoyed one another, were even lovers. Different than back home.

The issue of aid, support and concern for one another is real; if my considerations seem peculiar, wrong-headed, that is a measure of my exclusion—or qualified inclusion—and its crippling effects. Of course, for all those years Jim & I shared, cared and took energy, direction from one another. There were a few close and carefully attentive friends. It was the poets who really responded, gave me confirmation, made sense of my work as I had hoped it could be . . . and through those early weavings of construction, expanding materials, the nude, film, establishing my own theater . . . it was those poets, women and men, who saw, spoke with me, cared and wherever possible helped the work and my intentions into the world.

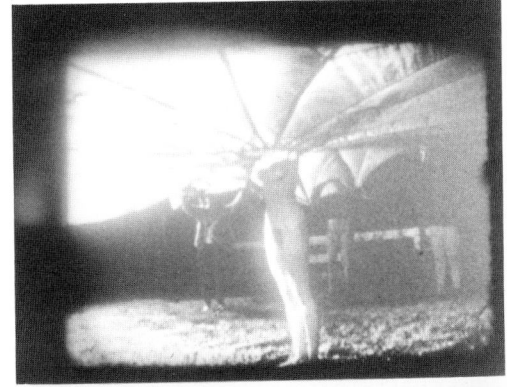

So, again I'm touched by your letter of welcome-back. When I went into a breakdown ('69), I had to leave my own territory . . . . . I could only save myself apart from the people I knew . . . . . because the way they related to me was rooted on my strength in persevering from an inner core—self-sustaining conviction & independence; no matter how small the direct communication with surrounding artists. My culture had frozen me into its image of my effectiveness, I could no longer manage so much with so little . . . . . . .there was no strengthening contact I could hope to find out of my weakness, disorder. (The poet Clayton Eshleman gave me a ticket to France, to Cannes, where *Fuses* was a special jury selection. I took my 13 year old cat—now 18 years old!—and some films. Four years passed before I was able to return.)

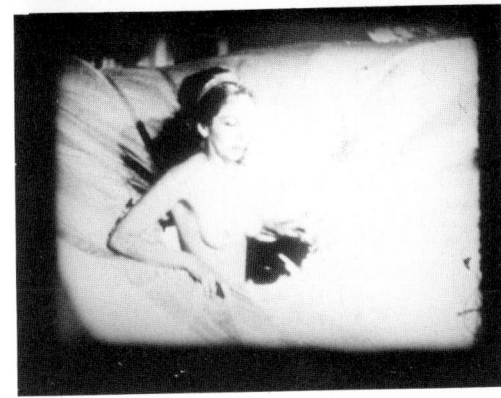

To persist, to persevere. Now we women reach to each other. Before we were isolated in the wake of the men. Scattered in their drift. I often think of Dorothea (Rockburne), persevering for years, veiled (because "they" couldn't see Her) hierarchic Woman Artist Mother penniless servant—locked into one position at a time—barely a flicker of estimation, heightening open regard from the successful artists for whom she worked & witnessed, that it SHOULD or COULD be otherwise. So much more satisfying & amazing

Birth of the Flag by Claes Oldenburg. Parachute Solo, from the film by Stan Vanderbeek, courtesy C. Oldenburg.

that her work can dominate our imagination & perceptions now. No man could have done it all! Alone.

Or as Jill (Johnston) had to go so utterly bananas/tipping the scales, carts, we projected as her own weights & balances for our threatened borders. Speeding Greek dance, all eyes on us, her short dress, black boots. Vast smile another mad girl mother fatherless buried alive burning into the clarity of female orphan madness. WE WERE THE GUESTS IN OUR OWN WORLDS! Flattered that Rauschenberg & Paxton phoned me in the country summer 65? saying Jill has really gone over the edge.....thinks she is Freud's daughter... can you suggest anything? Alas...it was too soon to recognize each other.....or Give Praise to Each Other Mother Cunt Art Maker. We have come through together! (And lost many on the way—which was the patriarchal tradition.)

What do you think of it all? I will send this to both you and Vaughan—now that makes sense. with love,

---

WOMAN IN THE YEAR 2000

By the year 2000 no young woman artist will meet the determined resistance and constant undermining which I endured as a student. Her Studio and Istory courses will usually be taught by women; she will never feel like a provisional guest at the banquet of life; or a monster defying her "God-given" role; or a belligerent whose devotion to creativity could only exist at the expense of a man, or men and their needs. Nor will she go into the "art world," gracing or disgracing a pervading stud club of artists, historians, teachers, museum directors, magazine editors, gallery dealers—all male, or committed to masculine preserves. All that is marvelously, already falling around our feet.

She will study Art Istory courses enriched by the inclusion, discovery, and re-evaluation of works by women artists: works (and lives) until recently buried away, willfully destroyed, ignored, or re-accredited (to male artists with whom they were associated). Our future student will be in touch with a continuous feminine creative istory—often produced against impossible odds—from her present, to the Renaissance and beyond. In the year 2000 books and courses will only be called "Man and His Image," "Man and His Symbols," "Art History of Man," to probe the source of dis-ease and man-ia which compelled patriarchial man to attribute to himself and his masculine forebearers every invention and artifact by which civilization was formed for over four millennia! Our woman will have courses and books on "The Invention of Art by Woman," "Woman—The

Source of Creation," "The Gynocratic Origins of Art," "Woman and Her Materials." Her studies of ancient Greece and Egypt will reconcile manipulations in translation, interpretation, and actual content of language and symbolic imagery with the protracted and agonizing struggle between the integral, cosmic principles of Gynocracy and the aggressive man-centered cultures gathered as the foundations of Judeo-Christian religion in the Western world.

Fifteen years ago I told my Art Istory professor I thought the bare breasted women bull jumpers, carved in ivory, painted in frescos about 1600 B.C. in Crete, could have been made by women depicting women. And I considered that the preponderant neolithic fertility figurines might have been crafted by women for themselves—to accompany them through pregnancy and birth-giving. And I wondered if the frescos of the Mysteries, Pompeii—almost exclusively concerned with feminine gestures and actions—could have been painted by women. He was shocked and annoyed, saying that there was absolutely no authority to support such ideas. Since then I have given myself the authority to support and pursue these insights. By the year 2000 feminist archeologists, etymologists, egyptologists, biologists, sociologists, will have established beyond question my contention that women determined the forms of the sacred and the functional—the divine properties of material, its religious and practical formations; that she evolved pottery, sculpture, fresco, architecture, astronomy and the laws of agriculture—all of which belonged implicitly to the female realms of transformation and production.

The shadowy notions of a harmonious core of civilization under the aegis of the Great Mother Goddess, where the divine unity of female biological *and* imaginative creation was normal and pervasive, where the female was the source of all living and created images, will once again move to clarify our own conscious desires. The sacred rituals of forming materials to embody life energies will return to the female source.

One further change will be the assembling of pioneer istorians—themselves discredited or forgotten by traditional masculist authority. In the year 2000 they will be on the required reading lists! What a joy to welcome: Helen Diner, J.J. Bachofen, Michelet, Rilke, Gould-Davis, Jane Ellen Harrison, Robert Graves, Jacquetta Hawkes, Ruth Benedict, Robert Briffault, Erich Neumann, H.D., Marie de LeCourt, Ruth Herschberger, Bryher, H.R. Hays, Minna Mosdherosch Schmidt, Clara E.C. Waters (1904), Elizabeth F. Ellet (1859)!

The negative aspect is simply that the young woman coming to these vital studies will never really believe that we in our desperate ground work, were so crippled and isolated; that a belief and dedication to a feminine istory of art was designed by those who might have taught it, and considered heretical and false by those who should have taught it. That our deepest energies were nurtured in secret, with precedents we kept secret—our lost women. Now found and to be found again.   *1975*

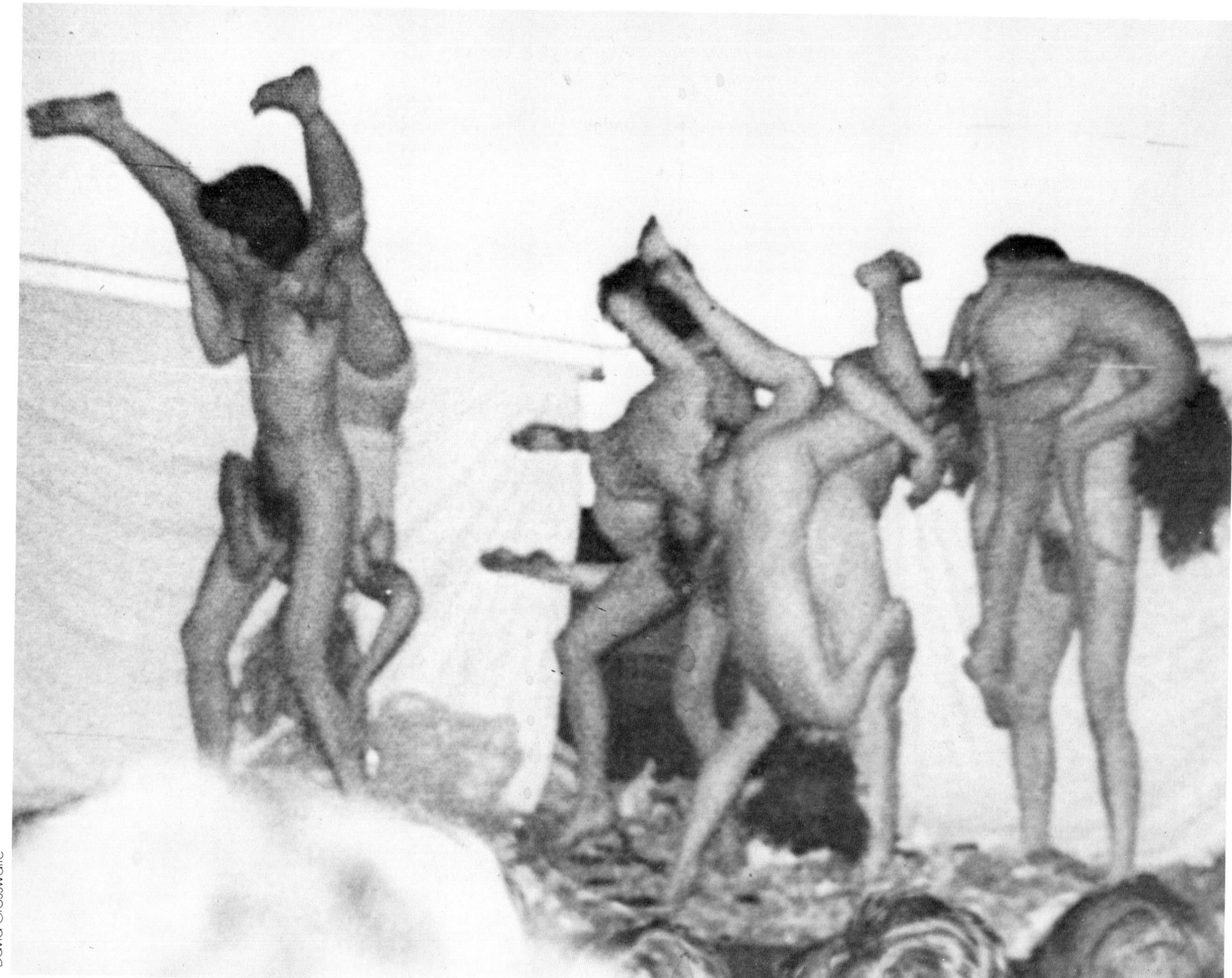

An "Expanded Cinema Event" for the International Underground Film Festival at the London National Film Theater on the banks of the Thames. Organized by David Curtis, the Festival ran for a week with programs of independent films shown daily from 10:30 in the morning to midnight. This marathon assembled filmmakers from all over the world. In addition to 16mm, 8mm, and super 8 films, multiscreen showings, European premieres of Mekas' "Notes, Diaries, and Sketches" (3 hours long), David Larcher's "Mare's Tail" (2 1/2 hours long), representative films from every known film co-op, and an international forum of sixty filmmakers (seven of them women), there were three events: actions by Peter Weibel, Valie Export & Hans Scheugl; Jeff Keen's "Rayday" film cycle; and my **Thames Crawling.**

This work was conceived as another form of "farewell"; I intended it to be the last large-group work I would do, and the performance actions were built within a retrospective showing of my films, including "Meat Joy," "Red News," "Water Light/Water Needle," and "Snows." It was also a "Meat Systems" event, conceived and realized with John Lifton, who designed the inflatables as well as the sound and projection system. Again there were intensive rehearsals with a group of eight non-performers, most of them friends. By this time I was familiar with the resistances and usual hostility of an English audience to physical enactments, and that influenced our plans for the space—for inflatable forms which would enlarge until they actually covered the audience. Since the audience hostility was usually passive or verbal we were unprepared to have our paper wrappings and underclothes ripped off at the very beginning of the performance by men in the audience.

THAMES CRAWLING

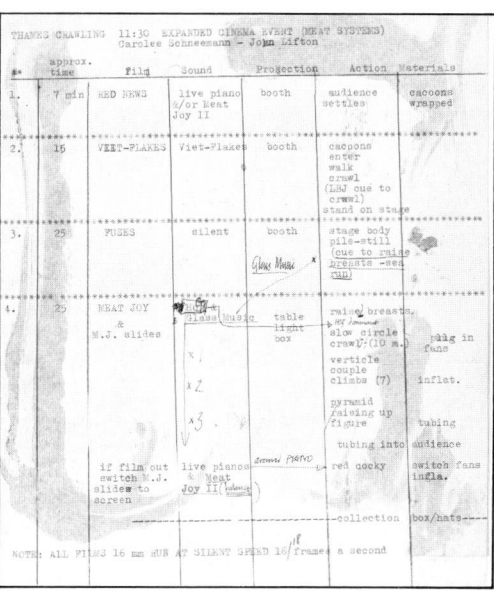

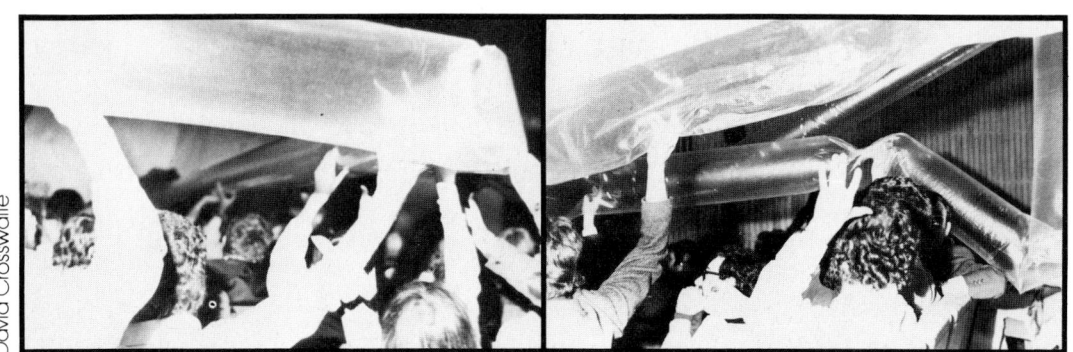

David Crosswaite

ELECTRONIC ACTIVATION ROOM

November 1970-January 1971
  Happenings & Fluxus Retrospective
  Kölnischer Künstverein, Köln

HARALD SZEEMANN, my favorite Museum Director At Large invites me to participate in a retrospective "Happenings and Fluxus" exhibit at the Köln Museum, November 1970. Since early fall John Lifton and I have been collaborating on ideas for an electronic-activation environment. He is an artist trained in architecture and electronics and has created "cybernetic environments in which audience responses have directly interacted with information media systems." The previous fall I had designed a work for audience activation called "The Divine Playhouse" in which the movement and proximity of the audience would trigger feedback systems of lights, slides, film, sound, and the motion of pulleys carrying soft materials. Designs and systems were underway with the help of an architect, Jonathan Park, until lack of funds forced us to suspend the project. John Lifton and I have named our projective collaborative works "Meat Systems" and send a proposal to Szeemann for an environmental room which would consist of banks of slides and film documenting three major Kinetic theater works, with sound and materials all to be activated by the presence of the audience. The budget from Köln is barely enough, but Lifton and I begin, in September, our home-made electronic systems for the Köln Exhibit. As usual the funds for work are not sufficient for living and we are part of a group of artists living in the vast, cold warehouse which is base to the London Filmmakers Cooperative. John has constructed a workshop and a bunk bed covered in plastic sheeting to hold any

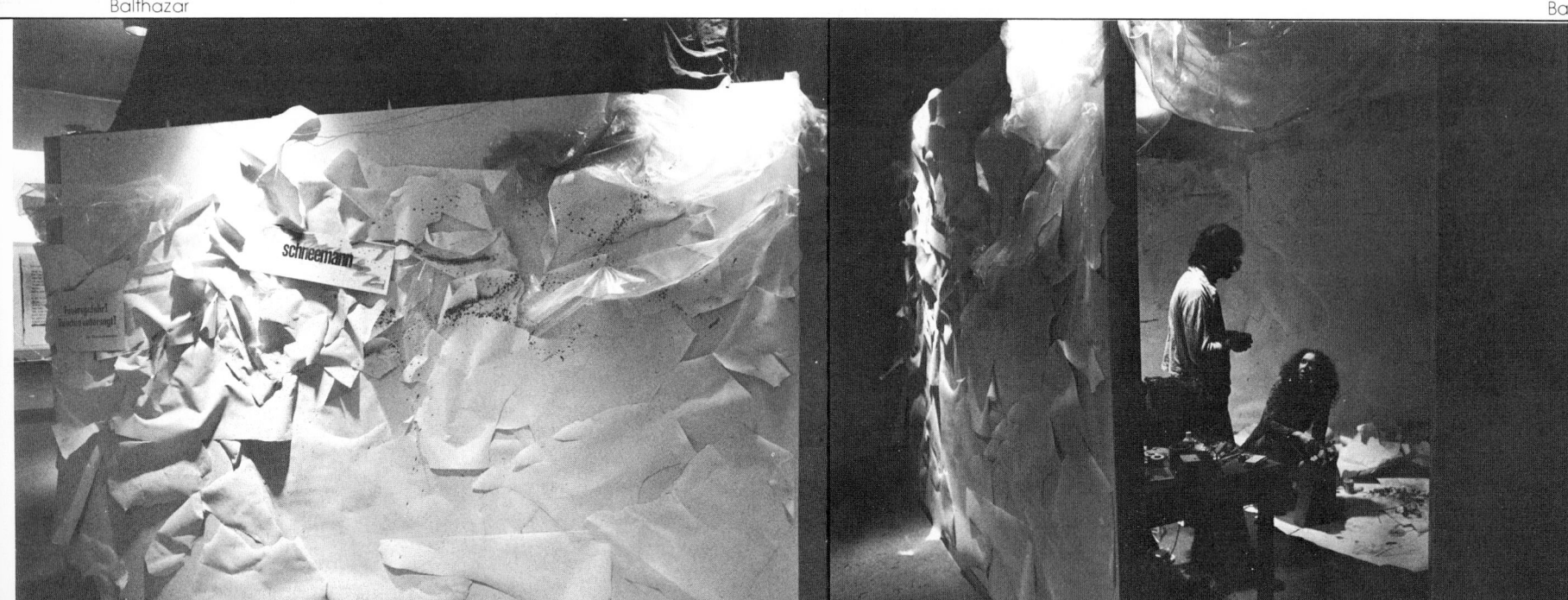

human warmth. Jobs for adventurous artists in new media are extremely limited; on the second floor—above the film screening and public rooms—a warren of artists share a cold faucet to wash, an inoperable toilet; they have arranged mattresses and plastic sheets, wooden partitions and work spaces.

Our collaboration is intensive, we work constantly. It's invigorating, our creative and tecnical experiences re-enforce one another. For instance, I wanted three slide relays to pulse and overlap, to alternate figure and ground, to concentrate and break apart the images. John designed a diaphram with a unit of servo motors set to a variable electronic program. Then we designed mirrored screens on the diaphram which would pulse in reaction to the movement of spectators— slide projectors focused into the mirrors run by the servo motors. We began to evolve a 180° panorama in which overlays of images on the slides would dissolve depth perspective, superimposing alternating fields. Audio and visual circuits would respond to both movement, position in space, and heat of the spectators' bodies. We re-filmed and sequenced three carousels of 80 slides coordinated to double track half hour sound tapes. The entire circuitry was built by Lifton on a small computer deck which he found, thrown out, behind a supermarket. The relays of the system would automatically stop when no one was in the room, and begin as soon as anyone entered.

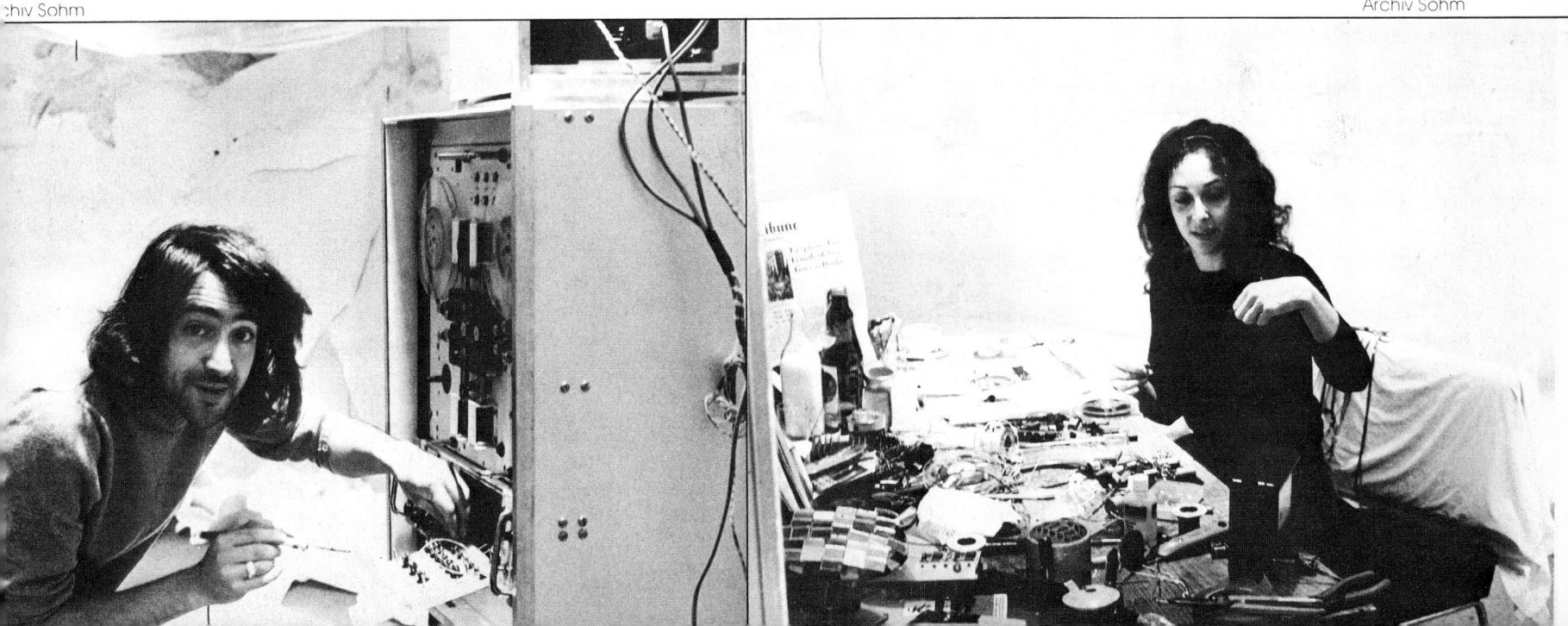

I planned a dome of plastic sheeting, overlapping layers, filled with soap flakes to defract and reflect the slide and film imagery as its pulsations swung across the ceiling; the walls of the room were covered in large irregular layers of white paper—a painstaking collage, since the shapes of the paper formed an overall rhythmic layer which further spread and split the imagery.

Once in Köln we discovered our entire budget had been used on the circuitry and we couldn't afford a hotel. To the horror and outrage of the museum guards, we moved into our environment. The remaining work to be done was as overwhelming for Szeemann as it was for us: he slept outside our "tent" on a cot. One museum trustee was the manufacturer of "Persil"—the "Ivory" of Europe. Our big break was the gross of soap flakes boxes delivered to me in the Museum, completing the details of the environment and contributing to our cleanliness. I remember washing Harald's, John's and my socks and underwear in the Museum toiletten and hanging it all to dry under our plastic ceiling. In revenge for this and greater crimes, the guards began to lock us all in or out of the Museum. The entire exhibit was condemned by the fire marshalls, the ministers of Köln (Nitsch's wall hanging of bloodied priests' raiments), the health department, the veterinarian and agricultural departments (Vostell's pregnant cow in a pen), the museum trustees and finally by the museum director himself. (Szeemann was guest curator). Nevertheless. . .it happened.

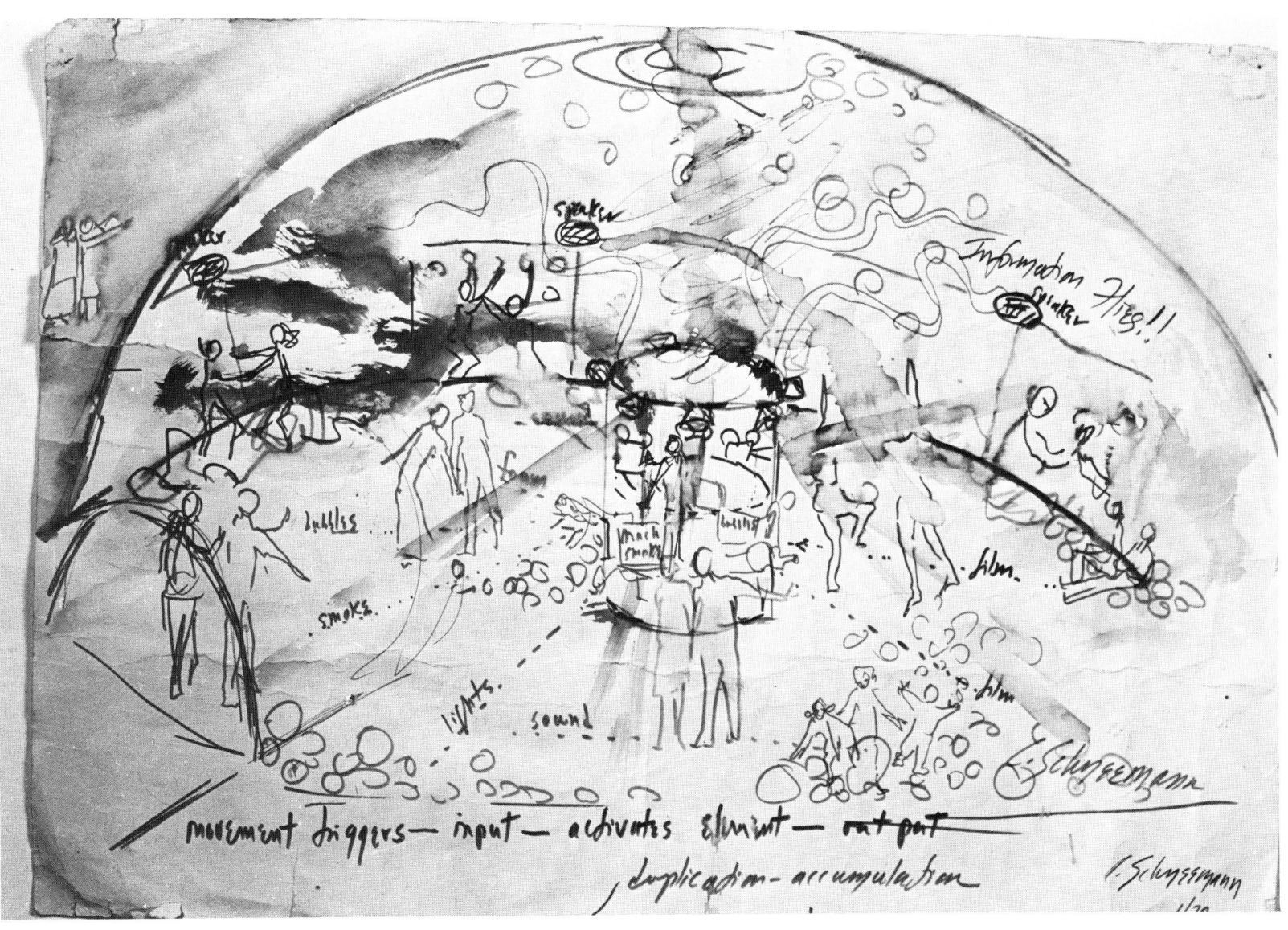

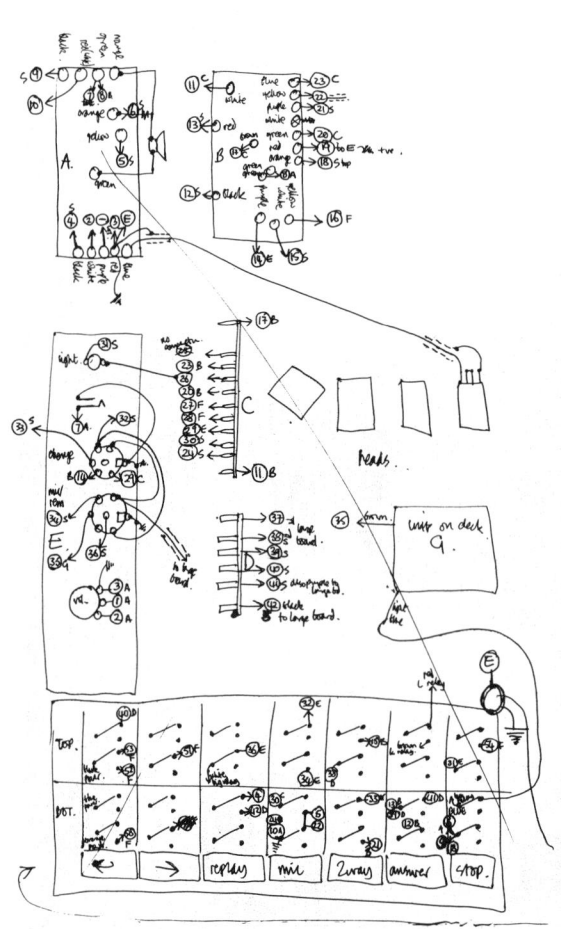

SLIDES

snows

meat joy

water light/
water needle

Meat Systems drawing of circuitry by John Lifton. 1970 Ink. 14'' x 9''

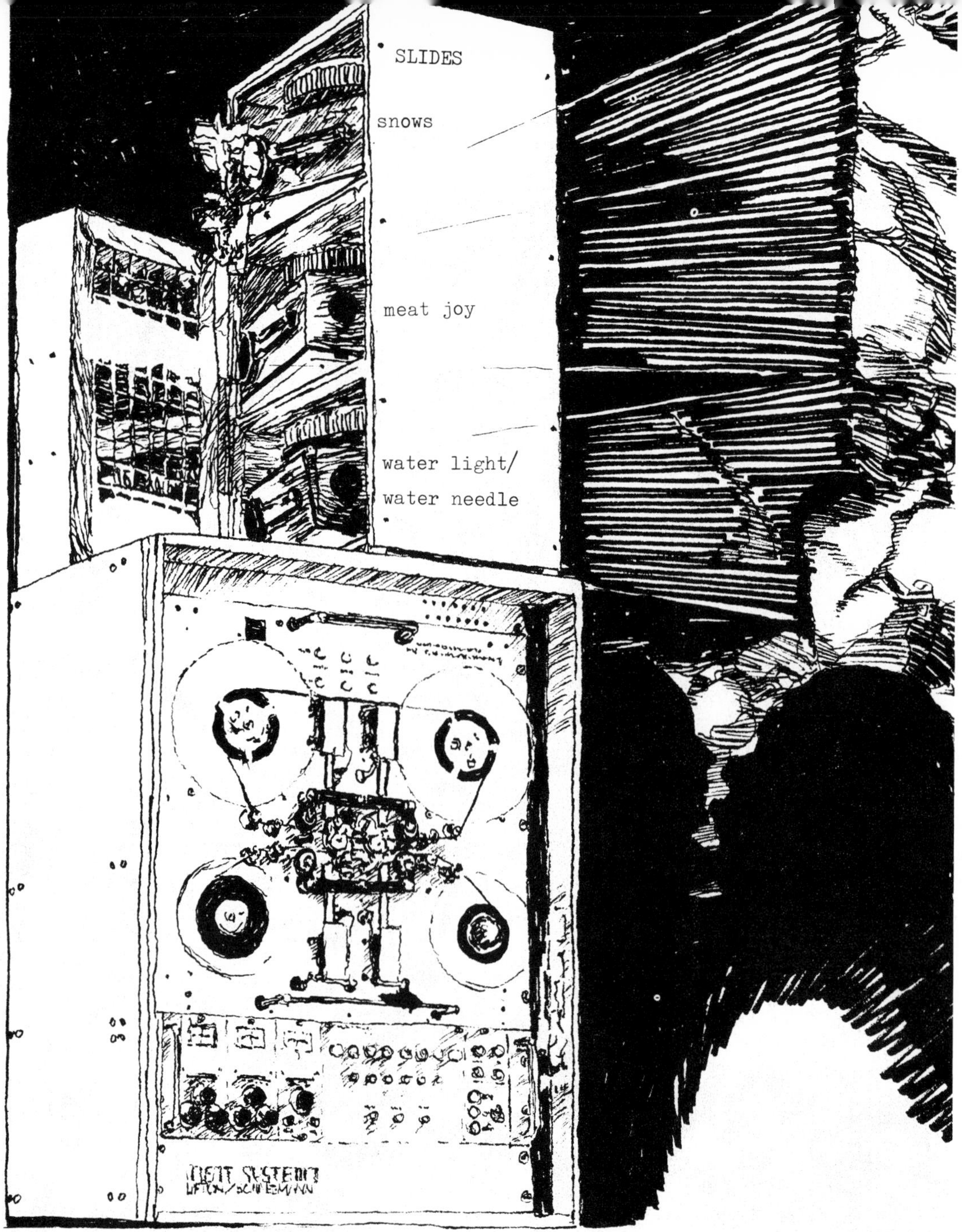

Meat Systems drawing by John Lifton for "Happenings and Fluxus Retrospective" Köln Künstverein 1970. Ink. 9'' x 14''

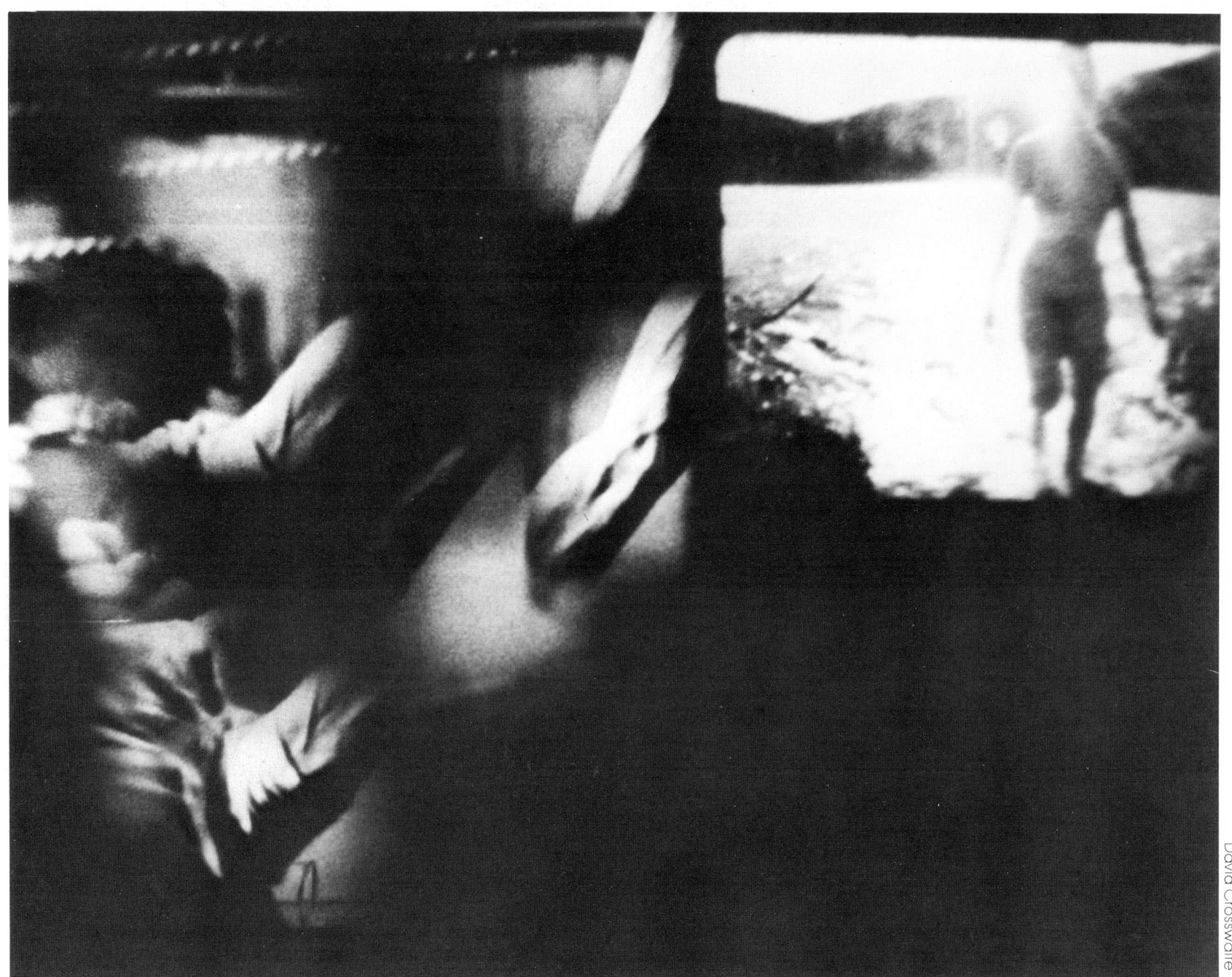

David Crosswaite

SCHLAGET AUF

November 14 1970 Fluxus Fluxorum
Festival Forum Theater Berlin

The Forum theater a little island within the island of the city, islanded within its own country. Observing things the Berliners told me not to bother with: how many of the old stone apartment houses in center Berlin were scarred with bullet holes, shrapnal; sections of the city like relics from the past surviving in expanses of the anonymous symmetries of post WWII building. It was winter and many people seemed crazy— different from New York City—hostile crazy: I was pushed and shoved on and off buses; salespeople screamed at me in Department Stores for putting my hands on a package of undershirts, for touching a jar of face cream. I understood one saleswoman yelling at me in German: "Red or Yellow! You don't know which! Don't come back here until you can speak properly." There were many artists on special scholarships from central and eastern Europe, mixed with the German artists in Berlin, and the contrary range and attitudes each represented were brought into some harmonious personal tolerance, even appreciation—as if accepting one another and having a communication or a good time was more essential than the aesthetic differences. So I enjoyed the artists getting along and felt welcome among them. Most of the Germans had been through experiences in the war which were beyond communicating. One impoverished poet who nightly ate from the plates of friends in the bar, took me to the roof top of a building from which we could see East Berlin. He pointed to a haze of factory chimneys and hills beyond and said "All that we can see from here was my grandfather's and my father's." At night we all hung out in bars where the convivial atmosphere was somehow strange and I described the people as having "reconstituted their psyches"—having had to go so far off in personal space they had emerged with an integrity whose alchemy was unrecognizable to me.

Uneasy. Tension. I wanted to make a work which relieved the containment, a circular hollow ring I began to hear in the Berlin night. There were many strands activated: my German name—a source of paradoxes, analogues, puns used in my work; not speaking German with the exception of phrases learned from Bach cantatas, the consistent importance of Bach in my own work; growing up, for the most part, in an all German rural community in Pennsylvania.

One of the people I met in the all-night bar was a poet and translator, dressed severely in black Victorian clothes, his hair and moustache meticulously trimmed, his glasses polished and his hands cold, white. To my eyes he was classically rigid, humorless, solemn, and he sparked something essential for the improvisation I was planning— contrast, accompaniment. Anastas spoke a careful precise English. I asked if he would be the translator for me—that the duration and tempo of my actions would build on a translation reiteration as I improvised a "lecture." Could he do an immediate translation of whatever I said into a medieval form of poetic German? He wanted to be helpful but was mistrustful and asked repeatedly: "Will I be laughed at? Will I seem foolish? I will not help you if I will seem foolish and be laughed at."...As I envisioned the piece we **would** be laughed at—my actions, their references to art istorical shibboliths...In the actual event everyone **was** laughing; Anastas himself discovered the unexpected satisfaction of provoking hilarity, heightening my naked demonstration of "gestalt movement" by stopping his translations to ask: "Do you mean this concept in the subjective or the archaic reflexive?"

He further surprised me when I came into the theater on the performance evening, insisting severely "You **must** come with me, here into the back." He opened the door to a tiny dressing room and for the first time, smiled. There was a huge Turkish hookah on a doily and a large lump of hashish.

Offering the pastry to the audience for the "cake attack": it seemed to me the communal pleasure in Berlin was composed of oral rewards, quantities of alcohol, sausages, and treats of incredibly rich and sugary sweets. I thought being attacked with the classical Berlin substance would enlarge the oral fixity of this pleasure to a more active physical one; notwithstanding the affront to the sanctity of "Viennese" baking—still, it was an avant-garde sort of audience and they took the transmutation in hand..

"Schlaget Auf" is a mishearing of Cantata #53: "Schlage doch, gewunschte stunde." This favorite record was given to me by Jim when we were snowbound in Vermont; the clear striking of the bells against strings, continuo and the sonorous aria sung by Hilde Roessel-Majden. "Schlage" is to hit, strike, bang, chip, heartbeat, and has implications—physical and temporal—taken out of the context of the Cantata. The recording of the Cantata, a very old turntable and speaker, were at the side of the stage. Ludwig Gosewitz had instructions to repeatedly play the bells section of the Cantata and to drop the needle onto the record at intervals he found appropriate.

René Block organized this Theater Festival with enthusiasm, inviting artists who had participated in the "Happenings and Fluxus" exhibit in Koln. I don't remember all the other events, but a roll-call of those performing included: Al Hansen, Valarie Herouvis, Eric Andersen, Marianne Filliou, Robert Filliou, Dick Higgins, Tot and Addy Koepcke, Charlotte Moorman, Robin Page, Tomas Schmit, Emmett Williams. And among the audience: Harald Szeemann, Hans Sohm, Maruta Schmit, Mark Brusse, Dorothy Iannone, Dieter Rot, Margaret Raspé, Michael Büthe, Gerhardt Richter, Christos Joachamides, Mary Kaplan, Carol Paige, Earle Brown, Bazen Bröck, Inge Böcker, Stefan & Ingrid Werwerke, Otto Müehl.

In Berlin's most auspicious theater, before a tumultuous crowd... Schneemann in a rare solo event, assisted by Dr. Annastas, German's renowned scholar of medieval poetry (stoned out of his head).... A hidden battery of technicians await secret signals for lights! slides! sound!

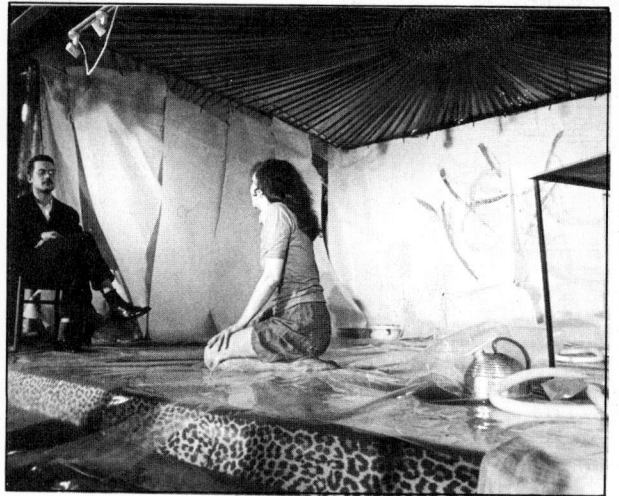

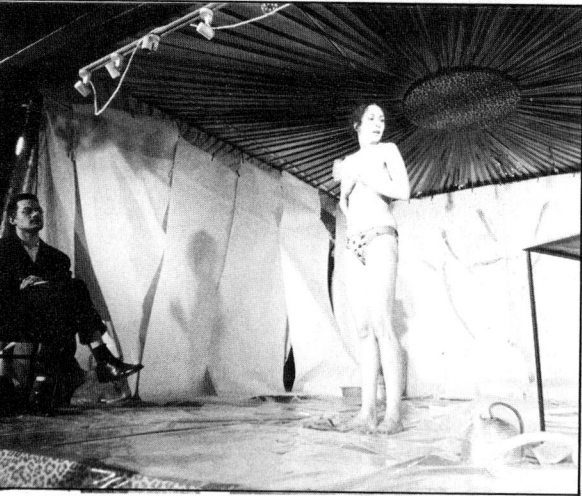

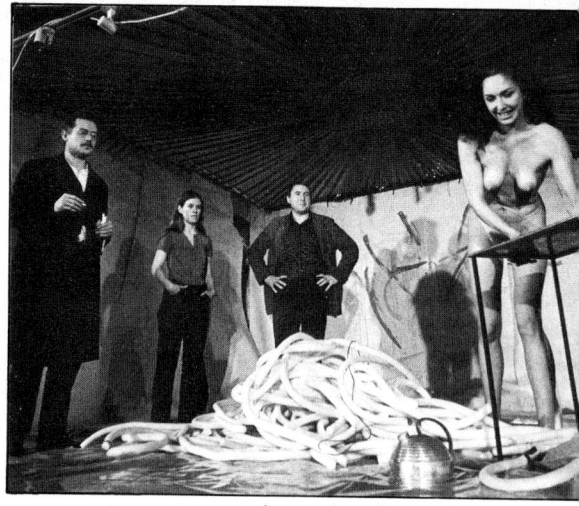

"Whatever I say you will please to translate."

"Was immer Ich sage wirst Du bitte übersetzen."

"Using my body as a tranformable energy system I will demonstrate some recent tendencies of the inter-relatedness between material and movement."

"Indem ich meinen Körper als übertragbares Energiesystem benütze, demonstriere ich jetzt einige neuere Tendenzen in der Wechselbeziehung von Material und Bewegung."

"Our ingredients tonight are a pile of foam rubber strips from the boiler room. Also pints of red, white, yellow grease paint. A dozen Viennese

pastries, a cream cake, a chocolate cake, a meringue."

"Unsere Zutaten sind heute abend ein Haufen Schaumgummistreifen aus dem Kesselraum. Ausserdem Dosen mit roter, weisser & gelber Schminke. Ein Dutzend Wiener Gebäck, eine Sahnetorte, eine Schokoladetorte, eine Meringue."

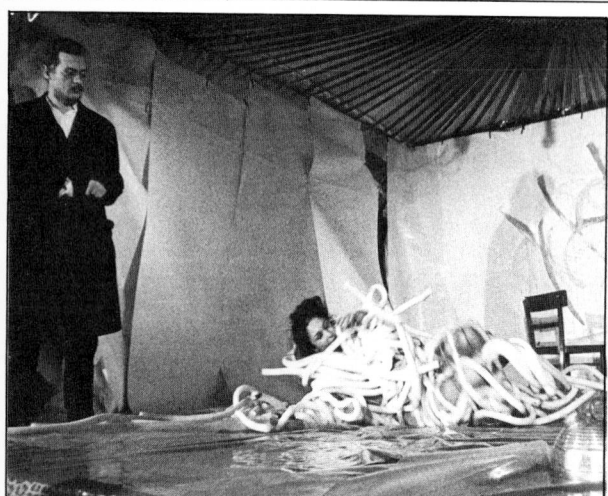

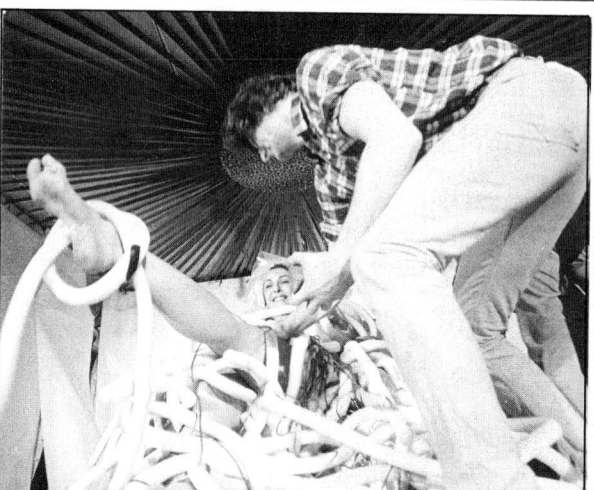

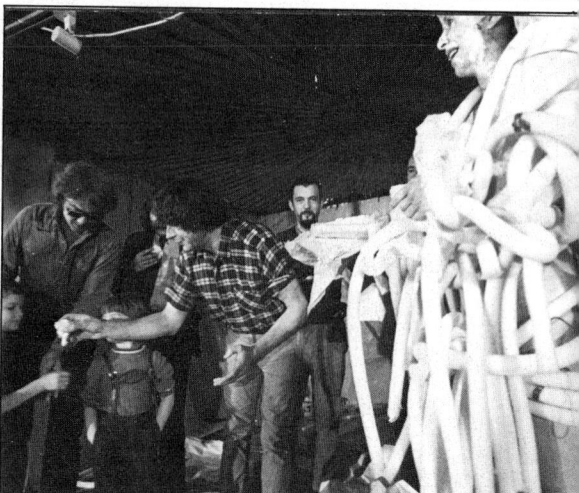

"A muscular impulse, in order for the energy of falling to begin moving."

"Ein Muskelimpuls, um die Energie des Fallens ins Rollen zu bringen."

"The foam rubber bounces. Another tangible

element which will change the possibilities of movement.....Could I have another volunteer for this grease?"   (Otto Muehl obliges.)

"Das Schaumgummie prallt. Ein weiter greifbares Element, das die Möglichkeiten von

Bewegung verändern wird... Dürfte ich bitte einen anderen Freiwilligen haben für diese Schmiere?"

"Everyone pick a cake! I will start running, you each try to slap a cake on me. Thank you. Music! Lights!"

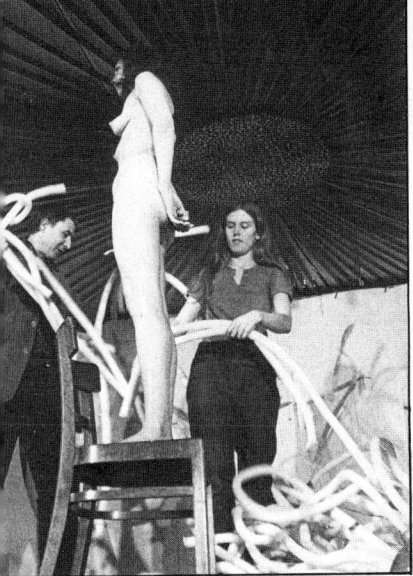
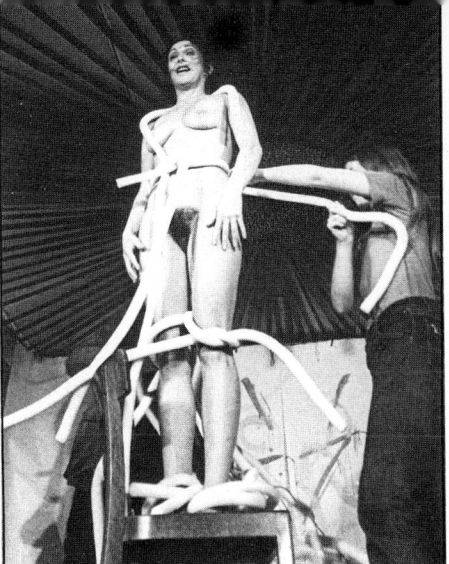
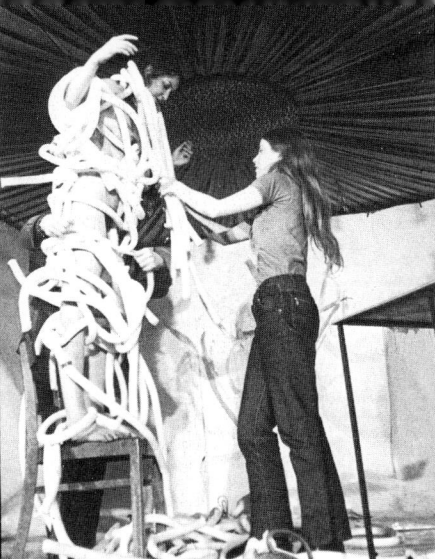

"Please may I have some volunteers? Thank you."

"Könnte ich bitte einige Freiwillige bekommen? Danke Schön."

"Notice the initial configurations are linear."

"Beachtet, dass die Figuren (Konfigurationen) linear beginnen."

"Increasing density of material-organic, rhythmic forms.... Because my legs and arms are tied up I will have to throw myself off this chair!"

"Zunehmende Dichte der material-organischen, rhythmischen Formen... Da meine Beine und Arme gebunden sind, muss ich mich von diesem Stuhl werfen."

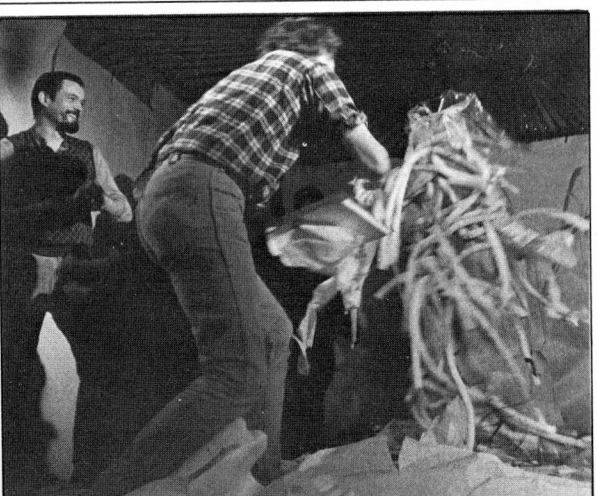
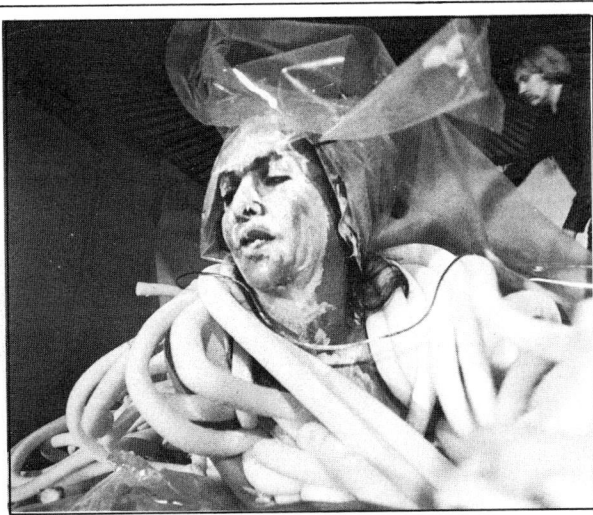

"Jeder greife eine Torte! Wenn ich anfange zu laufen, sollt Ihr versuchen mich zu treffen. Danke Schön. Musik! Beleuchtung!"

The running form.   *Die laufende Form.*

...schlaget gestalten...!

...schlaget gestalten...

photos by Hermann Kiessling

POSTCARDS

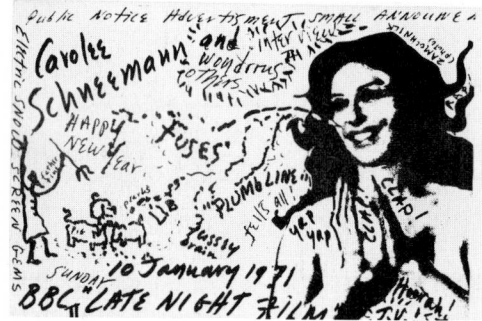

The post card series occurred over a period of two years in London. The first card was to announce a BBC program during which clips from my films were shown. With this card in hand, Anthony McCall first came to visit me. Subsequent cards relate to our life together.

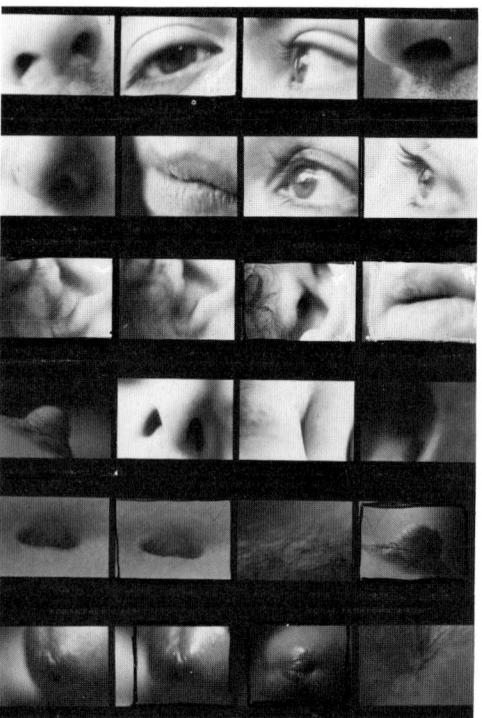

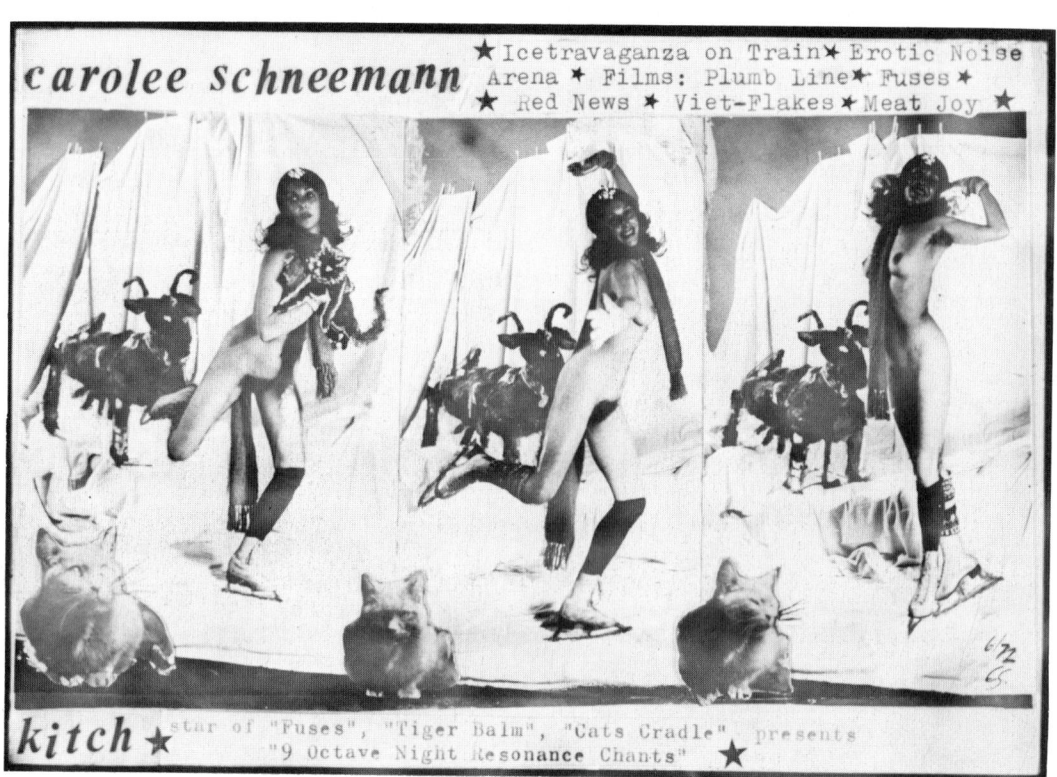

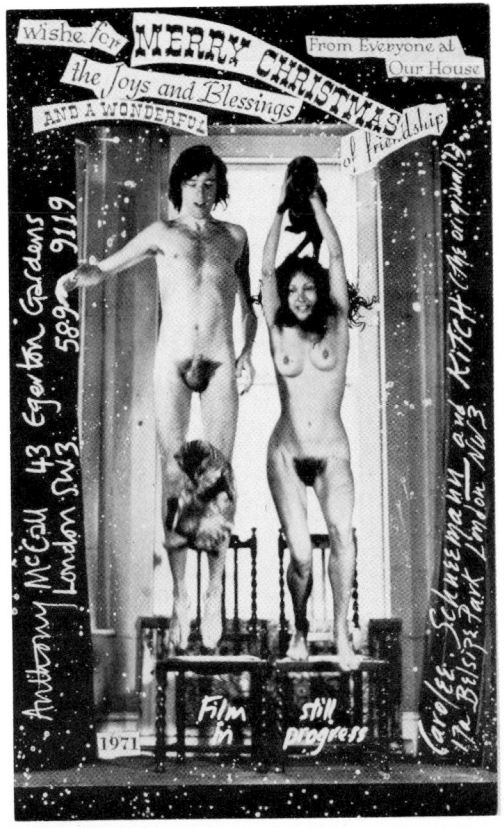

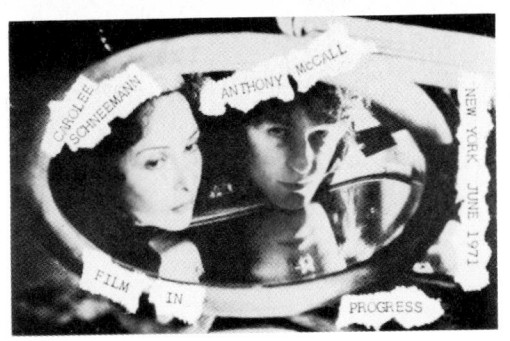

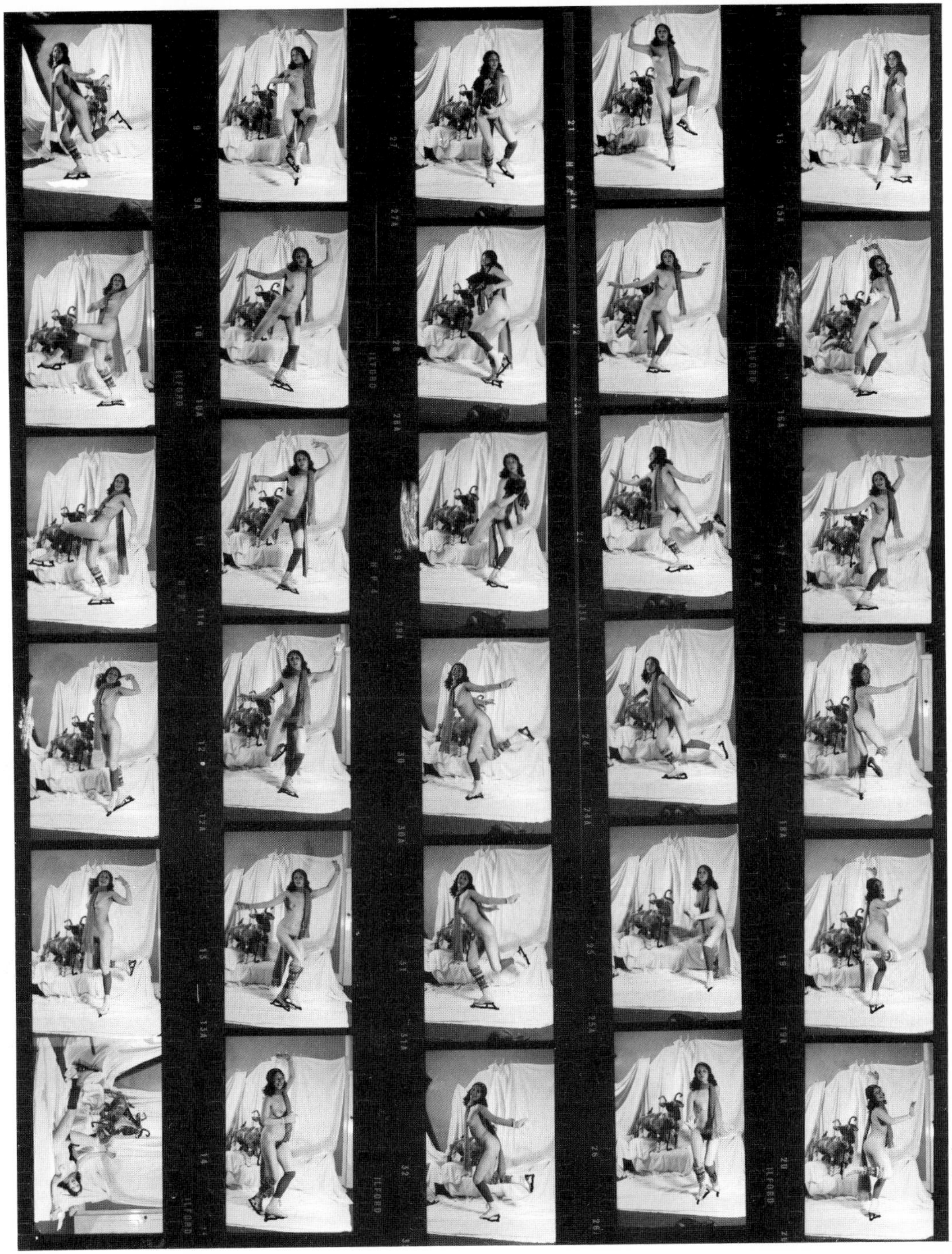

213

RAINBOW BLAZE

September 1971 Avant Garde Festival
  The Armory NY

A ritual painting event to enclose/expand, to sanctify and purify the Armory, its contradictory functions: to douse it with a natural referrent—the rainbow. A group cooperation. I sent Charlotte Moorman diagrams and instructions from London. I no longer have a copy…something like this: The bands of a rainbow spectrum blue, rose, green, yellow, violet are to be sequentially painted in wide strips around the Armory during the course of the Avant-Garde Festival. The first circle begins at the front door; increasing lengths of semi-circular colored bands are painted until the steps, pavement, street, cars and objects in the path of the band are covered. Spaces left unpainted when cars or persons move are filled in during the subsequent days. The rainbow band seems to penetrate the armory and comes out on all sides full circle.

Charlotte wrote me that a group of art students painted the rainbow blaze during the course of the festival.

ROAD ANIMATION FOR REYKJAVIK

June-July 1972 Reykjavik Art-Festival

Outside of New York, an art "center" can be wherever artists reach each other through the mail. This work was performed by Icelandic artists during an exhibit by Galerie SUM of performance art documentation which included many Scandinavian artists and, as I later discovered in the catalog, Acconci, Attalai, Ehrenberg, Filliou, Gibbs, Latham, McCall, Oppenheim, and Rot.

I. The participants collect dirty rags—which range in size from small to large as a sheet or blanket. Some bring wrinkled paper bags & sheets of newspaper.

The event is set off from the roof or upper windows of a building and in the street.

Choose a street in central Reykjavik where traffic is not constant.

1. one rag or paper is thrown down into the street from the roof. one rag or paper is laid in the street. if the rag or paper is run over the participants scream.
2. tie a long string to a rag & place it in the street. stand out of sight. if a car is about to run over it it is pulled away.
3. several rags on strings are laid in the street. when a car is about to run over them they are pulled away.
4. put all the rags & papers in the street. ask curious people to help—they can stop cars until the materials are positioned. let the rags & papers be run over by the traffic.
5. photograph the changes & interactions. photograph the rags & papers before & after they are run over.

February 1972 (& March thanks to Anthony McCall's "Road Work")

Both **Schlaget Aug** and **Ices Strip** are comic works—droll, testy, iconclastic. Here I took on Wittgenstein, compacting phrases from *Tractatus Logico-Philosophicus* as my thesis for a strip tease performed on a dining table of a train travelling from London to Edinburgh.

The train was open to the public as well as members of the Ices Festival—an international gathering of artists organized by Harvey Matusow and Annea Lockwood to give London's bitter-sweet, dreamy merger of energized exiles and receptive natives an art binge (and to provide every avant-gardist tendency in Europe a chance to surface for a week of events at the Round House).

The departure of the train was heralded by the Marilyn Wood dancers, and musicians performing amidst the commutor rush at Paddington Station. Our train had its own "instant" newspaper, (run off the Beau Geste Press Gestetener in a cattle car) by Felipe Eherenberg, Marthe Hellion, their children, David Mayor, Alan & Elaine Fisher, and others associated with Collumpton commune. Poets of assorted nationalities composed communications for printing, so that any sort of event or work in one car quickly became community knowledge. There were also cars with film and video showings. And our food (alas) was part of the art: the dining car had a buffet of purple (white) bread, cold green hot dogs, black mustard, magenta spaghetti, violet pound cake, and blue milk. The waiters on our train comprised an anarchist performance troupe from Liverpool, dressed in white medical coats with greyed jockey shorts and carrying trays of miniature wooden animals. (They handed you a regular menu; if you asked for hamburger, a tiny wooden bull was set down). On arriving in Edinburgh the "normal" people fled the train and the rest of us branched out as auxiliaries to the Edinburgh Festival. Charlotte performed the "T.V. Bra" and Anthony smoke-bombed the De Marco Gallery with "Smoke Without Fire". . .he had just come back from filming for the IRA in Londonderry. And we all had a chance to see the amazing Thadusz Kantor performance (from Poland), an intricate structure of seeming-chaos in a turmoil of disruptions/interferences—close to my heart.

ICES STRIP

August 21 1972 Ices Festival Train,
London-Edinburgh

ISIS TAKES YOU FOR A RIDE

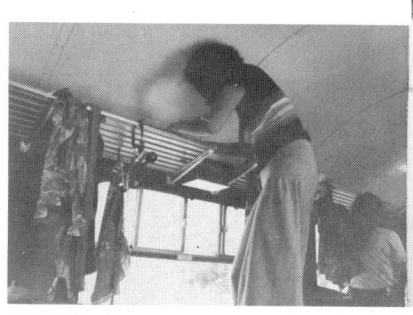
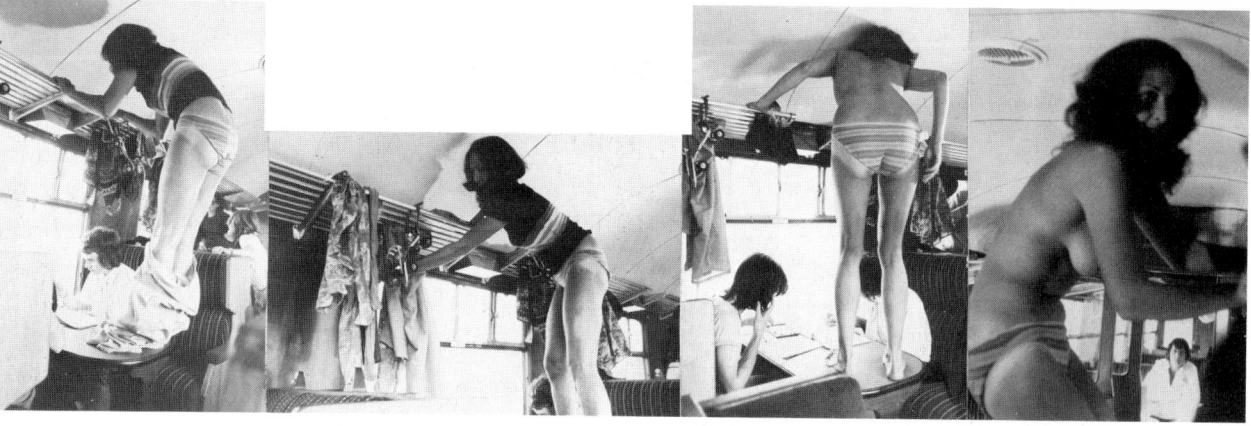

Schneemann redresses on dining car table in preparation to roller skate the length of the Ices Festival Train hurtling 133 kph from London to Edinburgh. August 1972.

3:11 We use the perceptible sign of a proposition (spoken or written etc.) as a projection of a possible situation.

3:13 Therefore, though what is projected is not itself included, its possibility is.

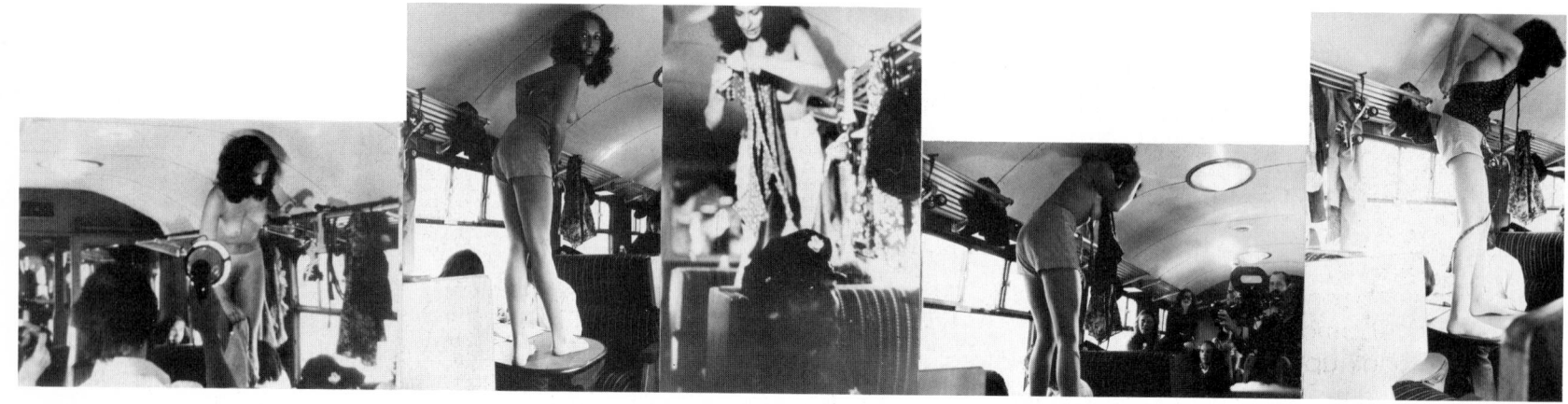

3:38 If a sign is useless, it is meaningless. That is the point of Occam's maxim.

4:02 Language disguises thought, so much so, that from the outward form of the clothing it is impossible to infer the form of the thoughts beneath it, because the outward form of the clothing is not designed to reveal the form of the body, but for entirely different purposes.

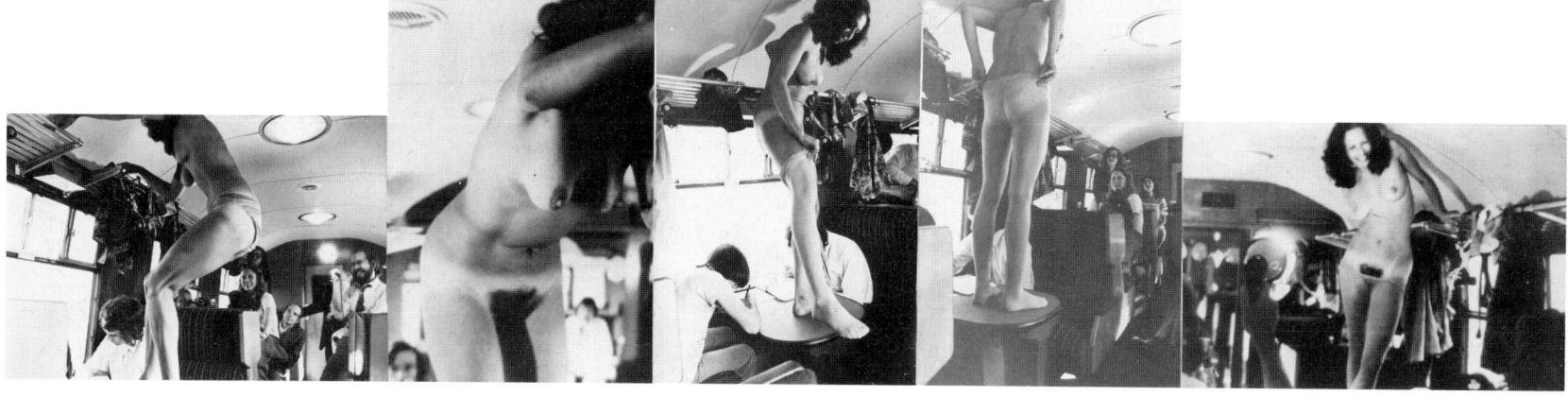

3:20 I call such elements 'simple signs', and such a proposition 'completely analyzed'.

3:26 The meanings of primitive signs can be explained by means of elucidations. Elucidations are primitive signs.

3:32 In this way the most fundamental confusions are easily produced, (the whole of philosophy is full of them).

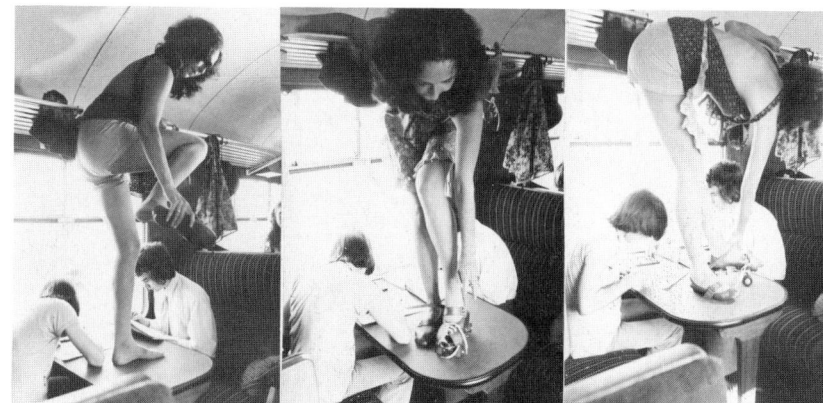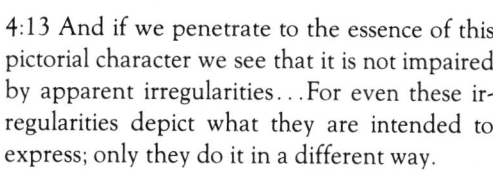

4:12 It is obvious that a proposition of the form 'aRb' strikes us as a picture.

4:13 And if we penetrate to the essence of this pictorial character we see that it is not impaired by apparent irregularities...For even these irregularities depict what they are intended to express; only they do it in a different way.

4:14 (Like the two young women in the fairy tale, their two horses, and their lilies. They are all in a certain sense one.)

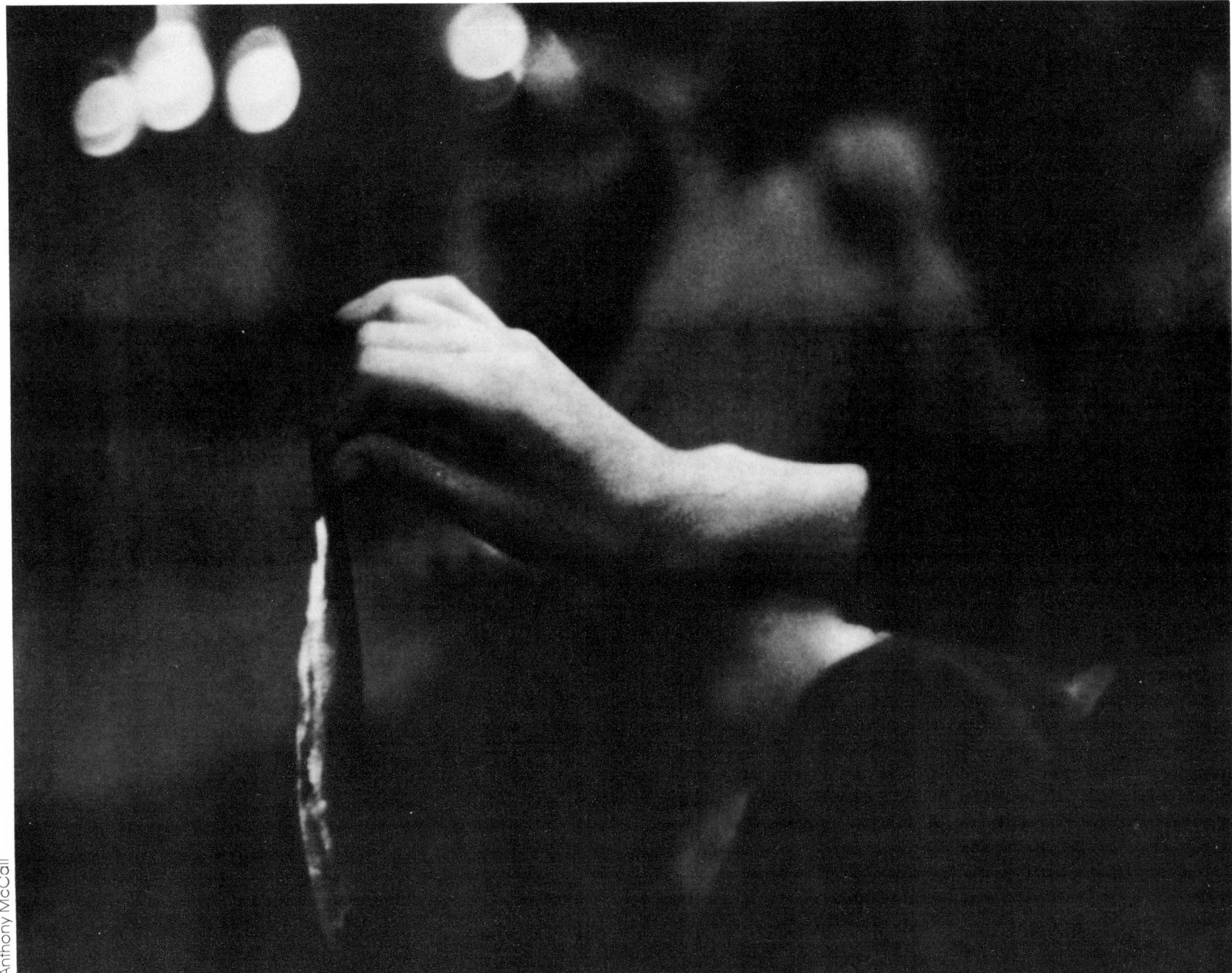

COOKING WITH APES

September 2 1973 Fylkingen Festival

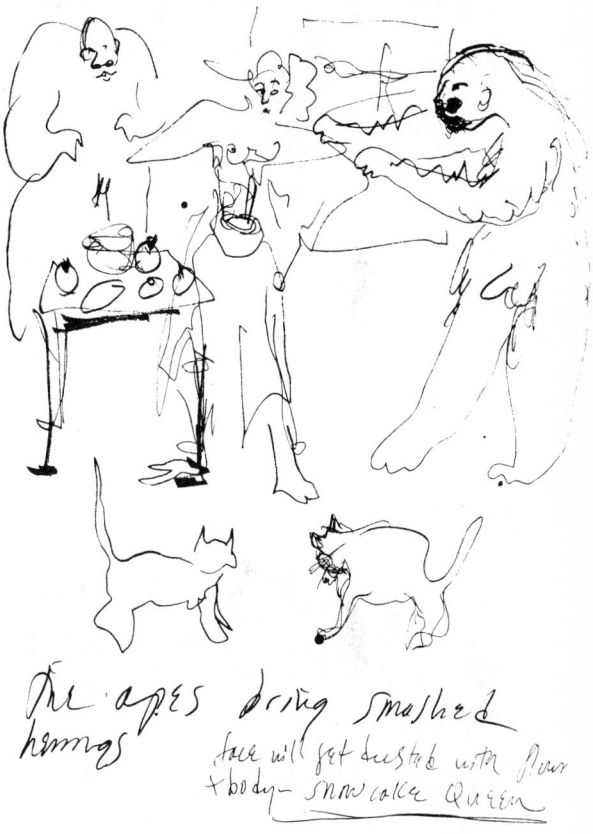

the apes driving smashed
herrings!   face will get dusted with flour
+ body— snow cake Queen

Cooking With Apes was created for the Flykingen Festival in Stockholm, and was performed only once, September 2, 1973. For the occasion I made a cooking-performance score of my recipe, "Americana I Ching Apple Pie," involving movement and sound sequences, and then allowed chance meetings, opportunities for materials, to become incorporated into the work. Two distinguished Swedish artists (composer Lars Gunnar-Bodin and poet Bengt Emil Johnson) wore gorilla suits: their movement instructions were linked with a petite Russian ballerina who appeared at the first rehearsal expressing a willingness to try new forms of dance. She spoke only Russian, making "cues" a matter of unpredictable negotiation. In the Stockholm subway I became fascinated by a young violinist dressed in white playing melancholy tunes and passing a large wicker basket for his future studies at the conservatory. Since our budget was able (barely) to meet his projected income for two nights in the subway, he joined the group. Two Swedish dancers (who were coming to New York to study with Cunningham) became the assistant cooks, dressed in abbreviated night gowns and nurses' caps. Susie Valentine (founder of L'Etoile du Nord) gave the recipe instructions in Swedish and English through a bullhorn from atop a high platform while wearing the bottom of a swan costume and a baseball cap. Sven Hansen—composer and the Director of Fylkingen—assisted by relaying the instructions into Finnish. He was naked except for socks, roller skates, a scarf, and a shepherd's staff (to aid his skating).

From the Score: As the audience enters the hallway each person is handed a raw herring by a Gorilla hanging from the iron stairs. Near dark. The other Gorilla rolls up and down the floor, so the audience must step around. The violinist plays darkly in dark corners. Inside is heard the amplified sound of a dying bee. At the door each audience member is given a little plastic bag for the herring when they pay their ticket. Inside the large, open performance space the Russian ballerina (wearing a Baverian cocktail waitress minidress) "measures the space," dancing while swinging bags of paprika, adjusting her movements as the room fills and explaining her dance and the measurements in Russian. As people are seated the Gorillas and the Cook shake whips dangling herrings at them, changing the space to suit the performance.

As cook my activities were centered around a glass table on wheels, five feet high and seven feet long. I was able to lie, stand, sit, crawl onto and off of it, and

Dramatis Personae	
Translator I (Swan)	Violinist
Cook	Translator II (on roller skates)
2 Assistant Cooks	Gorilla I
Russian Ballerina	Gorilla II 16 cats

FROM THE LIBERATED COCK BOOK FOR WOMEN AND OTHERS
FROM THE LIBERATED COOK BOOK FOR WOMEN AND OTHERS

Go into the kitchen with defiant joyful anger. On this scruffy battleground you will lay down the cookbook forever. You will cease competition with untold legions of sublimated self-satisfied female psyches engaged over the centuries in a pursuit of excellence through flour grease onion turnips blenders collander strainer boilers mincers graters choppers whiskers mincers beaters

DESIST DESIST STOP. STOP NOW!

Put on an apron and…

Liberation Through Joyous Aggression. (I Ching)

The Abandonment of False Illusions.

You are in this kitchen because you do not have a penis. Keep this in mind as you crush the garlic with the heel of your shoe. You are in this kitchen because you have or might have a baby.

Apple Pie As Direct Contact With Materials. A recipe based on my principles of Kinetic Theater (circa 1962 but good forever). This pie offers self-realization. You will be The Best Woman In The World. AMERICAN AS APPLE PIE. JUST LIKE MUM'S. Remember: The over is your womb! Let's do it right!

INGREDIENTS: apples   1 sack of whole wheat flour (100% stone ground) barbados sugar   egg yolks   safflower oil   butter   honey   cinnamon   lemon

Open the flour sack with yr right hand & scoup up 3 handfuls, drop into a bowl. Pinch off a big lump of butter, drop in bowl. Pour in 2 quick turns of oil. Add small pile brown sugar. Use both hands to scrunch it all up in yr finger tips to a nice crumby mass soft. Sprinkle a few drops of cold water on top, mix again. Now it is sticky & ready to be patted into a baking dish…or two. Might as well make two pies. Slide hunk of butter all over baking dishes.

Wash apples (don't peel if organically grown). Pat pastry all over the dish. Use small lumps which you press flat until they all mesh & cover the dish. Now you can make those cute finger indentations along the top. Slice apples right onto pastry, very thin until they reach the top! Sprinkle with cinnamon, bits of sugar, butter bits, lemon juice, drips of honey. If you have some yogurt or sour cream about, take yr fingers & smear it over apple tops.

(Have Faith!) Note: if any ingredients fall on the floor just pick them up & put where they should have gone. My father always said: "People eat about three lbs. of dirt every year."

Now for the butterfly! Take bits of remaining pastry in yr fingers & flatten out — make a vague sort of butterfly shape. Lay these over apples; pinch them onto edge of pastry on sides of baking dish. Keep laying the bits out until the top is covered. THAT'S ALL. Stick in oven.

I do not "preheat" the oven because I think it gives a cruel shock to the apples & flour & the dish. Rather a nice gradual baking. Baking is like waiting for pubic hair to grow when yr twelve yrs old. Put it in & go away. Pretend nothing is happening. You will suddenly remember pies in the oven! Just in time to run, look, find they are still raw. Be patient and haughty. After a time you will see butter bubbling, smell absolute evidence………. check pastry at bottom for crispness. Sample some. Amazing! Verdict: very sensuous and easy to do. Not up-tight making. A True Apple Pie. Archetypal. Most interestingly for some reason it tastes of coconut. Serve to friends whose adoration you wish to bind forever.

Tested in the Belsize Park Kitchens, U.K.

Gorilla I LARS GUNNAR	Gorilla II BENGT EMIL	Russian Ballerina DORIS	Assistant Cooks ANNA Gird	Cook CAROLEE	TRANS. (SWAH SUSIE + STENSKRE)	Sound TAPE/SONG VIOLIN	Film Slides	Opaque Projector	Lights
raise Susie to platform		paprika space measure	carry in utensils	READS + COOKS	Susie on platform	violinist plays outside	film	X	dim Side (6)
try on clothing from audience	crawl around the cooks	↓	turn on projector	pushing table in circles	sten naked roller skating	Dying BEE + tape		on	↓
at rear window	shamelessly	↓	lay out herrings in project	peel apples	argue other trans. floor/plat.	violinist walks film space plays	slides	on herrings	X
masturbate on ladder SLEEP	at rear window climb to SWAN	↓	project peels	exhibit ingredients	surbash	TAPE-letter to flyKing	↓	on peels	dim sides (2)(3)(5)
dance with Doris	dance with STEN	dance with LARS	project flour	RUN-throw eggs on ceiling	German	THUNDER TAPE	X	X	CIRCLES
"DANCE" with DORIS	riding gorillas	feed the cats PROJECT broken eggs	catch in bowl	surbash	gay violin thunder tape	X	X	on eggs	dim side (4)(5)(7)(6)
under table assist cook roll table as she stands	EXITS shaking whip at audience	baking dish projected	reads + revolving	→	↓	slides	baking dish	X	dim overhead ↓
eat raw ingredients	uncertain solo		slap pastry into dishes	discussion of a personal nature	X	X	↓	↓	
take assistant cooks away	EXITS X	grabbed by gorillas		surbash	X	film ↓	X X	X X	
pick up look-carry away	X		carried away as reading	sounth etc	gay traditional song	↓	X	X	
return cook to top of table undress + exchange gorilla suits	bring in water buckets mop	pie projected bubbles	squat on table organize cooking debris	↓	with metronome one phrase	X	on pie pie	dim side (3)(7)(5)
sing with violinist			yelling						
continue to sing + drop	dump bucket of water on gorillas mop	image steams	lies down in cooking debris on table	sten-wheel off cook on table	over over	↓	pie	dim side (3)(1)(4)(5) med side

push it around the area. During the performance I prepared and cooked an apple pie according to the instructions (of three languages). All eight performers and three technical assistants took cues from specific words of the recipe. The violinist was also coordinated to three tape recordings I made: a bee caught in a spider's web, a thunder storm, and a Letter to Flykingen (describing the country chores and personal projects which made it ''impossible'' for me to come to Sweden)...Slides of myself and Anthony engaged in these activities were projected during the letter tape. The assistant cooks were responsible for inserting ingredients of the pie, as I accumulated them, into an opaque projector which hugely magnified them on the white wall behind us. A film of Arctic tundra was projected occasionally throughout the performance.

From the Score: At the phrase ''you are in this kitchen because you do not have a penis,'' Gorilla I ''masturbates'' on a ladder, then falls asleep. Gorilla II picks up the Cook and carries her to an undetermined location. The Russian ballerina mops the floor. Translator II skates and translates. The assistant cooks are projecting ingredients. The violinist plays an ''unrecognizable traditional song.''

One further environmental element (which registered some particularity of Sweden for me) was a cat house composed from two ice hockey goals. We invited everyone we knew to bring stray or pet cats which could observe our cooking from within the goals and eat the herrings. About sixteen cats participated.

From the Score: At the conclusion of **Cooking With Apes,** slices of pies baked in rehearsals are given to the audience. Without further instructions the pies are devoured.

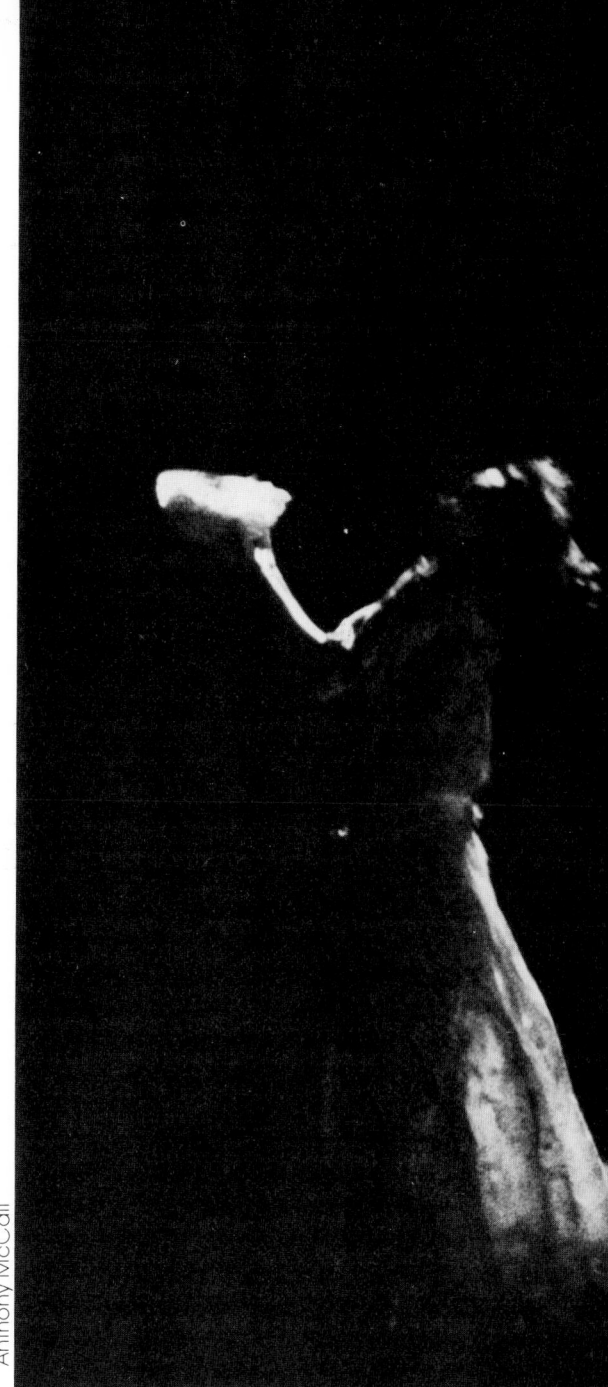

Anthony McCall

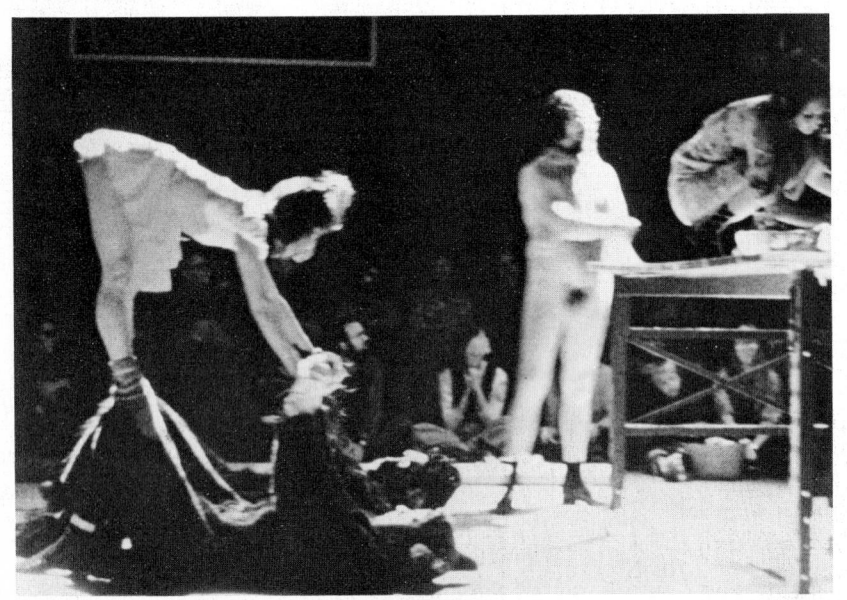
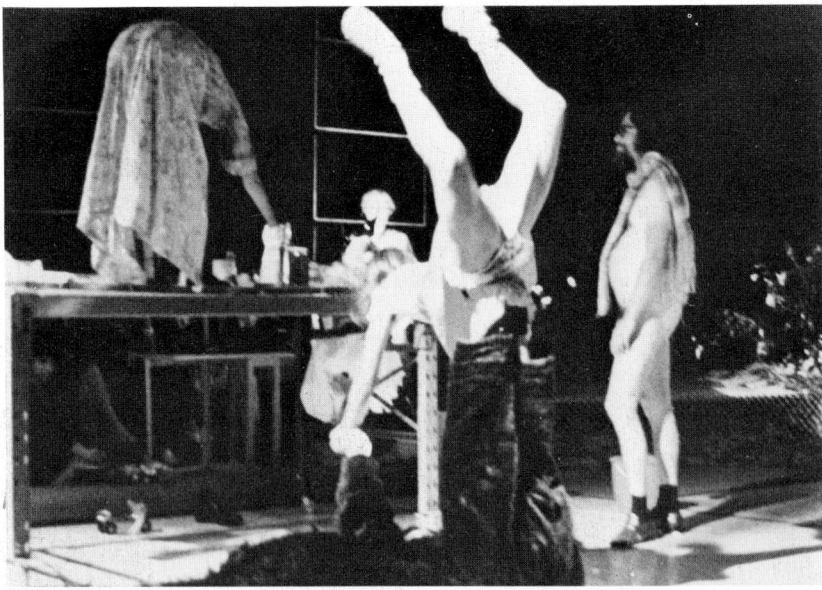
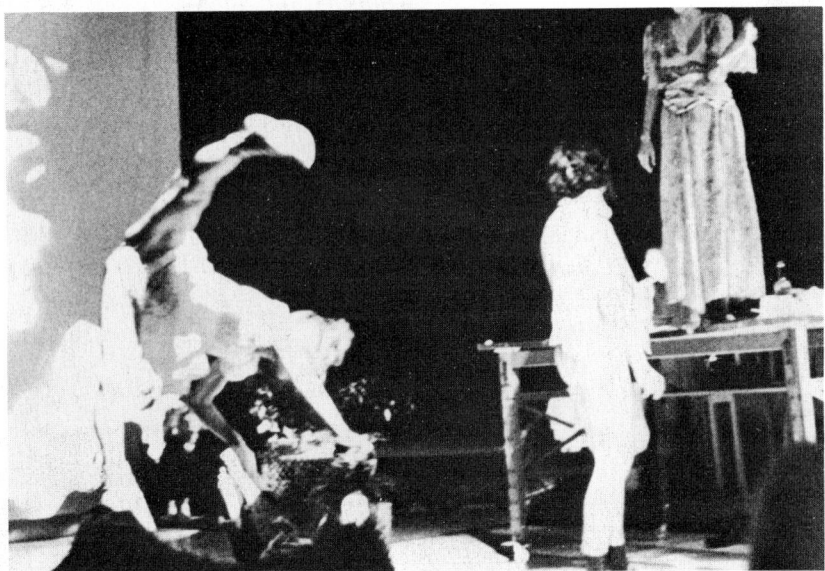
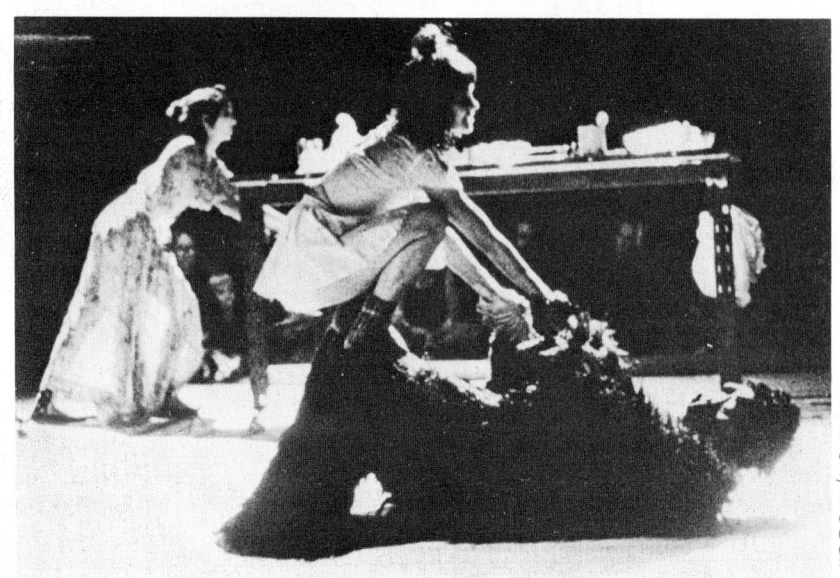

Anthony McCall

222

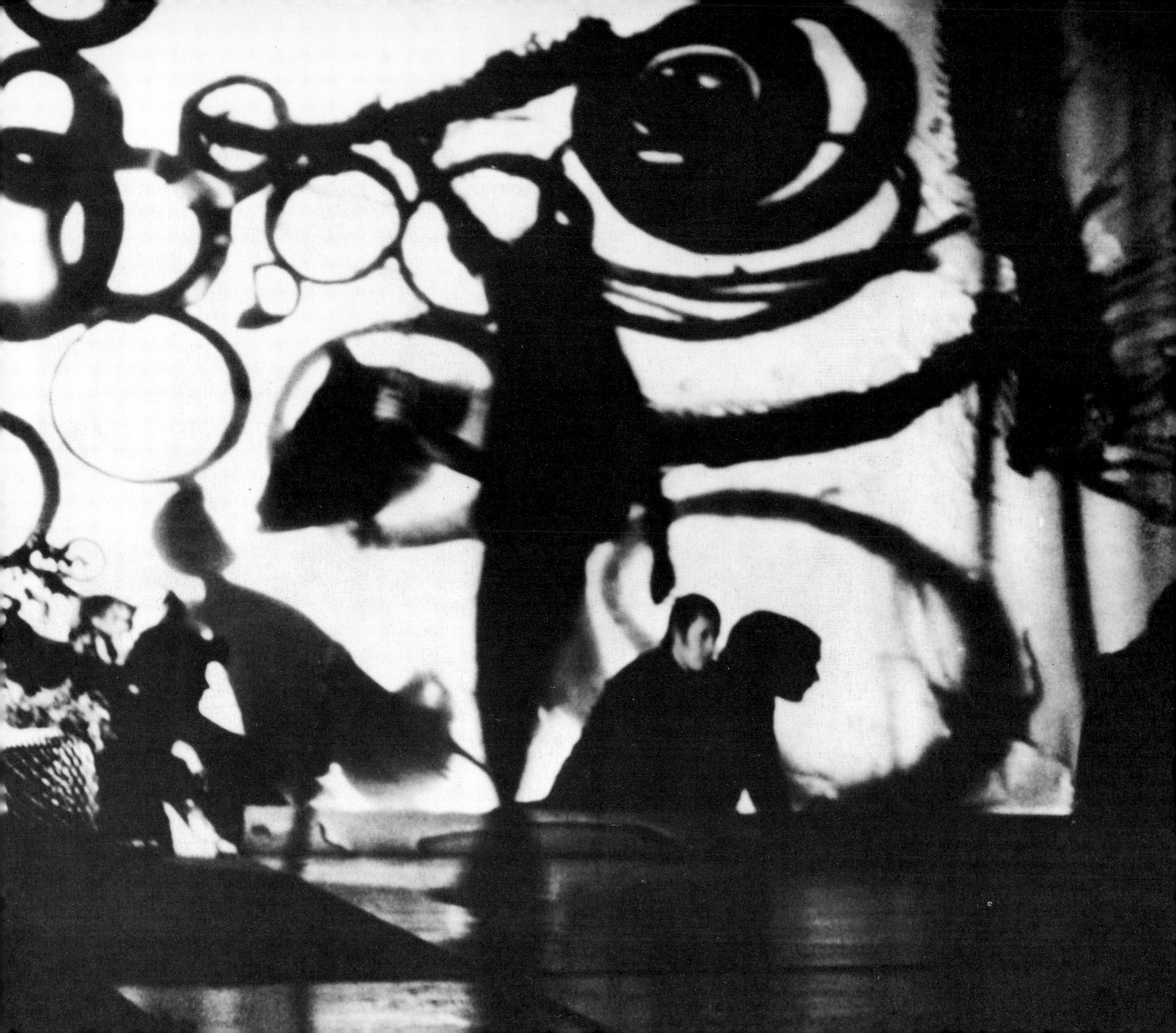

UP TO
AND
INCLUDING
HER LIMITS

("Trackings")
December 1973 Avant Garde Festival
  Grand Central Station NY

April 11 1974 University Art Museum
  Berkeley California (Performance-
  Installation)

June 18 1974 Arts Meeting Place,
  London (Performance-Installation)

June 19 1974 London Filmmakers
  Cooperative

December 1 1974 Artists Space NY

December 12 13 1974 Anthology Film
  Archive NY

February 13 14 1976 The Kitchen NY
  (Performance-Installation)

June 10 1976 Studiogalerie Berlin
  (Installation June 10-25)

June 13-20 1976 Basle Art Fair
  (Installation)

In January 1973 the England to South Africa cruise ship SS Canberra changed itinerary and made a winter crossing from London to New York City to pick up passengers before heading south. A one class, one fare ($150—with baggage) ticket was offered in an attempt to partially fill the ship, which would carry its full crew, and function like a small city with its newspaper, bakery, cabarets, beauty salon, sauna, games room, bars and sumptuous meals served in a huge dining hall by elegant young British ensigns in well tailored uniforms, and by Goanese waiters dressed in ill fitting uniforms. This unlikely offering made it possible for Anthony McCall and me to shift our life together from London to New York; we loaded up our trunks of books and art work, and managed to smuggle Kitch on board (animals are forbidden on British ships).

The ship was half-full and very luxurious for us. The passengers were a "slice of life" including David Bowie and retinue, draft-resisters, large family groups, artists, newlyweds, European tourists, Indian emigrants. A group of passengers went to the captain and told him they smoked marijuana and didn't want to disturb any of the other passengers, would he give them a room. They were offered the wicker-work outdoor terrace cafe, "Alice Springs," overlooking the empty swimming pool and the churning sea beyond. A convivial group wrapped in blankets assembled there before lunch, joined by the idle pool attendant. The first morning out at sea the ship's newspaper was passed under our stateroom door, the headline "War in Vietnam Ends". (The day before departure L.B.J. died.) (There was also the "Crystal Writing Room," where stationery, envelopes, pens and ink were provided. Passengers wrote home assiduously and put their letters in the ship's "mail box"!) We landed at 42nd Street on the tail of an ice storm.

The loft I had worked in since 1963 had been sublet for four years and Anthony and I began the arduous and exciting re-organization of our life. Friends helped us find lectures and film-showings. For me it was beginning again in once familiar territory; for Anthony it was beginning anew. In those first months I had film showings and lectures at Rutgers, School of Visual Arts, NYU, University of Mass., SUNY Buffalo, Moore College of Art, a radio interview on WBAI, and a film retrospective at the Whitney Museum.

I had sold all my film equipment and after a lecture and film showing at the New School, a man in the class asked "what do you film with?" I had to answer "with anything I can borrow." He generously offered to lend me his camera. I had visions of a Beaulieu, or a Bolex, and was surprised to open a little box and find a small cast iron camera—Super 8! "Kitch's Last Meal" took its form due to the nature of the Super 8: close to the body, compact, cheap film, three minute cartridges—immediacy and simplicity, fixed durations.

"Fuses" and "Plumb Line" had been made—in a certain sense—to celebrate and make visible the relation, the intimacy of a shared life underlying my performance (public) works; to turn the experiences behind the working processes into a content of the work itself. In each of the films the core relationship had ended unexpectedly: as the film was completed ("Fuses"), or as the visual material was being gathered ("Plumb Line"). At the London Institute for Contemporary Art showing of "Fuses," in '68, a stranger (Jo Durden-Smith, later to become a friend), astonished me by saying "I assume the relationship in "Fuses" terminated, is that true?" I said yes, and asked why he would think that. He said "well, I work with film and that is one of the things it does.....it absorbs the life into itself."

The remark haunted me. I decided to creep around this mystical determinism and center a super 8 diary film of Anthony's and my daily life on our cat Kitch—my companion of seventeen years. The final outcome of the film seemed, in this manner, to both include and over-ride the inevitable loss of my "subject." But the unpredicted outcome of this film was that in the month after Kitch died (on 3 February, 1976, 20 years old, while eating her breakfast), I lost my teaching job at Rutgers, and Anthony decided to find his own loft and establish a separate life.

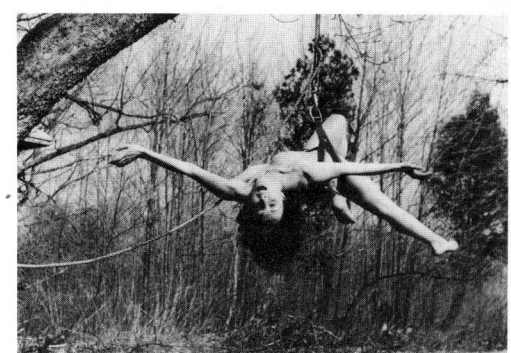

The premise of the film took this form:
To shoot one meal a week of Kitch eating, so long as she lived; and to film what I saw her observing in the course of our daily life. The structure of "Kitch's Last Meal" is based on the continuous texture of a shared daily life of a couple—both artists—living in the country. The visual imagery touches on the practical efforts which actually surround art practice—in this case: gardening, chopping wood, cleaning, grounds work, cooking, typing, jobs, reading, travels, the appearance of friends, the movements of the cat through the center of the home and grounds, and the recurrent passage of a train which runs close behind the house. Two simultaneous film reels are organized by the super 8 three minute durations, edited both disjunctively and in syncronization. The sound parallels the double film projection by exploring a range of complex personal and cultural themes

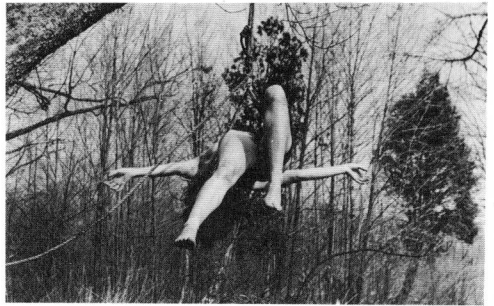

Anthony McCall

spoken from "interior" thought against the passage of "present" film time and references to past experience.

There are also textures of "found" sound of the household gathered by placing a microphone near the positions taken by the cat: noises of cooking, filming, interior movements, conversations of the couple in adjacent spaces, and the rumble of the train.

The ordinariness of the seasonal activities of the couple, in association with the complex sound, builds toward a disconcerting combustion: the death of the cat and the unpredicted separation of the couple became the unanticipated resolution of the film.

Our first year back in the states we spent part of every week in the country where the filming took place. One spring day in '73 a new neighbor came to prune an old apple tree. He had a harness and ropes by which he raised and lowered himself and tools through the branches. Kitch went out and watched him and so I filmed Dwight at work. It was a chilly day in April but he sat down to eat lunch under the tree. Since **Water Light/Water Needle**, ropes and pulleys had remained irresistable to me and I asked him if I could try them. He said fine, and was perhaps as surprised as I was when the impulse to float naked in the harness took effect. Then Anthony came and took some footage of my free float. Once suspended in the harness—free of normal gravity— something started which was to slowly evolve into a new performance work over the next four years—paralleling and then including the footage of "Kitch's Last Meal" (which in turn included these first images of "flying" in the tree).

That summer Anthony and I were invited to the Fylkingen performance festival in Stockholm; he did a spacious version of his "Fire Cycles" high on a hill overlooking Stockholm (until police closed the event); I presented **Cooking With Apes** (which had no rope work).

Once home I rigged a rope in the apple tree and began to discover a form of strengthening exercise which was also a meditation. When Charlotte Moorman sent out the call of the Avant Garde Festival #10 for December, I thought the best thing I could do would be to simply hang up my rope. She had organized this festival in Grand Central Station along a platform lined with two rows of open

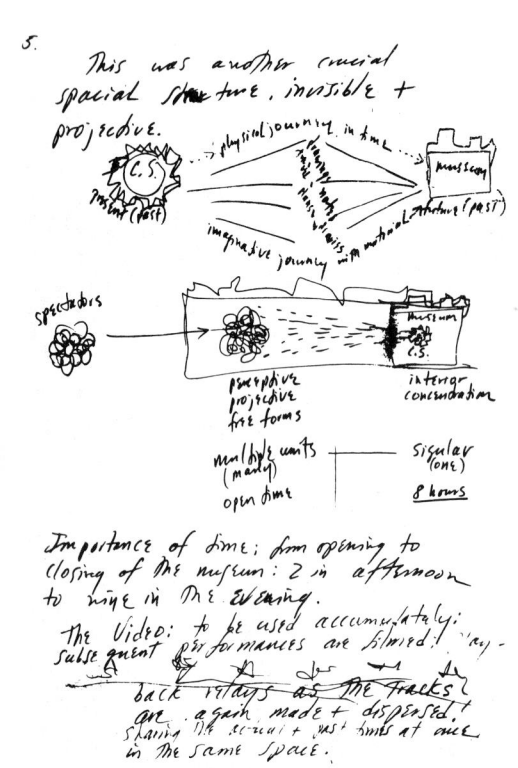

boxcars: all the performances were simultaneous, taking place in railroad cars, and spectators walked from one open freight car to another following the linear string, sampling this or that event at will, somewhat like a state fair.

It was extremely cold in the box cars; the ceiling was too low to use the harness, too cold to be naked. But once the rope was attached to the ceiling I found that tying parts of my body—a leg, arm, torso—could produce sufficient suspension and torsion to permit the concentration, the inward connection to the subtle response and shift of the rope which resulted in the meditation (and a process of what Cage calls "self-alteration"), in no way performed to an audience, but which they could witness. At this time the work was called **Trackings;** I held a chalk in one hand extended, so that changes in weight, position, motion were charted by the free motion of the hand on the perimeter of the walls & floor it touched. The underlying physical principle came to mind as a seismograph or Ouija Board.

Both **Trackings** in its evolution of **Up To And Including Her Limits,** and the concurrent "Kitch's Last Meal" deal with experiences and processes usually not "visible": a private movement meditation, the private life of the artist made public. The embedded relations are also non-sequential/non-linear: time forward, backward, recurrent.

The solitariness of these works depended on my stripping away forms and dimensions I had previously worked with. As **Up To And Including Her Limits** developed into a solo work incorporating film and the random presence of spectators, I realized my intentions were TO DO AWAY WITH:

1. Performance
2. A Fixed Audience
3. Rehearsals
4. Performers
5. Fixed Durations

6. Sequences
7. Conscious Intention
8. Improvisation
9. Technical Cues
10. A Central Metaphor or Theme.

What was left?

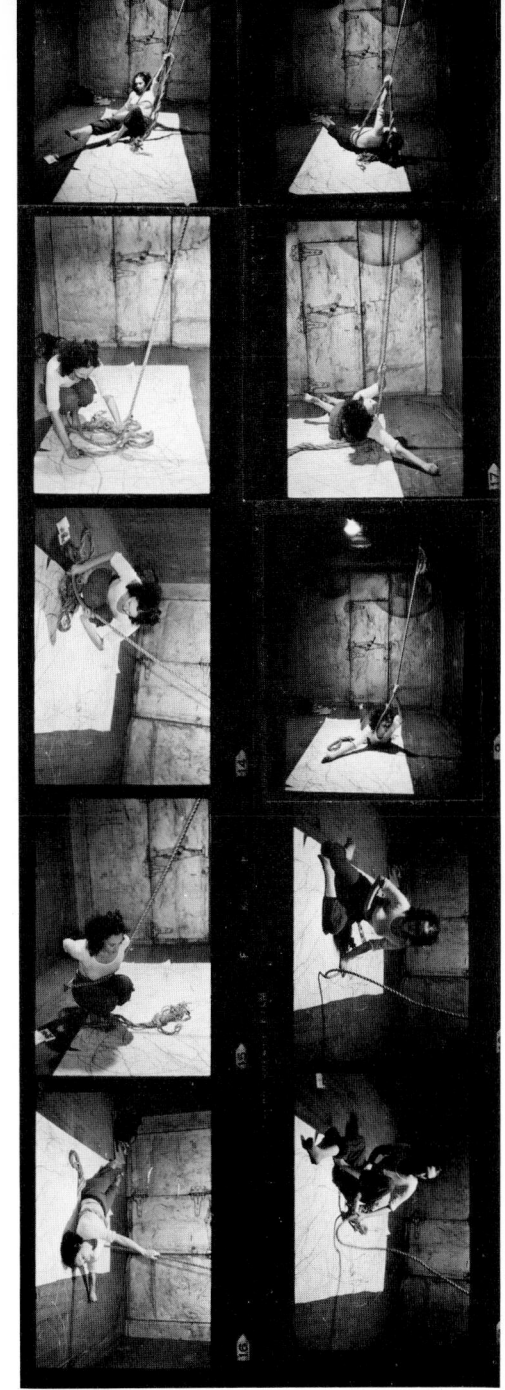

Peter Moore

227

BERKELEY NOTES

Structural concept of the actions.

I. TRACKINGS: tracks in space map a
. time process

Marks referential to actions producing
them—both visible and invisible,
durable and non-durable

Suspended on the rope, the "automatic drawing" maps time process
and the time process is "charted"
(factored) by spatial signs

II. The architectural space of the museum: political and personal

1. what it imposes, provokes, permits
what I discover, adapt to, change:
embedded modes of behavior and
an aesthetic ideal taken for granted—
invisible cultural assumptions

2. drawings and notes before seeing
the actual space, a "pre-view," projective (like automatic writing)

preparatory work: imagining the architecture, geography, food, temperature, light, tonality inside and outside,
water sources, energy—my own and
the place (materials, dimensions,
containment of the body......)

3. first time in California
istory of the Museum—what is its community?

how is Berkeley distinctive?
when and why is a living artist invited
(acceptable) in a Museum?

III. Dismantling the fixity of museum pat-
terns/cultural sets

1. arrive at the Museum when it opens—
with the cleaners, guards, secretaries,
maintenance crew—remain until
closing

2. NO "performance": Museum
becomes my home, studio; my cat
Kitch lives there with me

Construct, arrange a "home," work
environment: kitty litter, table, chair,
bowls of water, food for Kitch, green
plants, clock, typewriter, change of
clothes, papers, books, drawing materials, rug, pillows

3. ON & OFF the canvas

the artist, the nude—at home, at work

still life elements: fruit, eggs, clothes,
dishes—use in actions of exploring
and organizing the space

aromas: off the canvas—rags soaked
in turpentine (old art odors); fresh oil
paint, palettes (not used)

IV. THE TRACKS

1. attaching rope from 25 foot high
ceiling   side of lower gallery
suspended on the rope—sustained

duration so long as concentration
endures
chalk in hand—motion of body by
tension/relaxation with the rope   mark
motions on floors, walls.......accumu-
lative

2. nude woman (artist) walks through
the Museum

3. Dejuner sur l'herbe: nude outside
on the grass has lunch
people gather to observe her
the cat walks in the grass
the people and the nude in conversation

4. Invisible tracks: dip my feet and the
cat's paw in pans of flour; we follow
each other across floors—cross tracks,
parallel, apart, etc.

5. typing a score as the events occur

6. floating eggs among the fish in the
garden pond

7. rolling eggs by elbow, knee, nose
through the museum   spectators
participate

8. Kitch's outdoor tracks; sustained
durations (filmic) as people observe
her movement out of museum, along
shrubbery; perimeters of walls and
garden defined—light and shadow,
covering foliage, open space

our relation to the fifty or so people
arriving in "our" garden

impression of the bodies remains in the grass

9. time intervals: pattern of the day on and off the rope, spatial intervals which bring people directly into spaces I inhabit they arrive down a long ramp. Our contact.

10. habitation materials: lunch and dinner grease, wine, peels, napkins, plates, cups, clothing, etc.

11. Video a team of three women has instructions to watch, wait and film actions at the moment they are most realized (unselfconscious). Their main attention is to my motions on the rope; the cat, spectators and related events are taped as well. Repetition, mirroring, replay.

V. The Exhibit—9 Walls

Wall 1. What Lies Behind: posters, exhibit flyers from past works

Wall 2. How Did You Get Here: index file of schools, museums, persons I wrote to arrange a tour in California; form letters I sent and the replies (or marked "no reply"). This resulted in several messages being made directly on the letters: "I'm sorry our budget was committed".... "Glad you got here," "Please write us again"....

Wall 3. Getting Here: tracks of arranging life details in order to leave home. Domestic work advice to partner: dust,

laundry, shale, straw, manure for garden, weeding, set out early sprouts. Bills to be paid/to be delayed. Letters to Calif.—museum, Millie Hodson, Tom Luddy/travel arrangements. Materials to take/preparatory drawings and scores.

Wall 4. Being Here Accumulated hand-written maps of Berkeley streets; find health food store, grocery, photography store; welcome note from host Tom Luddy: "your room is on the left... hope our cats get along...Kenneth Anger may be staying upstairs, I return on Thursday," etc........scraps of paper: phone numbers, names, assistance, meetings......

Wall 5. Messages Today On this wall (and on museum stand located near central reading & writing table) instructions notify the spectators to ring a bell if they wish to speak with me—thus determining the cycles of the rope suspension. Many people felt unable to intrude on my concentration but wrote messages on the wall, tacked up notes, letters, reactions........(Central table had a bell, notepaper, pens, books of my writings)

Wall 6. Slide relay of my early painting-constructions, collages.

Wall 7. an adjacent room, blacked out: continuous showings of the double projection super 8 "Kitch's Last Meal." (Daily domestic diary—where I am usually...).

Wall 8. A row of nails on which changes of clothes are hung.

Wall 9. Glass doors leading to the garden.

Components of UTAIHL at Artists Space, The Kitchen, Studiogalerie.

1) Walls at right angles covered with six feet of white paper; the rope attached to steel fittings in ceiling, 3½ feet between walls.

2) Continuous double screen projection (vertical) Super 8 "Kitch's Last Meal" (eight reels 1973-76) adjacent to performance area.

3) Sound tapes with film.

4) Three to six video monitors grouped together, showing tapes of the previous rope work and the current actions. (Tapes of each performance/installation are cumulative and finally replace the live action.)

5) A reading area, away from the rope and film projection; writings related to the work.

6) Continuous relay of slides relating to the work— image area no larger than 9" x 12".

7) Walls between the reading area and installation/performance with texts describing the components. (The components are adapted to each space; doors and windows are utilized as active environmental elements.)

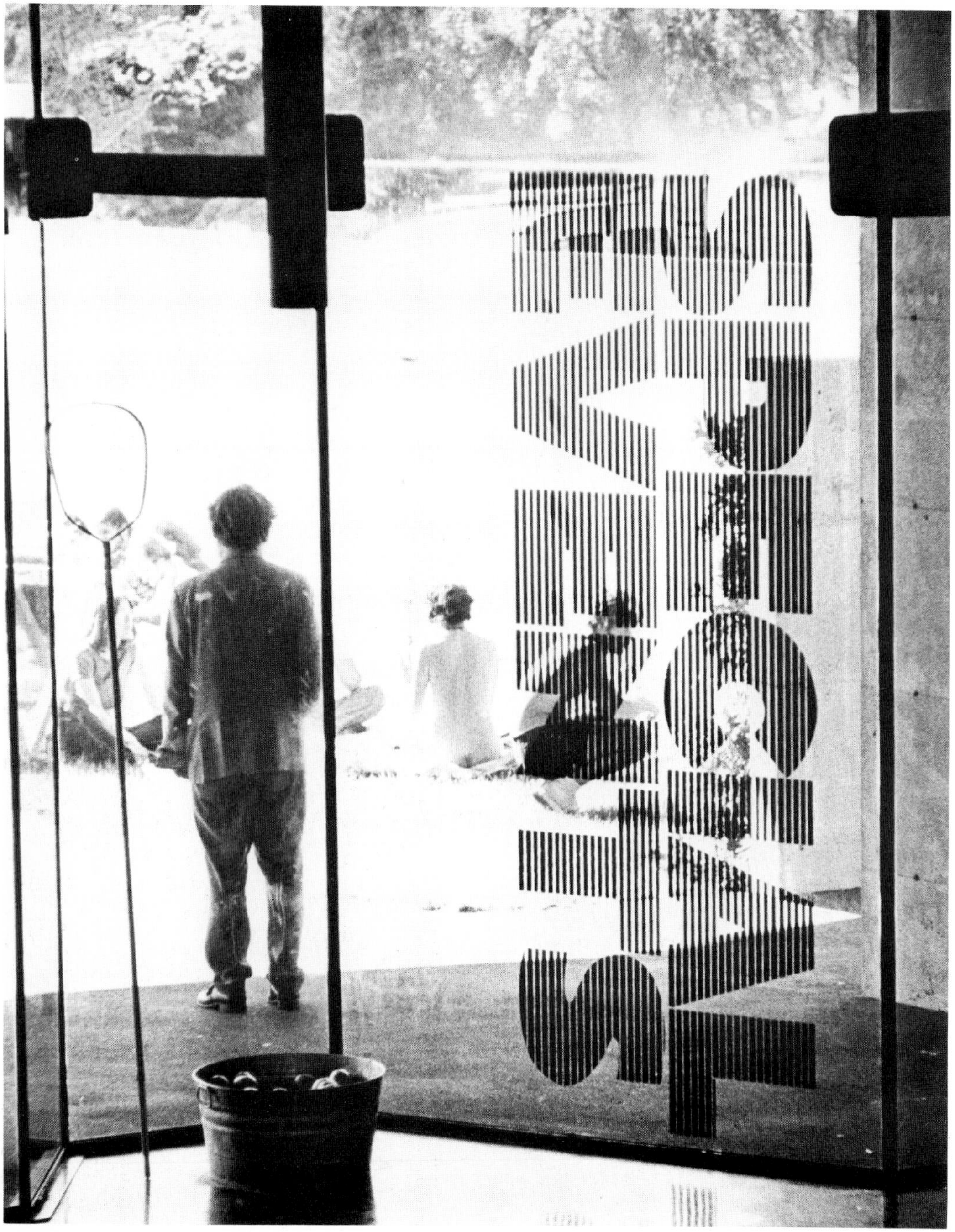

Berkeley Museum

Constellation of units organized by the spectator—impossible to see all the information at once (audience determines their physical position, duration of attention). Each unit further clarifies any other unit. Broken definitions of near/far, fixed rectangle, shifting frames; wavering line compresses time duration— line produced by volume of the body in space. Cyclic effect of rope turning, film/video repetitions, but synchronizations are always shifting. To overtly question the imbeddedness of perceptual expectations—how the spectator unifies referential material; questioning stratas of reality or actuality. The nude also artist; part of the work—it is but it isn't. To embody the reference and at the same time simply be (and enjoy) the freedom of the body shaping an environment.

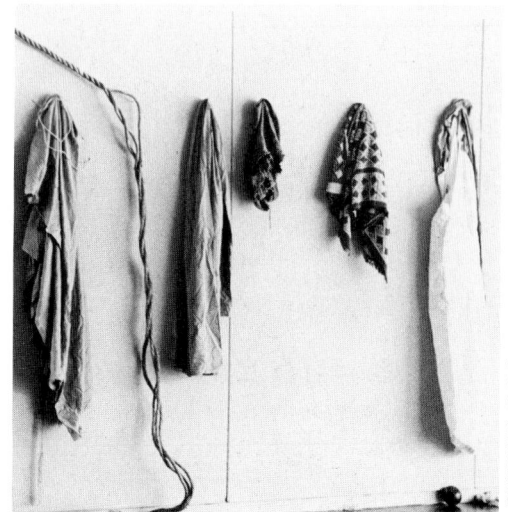

Anthology

Over the hours drawing accumulates as automatic writing or trance markings. The situation is personal—being nude, turning on the rope; my voice on the tapes, image in the film—but while my figure on the rope is actual it becomes less "real" than the woman of the film. Concentrated on the rope I may not know if there are spectators or not. The movements and gestures which produce the strokes occur through the torsion of my body wound, balanced with the rope. Only thought is to be an extension of the rope itself. Until discomfort or loss of concentration, I function as a pencil.

London

Film frames limits/boundaries, containment within which movement is temporal/fixed relativity. "Reality" of the film self-contained, repeatable. Body on the rope fixed span in light of a projector; self/body is consumed in the action ("used up"), finally leaves the space. Film and video continue. Attached window between performance/film area and spectators to a nylon thread so that current of wind would continually shift the "aperture," introduce the exterior environment—changing clouds over Camden Town roof tops. The light affecting the film density as window swung open and closed. A participatory influence on the interior "exposure" of live movement, film & video projection. Taking apart rectangles, their interpenetrations. Randomized synchronizations analogous to the film structure.

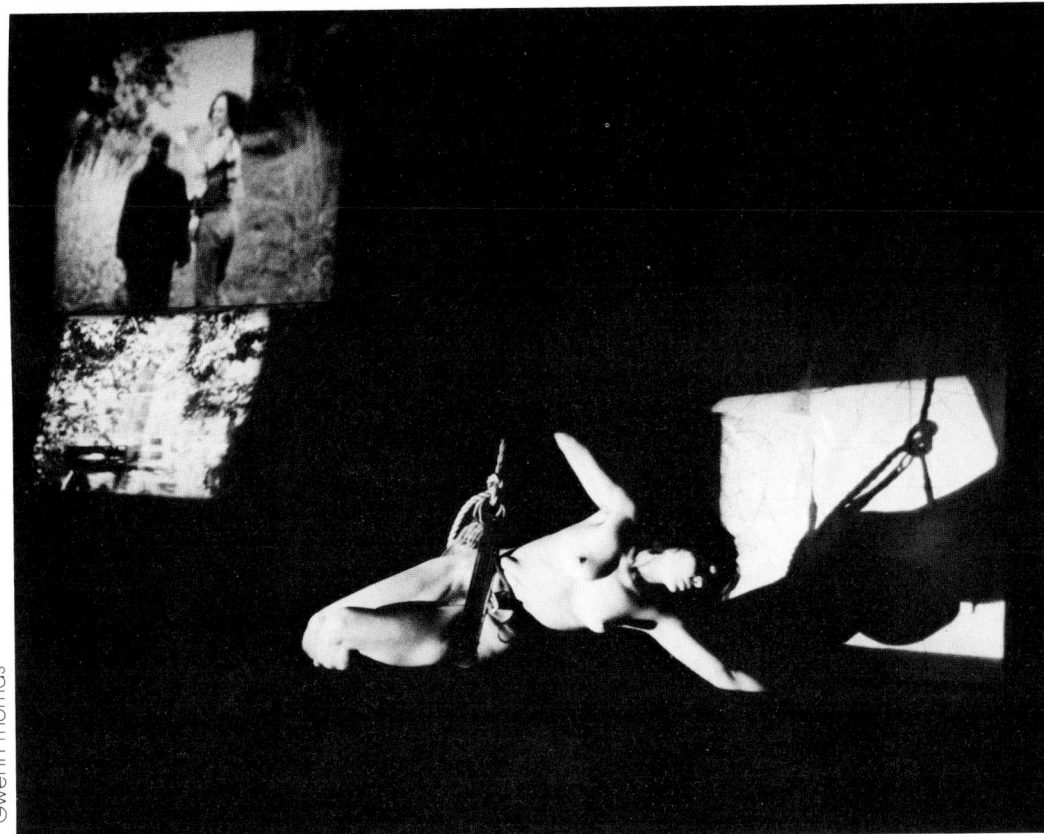

Gwenn Thomas

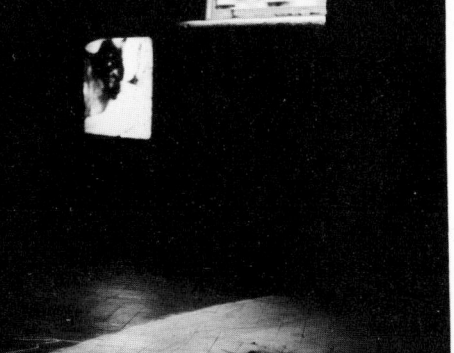

Alan Power

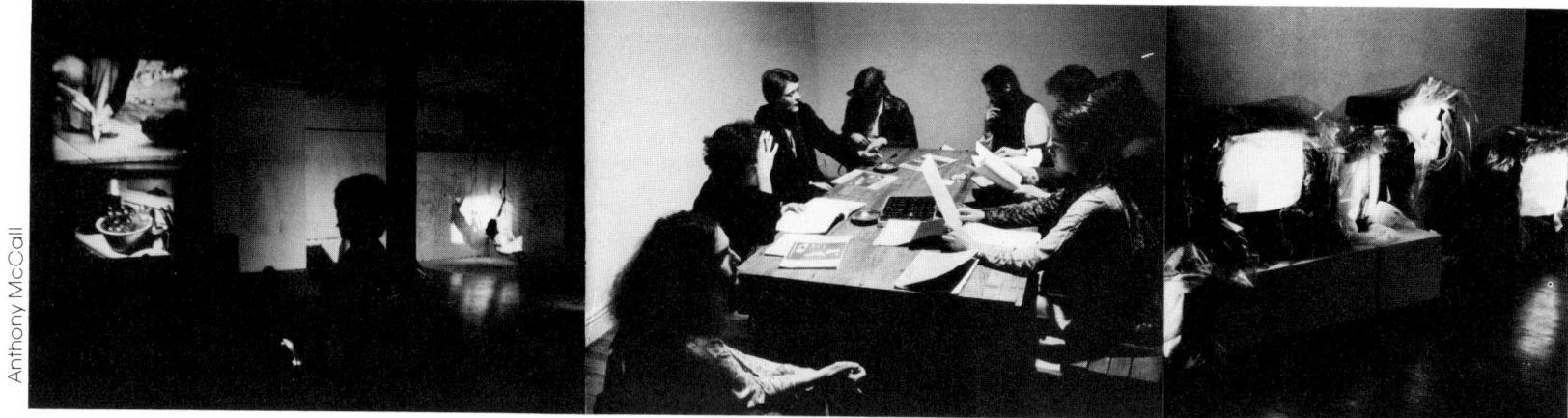

Anthony McCall

The Kitchen

Ritual community of the audience, ritual penetration of the space; communal investigation, organization of the elements. Participation in the death of the cat—funeral rite; integration of the dead cat body (live, active in the video and film). Suspension on the rope (plumb line) analogous to electromagnetic or gravitational field—the target of the perception is psychic traces. Relation of dream and psychic trace has to do with disparities and continuities in the seamless space and events: sense of dormant planes on which unexpected equivalences converge (jostle, flow, impinge, diverge, gather momentum, fade, shift... homologous to the body/rope/marking connections). Various units of UTAIHL—narrative, anecdote, instruction, temporal fixity, impermanence, repeated imagery—all in multiple, sensory contact points which emphasize contradictory needs for distance and contact, separation and mutuality. Transference of information-processing between performer and audience involves questions of telepathy, parapsychology—the insights which bind us during the course of an action extend our physical and conceptual expectations—a synesthetic touching on extrasensory processes—areas between conscious and unconscious (always active but unusually scattered.....).

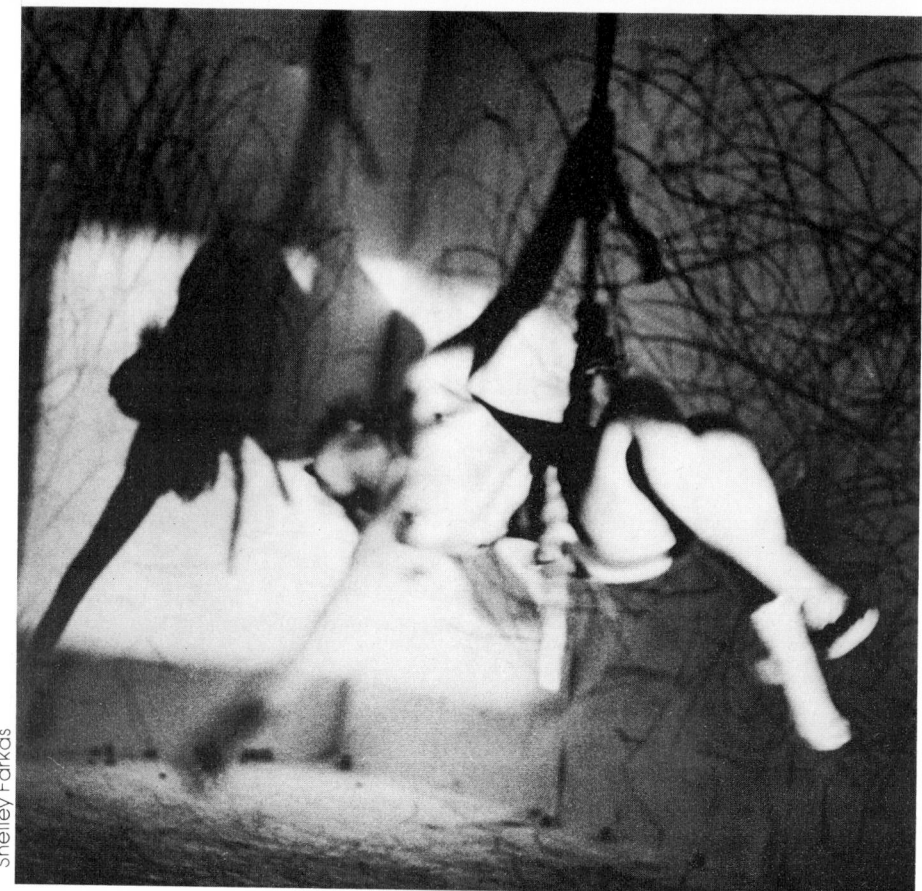

Shelley Farkas

Studiogalerie

Being taken over, possessed—not a process of will...force of the concentration is overwhelming...I move to "meet" it, to be submerged. Immediacy, unpredictable gains and losses, degree of preparation permits uninterrupted flow, absorbs scale of physical presences (large close crowd in Berlin).

Strength of the structural elements in the space contrasts with frailty of the body in live action. Film demonstrates tension between the thing-made and the person actually present. The video demonstrates tension between the immediate present and the relative past.

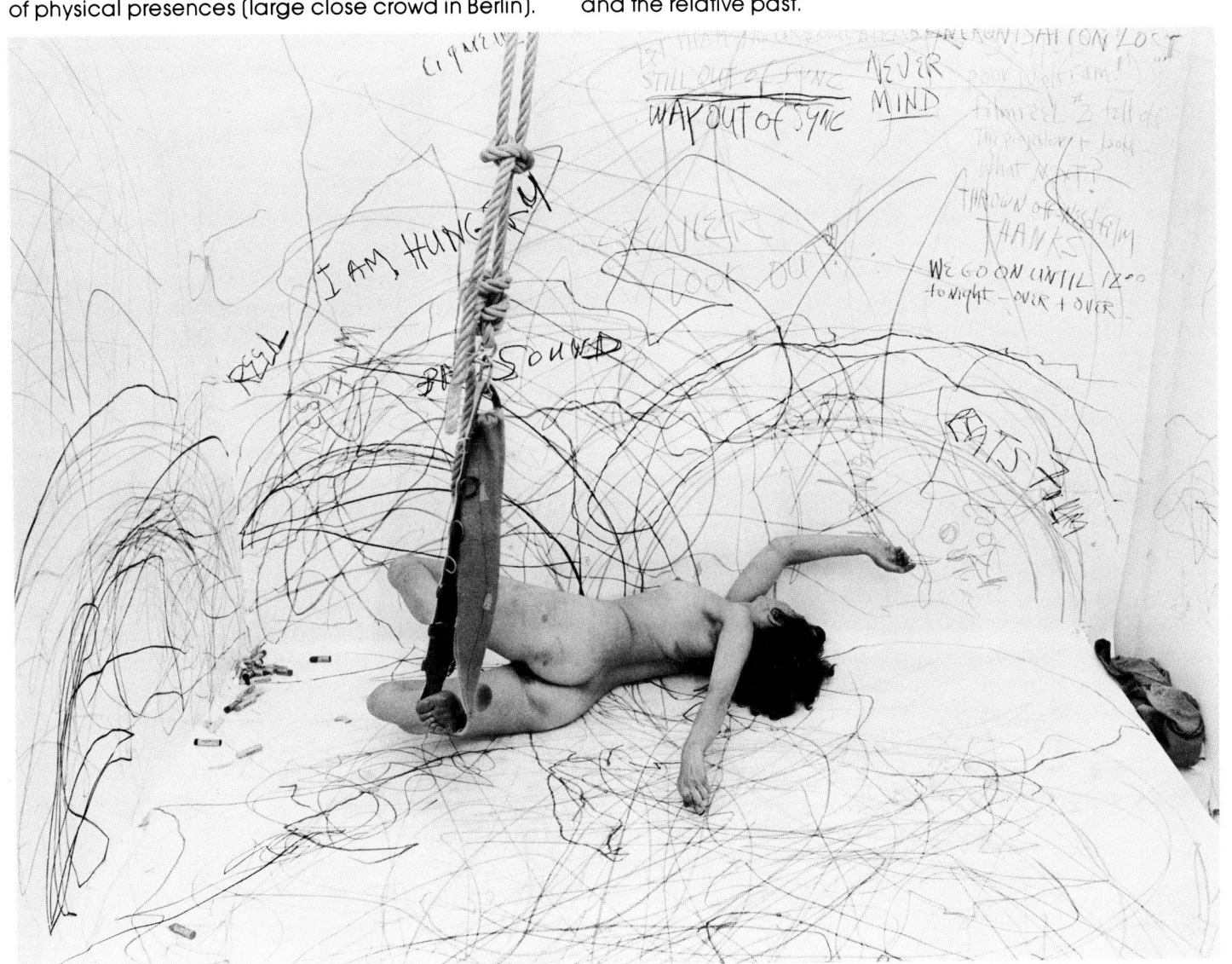

Henrik Gaard

233

INTERIOR SCROLL

August 29 1975 Women Here & Now
East Hampton L.I.

September 4 1977 Telluride Film Festival
Telluride Colorado

I first wrote about "vulvic space" in 1960 as a result of an art istory assignment on symbolism. I chose to do research on the "Transmigration of the Serpent," never suspecting that the transmutation of serpent symbolism in the wall paintings, carvings, inscriptions of ancient cultures—this traditionally "phallic" symbolism would lead me to a concept of vulvic space and this in turn to the disappearance and mis-attribution of Goddess artifacts and imagery, to a total inversion and re-interpretation of myth and symbol. Once begun my studies continued as a "secret project," for nothing at that time confirmed the inter-relations I saw and the fury and anguish they inspired (the relief of substantiation by Gould Davis, Gertrude Levy, H.R. Hays, Helen Diner, etc. ten or twelve years later was indescribable). Nevertheless it was usually the works of male scholars who first intensified my study—both by keys, links they established and by denials and obfuscations. In MacKenzie I read that: Cro-Magnon people believed in a Mother Earth Goddess; their cave paintings exaggerate the female sexual characteristics. Water and wind were of fundamental importance and were symbolized by natural spirals. The snake symbolized whirlpool, whirlwind, cosmic energy. Snakes originally symbolized the cosmic energy of the female womb which protected and nourished the embryo as they believed the ocean originally did the earth...(school notes from MacKenzie's The Migration of Symbols, 1926).

From my identification with the symbology of the female body I made the further assumption that carvings and sculptures of the serpent form were attributes of the Goddess and would have been made by women worshippers (artists) as analogous to their own physical, sexual knowledge. I thought of the vagina in many ways— physically, conceptually: as a sculptural form, an architectural referent, the source of sacred knowledge, ecstacy, birth passage, transformation. I saw the vagina as a translucent chamber of which the serpent was an outward model: enlivened by its passage from the visible to the invisible, a spiraled coil ringed with the shape of desire and generative mysteries, attributes of both female and male sexual powers. This source of "interior knowledge" would be symbolized as the primary index unifying spirit and flesh in Goddess worship. I related womb and vagina to "primary knowledge"; with strokes and cuts on bone and rock by which I believed my ancestor measured her menstrual cycles, pregnancies, lunar observations, agricultural notations—the origins of time factoring, of mathematical equivalences, of abstract relations. I assumed the carved figurines and incised female shapes of Paleolithic, Mesolithic artifacts were carved by women—the visual-mythic transmutation of self-knowledge to its integral connection with a cosmic Mother—that the experience and complexity of her personal body was the source of conceptualizing, of inter-acting with materials, of imagining the world and composing its images.

The message I read for **Interior Scroll** is from the feminist texts in "Kitch's Last Meal." The image occurred as a drawing; this image seemed to have to do with the power and possession of naming—the movement from interior thought to external signification, and the reference to an uncoiling serpent, to actual information (like a ticker tape, rainbow, torah in the ark, chalice, choir loft, plumb line, bell tower, the umbilicus and tongue).

I think the action was also influenced by two films seen at the "Women In Film and Video" conference (Buffalo University, Center for Media Study, February 74). First, Sharon Hennessey's "What I Want," in which she appears in a fixed frame shot for the duration it takes her to read from a paper endlessly unfolding like a scroll: the text is one simple statement after another of what a woman wants in her life—direct and full of rich contradiction. The other film was Anne Severson's "Near The Big Chakra," in which a continual relay of thirty or more different vaginas are filmed in close focus. Like "Fuses" it becomes a film about nature and confronts, dismantles the convention of the genital being "obscene," that is, forbidden to be seen. Our three films presented an ethic about knowledge itself—received from and in the body.

Interior Scroll was performed twice. Each "reading" required a ritual preparation for the action, a gradual inhabitation of the space, increasing concentration. For "Women Here and Now" I placed a long table under two dimmed spot lights, in a corner of the exhibition/performance hall of the old town meeting house. The audience was largely composed of other women artists who work during summers in East Hampton, and they assembled during the exhibit of paintings for a series of performance works. I approached the table dressed and carrying two sheets. I undressed, wrapped myself in one sheet, spread the other over the table and told the audience I would read from Cèzanne, She Was A Great Painter. I dropped the covering sheet and standing there painted large strokes defining the contours of my body and face. The reading was done on top of the table, taking a series of life model "action poses," the book balanced in one hand. At the conclusion I dropped the book and stood upright on the table. The scroll was slowly extracted as I read from it, inch by inch.

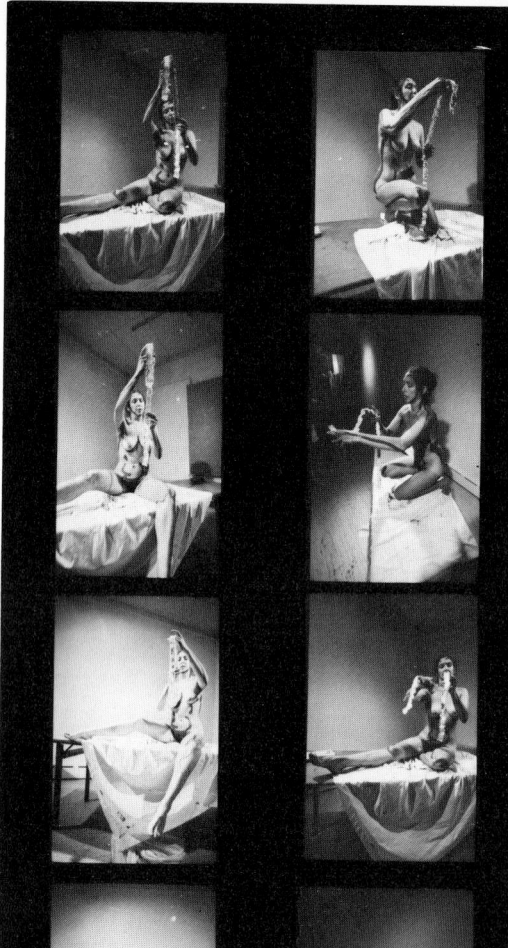

The last thing I wanted to do at the Telluide Film Festival was an "action." I was looking forward to seeing films, old friends, to being in Colorado again. Stan Brakhage had invited me to introduce a program of erotic films by women and together we made a selection. In the Festival brochure we were dismayed to read our program titled as "The Erotic Woman". I found myself stuck in the lodge facing the mountains, writing away at an introduction to explain my objections to the title of the film program, and to the film festival brochure itself. The cover had a drawing of a naked man in sunglasses, opening his coat (a flasher) to show "Fourth Telluride Film Festival" lettered across his chest; below the waist was a blank space—he had been deprived of genitals, but knees, socks and shoes had been granted.

Then the troublesome voice started nagging at me the day before the film program...I was saying "leave me alone I just want to have a nice time"; She was saying: "live body action steps into area of discrepancy between film which even in most intensive physical conviction remains in the minds-eye   permits the passive viewing separation projection an illusion   step into the fissure between live action and filmic images   the tension is there between the distancing of audience perception and fixity of projection   an actual reality triggering filmic reality as coherent present   the lens standing between us and the material embodiment   a live action beside illusionistic actions/images an antagonistic

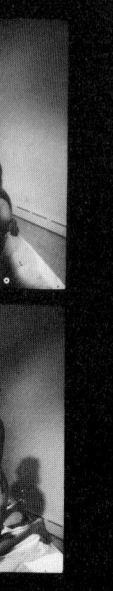
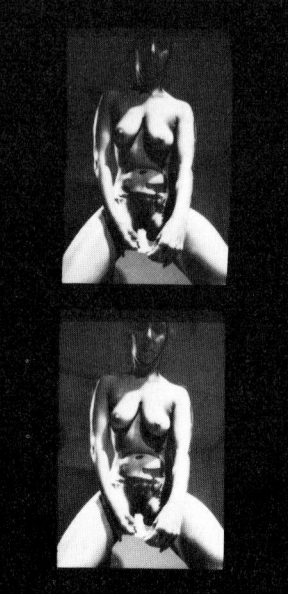
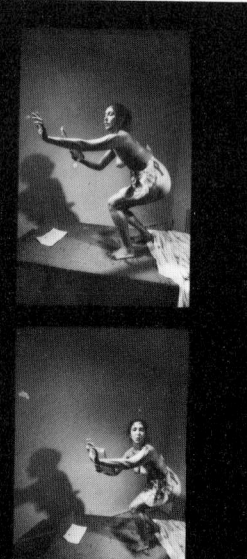
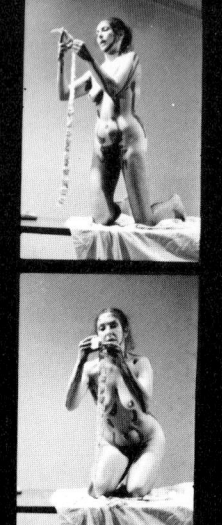
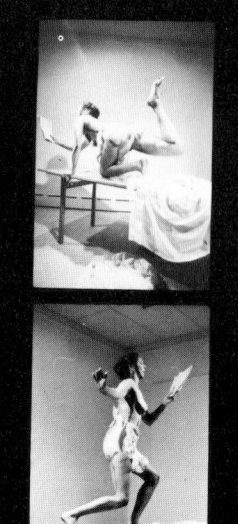

Peter Grass

Anthony McCall

field where the spectators must find their move   and to see it has to make sense and move thoroughly not just in twenty minute film segments for an evenings viewing   as filmmaker you must stand out step out of your frame....."

Stan introduced me to the film audience while I sat wrapped in a sheet on the small Victorian stage under its hand painted drop curtain and proscenium arches. I read my introductory statement which included:

> Having been described and proscribed by the male imagination for so long, no woman artist now wants to assume that she will define an "erotic woman" for other women—the very notion immediately reverts to the traditional stereo-types which this program of films vividly counters. Perhaps these films will re-define 'The Erotic Woman'; or to the contrary the films will be found to be anti-erotic, sub-erotic, non-erotic. Perhaps this 'erotic woman' will be seen as primitive, devouring, insatiable, clinical, obscene; or forthright, courageous, integral.

At the conclusion of the statement I unwrapped the sheeting and slowly applied stripes of mud to my body from a bowl filled from the Telluride mining stream. Then the scroll was extended and read. The film program followed: Agnes Varda's "L'Opera Mouffe," Marie Menken's "Orgia," Gunvor Nelson's "Schmeerguntz," Anne Severson's "Near The Big Chakra," and my films "Fuses" and "Plumb Line."

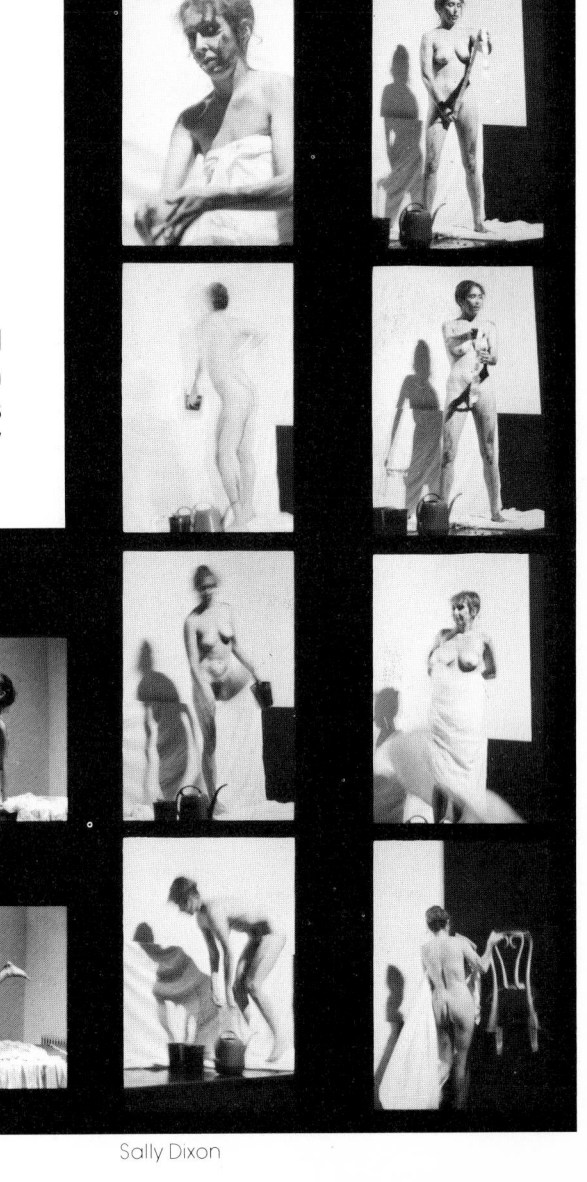

Sally Dixon

from tape 2 "Kitch's Last Meal"
(super 8 film 1973-77)

I met a happy man
a structuralist filmmaker
—but don't call me that
it's something else I do—
he said we are fond of you
you are charming
but don't ask us
to look at your films
we cannot
there are certain films
we cannot look at
the personal clutter
the persistence of feelings
the hand-touch sensibility
the diaristic indulgence
the painterly mess
the dense gestalt
the primitive techniques

(I don't take the advice
of men who only talk to
themselves)
PAY ATTENTION TO CRITICAL
AND PRACTICAL FILM LANGUAGE
IT EXISTS FOR AND IN ONLY
ONE GENDER

even if you are older than me
you are a monster I spawned
you have slithered out
of the excesses and vitality
of the sixties........

he said you can do as I do
take one clear process
follow its strictest
implications intellectually
establish a system of
permutations establish
their visual set.......

I said my film is concerned
with DIET AND DIGESTION

very well he said then
why the train?

the train is DEATH as there

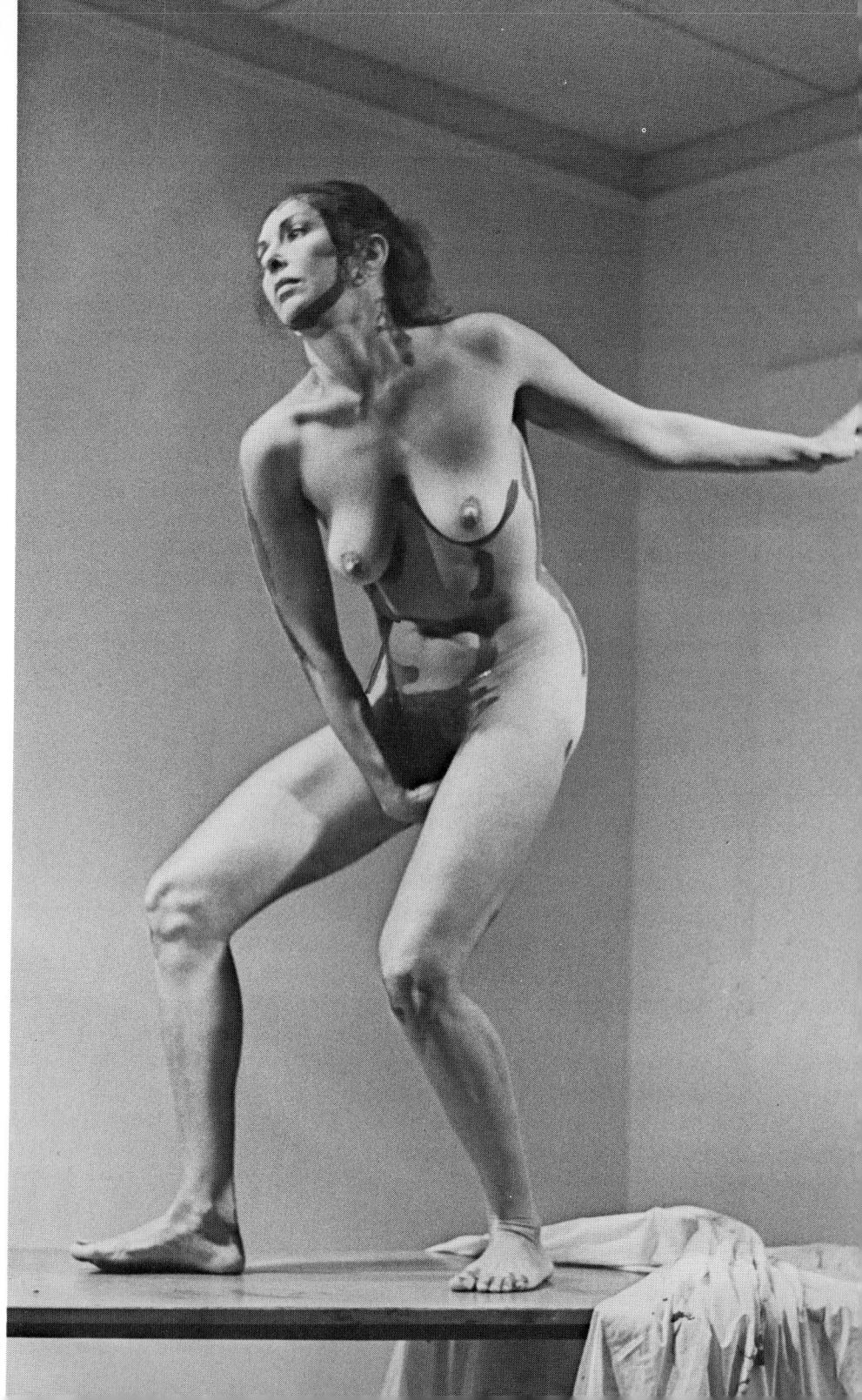

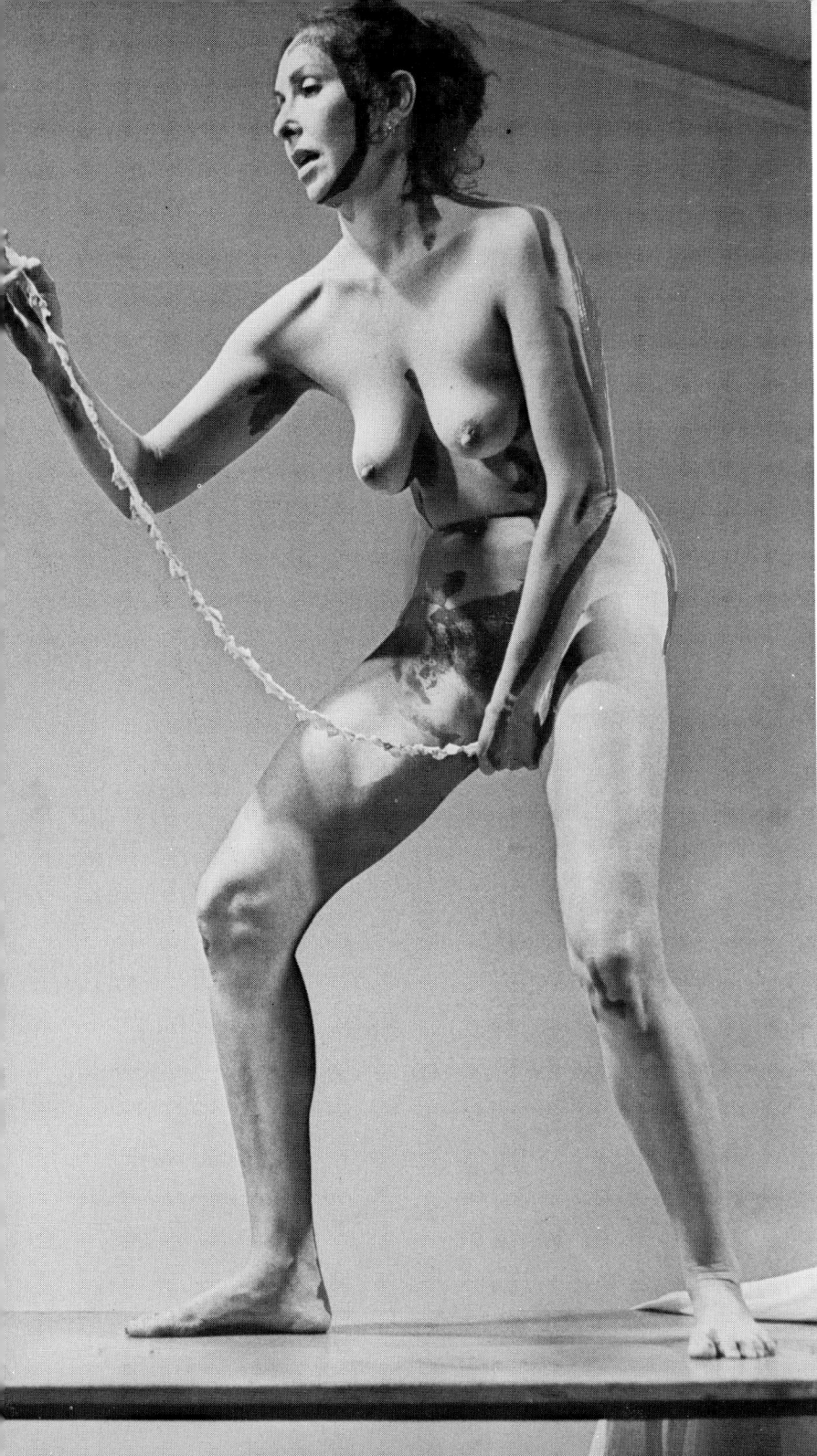

Anthony McCall

is die in diet and di in
digestion

then you are back to metaphors
and meanings
my work has no meaning beyond
the logic of its systems
I have done away with
emotion intuition inspiration—
those aggrandized habits which
set artists apart from
ordinary people—those
unclear tendencies which
are inflicted upon viewers.......

it's true I said when I watch
your films my mind wanders
freely................
during the half hour of
pulsing dots I compose letters
dream of my lover
write a grocery list
rummage in the trunk
for a missing sweater
plan the drainage pipes for
the root cellar...........
it is pleasant not to be
manipulated

he protested
you are unable to appreciate
the system the grid
the numerical rational
procedures—
the Pythagorean cues—

I saw my failings were worthy
of dismissal I'd be buried
alive my works lost.........

he said we can be friends
equally tho we are not artists
equally I said we cannot
be friends equally and we
cannot be artists equally

he told me he had lived with
a "sculptress" I asked does
that make me a "film-makeress"?

Oh No he said we think of you
as a dancer

MOON IN A TREE

In conjunction with an exhibit of works by Joseph Cornell at the Castelli Gallery, Jonas Mekas organized a series of programs in March 1976, at the Anthology Film Archives: "Films of Joseph Cornell. Conference on 'Working with Cornell'. Cornell's Sources and Materials." My event centered on Joseph's letters to me during our ten year friendship. It had been Stan Brakhage's suggestion in 1956 that Joseph and I should meet—because Stan saw qualities shared by Joseph's work and mine, and because Cornell took inspiration from particular young women.*

Stan had worked with him on a color film of the Third Avenue El (shortly before it was torn down). He told me that Joseph lived in an ordinary house on Utopia Parkway in Queens, with his mother and crippled brother; he described Cornell's mystical and sensitive presence and advised me that an innocent demeanor was necessary. For my first invitation to visit on a fine spring day, I dressed in a peasant blouse, a "ballerina" skirt, felt slippers and carried a bunch of daffodils for Joseph. We sat outside under the quince tree in the small yard; at a round table he fed me a doll's lunch of two sardines, two biscuits, a sprig of parsley and pink lemonade. He was extremely thin (and seemed old to me), but didn't eat anything himself. I understood that I might contribute to an enchantment, and was myself inspired by Joseph's deep connection to the gift of creative vision: the subtle immediacy of things observed and resonant for his "visioning" state, his rich and metaphoric erudition. And it was by his example that I first experienced a shaping humility and devotion—a preparedness to let an inner voice speak—prescient, timeless beyond will, determination or "personality".

When we walked through the house I met his mother, large and solid in the kitchen, complaining over some baking underway; his brother Robert, frail, confined to a wheel chair. Joseph thought I might work for him a few days each month, ordering his vast collection of materials—photographs, clippings and an overburdening personal archive of letters, works from other artists. (This work appealed to me as I had a part-time job for Edgar and Louise Varèse, collating

---

*It was a source of some irony and trepidation to me that Joseph's obsession with the ballet, with ballerinas who had lived in a distant past or were friends in present time, led him to a great curiosity about the Judson dancers; not their work itself but questions about the quality, the radiance, the presence, of my friends. Perhaps they would spark some rich image association, perhaps he could send them a small gift? (A sachet, a handkerchief, a letter.) And so he wrote to Yvonne Rainer, to Deborah Hay, to Arlene Rothlein. Arlene he quite rightly envisioned as a Russian princess, standing in the snow, dressed in a fur coat and holding a muff, and for a time they corresponded.

and preserving his files of letters, programs, reviews, etc.) It soon became apparent that many friends and admirers had introduced some too sharp aspect of worldly concerns into their association, and had to be discarded by Joseph, like discomforting dreams. I exclaimed over a de Kooning drawing; Joseph said, "Oh, don't look at that", and shuffled it under yellowing papers. There was an inscribed drawing from Max Ernst; Joseph again was agitated and said it was really too much to deal with. We went to the garage—his workshop—where I was entranced by stacks of boxes filled with collage materials: feathers, beads, pebbles, glitter, ribbons, flower decals, miniature wooden animals and birds. . . . and by boxes in various stages of completion.

It seemed that the substance of the communion to be shared would have to be based, in great part, on the tacit recognition that just as he selected or attracted materials imbued with fragile, intense significance, friendships had to carry and sustain specific but intangible generative value, and exclude those areas of expression which could be found disruptive. Our friendship was sustained over the years in so far as I was willing and able to present and to share only those aspects of my life and work congruent in Joseph's spiritual environment.

He had a magical way of phoning at provident moments and always when there was somehow time enough to speak at length. These conversations were inspiring to me—usually very long, punctuated by extended silences as he would build unexpected relations between fleeting sensations, practical observations, and imagistic metaphors. I would scribble rough phrases as he spoke—not as a record but as a tracing of the amazing roll and tumble of thought and texture— a physical and metaphysical journey—always much to think on. For instance these notes remain from a telephone conversation of 12 December 1963: the weather. . . . .the light in our rooms. . ."The nymph in the grotto" (he was making a box for me which I was too shy ever to collect). . . . ."a beauty patch and the mirror". . . ."the nude—sanguinity and spontaneity". . .Valéry, shadowy light. . . "an image of slipping a robe off your shoulders". . . .his wish for "an intimate, realistic sense in a little room. . . . .the background of a very complex situation which might change the course, is often a desperate state of mind for these sorts of things". . . . .would I mail him "some poetic after-thought, a little reminder of the heart of a women, the leaf and bramble". . . . . .but "don't be disappointed if it doesn't work out." Underlying the emphemera, these allusions, was a cached intimacy, an erotic quest.

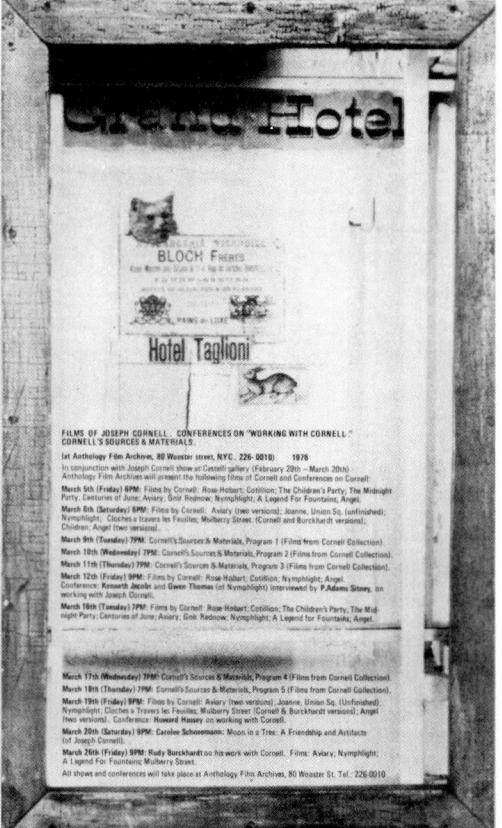

flyer by Jonas Mekas

letters

SLIDES	① C. SURROUND	② LETTERS	③ Joseph/TREE	
1	ptg / C. / ptg -3	— 1	1 Joseph	Nanmur May 56
2	C 1	1	2" hold works	May 56
3	S+S, J+L, J, S, K · 5	1	1 TREE	Sinsabaugh '56
4	- black -	1	1 " "	Aug 56
5	2 collage/ens	2 collage/ens	2 collage/ens ——— INSERT	
6	1, 1, 1, 1, 1, 6	"Rupfes" 1	1 - Rivir castle 1 - blank	Nov 58
7	Modeling 1	life model 1	" "	May 62
8	5 - C's window	1	1, 2, 3 JOS at window Schutte	Oct 62
9	↓ hold window	1, 2	↓ hold window	Nov 62
10	(25) ↓ K in snow	handwritten	↓ ———→ insert Stan Tape	May 63
11	1, 2, cms.	1 Nymph	Hotel l'étoile	my 63
12a	blank	1, 2 post card syntatic port."	JOSEPH 1/2 hed	Jan 64
12b	1, 2, 3 - 4 5 - didn't send	cms. 1, 2, 3. Grotto	TREE	'63
13	blank	Thank you	black	Jan 64
14	C+4 R, 1, 2, 3, studio	1 "Grotto nymph"	box	May 64
15	10 M. J.	1, 2, to PARIS	pipe/angel	June 64
16	"	1 rejecting letter	"	Aug 64
17	1 Construc.	1 making up	TREE	Aug 64
18	"	1 - sin card	"	Oct 65
19	"	1	"	Nov 65

letters

SLIDE	① C. surround	② letters	③ Joseph/Tree	
AP				
20	black	Leaf	black	Dec 65
21	"Maximus - em, 2, 3, 4, 5 ↓	1, 2 Venice	dance Loss.	Dec 65
22/22a	" " ↓	1	" "	Jan 66
23	← L'ABEILLE →	1 →	←	Jan 66
24	C nude	1, 2	JOSEPH	Feb 66
25	" "	1	" "	May 67
26	letter p. 1	letter p. 2	letter p. 3	April 69
27	little box	last card	little box	

Joseph was tender and formal, polite and tremulous. From the beginning he knew I lived with Jim Tenney, but it was several years before he would acknowledge him: send his regards, or say hello when Jim answered the phone. Later he would express interest in "Mr. Tenney's music," and finally inquire about "Tenney". It was as if this real and actual relation could deflect or intrude on the delicate strands of thought directed towards me. And Joseph could become quite fierce and abrupt or bitterly disappointed when tenuous and complex motions outwards from the web of this work were taken to a literal point, misunderstood. In 1961 he sent me a small packet with an image of "Ribera's daughter," herself a painter. Slowly over the years he formed the idea that I might teach him to draw from the nude figure, having often expressed regret that he was unable to draw from the nude. (He had seen some life drawings of mine, and photos of "Eye Body".) Joseph had asked me to describe in detail the small room off my main work area, where under the skylight there was a bed, a desk and a mirror; his thought developed around an image of this room: that one day when it was not too cold or too difficult to travel from Utopia Parkway to 29th St. we would have a drawing lesson in which we would both be model and artist—both nude and drawing each other. There was no sexual innuendo—it was about confronting a perception. This attraction and hesitation, this irresolute advance towards the immanent body, emerged thematically in the phone calls and letters. There are times when I believe we actually had our "drawing lesson" together.

For the Anthology event I made a setting to echo the little round table under the quince tree: I set the table with glass dishes, silverware and two glasses and two chairs, one for myself, the other for his presence. On the table I also had to manage controls for three slide carousels, a microphone, a penlight to read the letters and accompanying notes. The table and chairs were on a raised platform in front of the screen where three coordinated units of slides were projected simultaneously: the central images were of the 26 letters to me; to the left were photographs of myself, my work, and our friends at the time corresponding to each letter. On the right were slides of Joseph, his work, also correlated to the letter. An image of a single tree (by Art Sinsabaugh) was a recurrent motif.

I wore a flowered 40's dress found in a thrift shop. The pitcher of pink lemonade was spiked with vodka. The title occurred in a dream while preparing the slides. I felt throughout the reading and reminesences that I was speaking to Joseph, and had no awareness of the audience surrounding me.

Dearest Carolee, -

ry,mild maiden & friend. This gentle musing for a good

sleep& deep in dark covers disrobed maiden with
gesture gracious a wall-peg receiving her gesture
and covering & so denied the spectacle of her woman-
hood   In the early hours from deep

er of the maiden   That is, the image to the dream-
                        before this awakened to "candy" and
before that the naked youth in the room in innocence
with the young girls- he retained his composure through
out though losing the lovelyness though no matter again
it will come

                        The youth that of the maiden who
proffered her maidenliness & was falling into the
well of sleep again   no image but discourse obscure
with some distant maiden-"candy" she called outwhich
roused him once again - she meant that the plum had rip-
ened & that in all chaste candor I could so tell you
so of the glow   tell you so
reminders persisting but skirting the troublesome recall-
ing the covers once crawled into naked & wet the oceanic
dreams   related - natural gliding of the vessel/joy of
re-lease of joy sans dischargin cargo/ joy to girl from
boy to the grotto nymph jeune fille en fleurs & furs -

the above clear of course it is not - you know of course
who is the patient maiden & only from a distant does this
come   again

resurgent now - the great force of the original glimpse-
authenticity"solid vision"you could cut with a knife
must rejeunir,dedicate to evoke the wonder(s)   one
                                value   (grotto)
the ineffable)
            "Caliban" still seen, just outside.

    Joy to you, maiden !
      "   "   "   "

                        .L

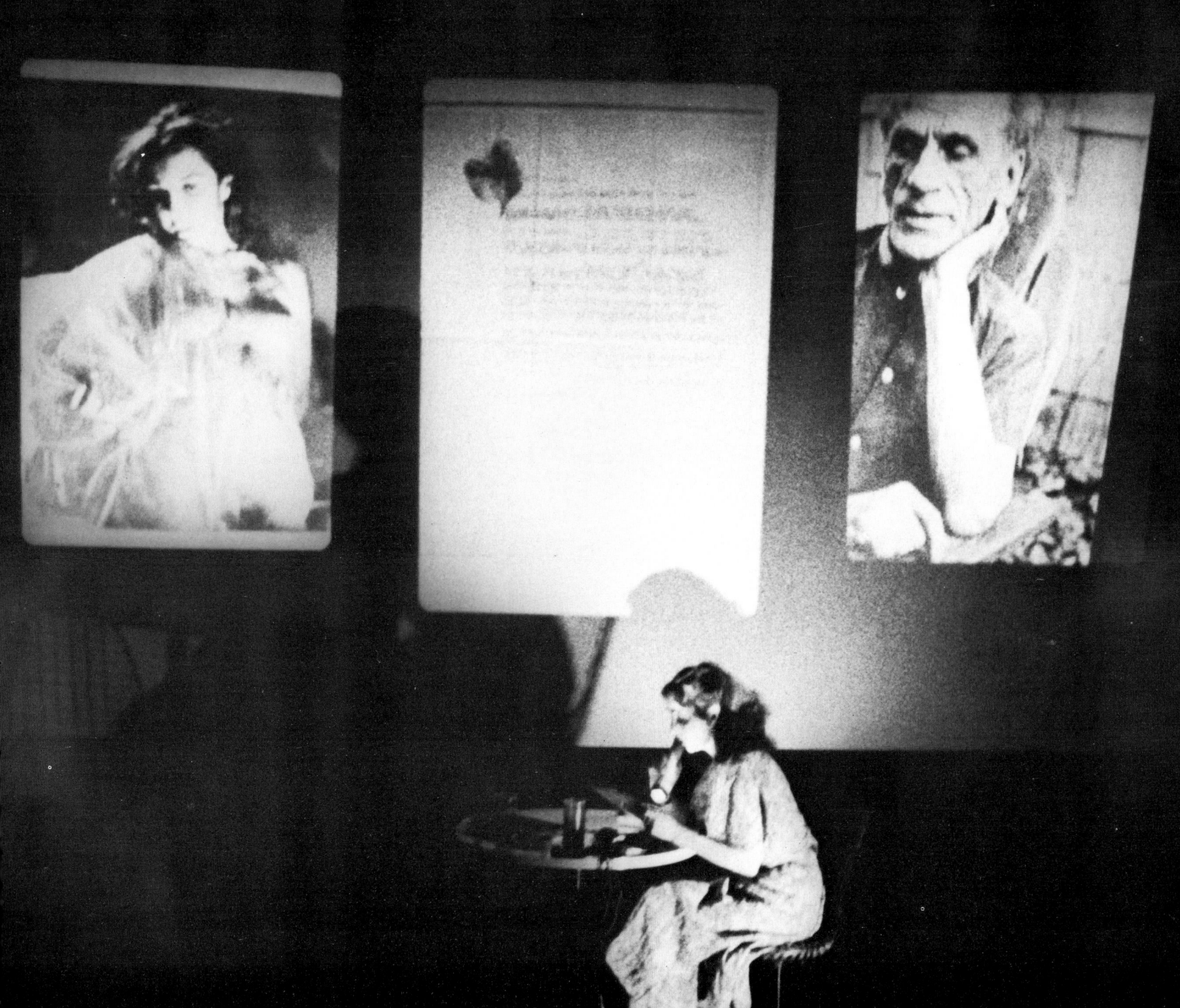

ABC —
WE
PRINT
ANYTHING
— IN THE CARDS

November 9 1976 Franklin Furnace NY

May 14 1977 "Discussion As An Art
   Form" New York University NY

June 3 4 1977 De Appel Gallery
   Amsterdam

June 9 1977 Festival of Performance Art
   Arnhem Holland

I received a phone call in May '76 from a man I had never met, Howard Hussey, an artist and friend of Joseph Cornell, who wanted to discuss the Cornell material I had presented that March at Anthology. He unexpectedly said: 'I can tell by your voice that your personal world seems to be falling apart; the vase is tipped upside down; the order and motion of your life is disrupted, but you have the chance to observe the change, to appreciate that what the vase contained must now flow out...' I added these observations to a list I had been keeping for over a year. If change and disruption in personal life was making it impossible for me to work, could charting confusion and despair become a work?

The list began as a form of accumulating advice from friends, comments overheard among artists about relationship, jealousy, love, work, sexual experience. Enlarging my personal queries, dilemmas in a social context I saw that each fragment of "wisdom" was contradicted by another, that in the puzzle of love, attachment, independence, fidelity, infidelity, each person had a piece of the puzzle and no solutions. The puzzle itself in the accumulating context became part of a larger social and cultural pattern. In order to "see," to externalize what was happening I also began to assemble extracts from my dreams which revealed underlying emotions and unconscious information. A third category of collation was made from comments and the related dreams of A.—the partner who was leaving, and B.—the partner who was arriving.

At different times I showed the lists to A. and B. A. said he could better understand what was occurring by reading these lists; B. further determined the course of the work by saying "put it all on cards, then you can shuffle" (which became one of the key cards). The three categories were then color coded onto index cards: pink—quotations from friends, acquaintances; yellow—extracts from dreams and diaries; blue—the remarks of A., B., and C.

Over the past few years I had done several reading/performances from my books Parts Of A Body House Book, and Cèzanne, She Was A Great Painter. ABC—We Print Anything—In the Cards developed as a book of cards which could be presented as a performance—rather than making a book from a performance work. It was first performed as a reading at Franklin Furnace with slides projecting the color of each text category. In May it was done at New York University as part of Annina Nosei Weber's "Art As Discussion" series. By this time I had made slides to project each color-coded text so the audience could read

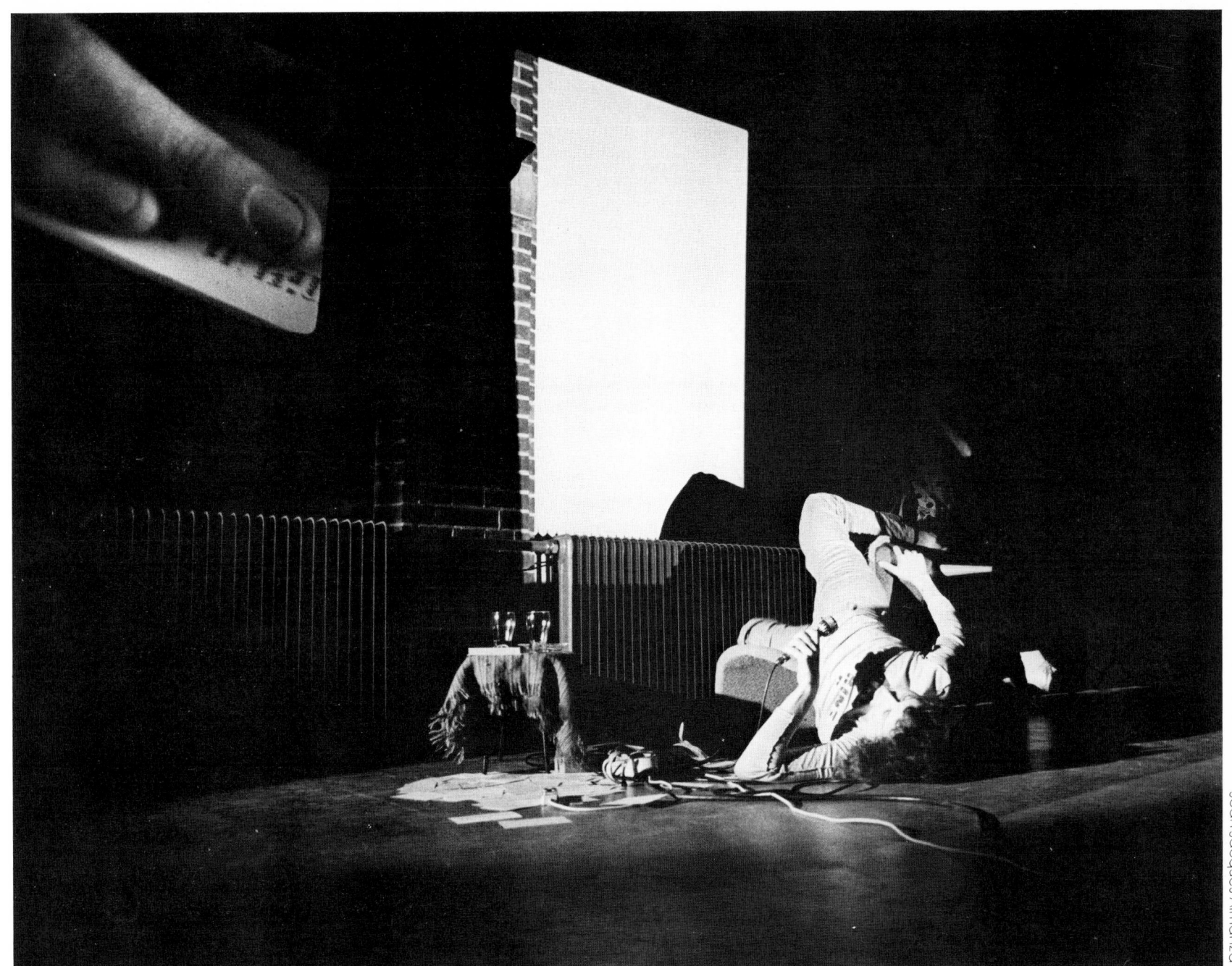

Jean Jacques Almanza

as well. Each card now had a complementary photograph (snapshots taken over the course of the year before there was any idea of incorporating casual imagery with the texts)—these images now enlarged the paradoxes of the cards. Slides made from the photographs depicted friends, A. and B. separately and together, parties, landscapes, travel shots, pets, nudes and archaic erotic sculpture. In the summer of '77 **ABC** was read at De Appel Gallery in Amsterdam. I was to present it later that month at the Arnhem Performance Art Festival; at this point I became dissatisfied with the static nature of the reading itself.

The first night in Arnhem I dreamt of a seedy upholstered grey chair with which I was engaged in a series of physical struggles: leaning, sliding, tumbling, falling, embracing, crawling, balancing on and under it. The next morning the organizer of the Festival, Jan Brand, took me to the performance space in an old town meeting hall. There on the stage was a seedy, red upholstered chair. It became my partner. I positioned three slide carousels to project between the arches of a long wall in the open space; the audience would be seated on the stage and around the floor. I returned to the principle of a solo improvisation

BLUE — Quotes from A., B., C.
PINK — Quotes from friends
YELLOW — From dreams & diaries
Collected from March to November 1976.

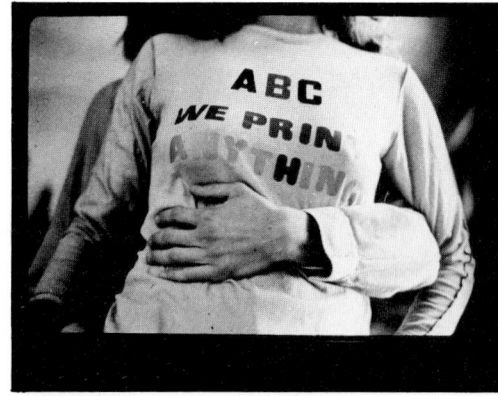

C.S.

B. told C., there are many kinds of affections & relations. A. asked C. about B. C. told A. about B., and told B. about A. C. asked A. about D. A. told D. about C.

B. told C. now he felt monogamous, more or less. C. told B. she was monogamous to him, except for A.

(blue)   6

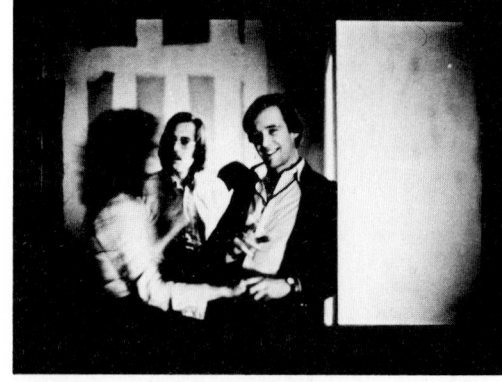

Bill Thompson

The women agreed their energies should be directed to their personal strengths and creative will, not to an idea of "happiness."

(pink)   41

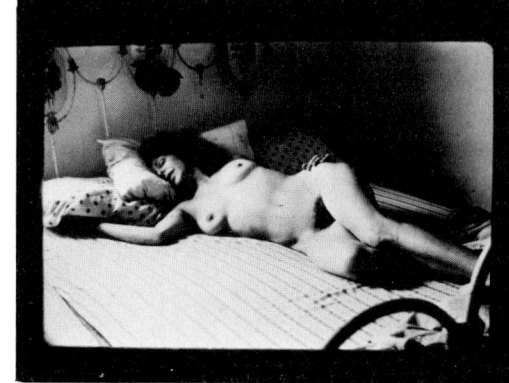

C.S.

The next morning the wall switch had been turned off, stopping the old electric clock B. had given C. When the switch was on the clock made an unhealthy, crunching noise. She began to cry, opened up the clock to adjust its parts. She told A.: you stopped the clock again. He was laughing & said: it's a hideous thing; you're going to get your period.

(yellow)   117

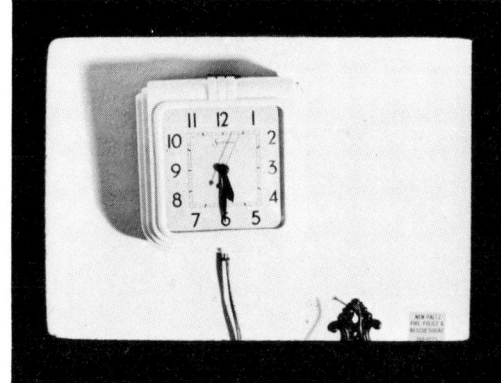

involving interferences: I controlled the three slide carousels on extension cords, a microphone, a penlight, and the spill of cards from which I read while sequencing the slides and struggling with the chair.

Among others, there are two sure signs that she has fallen in love: reverence & fascination for his genital, and for his handwriting.

(yellow)   47

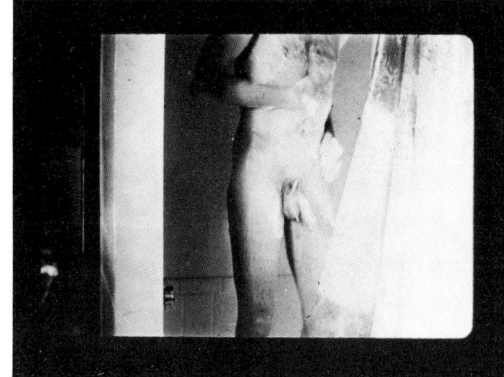

The artists realized their culture continued to fragment their relations by systems of economic rewards and notorieties; still, certain kinships took root as they shared ideas, equipment, spaces, friends, lovers, and each others diseases.

(pink)   113

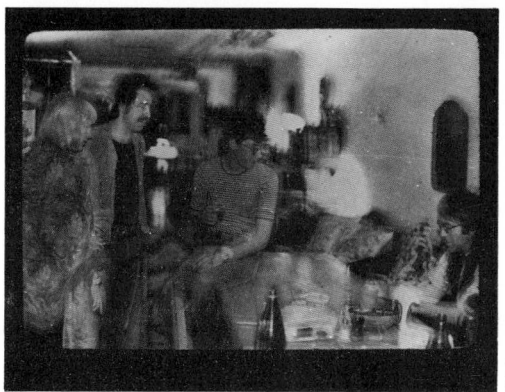

HOMERUNMUSE

November 20 1977 Brooklyn Museum of
Art NY

January 23 1978 Lions Walk Pittsburgh

A work-in-progress to explore derivations of the concept "muse": its form as museum—physical and aesthetic space, the images of a museum exhibit, "Women Artists 1550-1950"*—and the metaphoric implications of an artist herself performing in a museum.

Slide projections and pre-recorded or written texts are precisely scored; speech and live actions are improvised. There are four slide units:
1) details of the museum architecture and objects in its collection, juxtaposed with prehistoric artifacts.
2) double projections from the "Women Artists" exhibit.
3) images of my earlier performance actions having affinity to Cretan, Etruscan sculptures.
4) a free floating image of an Equatorial Island Owl Goddess.

These establish equivalences between architectural space, the objects/artifacts, and the body. Periodic runs through the museum break up the actions performed in relation to the slides and texts: video cameras positioned in selected corridors relay the runs onto monitors in front of the audience.

The following photographs and texts are from the Brooklyn Museum version which took place in a small gallery after being designed for the spacious Victorian rotunda.

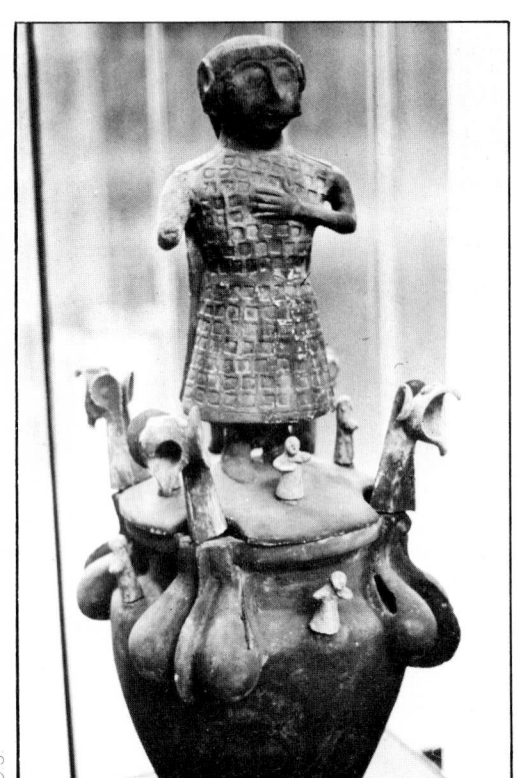

*Organized by Ann Sutherland Harris and Linda Nochlin/Los Angeles County Museum of Art; Brooklyn Museum installation October-November 1977.

improvise on texts

THE WHITE CHARTER HOUSE STONE
VAULT OF SACRED OBJECTS STOLEN
ADOPTED LOST TO THEIR NATURAL
SITES I HAVE NOTHING TO INVENT
TO SAY REMARK OUT OF THIS INWARD
LISTENING SPEAKING OUT LOUD A
SERPENT FORM NOT A POPULAR RELO
CATION SPIN OUT A TRUTH IN IM
MEDIACY AS IMMEDIACY MEANS OF
FINDING A TRUTH

I walk up to the muse image hold
microphone to her breast for heart
beat....turn & sit at her feet --
punctuate speaking with beats of
mic into mitt

OR IS SHE WHISPERING RUSTLING IN
THOSE LEAVES WHITE WOMAN YOU
DON'T KNOW ME WHITE WOMAN YOU
THINK BEING FEMALE & ALL YOU FEEL
OF MY ASPECT BRINGS ME WHOLE IN
YOUR SPACE

I jump up facing the image

ANYWAY I FOUND YOU IN A BOOK
YOU'RE ONLY A BLACK & WHITE IMAGE

tape of "When You Wish Upon A
Star" fades in....the muse image
disappears /on l. wall slides of
the Nubian corridor begin in slow
rotation with no companion images.
Stride back & forth in front of
audience as if caged, stymied.....
tape of ripping up roof...........

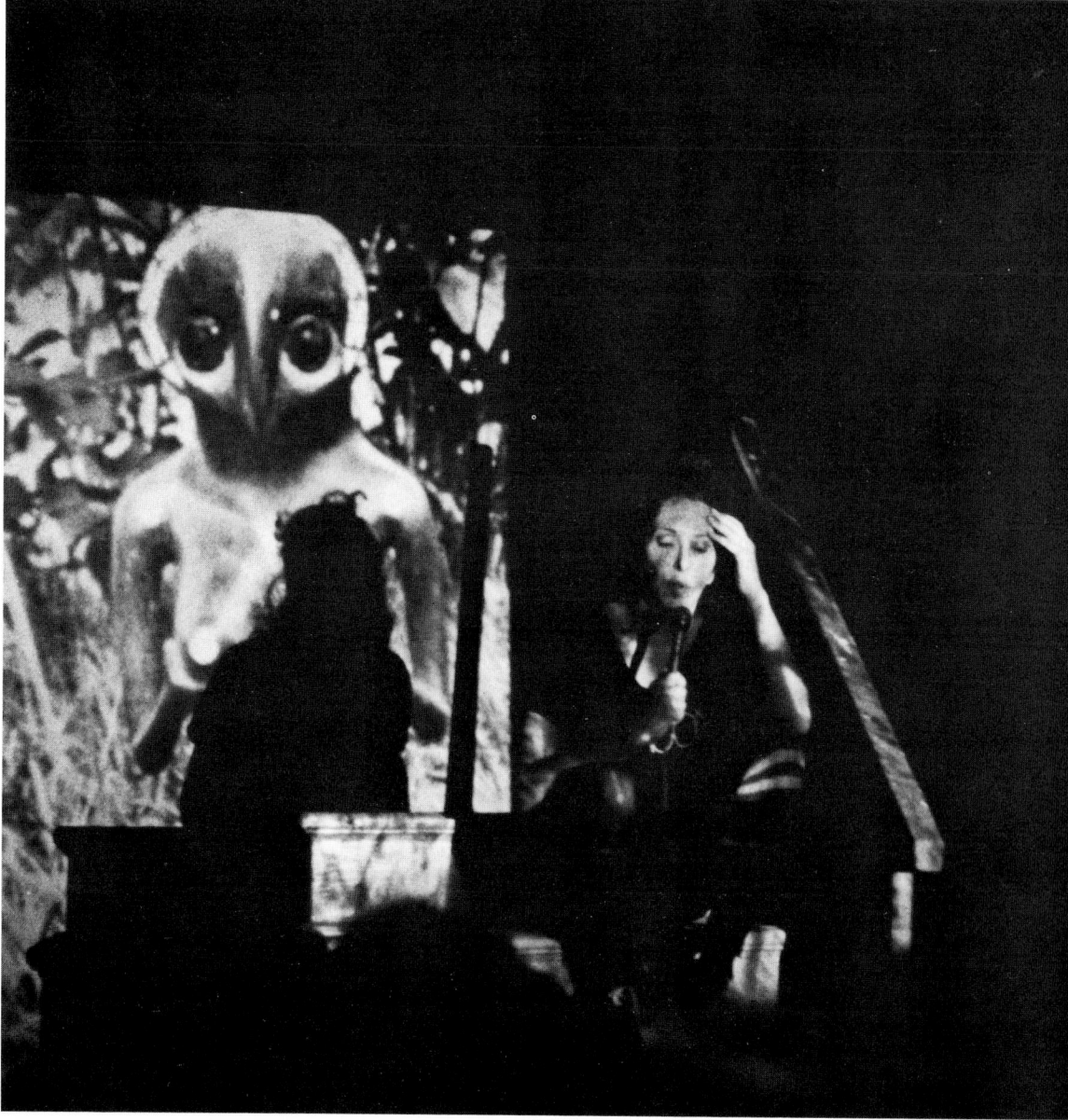

Bill Thompson

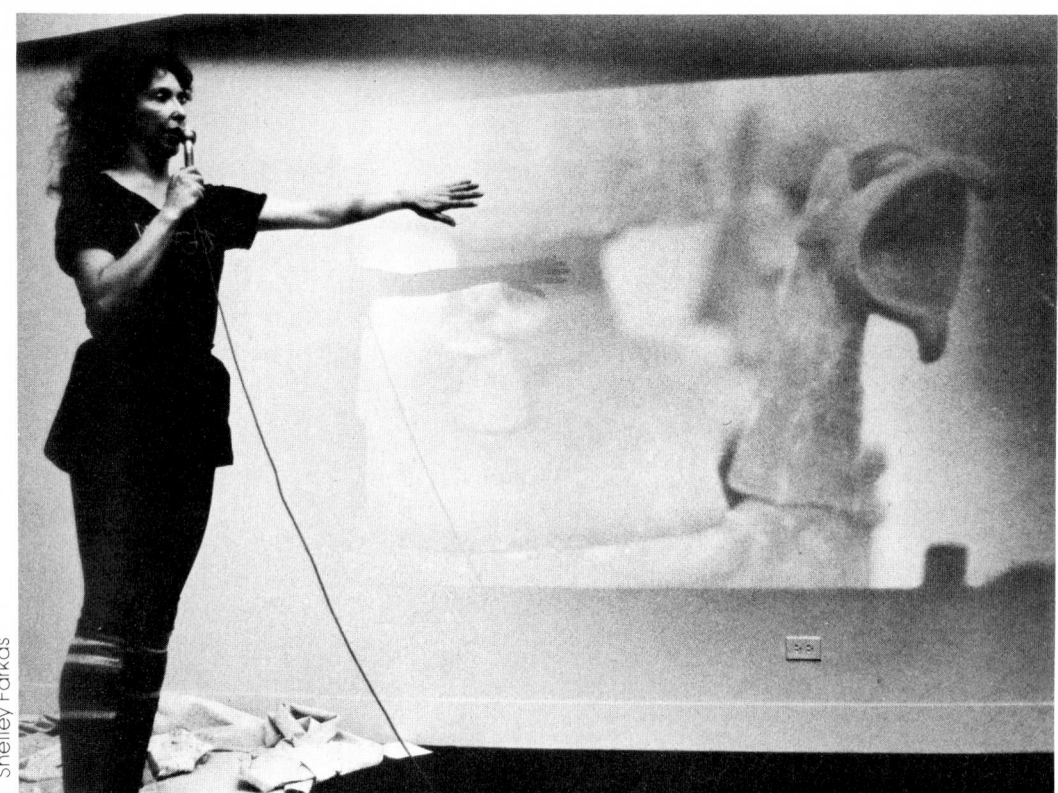

Shelley Farkas

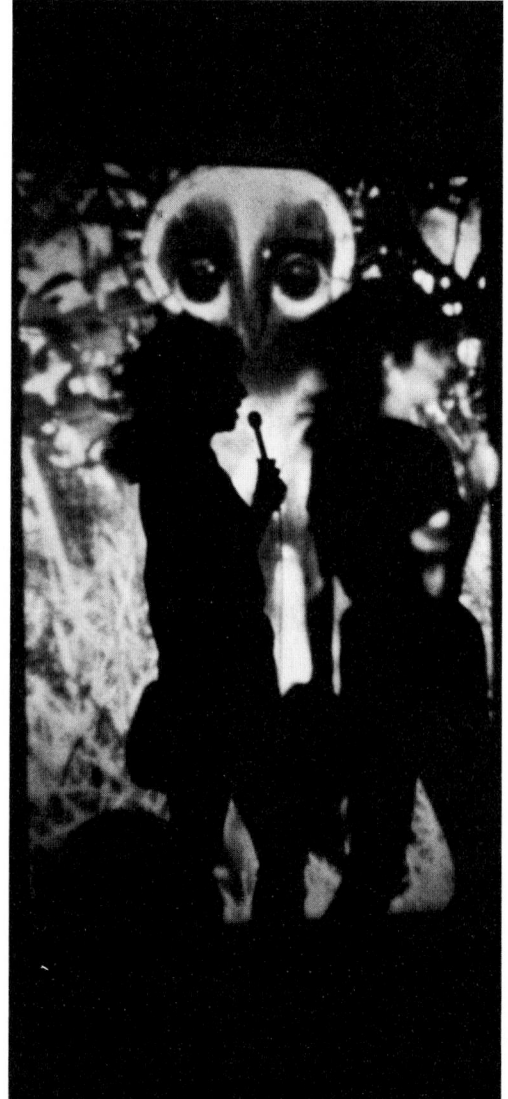

Bill Thompson

fade-out roof ripping tape/ muse slide floats on mirror/double
projection museum, prehistoric artifacts/improvise on text

........what am I doing?   well we'll show some things we've
made.....yes yes they're afraid I'll pull down my paints....
you know.....they suspect I get messages from my cunt & want
to exhibit them.....which?.......all the things are here......
no they don't know what they mean......but they might guess
something.....confused.....yes....passive?.....yes...spectators
......you know....it's all under glass....many of our things...
when? before we were raped murdered banished tricked lied
to abducted chased captured locked up starved tortured
....around that time....what?.....yes our things what we made
what they stole kidnapped hid denied were our yes under
glass....what? which? our bowls bones pots weavings masks.
vulva goddesses our phalli and slippers and coats and mittens
in leather and paint made from berries and leaves our holy
batons ivory horns calenders in stone our bells arrows shells
feathers thongs pebble images of our Mother........

(improvise between floor and stairway to nowhere)

......I was writing this letter to
my Black muse.....Bye Goddess...I
had a card from her to read....or
write.....when I looked up..didn't
know where I was headed...no sign
of Manhatten...I was the only white
pale face.....in the train...going
didn't know where.....losing time..
wondered Muse are you leading me
astray....lost did I find you......
how do we get to.....Manhatten.....

muse slide has appeared on center
wall; still hitting microphone into
baseball mitt, I turn to muse image.

AFTER ALL I DON'T KNOW WHO SHE IS
WAS PERHAPS CARVED BY A WOMAN TO
BANISH WHITE SPIRITS SEEN IN A
DREAM PALE & VORACIOUS I CHOOSE
HER FELT MUTUALITY   SOMETHING IS
AWRY
twirl microphone in the air slap it
repeatedly into mitt

PERHAPS IT IS NOT BETWEEN US BUT
BETWEEN HER PRESENCE   MINE THE
MUSEUM

slap microphone on the floor

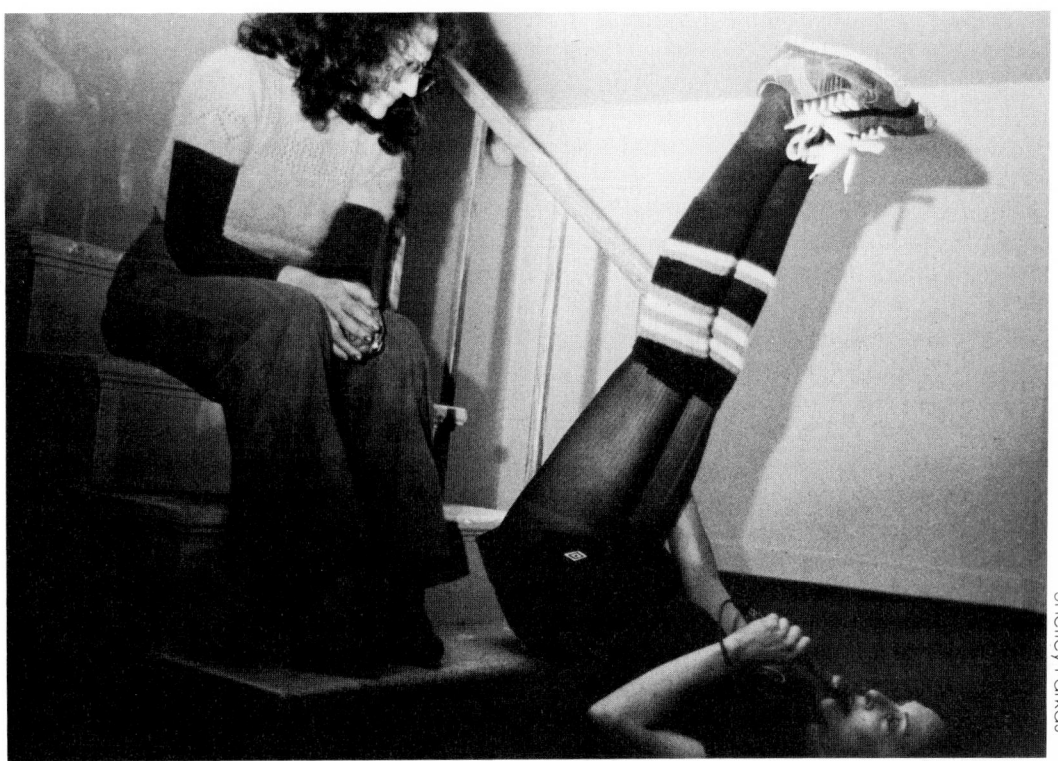

Shelley Farkas

freeze muse slide on wall behind stairway to nowhere/improvise

Look into audience "I need some help"....(called to Lynne)
"Would you come sit on these steps and ask me what happened?"
She comes and sits on top step. "I think if I lie upside down
on these steps I can tell the story better." Lynne asks "What
happened? You were working in the other space for quite awhile!"

...well, I couldn't do anything in the crypto-Egyptian lecture
hall....dinner party for Kissinger being given in rooms adjacent to the Nubian corridor....two weeks there...two days ago
they said we're sorry we don't want to upset you but we just
found out the waiters are setting up the dishes & drinks in
your rotunda......I said that's o.k. I'll work around the
waiters....they said actually that's not possible...you can not
.....you can't do that to me...pretence of a scene -- I'm leaving....for $75- bucks I'v got other work to do....or charming...
work must get done....I said well Kissinger can have his friends
and I'll have my friends....I know some of those bankers......
they know some of the artists......Kissinger is only a symbol....

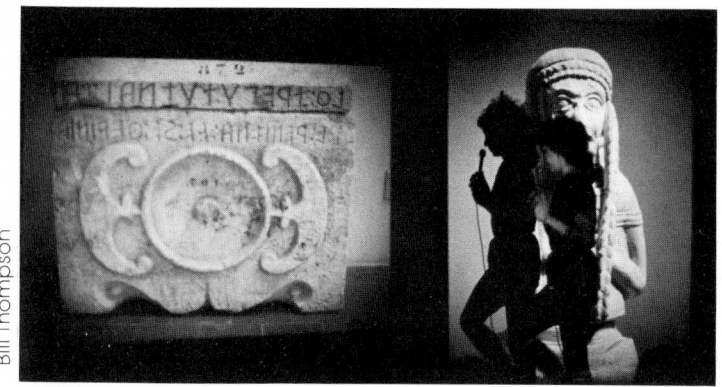

Bill Thompson

<u>dissolve muse slide/ full wall abutting slides</u>
<u>of "Women Artists", double projection scored</u>
<u>to recorded text/run in place with dumbells</u>

BIOLOGICAL SPIRITUAL & AESTHETIC UNITY --
PRIMAL UNITY OF CREATIVE ACTS HER INDENTIF
ICATION WITH MATERIAL IS IMMEDIATE BECAUSE
HER BODY'S FUNCTIONS ARE TRANSFORMATIVE
PERIODIC & UNDENIABLE. IT IS IN HER BODY
THAT EXTREME TRANSFORMATIONS OCCUR CHANGES
WHICH PARALLEL THOSE OF NATURE. FROM THE
KNOWLEDGE OF HER BODY SHE IS MOVED TO ACT
IVATE TO SHAPE & TO CREATE FORMS IN THE
WORLD WHICH SURROUNDS HER

THE CIRCLE OF MOONS IS SCRIPT

<u>bells on ankles...begin runs through museum</u>
<u>out of sight & reappearing....</u>

OR COURSE SHE IS NOT TO BE TAKEN LIGHTLY
MEN.DID NOT TRIVIALIZE THIS GUIDE IN ORDER
TO KEEP HER VALUE THEY MADE HER EXCLUSIVE
TO THEMSELVES THE CREATIVE FEMALE SPIRIT
WAS CO-OPTED SHE COULD ONLY SERVE MEN
SO SUPERIOR WAS SHE TO HER VERY GENDER
SOURCE THAT ONLY HE COULD ENCORPORATE HER
IN EFFECT SUCK HER BACK INTO HIS BODY A
REVERSAL ON THE CREATIVE ACT OF HIS ORIGINAL
BIOLOGICAL MOTHER   THE MUSE HAS SERVED
PATRIARCHIAL IMAGINATION AS ACCOMPLICE
COLLABORATOR TRAITOR DEFENDING & DEFINING
HIS CREATIVE TERRITORY APART FROM FEMALE
WILL & IMAGINATION

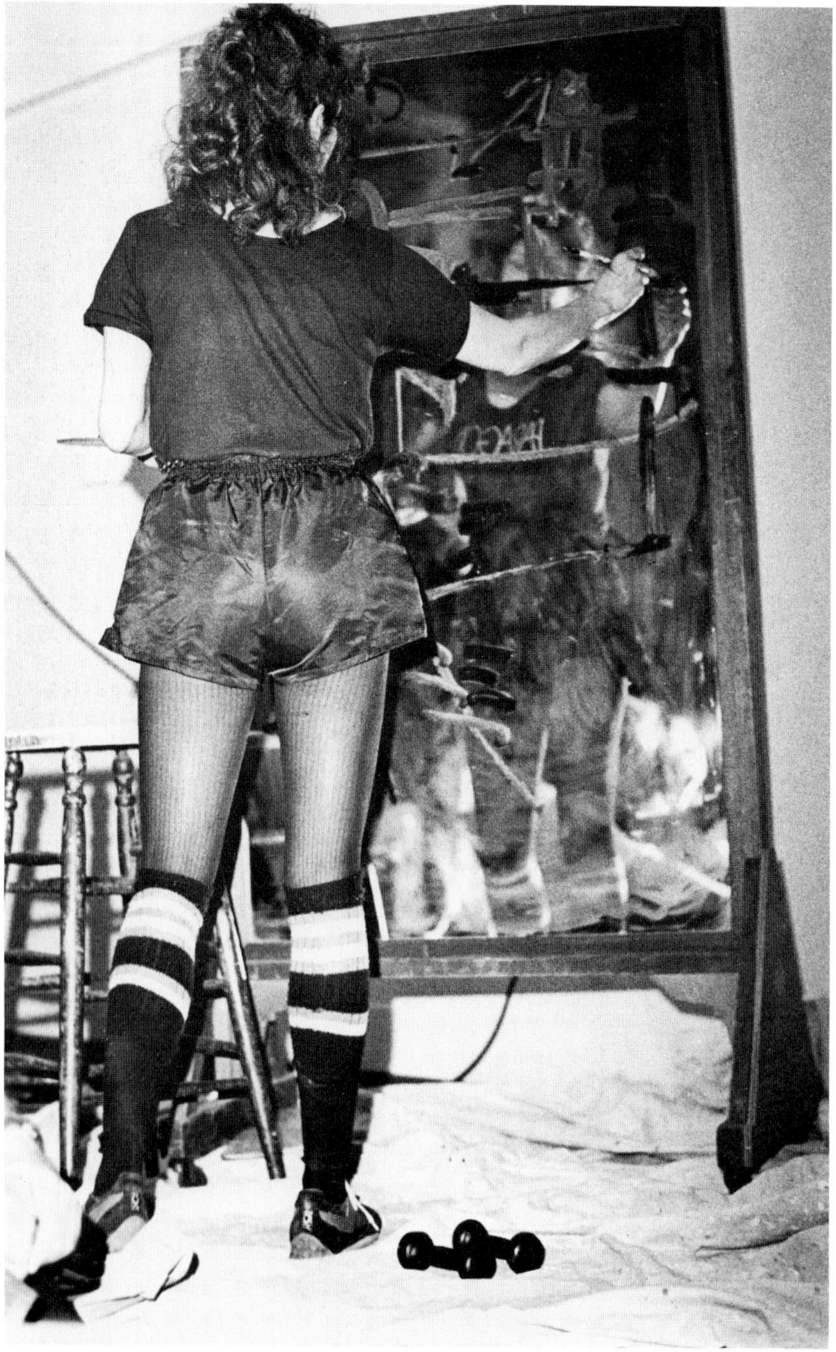

Shelley Farkas

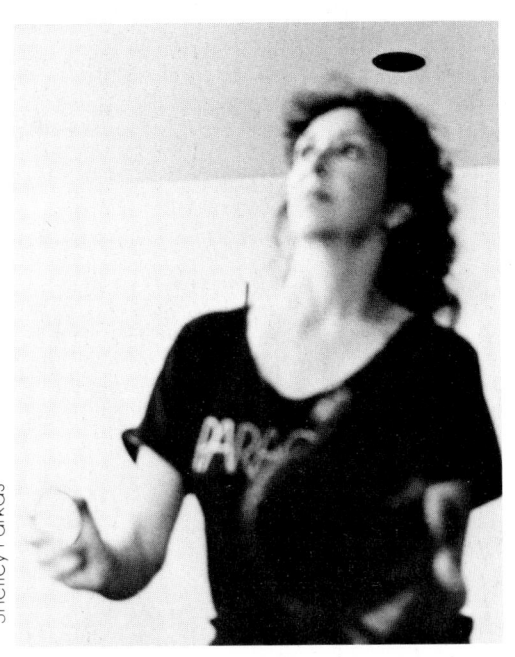

Shelley Farkas

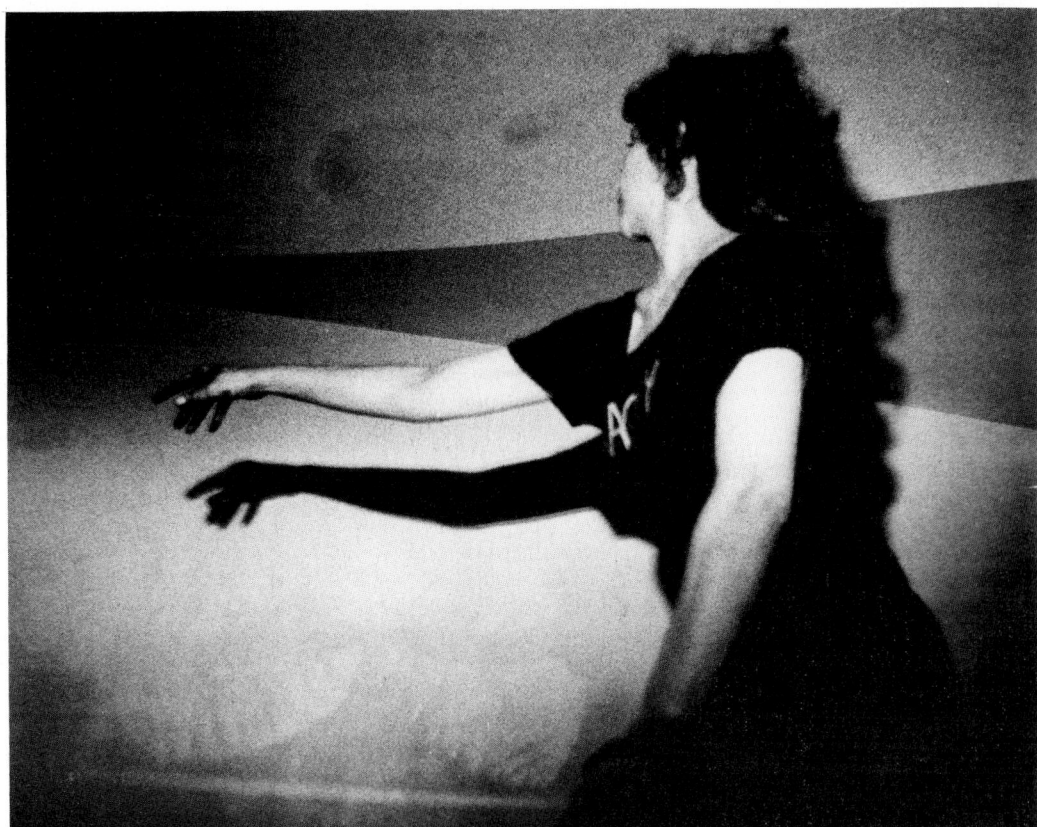

Shelley Farkas

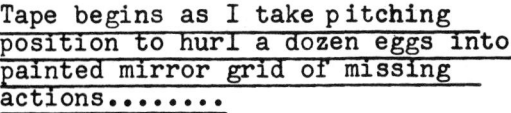

Tape begins as I take pitching
position to hurl a dozen eggs into
painted mirror grid of missing
actions........

TODAY IS NOVEMBER 20th SEVENTY
YEARS AGO ON NOVEMBER 20th 1907
IN WORPSWEDE GERMANY P AULA
MONDERSOHN-BECKER DIED   SHE
SUFFERED AN EMBOLISM AFTER GIVING
BIRTH TO HER DAUGHTER   HER LAST
WORDS WERE "WHAT A PITY"

slides of Becker's paint ings

Rilke one hoped to marry Becker, & was influenced as well by
his friendship with Lou Andreas Salomé. He spoke for equity
between male & female a rtists. At her death he wrote to Otto
Mondersohn, husband of Paula:

>"For that is guilt, if anything be guilt:
>   not to increase the freedom of a loved one
>By all the liberty within ourselves.
>We have but this to do, where once we love--
>To let each other be; to hold each other
>Comes easily to us, we need not learn it."

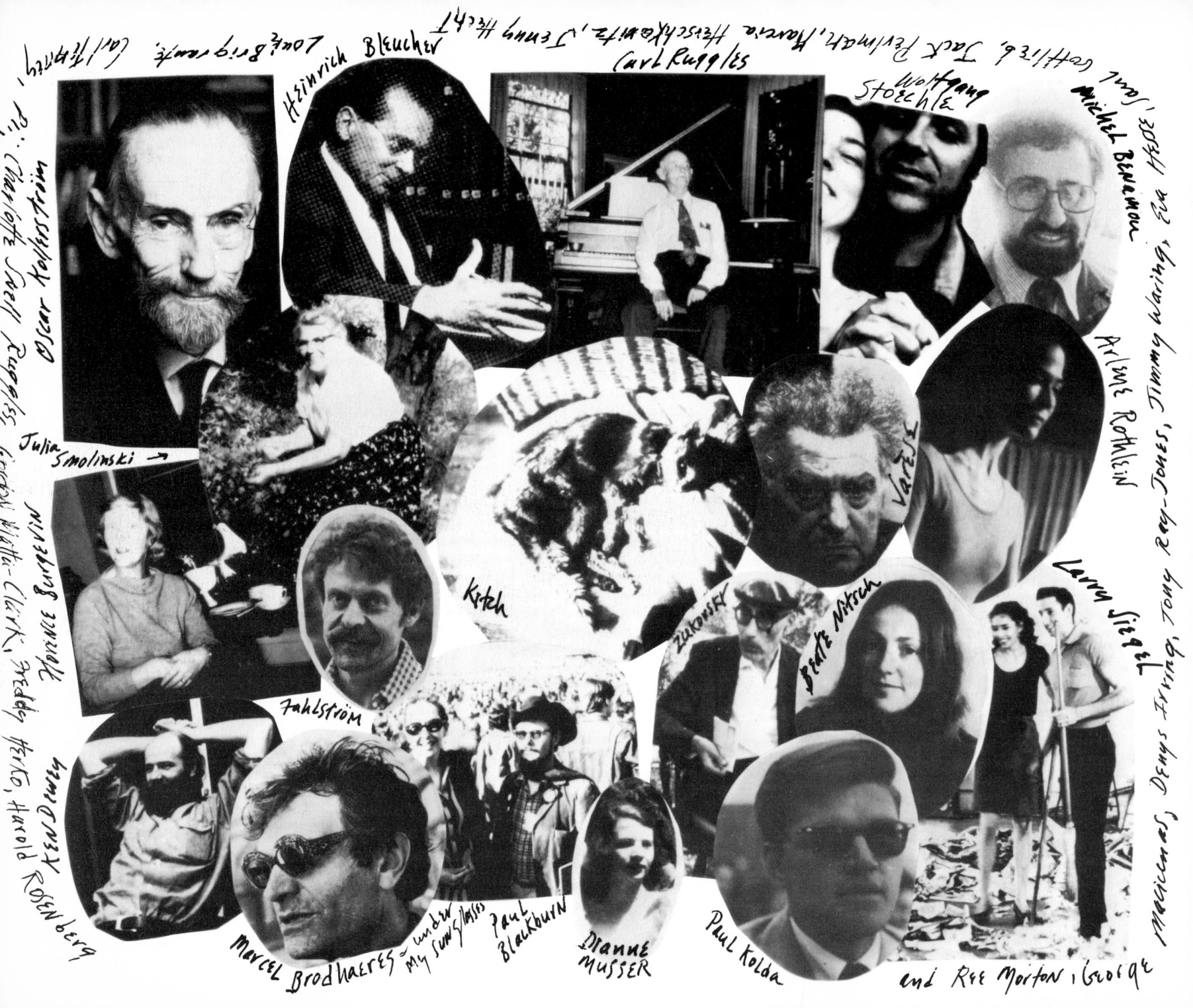

Oscar Kokoschka, Louis Bourgeois, (ca.) Heinrich Bleucher, Carl Ruggles, Wolfgang Stoehle, Iosef Pelikan, Franz, Jenny Holzer, Hetschkowitz, Jack Pelikan, Franz, Michel Benamou, Gottlieb, Louis, Arlene Rothlein, Charlotte Suell Ruggles, Gordon Matta-Clark, Freddy Herko, Harold Rosenberg, Florence Burgevin, Julia Smolinski →, Varèse, Larry Siegel, Zukofsky, Beate Nitsch, Fahlström, Kitch, Marcel Broodthaers – under my sunglasses, Paul Blackburn, Dianne Musser, Paul Kolda, Mercenaries, Denys Irving, Tony Rey-Jones, Timmy Waring, Eva and Ree Morton, George

appendix

UNPERFORMED WORKS

Partitions (for performers in a shelf/closet construction in a gallery) 1963

Water (for the Hartford Antheneum fountains) March 1964

Cunnilingus for Children (Red Riding Hood & Dog Event) 1965

Rituals Circular (sound & contact improvisation score) February 1965

Extrusions (performance for a cement truck) 1965

Contact duets (drawings) January 1965

Scrap/Shrapnel (outdoor night performance for St. Mark's Church in the Bowery) May 1966

Car Wreck Event (melodrama—live action) August 1966

Searchlight (night performance in landscape) 1966

Projections (A gallery environment of mirrors smashed by flashlights over the course of a week) September 1966

Parts Of A Body House (environment) 1957 & 1967

Solar System (performance for the NYC planetarium with Jerome Rothenberg) 1967

Acqua Notte (aerial performance over canals of Venice) 1966-68

Last Will & Testament (environments, events created by audience) 1968

Rope Ascensions (for clusters of performers vertically) 1968

Projection Tunnel (grant proposal) 1968

Time Passes (cameras on bodies-performance in a museum) December 1968

Brain Waves (projection environment of audience brain waves) December 1968

Amplified Sea & Fire On Water (summer event for Stockholm) 1969

Audience-Activated Environment (proposal to Los Angeles County Museum) 67-69

Open Spaces/Media (audience-activated environment; also called "Divine Playhouse") London 1970-71

Pignic for Artists (proposal for Art Spectrum London, Alexander Palace) 1971

Skyweb (outdoor aerial performance for Serpentine Gallery, London) 1972

Building Destruction (participation in the destruction of a building) London 1971

Beast (multi-media & performance for Institute of Contemporary Art, "Art and Body" series) London 1972

Summer Beast (a free circulation event with live animals for the Serpentine Gallery, Ices Festival) London 1972

SEARCHLIGHT 1966

For the deserted Havemayer Estate, MahWah, N.J. The grounds
include: thickets, open circle of pine trees, lilly pond, sand
quarry, lake, rough road track, dump, limed hills.

Drawings, notes plot areas of action and event: overlapping
sequences, images discovered in spotlights situated in opposite directions crossing fifty feet.

The audience/participants will have traveled to the site by bus
from NYC. In total darkness they slowly walk into areas of
possible event. The bursts of spotlights "run" through the
landscape illuminating actions, situations. The audience experiences physical changes within the unknown circumference. First
the long roadway lined with rhododendrons; circle of pine trees
which have lights in high branches on random-time switches. Intervals between lights 1½ minutes; illumination no longer than
six seconds. Performers are up in the branches -- near each
light --caught in a sudden motion or completely still.

The lily pond between the pine trees and paths to the lake:
rank, overgrown. From above sporatic yellow lights flash into
it --oranges and lemons float among the reeds.

Into the woods: quantities of pen lights active as fire flies --
guide lights, random but dense. The paths flicker, shadowed,
to the lake, sides of the lake, to the sand bar stretched out
towards the quarry under spot lights, the dune-like mounds to
which the spectators walk...and on, into....

From the dunes events within the landscape spotlighted in intervals: the wreckage of a tractor and old Oldsmobile. The dump
shimmering metal, glass. The shattered greenhouse. (Questions
of the "found" environment: luxury, order, aesthetic intentions
abandoned; inexplicable, violent accidents, decay.) Lights move
continually across the expanse of the lake. Lines of swimmers
appear, disappear.

Searchlights, flares suddenly silhouette a line of people in
the arch of the dunes -- struggling, carrying bodies between
them. The audience becomes part of an action or event which
has attracted them to it. To spectators in other areas their
intermittent position in the lights will determine the choice
of moves. Aromas of cooking meat become another guide; behind the sand-blasted roadway there is a cook-out. Quantities
of food and drink are discovered there.

The core group of twenty-six performers continue to inhabit
the landscape in a constant exchange of position, action-
clusters throughout the night. Those who begin in the trees
become cooks/ those who were cooking become figures swimming
in the lake/those who activated the lights become runners
through the woods creating an inconstant, unnerving sound texture of breaking twigs, crashing branches.

During the night all performers will have exchanged positions,
actions. All spectators will themselves have become subject
and witness.

---

8 June 1971
8 June 1971
DEAR TIM;
DEAR TIM I WANT TO MA KE A ROA SE PIG NICN
        I WANT TO MA KE A ROAST PIG PICNIC CALLED
PIG PICNIC IN AN OPEN OVAL TREES NEAR / BUDGET FOR FOOD
ENVIRONMENT GLUTTONY- EYE -EAR-ORA L-CHORAL. ALL VIBRANT
DECAY HERE. BACK 2 WKS.

"SLOTH" A PICNIC WITH MEDIA SLOPS
by Carolee Schneemann

for friends and their friends and their friends:.........

          GOBBLE SUCK CHOMP SLURP
EA CH BRING ONE THING TO EAT DRINK SMOKE SHA RE WITH 12
OTHERS   THIS IS NO JOKE BOUNEY AND JOY WILL ACCRUE
CAPTAIN ALPHONSE SMITZ ATE FREE FOR TWENTY DAYS!

This luck has been sent to you. It is no joke. Please do
n ot send money. Add your name to the bottom of this list.
Your faith will be rewarded!

     QUARENTEED FOR ONLY A MEASLEY £150-!!!
roast pigs flowing wine knives spoons forks serviettes
300 paper plates   breads cheeses butter and masks

3/4 inch manilla rope to climb = fifty feet of it
glimmering streamers
six speakers in trees: barrel organ and pig music
(pigs in n ormal converse as well as pain & ecstasy (of pigs))

apples   bananas peaches
trip to the country a van a driver flares   telephone call
the six speakers cable tape recorder a ssistents

a mailing of 600 postcards ingeniously designed & colored

A ONE AND ONLY FIRST AND LAST CHANCE ALEXANDER PALACE
SUMMER CONFLAGRATION FOR LONDON A UGUST 1971

               from C. Schneemann
               17a Belsize Park n.w. 3

to Tim Hilton, "Museum Tavern" (Pub near Grt. Russell St.)
London W.c. 1

ACQUA NOTTE

A Kinetic Theater work in Venice.
Images for this event began at the 1964 Venice Biennale,
developed into an aerial performance Water Light/WaterNNeedle
presented in 1965 at St, Mark's Church in the Bowerie. My
proposal now is to realize the imagery at its source.

MATERIALS & PARTICIPANTS
the spectators
8-10 performers (artists attending the Biennale '66)
technical assistents: lights and sound
                       rope suspension, harness construction
                       illuminated plastic tubeing

10 gondolas
1 small barge
3 bales pink polyurethene (extrusion scrap)
pile of wooden poles or wood pileings
125 feet of 3/4 inch manilla rope
industrial steel bolts eye hooks pulleys

10 canvas harnesses
50 Venetian flags
40 flashlights
100 candles
80 small brass bells

roll of medium weight transparent plastic
1 bale shredded colored cellophane
8 spot lights
4 sets of amplifiers and speakers
2 orchestras

SITUATION
Near a bridge across the Grand Canal

the bridge crowds water surrounding buildings & streets

Over the water by the bridge heavy manilla ropes are anchored
and raised on pulleys. Red spot lights, speakers, amplifiers
are situated in buildings on either side of the bridge.

Spectators line the sides of the canal. Flashlights, bells,
flags are distributed among them. They receive an outline of
the events from which they make choices as to when and how to
use their lights, bells and flags. Two particular groups
have rehearsed moving the pulleys, loading performers on and
off the harnesses and into the gondolas.

Each side of the canal is marked with a row of candles.

ACTIONS/ACTIVATIONS

Flickering lights. Small bells. The random Church bells.
Spectators use their lights, bells and flags in a relay of
brief, attenuated gestures. They listen for gondolas --
heard and unseen. Reflections, duplications.

Harness relay. Spectators adjust empty harnesses on the
ropes in random configurations. The harnesses are "flown"
back and forth across the water, illuminated by intermittent
spotlights worked from adjacent buildings. Other participants flash their lights on the harnesses and into the water
way where Gondolas are circling. Some of the lights are on
ropes which are thrown out towards the water in vertical and
horizontal strokes.

Body relay. An empty harness is pulled to the edge of the
pier and loaded with a performer who is then moved out over
the water on the pulley in juxtaposition to empty harnesses
shifting above the water. One by one the remaining performers
are placed in a harness and travel on the pulleys. They have
various movements: twisting, turning, flying, stretching,
reaching, suspensions....Spotlights are directed back and
forth over them. Spectators set up rhythms of shaking lights,
bells, flags.

After four or five relays the participants unload the performers and carry them to gondolas which have assembled on
either side of the canal. The performers are wrapped in
plastic, spread out in the gondolas. Spectators who are
not wrapping, light the gondolas. Others throw colored
cellophane over the bodies, filling the gondolas.

From opposite sides of the canal two orchestras suddenly
begin to play different songs. The gondolas move off with
the body piles. Tied to the back of each gondola are lengths
of illuminated plastic tubeing with piles of fat polyurethene
foam stretched out, floating. The gondolas follow the small
barge loaded with wood pilings. Spotlights flash over the
spectators, their bells, flags until the gondolas are out of
sight. From a nearby building a Vivaldi concerto is amplified,
mixing with the songs of the orchestra.

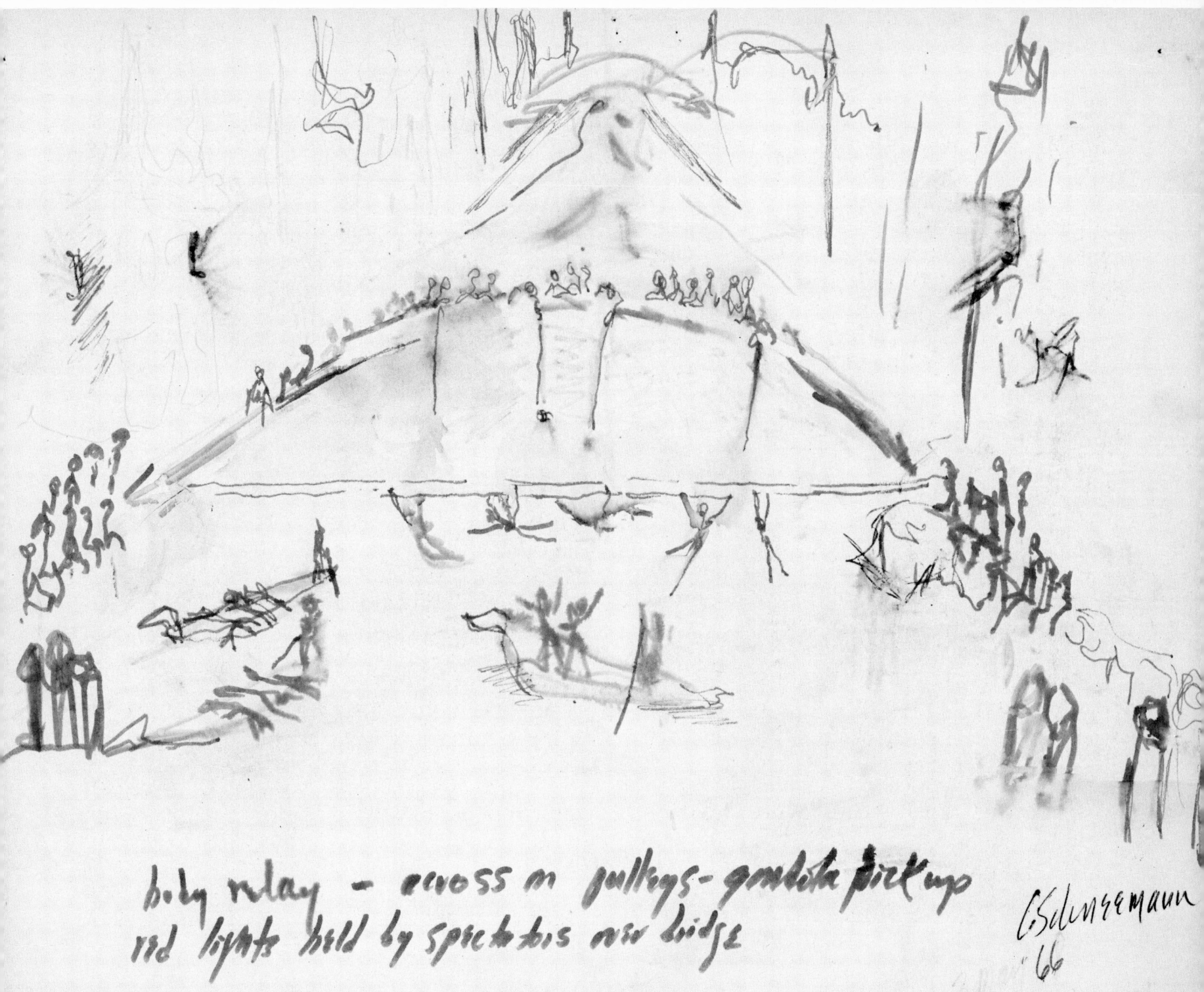

body relay — across on pulleys — gondola pick up
red lights held by spectators over bridge

C Schneemann
'66

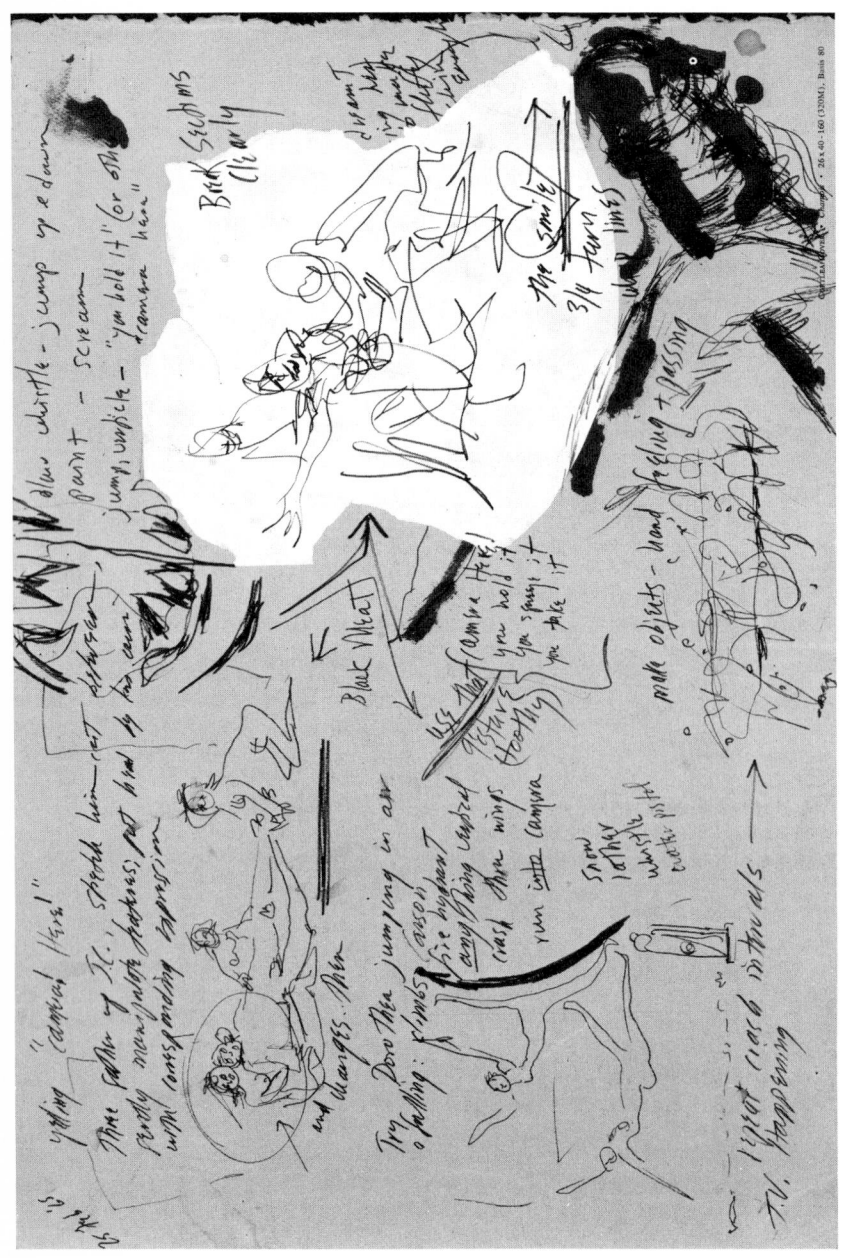

OPEN SPACES/MEDIA: public access mutable environment.
(Prototype for HOME SPACES/MEDIA) London 1970

1. An environment which demands physical action and response in
its inception as well as in the perception of it. There are no
"spectators", no "performers". Anyone present may produce
effects, organize materials, and physically move with the spatial
and tactile elements which compose the environment.

Materials: massed, tunneled, hung, piled. Selection and placement of lights, sound (speakers), film, slide images; rigging
ropes. Spontaneous and intensive organization.

As a group builds this environment their social and esthetic
considerations merge. Group intentions are shaped by individual
skills and imagination. Individuals find themselves in contact
improvisation with one another and the materials; the tactile
interactions determine the disposition of elements. Energies
are concentrated and flexible -- directed in towards a common
center, rather than out and away from a common center (which
characterizes usual social patterns of most families,work groups).

The time structure of the environment may be keyed to films,
slides, audio tapes which depict previous groups building in
the space. This reference can be absorbed into a disimiliar
result or provide basic organizational information.

2. The components of OPEN SPACES/MEDIA are coordinated in an
"information core" placed in the center of the room. The core
includes time-lapse closed circuit television; light beams which
are activated by participants movements, which in turn trigger
films, sound, slides, lights through an SCR switching system;
smoke machine, bubble machine, speakers. A selection of super 8
cassettes and sound tapes relate previous activities in the
environment. The tactile materials include: bales of foam rubber
(varying densities, colors, shapes); manilla rope, bales of
shredded fire retadent paper, prisims, mirrors, hoops, balls,
skates, reflective cloth, revolving light stands, etc.

Randomizing factors in the "information core" introduce gaps
between input and output of the response sensing systems, Thus
the person who receives new sensory information may not have set
the circuit in motion but may activate another element then experienced by someone else. Randomizing factors help break down
conditioning to specific and conventional expectations between
the body, space and "normal" functional limits imposed on the
use of space and personal interrelations in public. Participants
surprise themselves in finding their own intentions enlarged as
a source of continuing invention.

3. I provide the technological system and its sensory scope;
the basic materials with which a cohesive environment can be
developed, while constantly variable, flexible, interchangable.

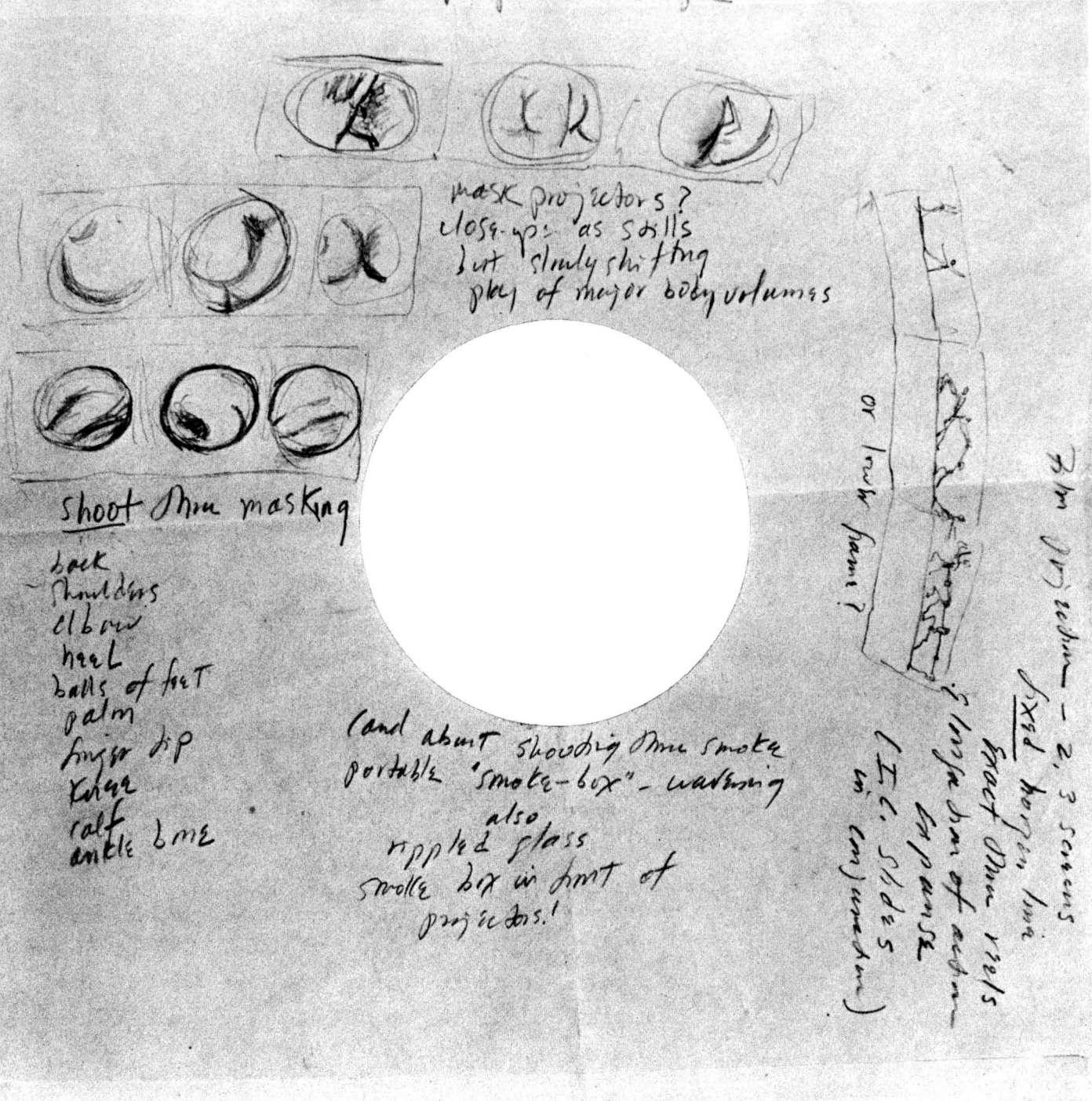

Schneemann: the work moves, for the years I've been watching it, always from [viewer's] lower left to upper right. Boxes, canvases, a wonderful frieze of watercolor paper she gave me a dozen years ago, with transfers & fuzzy enigmas transpiring upwards, always upwards, like cartoons becoming flesh becoming More Than That.

This philosophical direction is an Amerithing, a touch of Emerson, a clear honest yearning towards hanging the completed work right up there, on the chandelier (life an Irish party). It is innocent, and its rage to get there probably has scared many of the otherwise audience. When sophistication, that authentic Europe of the head, joins with the native urgency of her work in so many arts, there is a kind of shock or overload; the cheap machine of publicity freaks out & people stand around abashed at her shapely largeness.

I for one would not have it otherwise. Schneemann is a painter, filmmaker (apotheosis of that up-to-the-right movement in *Fuses*), dancer, embodiment in body meant of arts not yet culturally specified but factually, actually, in her work given. Schneemann is a writer, a diagnost of our malaises & a deft spokeswoman of the priority of *personal meaning* above all. Her written texts work vigorously as a fusion of personal *planh* & the most outrageous outward! social! invention!

Schneemann's work is in essence: a *problematic* of the arts. I would not want her work to veer ever from its own variegation of means (her Media are Many, not 'Mixed') or kaleidoscopic inward-ness of gesture; I would not want it less clamorous, good-humored, immense, complaining, generous, zealous, yeasty than it is.

There is a triumph to be made of circumstances. Comes to my mind a recollection of a theater piece years back, in a raunchy East Side theater: Schneemann on stage, upright & bare amidst a raft of literal garbage, the 'set' of that event. She stood like the pleistocene Lady of Beasts, but also like any artist, every artist, over the junk of one's life, here, for an instant, lifted with wit & power & decency into a luminous gesture.

Robert Kelly
2 May 77

I remember the smell of fish.

Nam June Paik

JUDSON, November 18, 1964/

Fish   slime
      rubbed all over the
          body
    stings, doesn't it, Jim?
    and itches to satisfy .

Carolee   Carolee
      she makes
    out of the dance
     her own sea

FISH

Paul Blackburn

Re: Carolee

    Her body — the body of body — is only one of her bodies: Meat Joy *celebrates it. But there are also the body of her thought (this book), the body of her magic and the body of her work.*

    Whole people are many things, a woman is many things (to herself and to others). This process of perception which goes beyond conception — how it feels to perceive her on a rope, implying how it feels to be on a rope — that is what, for me, most of her work is about. "Das Ewigweibliche, — hier wird's getan." (Goethe: untranslatable, alas: something like "The eternally-female, — here it is done.") But this lass is never done. Hers is a many-chambered house. Like her "Parts of a Body House," in my anthology, Fantastic Architecture. *Always new rooms to explore.*

Dick Higgins

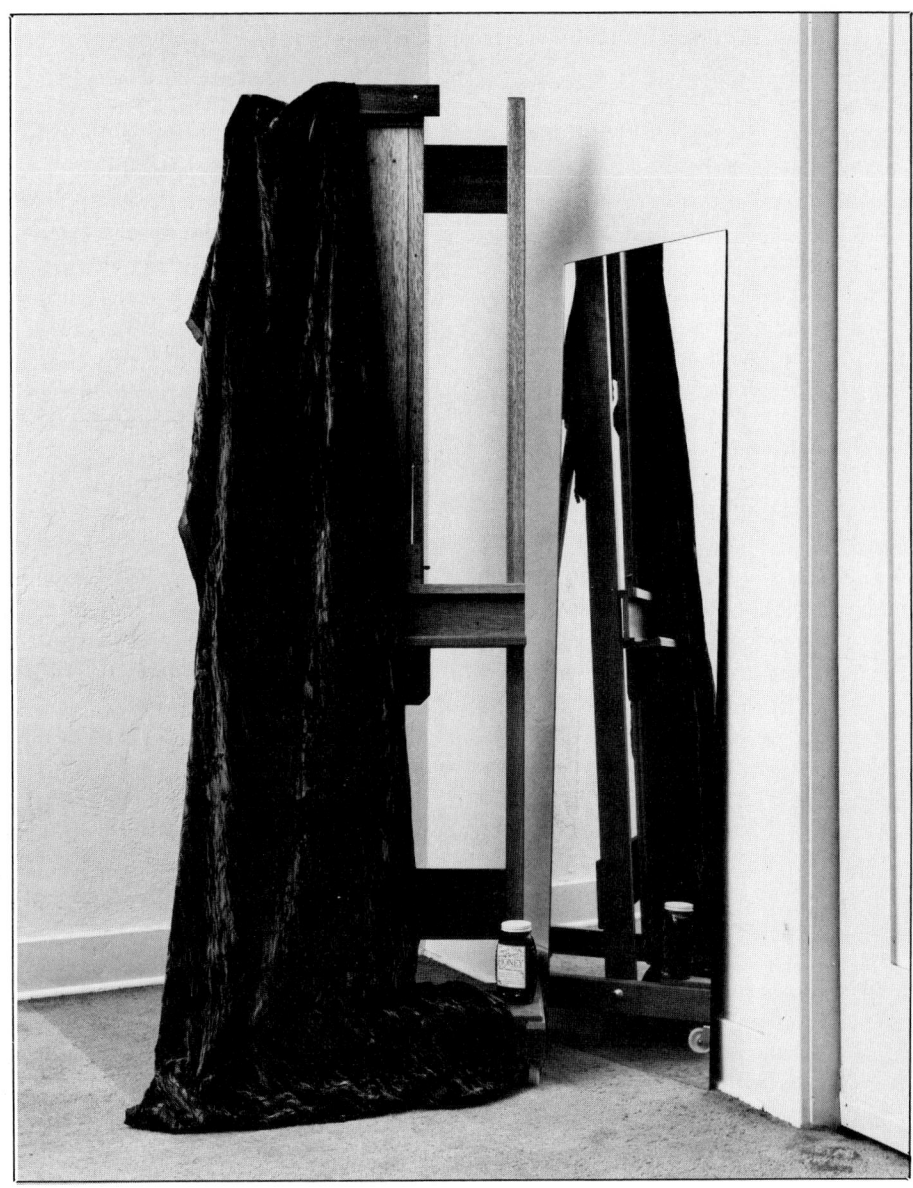

Portrait of Carolee Schneemann 1970
Studio Easel / Mirror / Crimson Crushed Velvet Throw / Jar of Honey with Comb
Eleanor Antin

BLOOD DUES

Considering the work of Carolee Schneemann, one begins with the image of her body; this is the center of her work, for few artists have concerned themselves so consistently with the epicurean, the fleshy, the corporeal. Throughout her career, the immediacy of *presence* has concretized her concerns. Through a wide variety of media, the possibilities of presentation have been explored in order to impart the vitality and vigor of experiential explication: Schneemann's inquiry has been to convert the aesthetic arena into a literalized space capable of responding to, and recording, the situation of the body. This phenomenological bias is a current which crossed through the period of Schneemann's artistic maturation; as a painter in the early 1960's, she was witness (in fact: participant) to the shift from the philosophical gesturalism of Abstract Expressionism to the epistemological concreteness of Pop, Minimal and Postminimal Art. By 1962, Schneemann already had moved from the impasted surface of gestural painting to the jagged dimensionalism of expressionist construction: she had included mechanized elements in a number of the assemblages in order to illuminate the correspondence between the place of art and the imperatives of movement, as well as to introduce the dimension of time. By enlarging her assemblages to the conditions of the environment, the logic of extension impelled Schneemann to performance; in 1962, *Glass Environment for Sound & Motion* and *Newspaper Event* were presented.

Since then, the prerogatives of performance have involved Schneemann in dance, theater, film, video, and writing.

The potentials of performance were exploited in that period by the Happenings of Kaprow, Whitman and Oldenberg, the Flux-events of Watts, Maciunas, Brecht, Higgins and Knowles, the music of Young, Corner and Maxfield. Though aligned to Happenings through her visual emphasis, the importance of gesturalism led Schneemann to become involved in the formation of the Judson Dance Theater. In *Meat Joy* there was a moment in which the paint applied to the body of the artist brough associations of menstrual blood; this image is emblematic. With typical irony, Robert Morris would underscore the resplendent physicality in his *Site* (1964); in addition, this physicality was presented in Stan Brakhage's film, *Loving* (1956): the young Schneemann and James Tenney represented Brakhage's mythos of the Romantic ideal. Yet the most uninhibited exploration is in her own erotic film, *Fuses* (1964-67).

In her insistence on the dictates of her body, particularly its sexual identity, Schneemann extolls a personalism evincing her response to the philosophical skepticism of history in this postnietzschean, postduchampian epoch. This physicality, all the more disturbing for its female derivation, has moved her work to the periphery of scandal: if at one extreme she mediates a powerful sense of transgression, Schneemann yet maintains the claim of "naturalism" for her often com-

plex imagery; if rooted in a Romantic apotheosis, her aesthetic yet stipulates an immanent materialism.

Dislocations and discontinuances have caused a *critical* neglect; since returning to New York City in 1973, she has applied her considerable intelligence, energy, and insight to an extensive repetoire, including the book *Cezanne, She Was a Great Painter*, the super-8 film epic *Kitch's Last Meal*, and the multimedia performance installation *Up To And Including Her Limits*. Only recently has revisionist criticism, reacting to formalist rigidity, begun to acknowledge this achievement: her work remains contemporary to the claims of current art practice, and her *oeuvre* deserves distinction in any objective consideration of the art of the past two decades.

Daryl Chin

A DREAM:

CAROLEE SITS FULLY CLOTHED WATCHING CAROLEE DISCLOSED — THE FINAL PANEL IS REMOVED & SHOWS US CAROLEE REVEALED RECLINING NAKEDLY SERENE.
©carl andré

Carolee, ah / yes _____ i remember

she was the first one i'd met who lived in a loft, not that that is should be
so important _____ except to give an idea or some feel of meeting her — then
—on 6th Avenue _____ she was with Jim Tenney at that time _____ and going over to this place in Chelsea _____ i had really just be been
could've known! turned on! to Jim too, by Malcolm (Goldstein) _____ don't think i knew)
precious that to-meet mutual-knowing was to be ' but a feel even then
of it, a hint and suspicion a desire to come _____ we went into this place which already had
this look of what her stage scene(s) were going to look like her style _____ look like /so rich
sensual yes never destroying the austere _____ made- but what to anyone else would'
her style an aristocracy of every day (made out? or shown? This
special revelation _____ midst accumulations flowing materials this traffic light — a real traffic lite — and she
laughing the story of repairmen come in said "so that's where the thing disappeared to!"
There's more sure to keep-us-together-thro-Time than that we've had to come to have to
live in lofts too It was (really; really?) Jim i was sposed to meet — i mean him
being a musician and all, so Carolee was —at that first— a "wife" along and so become
the first one very of those so many women wonderful women now i've met and worked with so as equals
and i've them always accept as equals and — wow she was (is That evening shared at
the Living theatre then the set-of many-to-follow-both-my own-creation'd-and-others'-played-in-
of-mix-means-soundmaking-with-visual-interest-by-musicians-working-sight-movers-
artists-dancer-many now
i have to stop to Pieces which have the full spectrum of so even the "non-musicians"
rethink if how much old play in them, naturally And, by that principle:
my later develop- Pieces which have no more artificial measures freeing the musicians too;
ments stimulated Pieces where the actions count as well for artistry, and
by specific that then HER Pieces where the place-where as an atmosphere at place
in which Yvonne could notice my rhythms stroking glass further in her set place.

Philip Corner

I was in *Meat Joy* and during *Meat Joy* there was a kind of indentification with Carolee which was so strong that even physically we started to look alike... and in the photographs not only of performance but also of the vacation of that summer which followed our images look alike (Carolee actually helped me apply for the grant by which I came to the States)...she offered even from then personal data as medium for her work so that her work rather than appearing as a collage of the expressions of the time, mostly was from her personal experience...personal experiences are collages but these called for identification and that identification provoked interest for me...there was less need of judging this work from a qualifying point of view, it was very much her own so that it possessed a special interest that did not have to fit with the various movements of the time...it had a quality of escaping the various movements of the time...they weren't really in the form of Happenings but her own forms, since each of the works, not only *Meat Joy* (*Water Light/Water Needle* for instance) and all the others were really marking paths of her life which in a way she shared. During the late '60's, despite the moralistic attitude of the artists who were mostly famous during those times (who were against an aesthetic, which was not an aesthetic but was a continous affirmation of the self and its sensibilities), despite that, Carolee continued working with groups and in a very sincere way for the time, so that even when she was in England I had news of her and the news was connected to her work—which was at some point always connected to the life. Somehow everyone was in contact with her and so she was really a part of their autobiography, and her influence and the infusion of her ideas was done first hand most of the time—it did not pass through publicity, or the media, or by the diffusion of ideas of our times which are done through movements, readings, writing articles about minimal art or sexual art or performance art...I didn't see any articles about Carolee Schneemann particularly except on her films, because they, whoever wrote on the films, considered the qualities of the movies but the films were just one of the parts of the continuous work (which was not being reviewed because it escaped the various movements) which was what was interesting for me...

The first day I arrived in New York she picked me up at the pier 42...I was very excited (I arrived by American export line Independence) although I'd been woken up at six by my cabin mates, they wanted to show me the Statue of Liberty... finally I got to New York and I saw on the deck Carolee and James Tenney, who was her husband at the time, the composer, student of Varèse, and I was so excited to be in New York which in fact made me slip on the pasarella (deck) and I landed in New York on my ass and I was picked up by two porters who stuck on my behind a tag of NY...but besides that, Carolee made me live in her loft, which was in the fur district, which was completely covered with the residual of furs which had been once trimmed there, which she used in her collage, which she used in her clothes, which she used as blankets...Then she and Jim had rented an old school house in Connecticut where I vacationed, and I learned for the first time about poison ivy...In London the theater got closed... Carolee remembers but I don't that at this time I told her that thinking of being over thirty I would not be able to exist...so I've been wrong now for nine years and I hope to be wrong for a few more...

When Carolee and I talked about clothes for instance I always thought she was totally out of fashion in that she would get dressed up or like something which was completely valuable for itself or for the way it looked on her but it certainly didn't have anything to do with a commercial idea or even a non-commerical idea of appearance, and I thought that this play of what one finds and what one uses and what one likes reflected also in her work. She selected things and subject matters out of a kind of naturalness for itself, but always by connection with herself rather than by connection to a special message that she wanted to have...it was always a personal connection of trying to explain the real and personal meaning of things. For instance her love for animals was not love for all animals but was love for her own pets, and in that way all the ideas of richness of affection or caring values did not matter very much, what mattered was the reality of her life and experience... and that seemed to me very interesting because it corresponded to a truth which was more real to me than cultural set-ups and seemed to be totally reasonable...in fact it seemed more reasonable and not "rational" in comparison with our friends—artists, writers, filmmakers— the openness and the personal feeling of Carolee's understanding had to do with the fact she did not make an appeal to rationality or to mind or to logic but to a deep common sense which belonged to life and that seemed to me very close to the idea of motherhood...which was also sisterhood, which was also a human unity which was particularly important because I'd never seen anyone else being a protagonist of that movement, of freedom, as she has been...because I've seen a lot of women artists concerned with feminist issues, but not so many artists concerned with the necessities of life...

People are very systematic and during the last ten years the repertories of people renew themselves according to trends, so while the repertories were renewing the trends, the trends were renewing the forms...some of the repertories and some of the trends are particularly meaningful but what's mostly meaningful is not something part of a repertory or part of a trend but something that is totally common sense with a common denominator...Another thing which always particularly inspired me about Carolee's quality was her type of energy, which was again a personal quality, a continuous energy which did not find sources from outside, constantly an inside energy... and talking about energy what I mean is

the possibility of coping with outside and inside situations in a meaningful way for her, so that things would enlarge experience...which is even more than dignity, which meant to really get to the meaning of the situation, a sense of humor too... And another thing is all through her life she's needed money and all around us our male friends, the artists, had lots of money...and I always thought between the figures of the artists of the American culture she definitely occupied a primary position, at least for me. She certainly didn't get the recognition she should have gotten, maybe because her work was specifically anti-movement or anti-male-movements...not because she intentionally did that: she did everything for the necessity of what she saw to do...Of course there are other female artists that have done the same and I always wonder how come they got the money...But she is of the caliber of somebody like Rauschenberg or Oldenburg for what she did for American culture, and that is not recognized. In my experience I have a very clear position for her work, it is a major position...and also she's not accompanied by anyone. Also she is a painter, not just a creator of performances. They have been a part of a whole series of conceptual works...of a collage aesthetic... and also her personal connection with the writers, with the filmmakers, with Jonas Mekas, Stan Brakhage, even Joseph Cornell...and her influence on Oldenburg, on Rauschenberg, on Whitman, on Brakhage, has been major...she has not

been recognized for that; it's not that she has a volume production compared to those people, but she has an energy and a meaning in her work...Carolee has formed discussion, objects, performance, film, but she has not made one specific form of art, she did not specialize...she does not identify or put her subjectivity as secondary to a problem...culture and the whole scene...

Annina Nosei Weber
(excerpted from a taped conversation)

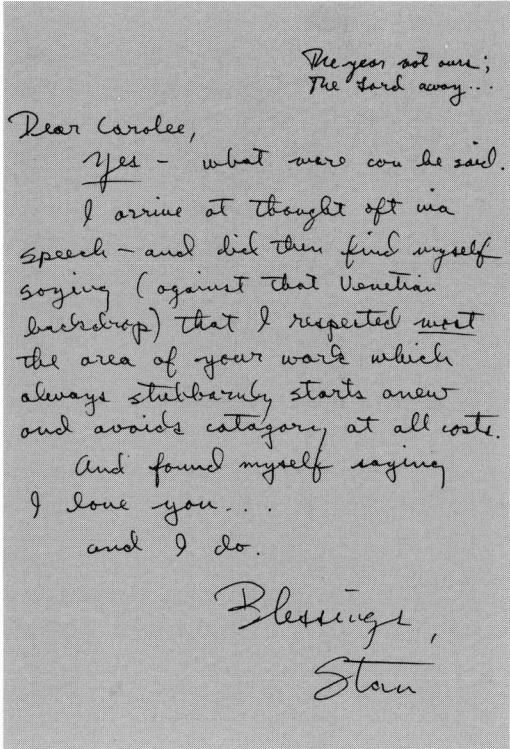

269

Dear Carolee,

I have been told that our word *theater* (or *theatre*) comes from the Greek word *theatron*, first used in the sixth century with the beginning of the theater to mean "a place for seeing." This, in turn, is derived from the verb *theasmai*, which, in the work of Isocrates (the pre-Socratic philosopher) is used to mean "viewing, as spectators." In Plato, the word has the slightly different connotation, "to contemplate."

Also derived from *theasmai* is our word *theory*, via *theoria*, which—at earliest—meant "a place for seeing." In the sixth century Diogenes Laertius, in his life of Pythagoras, categorizes three types of participants at the Olympic Games: those who go to sell peanuts, those who compete, and those who go to contemplate the spectacle—the *theoroi*. In Plato the word means "contemplation or consideration," and Aristotle uses it in the *De Memoria* to mean "an object of contemplation," and in the *Metaphysics* as "speculation."

I can think of no better way to describe the apparent *polarity* but fundamental *unity* (through complementarity) of our processes (yours and mine, during the dozen-or-so years of our "collaborations") than is suggested by the evolution of these words. That is, both *theater* and *theory* are derived from the same root verb, *theasmai* which, in Herodotus, the *Illad* and the *Odyssey* is used to mean "to gaze at or behold with wonder."

With love,
Jim

WATER LIGHT/WATER NEEDLE

"...we are stretched horizontally on a shifting gravity. Our attention is always on the ropes—as an extension of our bodies and our physical intentions—and on one another. Each meeting is a unique encounter by which our journey is shaped. Each body is a confirmation of our situation in space...."

—Schneemann

I have seen the realm of the human backbone; how rich and soft the whole body is when it perceives its nature as it was first made. Water Light/Water Needle *moves out of a source of energy to the place which existed before, before the separation of the divine consciousness of human experience; the place where in his animal soul man wonders and exults, has no straining intentions, and no lordship over nature.*

The audience was led in by guides; we sat on crumpled newspapers in a semicircle around ropes which were suspended from the walls in a four-sided figure on three horizontal, not quite parallel, levels. One segment, directly before the audience, was attached to pulleys; there was soft murky green and blue lighting. The ten performers were hidden in cupboards; a curtain hung over the top rope hiding the cupboards. Carolee and a young man entered carrying trays of crumpled paper. They went to the fans, knelt down, turned them on, and listened to them ... began blowing papers, filling the center aisle with heaps of paper. They turned the fans off and pushed them to the side. The performers began to come out of the cupboards, fell out in architectural patterns of body; they climbed the ropes, walked and swung on the ropes functionally. The character of movement was not acrobatic or balletic but as natural as that of monkeys. I was fascinated by lovely human bodies moving with the skill and innocence of monkeys, making natural faces and sounds while doing physical actions; their spontaneity was delightful! Various sounds happened: hammering on wood and metal, glass breaking, Bach and Vivaldi, scratching of fingernails on windows. The apparent disorder of various seemingly alien noises was revealed in order. And while the people walked and hung they showed the hidden, the magical, joining of spirit and body. As I watched I was happily pulled away from earth-bound realism and made to be more aware of the earth. What is above and what is below? seemed to be the question which was sung out from the males and females as they moved and embraced each other. They were cosmic beings moving through the outermost to the innermost, restoring things and saving themselves from artificial actions, telling the story of the birth of the soul and linking together the forces of life, drifting us along with them to show us passion and the essence of our being.

Rochelle Owens
March 1966

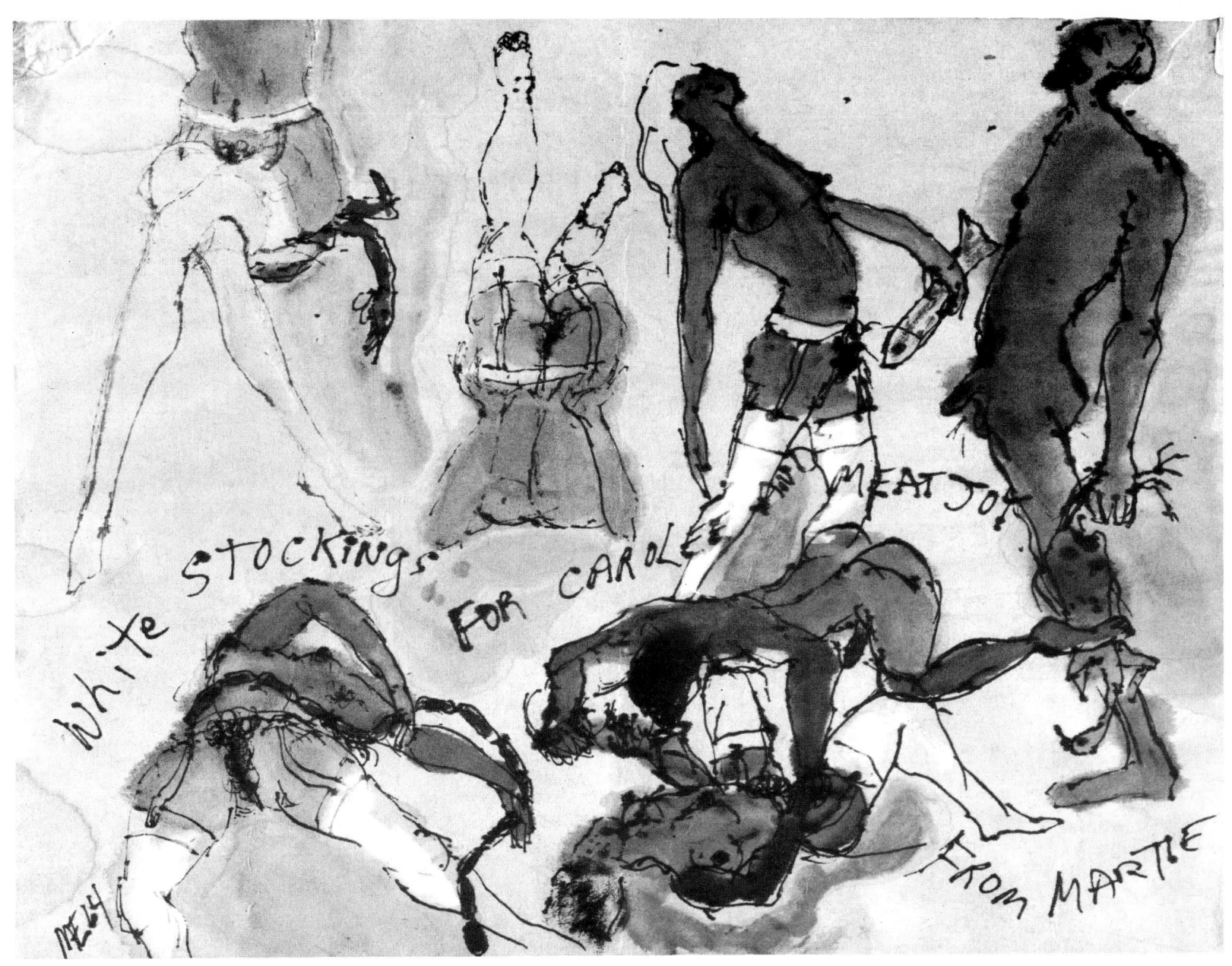

White Stockings for Carolee

Meat Joy

From Martie

Martie Edelheit

271

ENERGY VISIONS

Carolee Schneemann's kinetic performance pieces use blood-into-paint, bodies as sculptural media, war-sounds and news-reports as music; she is visio-painterly without the confinement of canvas, substantively sculptural without needing earthy staticity (well before earthworks or conceptual art). She was one of the first artists to move from traditional specificity in aesthetics. She gives the next leap beyond Oskar Schlemmer: "incorporation," including the *body*—evocative, provocative, sensual and sexual, outspoken, insisting on moving people from one emotional space to another—the need to cause this transmutation: her commitment, an excitement with using all available materials.

In denial of the traditional passivity of art, she has fought the insulation/isolation of body/sense, as DH Lawrence did by discussing the dark of the blood as that area between men and women (after Victorian tension). Her work is perceived in time & space (viz. Hundertwasser's students drawing a line to cover the interior of a classroom, extend into hallway and cover it, whereupon he is fired—or Charles Olson, Vancouver 1963, scowling & gleaming "spin me" about Hittites & Summerians, Langue d'oc or d'or &c. in wildness across blackboard till enthu-

siasm moves him off & onto the wall, stopped only by the barrier of post-&-lintel doorway)—she moves over an edge & out, keeping it in motion, shining. An eloquence expressing what many people felt about being alive in the 60's, products of several wars, pull-&-tug of nations which ignored &/or mutilated art—bombing of Dresden, Cologne, Paris, desecration of history's values, deaths of faces well-loved, until the artists wept & cringed.

She came through dance & paint in the Sixties, part of the enthusiasts insisting art would be all previous expressions melded: bodies, materials, spaces, emotion—her work shone as startlingly original, among her confreres: Kaprow, Dick Higgins, Rauschenberg, Oldenburg, Johns, Malina & Beck, Cage, George Segal, Feldman, Mac Low, Vanderbeek, Knowles, Hansen—all innovators. Schneemann, blending sculpture, painting, sound, light, painted flesh and politics, adding one new vital element: sensuality. MEAT JOY, at Judson Church, began the exploration into statements by art about joy, sex, violence & horror; it was an expression of De-Kooning's screaming women, precursor to flat Bacon distortions made three-dimensional and to Warhol's BAD. It fit near Living Theater's FRANKENSTEIN in involving audiences, who reacted to her use of live bodies writhing in juxtaposition to bloody dead animals. Bob Brown's chicken-killing and Ralph Ortiz'

scenarios developed near & after MEAT JOY. Non-artists were shocked; *we* were excited, impressed, and jolted into new modes. My "Watch Out For Children," collage writing dealing with violence and love, happened after and because of MEAT JOY.

Lebel said, "We don't have to paint with paintbrushes...paint with people, with visions, with movies, with objects, with anything." Schneemann's powerful capacity added a delicate, sensual horror: rooms grew thick with activity/reaction, the proscenium arch vanished, no way to escape from the art being presented. Anyone viewing or participating in works by Schneemann, Mac Low, Higgins, Beck & Malina emerged changed, an extension of the excitement at seeing and becoming part of a Pollock painting. Her work moved between delicacy/aestheticism (fine rhythmic lines & purity of WATER LIGHT/WATER NEEDLE) and deep bloody horror (SNOWS). WATER LIGHT/WATER NEEDLE's "dancers" moved on heavy rope through air like romantic animals, making a musical score without sounds. A glamorous piece surprisingly unlike MEAT JOY or SNOWS but more like THE QUEEN'S DOG. King, Neville, Rainer and Meredith Monk were also making pieces nearby which showed new motions of body-in-space. SNOWS is in context with her "box art" first seen when Carolee, Jim Tenney, I and others shared a house in New Paltz. Quite her own, the boxes, related to

Cornell's, jumped tougher: made with torn metal & broken glass, ragged wood and smeared paint, they spoke harshly. SNOWS, war-scenes, ice, odd voice-overs, anger, war, was also like Paik's destruction of a piano onstage at Town Hall: importance of not taking for granted. We all worked with *I Ching*, seeking to speak about the unclear: struggle, wars, loss, the attempts to be loved and admired.

The years 1962-1969: excitement, energy, motion, reaction, response, growth: rich intensity of those involved in changing art. Amalgam: blood, spit, come, wood, linen, glass, film-celluloid, bones—designs shattering like splatter of war across a culture. Higgins' filmloop: peaceful lakes/hills, sunset, exquisite and hypnotic: called FOR THE DEAD. Ray Johnson, dinner at Cavanagh's for an Art Auction, seeing me preen next to my date Diter Rot, sings out "Carole Bergé will die some day" and thus enlightening. Charlotte Moorman playing the cello underwater in the Avant Garde Festival she organized and keeps alive. I stayed largely linear, alongside being in works by Paik, Mac Low, Higgins: writing pieces about film, sculpture, painting. Schneemann's work moved me to poetry, writ by one Libran woman artist for, about & during performances: exchange of affection, excitement, delight in her sinister, sinuous qualities—my piece NIGHTSCENE conveys her Mystery into another ɔrm. Libra the Catalyst, through whom people pass to change and become.

NIGHTSCENE #3

for Carolee Schneemann

Possibly having arrived from Italy. Having perhaps arrived from Italia, crated, more or less jam-packed and now free: the huge dog. walking slowly

through jelly air, the dog sniffs a live body, or live bodies.
No. Walking the jelly night lawn, the huge dog sniffs: bodies on the thick air.
No. Walking slowly through jelly air, the huge dog sniffs rigid live bodies. Yes.
Which writhe. Yes.
Okay. The quick brown dog jumps over the
NO.
The big heavy white dog sniffles the live rigid small bodies of females. Yes?
The air is night, in perhaps the Villa Borghese. No. Buckingham. No. Maybe. Midnight in the gardens of Boboli, there is suddenly slowly a huge dog, he is not loose, or rather he is loosely connected to his magician, he is attended by his own magician. And he is sniffing the statues as they are set in formal pedestal columns alongside the steps down the dark hillside with dark pines nearby. No.
The muffled dark alive bodies stacked idly like kindling
the dog sniffing the statue bodies as the guard or magician moves them to his taste. No. The man is his keeper
he shall not want.
Tithes and taxes the shape of flesh. His keeper places the somnolent statues for him to
for him to

to snuffle . . . to
All right. Night. Clearly a dark night and probably an Italianate night, Anglicized, with the texture of jelly. Or as the blood congeals, hackles rise. So then the quick brown fox
NO. The big dog, male, moves lazily around the writhing females. His keeper a man like any other and he himself is merely an ordinary unroyal dog. But so much larger. Yes. Larger. Yes.

1965

Carolee: reviews, crowds, hysteria, cops, applause, shock, imitators, poems, changes—no one unmoved—Germany, England, Canada, Sweden—concepts of fluids, time, magical theories as explanations of what ought to work and doesn't in the life—when a Girl-Child becomes Woman nowadays, what are the inculcated values? What is permissible-correct-proper? Her book, CEZANNE, SHE WAS A GREAT PAINTER, concerns the experience of being a *woman* artist. We didn't *know* for sure we were being victims till Women's Liberation sharpened our perceptions; Schneemann is "angry," resentful, outraged and outrageous, and *completely correct*: NO SUCH THING AS BEING TOO INTENSE, YOU'RE EITHER INTENSE OR YOU'RE TAKING THINGS FOR GRANTED. In her book is a beautiful, wistful, funny piece, "Americana I Ching Apple Pie," instructions/recipe a la Schneemann, commentary on a classic item in our culture, a mockery of cookbooks, perfect satire, casual and sensual rather than precise and mechanical; I published it in my magazine CENTER, where it drew comment and smirks. One could "bake" as one created art, using her guide: a pie would be one's own, as in artistry. Last year I saw her *perform* "Americana I Ching Apple Pie" at a benefit for EAR Magazine: enormously funny, she clattered, using rocks & pebbles to symbolize flour & crust & apples; old broken bottles were utensils, boxes were pans—her hair bound back with an evil old rag; the whole scene anything but the sanitary, cold, bloodless, calculated Germanic tidiness we knew as kitchen ambience in girlhood—she had to bring back some Gemutlichkeit, restore the beloved chaos established in any creative act—ceremonial for the body—if good food is to transmute into body, let it be done with joy—meat joy—.

We are who our good friends are, and what we become intertwines with them;

Carolee has been a constant in my life's learning; it would be impossible to consider Nauman's or Hesse's or Hoffman's work sentiently without knowing Schneemann's or to consider that Acconci or Oppenheim made art without her groundwork. In *communitas* we all exchange energy visions till the individual art emerges from each, strong and power-loaded, crowded with verve, outrageously ahead of the day it appears, in synch with our pasts, demanding response and involvement. The artist who moves me out is a genius-at-large, heavier than those who merely mirror the society, shunting it forward where elements are almost too thin to support body-weight, moving into the unexpected. I need no notes to talk about Schneemann's work: it's *memorable,* vivid in the space of the mind. It has weight in history.

Carol Bergé

CAROLEE • I NEVER HAD A SISTER • WOULD YOU MIND • I HOPE NOT • BECAUSE THATS HOW I FEEL YOUR IMAGINATION GREW UP WITH MINE • I THINK MAYBE YOU REALLY KNOW SOMETHING ABOUT LIVING-WORKING—THAT CHICKEN & EGG THING • ALONG WITH LOVE I RESPECT YOU •
Lee Breuer

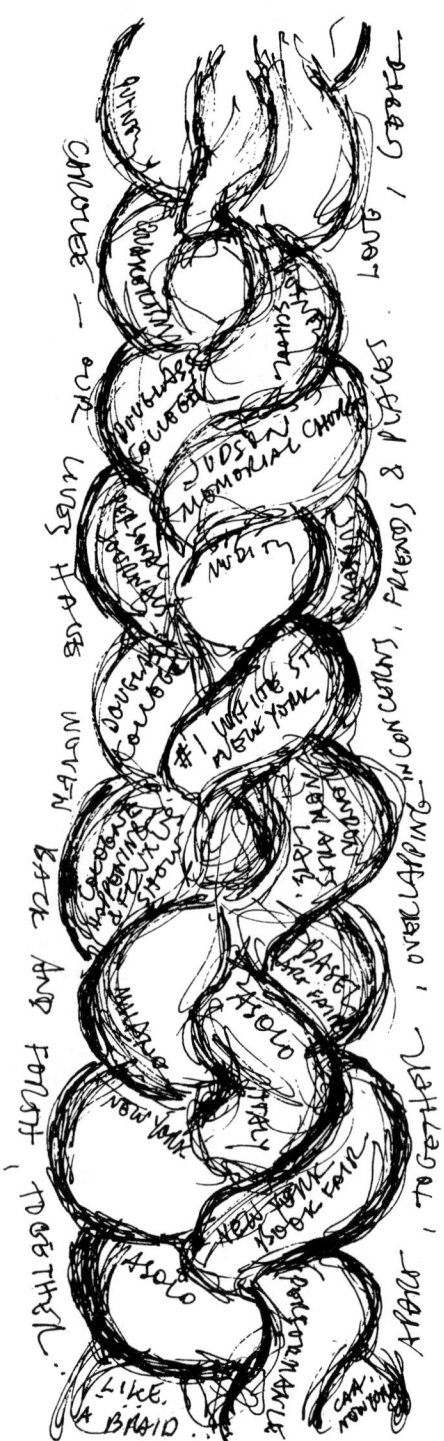

Geoff Hendricks

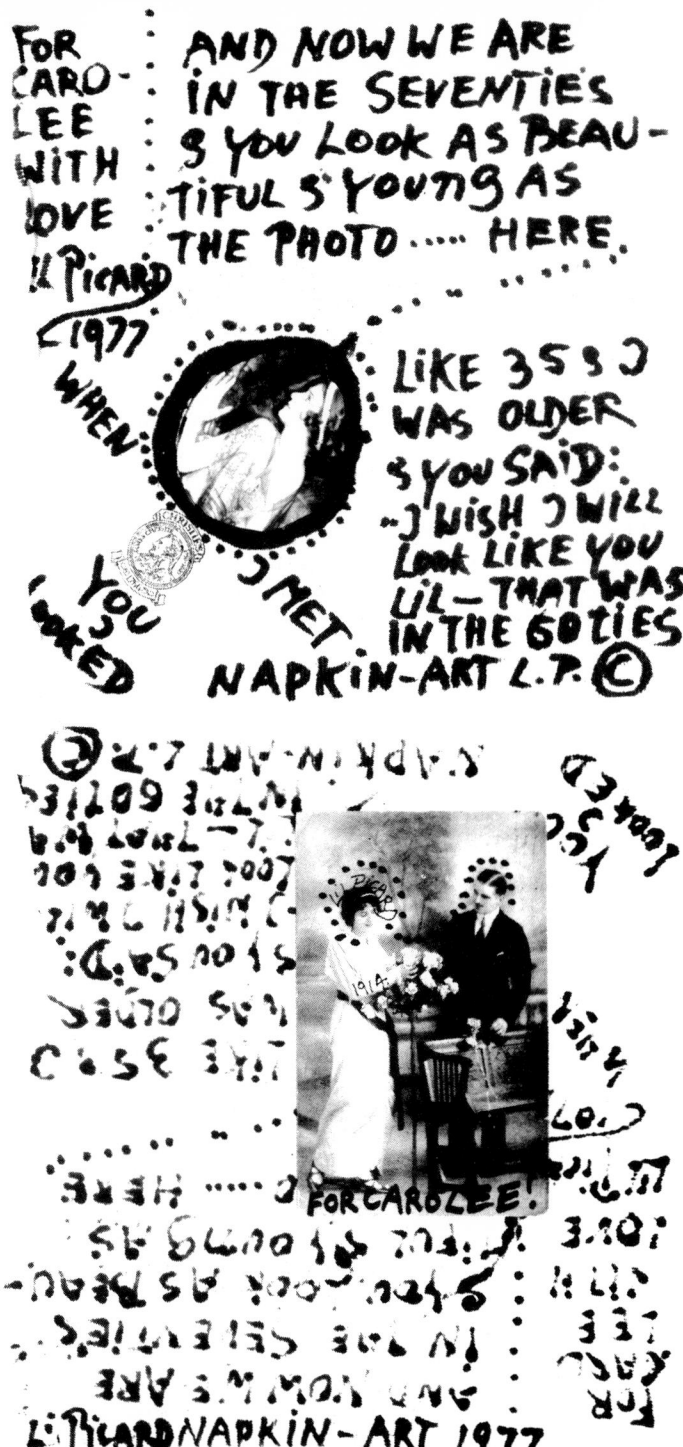

FOR CARO-
LEE WITH
LOVE
l. Picard
1977

WHEN
YOU
I MET
looked

AND NOW WE ARE
IN THE SEVENTIES
& YOU LOOK AS BEAU-
TIFUL & YOUNG AS
THE PHOTO ..... HERE.

· LIKE 35 &
WAS OLDER
& YOU SAID:
—I WISH I WILL
LOOK LIKE YOU
LIL — THAT WAS
IN THE 60TIES
NAPKIN-ART L.P. ©

FOR CAROLEE.

L. PICARD NAPKIN-ART 1977

Carolee Kinetic

Carolee bending light sensual
under the rainbow in the sky
taken from her mother's purse
her long white arm caresses the
umbilical cord twisting in the
night air dances the first joy
black hair flowing along the
wooden floor the light breaks
on the quartz stones opening her
eyes to the legs torso the child
alone in the daughter's bed
breathes dreams softly to her
drifting down opens the snow flakes
gliding along the silver stage
behind the womb of her theater
electrical breakers in the sea
locks the light bringing in the
audience's birth

Carolee bending light sensual
from her body each dance notes
a muses measure —
the day was red covered Vietnam
flower beds grew under her eye
staring while each murdered face
smiled under them a face mask
silver foiled mirrored her dreams back
against the fool the soldier stood up with
the knife in his back the movies flickered in
the naval ships "Schlissen ihm, Hans, Schlissen ihm"
caught in his throat his stomach retrieved the food from
the night each body dropping down passing through Carolee's
face a virgin mary's orifice mouth opening up between her hands
he kisses her body and her wetness dries the droplets of water
from the frozen ice covering their bodies rolling under the earth

Carolee bending light sensual
in water light ropes against the sky in her eyes
seeing for the first time each crevice of his form the
shadows under his beard the tongue under the cheek the breast
under the neck the necklace of his love in her hand wetting each
eyelash on her face
she waited to climb the snow mountain
before the daylight refracted in her eyes
the manship womanplane cutting her garments
open to the air pairing red hearts her hand
mirror reflected her face revolving trees in
moving windows

Locomotion illinois lilting
arteries outside the skin
karma sutra sutures Carolee's tales

Carolee bending light sensual
eyes pass through the spectrum of her
rainbow light her voice pulsing quasars
in time continuing in space
Carolee living in the Ice Palace
burning night tracks
her kinship with her brother
her one person bending shadows
over the rainbow's halo
the child's crescent
the gift left at the open
door

Larry Warshaw   May 1977

275

IN PRAISE OF THE SURFACE

So much has been said about the "essence" of things and men that you'll forgive me if I'll say a few words in praise of the surface.

I was provoked by this sentence: "Schneemann abstracts, removes all social context, alters and distorts reality instead of moving toward its essence." (Michael Smith, V. Voice, Nov. 26, 1964 in his review of *Meat Joy*.)

Arts have been always rebelling against prescribed "essences," against "social significances"—for those terms mean and imply either the Old (comfortable) essence & significance (a trick to protect oneself from anything that may upset the status quo) or simply it means nothing (or nobody knows what it means). So the artists junked everything that had been known as essence & significance and began searching for it, from scratch.

In painting, in sculpture, for a decade now the artist has been exploring new textures, materials, surfaces, junk, garbage, things around us, putting them in/on canvasses until they swell (& smell), until they are no longer paintings but things—striving, hoping this way to escape the prescribed meanings, forms, perspectives, contexts.

In Cinema: Smith, Warhol, Brakhage, Markopoulos, Rubin, Jacobs are going directly to the surface (impactness) of things, of person, textures, faces & bodies, and exploring the eye that sees it and the means and ways by which it sees. Things that surround us, the human body itself has become invisible during last two centuries. Two centuries of industry, rationalism and materialism succeeded in making the material world invisible to our eyes. It was Warhol who demonstrated to us that a Campbell Soup Can can be visible. That the Empire State Building can be seen. Smith, like a magician, opens to us the world of color and texture in simplest materials around us, colors we keep looking at every day without seeing, without perceiving them. Brakhage and Markopoulos are demonstrating to us that there is LIGHT, and that we have EYES, and that there is human body. Ken Jacobs shows us that shadows exist. Nam June Paik even shows that DUST exists and falls on everything, including film. Nothing can be taken for granted: we are basically blind. We see nothing unless

Music: La Monte Young goes beyond all melody, his music becomes one uninterrupted sound, all sounds fade into one, and then you listen to the very surface of sound and you discover most fantastic harmonies, you hear the sound for the first time, you hear the music of the spheres.

The Kinetic Theater, Carolee Schneemann's *Meat Joy* brings us back to the touch, smell, to the surfaces of things and bodies; it accepts, with love, everything that our insistence on ideas (certain ideas) kept us away from; even what was "repellent," like "raw" meat, or chicken **guts, what we usually dread & fear to touch**—glittery, vomity substances (under the excuse of our own "delicateness," the delicateness of our natures...).

Eh, the walls of puritanism and rationalism and false idealism are shaking, we are beginning to feel the surface again, although our touch, our senses are still numb.

What an irony, we must admit, that we have to find our depths *via* the object, *via* the surface world, through the phenomenal world. Our pomposity in us still denies this, we still insist on "importance," on "essence" the way we know and understand it; we reject the sensuous world of *Meat Joy* as lacking social "essence." We'd like to go directly to heaven without going through earth—we'd like to be saintlier than God Jesus Christ Himself. What pompous asses we are.

Yes, Schneemann removes the social context or, rather, the familiar social contexts, to break us open, to expose our senses, to bring us back to our senses—and to get rid of prescribed meanings.

I remember my father, taking & mixing cow's dung in a pail, and, with his bare hands applying the mixture to the roots of young seedling trees. I watched him with a sort of disgust, I remember, and although, like all other boys that I grew up with, I used to step into the hot cow dung in cold autumn days, to warm up my feet—I felt simultaneously a disgust and a wonderment seeing my father working with it so casually as if it were no different from touching the corn, or tending the horses, or stroking the wheat stems, or looking at an approaching rain cloud.

But now some of my childhood riddles begin to unravel themselves under different circumstances, and so when I watch *Meat Joy* and I see the performers throw themselves into the immediate experience of meat and chicken gut and paint and sweat and touch of bodies and grease—I know that this is not an empty gesture devoid of essence but, just the opposite: it's touching the very essence; the long held-back need to be one with all things, to return down to earth, down to the surface of matter; we realize that we can't look disdainfully at the meat world without somehow somewhere deeper in ourselves condemning our own meat, our own body, our own soul. So that *Meat Joy* becomes an act of liberation and an act of contact with the essence; a philosophical (or religious?) essay on Essence, Matter & Being.

Therefore, dear reader, don't blame Andy Warhol for showing you eight hours of Empire State Building or Schneemann for "exposing" you to the feeling and touch of meat . . . Blame the Western Civilization for making the reality invisible to you, numbing your senses. Thank the Artist for bringing the surface reality of things, and all kinds of phenomena that surround us and make us what we are, to our senses and to our consciousness. Praise the artist for enabling us to see again, to feel, to hear again: for giving us EYES, EARS, TOUCH. We are waking up and the world around us is waking up with us.

Or is this only my Spring Dream? Tell me, dear Carolee.

Jonas Mekas
(from the Diaries, March 1965)

Schneemann   Duchamp

off with our Clothes!
so thAt
we may be, as you are, undRessed
Of
aLl
idEas
(marcEl).

John Cage

---

richness of exquisite excess:
loft filled with textures, wood boxes
images (pictures, objects, the   shattered glass/echoes
        paint dripping   reflected
        her life together   in a concert of music boxes
                                singing and dancing in a sky
        Tone Roads (her collages/Geo. Washington   of mirrors.
                        Kitch painting) concerts
                of a NEW [American] music; Ives, Cage, Varése
                and the wonderful rock n' roll dancing parties after.
                        blue fish and bodies
                        flailing upon the Judson Church floor,
        her nude whiteness/Manet reclining
                        . . . and, in Viet Flakes, crying
                out for all that lives.

Malcolm Goldstein

film

Fuses, a film of cats and couples clowning in the hormone circus, was
the first erotic/I ever saw. Behind a large curtain in one of the ~~a stream of~~
cloisters of the Roundhouse ~~during the xxxx~~ I felt/beckoning pheromones
~~and xx~~ heard a whirring projector and stole into a private viewing.

Is this Blitz Heaven or another skit from the mango factory? how strange
it compared with the black and white aquarian stalinists ranting and
raving from the platform at the Dialectics of Liberation 1968. That was
the soundtrack in the background. The images ~~with~~ Reichian Sex-Pol. We *were*
must fuck one another or die! We are all one flesh!! the sexual
revolution is the third world war!! No one speaking in the background *of the building*
had caught up with it. No one was naked. It was a strong ingredient
in my body-brain for Suck a paper of passion started by Germaine, Bill
Levy & Jim Haynes, ~~xxxx~~ and fused its manifesto: "Suck ~~x~~ gives the
shadows genitals, Suck is a reactor for a cum atom, Suck is a ~~xx~~
synergetic brothel instead of a pub at every street corner, Suck is
toilet paper for an orgone chamber, Suck is all sex is good sex, Suck
is crucial shit, Suck is a filthy tabloid because art has tried to
steal your erections, Suck is an orgasm in every pore, on the hour,
every hour and lasting an hour. Suck is free to all groups low on
sexual resonance. Suck is group sex, police sex, animal sex, one-armed
bandit sex, geriatric sex and cosmic sex. Suck builds a rubber bridge
from England to Atlantis. Suck is a cover story for the Armed Love
Conspiracy. Suck is ~~xx~~ galvanising pussy power into bombing the playboy
club & seizing the ~~xxxxx~~ site for Suck City. Suck is sex all over
the body; genital sex is bombs and car accidents. Suck is schoolchildren
rising up and demanding a sexual relationship with their teachers to
get information, sparking the gap purely. Suck is a hairy, sperm laden
beaver for Fleet Street's ~~xxxx~~ ingrowing pubis. Suck sucks up
all your bodily fluids and mingles them with 20,000 others and returns
them to you at interest (20,000 being the hoped for readership). Suck is Stalin's
flying wang being stroked by Nijinsky. Suck destroys jealousy with group
sex, Suck smashes sexual elitism with photoes of old people making it
beautifully. Suck wipes out the energy fetishism of romance and privacy
and virility. Suck saws up the crutches of a biological cripple: The Family.
Suck covers your whole ~~xxxxx~~ body with a layer of brain cells.. ~~xxxxxx~~ \\
~~xxxxxxxxxxxxxxxxxxxxxxxxxxxxxxxxxxxxxxxxxx~~ (sometimes there was much more
~~xxxxx~~ Suck lived up and down to the manifesto and in and out of it. / meat than joy)
Five years later after its demise, and after everyone had grown a little
older and realized perhaps that it was impossible to fuck everyone in
the world, and that nature had ~~xxxxxx~~ sold us a little short on orofices,
I saw Fuses again. In a little village in Norfolk the local garage owner
had a cinema club where he showed mainly his own films of railway engines.
The cinema club was in the vicarage. Someone had heard that Carolee was
staying in the village and invited her to show any films she had. She
brazenly projected Fuses to the vicar, his wife, and the local Derby &
Joan club ~~and women xxxxxxxxx~~ offering during the ~~xx~~ stunned ~~xxxx~~
silence that followed, to explain it. None of them were shocked, just
dazed, but maybe one was amazed and wobbled off down a country lane
his head reeling with slogans determined to see that Love was
re-interpreted in the parish magazine. "I would adorn and be adorned.
I would be born and I would bear. I would be washed and I would wash.
Whose danceth not knoweth not what cometh to pass. Thou ~~xxx~~ hast me
as a bed, rest on me." J.C. in the Acts of John.

If not now, when?

Heathcote Williams.

As founder and Director of Cinema 16 (America's largest film society, 1947-1963) and as founder-Director of the New York Film Festival at Lincoln Center (1963-68), I have, over a 30-year period, seen more than 30,000 films, American and foreign. Amidst this welter of material, Carolee Schneemann's work stands out, both in terms of films and live performances. I consider her, unquestionably, one of the great and seminal creators of our day. Her originality, depth of perception and her humanity have touched me on the deepest levels, as she has been able to tap our collective unconscious. Into an unfortunate world and decaying civilization, founded on consumerism, profiteering, cut-throat competition, death-dealing ugliness and rampant technology, she has re-introduced that most marvelous of all gifts: the gift of magic, the gift of the inexplicable.

Amos Vogel

Annenberg School of Communications,
 University of Pennsylvania

Carolee Schneemann landed on our Rive Gauche horizon in 1964, at the peak hour of the Nouveaux Réalistes (New Realists) wave. Yves Klein had died two years ago and he was becoming the God of his own "Monochrome" and "living brushes" legend. Christo had just decided to leave Paris for New York. Tinguely and Arman were spending all their time along the Atlantic, commuting between the Chelsea Hotel and Jean Larcade's Gallery. César was the european king of junk sculpture.

The N.R. actions and public projects had already opened the way to the Vostell-Ben Fluxus confusing campaign. For a whole week in May 1964 J.J. Lebel, the european introducer of happenings as an artform of protest, had organized a "Festival/Workshop of Free Expression" to be held at the American Students Center (Boulevard Raspail) — one year after the Bon Marché Happening, first event of Kaprow to have taken place in Paris.

Carolee Schneemann's Meat Joy was programmed among other performance pieces. Her Kinetic Theater demonstration was a tremendous success, at the edge of the scandal, on the fringe of "moral" reprobation! She was beautiful, sensual, energetic, quoting Wilhelm Reich every second sentence she would pronounce in front of an audience: "the human mind is only an executive organ of investigating, living plasma feeling out its environment..."

Schneemann performed the role of the Central Woman in Meat Joy, the Independent Woman being played by Rita Renoir, former superstar of Alain Bernardin's world famous Crazy Horse (Striptease) Saloon.

Bernardin was curious to see Rita acting in the (semi)nude in a totally different kind of environment. We went together to the Students Center: human flesh all around, inundated with fish and chickens, in a musical cocktail of rock songs and Parisian street noises.

I remember two highly emotional moments very close to each other: Carolee sucking fish — and a man handling a fish and following with it the contours of Rita's body, undulating first tenderly and then wildly.

At the end of the performance I told Bernardin that I had been sexually aroused by Meat Joy in a real orgiastic way, sex stimulation acting as a synthesis of all active senses. He admitted he had been too, adding that an orgy of perceptions should always be the natural reward for using human body as raw material on stage.

Schneemann has written in some Notes of 1962 "The body is in the eye: sensations received visually take hold in the total organism. Perception moves the total personality to excitation." Meat Joy made me realize what she meant by "moving the total personality to excitation": if the body is in the eye, sex is the body's eye. Carolee's statement was not new, but it proved to be quite efficient when applied to her Kinetic Theater. No wonder she calls it kinetic, since she deals with sex as a basic catalyzer of sensorial response: which other organ could be more sensitive to functional kinetism?

Since that day of May 1964 I am tempted to consider Schneemann as a guru of non-verbal communication. From time to time I hear from her and her career. We meet also, rarely, in different places throughout the world. I feel always then this solemn and pantheistic joy — which is supposed to invade the soul of the primitive, when he suspects in his neighbour the talents and the powers of a shaman.

Pierre Restany
Paris, Sept. 24, 1977

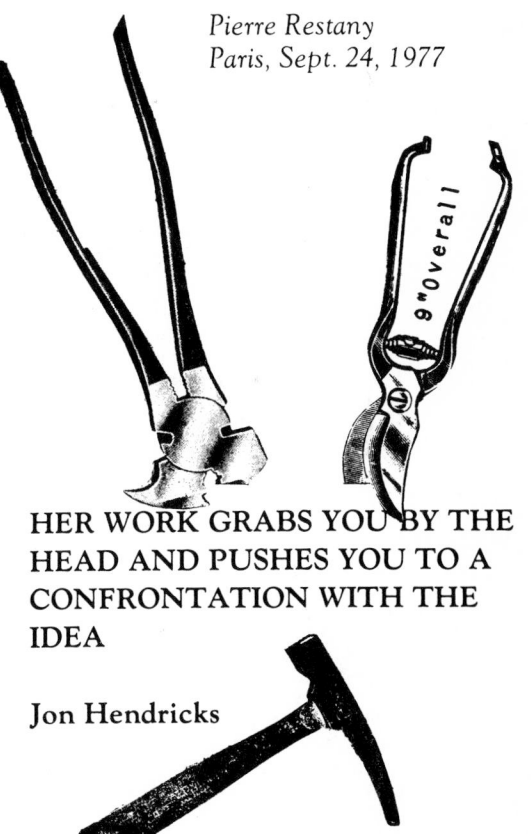

9"overall

HER WORK GRABS YOU BY THE HEAD AND PUSHES YOU TO A CONFRONTATION WITH THE IDEA

Jon Hendricks

When Carolee and I meet we talk about women, men, animals, beans, occasionally art or politics. The following Carolee bean sprouting recipe she gave me in 1963 in the Myersville, N.J. country house. There was laughter and vigor and sunshine there as one sees in the art — in the slides. There is much to sprout as revolutionary and american and woman. So let us get on to our beans and apple pie . . . fresh iron every day and thanks to Carolee.

Alison Knowles

1. Quality beans (or seeds) is most important; many commercial beans are treated in some way so that the "life element" is destroyed. Organically grown, new-crop beans are ideal sprouters.

2. Discard all except clean, whole beans.

3. Wash the beans and place them in a one or two-quart fruit jar. The sprouting beans will increase about 6 times original volume.

4. Cover seed with 4 times volume of lukewarm water and let them stand overnight until swollen (no longer).

5. Pour off the water and rinse thoroughly. (The soaking water can be used for soup stock or in juices; it contains the water-soluble vitamins and minerals.)

6. Cover the jar top with cheesecloth and tie it securely.

7. Invert the jar in a porcelin or glass pan and place in cupboard or dark place, in a slightly tilted position, so that excess water can drain away.

8. The seeds must be kept damp; at least three times a day, place the jar under a water tap or pour on plenty of cool water to wash away any bacteria which may have developed. Return the jar to inverted position.

9. In three to four days, at room temperature, the sprouts will be from one to two inches long and ready for use. Rinse them in cold water.

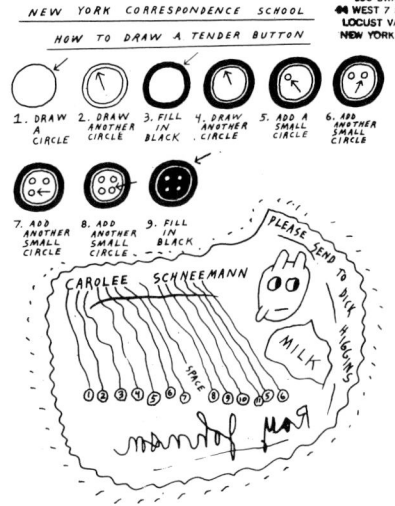

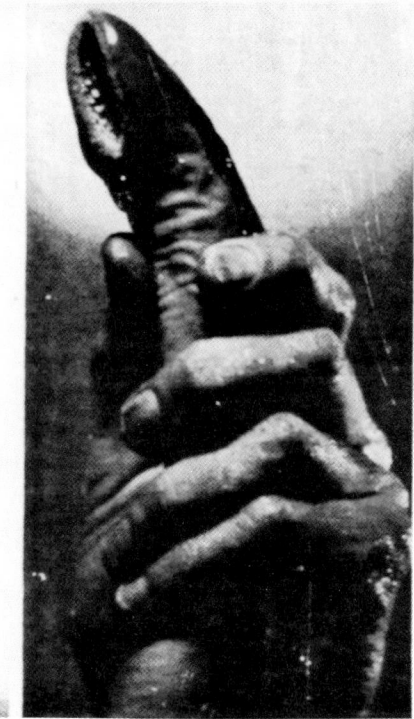

CAROLEE NAKED AND MAENADIAN. *An early memory from my early years in New York. Maybe at Judson. Lights flashing. I was strictly awed in the audience. In Philadelphia years later, on a platform together. Carolee elegant and articulate and witty. Claus Oldenburg had recommended her for this feminist panel because she had "the best body in New York."*

I'm still a little intimidated by Carolee. She has a regal poise. Something archaic about her. She is confident enough to make messes. She knows that life strikes in fragments. Even while I'm drawing back from that sometimes tedious eventfulness, that chain of out-of-focus images, I'm admiring her courageous chaos and random humor, loving her welter of associations and nonchalantly intelligent body with its long-limbed reach and direct access to the mind.

How come she's not afraid of the depths? How come she leaps out of the frame so easily? How come she doesn't drown or get bitten by the water guardians? How come she swings back and forth, making her mark no matter how the rope turns? What limits?

Carolee is not officially welcomed by the art world for good reason. She threatens mythological revolution, an anarchy that is neither economically feasible nor socially acceptable. As an emissary from the Goddess she bodes no good for the tightassed backbiting esthetic status quo. Years ago, with snakes on her belly, she reclaimed phallic imagery. She smiles from the loathsome mouth of the cave. She is an abominable snowwoman, coolly surveying the wreckage and planning new storms.

Lucy R. Lippard

I had heard about her first from Kelly & other poets of my New York acquaintance, circa 1962 or 63, & in the typical way of the talk of that time the report of an artistic intelligence was almost obscured by description of her physical presence: a young and beautiful woman who does art & is interested as well in the work of poets.

All of that made a friendly combination but told me little except the name which stuck in mind & then the face too & the voice met at readings of poetry she attended; maybe parties also. So I wouldn't say that I really knew her — & surely not her work — until the New York/Judson performance of *Meat Joy* very nearly turned my head around & she became for me one of the germinal masters of a new art that I had only dreamed before.

I want to stick with the memory of that as it exists for me now, some 12 or 13 years beyond it. There had been "happenings" before it & other possibilities of "new performance" & "environmental art," etc. But I was even so unprepared for the sensual/kinetic intensity of her work ("I work towards metaphors of sensation," she wrote: ". . . an intensification of all faculties simultaneously," etc.): the remarkable sense not only that things could be juxtaposed (which we had learned before) but that the juxtaposition ("the images are realized by a process that unites visual obsessions & precise physical action") could be organized & moved towards particular ends, in the service of both mind & body.

There is an image I carry of coming into a room of sounds, a large room in which the performers were already present, working their way into the picture, while a double-barrelled tape shot words at us in different languages. The room is very cool (a coolness of the air that I remember also from her other works) & the bodies of the "dancers" are only shadows now that once were visible & held attention in that first near-nakedness of early 1960s. (She had managed the nakedness in Paris; New York was still a way to go.) But the bodies were central to all those acts: living bodies upon which materials were sent to work, beautiful or shocking/painful. Bodies among rolls of paper, packaged, papers pressed against their legs, their hips; or bodies under plastic sheets, a play of flashlights over them; or bodies paintings bodies, dripping sponges of wet paint; or bodies moving, tying bodies; or bodies living, holding the remains of other bodies: chicken, fish & sausages, the raw meat that we become. But it was beautiful for all of that, almost austere & not an imposition, an exploitation of dead flesh, like a "mere cruelty" — but tender (I mean joyful & forlorn at once) in its proposition "that we become what we see what we touch" & what she elsewhere wrote: "a certain tenderness or empathy is pervasive even to the most violent action." And to the perception that a body under plastic is a body under plastic, in a theater or in the white counter of the supermarket butcher — for "we are a part of nature & of all visible & invisible forms."

It was not only that it conformed to my own vision, circa 1960, of "white butchershops" etc. but that she had so rightly brought it into ritual: down to the very reverence & terror of the enactment of our dreams, & to a degree I hadn't seen it done before. Body is beautiful & fragile/powerful, & body dies & forms another beauty we can barely reach. The work is celebration: therefore it transforms us. That much was evident & if it was, it was an art that was no longer art but the *precision* born of art directed now towards life. With that "precision" & that "direction" nothing proves "too much" but the "total sensibility" is in fact "alerted" — as she would then have said. And as she was (in setting the parameters of a new performance that would truly be performance) indeed the first to show us.

Jerome Rothenberg
San Diego   1977

Performance Chronology

Labyrinths
June 1960 Sidney, Illinois

Banana Hands
Original score 1962
Revised score 1969
Performed March 23 1970 New Milton
    Drama Center   The Castle,
    Winchester, England

**Glass Environment for Sound and
Motion**
May 1 2 1962 Living Theater NY

Newspaper Event
January 29 1963 Judson Dance
    Theater NY

Chromelodeon
June 24   1963 Judson Dance Theater
    NY

Lateral Splay
November 19 20 1963 Judson Dance
    Theater NY

Eye Body
December 1963 NY

Looseleaf
January 21 1964 Judson Dance Theater
    Workshop NY

June 8 9 1966 Bridge Theater Festival
    NY

Music Box Music
April 4 1964 From Pitt St NY
April 24 1964 Tone Roads The New
    School NY
November 21 1965 Bridge Theater NY

Meat Joy
May 29 1964 Festival de La Libre
    Expression, Paris

June 8 1964 Dennison Hall, London

November 16 17 18 1964 Judson
    Church NY

The Queen's Dog
April 21 22 1965 Judson Dance Theater
    NY

Noise Bodies
August 28 1965 Avant Garde Festival
    Judson Hall NY

November 28 30 1965 Bridge Theater
    NY

Ghost Rev
November 17 18 1965 New Cinema
    Festival I, Cinematheque (Astor Place
    Theater) NY

**Water Light
Water Needle**
March 17 18 19 20 1966 St. Mark's
    Church NY

May 29 1966 Havemayer Estate
    MahWah NJ

Snows
January 21 22 27 28 29 February 3 4 5
    1967 Martinique Theater NY

Round House
July 29 1967 Congress of the Dialectics
    of Liberation London

Ordeals
29 August 1967 Judson Church NY

**Night Crawlers
(Rampants de la Nuit)**
Spetember 8 1967 Expo 67 Pavillon de
    la Jeunesse, Montreal

Snug Harbor
September 1967 Avant Garde Festival
    Staten Island Ferry NY

Divisions and Rubble
October 19 1967 Judson Gallery NY

Body Collage
December 20 1967 NY

Illinois Central
January 26 27 28 1968 Museum of
    Contemporary Art Chicago

Illinois Central Transposed
February 20 1968 SUNY Stony Brook L.I.

March 8 1968 Brooklyn Academy of
    Music

March 16 1968 SUNY Rochester

March 18 1968 SUNY Buffalo, Spring Arts
    Festival

March 26 1968 SUNY Nassau L.I.

16 March 1969 The Ark Boston

Naked Action Lecture
June 27 1968 Institute of Contemporary
    Art London

Expansions
April 24 1969 New Poets Theater NY

Thames Crawling
September 17 1970 International
    Underground Film Festival London

Electronic Activations Room
November 1970-January 1971
    Happenings & Fluxus Retrospective
    Kölnischer Künstverein, Köln

Schlaget Auf
November 14 1970 Fluxus Fluxorum
    Festival Forum Theater Berlin

Rainbow Blaze
September 1971 Avant Garde Festival
    The Armory NY

Road Animation for Reykjavik
June-July 1972 Reykjavik Art-Festival

Ices Strip
August 21 1972 Ices Festival Train,
    London-Edinburgh

Cooking With Apes
September 2 1973 Fylkingen Festival
    Stockholm

**Up To And Including Her Limits
("Trackings")**
December 1973 Avant Garde Festival
    Grand Central Station NY

April 11 1974 University Art Museum
    Berkeley California (Performance-
    Installation)

June 18   1974 Arts Meeting Place,
    London (Performance-Installation)

June 19 1974 London Filmmakers
    Cooperative

December 1 1974 Artists Space NY

December 12 13 1974 Anthology Film
    Archive NY

February 13 14 1976 The Kitchen NY
    (Performance-Installation)

June 10 1976 Studiogalerie Berlin
    (Installation June 10-25)

June 13-20 1976 Basle Art Fair
    (Installation)

Interior Scroll
August 29 1975 Women Here & Now
    East Hampton L.I.

September 4 1977 Telluride Film Festival
    Telluride Colorado

Americana I Ching Apple Pie
February 26 1977 Heresies **Benefit 112**
    Greene St NY

March 1 1977 Ear Benefit Washington
    Square Church NY

Moon In A Tree
March 20 1976 Anthology Film Archives,
    NY

ABC—We Print Anything—In The Cards
November 9 1976 Franklin Furnace NY

May 14 1977 "Discussion As An Art
    Form" New York University NY

June 3 4 1977 De Appel Gallery
    Amsterdam

June 9 Festival of Performance Art
    Arnhem Holland

HOMERUNMUSE
November 20 1977 Brooklyn Museum of
Art NY

January 23 1978 Lions Walk Pittsburgh

As Participant / Performer

1956
Stan Brakhage "Loving" (film, with
James Tenney)

1959
Stan Brakhage "Cat's Cradle" (film, with
Kitch, J.T., and Jane Brakhage)

1962
Claes Oldenburg "Store Days"

1960's
Fluxus concerts (Corner, Watts, Mac
Low, Higgins, Knowles)

Tone Roads music concerts (Corner,
Goldstein, Tenney)

1964
Robert Morris "Site (Stage 73, Pocket
Theater, Judson Church)

Stan Vanderbeek film of "Site"

Wolf Vostell "You"

1965
Ken Dewey "Confederate Memorial
Day"

Claes Oldenburg "Birth of the Flag"

Avant Garde Festival Stockhausen's
"Originale" ("Beast Event")

Allan Kaprow "Push & Pull" (director)

James Tenney "Second Thermocouple"

1966
Rochelle Owens "Beclech"
(consultant)

1968
Michael Benedikt "Tear Poem"

Avant Garde Festival Parade "Flying
Blue Glue Float"

1969
Claes Oldenburg "Nude Bride"

1970
"Chicago Festival of Life—London"
(director)

Steve Dwoskin "Times Four"

1971-73
Anthony McCall "Circulation Figures,"
"Landscape for Fire"

1975
Lee Breuer collaborative reading, St.
Mark's Church

Filmography

All film & video rights retained by C.S.
Films in all caps are original works by
C.S.

1963
CARL RUGGLES' CHRISTMAS BREAKFAST
(8mm enlarged to 16mm, sepia toned,
separate sound) 3 1/2 & 7 minute versions

1964
Meat Joy
(16mm color sound) 12-minute version
edited by Bob Giorgio. Longer version held
by Schneemann. Filmed by Pierre
Dominique Gaisseau. Documentation

1965
VIET-FLAKES
(16mm b/w toned, sound collage by
James Tenney) 11 minutes.

Water Light/Water Needle
Documentations
1) (16mm color sound) Filmed by John
Jones, edited by Jones & C.S., sound
by C.S., 12 minutes.
2) (16mm color) Filmed by Sheldon
Rocklin, edited by C.S. 20 minutes.
Original stolen—no print.
3) (16mm b/w) Filmed by Elaine
Summers. 15 minutes. Unedited.

1966
Red News
(16mm b/w red toned silent) Found
footage. 6 minutes.

1967
FUSES
(16mm color silent) Part I of "Autobiographical Trilogy." 22 minutes. Filming
began in 1964.

Falling Bodies (or Body Rotations)
(16mm b/w silent) Filmed by Peter Whitehead. c. 6 minutes. Contact improvisation: C.S. & J. Tenney. Documentation.

Snows
(16mm b/w silent) Filmed by Alphonse
Shilling. c. 24 minutes. Unedited.
Documentation.

Body Collage
(16mm b/w silent) Filmed by Gideon
Bachmann. c. 6 minutes.
Documentation.

1968
Illinois Central
(16mm color silent) Filmed by John
Heinz. c. 10 minutes. Documentation

Illinois Central Transposed
(16mm color silent) Filmed by Robert
Dacey. 800 ft. unedited.
Documentation.

1971
PLUMB LINE
(s8 step printed to 16mm color sound)
Part II of "Autobiographical Trilogy." 18
minutes. Sound by C.S. Filming began in
1968.

1971-72
Reel Time
(16mm color sound 1 hr.) Uncompleted
mutual film diary with Anthony McCall.

1972
Americana I Ching Apple Pie
(16mm color sound) 20 minutes.
(Footage withheld by Richard Chase.)

Ices Strip Train Skating
(16mm color sound) 12 minutes.
(Footage withheld by Leslie Elliot.)
Documentation.

1973
Acts of Perception
(s8 b/w separate sound) 11 minutes.
Group film as process of workshop.

1973-78
KITCH'S LAST MEAL
(s8 color dual projection separate
sound) Variable units: 20 minutes to 2
hours. Part III of "Autobiographical
Trilogy."

1976-77
ABC—We Print Anything—In The Cards
(s8 color sound) Filmed by Paul Sharits
and Tony Morgan. Unedited.

Video Tapes

1974-77
Up To And Including Her Limits
(b/w sound)
Edited to one hour, mixed in five permu-
tations. Performances at University Art
Museum, Berkeley; London Filmmakers'
Cooperative (by John Hopkins); Artists
Space, New York (by Al Rossi); Anthology
Film Archives, New York; The Kitchen,
New York (by J. Nichols, J. McLaughlin, S.
Clarke); Studiogalerie, Berlin (by Mike
Steiner).

1975
Interior Scroll
(b/w) 40 minutes. Taped & withheld by
Dorothy Beskind.

1976-77
ABC—We Print Anything—In The Cards
(b/w sound) Three tapes. New York Uni-
versity (by Paul Shavelson); Franklin
Furnace, New York (by Jackie Ochs); De
Appel, Amsterdam (by M. Cardenas).

1977
HOMERUNMUSE
(b/w sound) 60 minutes. Taped by Ricky
Slater.

BIBLIOGRAPHY

1. About & in reference to works

Anderson, Jack. "What Happens at a Happening?" *Dance Magazine* (1967).

Aue, Walter. *Project, Concept, Action*, Dumont, Koln (1971).

Baxandall, Lee. "The New Theater" *Studies on the Left* (1966).

Benedikt, Michael. "What's Happening with Happenings" *Story* (1967).

Berke, Joseph, ed. *Counter Culture*, Peter Owen Ltd., London (1970).

Brakhage, Stan. *Film Culture Reader*, p. 207. Praeger, New York (1970).

Brakhage, Stan. *Metaphors on Vision*, ed. P. Adams Sitney. *Film Culture #30* (1963).

Burnside, Madeleine. "ABC—We Print Anything" *Soho Weekly News* (Nov. 18, 1976).

Cage, John. *Notations*, Something Else Press, New York (1967).

Cott, Jonathan. "Play Power in London" *Rolling Stone* (March 19, 1970).

Creative Camera (October 1970) "Carolee Schneemann—Image as Process".

Dance Magazine (June 1965) "Unexpected Assemblage".

de Miro d'Ajeta, Esta Carla. *Spettacoli & Societa* (Milan, March 1976) "Cultura & Commuicazione Alternativa".

Der Spiegel (No. 26, 1976) "Carolee Schneemann multimedial."

Export, Valie. "Eye Body—Meat Joy" *Heute Kunst* (September 1975).

France Observateur (4 Juin 1964) "En Attendant Le Happening".

Gibbs, Michael. "Everything in the art world exists in order to end up as a book" *Art Communication* (July 1977).

Gidal, Peter. "Books" *Art and Artists* (August 1972).

Goldberg, Roselee. A book on performance art to be published by Thames & Hudson, London (1978).

Hansen, Al. *A Primer of Happenings and Time/Space Art*, Something Else Press, New York (1966).

Henri, Adrian. *Total Art: Environments, Happenings, Performance*, Thames & Hudson, London (1974).

Holbrook, Peter. "The Chicago Saga of Carolee Schneemann" *Art Scene* (March 1968).

Hutchinson, Peter. "Moving Paintings" *Art in America* (1967).

Johnston, Jill. "Den Nya Dansen", and Lebel, Jean-Jacques. "Fran Malad Bild Till Happening" *Konstrevy*, nr. 4-5 (1965).

Kozloff, Max. "Body Art" *Art Forum* (November 1975).

Kostelanetz, Richard. *Theater of Mixed Means*, Dial Press, New York (1970).

Kultermann, Udo. *Art-Events and Happenings*, Mathews Miller Dunbar, London (1971).

L'Esspresso Roma (14 Guigno 1964) " 'Meat Joy' Un Happening Che Si Tacoli Surrealisti".

LeGrice, Malcolm. *Abstract Film and Beyond*, MIT Press (1977).

Lebel, Jean-Jacques. *Le Happening*, Denoel, Paris (1966).

Lester, Elenore. "Intermedia: Tune In, Turn On—And Walk Out?" *New York Times Magazine* (May 12, 1968).

Lippard, Lucy R. "Quite Contrary: Body, Nature, Ritual in Women's Art" *Chrysalis 2*, (1977).

Lippard, Lucy R. "Women's Body Art" *Art in America* (June 1976).

Lord, Jeffrey P. "Kitch's Last Meal" *Field of Vision #4*, Pittsburgh (1978).

McDonagh, Don. *Complete Guide to Modern Dance*, Doubleday, Garden City, N.Y. (1976).

Mekas, Jonas. "Movie Journal" *Village Voice* (December 30, 1974).

Nabakowski, Gislind. "Up To And Including Her Limits" *Heute Kunst* (#9, Feb-March 1976).

Picard, Lil. "Art" ("Schneemann Models Oldenburg's Invisible Bridal Gown" illus. caption) *East Village Other* (Jan. 24, 1969).

Penthouse (Vol. 3, No. 10, 1968) "Happenings—The Sticking Point".

Robillard, Yves. "D'Un Happening, De La Fete Et Des Bonbons" *La Presse Montreal* (16 Sept. 1967).

Rothenberg, Jerome, ed. *Technicians of the Sacred*, Doubleday/Anchor, Garden City, N.Y. (1967).

Schapp, Dick. "What's Happening" *New York Herald Tribune* (Jan. 24, 1966).

Sherman, Susan. "The Dialiectics of Liberation" *I-KON* (#4, October 1967).

Smith, Michael. "Theater Journal" *Village Voice* Jan. 26, 1967).

Szeemann, Harald, and Sohm, Hans. *Happenings and Fluxus*, Koelnischer Kunstverein, Koln (1970).

Vogel, Amos. *Film as a Subversive Art*, Random House, New York (1974).

Wikarska, Carol. "Schneemann's 'Plumb Line' " *Women and Film* (Vol. 12, No. 7, 1976).

Wooster, Ann-Sargent. "Up To And Including Her Limits" *Art Forum* (May 1976).

Youngblood, Gene. *Expanded Cinema*, Dutton, New York (1970).

2. Writings by C.S.

"Americana I Ching Apple Pie" *Center*, Berge, Carol, ed., #8 1975.

"Aspects of EAT in the Making of SNOWS" *Experiments in Art and Technology Newsletter*, June 1, 1967.

"Banana Hands" *Plays for Children to Direct*, Heinemann, London, 1970.

"Be Prepared" and "Missing Gender" *Earth Ship*, Hemensley, Chris, ed., #12 1972.

"Divisions and Rubble" *Manipulations*, Hendricks, Jon, ed., Judson Publications, 1967.

"Dreams From Now And Again", *Tracks* ed. George, Herbert (1976).

"Fish Love Notes" and "A Body Montage". *Wipe Poetry Package*. ed., Finestein, M. London (1970).

"Free Form Recollections of New York" *National Film Theater Expanded Cinema Journal*, London, November 1970.

"From the Diaries" (with Anthony McCall) *Fetter Lane Review*, Hewison, Robert, ed., London, #7 November 1971.

"from ABC—We Print Anything—In the Cards" *Arnhem Performance Art Festival*, Wijers, Louwrien & Brand, Jan, eds., Brummense de Luxe Werkes, Holland 1978. (Includes interview and illustrations.)

"Hormones Circling" *Matter*, Kelly, Robert, ed., 1963.

"I Assume the Senses Crave . . ." *Eddy*, Borek, T., ed., #3 April 1974.

"I Met a Happy Man . . ." *Cinemabook*, Schact, R., ed., Spring 1976.

"In, On, and About My Premises" *Sixpack*, Prescott, W. and Joris, P., eds., #7/8 1974.

"Introduction to 'Erotic Films by Women' " *Deciphering America*, Gibbs, Michael, ed., Kontexts Publications, Amsterdam 1978.

"Kenneth Anger's 'Scorpio Rising' " *Film Culture* #34, Spring 1964, and *Film Culture Reader*, Praeger, New York, 1970.

"Love Paint Ritual" (from Meat Joy) *Technicians of the Sacred*, Rothenberg, Jerome, ed., Doubleday, 1968.

"Meat Joy" and "Notes as Prologue" *Some/Thing*, Antin, David & Rothenberg, Jerome, eds., #2 1965.

"Meat Joy" and "Notes as Process" *Theatre Experiment*, Benedikt, Michael, ed., Doubleday, 1967.

"Meat Joy" *Mirrors for Man: 26 Plays of the World Drama*, Ashley, L.N., ed., Winthrop 1974.

"Mixed-Up Dreams Today" *The Ices '72 Brain Drain Music Train*, Beau Geste Press, Devon, England, 1972.

"Mystical Affinities" *Chrysalis*, Summer 1978. *Extracts from HOMERUNMUSE.*

"Notations" *Caterpillar*, Eshleman, Clayton, ed., #8/9 1969, and *A Caterpillar Anthology*, Eshleman, C., ed., Doubleday, 1971.

"On Creative Liberation" *Hello, Je T'aime*, Pasle-Green & Haynes, eds., Almonde, Paris, 1975.

"On Creativity & Violence" *Heresies* #6, Fall 1978. ("Women and Violence" issue.)

"Parts Of A Body House" *Caterpillar*, Eshleman, C., ed., #3/4 1968.

——————————— *Earth Ship*, Hemensley, C., ed., #10/11 1972. (Excerpts.)

——————————— *Fantastic Architecture*, Vostell, W. & Higgins, D., eds., Something Else Press, 1969.

"Permission to Dream" *The Dream Book*, Coxhead, D. & Hiller, S., eds., Thames and Hudson, London 1975.

"Road Animation for Reykjavik" *Sùm: A Listaijatid I Treykjavik*, Sùm Galerie, Iceland 1972.

"Second Thermocouple" (James Tenney with C.S.), *Some/Thing*, Antin, D. & Rothenberg, J., eds., #3 1966.

"Schlaget Auf" *Flash Art*, Summer 1978. (George Maciunas Memorial Issue.)

"Snows" *I-KON*, Sherman, Susan, ed., #5 1968.

"Snows (sequence 4-7)" *Notations*, Cage, John. Something Else Press, 1967. (Drawing.)

"The Loaves and the Fishes" *A Voice in the Village*, Kuhn, Annette, ed., Judson Church Publication, 1977.

The Museum of Drawers, ed. Distel, Herbert. Kunsthaus, Zurich (1978).

"The Pronoun Tyranny" *The Fox*, #3 1976.

Time and Space Concepts II, Belford, Marilyn & Herman, Jerry, eds., Pleiades Gallery, New York 1977. *Panel discussion.*

"Uber Sexualles" *Americans Abroad*, Tillman, Lynne, ed., Cold Turkey Press, Rotterdam 1978.

"Untitled" *Performing Arts Journal*, Marranca, B. & Dasgupta, G., eds., Vol. II. #2, 1977. *Statement in "American Experimental Theater Then and Now" section.*

"Vision is not a fact . . ." *Expanded Cinema*, Youngblood, Gene. Dutton, 1970. (Statement.)

"When No One Was Looking" *Book of the Goat*, Beau Geste Press, Devon, England 1972.

"Woman Artist &" *Elima*, Gottlieb, Annie, ed., #1 1973.

BOOKS

Parts Of A Body House Book. Beau Geste Press,
Devon, England. Hand made edition of 75, illus.
35 pages, slipcase. Facsimile edition of 300.
(January 1972).

Cézanne, She Was A Great Painter. Tresspass
Press, N.Y. 40 pages. Three editions, 1,300
copies. (1974, 75, 76).

ABC — We Print Anything — In The Cards.
Brummense Uitgeverij Van Luxe Werkjes,
Beuningen, Holland. 158 cards, photos & text,
boxed. Edition of 151. December 1977.

Design by Bruce McPherson. Collages by Carolee Schneemann. Typeset by Lynn Whittaker at Open Studio. Printed at The Book Press. First edition: 2000 clothbound copies; one hundred copies specially bound, numbered and signed; forty lettered autograph copies.

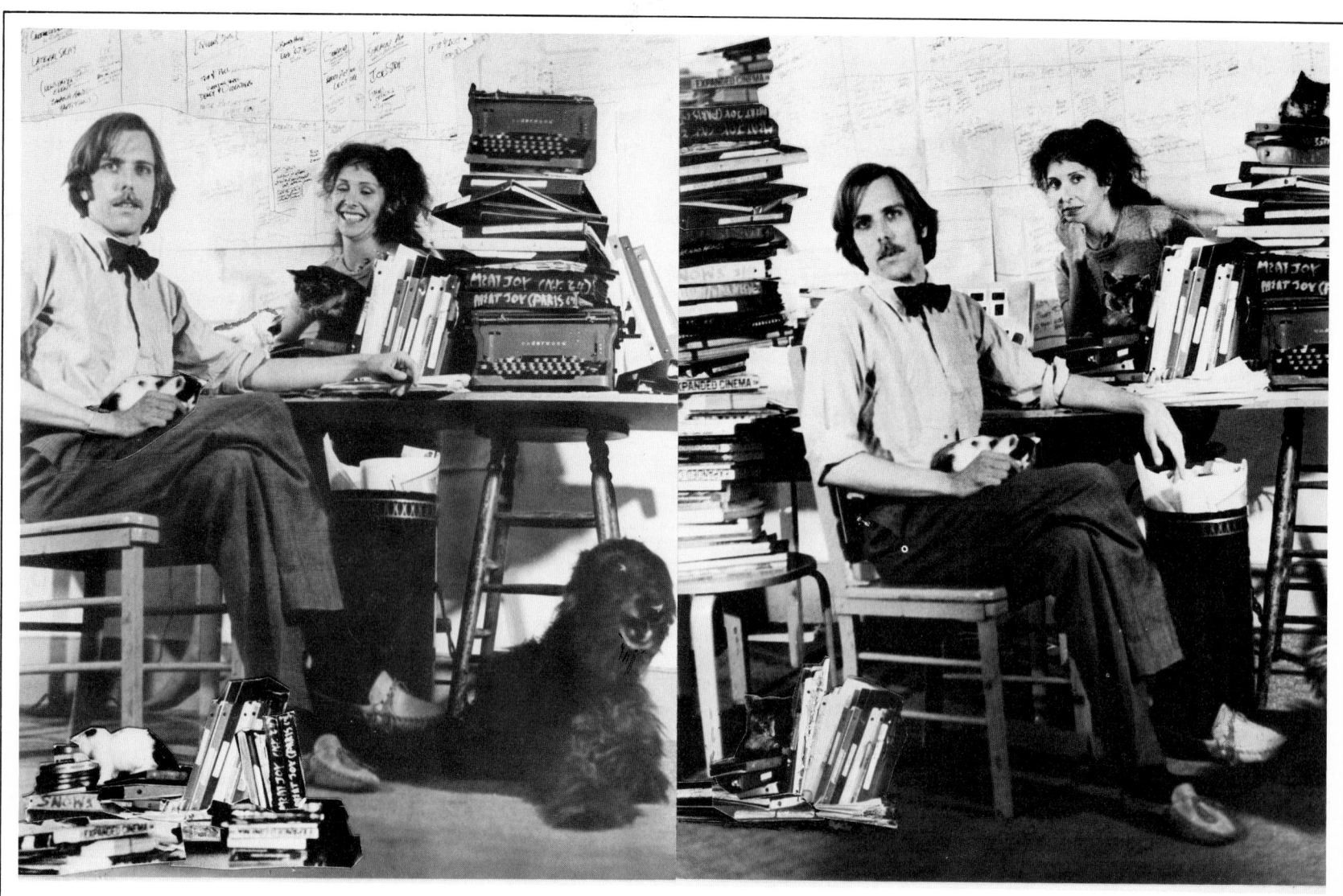

Photos: Mary Ellen Morrow. Collage: C.S.